PRAXIS I
PPST
Pre-Professional Skills Tests

by the staff of
Research & Education Association
Dr. M. Fogiel, Director

Research & Education Association
61 Ethel Road West
Piscataway, New Jersey 08854

The Best Test Preparation for the
The PRAXIS SERIES™ PPST® Tests
Pre-Professional Skills Tests

Year 2004 Printing

Copyright © 2003, 2000, 1999, 1998, 1996
by Research & Education Association. All rights
reserved. No part of this book may be reproduced
in any form without permission of the publisher.

Printed in the United States of America

Library of Congress Control Number 2002115353

International Standard Book Number 0-87891-867-1

Research & Education Association
61 Ethel Road West
Piscataway, New Jersey 08854

About the Praxis Series

The Praxis Series: Professional Assessments for Beginning Teachers® is a group of tests developed and administered by Educational Testing Service (ETS). Depending on where you wish to teach, you may be asked to take one or more of the Praxis Series exams in order to be certified to teach in that state. In most cases, however, you will be required to take only one exam, and that exam will come under one of the following three headings:

Praxis I embraces the Academic Skills Assessments, including the paper-based Pre-Professional Skills Tests (PPST®)—which we cover in this book—and the Praxis I Computer-Based Tests (CBT). Both the paper- and computer-based exams measure your reading, mathematics, and writing skills.

Praxis II includes the Subject Assessments/Specialty Area tests, the Multiple Subjects Assessment for Teachers (MSAT), and the Principles of Learning and Teaching Tests (PLT).

Praxis III moves from multiple-choice and essay tests to the classroom, where ETS-trained observers evaluate your performance while you are teaching. These observers use uniform criteria developed by ETS to evaluate you, and may videotape your lesson so that they may compare their critique with teaching experts.

To find out which of the Praxis assessments you will be required to take, contact your state department of education.

The Praxis Series at a Glance		
Praxis I	**Praxis II**	**Praxis III**
• PPST (paper-based) • Praxis I Computer-Based Tests • Listening Skills Test	• MSAT • Subject Assessments/Specialty Area Tests • Principles of Learning and Teaching Tests	• Classroom Performance Assessments

Praxis I: Academic Skills Assessments

PPST — Pre-Professional Skills Tests (paper-based)

Measures proficiency in reading, mathematics, and writing.

> **Reading** — 40 questions based on passages. 60 minutes.
> **Mathematics** — 40 questions. 60 minutes.
> **Writing** — 45 questions, 30 minutes. 1 essay, 30 minutes.

CBT — Computer-Based Testing

Same subject matter as the PPST, only in an adaptive environment; the test modifies itself based on your individual performance. The test includes so-called pretest questions that won't count toward your score. You won't be told which ones they are. Offered year-round at select testing centers. Its format is as follows:

Reading — 36 questions based on passages. 95 minutes.
Mathematics — 29 questions. 65 minutes.
Writing — 35 questions, 30 minutes. 1 essay, 40 minutes.

Listening Skills Test

This paper-based one-hour test features multiple-choice questions that reference recorded segments. The test requires much of the same knowledge and many of the same skills previously assessed by the defunct Praxis II: Core Battery Communication Skills test listening section.

Praxis II: MSAT, PLT, Subject Assessments/ Specialty Area Tests

MSAT— Multiple Subjects Assessment for Teachers (California, Oregon only)

120 multiple-choice questions, 18 short-essay questions in 7 subject areas; 5 hours.

Literature & Language Studies — 24 multiple-choice items, 3 short-essay items.
Mathematics — 24 multiple-choice items, 3 short-essay items.
History & Social Studies — 22 multiple-choice items, 3 short-essay items.
Science — 22 multiple-choice items, 3 short-essay items.
Visual & Performing Arts — 12 multiple-choice items, 2 short-essay items.
Human Development — 8 multiple-choice items, 2 short-essay items.
Physical Education — 8 multiple-choice items, 2 short-essay items.

PLT— Principles of Learning and Teaching Tests

These tests use a case-study approach to gauge general pedagogical knowledge at the K–6, 5–9, and 7–12 grade levels. The PLT is made up of a combination of constructed-response and multiple-choice items.

Subject Assessments/Specialty Area Tests

The Specialty Area Tests measure proficiency in individual subject areas for the purpose of obtaining special subject certification. They also measure general and specific skills relating to pedagogy itself. More than 140 individual content tests are in this category. Subject tests vary in length and format.

Praxis III: Classroom Performance Assessments

There is no specific test for Praxis III. Instead, trained local observers employed by Educational Testing Service evaluate teachers in the classroom environment. These observers use uniform criteria, created by ETS, measuring a teacher's sensitivity to multicultural issues, the needs of individual students, and the changing requirements of diverse subject areas.

CONTENTS

CHAPTER 3

CHAPTER 4

PRACTICE TESTS

ABOUT RESEARCH & EDUCATION ASSOCIATION

Research & Education Association (REA) is an organization of educators, scientists, and engineers specializing in various academic fields. Founded in 1959 with the purpose of disseminating the most recently developed scientific information to groups in industry, government, and universities, REA has since become a successful and highly respected publisher of study aids, test preps, handbooks, and reference works.

REA's Test Preparation series includes study guides for all academic levels in almost all disciplines. Research & Education Association publishes test preps for students who have not yet completed high school, as well as high school students preparing to enter college. Students from countries around the world seeking to attend college in the United States will find the assistance they need in REA's publications. For college students seeking advanced degrees, REA publishes test preps for many major graduate school admission examinations in a wide variety of disciplines, including engineering, law, and medicine. Students at every level, in every field, with every ambition can find what they are looking for among REA's publications.

While most test preparation books present only a few practice tests which bear little resemblance to the actual exams, REA's series presents tests which accurately depict the official exams in both degree of difficulty and types of questions. REA's practice tests are always based upon the most recently administered exams, and include every type of question that can be expected on the actual exams.

REA's publications and educational materials are highly regarded and continually receive an unprecedented amount of praise from professionals, instructors, librarians, parents, and students. Our authors are as diverse as the subjects represented in the books we publish. They are well-known in their respective fields and serve on the faculties of prestigious high schools, colleges, and universities throughout the United States and Canada.

ACKNOWLEDGMENTS

We would like to thank Dr. Max Fogiel, President, for his overall guidance, which brought this publication to completion; John Paul Cording, Manager of Educational Software, for coordinating development of the book; Larry B. Kling, Quality Control Manager of Books in Print, for his supervision of revisions; Michael Tomolonis, Assistant Managing Editor for Production, and Catherine Battos, Editorial Assistant, for coordinating revisions; and Marty Perzan for typesetting the manuscript.

PPST INDEPENDENT STUDY SCHEDULE

The following study schedule allows for thorough preparation for the PPST. Although it is designed for 8 weeks, it can be condensed into a four week course by condensing two weeks into one. If you are not enrolled in a structured course, be sure to set aside enough time, at least two or three hours each day, to study. But no matter which study schedule works best for you, the more time you spend studying, the more prepared and relaxed you will feel on the day of the exam.

Week	Activity
1	Take the first exam as a diagnostic exam. Your score will be an indication of your strengths and weaknesses. Carefully review the explanations for the questions you answered incorrectly.
2	Study REA's PPST review material and answer the drill questions provided. Highlight key terms and information. Take notes on the important theories and key concepts since writing will aid in the retention of information.
3 and 4	Review your references and sources. Use any other supplementary material which your education instructors might recommend.
5	Condense your notes and findings. You should have a structured outline detailing specific facts. You may want to use index cards to help you in memorizing important facts and concepts.
6	Test yourself using the index cards. You may want to have a friend or colleague quiz you on key facts and items. Take the second full-length exam. Review the explanations for the questions you answered incorrectly.
7	Study any areas you consider to be your weaknesses by using your study materials, references, and notes. Take the third full-length exam. Review the explanations for the questions you answered incorrectly.
8	Take the final full-length exam. Review the explanations for the questions you answered incorrectly.

PPST
Pre-Professional Skills Tests

Chapter 1
Passing the PPST

Chapter 1

PASSING THE PPST

ABOUT THIS BOOK

This book provides a complete and accurate representation of the Praxis® I: Pre-Professional Skills Tests (PPST®). Our comprehensive review material covers every aspect of the test and is designed to provide all the information you will need to achieve a high score on this challenging exam. You are given three hours to take the actual exam, and the same amount of time is allotted to take each of our practice tests. REA's tests contain every type of question that you can expect to see on the actual exam, and following each practice test are answer keys accompanied by detailed explanations of every question and sample responses to every essay to help you master the test material.

ABOUT THE TEST

Who Takes the Test and What Is it Used for?

The PPST is a set of teacher certification exams required by several states and is part of the Praxis Series: Professional Assessments for Beginning Teachers. The PPST falls under Praxis I: Academic Skills Assessments and is designed to test the reading, writing, and mathematics skills of its candidates.

If you do not achieve a passing score on the PPST, don't panic. The test can be taken again, so you can work on improving your score in preparation for your next administration.

Who Administers the Test?

Like all Praxis Series tests, the PPST is administered by Educational Testing Service (ETS) and involves the assistance of educators throughout

the country. The test development process is designed and implemented to ensure that the content and difficulty level of the test are appropriate.

When Should the PPST be Taken?

The PPST is usually taken immediately before the completion of a teacher certification program at a college or university. This gives candidates enough time to retake the test if they are not pleased with their score. Our practice tests will familiarize you with the format of the exam so that you do not have to go through the anxiety of learning about the PPST during the actual exam.

When and Where Is the Test Given?

The PPST is administered six times a year at schools throughout the United States. Tests are usually administered on a Saturday; however, the test may be taken on an alternate day if some conflict, such as a religious obligation, exists.

When you register for the PPST, your registration bulletin will contain test dates and administration sites. You may obtain a registration bulletin by contacting:

Educational Testing Service
Rosedale Road
Princeton, NJ 08541
Phone: (609) 921-9000
Website: www.ets.org

Is There a Registration Fee?

Yes, you must pay a fee to take the PPST. Fee waivers are available for candidates who are unable to afford registration. You must be enrolled in a college undergraduate program and prove that you are required to take the exam by a registered score recipient. Details regarding income eligibility levels are contained in the registration bulletin.

HOW TO USE THIS BOOK

What Should I Study First?

Read over our review material, and then take the first practice test. This will help you assess your areas of weakness. Study those sections in which you had the most difficulty first, and then move on to those areas which presented less of a challenge to you.

When Should I Start Studying?

It is never too early to begin studying for the PPST. The earlier you begin, the more time you will have to sharpen your skills. Do not procrastinate! Cramming is not an effective way to study. Give yourself enough time to become familiar with the format of the test and the material it covers. The sooner you learn the format of the exam, the more comfortable and confident you will be on the day of the test.

FORMAT OF THE PPST

The PPST is divided into three sections:

The Reading Comprehension Test

The Reading Test measures your ability to understand and analyze written information. The test consists of several written passages and 40 multiple-choice questions to test your understanding of those passages. You have one hour to complete this section of the exam.

The Mathematics Test

The Mathematics Test measures competency in mathematical skills that an educated adult will require. It focuses on the ability to solve problems in a quantitative context. Several problems involve the integration of several skills into one problem solving situation. The test consists of 40 multiple-choice questions, which you have one hour to complete.

The Writing Test

The Writing Test assesses the ability to communicate in written form using appropriate language and grammar. There are two separately timed sections in the writing test. The first consists of 45 multiple-choice questions testing your facility with the use of standard English, and you have 30 minutes to complete it. The second section consists of an essay on an assigned topic to be written in 30 minutes.

ABOUT THE REVIEW SECTIONS

The Reading Comprehension Review

The Reading Comprehension Review is designed to enhance the reading comprehension skills necessary to achieve a high score on the PPST. Strategies for attacking reading comprehension questions are thoroughly explained, and a four-step approach to answering the test questions is completely outlined. In addition, a vocabulary enhancer is included to help you better understand the passages on the test.

The Basic Math Skills Review

The Mathematics Review will help you reinforce the arithmetic, algebraic, and geometric concepts that will be tested on the PPST. Drill questions are included that will help you sharpen your mathematical skills. A valuable reference table offers quick access to important formulae and an index of mathematical symbols. Careful review of this section should give you all the information you need to pass this section of the PPST.

The Writing Skills Review

The Writing Skills Review contains a wealth of information concerning the structure, content, and form of the PPST essay. Regardless of the topic you are assigned on the exam, a concise, well-constructed essay is essential to achieve a passing score. Careful study of the Essay Writing Review will hone your essay writing abilities, so that you will be able to write your essay with confidence.

SCORING YOUR PRACTICE TESTS

How Do I Score My Practice Tests?

Educational Testing Service does not set the passing scores for the PPST. Scores considered passing are set by the institutions that require the test. Each test is scored separately, and a conversion table is included in this section that will help you convert your raw score (the number of questions answered correctly) into your scaled score (the score that a given institution will use to determine whether or not you've passed).

PPST Reading Test Conversion Table

Number Correct	Scaled Score	Number Correct	Scaled Score
40	187	19	168
39	186	18	168
38	186	17	167
37	185	16	166
36	184	15	165
35	183	14	164
34	182	13	163
33	181	12	162
32	180	11	161
31	179	10	160
30	178	9	159
29	177	8	159
28	177	7	158
27	176	6	157
26	175	5	156
25	174	4	155
24	173	3	154
23	172	2	153
22	171	1	152
21	170	0	151
20	169		

PPST Mathematics Test Conversion Table

Number Correct	Scaled Score	Number Correct	Scaled Score
40	190	19	169
39	189	18	168
38	188	17	167
37	187	16	166
36	186	15	165
35	185	14	164
34	184	13	163
33	183	12	162
32	182	11	161
31	181	10	160
30	180	9	159
29	179	8	158
28	178	7	157
27	177	6	155
26	176	5	154
25	175	4	153
24	174	3	152
23	173	2	151
22	172	1	150
21	171	0	150
20	170		

PPST Writing Test Conversion Table

Multiple-Choice Section (# Right)	Essay Score (Sum of Two Readings)												
	0	1	2	3	4	5	6	7	8	9	10	11	12
0–2	150	152	154	155	157	159	160	162	163	165	167	168	170
3	150	152	154	155	157	159	161	162	164	166	167	169	170
4	151	153	154	156	158	159	161	162	164	166	168	169	171
5	151	153	155	156	158	160	162	163	165	166	168	170	171
6	152	154	155	157	158	160	162	163	165	167	169	170	172
7	152	154	156	157	159	161	162	164	166	167	169	170	172
8	153	154	156	158	159	161	163	164	166	168	170	171	173
9	153	155	157	158	160	162	163	165	166	168	170	171	173
10–11	154	155	157	158	160	162	164	165	167	169	170	172	174
12	154	156	158	159	161	162	164	166	167	169	171	172	174
13	154	156	158	159	161	163	165	166	168	170	171	173	174
14	155	157	158	159	161	163	165	166	168	170	171	173	174
15	155	157	159	160	162	164	166	167	169	170	172	174	175
16	156	158	159	161	162	164	166	167	169	171	173	174	176
17	156	159	160	161	163	165	166	168	170	171	173	174	176
18	157	158	160	162	163	165	167	168	170	172	174	175	177
19	157	159	161	162	164	166	167	169	170	172	174	175	177
20	158	159	161	162	164	166	168	169	171	173	174	176	178
21	158	160	162	163	165	166	168	170	171	173	175	176	178
22	158	160	162	163	165	167	169	170	172	174	175	177	178
23	159	161	162	164	166	167	169	170	172	174	176	177	179
24	159	161	163	164	166	168	170	171	173	174	176	178	179
25	160	162	163	165	166	168	170	171	173	175	177	178	180
26	160	162	164	165	167	169	170	172	174	175	177	178	180
27	161	162	164	166	167	169	171	172	174	176	178	179	181
28–29	161	163	165	166	168	170	171	173	174	176	178	179	181
30	162	163	165	166	168	170	172	173	175	177	178	180	182
31	162	164	166	167	169	170	172	174	175	177	179	180	182
32	162	164	166	167	169	171	173	174	176	178	179	181	182
33	163	165	166	168	170	171	173	174	176	178	180	181	183
34	163	165	167	168	170	172	174	175	177	179	180	182	183
35	164	166	167	169	170	172	174	175	177	179	181	182	184
36	164	166	168	169	171	173	174	176	178	179	181	182	184
37	165	166	168	170	171	173	175	176	178	180	182	183	185
38	165	167	169	170	172	174	175	177	178	180	182	183	185
39	166	167	169	170	172	174	176	177	179	181	182	184	186
40	166	168	170	171	173	174	176	178	179	181	182	184	186
41	166	168	170	171	173	175	177	178	180	182	183	185	186
42	167	169	170	172	174	175	177	178	180	182	184	185	187
43	167	169	171	172	174	176	178	179	181	182	184	186	187
44	168	170	171	173	174	176	178	179	181	183	185	186	187
45	168	170	172	173	175	177	178	180	182	183	185	186	188

The multiple-choice section of the PPST Writing Test is scored very much the same as the other sections. However, the essay portion of the exam is read and rated by two writing experts. The essays are scored on a six-point scale, with six being an exceptional essay and one being an unsatisfactory essay. Zero is used for essays that are completely off-topic. Therefore, provided that you respond to the topic, your score will be between 2 and 12. You may use the table above to determine your scaled score by locating the number of questions you've answered correctly in the first column, and following that to the row represented by your essay score.

Recently reported average scores for the PPST are as follows:

Reading Test: 177

Mathematics Test: 178

Writing Test: 176

STUDYING FOR THE PPST

Everyone has a different learning environment that works best for them, and it is very important that you find the one that works best for you. Some students prefer to set aside a few hours every morning to study, while others prefer to study at night before going to sleep. Some students are capable of studying while waiting on line, or even while eating lunch. Other students require absolute silence in a well-lit room to study. Only you can determine what works best for you, but be consistent and use your time wisely. Develop a routine that works for you and stick to it.

When you are taking the practice tests, you should try to duplicate the testing conditions as closely as possible. Turn off the television and radio, and sit down in a quiet area as free from distraction as possible. Make sure to time yourself, and allow yourself no more time for the practice tests than you would have on the actual exam. Start off by setting a timer for the time that is allotted to each section of the exam, and be sure to reset it for the appropriate amount of time whenever you start a new section.

As you complete each practice test, score your exam and thoroughly review the detailed explanations to all the questions you answered incorrectly. Concentrate on one question at a time by reviewing the question and the explanation, and by studying the appropriate review material until you are confident that you completely understand the material.

Keep track of your scores on the individual practice tests. By doing this, you will be able to gauge your progress and discover general weak-

nesses in particular sections. You should carefully study the review sections that cover your areas of difficulty to help reinforce your skills in those areas.

TEST-TAKING TIPS

You have probably taken standardized tests like the PPST before, however you may still be experiencing some anxiety about the exam. This is perfectly normal and there are several ways to help alleviate it listed below.

- **Become comfortable with the format of the PPST.** When you are taking the practice tests, simulate the testing conditions as closely as possible. Stay calm and pace yourself. After simulating the test a few times, you will boost your chances of doing well. The test-taking experience will not be unfamiliar to you, and this will allow you to take the PPST with much more confidence.

- **Read all of the possible answers.** Just because you think you have found the correct response, do not automatically assume that it is the best answer. Read all the answer choices so that you do not make a mistake by jumping to conclusions.

- **Use the process of elimination.** Go through all the answer choices and eliminate obviously incorrect answers immediately. If you are able to eliminate one or two answer choices, you will be able to make an educated guess.

- **Work quickly and steadily.** You only have one hour for each section, so pace yourself carefully. Do not spend too much time on any one question. By taking the practice tests included in this book, you will become better able to manage your time.

- **Learn the directions and format of each test section.** Familiarizing yourself with the directions and format of each section will not only save time, but also help you avoid nervousness and the mistakes that nervousness can cause.

- **Be sure that the answer oval you are marking corresponds to the number of the question in the test booklet.** Since the multiple-choice sections of the PPST are graded by a machine, misplacing one response can throw off your entire score. Periodically check to be sure that you have not unintentionally left a space blank, or filled in two answer choices for a single question.

- **Guess, guess, guess.** You are not penalized for incorrect responses on the PPST. Your score is based on the number of questions you have answered correctly. Therefore, even if you have absolutely no idea what the answer to a given question might be, you still have a 20 percent chance of being right. If you are able to eliminate even one or two of the answer choices, your chances of guessing correctly are greatly increased.

THE DAY OF THE TEST

Before the Test

On the day of the test, you should wake up early after a good night's rest. You should have a good breakfast and dress in layers that can be removed or added as the conditions in the testing center require. You do not want to be distracted by hunger, or by being too cold or too warm. Plan to arrive at the testing center early. This will allow you to relax and collect your thoughts before the test, and will also spare you the anguish that comes with being late. As an added incentive to make sure that you arrive early, keep in mind that NO ONE WILL BE ADMITTED INTO THE TESTING CENTER AFTER THE TEST HAS BEGUN.

Before you leave for the testing center, make sure that you have your admission ticket and another form of identification, which must contain a recent photograph, your name, and signature (i.e., your driver's license, student identification card, or alien registration card). You will not be admitted to the testing center if you do not have proper identification.

YOU MUST ALSO BRING SEVERAL SHARPENED NUMBER 2 PENCILS, AS NONE WILL BE PROVIDED AT THE TESTING CENTER.

If you like, you may wear a watch to the testing center. However, you should not wear a watch that has an audible alarm or signal, as it may distract the other candidates. No dictionaries, notebooks, briefcases, or packages will be permitted into the testing center. Drinking, smoking, and eating are also prohibited in the testing center.

During the Test

Once you enter the test center, follow all the rules and instructions given by the test supervisor. If you do not, you risk being dismissed from the testing center and having your scores canceled.

When all the testing materials have been distributed, the test supervisor will give you directions for filling out your answer sheet. You must fill out this sheet carefully, since this information will be printed on your score report. Fill out your name exactly as it appears on the admission ticket, unless otherwise instructed.

Remember that you can write in your test booklet, and no scrap paper will be provided. Mark your answers in the appropriate spaces on the answer sheet. Each numbered row will contain five ovals corresponding to each answer choice for that question. Fill in the oval which corresponds to your answer darkly, completely, and neatly. You may change your answer, but remember to remove the old answer completely. Only one answer should be marked for each question. This is very important, because the answer sheets are machine scored, and stray marks could cause the machine to score your answers incorrectly.

PPST
Pre-Professional Skills Tests

Chapter 2
Reading
Comprehension
Review

Chapter 2

READING COMPREHENSION REVIEW

    I. STRATEGIES FOR THE READING SECTION

    II. A FOUR-STEP APPROACH

    III. VOCABULARY ENHANCER

This review was developed to prepare you for the Reading Section of the PPST. You will be guided through a step-by-step approach to attacking reading passages and questions. Also included are tips to help you quickly and accurately answer the questions which will appear in this section. By studying our review, you will greatly increase your chances of achieving a passing score on the Reading Section of the PPST.

Remember, the more you know about the skills tested, the better you will perform on the test. In this section, the skills you will be tested on are

- determining what a word or phrase means;

- determining main ideas;

- recognizing supporting details;

- determining purpose;

- determining point of view;

- organizing ideas in the passage; and

- evaluating the validity of the author's argument.

To help you master these skills, we present examples of the types of questions you will encounter and explanations of how to answer them. A drill section is also provided for further practice. Even if you are sure you will perform well on this section, make sure to complete the drills, as they will help sharpen your skills.

THE PASSAGES

The eight reading passages in the Reading Section are specially designed to be on the level of the types of material that you will encounter in college textbooks. They will present you with very diverse subjects. Although you will not be expected to have prior knowledge of the information presented in the passages, you will be expected to know the fundamental reading comprehension techniques presented in this chapter. Only your ability to read and comprehend material will be tested.

THE QUESTIONS

Each passage will be followed by a number of questions, with the total number appearing in the section being 40 questions. The questions will ask you to make determinations based on what you have read. You will encounter 9 main types of questions in this test. These questions will ask you to

1. determine which of the given answer choices best expresses the main idea of the passage;

2. determine the author's purpose in writing the passage;

3. determine which fact best supports the writer's main idea;

4. know the difference between fact and opinion in a statement;

5. organize the information in the passage;

6. determine which of the answer choices best summarizes the information presented in the passage;

7. recall information from the passage;

8. analyze cause-and-effect relationships based on information in the passage;

9. determine the definition of a word as it is used in the passage.

I. STRATEGIES FOR THE READING SECTION

You should follow this plan of attack when answering Reading Section questions.

Before the test, this is your plan of attack:

| ➤ Step 1 | Study our review to build your reading skills. |

| ➤ Step 2 | Make sure to study and learn the directions to save yourself time during the actual test. You should simply skim them when beginning the section. The directions will read similar to the following. |

DIRECTIONS: You will encounter eight passages in this section of the test, each followed by a number of questions. Only **ONE** answer to each question is the **best** answer, although more than one answer may appear to be correct. There are 40 multiple-choice questions in this section. Choose your answers carefully and mark them on your answer sheet. Make sure that the space you are marking corresponds to the answer you have chosen.

When reading the passage, this is your plan of attack:

| ➤ Step 1 | Read quickly while keeping in mind that questions will follow. |

| ➤ Step 2 | Uncover the main idea or theme of the passage. Many times it is contained within the first few lines of the passage. |

| ➤ Step 3 | Uncover the main idea of each paragraph. Usually it is contained in either the first or last sentence of the paragraph. |

| ➤ Step 4 | Skim over the detailed points of the passage while circling key words or phrases. These are words or phrases such as *but, on the other hand, although, however, yet,* and *except.* |

When answering the questions, this is your plan of attack:

| ➤ Step 1 | Attack each question one at a time. Read it carefully. |

> ► Step 2   If the question is asking for a general answer, such as the main idea or the purpose of the passage, answer it immediately.

> ► Step 3   If the question is asking for an answer that can only be found in a specific place in the passage, save it for last since this type of question requires you to go back to the passage and therefore takes more of your time.

> ► Step 4   For the detail-oriented questions, try to eliminate or narrow down your choices before looking for the answer in the passage.

> ► Step 5   Go back into the passage, utilizing the key words you circled, to find the answer.

> ► Step 6   Any time you cannot find the answer, use the process of elimination to the greatest extent and then guess.

ADDITIONAL TIPS

- Look over all the passages first and then attack the passages that seem easiest and most interesting.

- Identify and underline what sentences are the main ideas of each paragraph.

- When a question asks you to draw inferences, your answer should reflect what is implied in the passage, rather than what is directly stated.

- Use the context of the sentence to find the meaning of an unfamiliar word.

- Identify what sentences are example sentences and label them with an "E." Determine whether or not the writer is using facts or opinions.

- Circle key transitions and identify dominant patterns of organization.

- Make your final response and move on. Don't dawdle or get frustrated by the really troubling passages. If you haven't gotten answers after two attempts, answer as best you can and move on.

- If you have time at the end, go back to the passages that were difficult and review them again.

II. A FOUR-STEP APPROACH

When you take the Reading Section of the PPST, you will have two tasks:

1. to read the passage and

2. to answer the questions.

Of the two, carefully reading the passage is the most important; answering the questions is based on an understanding of the passage. Here is a four-step approach to reading:

Step 1: preview,

Step 2: read actively,

Step 3: review the passage, and

Step 4: answer the questions.

You should study the following exercises and use these four steps when you complete the Reading Section of the PPST.

STEP 1: Preview

A preview of the reading passage will give you a purpose and a reason for reading; previewing is a good strategy to use in test-taking. Before beginning to read the passage (usually a four-minute activity if you preview and review), you should take about 30 seconds to look over the passage and questions. An effective way to preview the passage is to read quickly the first sentence of each paragraph, the concluding sentence of the passage, and the questions — not all the answers — following the passage. A passage is given below. Practice previewing the passage by reading the first sentence of each paragraph and the last line of the passage.

PASSAGE

1   That the area of obscenity and pornography is a difficult one for the Supreme Court is well documented. The Court's numerous attempts to define obscenity have proven unworkable and left the decision to the subjective preferences of the justices. Perhaps Justice

5   Stewart put it best when, after refusing to define obscenity, he declared, "But I know it when I see it." Does the Court literally have to see it to know it? Specifically, what role does the fact-pattern, including the materials' medium, play in the Court's decision?

Several recent studies employ fact-pattern analysis in modeling
10 the Court's decision making. These studies examine the fact-pattern
or case characteristics, often with ideological and attitudinal factors,
as a determinant of the decision reached by the Court. In broad terms,
these studies owe their theoretical underpinnings to attitude theory.
As the name suggests, attitude theory views the Court's attitudes as
15 an explanation of its decisions.

These attitudes, however, do not operate in a vacuum. As Spaeth
explains, "the activation of an attitude involves both an object and the
situation in which that object is encountered." The objects to which
the court directs its attitudes are litigants. The situation — the subject
20 matter of the case — can be defined in broad or narrow terms. One
may define the situation as an entire area of the law (e.g., civil liber-
ties issues). On an even broader scale the situation may be defined as
the decision to grant certiorari or whether to defect from a minimum-
winning coalition.

25 Defining the situation with such broad strokes, however, does
not allow one to control for case content. In many specific issue
areas, the cases present strikingly similar patterns. In examining the
Court's search and seizure decisions, Segal found a relatively small
number of situational and case characteristic variables explain a high
30 proportion of the Court's decisions.

Despite Segal's success, efforts to verify the applicability of
fact-pattern analysis in other issue areas and using broad-based factors have been slow in forthcoming. Renewed interest in obscenity
and pornography by federal and state governments, the academic
35 community, and numerous antipornography interest groups indicates
the Court's decisions in this area deserve closer examination.

The Court's obscenity and pornography decisions also present
an opportunity to study the Court's behavior in an area where the
Court has granted significant decision-making authority to the states.
40 In *Miller vs. California* (1973) the Court announced the importance
of local community standards in obscenity determinations. The
Court's subsequent behavior may suggest how the Court will react in
other areas where it has chosen to defer to the states (e.g., abortion).

QUESTIONS

1. The main idea of the passage is best stated in which of the following?

   (A) The Supreme Court has difficulty convicting those who violate
   obscenity laws.

(B) The current definitions for obscenity and pornography provided by the Supreme Court are unworkable.

(C) Fact-pattern analysis is insufficient for determining the attitude of the Court toward the issues of obscenity and pornography.

(D) Despite the difficulties presented by fact-pattern analysis, Justice Segal found the solution in the patterns of search and seizure decisions.

2. The main purpose of the writer in this passage is to

(A) convince the reader that the Supreme Court is making decisions about obscenity based on their subjective views only.

(B) explain to the reader how fact-pattern analysis works with respect to cases of obscenity and pornography.

(C) define obscenity and pornography for the layperson.

(D) demonstrate the role fact-pattern analysis plays in determining the Supreme Court's attitude about cases in obscenity and pornography.

3. Of the following, which fact best supports the writer's contention that the Court's decisions in the areas of obscenity and pornography deserve closer scrutiny?

(A) The fact that a Supreme Court Justice said, "I know it when I see it."

(B) Recent studies that employ fact-pattern analysis in modeling the Court's decision-making process.

(C) The fact that attitudes do not operate in a vacuum.

(D) The fact that federal and state governments, interest groups, and the academic community show renewed interest in the obscenity and pornography decisions by the Supreme Court.

4. Among the following statements, which states an opinion expressed by the writer rather than a fact?

(A) That the area of obscenity and pornography is a difficult one for the Supreme Court is well documented.

(B) The objects to which a court directs its attitudes are the litigants.

(C) In many specific issue areas, the cases present strikingly similar patterns.

(D) The Court's subsequent behavior may suggest how the Court will react in other legal areas.

5. The list of topics below that best reflects the organization of the topics of the passage is

(A)   I.   The difficulties of the Supreme Court

        II.   Several recent studies

       III.   Spaeth's definition of "attitude"

       IV.   The similar patterns of cases

        V.   Other issue areas

       VI.   The case of *Miller vs. California*

(B)   I   The Supreme Court, obscenity, and fact-pattern analysis

        II.   Fact-pattern analyses and attitude theory

       III.   The definition of "attitude" for the Court

       IV.   The definition of "situation"

        V.   The breakdown in fact-pattern analysis

       VI.   Studying Court behavior

(C)   I.   Justice Stewart's view of pornography

        II.   Theoretical underpinnings

       III.   A minimum-winning coalition

       IV.   Search and seizure decisions

        V.   Renewed interest in obscenity and pornography

       VI.   The importance of local community standards

(D)   I.   The Court's numerous attempts to define obscenity

        II.   Case characteristics

       III.   The subject matter of cases

       IV.   The Court's proportion of decisions

        V.   Broad-based factors

       VI.   Obscenity determination

6. Which paragraph below is the best summary of the passage?

(A) The Supreme Court's decision-making process with respect to obscenity and pornography has become too subjective. Fact-pattern analyses, used to determine the overall attitude of the Court, reveal only broad-based attitudes on the part of the Court toward the situations of obscenity cases. But these patterns cannot fully account for the Court's attitudes toward case content. Research is not conclusive that fact-pattern analyses work when applied to legal areas. Renewed public and local interest suggests continued study and close examination of how the Court makes decisions. Delegating authority to the states may reflect patterns for Court decisions in other socially sensitive areas.

(B) Though subjective, the Supreme Court decisions are well documented. Fact-pattern analyses reveal the attitude of the Supreme Court toward its decisions in cases. Spaeth explains that an attitude involves both an object and a situation. For the Court, the situation may be defined as the decision to grant certiorari. Cases present strikingly similar patterns, and a small number of variables explain a high proportion of the Court's decisions. Segal has made an effort to verify the applicability of fact-pattern analysis with some success. The Court's decisions on obscenity and pornography suggest weak Court behavior, such as in *Miller vs. California.*

(C) To determine what obscenity and pornography mean to the Supreme Court, we must use fact-pattern analysis. Fact-pattern analysis reveals the ideas that the Court uses to operate in a vacuum. The litigants and the subject matter of cases is defined in broad terms (such as an entire area of law) to reveal the Court's decision-making process. Search and seizure cases reveal strikingly similar patterns, leaving the Court open to grant certiorari effectively. Renewed public interest in the Court's decisions proves how the Court will react in the future.

(D) Supreme Court decisions about pornography and obscenity are under examination and are out of control. The Court has to see the case to know it. Fact-pattern analyses reveal that the Court can only define cases in narrow terms, thus revealing individual egotism on the part of the Justices. As a result of strikingly similar patterns in search and seizure cases, the Court should be studied further for its weakness in delegating authority to state courts, as in the case of *Miller vs. California.*

7. Based on the passage, the rationale for fact-pattern analyses arises out of what theoretical groundwork?

    (A) Subjectivity theory

    (B) The study of cultural norms

    (C) Attitude theory

    (D) Cybernetics

8. Based on data in the passage, what would most likely be the major cause for the difficulty in pinning down the Supreme Court's attitude toward cases of obscenity and pornography?

    (A) The personal opinions of the Court Justices

    (B) The broad nature of the situations of the cases

    (C) The ineffective logistics of certiorari

    (D) The inability of the Court to resolve the variables presented by individual case content

9. In the context of the passage, *subjective* might be most nearly defined as

    (A) personal.

    (B) wrong.

    (C) focused.

    (D) objective.

By previewing the passage, you should have learned the following:

- The fact that the area of obscenity and pornography is a difficult one for the Supreme Court is well documented.

- Several recent studies employ fact-pattern analysis in modeling the Court's decision making.

- These attitudes are not formed and expressed in a vacuum.

- Defining the situation with such broad strokes does not allow one to control for case content.

- Despite Segal's success, efforts to verify the applicability of fact-pattern analysis in other issue areas and using broad-based factors have been slow in coming.

- The Court's obscenity and pornography decisions also present an opportunity to study the Court's behavior in an area where the Court has granted significant decision-making authority to the states.

- The Court's subsequent behavior may suggest how the Court will react in other areas where it has chosen to defer to the states (e.g., abortion).

These few sentences tell you much about the entire passage.

As you begin to examine the passage, you should first determine the main idea of the passage and underline it, so that you can easily refer back to it if a question requires you to do so (see question 1). The main idea should be found in the first paragraph of the passage, and may even be the first sentence. From what you have read thus far, you now know that the main idea of this passage is that: the Supreme Court has difficulty in making obscenity and pornography decisions.

In addition, you also know that recent studies have used fact-pattern analysis in modeling the Court's decision. You have learned also that attitudes do not operate independently and that case content is important. The feasibility of using fact-pattern analysis in other areas and broad-based factors have not been quickly verified. To study the behavior of the Court in an area in which they have granted significant decision-making authority to the states, one has only to consider the obscenity and pornography decisions. In summary, the author suggests that the Court's subsequent behavior may suggest how the Court will react in those other areas in which decision-making authority has previously been granted to the states. As you can see, having this information will make the reading of the passage much easier.

You should have also looked at the stem of the question in your preview. You do not necessarily need to spend time reading the answers to each question in your preview. The stem alone can help to guide you as you read.

The stems in this case are:

1. The main idea of the passage is best stated in which of the following?

2. The main purpose of the writer in this passage is to

3. Of the following, which fact best supports the writer's contention that the Court's decisions in the areas of obscenity and pornography deserve closer scrutiny?

4. Among the following statements, which states an opinion, rather than a fact, expressed by the writer?

5. The list of topics below that best reflects the organization of the topics of the passage is

6. Which paragraph below is the best summary of the passage?

7. Based on the passage, the rationale for fact-pattern analyses arises out of what theoretical groundwork?

8. Based on data in the passage, what would most likely be the major cause for the difficulty in pinning down the Supreme Court's attitude toward cases of obscenity and pornography?

9. In the context of the passage, *subjective* might be most nearly defined as

STEP 2: Read Actively

After your preview, you are now ready to read actively. This means that as you read, you will be engaged in such things as underlining important words, topic sentences, main ideas, and words denoting tone of the passage. If you think underlining can help you save time and help you remember the main ideas, feel free to use your pencil.

Read carefully the first sentence of each paragraph since this often contains the topic of the paragraph. You may wish to underline each topic sentence.

During this stage, you should also determine the writer's purpose in writing the passage (see question 2), as this will help you focus on the main points and the writer's key points in the organization of a passage. You can determine the author's purpose by asking yourself, Does *the relationship* between the writer's main idea plus evidence the writer uses answer one of four questions?

* What is the writer's overall primary goal or objective?

* Is the writer trying primarily to persuade you by proving or using facts to make a case for an idea? (P)

* Is the writer trying only primarily to inform and enlighten you about an idea, object, or event? (I)

* Is the writer attempting primarily to amuse you? To keep you fascinated? To keep you laughing? (A)

Read these examples and see if you can decide what the primary purpose of the following statements might be.

(A) Jogging too late in life can cause more health problems than it solves. I will allow that the benefits of jogging are many: lowered blood pressure, increased vitality, better cardiovascular health, and better muscle tone. However, an older person may have a history of injury or chronic ailments that makes jogging counterproductive. For example, the elderly jogger may have hardening of the arteries, emphysema, or undiscovered aneurysms just waiting to burst and cause stroke or death. Chronic arthritis in the joints will only be aggravated by persistent irritation and use. Moreover, for those of us with injuries sustained in our youth — such as torn Achilles' tendons or torn knee cartilage — jogging might just make a painful life more painful, cancelling out the benefits the exercise is intended to produce.

(B) Jogging is a sporting activity that exercises all the main muscle groups of the body. That the arms, legs, buttock, and torso voluntary muscles are engaged goes without question. Running down a path makes you move your upper body as well as your lower body muscles. People do not often take into account, however, how the involuntary muscle system is also put through its paces. The heart, diaphragm, even the eye and face muscles, take part as we hurl our bodies through space at speeds up to five miles per hour over distances as long as 26 miles.

(C) It seems to me that jogging styles are as identifying as fingerprints! People seem to be as individual in the way they run as they are in personality. Here comes the Duck, waddling down the track, little wings going twice as fast as the feet in an effort to stay upright. At about the quarter mile mark, I see the Penguin, quite natty in the latest jogging suit, body stiff as a board from neck to ankles and the ankles flexing a mile a minute to cover the yards. And down there at the half-mile post — there comes the Giraffe — a tall fellow in a spotted electric yellow outfit, whose long strides cover about a dozen yards each, and whose neck waves around under some old army camouflage hat that probably served its time in a surplus store in the Bronx rather than in Desert Storm. Once you see the animals in the jogger woods once, you can identify them from miles away just by seeing their gait. And by the way, be careful whose hoof you're stepping on, it may be mine!

In (A) the writer makes a statement that a number of people would debate and which isn't clearly demonstrated in science or common knowledge. In fact, common wisdom usually maintains the opposite thesis. Many would say that jogging improves the health of the aging — even slows down the aging process. As soon as you see a writer point to or identify *an issue open to debate* and standing in need of proof, s/he is setting out to persuade you of one side or the other. You'll notice, too, that the writer in this case takes a stand, here. It's almost as if s/he is saying, "I have concluded that . . ." But a thesis or arguable idea is only a *hypothesis* until evidence is summoned by the writer to prove it. Effective arguments are based on serious, factual, or demonstrable evidence, not opinion.

In (B) the writer is just stating a fact. This is not a matter for debate. From here, the writer's evidence is to *explain* and *describe* what is meant by the fact. S/he proceeds to *analyze* (break down into its elements) the way the different muscle groups come into play or do work when jogging, thus explaining the fact stated as a main point in the opening sentence. That jogging exercises all the muscle groups is not in question or a matter of debate. Besides taking the form of explaining how something works, what parts it is made of (for example, the basic parts of a bicycle are...), writers may show how the idea, object, or event functions. A writer may use this information to prove something. But if s/he doesn't argue to prove a debatable point, then the purpose must be either to inform (as here) or to entertain.

In (C) the writer is taking a stand, but s/he is not attempting to prove anything, merely pointing to a lighthearted observation. Moreover, all of the examples s/he uses to support the statement are either fanciful, funny, odd, or peculiar to the writer's particular vision. Joggers aren't really animals, after all.

Make sure to examine all of the facts that the author uses to support his/her main idea. This will allow you to decide whether or not the writer has made a case, and what sort of purpose s/he supports. Look for supporting details — facts, examples, illustrations, the testimony or research of experts, that are about the topic in question and *show* what the writer *says* is so. In fact, paragraphs and theses consist of *show* and *tell*. The writer *tells* you something is so or not so and then *shows* you facts, illustrations, expert testimony, or experience to back up what s/he says is or is not so. As you determine where the author's supporting details are, you may want to label them with an "S" so that you can refer back to them easily when answering questions (see question 3).

It is also important for you to be able to recognize the difference

between the statements of fact presented and statements of the author's opinion. You will be tested on this skill in this section of the test (see question 4). Let's look at the following examples. In each case ask yourself if you are reading a fact or an opinion.

1. Some roses are red.

2. Roses are the most beautiful flower on earth.

3. After humans smell roses, they fall in love.

4. Roses are the worst plants to grow in your backyard.

Number 1 is a fact. All you have to do is go look at the evidence. Go to a florist. You will see that number 1 is true. A fact is anything which can be demonstrated to be true in reality or which has been demonstrated to be true in reality and is documented by others. For example, the moon is in orbit about 250,000 miles from the earth.

Number 2 is an opinion. The writer claims this as truth, but since it is an abstract quality (beauty), it remains to be seen. Others will hold different opinions. This is a matter of taste, not fact.

Number 3 is an opinion. There is probably some time-related coincidence between these two, but there is no verifiable or repeatable and observable evidence that this is always true — at least not the way it is true that if you throw a ball into the air, it will always come back down to earth if left on its own without interference. Opinions have a way of sounding absolute, are held by the writer with confidence, but are not backed up by factual evidence.

Number 4, though perhaps sometimes true, is a matter of opinion. Many variables contribute to the health of a plant in a garden: soil, temperature range, amount of moisture, number, and kinds of bugs. This is a debatable point that the writer would have to prove.

As you read, you should note the structure of the passage. There are several common structures for the passages. Some of these structures are described below.

Main Types of Paragraph Structures

1. The structure is a main idea plus supporting arguments.

2. The structure is a main idea plus examples.

3. The structure includes comparisons or contrasts.

4. There is a pro and a con structure.

5. The structure is chronological.

6. The structure has several different aspects of one idea. For example, a passage on education in the United States in the 1600s and 1700s might first define education, then describe colonial education, then give information about separation of church and state, and then outline the tax opposition and support arguments. Being able to recognize these structures will help you recognize how the author has organized the passage.

Examining the structure of the passage will help you answer questions that ask you to organize (see question 5) the information in the passage, or to summarize (see question 6) the information presented in that passage.

For example, if you see a writer using a transitional pattern that reflects a sequence moving forward in time, such as "In 1982 . . . Then, in the next five years . . . A decade later, in 1997, the xxxx will . . ." chances are the writer is telling a story, history, or the like. Writers often use transitions of classification to analyze an idea, object, or event. They may say something like, "The first part . . . Secondly . . . Thirdly . . . Finally." You may then ask yourself what is this analysis for? To explain or to persuade me of something? These transitional patterns may also help reveal the relationship of one part of a passage to another. For example, a writer may be writing "on the one hand, . . . on the other hand . . ." This should alert you to the fact that the writer is comparing two things or contrasting them. What for? Is one better than the other? Worse?

By understanding the *relationship* among the main point, transitions, and supporting information, you may more readily determine the pattern of organization as well as the writer's purpose in a given piece of writing.

As with the paragraph examples above showing the difference among possible purposes, you must look at the relationship between the facts or information presented (that's the show part) and what the writer is trying to point out to you (that's the tell part) with that data. For example, in the data given in number 6 above, the discussion presented about education in the 1600s might be used

- to prove that it was a failure (a form of argument),

- to show that it consisted of these elements (an analysis of the status of education during that time), or

- to show that education during that time was silly.

To understand the author's purpose, the main point and the evidence

that supports it must be considered together to be understood. In number 6, no statement appears which controls these disparate areas of information. To be meaningful, a controlling main point is needed. You need to know that that main point is missing. You need to be able to distinguish between the writer showing data and the writer telling or making a point.

In the two paragraphs below, consider the different relationship between the same data above and the controlling statement, and how that controlling statement changes the discussion from explanation to argument:

(A) Colonial education was different than today's and consisted of several elements. Education in those days meant primarily studying the three "r's" (reading, writing, and arithmetic) and the Bible. The church and state were more closely aligned with one another — education was, after all, for the purpose of serving God better, not to make more money.

(B) Colonial "education" was really just a way to create a captive audience for the Church. Education in those days meant studying the three "r's" in order to learn God's word — the Bible — not commerce. The Church and state were closely aligned with one another, and what was good for the Church was good for the state — or else you were excommunicated, which kept you out of Heaven for sure.

The same information areas are brought up in both cases, but in (A) the writer treats it analytically (. . ."consisted of several elements" . . .), not taking any real debatable stand on the issue. What is, is. However, the controlling statement in (B) puts forth a volatile hypothesis, and then uses the same information to support that hypothesis.

STEP 3: Review the Passage

After you finish reading actively, take 10 or 20 seconds to look over the main idea and the topic sentences that you have underlined, and the key words and phrases you have marked. Now you are ready to enter Step 4 and answer the questions.

STEP 4: Answer the Questions

In Step 2, Read Actively, you gathered enough information from the passage to answer questions dealing with main idea, purpose, support, fact vs. opinion, organization, and summarization. Let's look again at these questions.

Main Idea Questions

Looking back at the questions which follow the passage, you see that question 1 is a "main idea" question:

1. The main idea of the passage is best stated in which of the following?

   (A) The Supreme Court has difficulty convicting those who violate obscenity laws.

   (B) The current definitions for obscenity and pornography provided by the Supreme Court are unworkable.

   (C) Fact-pattern analysis is insufficient for determining the attitude of the Court toward the issues of obscenity and pornography.

   (D) Despite the difficulties presented by fact-pattern analysis, Justice Segal found the solution in the patterns of search and seizure decisions.

In answering the question, you see that answer choice (C) is correct. The writer uses the second, third, fourth, and fifth paragraphs to show how fact-pattern analysis is an ineffective determinant of Court attitude toward obscenity and pornography.

Answer (A) is incorrect. Nothing is ever said directly about "convicting" persons accused of obscenity, only that the Court has difficulty defining it.

Choice (B) is also incorrect. Though it is stated as a fact by the writer, it is only used as an effect that leads the writer to examine how fact-pattern analysis does or does not work to reveal the "cause" or attitude of the Court toward obscenity and pornography.

Finally, answer choice (D) is incorrect. The statement is contrary to what Segal found when he examined search and seizure cases.

Purpose Questions

In examining question 2, you see that you must determine the author's purpose in writing the passage:

2. The main purpose of the writer in this passage is to

   (A) convince the reader that the Supreme Court is making decisions about obscenity based on their subjective views only.

   (B) explain to the reader how fact-pattern analysis works with respect to cases of obscenity and pornography.

(C) define obscenity and pornography for the layperson.

(D) demonstrate the role fact-pattern analysis plays in determining the Supreme Court's attitude about cases in obscenity and pornography.

Looking at the answer choices, you see that choice (D) is correct. Though the writer never states it directly, s/he summons data consistently to show that fact-pattern analysis only gives us part of the picture, or "broad strokes" about the Court's attitude, but cannot account for the attitude toward individual cases.

Choice (A) is incorrect. The writer doesn't try to convince us of this fact, but merely states it as an opinion resulting from the evidence derived from the "well-documented" background to the problem.

(B) is also incorrect. The writer does more than just explain the role of fact-pattern analysis, but rather shows how it cannot fully apply.

The passage is about the Court's difficulty in defining these terms, not the man or woman in the street. Nowhere do definitions for these terms appear. Therefore, choice (C) is incorrect.

Support Questions

Question 3 requires you to analyze the author's supporting details:

3. Of the following, which fact best supports the writer's contention that the Court's decisions in the areas of obscenity and pornography deserve closer scrutiny?

    (A) The fact that a Supreme Court Justice said, "I know it when I see it."

    (B) Recent studies that employ fact-pattern analysis in modeling the Court's decision-making process.

    (C) The fact that attitudes do not operate in a vacuum.

    (D) The fact that federal and state governments, interest groups, and the academic community show renewed interest in the obscenity and pornography decisions by the Supreme Court.

To answer this question, let's look at the answer choices. Choice (D) must be correct. In the fifth paragraph, the writer states that the "renewed interest" — a real and observable fact — from these groups "indicates the Court's decisions . . . deserve closer examination," another way of saying scrutiny.

Answer (A) is incorrect. The writer uses this remark to show how the Court cannot effectively define obscenity and pornography, relying on "subjective preferences" to resolve issues.

In addition, choice (B) is incorrect because the writer points to the data in (D), not fact-pattern analyses, to prove this.

(C), too, is incorrect. Although it is true, the writer makes this point to show how fact-pattern analysis doesn't help clear up the real-world "situation" in which the Court must make its decisions.

Fact vs. Opinion Questions

By examining question 4, you can see that you are required to know the difference between fact and opinion:

4. Among the following statements, which states an opinion expressed by the writer rather than a fact?

    (A) That the area of obscenity and pornography is a difficult one for the Supreme Court is well documented.

    (B) The objects to which a court directs its attitudes are the litigants.

    (C) In many specific issue areas, the cases present strikingly similar patterns.

    (D) The Court's subsequent behavior may suggest how the Court will react in other legal areas.

Keeping in mind that an opinion is something that cannot be proven to hold true in all circumstances, you can determine that choice (D) is correct. It is the only statement among the four for which the evidence is yet to be gathered. It is the writer's opinion that this may be a way to predict the Court's attitudes.

(A), (B), and (C) are all taken from data or documentation in existence already in the world, and are, therefore, incorrect.

Organization Questions

Question 5 asks you to organize given topics to reflect the organization of the passage:

5. The list of topics below that best reflects the organization of the topics of the passage is

    (A)   I.   The difficulties of the Supreme Court

II.   Several recent studies

III. Spaeth's definition of "attitude"

IV.   The similar patterns of cases

V.   Other issue areas

VI.   The case of *Miller vs. California*

(B)   I.   The Supreme Court, obscenity, and fact-pattern analysis

II.   Fact-pattern analyses and attitude theory

III. The definition of "attitude" for the Court

IV.   The definition of "situation"

V.   The breakdown in fact-pattern analysis

VI.   Studying Court behavior.

(C)   I.   Justice Stewart's view of pornography

II.   Theoretical underpinnings

III. A minimum-winning coalition

IV.   Search and seizure decisions

V.   Renewed interest in obscenity and pornography

VI.   The importance of local community standards

(D)   I.   The Court's numerous attempts to define obscenity

II.   Case characteristics

III. The subject matter of cases

IV.   The Court's proportion of decisions

V.   Broad-based factors

VI.   Obscenity determination

After examining all of the choices, you will determine that choice (B) is the correct response. These topical areas lead directly to the implied thesis that the "role" of fact-pattern analysis is insufficient for determining the attitude of the Supreme Court in the areas of obscenity and pornography. (See question 1.)

Answer (A) is incorrect because the first topic stated in the list is not the topic of the first paragraph. It is too global. The first paragraph is about the difficulties the Court has with defining obscenity and how fact-pattern

analysis might be used to determine the Court's attitude and clear up the problem.

(C) is incorrect because each of the items listed in this topic list are supporting evidence or data for the real topic of each paragraph. (See the list in (B) for correct topics.) For example, Justice Stewart's statement about pornography is only cited to indicate the nature of the problem with obscenity for the Court. It is not the focus of the paragraph itself.

Finally, (D) is incorrect. As with choice (C) these are all incidental pieces of information or data used to make broader points.

Summarization Questions

To answer question 6, you must be able to summarize the passage:

6. Which paragraph below is the best summary of the passage?

(A) The Supreme Court's decision-making process with respect to obscenity and pornography has become too subjective. Fact-pattern analyses, used to determine the overall attitude of the Court, reveal only broad-based attitudes on the part of the Court toward the situations of obscenity cases. But these patterns cannot fully account for the Court's attitudes toward case content. Research is not conclusive that fact-pattern analyses work when applied to legal areas. Renewed public and local interest suggests continued study and close examination of how the Court makes decisions. Delegating authority to the states may reflect patterns for Court decisions in other socially sensitive areas.

(B) Though subjective, the Supreme Court decisions are well documented. Fact-pattern analyses reveal the attitude of the Supreme Court toward its decisions in cases. Spaeth explains that an attitude involves both an object and a situation. For the Court, the situation may be defined as the decision to grant certiorari. Cases present strikingly similar patterns, and a small number of variables explain a high proportion of the Court's decisions. Segal has made an effort to verify the applicability of fact-pattern analysis with some success. The Court's decisions on obscenity and pornography suggest weak Court behavior, such as in *Miller vs. California.*

(C) To determine what obscenity and pornography mean to the Supreme Court, we must use fact-pattern analysis. Fact-pattern analysis reveals the ideas that the Court uses to operate in a vacuum. The litigants and the subject matter of cases is defined in broad terms (such as an entire area of law) to reveal the

Court's decision-making process. Search and seizure cases reveal strikingly similar patterns, leaving the Court open to grant certiorari effectively. Renewed public interest in the Court's decisions proves how the Court will react in the future.

(D) Supreme Court decisions about pornography and obscenity are under examination and are out of control. The Court has to see the case to know it. Fact-pattern analyses reveal that the Court can only define cases in narrow terms, thus revealing individual egotism on the part of the Justices. As a result of strikingly similar patterns in search and seizure cases, the Court should be studied further for its weakness in delegating authority to state courts, as in the case of *Miller vs. California*.

The paragraph that best and most accurately reports what the writer demonstrated based on the implied thesis (see question 1) is answer choice (C) which is correct.

Choice (A) is incorrect. While it reflects some of the evidence presented in the passage, the passage does not imply that all Court decisions are subjective, just the ones about pornography and obscenity. Similarly, the writer does not suggest that delegating authority to the states as in *Miller vs. California* is a sign of some weakness, but merely that it is worthy of study as a tool for predicting or identifying the Court attitude.

Response (B) is also incorrect. The writer summons information over and over to show how fact-pattern analysis cannot pin down the Court's attitude toward case content.

(D) is incorrect. Nowhere does the writer say or suggest that the justice system is "out of control" or that the justices are "egotists," only that they are liable to be reduced to being "subjective" rather than based on an identifiable shared standard.

At this point, the four remaining question types must be discussed: recall questions (see question 7), cause/effect questions (see question 8), and definition questions (question 9). They are as follows:

Recall Questions

To answer question 7, you must be able to recall information from the passage:

7. Based on the passage, the rationale for fact-pattern analyses arises out of what theoretical groundwork?

(A) Subjectivity theory

(B) The study of cultural norms

(C) Attitude theory

(D) Cybernetics

The easiest way to answer this question is to refer back to the passage. In the second paragraph, the writer states that recent studies using fact-pattern analyses, "owe their theoretical underpinnings to attitude theory." Therefore, we can conclude that response (C) is correct.

Answer choices (A), (B), and (D) are incorrect, as they are never discussed or mentioned by the writer.

Cause/Effect Questions

Question 8 requires you to analyze a cause-and-effect relationship:

8. Based on data in the passage, what would most likely be the major cause for the difficulty in pinning down the Supreme Court's attitude toward cases of obscenity and pornography?

(A) The personal opinions of the Court Justices

(B) The broad nature of the situations of the cases

(C) The ineffective logistics of certiorari

(D) The inability of the Court to resolve the variables presented by individual case content

Choice (D) is correct, as it is precisely what fact-pattern analyses cannot resolve.

Response (A) is incorrect because no evidence is presented for this, only that they do make personal decisions.

Answer choice (B) is incorrect because this is one way in which fact-pattern analysis can be helpful.

Finally, (C) is only a statement about certiorari being difficult to administer, and this was never claimed about them by the writer in the first place.

Definition Questions

Returning to question 9, we can now determine an answer:

9. In the context of the passage, *subjective* might be most nearly defined as

(A) personal.

(B) wrong.

(C) focused.

(D) objective.

Choice (A) is best. By taking note of the example of Justice Stewart provided by the writer, we can see that Justice Stewart's comment is an example not of right or wrong. (He doesn't talk about right or wrong. He uses the verb "know" — whose root points primarily to *know*ledge, understanding, and insight, *not* ethical considerations.) He probably doesn't mean "focused by" since the focus is provided by the appearance or instance of the case itself. By noting the same word ending and the appearance of the root "object" — meaning an observable thing existing outside of ourselves in time and space, and comparing it with the root of subjective, "subject" — often pointing to something personally studied, we can begin to rule out "objective" as the opposite of "subjective." Usually when we talk about people's "preferences," we are referring to matters of taste or quality; preferences don't usually result from scientific study or reasoning but instead arise out of a combination of personal taste and idiosyncratic intuitions. Thus, (A) becomes the most likely choice.

(C) is incorrect because the Court's focus is already in place — obscenity and pornography.

Answer (B) is incorrect. Nothing is implied or stated about the rightness or wrongness of the decisions themselves. Rather, it is the definition of obscenity that seems "unworkable."

(D) is also incorrect. "Objective" is the direct opposite of "subjective." To reason based on the object of study is the opposite of reasoning based upon the beliefs, opinions, or ideas of the one viewing the object, rather than consideration of the evidence presented by the object itself *independent* of the observer.

You may not have been familiar with the word "subjective," but from your understanding of the writer's intent, you should have been able to figure out what s/he was after. Surrounding words and phrases almost always provide clues in determining a word's meaning. In addition, any examples that appear in the text may also provide some hints.

III. VOCABULARY ENHANCER

It is important to understand the meanings of all words — not just the ones you are asked to define. A good vocabulary is a strength that can help you perform well on all sections of this test. The following information will build your skills in determining the meanings of words.

SIMILAR FORMS AND SOUNDS

The complex nature of language sometimes makes reading difficult. Words often become confusing when they have similar forms and sounds. Indeed the author may have a correct meaning in mind, but an incorrect word choice can alter the meaning of the sentence or even make it totally illogical.

NO: Martha was always part of that *cliché*.

YES: Martha was always part of that *clique*.

(A *cliché* is a trite or hackneyed expression; a *clique* is an exclusive group of people.)

NO: The minister spoke of the soul's *immorality*.

YES: The minister spoke of the soul's *immortality*.

(*Immorality* means wickedness; *immortality* means imperishable or unending life.)

NO: Where is the nearest *stationary* store?

YES: Where is the nearest *stationery* store?

(*Stationary* means immovable; *stationery* is paper used for writing.)

Below are groups of words that are often confused because of their similar forms and sounds.

1.   accent – *v.* – to stress or emphasize (You must *accent* the last syllable.)

   ascent – *n.* – a climb or rise (John's *ascent* of the mountain was dangerous.)

   assent – *n.* – consent; compliance (We need your *assent* before we can go ahead with the plans.)

2.   accept – *v.* – to take something offered (She *accepted* the gift.)

   except – *prep.* – other than; but (Everyone was included in the plans *except* him.)

3.   advice – *n.* – opinion given as to what to do or how to handle a situation (Her sister gave her *advice* on what to say at the interview.)

advise – *v.* – to counsel (John's guidance counselor *advised* him on which colleges to apply to.)

4.   affect – *v.* – to influence (Mary's suggestion did not *affect* me.)

effect – 1. *v.*– to cause to happen (The plan was *effected* with great success.); 2. *n.* – result (The *effect* of the medicine is excellent.)

5.   allusion – *n.* – indirect reference (In the poem, there are many biblical *allusions*.)

illusion – *n.* – false idea or conception; belief or opinion not in accord with the facts (Greg was under the *illusion* that he could win the race after missing three weeks of practice.)

6.   already – *adv.* – previously (I had *already* read that novel.)

all ready – *adv.* + *adj.* – prepared (The family was *all ready* to leave on vacation.)

7.   altar – *n.* – table or stand used in religious rites (The priest stood at the *altar*.)

alter – *v.* – to change (Their plans were *altered* during the strike.)

8.   capital – 1. *n.* – a city where the government meets (The senators had a meeting in Albany, the *capital* of New York.); 2. money used in business (They had enough *capital* to develop the industry.)

capitol – *n.* – building in which the legislature meets (Senator Brown gave a speech at the *capitol* in Washington.)

9.   choose – *v.* – to select (Which camera did you *choose*?)

chose – (past tense, *choose*) (Susan *chose* to stay home.)

10.   cite – *v.* – to quote (The student *cited* evidence from the text.)

site – *n.* – location (They chose the *site* where the house would be built.)

11.   clothes – *n.* – garments (Because she got caught in the rain, her *clothes* were wet.)

cloths – *n.* – pieces of material (The *cloths* were used to wash the windows.)

12.   coarse – *adj.* – rough; unrefined (Sandpaper is *coarse*.)

course – 1. *n.* – path of action (She did not know what *course* would

solve the problem.); 2. passage (We took the long *course* to the lake.); 3. series of studies (We both enrolled in the physics *course*.); 4. part of a meal (She served a five *course* meal.)

13. consul – *n.* – a person appointed by the government to live in a foreign city and represent the citizenry and business interests of his native country there (The *consul* was appointed to Naples, Italy.)

    council – *n.* – a group used for discussion, advisement (The *council* decided to accept his letter of resignation.)

    counsel – *v.* – to advise (Tom *counsels* Jerry on tax matters.)

14. decent – *adj.* – proper; respectable (He was very *decent* about the entire matter.)

    descent – 1. *n.* – moving down (In Dante's *Inferno*, the *descent* into Hell was depicted graphically.); 2. ancestry (He is of Irish *descent*.)

15. device – 1. *n.* – plan; scheme (The *device* helped her win the race.); 2. invention (We bought a *device* that opens the garage door automatically.)

    devise – *v.* – to contrive (He *devised* a plan so John could not win.)

16. emigrate – *v.* – to go away from a country (Many Japanese *emigrated* from Japan in the late 1800s.)

    immigrate – *v.* – to come into a country (Her relatives *immigrated* to the United States after World War I.)

17. eminent – *n.* – prominent (He is an *eminent* member of the community.)

    imminent – *adj.* – impending (The decision is *imminent*.)

    immanent – *adj.* – existing within (Maggie believed that religious spirit is *immanent* in human beings.)

18. fair – 1. *adj.* – beautiful (She was a *fair* maiden.); 2. just (She tried to be *fair*.); 3. *n* – festival (There were many games at the *fair*.)

    fare – *n.* – amount of money paid for transportation (The city proposed that the subway *fare* be raised.)

19. forth – *adv.* – onward (The soldiers moved *forth* in the blinding snow.)

    fourth – *n., adj.* – 4th (She was the *fourth* runner-up in the beauty contest.)

20. its – possessive form of *it* (Our town must improve *its* roads.)

   it's – contraction of it is (*It's* time to leave the party.)

21. later – *adj., adv.* – at a subsequent date (We will take a vacation *later* this year.)

   latter – *n.* – second of the two (Susan can visit Monday or Tuesday. The *latter,* however, is preferable.)

22. lead – 1. *n.* – (led) a metal (The handgun was made of *lead.*); 2. *v.t.* – (leed) to show the way (The camp counselor *leads* the way to the picnic grounds.)

   led – past tense of *lead* (#2 above) (The dog *led* the way.)

23. loose – *adj.* – free; unrestricted (The dog was let *loose* by accident.)

   lose – *v.* – to suffer the loss of (He was afraid he would *lose* the race.)

24. moral – 1. *adj.* – virtuous (She is a *moral* woman with high ethical standards.); 2. *n.* – lesson taught by a story, incident, etc. (Most fables end with a *moral.*)

   morale – *n.* – mental condition (After the team lost the game, their *morale* was low.)

25. of – *prep.* – from (She is *of* French descent.)

   off – *adj.* – away; at a distance (The television fell *off* the table.)

26. passed – *v.* – having satisfied some requirement (He *passed* the test.)

   past – 1. *adj.* – gone by or elapsed in time (His *past* deeds got him in trouble.); 2. *n.* – a period of time gone by (His *past* was shady.); 3. *prep.* – beyond (She ran *past* the house.)

27. personal – *adj.* – private (Jack was unwilling to discuss his childhood; it was too *personal.*)

   personnel – *n.* – staff (The *personnel* at the department store was made up of young adults.)

28. principal – *n.* – head of a school (The *principal* addressed the graduating class.)

   principle – *n.* – the ultimate source, origin, or cause of something; a law, truth (The *principles* of physics were reviewed in class today.)

29. prophecy – *n.* – prediction of the future (His *prophecy* that he would become a doctor came true.)

prophesy – *v.* – to declare or predict (He *prophesied* that we would win the lottery.)

30. quiet – *adj.* – still; calm (At night all is *quiet*.)

   quite – *adv.* – really; truly (She is *quite* a good singer.)

   quit – *v.* – to free oneself (Peter had little time to spare so he *quit* the chorus.)

31. respectfully – *adv.* – with respect, honor, esteem (He declined the offer *respectfully*.)

   respectively – *adv.* – in the order mentioned (Jack, Susan and Jim, who are members of the club, were elected president, vice-president, and secretary *respectively*.)

32. stationary – *adj.* – immovable (The park bench is *stationary*.)

   stationery – *n.* – paper used for writing (The invitations were printed on yellow *stationery*.)

33. straight – *adj.* – not curved (The road was *straight*.)

   strait – 1. *adj.* – restricted; narrow; confined (The patient was put in a *strait* jacket.); 2. *n.* – narrow waterway (He sailed through the *Straits* of Magellan.)

34. than – *conj.* – used most commonly in comparisons (Maggie is older *than* I.)

   then – *adv.* – soon afterward (We lived in Boston, *then* we moved to New York.)

35. their – possessive form of *they* (That is *their* house on Tenafly Drive.)

   they're – contraction of they are (*They're* leaving for California next week.)

   there – *adv.* – at that place (Who is standing *there* under the tree?)

36. to – *prep.* – in the direction of; toward; as (She made a turn *to* the right on Norman Street.)

   too – 1. *adv.* – more than enough (She served *too* much for dinner.); 2. also (He is going to Maine *too*.)

   two – *n.* – 2; one and one (We have *two* pet rabbits.)

37. weather – *n.* – the general condition of the atmosphere (The *weather* is expected to be clear on Sunday.)

whether – *conj.* – if it be a case or fact (We don't know *whether* the trains are late.)

38. who's – contraction of who is or who has (*Who's* willing to volunteer for the night shift?)

    whose – possessive form of *who* (*Whose* book is this?)

39. your – possessive form of *you* (Is this *your* seat?)

    you're – contraction of you and are (I know *you're* going to do well on the test.)

MULTIPLE MEANINGS

In addition to words that sound alike, you must be careful when dealing with words that have multiple meanings. For example:

> The boy was thrilled that his mother gave him a piece of chewing *gum*.

> Dentists advise people to floss their teeth to help prevent *gum* disease.

As you can see, one word can have different meanings depending on the context in which it is used.

CONNOTATION AND DENOTATION

Language can become even more complicated. Not only can a single word have numerous definitions and subtle meanings, it may also take on added meanings through implication. The **connotation** is the idea suggested by its place near or association with other words or phrases. The **denotation** of a word is the direct explicit meaning.

Connotation

Sometimes, you will be asked to tell the meaning of a word in the context of the paragraph. You may not have seen the word before, but from your understanding of the writer's intent, you should be able to figure out what it is s/he's after. For example, read the following paragraph:

> Paris is a beautiful city, perhaps the most beautiful on earth. Long, broad avenues are lined with seventeenth and eighteenth century apartments, office buildings, and cafes. Flowers give the city a

rich and varied look. The bridges and the river lend an air of lightness and grace to the whole urban landscape.

1. In this paragraph, "rich" most nearly means

    (A) wealthy.

    (B) polluted.

    (C) colorful.

    (D) dull.

If you chose "colorful" you would be right. Although "rich" literally means "wealthy" (that is its *denotation*, its literal meaning), here the writer means more than the word's literal meaning, and seems to be highlighting the variety and color that the flowers add to the avenues, that is, richness in a figurative sense.

The writer is using a non-literal meaning, or *connotation* that we associate with the word "rich" to show what s/he means. When we think of something "rich," we usually also think of abundance, variety, color, and not merely numbers.

Denotation

Determining the denotation of a word is different from determining a word's connotation. Read this paragraph:

Many soporifics are on the market to help people sleep. Take a glass of water and two *Sleepeze* and you get the "zzzzz" you need. *Sominall* supposedly helps you get the sleep you need so you can go on working. With *Morpho*, your head hits the pillow and you're asleep before the light goes out.

1. From this paragraph, a "soporific" is probably

    (A) a drug that stimulates you to stay awake.

    (B) a kind of sleeping bag.

    (C) a kind of bed.

    (D) a drug that helps you sleep.

What is a soporific? You can figure out what it means by looking at what is said around it. People take these "soporifics" to go to sleep, not to wake up. So it can't be (A). You can't take two beds and a glass of water

to go to sleep, either. So, it can't be (C). Anyway, you might be able to identify what a soporific is because you recognize the brand names used as examples. So, it must be some sort of pill that you take to sleep. Well, pills are usually drugs of some kind. Therefore, the answer is (D).

VOCABULARY BUILDER

Although the context in which a word appears can help you determine the meaning of the word, one sure-fire way to know a definition is to learn it. By studying the following lists of words and memorizing their definition(s), you will be better equipped to answer Reading Section questions that deal with word meanings.

To benefit most from this vocabulary list, study the words and their definitions, then answer all of the drill questions making sure to check your answers with the answer key that appears at the end of the review.

Group 1

abstract – *adj.* – not easy to understand; theoretical

acclaim – *n.* – loud approval; applause

acquiesce – *v.* – agree or consent to an opinion

adamant – *adj.* – not yielding; firm

adversary – *n.* – an enemy; foe

advocate – 1. *v.* – to plead in favor of; 2. *n.* – supporter; defender

aesthetic – *adj.* – showing good taste; artistic

alleviate – *v.* – to lessen or make easier

aloof – *adj.* – distant in interest; reserved; cool

altercation – *n.* – controversy; dispute

altruistic – *adj.* – unselfish

amass – *v.* – to collect together; accumulate

ambiguous – *adj.* – not clear; uncertain; vague

ambivalent – *adj.* – undecided

ameliorate – *v.* – to make better; to improve

amiable – *adj.* – friendly

amorphous – *adj.* – having no determinate form

anarchist – *n.* – one who believes that a formal government is unnecessary

antagonism – *n.* – hostility; opposition

apathy – *n.* – lack of emotion or interest

appease – *v.* – to make quiet; to calm

apprehensive – *adj.* – fearful; aware; conscious

arbitrary – *adj.* – based on one's preference or whim

arrogant – *adj.* – acting superior to others; conceited

articulate – 1. *v.* – to speak distinctly; 2. *adj.* – eloquent; fluent; 3. *adj.* – capable of speech; 4. *v* – to hinge; to connect; 5. *v.* – to convey; to express effectively

☞ Drill 1

DIRECTIONS: Match each word in the left column with the word in the right column that is most *opposite* in meaning.

Word				Match			
1. ___ articulate	6. ___ abstract	A. hostile	F. disperse
2. ___ apathy	7. ___ acquiesce	B. concrete	G. enthusiasm
3. ___ amiable	8. ___ arbitrary	C. selfish	H. certain
4. ___ altruistic	9. ___ amass	D. reasoned	I. resist
5. ___ ambivalent	10. ___ adversary	E. ally	J. incoherent

DIRECTIONS: Match each word in the left column with the word in the right column that is most *similar* in meaning.

Word			Match		
11. ___ adamant	14. ___ antagonism	A. afraid	D. insistent
12. ___ aesthetic	15. ___ altercation	B. disagreement	E. hostility
13. ___ apprehensive		C. tasteful	

Group 2

assess – *v.* – to estimate the value of

astute – *adj.* – cunning; sly; crafty

atrophy – *v.* – to waste away through lack of nutrition

audacious – *adj.* – fearless; bold

augment – *v.* – to increase or add to; to make larger

austere – *adj.* – harsh; severe; strict

authentic – *adj.* – real; genuine; trustworthy

authoritarian – *adj.* – acting as a dictator; demanding obedience

banal – *adj.* – common; petty; ordinary

belittle – *v.* – to make small; to think lightly of

benefactor – *n.* – one who helps others; a donor

benevolent – *adj.* – kind; generous

benign – *adj.* – mild; harmless

biased – *adj.* – prejudiced; influenced; not neutral

blasphemous – *adj.* – irreligious; away from acceptable standards

blithe – *adj.* – happy; cheery; merry

brevity – *n.* – briefness; shortness

candid – *adj.* – honest; truthful; sincere

capricious – *adj.* – changeable; fickle

caustic – *adj.* – burning; sarcastic; harsh

censor – *v.* – to examine and delete objectionable material

censure – *v.* – to criticize or disapprove of

charlatan – *n.* – an imposter; fake

coalesce – *v.* – to combine; come together

collaborate – *v.* – to work together; cooperate

☞ Drill 2

DIRECTIONS: Match each word in the left column with the word in the right column that is most *opposite* in meaning.

Word		Match	
1. ____ augment	6. ____ authentic	A. permit	F. malicious
2. ____ biased	7. ____ candid	B. religious	G. neutral
3. ____ banal	8. ____ belittle	C. praise	H. mournful
4. ____ benevolent	9. ____ blasphemous	D. diminish	I. unusual
5. ____ censor	10. ____ blithe	E. dishonest	J. ersatz

DIRECTIONS: Match each word in the left column with the word in the right column that is most *similar* in meaning.

Word		Match	
11. ____ collaborate	14. ____ censure	A. harmless	D. cooperate
12. ____ benign	15. ____ capricious	B. cunning	E. criticize
13. ____ astute		C. changeable	

Group 3

compatible – *adj.* – in agreement; harmonious

complacent – *adj.* – content; self-satisfied; smug

compliant – *adj.* – yielding; obedient

comprehensive – *adj.* – all-inclusive; complete; thorough

compromise – *v.* – to settle by mutual adjustment

concede – 1. *v.* – to acknowledge; admit; 2. to surrender; to abandon one's position

concise – *adj.* – in few words; brief; condensed

condescend – *v.* – to come down from one's position or dignity

condone – *v.* – to overlook; to forgive

conspicuous – *adj.* – easy to see; noticeable

consternation – *n.* – amazement or terror that causes confusion

consummation – *n.* – the completion; finish

contemporary – *adj.* – living or happening at the same time; modern

contempt – *n.* – scorn; disrespect

contrite – *adj.* – regretful; sorrowful

conventional – *adj.* – traditional; common; routine

cower – *v.* – crouch down in fear or shame

defamation – *n.* – any harm to a name or reputation; slander

deference – *n.* – a yielding to the opinion of another

deliberate – 1. *v.* – to consider carefully; weigh in the mind; 2. *adj.* – intentional

denounce – *v.* – to speak out against; condemn

depict – *v.* – to portray in words; present a visual image

deplete – *v.* – to reduce; to empty

depravity – *n.* – moral corruption; badness

deride – *v.* – to ridicule; laugh at with scorn

☞ Drill 3

> **DIRECTIONS:** Match each word in the left column with the word in the right column that is most *opposite* in meaning.

	Word				Match		
1.	____ deplete	6.	____ condone	A.	unintentional	F.	support
2.	____ contemporary	7.	____ conspicuous	B.	disapprove	G.	beginning
3.	____ concise	8.	____ consummation	C.	invisible	H.	ancient
4.	____ deliberate	9.	____ denounce	D.	respect	I.	virtue
5.	____ depravity	10.	____ contempt	E.	fill	J.	verbose

> **DIRECTIONS:** Match each word in the left column with the word in the right column that is most *similar* in meaning.

Word		**Match**	
11. ____ compatible	14. ____ comprehensive	A. portray	D. thorough
12. ____ depict	15. ____ complacent	B. content	E. common
13. ____ conventional		C. harmonious	

Group 4

desecrate – *v.* – to violate a holy place or sanctuary

detached – *adj.* – separated; not interested; standing alone

deter – *v.* – to prevent; to discourage; hinder

didactic – 1. *adj.* – instructive; 2. dogmatic; preachy

digress – *v.* – stray from the subject; wander from topic

diligence – *n.* – hard work

discerning – *adj.* – distinguishing one thing from another

discord – *n.* – disagreement; lack of harmony

discriminating – 1. *v.* – distinguishing one thing from another; 2. *v.* – demonstrating bias; 3. *adj.* – able to distinguish

disdain – 1. *n.* – intense dislike; 2. *v.* – look down upon; scorn

disparage – *v.* – to belittle; undervalue

disparity – *n.* – difference in form, character, or degree

dispassionate – *adj.* – lack of feeling; impartial

disperse – *v.* – to scatter; separate

disseminate – *v.* – to circulate; scatter

dissent – *v.* – to disagree; differ in opinion

dissonance – *n.* – harsh contradiction

diverse – *adj.* – different; dissimilar

document – 1. *n.* – official paper containing information; 2. *v.* – to support; substantiate; verify

dogmatic – *adj.* – stubborn; biased; opinionated

dubious – *adj.* – doubtful; uncertain; skeptical; suspicious

eccentric – *adj.* – odd; peculiar; strange

efface – *v.* – wipe out; erase

effervescence – 1. *n.* – liveliness; spirit; enthusiasm; 2. bubbliness

egocentric – *adj.* – self-centered

☞ Drill 4

DIRECTIONS: Match each word in the left column with the word in the right column that is most *opposite* in meaning.

Word

1. ____ detached	6. ____ dubious	A. agree	F. respect	
2. ____ deter	7. ____ diligence	B. certain	G. compliment	
3. ____ dissent	8. ____ disdain	C. lethargy	H. sanctify	
4. ____ discord	9. ____ desecrate	D. connected	I. harmony	
5. ____ efface	10. ____ disparage	E. assist	J. restore	

Match

DIRECTIONS: Match each word in the left column with the word in the right column that is most *similar* in meaning.

Word

11. ____ effervescence	14. ____ document	A. stubborn	D. liveliness
12. ____ dogmatic	15. ____ eccentric	B. distribute	E. odd
13. ____ disseminate		C. substantiate	

Match

Group 5

elaboration – *n.* – the act of clarifying or adding details

eloquence – *n.* – the ability to speak well

elusive – *adj.* – hard to catch; difficult to understand

emulate – *v.* – to imitate; copy; mimic

endorse – *v.* – support; to approve of; recommend

engender – *v.* – to create; bring about

enhance – *v.* – to improve; compliment; make more attractive

enigma – *n.* – mystery; secret; perplexity

ephemeral – *adj.* – temporary; brief; short-lived

equivocal – *adj.* – doubtful; uncertain

erratic – *adj.* – unpredictable; strange

erroneous – *adj.* – untrue; inaccurate; not correct

esoteric – *adj.* – incomprehensible; obscure

euphony – *n.* – pleasant sound

execute – 1. *v.* – put to death; kill; 2. to carry out; fulfill

exemplary – *adj.* – serving as an example; outstanding

exhaustive – *adj.* – thorough; complete

expedient – *adj.* – helpful; practical; worthwhile

expedite – *v.* – speed up

explicit – *adj.* – specific; definite

extol – *v.* – praise; commend

extraneous – *adj.* – irrelevant; not related; not essential

facilitate – *v.* – make easier; simplify

fallacious – *adj.* – misleading

fanatic – *n.* – enthusiast; extremist

☞ Drill 5

> **DIRECTIONS:** Match each word in the left column with the word in the right column that is most *opposite* in meaning.

Word   ### Match

1. ____ extraneous	6. ____ erratic	A. incomplete	F. eternal
2. ____ ephemeral	7. ____ explicit	B. delay	G. condemn
3. ____ exhaustive	8. ____ euphony	C. dependable	H. relevant
4. ____ expedite	9. ____ elusive	D. comprehensible	I. indefinite
5. ____ erroneous	10. ____ extol	E. dissonance	J. accurate

> **DIRECTIONS:** Match each word in the left column with the word in the right column that is most *similar* in meaning.

Word   ### Match

11. ____ endorse	14. ____ fallacious	A. enable	D. worthwhile
12. ____ expedient	15. ____ engender	B. recommend	E. deceptive
13. ____ facilitate		C. create	

Group 6

fastidious – *adj.* – fussy; hard to please

fervor – *n.* – passion; intensity

fickle – *adj.* – changeable; unpredictable

fortuitous – *adj.* – accidental; happening by chance; lucky

frivolity – *n.* – giddiness; lack of seriousness

fundamental – *adj.* – basic; necessary

furtive – *adj.* – secretive; sly

futile – *adj.* – worthless; unprofitable

glutton – *n.* – overeater

grandiose – *adj.* – extravagant; flamboyant

gravity – *n.* – seriousness

guile – *n.* – slyness; deceit

gullible – *adj.* – easily fooled

hackneyed – *adj.* – commonplace; trite

hamper – *v.* – interfere with; hinder

haphazard – *adj.* – disorganized; random

hedonistic – *adj.* – pleasure seeking

heed – *v.* – obey; yield to

heresy – *n.* – opinion contrary to popular belief

hindrance – *n.* – blockage; obstacle

humility – *n.* – lack of pride; modesty

hypocritical – *adj.* – two-faced; deceptive

hypothetical – *adj.* – assumed; uncertain

illuminate – *v.* – make understandable

illusory – *adj.* – unreal; false; deceptive

☞ Drill 6

> **DIRECTIONS:** Match each word in the left column with the word in the right column that is most *opposite* in meaning.

Word

1. ____ heresy
2. ____ fickle
3. ____ illusory
4. ____ frivolity
5. ____ grandiose
6. ____ fervent
7. ____ fundamental
8. ____ furtive
9. ____ futile
10. ____ haphazard

Match

A. predictable
B. dispassionate
C. simple
D. extraneous
E. real
F. beneficial
G. orthodoxy
H. organized
I. candid
J. seriousness

> **DIRECTIONS:** Match each word in the left column with the word in the right column that is most *similar* in meaning.

Word		**Match**	
11. ____ glutton	14. ____ hackneyed	A. hinder	D. overeater
12. ____ heed	15. ____ hindrance	B. obstacle	E. obey
13. ____ hamper		C. trite	

Group 7

immune – *adj.* – protected; unthreatened by

immutable – *adj.* – unchangeable; permanent

impartial – *adj.* – unbiased; fair

impetuous – 1. *adj.* – rash; impulsive; 2. forcible; violent

implication – *n.* – suggestion; inference

inadvertent – *adj.* – not on purpose; unintentional

incessant – *adj.* – constant; continual

incidental – *adj.* – extraneous; unexpected

inclined – 1. *adj.* – apt to; likely to; 2. angled

incoherent – *adj.* – illogical; rambling

incompatible – *adj.* – disagreeing; disharmonious

incredulous – *adj.* – unwilling to believe; skeptical

indifferent – *adj.* – unconcerned

indolent – *adj.* – lazy; inactive

indulgent – *adj.* – lenient; extravagant

inevitable – *adj.* – sure to happen; unavoidable

infamous – *adj.* – having a bad reputation; notorious

infer – *v.* – form an opinion; conclude

initiate – 1. *v.* – begin; admit into a group; 2. *n.* – a person who is in the process of being admitted into a group

innate – *adj.* – natural; inborn

innocuous – *adj.* – harmless; innocent

innovate – *v.* – introduce a change; depart from the old

insipid – *adj.* – uninteresting; bland

instigate – *v.* – start; provoke

intangible – *adj.* – incapable of being touched; immaterial

☞ Drill 7

> **DIRECTIONS:** Match each word in the left column with the word in the right column that is most *opposite* in meaning.

Word		**Match**	
1. ____ immutable	6. ____ innate	A. intentional	F. changeable
2. ____ impartial	7. ____ incredulous	B. articulate	G. avoidable
3. ____ inadvertent	8. ____ inevitable	C. gullible	H. harmonious
4. ____ incoherent	9. ____ intangible	D. material	I. learned
5. ____ incompatible	10. ____ indolent	E. biased	J. energetic

> **DIRECTIONS:** Match each word in the left column with the word in the right column that is most *similar* in meaning.

Word		**Match**	
11. ____ impetuous	14. ____ instigate	A. lenient	D. conclude
12. ____ incidental	15. ____ indulgent	B. impulsive	E. extraneous
13. ____ infer		C. provoke	

Group 8

ironic – *adj.* – contradictory; inconsistent; sarcastic

irrational – *adj.* – not logical

jeopardy – *n.* – danger

kindle – *v.* – ignite; arouse

languid – *adj.* – weak; fatigued

laud – *v.* – to praise

lax – *adj.* – careless; irresponsible

lethargic – *adj.* – lazy; passive

levity – *n.* – silliness; lack of seriousness

lucid – 1. *adj.* – shining; 2. easily understood

magnanimous – *adj.* – forgiving; unselfish

malicious – *adj.* – spiteful; vindictive

marred – *adj.* – damaged

meander – *v.* – wind on a course; go aimlessly

melancholy – *n.* – depression; gloom

meticulous – *adj.* – exacting; precise

minute – *adj.* – extremely small; tiny

miser – *n.* – penny pincher; stingy person

mitigate – *v.* – alleviate; lessen; soothe

morose – *adj.* – moody; despondent

negligence – *n.* – carelessness

neutral – *adj.* – impartial; unbiased

nostalgic – *adj.* – longing for the past; filled with bittersweet memories

novel – *adj.* – new

☞ Drill 8

DIRECTIONS: Match each word in the left column with the word in the right column that is most *opposite* in meaning.

	Word			Match		
1. ___ irrational		6. ___ magnanimous	A. extinguish		F. ridicule	
2. ___ kindle		7. ___ levity	B. jovial		G. kindly	
3. ___ meticulous		8. ___ minute	C. selfish		H. sloppy	
4. ___ malicious		9. ___ laud	D. logical		I. huge	
5. ___ morose		10. ___ novel	E. seriousness		J. stale	

> **DIRECTIONS:** Match each word in the left column with the word in the right column that is most *similar* in meaning.

	Word			**Match**	
11. ___ ironic		14. ___ jeopardy	A. lessen	D. carelessness
12. ___ marred		15. ___ negligence	B. damaged	E. danger
13. ___ mitigate			C. sarcastic	

Group 9

nullify – *v.* – cancel; invalidate

objective – 1. *adj.* – open-minded; impartial; 2. *n.* – goal

obscure – *adj.* – not easily understood; dark

obsolete – *adj.* – out of date; passe

ominous – *adj.* – threatening

optimist – *n.* – person who hopes for the best; sees the good side

orthodox – *adj.* – traditional; accepted

pagan – 1. *n.* – polytheist; 2. *adj.* – polytheistic

partisan – 1. *n.* – supporter; follower; 2. *adj.* – biased; one sided

perceptive – *adj.* – full of insight; aware

peripheral – *adj.* – marginal; outer

pernicious – *adj.* – dangerous; harmful

pessimism – *n.* – seeing only the gloomy side; hopelessness

phenomenon – 1. *n.* – miracle; 2. occurrence

philanthropy – *n.* – charity; unselfishness

pious – *adj.* – religious; devout; dedicated

placate – *v.* – pacify

plausible – *adj.* – probable; feasible

pragmatic – *adj.* – matter-of-fact; practical

preclude – *v.* – inhibit; make impossible

predecessor – *n.* – one who has occupied an office before another

prodigal – *adj.* – wasteful; lavish

prodigious – *adj.* – exceptional; tremendous

profound – *adj.* – deep; knowledgeable; thorough

profusion – *n.* – great amount; abundance

☞ Drill 9

> **DIRECTIONS:** Match each word in the left column with the word in the right column that is most *opposite* in meaning.

Word			Match		
1. ___ objective	6. ___ plausible		A. scantiness	F. minute	
2. ___ obsolete	7. ___ preclude		B. assist	G. anger	
3. ___ placate	8. ___ prodigious		C. mundane	H. pessimism	
4. ___ profusion	9. ___ profound		D. biased	I. modern	
5. ___ peripheral	10. ___ optimism		E. improbable	J. central	

> **DIRECTIONS:** Match each word in the left column with the word in the right column that is most *similar* in meaning.

Word		Match	
11. ___ nullify	14. ___ pernicious	A. invalidate	D. threatening
12. ___ ominous	15. ___ prodigal	B. follower	E. harmful
13. ___ partisan		C. lavish	

Group 10

prosaic – *adj.* – tiresome; ordinary

provincial – *adj.* – regional; unsophisticated

provocative – 1. *adj.* – tempting; 2. irritating

prudent – *adj.* – wise; careful; prepared

qualified – *adj.* – experienced; indefinite

rectify – *v.* – correct

redundant – *adj.* – repetitious; unnecessary

refute – *v.* – challenge; disprove

relegate – *v.* – banish; put to a lower position

relevant – *adj.* – of concern; significant

remorse – *n.* – guilt; sorrow

reprehensible – *adj.* – wicked; disgraceful

repudiate – *v.* – reject; cancel

rescind – *v.* – retract; discard

resignation – 1. *n.* – quitting; 2. submission

resolution – *n.* – proposal; promise; determination

respite – *n.* – recess; rest period

reticent – *adj.* – silent; reserved; shy

reverent – *adj.* – respectful

rhetorical – *adj.* – having to do with verbal communication

rigor – *n.* – severity

sagacious – *adj.* – wise; cunning

sanguine – 1. *adj.* – optimistic; cheerful; 2. red

saturate – *v.* – soak thoroughly; drench

scanty – *adj.* – inadequate; sparse

☞ Drill 10

DIRECTIONS: Match each word in the left column with the word in the right column that is most *opposite* in meaning.

Word				Match		
1. ___ provincial	6.	___ remorse	A. inexperienced	F. affirm
2. ___ reticent	7.	___ repudiate	B. joy	G. extraordinary
3. ___ prudent	8.	___ sanguine	C. pessimistic	H. sophisticated
4. ___ qualified	9.	___ relevant	D. unrelated	I. forward
5. ___ relegate	10.	___ prosaic	E. careless	J. promote

DIRECTIONS: Match each word in the left column with the word in the right column that is most *similar* in meaning.

Word			Match	
11. ___ provocative	14.	___ rescind	A. drench	D. severity
12. ___ rigor	15.	___ reprehensible	B. tempting	E. blameworthy
13. ___ saturate			C. retract	

Group 11

scrupulous – *adj.* – honorable; exact

scrutinize – *v.* – examine closely; study

servile – *adj.* – slavish; groveling

skeptic – *n.* – doubter

slander – *v.* – defame; maliciously misrepresent

solemnity – *n.* – seriousness

solicit – *v.* – ask; seek

stagnant – *adj.* – motionless; uncirculating

stanza – *n.* – group of lines in a poem having a definite pattern

static – *adj.* – inactive; changeless

stoic – *adj.* – detached; unruffled; calm

subtlety – 1. *n.* – understatement; 2. propensity for understatement; 3. sophistication; 4. cunning

superficial – *adj.* – on the surface; narrow-minded; lacking depth

superfluous – *adj.* – unnecessary; extra

surpass – *v.* – go beyond; outdo

sycophant – *n.* – flatterer

symmetry – *n.* – correspondence of parts; harmony

taciturn – *adj.* – reserved; quiet; secretive

tedious – *adj.* – time-consuming; burdensome; uninteresting

temper – *v.* – soften; pacify; compose

tentative – *adj.* – not confirmed; indefinite

thrifty – *adj.* – economical; pennywise

tranquility – *n.* – peace; stillness; harmony

trepidation – *n.* – apprehension; uneasiness

trivial – *adj.* – unimportant; small; worthless

☞ Drill 11

> **DIRECTIONS:** Match each word in the left column with the word in the right column that is most *opposite* in meaning.

Word		**Match**	
1. ___ scrutinize	6. ___ tentative	A. frivolity	F. skim
2. ___ skeptic	7. ___ thrifty	B. enjoyable	G. turbulent
3. ___ solemnity	8. ___ tranquility	C. prodigal	H. active
4. ___ static	9. ___ solicit	D. chaos	I. believer
5. ___ tedious	10. ___ stagnant	E. give	J. confirmed

> **DIRECTIONS:** Match each word in the left column with the word in the right column that is most *similar* in meaning.

Word		Match	
11. ____ symmetry	14. ____ subtle	A. understated	D. fear
12. ____ superfluous	15. ____ trepidation	B. unnecessary	E. flatterer
13. ____ sycophant		C. balance	

Group 12

tumid – *adj.* – swollen; inflated

undermine – *v.* – weaken; ruin

uniform – *adj.* – consistent; unvaried; unchanging

universal – *adj.* – concerning everyone; existing everywhere

unobtrusive – *adj.* – inconspicuous; reserved

unprecedented – *adj.* – unheard of; exceptional

unpretentious – *adj.* – simple; plain; modest

vacillation – *n.* – fluctuation

valid – *adj.* – acceptable; legal

vehement – *adj.* – intense; excited; enthusiastic

venerate – *v.* – revere

verbose – *adj.* – wordy; talkative

viable – 1. *adj.* – capable of maintaining life; 2. possible; attainable

vigor – *n.* – energy; forcefulness

vilify – *v.* – slander

virtuoso – *n.* – highly skilled artist

virulent – *adj.* – deadly; harmful; malicious

vital – *adj.* – important; spirited

volatile – *adj.* – changeable; undependable

vulnerable – *adj.* – open to attack; unprotected

wane – *v.* – grow gradually smaller

whimsical – *adj.* – fanciful; amusing

wither – *v.* – wilt; shrivel; humiliate; cut down

zealot – *n.* – believer; enthusiast; fan

zenith – *n.* – point directly overhead in the sky

☞ Drill 12

> **DIRECTIONS:** Match each word in the left column with the word in the right column that is most *opposite* in meaning.

Word			Match	
1. ____ uniform	6. ____ vigorous	A. amateur	F. support
2. ____ virtuoso	7. ____ volatile	B. trivial	G. constancy
3. ____ vital	8. ____ vacillation	C. visible	H. lethargic
4. ____ wane	9. ____ undermine	D. placid	I. wax
5. ____ unobtrusive	10. ____ valid	E. unacceptable	J. varied

> **DIRECTIONS:** Match each word in the left column with the word in the right column that is most *similar* in meaning.

Word		Match	
11. ____ wither	14. ____ vehement	A. intense	D. possible
12. ____ whimsical	15. ____ virulent	B. deadly	E. shrivel
13. ____ viable		C. amusing	

Additional Vocabulary

The following words comprise additional vocabulary terms which may be found on the PPST.

abandon – 1. *v.* – to leave behind; 2. *v.* – to give something up; 3. *n.* – freedom; enthusiasm; impetuosity

abase – *v.* – to degrade; humiliate; disgrace

abbreviate – *v.* – to shorten; compress; diminish

aberrant – *adj.* – abnormal

abhor – *v.* – to hate

abominate – *v.* – to loathe; to hate

abridge – 1. *v.* – to shorten; 2. to limit; to take away

absolve – *v.* – to forgive; to acquit

abstinence – *n.* – self-control; abstention; chastity

accede – *v.* – to comply with; to consent to

accomplice – *n.* – co-conspirator; partner; partner-in-crime

accrue – *v.* – collect; build up

acrid – *adj.* – sharp; bitter; foul smelling

adept – *adj.* – skilled; practiced

adverse – *adj.* – negative; hostile; antagonistic; inimical

affable – *adj.* – friendly; amiable; good-natured

aghast – 1. *adj.* – astonished; amazed; 2. horrified; terrified; appalled

alacrity – 1. *n.* – enthusiasm; fervor; 2. liveliness; sprightliness

allocate – *v.* – set aside; designate; assign

allure – 1. *v.* – to attract; entice; 2. *n.* – attraction; temptation; glamour

amiss – 1. *adj.* – wrong; awry; 2. *adv.* – wrongly; mistakenly

analogy – *n.* – similarity; correlation; parallelism; simile; metaphor

anoint – 1. *v.* – to crown; ordain; 2. to smear with oil

anonymous – *adj.* – nameless; unidentified

arduous – *adj.* – difficult; burdensome

awry – 1. *adj., adv.* – crooked(ly); uneven(ly); 2. wrong; askew

baleful – *adj.* – sinister; threatening; evil; deadly

baroque – *adj.* – extravagant; ornate

behoove – *v.* – to be advantageous; to be necessary

berate – *v.* – scold; reprove; reproach; criticize

bereft – *adj.* – hurt by someone's death

biennial – 1. *adj.* – happening every two years; 2. *n.* – a plant which blooms every two years

blatant – 1. *adj.* – obvious; unmistakable; 2. crude; vulgar

bombastic – *adj.* – pompous; wordy; turgid

burly – *adj.* – strong; bulky; stocky

cache – 1. *n.* – stockpile; store; heap; 2. hiding place for goods

calamity – *n.* – disaster

cascade – 1. *n.* – waterfall; 2. *v.* – pour; rush; fall

catalyst – *n.* – anything which creates a situation in which change can occur

chagrin – *n.* – distress; shame

charisma – *n.* – appeal; magnetism; presence

chastise – *v.* – punish; discipline; admonish; rebuke

choleric – *adj.* – cranky; cantankerous

cohesion – *n.* – the act of holding together

colloquial – *adj.* – casual; common; conversational; idiomatic

conglomeration – *n.* – mixture; collection

connoisseur – *n.* – expert; authority (usually refers to a wine or food expert)

consecrate – *v.* – sanctify; make sacred; immortalize

craven – *adj.* – cowardly; fearful

dearth – *n.* – scarcity; shortage

debilitate – *v.* – deprive of strength

deign – *v.* – condescend; stoop

delineate – *v.* – to outline; to describe

demur – 1. *v.* – to object; 2. *n.* – objection; misgiving

derision – *n.* – ridicule; mockery

derogatory – *adj.* – belittling; uncomplimentary

destitute – *adj.* – poor; poverty-stricken

devoid – *adj.* – lacking; empty

dichotomy – *n.* – branching into two parts

disheartened – *adj.* – discouraged; depressed

diverge – *v.* – separate; split

docile – *adj.* – manageable; obedient

duress – *n.* – force; constraint

ebullient – *adj.* – showing excitement

educe – *v.* – draw forth

effervescence – *n.* – bubbliness; enthusiasm; animation

emulate – *v.* – to follow the example of

ennui – *n.* – boredom; apathy

epitome – *n.* – model; typification; representation

errant – *adj.* – wandering

ersatz – *adj.* – artificial

ethnic – *adj.* – native; racial; cultural

evoke – *v.* – call forth; provoke

exotic – *adj.* – unusual; striking

facade – *n.* – front view; false appearance

facsimile – *n.* – copy; reproduction; replica

fathom – *v.* – comprehend; uncover

ferret – *v.* – drive or hunt out of hiding

figment – *n.* – product; creation

finite – *adj.* – measurable; limited; not everlasting

fledgling – *n.* – inexperienced person; beginner

flinch – *v.* – wince; draw back; retreat

fluency – *n.* – smoothness of speech

flux – *n.* – current; continuous change

forbearance – *n.* – patience; self-restraint

foster – *v.* – encourage; nurture; support

frivolity – *n.* – lightness; folly; fun

frugality – *n.* – thrift

garbled – *adj.* – mixed up

generic – *adj.* – common; general; universal

germane – *adj.* – pertinent; related; to the point

gibber – *v.* – speak foolishly

gloat – *v.* – brag; glory over

guile – *n.* – slyness; fraud

haggard – *adj.* – tired looking; fatigued

hiatus – *n.* – interval; break; period of rest

hierarchy – *n.* – body of people, things, or concepts divided into ranks

homage – *n.* – honor; respect

hubris – *n.* – arrogance

ideology – *n.* – set of beliefs; principles

ignoble – *adj.* – shameful; dishonorable

imbue – *v.* – inspire; arouse

impale – *v.* – fix on a stake; stick; pierce

implement – *v.* – begin; enact

impromptu – *adj.* – without preparation

inarticulate – *adj.* – speechless; unable to speak clearly

incessant – *adj.* – uninterrupted

incognito – *adj.* – unidentified; disguised; concealed

indict – *v.* – charge with a crime

inept – *adj.* – incompetent; unskilled

innuendo – *n.* – hint; insinuation

intermittent – *adj.* – periodic; occasional

invoke – *v.* – ask for; call upon

itinerary – *n.* – travel plan; schedule; course

jovial – *adj.* – cheery; jolly; playful

juncture – *n.* – critical point; meeting

juxtapose – *v.* – place side by side

knavery – *n.* – rascality; trickery

knead – *v.* – mix; massage

labyrinth – *n.* – maze

laggard – *n.* – a lazy person; one who lags behind

larceny – *n.* – theft; stealing

lascivious – *adj.* – indecent; immoral

lecherous – *adj.* – impure in thought and act

lethal – *adj.* – deadly

liaison – *n.* – connection; link

limber – *adj.* – flexible; pliant

livid – 1. *adj.* – black-and-blue; discolored; 2. enraged; irate

lucrative – *adj.* – profitable; gainful

lustrous – *adj.* – bright; radiant

malediction – *n.* – curse; evil spell

mandate – *n.* – order; charge

manifest – *adj.* – obvious; clear

mentor – *n.* – teacher

mesmerize – *v.* – hypnotize

metamorphosis – *n.* – change of form

mimicry – *n.* – imitation

molten – *adj.* – melted

motif – *n.* – theme

mundane – *adj.* – ordinary; commonplace

myriad – *adj.* – innumerable; countless

narcissistic – *adj.* – egotistical; self-centered

nautical – *adj.* – of the sea

neophyte – *n.* – beginner; newcomer

nettle – *v.* – annoy; irritate

notorious – *adj.* – infamous; renowned

obdurate – *adj.* – stubborn; inflexible

obligatory – *adj.* – mandatory; necessary

obliterate – *v.* – destroy completely

obsequious – *adj.* – slavishly attentive; servile

obstinate – *adj.* – stubborn

occult – *adj.* – mystical; mysterious

opaque – *adj.* – dull; cloudy; nontransparent

opulence – *n.* – wealth; fortune

ornate – *adj.* – elaborate; lavish; decorated

oust – *v.* – drive out; eject

painstaking – *adj.* – thorough; careful; precise

pallid – *adj.* – sallow; colorless

palpable – *adj.* – tangible; apparent

paradigm – *n.* – model; example

paraphernalia – *n.* – equipment; accessories

parochial – *adj.* – pertaining to a parish; narrow-minded

passive – *adj.* – submissive; unassertive

pedestrian – *adj.* – mediocre; ordinary

pensive – *adj.* – reflective; contemplative

percussion – *n.* – the striking of one object against another

perjury – *n.* – the practice of lying

permeable – *adj.* – porous; allowing to pass through

perpetual – *adj.* – enduring for all time

pertinent – *adj.* – related to the matter at hand

pervade – *v.* – to occupy the whole of

petty – *adj.* – unimportant; of subordinate standing

phlegmatic – *adj.* – without emotion or interest

phobia – *n.* – morbid fear

pittance – *n.* – small allowance

plethora – *n.* – condition of going beyond what is needed; excess; over-abundance

potent – *adj.* – having great power or physical strength

privy – *adj.* – private; confidential

progeny – *n.* – children; offspring

provoke – *v.* – to stir action or feeling; arouse

pungent – *adj.* – sharp; stinging

quaint – *adj.* – old-fashioned; unusual; odd

quandary – *n.* – dilemma

quarantine – *n.* – isolation of a person to prevent spread of disease

quiescent – *adj.* – inactive; at rest

quirk – *n.* – peculiar behavior; startling twist

rabid – *adj.* – furious; with extreme anger

rancid – *adj.* – having a bad odor

rant – *v.* – to speak in a loud, pompous manner; rave

ratify – *v.* – to make valid; confirm

rationalize – *v.* – to offer reasons for; account for

raucous – *adj.* – disagreeable to the sense of hearing; harsh

realm – *n.* – an area; sphere of activity

rebuttal – *n.* – refutation

recession – *n.* – withdrawal; depression

reciprocal – *n.* – mutual; having the same relationship to each other

recluse – *n.* – solitary and shut off from society

refurbish – *v.* – to make new

regal – *adj.* – royal; grand

reiterate – *v.* – repeat; to state again

relinquish – *v.* – to let go; abandon

render – *v.* – deliver; provide; to give up a possession

replica – *n.* – copy; representation

resilient – *adj.* – flexible; capable of withstanding stress

retroaction – *n.* – an action elicited by a stimulus

reverie – *n.* – the condition of being unaware of one's surroundings; trance

rummage – *v.* – search thoroughly

rustic – *adj.* – plain and unsophisticated; homely

saga – *n.* – a legend; story

salient – *adj.* – noticeable; prominent

salvage – *v.* – rescue from loss

sarcasm – *n.* – ironic, bitter humor designed to wound

satire – *n.* – a novel or play that uses humor or irony to expose folly

saunter – *v.* – walk at a leisurely pace; stroll

savor – *v.* – to receive pleasure from; enjoy

seethe – *v.* – to be in a state of emotional turmoil; to become angry

serrated – *adj.* – having a sawtoothed edge

shoddy – *adj.* – of inferior quality; cheap

skulk – *v.* – to move secretly

sojourn – *n.* – temporary stay; visit

solace – *n.* – hope; comfort during a time of grief

soliloquy – *n.* – a talk one has with oneself (esp. on stage)

somber – *adj.* – dark and depressing; gloomy

sordid – *adj.* – filthy; base; vile

sporadic – *adj.* – rarely occurring or appearing; intermittent

stamina – *n.* – endurance

steadfast – *adj.* – loyal

stigma – *n.* – a mark of disgrace

stipend – *n.* – payment for work done

stupor – *n.* – a stunned or bewildered condition

suave – *adj.* – effortlessly gracious

subsidiary – *adj.* – subordinate

succinct – *adj.* – consisting of few words; concise

succumb – *v.* – give in; yield; collapse

sunder – *v.* – break; split in two

suppress – *v.* – to bring to an end; hold back

surmise – *v.* – draw an inference; guess

susceptible – *adj.* – easily imposed; inclined

tacit – *adj.* – not voiced or expressed

tantalize – *v.* – to tempt; to torment

tarry – *v.* – to go or move slowly; delay

taut – *adj.* – stretch tightly

tenacious – *adj.* – persistently holding to something

tepid – *adj.* – lacking warmth, interest, enthusiasm; lukewarm

terse – *adj.* – concise; abrupt

thwart – *v.* – prevent from accomplishing a purpose; frustrate

timorous – *adj.* – fearful

torpid – *adj.* – lacking alertness and activity; lethargic

toxic – *adj.* – poisonous

transpire – *v.* – to take place; come about

traumatic – *adj.* – causing a violent injury

trek – *v.* – to make a journey

tribute – *n.* – expression of admiration

trite – *adj.* – commonplace; overused

truculent – *adj.* – aggressive; eager to fight

turbulence – *n.* – condition of being physically agitated; disturbance

turmoil – *n.* – unrest; agitation

tycoon – *n.* – wealthy leader

tyranny – *n.* – absolute power; autocracy

ubiquitous – *adj.* – ever present in all places; universal

ulterior – *adj.* – buried; concealed

uncanny – *adj.* – of a strange nature; weird

unequivocal – *adj.* – clear; definite

unique – *adj.* – without equal; incomparable

unruly – *adj.* – not submitting to discipline; disobedient

unwonted – *adj.* – not ordinary; unusual

urbane – *adj.* – cultured; suave

usurpation – *n.* – act of taking something for oneself; seizure

usury – *n.* – the act of lending money at illegal rates of interest

utopia – *n.* – imaginary land with perfect social and political systems

vacuous – *adj.* – containing nothing; empty

vagabond – *n.* – wanderer; one without a fixed place

vagrant – 1. *n.* – homeless person; 2. *adj.* – rambling; wandering; transient

valance – *n.* – short drapery hanging over a window frame

valor – *n.* – bravery

vantage – *n.* – position giving an advantage

vaunted – *adj.* – boasted of

velocity – *n.* – speed

vendetta – *n.* – feud

venue – *n.* – location

veracious – *adj.* – conforming to fact; accurate

verbatim – *adj.* – employing the same words as another; literal

versatile – *adj.* – having many uses; multifaceted

vertigo – *n.* – dizziness

vex – *v.* – to trouble the nerves; annoy

vindicate – *v.* – to free from charge; clear

vivacious – *adj.* – animated; gay

vogue – *n.* – modern fashion

voluble – *adj.* – fluent

waft – *v.* – move gently by wind or breeze

waive – *v.* – to give up possession or right

wanton – *adj.* – unruly; excessive

warrant – *v.* – justify; authorize

wheedle – *v.* – try to persuade; coax

whet – *v.* – sharpen

wrath – *n.* – violent or unrestrained anger; fury

wry – *adj.* – mocking; cynical

xenophobia – *n.* – fear of foreigners

yoke – *n.* – harness; collar; bond

yore – *n.* – former period of time

zephyr – *n.* – a gentle wind; breeze

☞ Drill 13

DIRECTIONS: Each of the following questions provides a given word in capitalized letters followed by five word choices. Choose the word which is *opposite* in meaning to the given word.

1. AUTHENTIC:
   - (A) cheap
   - (B) competitive
   - (C) false
   - (D) biased
   - (E) irrational

2. MISERLY:
   - (A) unhappy
   - (B) generous
   - (C) optimistic
   - (D) reticent
   - (E) golden

3. DILIGENT:
   - (A) lethargic
   - (B) morose
   - (C) silly
   - (D) nostalgic
   - (E) poor

4. PRECLUDE:
   - (A) commence
   - (B) include
   - (C) produce
   - (D) perpetuate
   - (E) enable

5. EXTOL:
   - (A) criticize
   - (B) expedite
   - (C) pay
   - (D) deport
   - (E) defer

6. DIVERSE:
   - (A) solo
   - (B) furtive
   - (C) jovial
   - (D) wrinkled
   - (E) similar

7. DISPERSE:
   - (A) despair
   - (B) belittle
   - (C) renew
   - (D) renege
   - (E) amass

8. ENDURING:

   (A) fallacious   (B) temporal   (C) dismal

   (D) minute   (E) disseminating

9. BREVITY:

   (A) gravity   (B) gluttony   (C) cowardice

   (D) authenticity   (E) verbosity

10. DEMUR:

   (A) assemble   (B) bereave   (C) approve

   (D) add   (E) ascribe

11. UNWONTED:

   (A) perceptive   (B) ordinary   (C) tepid

   (D) desirable   (E) qualified

12. CHASTISE:

   (A) repudiate   (B) immortalize   (C) endorse

   (D) virility   (E) congratulate

13. INFAMOUS:

   (A) revered   (B) resolute   (C) obscure

   (D) contiguous   (E) unknown

14. DISPASSIONATE:

   (A) resigned   (B) profound   (C) fanatical

   (D) torrid   (E) prudent

15. SCANTY:

   (A) redundant   (B) mediocre   (C) calming

   (D) profuse   (E) partisan

16. PROSAIC:
    - (A) poetic
    - (B) unique
    - (C) rabid
    - (D) disdainful
    - (E) condescending

17. DIDACTIC:
    - (A) dubious
    - (B) imbecilic
    - (C) punctual
    - (D) rhetorical
    - (E) reverent

18. COLLOQUIAL:
    - (A) poetic
    - (B) separate
    - (C) formal
    - (D) analogical
    - (E) anonymous

19. COHESIVE:
    - (A) adhesive
    - (B) opposed
    - (C) smooth
    - (D) adverse
    - (E) fragmented

20. OBLIGATORY:
    - (A) promising
    - (B) permissible
    - (C) heaven
    - (D) optional
    - (E) responsible

21. OPAQUE:
    - (A) permeable
    - (B) similar
    - (C) visible
    - (D) opulent
    - (E) translucent

22. SUNDER:
    - (A) unite
    - (B) create noise
    - (C) oust
    - (D) rise above
    - (E) freeze

23. NARCISSISTIC:
    - (A) flowery
    - (B) detrimental
    - (C) gentle
    - (D) modest
    - (E) polite

24. FOSTER:

   (A) destroy   (B) relate   (C) parent

   (D) abort   (E) revere

25. LIVID:

   (A) homeless   (B) bright   (C) calm

   (D) elusive   (E) opulent

26. SUPPRESS:

   (A) justify   (B) advocate   (C) free

   (D) level   (E) immunize

27. DESTITUTE:

   (A) organized   (B) ornate   (C) moral

   (D) wealthy   (E) obsequious

28. PAINSTAKING:

   (A) healthful   (B) sordid   (C) careless

   (D) sadistic   (E) lethal

29. PAROCHIAL:

   (A) melancholy (B) blasphemous (C) sporting

   (D) irreligious (E) broad-minded

30. MANDATE:

   (A) emphasis   (B) sophism   (C) pinnacle

   (D) request   (E) meander

31. LUCID:

   (A) obscure   (B) tedious   (C) calm

   (D) frightening (E) intelligent

32. IGNOBLE:
    - (A) brave
    - (B) honorable
    - (C) royal
    - (D) attentive
    - (E) informal

33. PERTINENT:
    - (A) respectful
    - (B) detailed
    - (C) dreary
    - (D) blatant
    - (E) irrelevant

34. ABSTINENCE:
    - (A) indulgence
    - (B) concurrence
    - (C) hedonism
    - (D) diligence
    - (E) alcoholism

35. FRUGAL:
    - (A) unplanned
    - (B) temperamental
    - (C) regal
    - (D) ethical
    - (E) extravagant

36. FORTUITOUS:
    - (A) lethargic
    - (B) unprotected
    - (C) weak
    - (D) unlucky
    - (E) antagonistic

37. UNEQUIVOCAL:
    - (A) versatile
    - (B) equal
    - (C) noisy
    - (D) unclear
    - (E) truthful

38. CONTEMPT:
    - (A) respect
    - (B) pettiness
    - (C) politeness
    - (D) resistance
    - (E) compliance

39. GRAVITY:
    - (A) antipathy
    - (B) derision
    - (C) buoyancy
    - (D) eloquence
    - (E) effervescence

40. AUSTERE:

    (A) measurable   (B) resilient   (C) indulgent

    (D) indirect   (E) destitute

41. PASSIVE:

    (A) thoughtless   (B) supportive   (C) retentive

    (D) contemporary   (E) assertive

42. STAGNANT:

    (A) celibate   (B) active   (C) effluent

    (D) feminine   (E) polluted

43. ADVERSE:

    (A) friendly   (B) quiescent   (C) poetic

    (D) burly   (E) petty

44. CRAVEN:

    (A) difficult   (B) reptilian   (C) pungent

    (D) birdlike   (E) courageous

45. HEED:

    (A) adjust   (B) resist   (C) attend

    (D) encourage   (E) order

46. IMPARTIAL:

    (A) biased   (B) complete   (C) eternal

    (D) articulate   (E) raucous

47. VINDICATE:

    (A) remove   (B) absolve   (C) evoke

    (D) accuse   (E) ferret

48. DERISION:

   (A) elimination   (B) attention   (C) praise

   (D) entrance   (E) recession

49. REPREHENSIBLE:

   (A) released   (B) aghast   (C) awry

   (D) incidental   (E) commendable

50. RELEGATE:

   (A) promote   (B) nullify   (C) include

   (D) obliterate   (E) placate

51. VAIN:

   (A) addicted   (B) modest   (C) unscented

   (D) proud   (E) choleric

52. LAGGARD:

   (A) haggard   (B) lustrous   (C) haphazard

   (D) advanced   (E) industrious

53. LABYRINTHINE:

   (A) inconsistent   (B) amazing   (C) direct

   (D) incredulous   (E) mythological

54. SLANDER:

   (A) praise   (B) comfort   (C) discipline

   (D) risk   (E) digress

55. PITTANCE:

   (A) mound   (B) plethora   (C) quirk

   (D) grandeur   (E) phlegm

56. SOLACE:

   (A) lunation   (B) turmoil   (C) distress

   (D) valance   (D) spontaneity

57. DEFERENT:

   (A) current   (B) constructive   (C) erratic

   (D) unyielding   (E) applicant

58. FICKLE:

   (A) bland   (B) cascading   (C) caustic

   (D) dubious   (E) faithful

59. EXOTIC:

   (A) ethnic   (B) diverse   (C) realistic

   (D) mundane   (E) enigmatic

60. THWART:

   (A) imprison   (B) mystify   (C) assist

   (D) fluctuate   (E) saturate

KNOWING YOUR WORD PARTS

Memorization and practice are not the only ways to learn the meanings of new words. While taking this test, you will have nothing but your own knowledge and context clues to refer to when you come into contact with unfamiliar words. Even though we have provided you with a comprehensive list of words, there is a very good chance that you will come across words that you still do not know. Therefore, you will need to study our list of prefixes, roots, and suffixes in order to be prepared. Learning the meanings of these prefixes, roots, and suffixes is essential to a strong vocabulary and, therefore, to performing well on the Reading Section, as well as the entire PPST exam.

Prefix

Prefix	Meaning	Example
ab-, a-, abs-	away, from	absent – away, not present abstain – keep from doing, refrain
ad-	to, toward	adjacent – next to address – to direct towards
ante-	before	antecedent – going before in time anterior – occurring before
anti-	against	antidote – remedy to act against an evil antibiotic – substance that fights against bacteria
be-	over, thoroughly	bemoan – to mourn over belabor – to exert much labor upon
bi-	two	bisect – to divide biennial – happening every two years
cata-, cat-, cath-	down	catacombs – underground passage ways catalogue – descriptive list
circum-	around	circumscribe – to draw a circle around circumspect – watchful on all sides
com-	with	combine – join together communication – to have dealing with
contra-	against	contrary – opposed contrast – to stand in opposition
de-	down, from, away	decline – to slope downward decontrol – to remove control from
di-	two	dichotomy – process of dividing into two groups or entities diarchy – system of government with two authorities

Prefix	Meaning	Example
dis-, di-	apart, away	discern – to distinguish as separate
		digress – to turn away from the subject of attention
epi-, ep-, eph-	upon, among	epidemic – happening among a disproportionately large number of individuals
		epicycle – circle whose center moves round in the circumference of a greater circle
ex-, e-	from, out	exceed – go beyond the limit
		emit – to send forth
extra-	outside, beyond	extraordinary – beyond or outside conventional means
		extrasensory – beyond the ordinary senses
hyper-	beyond, over	hyperactive – over the normal activity level
		hypercritic – one who is critical beyond measure
hypo-	beneath, down	hypodermic – beneath the skin
		hypoglycemia – abnormally low glucose level in the blood
in-, il-, im-, ir-	not	inactive – not active
		irreversible – not reversible
in-, il-, im-, ir-	in, on, into	instill – to put in slowly
		impose – to lay on
inter-	among, between	intercom – to exchange conversations between people
		interlude – performance given between parts in a play
intra-	within	intravenous – within a vein
		intramural – being or happening within the confines of a community, group, or institution

Prefix	Meaning	Example
meta-	beyond, over, along with	metamorphosis – change over in form or nature metatarsus – part of foot beyond the flat of the foot
mis-	badly, wrongly	misconstrue – to interpret wrongly misappropriate – to use wrongly
mono-	one	monogamy – to be married to one person at a time monotone – a single, unvaried tone
multi-	many	multiple – of many parts multitude – a great number
non-	no, not	nonsense – lack of sense nonentity – not existing
ob-	against	obscene – offensive to modesty obstruct – to hinder the passage of
para-, par-	beside	parallel – continuously at equal distance apart parenthesis – sentence inserted within a passage
per-	through	persevere – to maintain an effort permeate – to pass through
poly-	many	polygon – a plane figure with many sides or angles polytheism – belief in existence of many gods
post-	after	posterior – coming after postpone – to put off till a future time
pre-	before	premature – ready before the proper time premonition – a previous warning

Prefix	Meaning	Example
pro-	in favor of, forward	prolific – bringing forth offspring project – throw or cast forward
re-	back, against	reimburse – pay back retract – to draw back
semi-	half	semicircle – half a circle semiannual – half-yearly
sub-	under	subdue – to bring under one's power submarine – travel under the surface of the sea
super-	above	supersonic – above the speed of sound superior – higher in place or position
tele-, tel-	across	telecast – transmit across a distance telepathy – communication between mind and mind at a distance
trans-	across	transpose – to change the position of two things transmit – to send from one person to another
ultra-	beyond	ultraviolet – beyond the limit of visibility ultramarine – beyond the sea
un-	not	undeclared – not declared unbelievable – not believable
uni-	one	unity – state of oneness unison – sounding together
with-	away, against	withhold – to hold back withdraw – to take away

Root

Root	Meaning	Example
act, ag	do, act, drive	activate – to make active agile – having quick motion
alt	high	altitude – height alto – highest male singing voice
alter, altr	other, change	alternative – choice between two or more things of which just one may be picked altruism – living for the good of others
am, ami	love, friend	amiable – worthy of affection amity – friendship
anim	mind, spirit	animated – spirited animosity – intense hostility
annu, enni	year	annual – occurring every year centennial – a 100-year anniversary
aqua	water	aquarium – tank for water animals and plants aquacade – swimming or diving exhibition
arch	principal, first	archenemy – principal enemy archetype – original pattern from which things are copied
aud, audit	hear	audible – capable of being heard audience – assembly of listeners or spectators
auto	self	automatic – self-acting autobiography – a story whose subject and author are one and the same
bell	war	belligerent – a nation or state waging war bellicose – favoring or inclined toward hostility

Root	Meaning	Example
ben, bene	good	benign – kindly disposition beneficial – advantageous
bio	life	biotic – relating to life biology – the science of life
brev	short	abbreviate – make shorter brevity – shortness
cad, cas	fall	cadence – fall in voice casualty – loss caused by death
capit, cap	head	captain – the head or chief decapitate – to cut off the head
cede, ceed, cess	to go, to yield	recede – to move or fall back proceed – to move onward
cent	hundred	century – hundred years centipede – insect with a hundred legs
chron	time	chronology – science dealing with historical dates chronicle – register of events in order of time
cide, cis	to kill, to cut	homicide – a killing of one person by another; the killer of another person incision – a cut
clam, claim	to shout	acclaim – receive with applause proclamation – announce publicly
cogn	to know	recognize – to know again cognition – awareness
corp	body	incorporate – combine into one body corpse – dead body
cred	to trust, to believe	incredible – unbelievable credulous – too prone to believe
cur, curr, curs	to run	current – flowing body of air or water excursion – short trip

Root	Meaning	Example
dem	people	democracy – government formed for the people epidemic – affecting all people
dic, dict	to say	dictate – to read aloud for another to transcribe verdict – decision of a jury
doc, doct	to teach	docile – easily instructed indoctrinate – to instruct
domin	to rule	dominate – to rule dominion – territory of rule
duc, duct	to lead	conduct – act of guiding induce – to overcome by persuasion
eu	well, good	eulogy – speech or writing in praise euphony – pleasantness or smoothness of sound
fac, fact, *fect, fic*	to do, to make	factory – location of production fiction – something invented or imagined
fer	to bear, to carry	transfer – to move from one place to another refer – to direct to
fin	end, limit	infinity – unlimited finite – limited in quantity
flect, flex	to bend	flexible – easily bent reflect – to throw back
fort	luck	fortunate – lucky fortuitous – happening by chance
fort	strong	fortify – strengthen fortress – stronghold

Root	Meaning	Example
frag, fract	break	fragile – easily broken fracture – break
fug	flee	fugitive – fleeing refugee – one who flees to a place of safety
gen	class, race	engender – to breed generic – of a general nature in regard to all members
grad, gress	to go, to step	regress – to go back graduate – to divide into regular steps
gram, graph	writing	telegram – message sent by telegraph autograph – person's handwriting or signature
ject	to throw	projectile – capable of being thrown reject – to throw away
leg	law	legitimate – lawful legal – defined by law
leg, lig, lect	to choose, gather, read	illegible – incapable of being read election – the act of choosing
liber	free	liberal – favoring freedom of ideals liberty – freedom from restraint
log	study, speech	archaeology – study of human antiquities prologue – address spoken before a performance
luc, lum	light	translucent – slightly transparent illuminate – to light up
magn	large, great	magnify – to make larger magnificent – great
mal, male	bad, wrong	malfunction – to operate incorrectly malevolent – evil

Root	Meaning	Example
mar	sea	marine – pertaining to the sea submarine – below the surface of the sea
mater, matr	mother	maternal – motherly matriarch – government exercised by a mother
mit, miss	to send	transmit – to send from one person or place to another mission – the act of sending
morph	shape	metamorphosis – a changing in shape anthropomorphic – having a human shape
mut	change	mutable – subject to change mutate – to change a vowel
nat	born	innate – inborn native – a person born in a place
neg	deny	negative – expressing denial renege – to deny
nom	name	nominate – to put forward a name anonymous – no name given
nov	new	novel – new renovate – to make as good as new
omni	all	omnipotent – all powerful omnipresent – all present
oper	to work	operate – to work on something cooperate – to work with others
pass, path	to feel	pathetic – affecting the tender emotions passionate – moved by strong emotion

Root	Meaning	Example
pater, patr	father	paternal – fatherly
		patriarch – government exercised by a father
ped, pod	foot	pedestrian – one who travels on foot
		podiatrist – foot doctor
pel, puls	to drive, to push	impel – to drive forward
		compulsion – irresistible force
phil	love	philharmonic – loving harmony or music
		philanthropist – one who loves and seeks to do good for others
port	carry	export – to carry out of the country
		portable – able to be carried
psych	mind	psychology – study of the mind
		psychiatrist – specialist in mental disorders
quer, ques, quir, quis	to ask	inquiry – to ask about
		question – that which is asked
rid, ris	to laugh	ridiculous – laughable
		derision – to mock
rupt	to break	interrupt – to break in upon
		erupt – to break through
sci	to know	science – systematic knowledge of physical or natural phenomena
		conscious – having inward knowledge
scrib, script	to write	transcribe – to write over again
		script – text of words
sent, sens	to feel, to think	sentimental – feel great emotion
		sensitive – easily affected by changes

Root	Meaning	Example
sequ, secut	to follow	sequence – connected series consecutive – following one another in unbroken order
solv, solu, solut	to loosen	dissolve – to break up absolute – without restraint
spect	to look at	spectator – one who watches inspect – to look at closely
spir	to breathe	inspire – to breathe in respiration – process of breathing
string, strict	to bind	stringent – binding strongly restrict – to restrain within bounds
stru, struct	to build	misconstrue – to interpret wrongly construct – to build
tang, ting, tact, tig	to touch	tangent – touching, but not intersecting contact – touching
ten, tent, tain	to hold	tenure – holding of office contain – to hold
term	to end	terminate – to end terminal – having an end
terr	earth	terrain – tract of land terrestrial – existing on earth
therm	heat	thermal – pertaining to heat thermometer – instrument for measuring temperature
tort, tors	to twist	contortionist – one who twists violently torsion – act of turning or twisting

Root	Meaning	Example
tract	to pull, to draw	attract – draw toward distract – to draw away
vac	empty	vacant – empty evacuate – to empty out
ven, vent	to come	prevent – to stop from coming intervene – to come between
ver	true	verify – to prove to be true veracious – truthful
verb	word	verbose – use of excess words verbatim – word for word
vid, vis	to see	video – picture phase of television vision – act of seeing external objects
vinc, vict, vang	to conquer	invincible – unconquerable victory – defeat of enemy
viv, vit	life	vital – necessary to life vivacious – lively
voc	to call	provocative – serving to excite or stimulate to action vocal – uttered by voice
vol	to wish, to will	involuntary – outside the control of will volition – the act of willing or choosing

Suffix

Suffix	Meaning	Example
-able, -ble	capable of	believable – capable of being believed legible – capable of being read
-acious, -icious, -ous	full of	vivacious – full of life wondrous – full of wonder

Suffix	Meaning	Example
-ant, -ent	full of	eloquent – full of eloquence expectant – full of expectation
-ary	connected with	honorary – for the sake of honor disciplinary – enforcing instruction
-ate	to make	ventilate – to make public consecrate – to make sacred
-fy	to make	magnify – to make larger testify – to make witness
-ile	pertaining to, capable of	docile – capable of being managed easily civil – pertaining to a city or state
-ism	principle or practice	conservatism – interest in preserving or restoring idiotism – foolish conduct or action
-ist	doer	artist – one who creates art pianist – one who plays the piano
-ose	full of	verbose – full of words grandiose – striking, imposing
-osis	condition	neurosis – nervous condition psychosis – psychological condition
-tude	state	magnitude – state of greatness multitude – state of quantity

FIGURES OF SPEECH

Figurative language helps to create imaginative and detailed writing. A figure of speech is used in the imaginative rather than the literal sense. It helps the reader to make connections between the writer's thoughts and the external world. Knowing the different types of figures of speech can help you determine the context in which a word is being used and,

thereby, help you determine the meaning of that word. The following are some commonly used figures of speech.

Simile

A simile is an explicit comparison between two things. The comparison is made by using *like* or *as*.

Her hair was *like* straw.

The blanket was *as* white as snow.

Metaphor

Like the simile, the metaphor likens two things. However, *like* or *as* are not used in the comparison.

"All the world's a stage." Shakespeare

Grass is nature's blanket.

A common error is the mixed metaphor. This occurs when a writer uses two inconsistent metaphors in a single expression.

The blanket of snow clutched the earth with icy fingers.

Hyperbole

A hyperbole is a deliberate overstatement or exaggeration used to express an idea.

I have told you a thousand times not to play with matches.

Personification

Personification is the attribution of human qualities to an object, animal, or idea.

The wind laughed at their attempts to catch the flying papers.

☞Drill 14: Reading Comprehension

> **DIRECTIONS:** Read the passage and answer the questions that follow.

Water

1   The most important source of sediment is earth and rock material carried to the sea by rivers and streams; the same materials may also have been transported by glaciers and winds. Other sources are volcanic ash and lava, shells and skeletons of organisms, chemical
5   precipitates formed in seawater, and particles from outer space.

Water is a most unusual substance because it exists on the surface of the earth in its three physical states: ice, water, and water vapor. There are other substances that might exist in a solid and liquid or gaseous state at temperatures normally found at the earth's
10   surface, but there are fewer substances which occur in all three states.

Water is odorless, tasteless, and colorless. It is the only substance known to exist in a natural state as a solid, liquid, or gas on the surface of the earth. It is a universal solvent. Water does not corrode, rust, burn, or separate into its components easily. It is chemically
15   indestructible. It can corrode almost any metal and erode the most solid rock. A unique property of water is that it expands and floats on water when frozen or in the solid state. Water has a freezing point of 0°C and a boiling point of 100°C. Water has the capacity for absorbing great quantities of heat with relatively little increase in tempera-
20   ture. When *distilled*, water is a poor conductor of electricity but when salt is added, it is a good conductor of electricity.

Sunlight is the source of energy for temperature change, evaporation, and currents for water movement through the atmosphere. Sunlight controls the rate of photosynthesis for all marine plants,
25   which are directly or indirectly the source of food for all marine animals. Migration, breeding, and other behaviors of marine animals are affected by light.

Water, as the ocean or sea, is blue because of the molecular scattering of the sunlight. Blue light, being of short wavelength, is
30   scattered more effectively than light of longer wavelengths. Variations in color may be caused by particles suspended in the water, water depth, cloud cover, temperature, and other variable factors. Heavy concentrations of dissolved materials cause a yellowish hue, while algae will cause the water to look green. Heavy populations of
35   plant and animal materials will cause the water to look brown.

1. Which of the following lists of topics best organizes the information in the selection?

   (A) I.   Water as vapor

        II. Water as ice

        III. Water as solid

   (B) I.   Properties of seawater

        II. Freezing and boiling points of water

        III. Photosynthesis

        IV. Oceans and seas

   (C) I.   Water as substance

        II. Water's corrosion

        III. Water and plants

        IV. Water and algae coloration

   (D) I.   Water's physical states

        II. Properties of water

        III. Effects of the sun on water

        IV. Reasons for color variation in water

2. According to the passage, what is the most unique property of water?

   (A) Water is odorless, tasteless, and colorless.

   (B) Water exists on the surface of the earth in three physical states.

   (C) Water is chemically indestructible.

   (D) Water is a poor conductor of electricity.

3. Which of the following best defines the word *distilled* as it is used in the last sentence of the third paragraph?

   (A) Free of salt content

   (B) Free of electrical energy

   (C) Dehydrated

   (D) Containing wine

4. The writer's main purpose in this selection is to

   (A) explain the colors of water.

   (B) examine the effects of the sun on water.

   (C) define the properties of water.

   (D) describe the three physical states of all liquids.

5. The writer of this selection would most likely agree with which of the following statements?

   (A) The properties of water are found in most other liquids on this planet.

   (B) Water should not be consumed in its most natural state.

   (C) Water might be used to serve many different functions.

   (D) Water is too unpredictable for most scientists.

DIRECTIONS: Read the passage and answer the questions that follow.

The Beginnings of the Submarine

1   A submarine was first used as an offensive weapon during the American Revolutionary War. The Turtle, a one-man submersible designed by an American inventor named David Bushnell and hand-operated by a screw propeller, attempted to sink a British man-of-war

5   in New York Harbor. The plan was to attach a charge of gunpowder to the ship's bottom with screws and explode it with a time fuse. After repeated failures to force the screws through the copper sheathing of the hull of H.M.S. *Eagle*, the submarine gave up and withdrew, exploding its powder a short distance from the *Eagle*. Although the

10   attack was unsuccessful, it caused the British to move their blockading ships from the harbor to the outer bay.

      On 17 February 1864, a Confederate craft, a hand-propelled submersible, carrying a crew of eight men, sank a Federal corvette that was blockading Charleston Harbor. The hit was accomplished by a

15   torpedo suspended ahead of the Confederate Hunley as she rammed the Union frigate *Housatonic*, and is the first recorded instance of a submarine sinking a warship.

      The submarine first became a major component in naval warfare during World War I, when Germany demonstrated its full potential.

20   Wholesale sinking of Allied shipping by the German U-boats almost

swung the war in favor of the Central Powers. Then, as now, the submarine's greatest advantage was that it could operate beneath the ocean surface where detection was difficult. Sinking a submarine was comparatively easy, once it was found — but finding it before it
25 could attack was another matter.

During the closing months of World War I, the Allied Submarine Devices Investigation Committee was formed to obtain from science and technology more effective underwater detection equipment. The committee developed a reasonably accurate device for
30 locating a submerged submarine. This device was a trainable hydrophone, which was attached to the bottom of the ASW ship, and used to detect screw noises and other sounds that came from a submarine. Although the committee disbanded after World War I, the British made improvements on the locating device during the interval be-
35 tween then and World War II, and named it ASDIC after the committee.

American scientists further improved on the device, calling it SONAR, a name derived from the underlined initials of the words <u>so</u>und <u>n</u>avigation and <u>r</u>anging.
40 At the end of World War II, the United States improved the snorkel (a device for bringing air to the crew and engines when operating submerged on diesels) and developed the Guppy (short for greater underwater propulsion power), a conversion of the fleet-type submarine of World War II fame. The superstructure was changed by
45 reducing the surface area, streamlining every protruding object, and enclosing the periscope shears in a streamlined metal fairing. Performance increased greatly with improved electronic equipment, additional battery capacity, and the addition of the snorkel.

6. The passage implies that one of the most pressing modifications needed for the submarine was to

   (A) streamline its shape.

   (B) enlarge the submarine for accommodating more torpedoes and men.

   (C) reduce the noise caused by the submarine.

   (D) add a snorkel.

7. It is inferred that

   (A) ASDIC was formed to obtain technology for underwater detection.

(B) ASDIC developed an accurate device for locating submarines.

(C) the hydrophone was attached to the bottom of the ship.

(D) ASDIC was formed to develop technology to defend U.S. shipping.

8. SONAR not only picked up the sound of submarines moving through the water but also

(A) indicated the speed at which the sub was moving.

(B) gave the location of the submarine.

(C) indicated the speed of the torpedo.

(D) placed the submarine within a specified range.

9. According to the passage, the submarine's success was due in part to its ability to

(A) strike and escape undetected.

(B) move swifter than other vessels.

(C) submerge to great depths while being hunted.

(D) run silently.

10. From the passage, one can infer

(A) David Bushnell was indirectly responsible for the sinking of the Federal corvette in Charlestown Harbor.

(B) David Bushnell invented the Turtle.

(C) the Turtle was a one-man submarine.

(D) the Turtle sank the *Eagle* on February 17, 1864.

READING DRILLS

ANSWER KEY

Drill 1
1.	(J)	9.	(F)
2.	(G)	10.	(E)
3.	(A)	11.	(D)
4.	(C)	12.	(C)
5.	(H)	13.	(A)
6.	(B)	14.	(E)
7.	(I)	15.	(B)
8.	(D)		

Drill 2
1.	(D)	9.	(B)
2.	(G)	10.	(H)
3.	(I)	11.	(D)
4.	(F)	12.	(A)
5.	(A)	13.	(B)
6.	(J)	14.	(E)
7.	(E)	15.	(C)
8.	(C)		

Drill 3
1.	(E)	9.	(F)
2.	(H)	10.	(D)
3.	(J)	11.	(C)
4.	(A)	12.	(A)
5.	(I)	13.	(E)
6.	(B)	14.	(D)
7.	(C)	15.	(B)
8.	(G)		

Drill 4
1.	(D)	9.	(H)
2.	(E)	10.	(G)
3.	(A)	11.	(D)
4.	(I)	12.	(A)
5.	(J)	13.	(B)
6.	(B)	14.	(C)
7.	(C)	15.	(E)
8.	(F)		

Drill 5
1.	(H)	9.	(D)
2.	(F)	10.	(G)
3.	(A)	11.	(B)
4.	(B)	12.	(D)
5.	(J)	13.	(A)
6.	(C)	14.	(E)
7.	(I)	15.	(C)
8.	(E)		

Drill 6
1.	(G)	9.	(F)
2.	(A)	10.	(H)
3.	(E)	11.	(D)
4.	(J)	12.	(E)
5.	(C)	13.	(A)
6.	(B)	14.	(C)
7.	(D)	15.	(B)
8.	(I)		

Drill 7

1.	(F)	9.	(D)
2.	(E)	10.	(J)
3.	(A)	11.	(B)
4.	(B)	12.	(E)
5.	(H)	13.	(D)
6.	(I)	14.	(C)
7.	(C)	15.	(A)
8.	(G)		

Drill 8

1.	(D)	9.	(F)
2.	(A)	10.	(J)
3.	(H)	11.	(C)
4.	(G)	12.	(B)
5.	(B)	13.	(A)
6.	(C)	14.	(E)
7.	(E)	15.	(D)
8.	(I)		

Drill 9

1.	(D)	9.	(C)
2.	(I)	10.	(H)
3.	(G)	11.	(A)
4.	(A)	12.	(D)
5.	(J)	13.	(B)
6.	(E)	14.	(E)
7.	(B)	15.	(C)
8.	(F)		

Drill 10

1.	(H)	9.	(D)
2.	(I)	10.	(G)
3.	(E)	11.	(B)
4.	(A)	12.	(D)
5.	(J)	13.	(A)
6.	(B)	14.	(C)
7.	(F)	15.	(E)
8.	(C)		

Drill 11

1.	(F)	9.	(E)
2.	(I)	10.	(G)
3.	(A)	11.	(C)
4.	(H)	12.	(B)
5.	(B)	13.	(E)
6.	(J)	14.	(A)
7.	(C)	15.	(D)
8.	(D)		

Drill 12

1.	(J)	9.	(F)
2.	(A)	10.	(E)
3.	(B)	11.	(E)
4.	(I)	12.	(C)
5.	(C)	13.	(D)
6.	(H)	14.	(A)
7.	(D)	15.	(B)
8.	(G)		

Drill 13

1.	(C)	16.	(B)	31.	(A)	46.	(A)
2.	(B)	17.	(B)	32.	(B)	47.	(D)
3.	(A)	18.	(C)	33.	(E)	48.	(C)
4.	(E)	19.	(E)	34.	(A)	49.	(E)
5.	(A)	20.	(D)	35.	(E)	50.	(A)
6.	(E)	21.	(E)	36.	(D)	51.	(B)
7.	(E)	22.	(A)	37.	(D)	52.	(E)
8.	(B)	23.	(D)	38.	(A)	53.	(C)
9.	(E)	24.	(A)	39.	(E)	54.	(A)
10.	(C)	25.	(C)	40.	(C)	55.	(B)
11.	(B)	26.	(B)	41.	(E)	56.	(C)
12.	(E)	27.	(D)	42.	(B)	57.	(D)
13.	(A)	28.	(C)	43.	(A)	58.	(E)
14.	(C)	29.	(E)	44.	(E)	59.	(D)
15.	(D)	30.	(D)	45.	(B)	60.	(C)

Drill 14: Reading Comprehension—Detailed Explanations of Answers

1. **(D)** The correct response is (D) because its precepts are summations of each of the composition's main paragraphs. (A) only mentions points made in the second paragraph. (B) and (C) only mention scattered points made throughout the passage, each of which does not represent a larger body of information within the passage.

2. **(B)** The second paragraph states that this is the reason that water is a most unusual substance. (A) and (C) list unusual properties of water, but are not developed in the same manner as the property stated in (B). (D) is not even correct under all circumstances.

3. **(A)** The sentence contrasts distilled water to that which contains salt, so (A) is correct. (B), (C), and (D) are not implied by the passage.

4. **(C)** The writer's didactic summary of water's properties is the only perspective found in the passage. (A) and (B) are the subjects of individual paragraphs within the passage, but hardly represent the entire passage itself. An in-depth discussion of the physical states of liquids (D) is not offered within the passage.

5. **(C)** The correct choice is (C) because of the many properties of water ascribed to it in the passage, each of which might serve one practical

purpose or another. (A) and (D) are contradicted within the passage, while (B) is not implied at all by the passage.

6. **(A)** Answer (A) is correct because of the importance of streamlining mentioned in the final paragraph. (B) and (C) are not suggested in the paragraph, and (D) is secondary in importance to (A).

7. **(D)** Since it may be inferred from the general purpose of underwater detection equipment, (D) is correct. While (A) and (B) are true statements, they are not inferences. (C) is not implied in the passage.

8. **(D)** Answer (D) is correct because the "R" in SONAR stands for "Ranging." (A), (B), and (C) are neither mentioned nor implied by the passage.

9. **(A)** As was mentioned in the third sentence of the third paragraph, (A) is correct. (B), (C), and (D) are not mentioned in the passage.

10. **(A)** It may be inferred that Bushnell's invention led to the success of the later version of the submarine. (B) and (C) are true, but are not inferences because they are directly stated in the first paragraph. (D) is not a true statement; the Turtle had no direct link to the 1864 incident.

PPST

Pre-Professional Skills Tests

Chapter 3
Basic Math Skills Review

Chapter 3

BASIC MATH SKILLS REVIEW

    I.   **ARITHMETIC**

   II.   **ALGEBRA**

  III.   **GEOMETRY**

  IV. **WORD PROBLEMS**

Are you ready to tackle the math section of the PPST? Well, the chances are that you will be, but only after some reviewing of basic concepts in arithmetic, algebra, and geometry. The more familiar you are with these fundamental principles, the better you will do on the math section of the PPST. Our math review represents the various mathematical topics that will appear on the PPST. You will not find any calculus, trigonometry, or even imaginary numbers in our math review. Why? Because these concepts are not tested on the math sections of the PPST. The mathematical concepts presented on the PPST are ones with which you are already familiar and simply need to review in order to score well.

Along with a knowledge of these topics, how quickly and accurately you can answer the math questions will have an effect upon your success. Therefore, memorize the directions in order to save time and decrease your chances of making careless mistakes. Then, complete the practice drills that are provided for you in our review. Even if you are sure you know your fundamental math concepts, the drills will help to warm you up so that you can go into the math section of the PPST with quick, sharp math skills.

REFERENCE TABLE

SYMBOLS AND THEIR MEANINGS

=	is equal to	≤	is less than or equal to
≠	is unequal to	≥	is greater than or equal to
<	is less than	||	is parallel to
>	is greater than	⊥	is perpendicular to

FORMULAS

DESCRIPTION	FORMULA
Area (A) of a:	
square	$A = s^2$; where s = side
rectangle	$A = lw$; where l = length, w = width
parallelogram	$A = bh$; where b = base, h = height
triangle	$A = \frac{1}{2} bh$; where b = base, h = height
circle	$A = \pi r^2$; where π = 3.14, r = radius
Perimeter (P) of a:	
square	$P = 4s$; where s = side
rectangle	$P = 2l + 2w$; where l = length, w = width
triangle	$P = a + b + c$; where a, b, and c are the sides
circumference (C) of a circle	$C = \pi d$; where π = 3.14, d = diameter = $2r$
Volume (V) of a:	
cube	$V = s^3$; where s = side
rectangular container	$V = lwh$; where l = length, w = width, h = height
Pythagorean Theorem	$c^2 = a^2 + b^2$; where c = hypotenuse, a and b are legs of a right triangle
Distance (d):	
between two points in a plane	$d = \sqrt{(x_2 - x_1)^2 + (y_2 - y_1)^2}$ where (x_1, y_1) and (x_2, y_2) are two points in a plane
as a function of rate and time	$d = rt$; where r = rate, t = time
Mean	$\text{mean} = \dfrac{x_1 + x_2 + \ldots + x_n}{n}$ where the x's are the values for which a mean is desired, and n = number of values in the series
Median	median = the point in an ordered set of numbers at which half of the numbers are above and half of the numbers are below this value
Simple Interest (i)	$i = prt$; where p = principal, r = rate, t = time
Total Cost (c)	$c = nr$; where n = number of units, r = cost per unit

I. ARITHMETIC

INTEGERS AND REAL NUMBERS

Most of the numbers used in algebra belong to a set called the **real numbers** or **reals**. This set can be represented graphically by the real number line.

Given the number line below, we arbitrarily fix a point and label it with the number 0. In a similar manner, we can label any point on the line with one of the real numbers, depending on its position relative to 0. Numbers to the right of 0 are positive, while those to the left are negative. Value increases from left to right, so that if a is to the right of b, it is said to be greater than b.

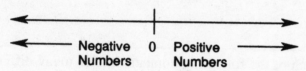

If we now divide the number line into equal segments, we can label the points on this line with real numbers. For example, the point 2 lengths to the left of 0 is – 2, while the point 3 lengths to the right of 0 is + 3 (the + sign is usually assumed, so + 3 is written simply as 3). The number line now looks like this:

These boundary points represent the subset of the reals known as the **integers**. The set of integers is made up of both the positive and negative whole numbers:

$$\{\ldots, -4, -3, -2, -1, 0, 1, 2, 3, 4, \ldots\}.$$

Some subsets of integers are:

Natural Numbers or Positive Numbers—the set of integers starting with 1 and increasing:

$$N = \{1, 2, 3, 4, \ldots\}.$$

Whole Numbers—the set of integers starting with 0 and increasing:

$$W = \{0, 1, 2, 3, \ldots\}.$$

Negative Numbers—the set of integers starting with − 1 and decreasing:

Z = { − 1, − 2, − 3, ...}.

Prime Numbers—the set of positive integers greater than 1 that are divisible only by 1 and themselves:

{2, 3, 5, 7, 11, ...}.

Even Integers—the set of integers divisible by 2:

{..., − 4, − 2, 0, 2, 4, 6, ...}.

Odd Integers—the set of integers not divisible by 2:

{..., − 3, − 1, 1, 3, 5, 7, ...}.

Consecutive Integers—the set of integers that differ by 1:

{n, n + 1, n + 2, ...} (n = an integer).

PROBLEM

Classify each of the following numbers into as many different sets as possible. Example: real, integer ...

(1) 0

(2) 9

(3) $\sqrt{6}$

(4) $\dfrac{1}{2}$

(5) $\dfrac{2}{3}$

(6) 1.5

SOLUTION

(1) 0 is a real number, an integer, and a whole number.

(2) 9 is a real number, an odd number, and a natural number.

(3) $\sqrt{6}$ is a real number.

(4) $\dfrac{1}{2}$ is a real number.

(5) $\dfrac{2}{3}$ is a real number.

(6) 1.5 is a real number and a decimal.

ABSOLUTE VALUE

The **absolute value** of a number is represented by two vertical lines around the number, and is equal to the given number, regardless of sign.

The absolute value of a real number A is defined as follows:

$$|A| = \begin{cases} A \text{ if } A \geq 0 \\ -A \text{ if } A < 0 \end{cases}$$

EXAMPLES

$$|5| = 5, |-8| = -(-8) = 8$$

Absolute values follow the given rules:

    (A) $|-A| = |A|$

    (B) $|A| \geq 0$, equality holding only if $A = 0$

    (C) $\left|\dfrac{A}{B}\right| = \dfrac{|A|}{|B|}$, $B \neq 0$

    (D) $|AB| = |A| \times |B|$

    (E) $|A|^2 = A^2$

Absolute value can also be expressed on the real number line as the distance of the point represented by the real number from the point labeled 0.

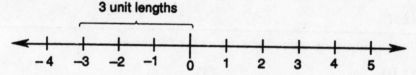

3 unit lengths

So $|-3| = 3$ because -3 is 3 units to the left of 0.

PROBLEM

Classify each of the following statements as true or false. If it is false, explain why.

    (1) $|-120| > 1$ (4) $|12 - 3| = 12 - 3$

    (2) $|4 - 12| = |4| - |12|$ (5) $|-12a| = 12|a|$

    (3) $|4 - 9| = 9 - 4$

SOLUTION

    (1) True

    (2) False, $|4 - 12| = |4| - |12|$

$$|-8| = 4 - 12$$

$$8 \neq -8$$

In general, $|a + b| \neq |a| + |b|$

(3) True

(4) True

(5) True

PROBLEM

Calculate the value of each of the following expressions:

(1) $||2 - 5| + 6 - 14|$

(2) $|-5| \times |4| + \dfrac{|-12|}{4}$

SOLUTION

Before solving this problem, one must remember the order of operations: parenthesis, multiplication and division, addition and subtraction.

(1) $||-3| + 6 - 14| = |3 + 6 - 14| = |9 - 14| = |-5| = 5$

(2) $(5 \times 4) + {}^{12}/_4 = 20 + 3 = 23$

PROBLEM

Find the absolute value for each of the following:

(1) 0

(2) 4

(3) $-\pi$

(4) a, where a is a real number

SOLUTION

(1) $|0| = 0$

(2) $|4| = 4$

(3) $|-\pi| = \pi$

(4) for $a > 0, |a| = a$

for $a = 0, |a| = 0$

for $a < 0, |a| = a$

i.e., $|a| = \begin{cases} a \text{ if } a > 0 \\ 0 \text{ if } a = 0 \\ -a \text{ if } a < 0 \end{cases}$

POSITIVE AND NEGATIVE NUMBERS

A) **To add two numbers with like signs,** add their absolute values and write the sum with the common sign. So,

$$6 + 2 = 8, (-6) + (-2) = -8$$

B) **To add two numbers with unlike signs,** find the difference between their absolute values, and write the result with the sign of the number with the greater absolute value. So,

$$(-4) + 6 = 2, 15 + (-19) = -4$$

C) **To subtract a number b from another number a,** change the sign of b and add to a. Examples:

$$10 - (3) = 10 + (-3) = 7 \tag{1}$$

$$2 - (-6) = 2 + 6 = 8 \tag{2}$$

$$(-5) - (-2) = -5 + 2 = -3 \tag{3}$$

D) **To multiply (or divide) two numbers having like signs,** multiply (or divide) their absolute values and write the result with a positive sign. Examples:

$$(5)(3) = 15 \tag{1}$$

$$(-6) \div (-3) = 2 \tag{2}$$

E) **To multiply (or divide) two numbers having unlike signs,** multiply (or divide) their absolute values and write the result with a negative sign. Examples:

$$(-2)(8) = -16 \tag{1}$$

$$9 \div (-3) = -3 \tag{2}$$

According to the law of signs for real numbers, the square of a positive or negative number is always positive. This means that it is impossible to take the square root of a negative number in the real number system.

PROBLEM

Calculate the value of each of the following expressions:

(1) $||2 - 5| + 6 - 14|$ (2) $|-8| \times 2 + \dfrac{|-12|}{4}$

SOLUTION

Before solving this problem, one must use the rules for the **order of operations.** Always work within the parentheses or with absolute values first while keeping in mind that multiplication and division are carried out before addition and subtraction.

$$(1) \quad ||-3|+6-14| = |3+6-14|$$
$$= |9-14|$$
$$= |-5|$$
$$= 5$$

$$(2) \quad (8 \times 2) + \frac{12}{4} = 16 + 3$$
$$= 19$$

ODD AND EVEN NUMBERS

When dealing with odd and even numbers, keep in mind the following:

Adding:

even + even = even

odd + odd = even

even + odd = odd

Multiplying:

even × even = even

even × odd = even

odd × odd = odd

☞ Drill: Integers and Real Numbers

Addition

1. Simplify $4 + (-7) + 2 + (-5)$.

(A) -6 (B) -4 (C) 0 (D) 6 (E) 18

2. Simplify $144 + (-317) + 213$.

(A) -357 (B) -40 (C) 40 (D) 257 (E) 674

3. Simplify $|4+(-3)|+|-2|$.

(A) -2 (B) -1 (C) 1 (D) 3 (E) 9

4. What integer makes the equation $-13 + 12 + 7 + ? = 10$ a true statement?

(A) -22 (B) -10 (C) 4 (D) 6 (E) 10

5. Simplify $4 + 17 + (-29) + 13 + (-22) + (-3)$.

(A) -44 (B) -20 (C) 23 (D) 34 (E) 78

Subtraction

6. Simplify $319 - 428$.

(A) -111 (B) -109 (C) -99 (D) 109 (E) 747

7. Simplify $91,203 - 37,904 + 1,073$.

(A) $54,372$ (B) $64,701$ (C) $128,034$ (D) $129,107$ (E) $130,180$

8. Simplify $|43 - 62| - |-17 - 3|$.

(A) -39 (B) -19 (C) -1 (D) 1 (E) 39

9. Simplify $-(-4 - 7) + (-2)$.

(A) -22 (B) -13 (C) -9 (D) 7 (E) 9

10. In the St. Elias Mountains, Mt. Logan rises from 1,292 meters above sea level to 7,243 meters above sea level. How tall is Mt. Logan?

(A) $4,009$ m   (B) $5,951$ m   (C) $5,699$ m   (D) $6,464$ m   (E) $7,885$ m

Multiplication

11. Simplify $(-3) \times (-18) \times (-1)$.

(A) -108 (B) -54 (C) -48 (D) 48 (E) 54

12. Simplify $|-42| \times |7|$.

(A) -294 (B) -49 (C) -35 (D) 284 (E) 294

13. Simplify $(-6) \times 5 \times (-10) \times (-4) \times 0 \times 2$.

(A) $-2,400$ (B) -240 (C) 0 (D) 280 (E) $2,700$

14. Simplify $-|-6 \times 8|$.

(A) -48 (B) -42 (C) 2 (D) 42 (E) 48

15. A city in Georgia had a record low temperature of $-3°F$ one winter. During the same year, a city in Michigan experienced a record low that was nine times the record low set in Georgia. What was the record low in Michigan that year?

(A) $-31°F$ (B) $-27°F$ (C) $-21°F$ (D) $-12°F$ (E) $-6°F$

Division

16. Simplify $(-24) \div 8$.

(A) -4 (B) -3 (C) -2 (D) 3 (E) 4

17. Simplify $(-180) \div (-12)$.

(A) -30 (B) -15 (C) 1.5 (D) 15 (E) 216

18. Simplify $|-76| \div |-4|$.

(A) -21 (B) -19 (C) 13 (D) 19 (E) 21.5

19. Simplify $|216 \div (-6)|$.

(A) -36 (B) -12 (C) 36 (D) 38 (E) 43

20. At the end of the year, a small firm has $2,996 in its account for bonuses. If the entire amount is equally divided among the 14 employees, how much does each one receive?

(A) $107   (B) $114   (C) $170   (D) $210   (E) $214

Order of Operations

21. Simplify $\dfrac{4 + 8 \times 2}{5 - 1}$.

(A) 4 (B) 5 (C) 6 (D) 8 (E) 12

22. $96 \div 3 \div 4 \div 2 =$

(A) 65 (B) 64 (C) 16 (D) 8 (E) 4

23. $3 + 4 \times 2 - 6 \div 3 =$

(A) -1 (B) $\dfrac{5}{3}$ (C) $\dfrac{8}{3}$ (D) 9 (E) 12

24. $[(4 + 8) \times 3] \div 9 =$

(A) 4 (B) 8 (C) 12 (D) 24 (E) 36

25. $18 + 3 \times 4 \div 3 =$

(A) 3 (B) 5 (C) 10 (D) 22 (E) 28

26. $(29 - 17 + 4) \div 4 + |-2| =$

(A) $2\dfrac{2}{3}$ (B) 4 (C) $4\dfrac{2}{3}$ (D) 6 (E) 15

27. $(-3) \times 5 - 20 \div 4 =$

(A) -75 (B) -20 (C) -10 (D) $-8\dfrac{3}{4}$ (E) 20

28. $\dfrac{11 \times 2 + 2}{16 - 2 \times 2} =$

(A) $\dfrac{11}{16}$ (B) 1 (C) 2 (D) $3\dfrac{2}{3}$ (E) 4

29. $|-8 - 4| \div 3 \times 6 + (-4) =$

(A) 20 (B) 26 (C) 32 (D) 62 (E) 212

30. $32 \div 2 + 4 - 15 \div 3 =$

(A) 0 (B) 7 (C) 15 (D) 23 (E) 63

FRACTIONS

The fraction, a/b, where the **numerator** is a and the **denominator** is b, implies that a is being divided by b. The denominator of a fraction can never be zero since a number divided by zero is not defined. If the numerator is greater than the denominator, the fraction is called an **improper fraction**. A **mixed number** is the sum of a whole number and a fraction, i.e.,

$$4\dfrac{3}{8} = 4 + \dfrac{3}{8}.$$

OPERATIONS WITH FRACTIONS

A) **To change a mixed number to an improper fraction**, simply multiply the whole number by the denominator of the fraction and add the numerator. This product becomes the numerator of the result and the denominator remains the same, e.g.,

$$5\frac{2}{3} = \frac{(5 \times 3) + 2}{3} = \frac{15 + 2}{3} = \frac{17}{3}$$

To change an improper fraction to a mixed number, simply divide the numerator by the denominator. The remainder becomes the numerator of the fractional part of the mixed number, and the denominator remains the same, e.g.,

$$\frac{35}{4} = 35 \div 4 = 8\frac{3}{4}$$

To check your work, change your result back to an improper fraction to see if it matches the original fraction.

B) **To find the sum of fractions having a common denominator**, simply add together the numerators of the given fractions and put this sum over the common denominator.

$$\frac{11}{3} + \frac{5}{3} = \frac{11 + 5}{3} = \frac{16}{3}$$

Similarly for subtraction,

$$\frac{11}{3} - \frac{5}{3} = \frac{11 - 5}{3} = \frac{6}{3} = 2$$

C) **To find the sum of two fractions having different denominators**, it is necessary to find the **lowest common denominator (LCD)** of the different denominators using a process called **factoring**.

To **factor** a number means to find two numbers that when multiplied together have a product equal to the original number. These two numbers are then said to be **factors** of the original number; e.g., the factors of 6 are

(1)   1 and 6 since $1 \times 6 = 6$.

(2)   2 and 3 since $2 \times 3 = 6$.

Every number is the product of itself and 1. A **prime factor** is a number that does not have any factors besides itself and 1. This is important when finding the LCD of two fractions having different

denominators.

To find the LCD of $^{11}/_6$ and $^5/_{16}$, we must first find the prime factors of each of the two denominators.

$$6 = 2 \times 3$$

$$16 = 2 \times 2 \times 2 \times 2$$

$$LCD = 2 \times 2 \times 2 \times 2 \times 3 = 48$$

Note that we do not need to repeat the 2 that appears in both the factors of 6 and 16.

Once we have determined the LCD of the denominators, each of the fractions must be converted into equivalent fractions having the LCD as a denominator.

Rewrite $^{11}/_6$ and $^5/_{16}$ to have 48 as their denominators.

$$6 \times ? = 48 \qquad\qquad 16 \times ? = 48$$

$$6 \times 8 = 48 \qquad\qquad 16 \times 3 = 48$$

If the numerator and denominator of each fraction is multiplied (or divided) by the same number, the value of the fraction will not change. This is because a fraction b/b, b being any number, is equal to the multiplicative identity, 1.

Therefore,

$$\frac{11}{6} \times \frac{8}{8} = \frac{88}{48} \qquad \frac{5}{16} \times \frac{3}{3} = \frac{15}{48}$$

We may now find

$$\frac{11}{6} + \frac{5}{16} = \frac{88}{48} + \frac{15}{48} = \frac{103}{48}$$

Similarly for subtraction,

$$\frac{11}{6} - \frac{5}{16} = \frac{88}{48} - \frac{15}{48} = \frac{73}{48}$$

D) **To find the product of two or more fractions,** simply multiply the numerators of the given fractions to find the numerator of the product and multiply the denominators of the given fractions to find the denominator of the product, e.g.,

$$\frac{2}{3} \times \frac{1}{5} \times \frac{4}{7} = \frac{2 \times 1 \times 4}{3 \times 5 \times 7} = \frac{8}{105}$$

E) **To find the quotient of two fractions**, simply invert (or flip-over) the divisor and multiply; e.g.,

$$\frac{8}{9} \div \frac{1}{3} = \frac{8}{9} \times \frac{3}{1} = \frac{24}{9} = \frac{8}{3}$$

F) **To simplify a fraction** is to convert it into a form in which the numerator and denominator have no common factor other than 1; e.g.,

$$\frac{12}{18} = \frac{12 \div 6}{18 \div 6} = \frac{2}{3}$$

G) A **complex fraction** is a fraction whose numerator and/or denominator is made up of fractions. To simplify the fraction, find the LCD of all the fractions. Multiply both the numerator and denominator by this number and simplify.

PROBLEM

If $a = 4$ and $b = 7$, find the value of $\dfrac{a + \frac{a}{b}}{a - \frac{a}{b}}$.

SOLUTION

By substitution,

$$\frac{a + \frac{a}{b}}{a - \frac{a}{b}} = \frac{4 + \frac{4}{7}}{4 - \frac{4}{7}}$$

In order to combine the terms, we must find the LCD of 1 and 7. Since both are prime factors, the LCD = $1 \times 7 = 7$.

Multiplying both the numerator and denominator by 7, we get

$$\frac{7\left(4 + \frac{4}{7}\right)}{7\left(4 - \frac{4}{7}\right)} = \frac{28 + 4}{28 - 4} = \frac{32}{24}$$

By dividing both the numerator and denominator by 8, $^{32}/_{24}$ can be reduced to $^{4}/_{3}$.

☞ Drill: Fractions

Changing an Improper Fraction to a Mixed Number

DIRECTIONS: Write each improper fraction as a mixed number in simplest form.

1. $\dfrac{50}{4}$

(A) $10\dfrac{1}{4}$ (B) $11\dfrac{1}{2}$ (C) $12\dfrac{1}{4}$ (D) $12\dfrac{1}{2}$ (E) 25

2. $\dfrac{17}{5}$

(A) $3\dfrac{2}{5}$ (B) $3\dfrac{3}{5}$ (C) $3\dfrac{4}{5}$ (D) $4\dfrac{1}{5}$ (E) $4\dfrac{2}{5}$

3. $\dfrac{42}{3}$

(A) $10\dfrac{2}{3}$ (B) 12 (C) $13\dfrac{1}{3}$ (D) 14 (E) $21\dfrac{1}{3}$

4. $\dfrac{85}{6}$

(A) $9\dfrac{1}{6}$ (B) $10\dfrac{5}{6}$ (C) $11\dfrac{1}{2}$ (D) 12 (E) $14\dfrac{1}{6}$

5. $\dfrac{151}{7}$

(A) $19\dfrac{6}{7}$ (B) $20\dfrac{1}{7}$ (C) $21\dfrac{4}{7}$ (D) $31\dfrac{2}{7}$ (E) $31\dfrac{4}{7}$

Changing a Mixed Number to an Improper Fraction

DIRECTIONS: Change each mixed number to an improper fraction in simplest form.

6. $2\dfrac{3}{5}$

(A) $\dfrac{4}{5}$ (B) $\dfrac{6}{5}$ (C) $\dfrac{11}{5}$ (D) $\dfrac{13}{5}$ (E) $\dfrac{17}{5}$

7. $4\dfrac{3}{4}$

(A) $\dfrac{7}{4}$ (B) $\dfrac{13}{4}$ (C) $\dfrac{16}{3}$ (D) $\dfrac{19}{4}$ (E) $\dfrac{21}{4}$

8. $6\dfrac{7}{6}$

(A) $\dfrac{13}{6}$ (B) $\dfrac{43}{6}$ (C) $\dfrac{19}{36}$ (D) $\dfrac{42}{36}$ (E) $\dfrac{48}{6}$

9. $12\dfrac{3}{7}$

(A) $\dfrac{87}{7}$ (B) $\dfrac{164}{14}$ (C) $\dfrac{34}{3}$ (D) $\dfrac{187}{21}$ (E) $\dfrac{252}{7}$

10. $21\dfrac{1}{2}$

(A) $\dfrac{11}{2}$ (B) $\dfrac{22}{2}$ (C) $\dfrac{24}{2}$ (D) $\dfrac{42}{2}$ (E) $\dfrac{43}{2}$

Adding Fractions with the Same Denominator

DIRECTIONS: Add and write the answer in simplest form.

11. $\dfrac{5}{12}+\dfrac{3}{12}=$

(A) $\dfrac{5}{24}$ (B) $\dfrac{1}{3}$ (C) $\dfrac{8}{12}$ (D) $\dfrac{2}{3}$ (E) $1\dfrac{1}{3}$

12. $\dfrac{5}{8}+\dfrac{7}{8}+\dfrac{3}{8}=$

(A) $\dfrac{15}{24}$ (B) $\dfrac{3}{4}$ (C) $\dfrac{5}{6}$ (D) $\dfrac{7}{8}$ (E) $1\dfrac{7}{8}$

13. $131\dfrac{2}{15}+28\dfrac{3}{15}=$

(A) $159\dfrac{1}{6}$ (B) $159\dfrac{1}{5}$ (C) $159\dfrac{1}{3}$ (D) $159\dfrac{1}{2}$ (E) $159\dfrac{3}{5}$

14. $3\dfrac{5}{18} + 2\dfrac{1}{18} + 8\dfrac{7}{18} =$

(A) $13\dfrac{13}{18}$ (B) $13\dfrac{3}{4}$ (C) $13\dfrac{7}{9}$ (D) $14\dfrac{1}{6}$ (E) $14\dfrac{2}{9}$

15. $17\dfrac{9}{20} + 4\dfrac{3}{20} + 8\dfrac{11}{20} =$

(A) $29\dfrac{23}{60}$ (B) $29\dfrac{23}{20}$ (C) $30\dfrac{3}{20}$ (D) $30\dfrac{1}{5}$ (E) $30\dfrac{3}{5}$

Subtracting Fractions with the Same Denominator

DIRECTIONS: Subtract and write the answer in simplest form.

16. $4\dfrac{7}{8} - 3\dfrac{1}{8} =$

(A) $1\dfrac{1}{4}$ (B) $1\dfrac{3}{4}$ (C) $1\dfrac{12}{16}$ (D) $1\dfrac{7}{8}$ (E) 2

17. $132\dfrac{5}{12} - 37\dfrac{3}{12} =$

(A) $94\dfrac{1}{6}$ (B) $95\dfrac{1}{12}$ (C) $95\dfrac{1}{6}$ (D) $105\dfrac{1}{6}$ (E) $169\dfrac{2}{3}$

18. $19\dfrac{1}{3} - 2\dfrac{2}{3} =$

(A) $16\dfrac{2}{3}$ (B) $16\dfrac{5}{6}$ (C) $17\dfrac{1}{3}$ (D) $17\dfrac{2}{3}$ (E) $17\dfrac{5}{6}$

19. $\dfrac{8}{21} - \dfrac{5}{21} =$

(A) $\dfrac{1}{21}$ (B) $\dfrac{1}{7}$ (C) $\dfrac{3}{21}$ (D) $\dfrac{2}{7}$ (E) $\dfrac{3}{7}$

20. $82\dfrac{7}{10} - 38\dfrac{9}{10} =$

(A) $43\dfrac{4}{5}$ (B) $44\dfrac{1}{5}$ (C) $44\dfrac{2}{5}$ (D) $45\dfrac{1}{5}$ (E) $45\dfrac{2}{10}$

Finding the LCD

DIRECTIONS: Find the lowest common denominator of each group of fractions.

21. $\frac{2}{3}, \frac{5}{9}$, and $\frac{1}{6}$

(A) 9   (B) 18   (C) 27   (D) 54   (E) 162

22. $\frac{1}{2}, \frac{5}{6}$, and $\frac{3}{4}$

(A) 2   (B) 4   (C) 6   (D) 12   (E) 48

23. $\frac{7}{16}, \frac{5}{6}$, and $\frac{2}{3}$

(A) 3   (B) 6   (C) 12   (D) 24   (E) 48

24. $\frac{8}{15}, \frac{2}{5}$, and $\frac{12}{25}$

(A) 5   (B) 15   (C) 25   (D) 75   (E) 375

25. $\frac{2}{3}, \frac{1}{5}$, and $\frac{5}{6}$

(A) 15   (B) 30   (C) 48   (D) 90   (E) 120

26. $\frac{1}{3}, \frac{9}{42}$, and $\frac{4}{21}$

(A) 21   (B) 42   (C) 126   (D) 378   (E) 4,000

27. $\frac{4}{9}, \frac{2}{5}$, and $\frac{1}{3}$

(A) 15   (B) 17   (C) 27   (D) 45   (E) 135

28. $\frac{7}{12}, \frac{11}{36}$, and $\frac{1}{9}$

(A) 12   (B) 36   (C) 108   (D) 324   (E) 432

29. $\frac{3}{7}, \frac{5}{21}$, and $\frac{2}{3}$

(A) 21   (B) 42   (C) 31   (D) 63   (E) 441

30. $\dfrac{13}{16}$, $\dfrac{5}{8}$, and $\dfrac{1}{4}$

(A) 4 (B) 8 (C) 16 (D) 32 (E) 64

Adding Fractions with Different Denominators

<u>DIRECTIONS</u>: Add and write the answer in simplest form.

31. $\dfrac{1}{3} + \dfrac{5}{12} =$

(A) $\dfrac{2}{5}$ (B) $\dfrac{1}{2}$ (C) $\dfrac{9}{12}$ (D) $\dfrac{3}{4}$ (E) $1\dfrac{1}{3}$

32. $3\dfrac{5}{9} + 2\dfrac{1}{3} =$

(A) $5\dfrac{1}{2}$ (B) $5\dfrac{2}{3}$ (C) $5\dfrac{8}{9}$ (D) $6\dfrac{1}{9}$ (E) $6\dfrac{2}{3}$

33. $12\dfrac{9}{16} + 17\dfrac{3}{4} + 8\dfrac{1}{8} =$

(A) $37\dfrac{7}{16}$ (B) $38\dfrac{7}{16}$ (C) $38\dfrac{1}{2}$ (D) $38\dfrac{2}{3}$ (E) $39\dfrac{3}{16}$

34. $28\dfrac{4}{5} + 11\dfrac{16}{25} =$

(A) $39\dfrac{2}{3}$ (B) $39\dfrac{4}{5}$ (C) $40\dfrac{9}{25}$ (D) $40\dfrac{2}{5}$ (E) $40\dfrac{11}{25}$

35. $2\dfrac{1}{8} + 1\dfrac{3}{16} + \dfrac{5}{12} =$

(A) $3\dfrac{35}{48}$ (B) $3\dfrac{3}{4}$ (C) $3\dfrac{19}{24}$ (D) $3\dfrac{13}{16}$ (E) $4\dfrac{1}{12}$

Subtracting Fractions with Different Denominators

<u>DIRECTIONS</u>: Subtract and write the answer in simplest form.

36. $8\dfrac{9}{12} - 2\dfrac{2}{3} =$

(A) $6\dfrac{1}{12}$ (B) $6\dfrac{1}{6}$ (C) $6\dfrac{1}{3}$ (D) $6\dfrac{7}{12}$ (E) $6\dfrac{2}{3}$

37. $185\frac{11}{15} - 107\frac{2}{5} =$

(A) $77\frac{2}{15}$　　(B) $78\frac{1}{5}$　　(C) $78\frac{3}{10}$　　(D) $78\frac{1}{3}$　　(E) $78\frac{9}{15}$

38. $34\frac{2}{3} - 16\frac{5}{6} =$

(A) 16　　(B) $16\frac{1}{3}$　　(C) 17　　(D) 17　　(E) $17\frac{5}{6}$

39. $3\frac{11}{48} - 2\frac{3}{16} =$

(A) $\frac{47}{48}$　　(B) $1\frac{1}{48}$　　(C) $1\frac{1}{24}$　　(D) $1\frac{8}{48}$　　(E) $1\frac{7}{24}$

40. $81\frac{4}{21} - 31\frac{1}{3} =$

(A) $47\frac{3}{7}$　　(B) $49\frac{6}{7}$　　(C) $49\frac{1}{6}$　　(D) $49\frac{5}{7}$　　(E) $49\frac{13}{21}$

Multiplying Fractions

DIRECTIONS: Multiply and reduce the answer.

41. $\frac{2}{3} \times \frac{4}{5} =$

(A) $\frac{6}{8}$　　(B) $\frac{3}{4}$　　(C) $\frac{8}{15}$　　(D) $\frac{10}{12}$　　(E) $\frac{6}{5}$

42. $\frac{7}{10} \times \frac{4}{21} =$

(A) $\frac{2}{15}$　　(B) $\frac{11}{31}$　　(C) $\frac{28}{210}$　　(D) $\frac{1}{6}$　　(E) $\frac{4}{15}$

43. $5\frac{1}{3} \times \frac{3}{8} =$

(A) $\frac{4}{11}$　　(B) 2　　(C) $\frac{8}{5}$　　(D) $5\frac{1}{8}$　　(E) $5\frac{17}{24}$

44. $6\frac{1}{2} \times 3 =$

(A) $9\frac{1}{2}$　　(B) $18\frac{1}{2}$　　(C) $19\frac{1}{2}$　　(D) 20　　(E) $12\frac{1}{2}$

45. $3\frac{1}{4} \times 2\frac{1}{3} =$

(A) $5\frac{7}{12}$　　(B) $6\frac{2}{7}$　　(C) $6\frac{5}{7}$　　(D) $7\frac{7}{12}$　　(E) $7\frac{11}{12}$

Dividing Fractions

DIRECTIONS: Divide and reduce the answer.

46. $\frac{3}{16} \div \frac{3}{4} =$

(A) $\frac{9}{64}$　　(B) $\frac{1}{4}$　　(C) $\frac{6}{16}$　　(D) $\frac{9}{16}$　　(E) $\frac{3}{4}$

47. $\frac{4}{9} \div \frac{2}{3} =$

(A) $\frac{1}{3}$　　(B) $\frac{1}{2}$　　(C) $\frac{2}{3}$　　(D) $\frac{7}{11}$　　(E) $\frac{8}{9}$

48. $5\frac{1}{4} \div \frac{7}{10} =$

(A) $2\frac{4}{7}$　　(B) $3\frac{27}{40}$　　(C) $5\frac{19}{20}$　　(D) $7\frac{1}{2}$　　(E) $8\frac{1}{4}$

49. $4\frac{2}{3} \div \frac{7}{9} =$

(A) $2\frac{24}{27}$　　(B) $3\frac{2}{9}$　　(C) $4\frac{14}{27}$　　(D) $5\frac{12}{27}$　　(E) 6

50. $3\frac{2}{5} \div 1\frac{7}{10} =$

(A) 2　　(B) $3\frac{4}{7}$　　(C) $4\frac{7}{25}$　　(D) $5\frac{1}{10}$　　(E) $5\frac{2}{7}$

DECIMALS

When we divide the denominator of a fraction into its numerator, the result is a **decimal**. The decimal is based upon a fraction with a denominator of 10, 100, 1,000, ... and is written with a **decimal point**. Whole numbers are placed to the left of the decimal point where the first place to the left is the units place; the second to the left is the tens; the third to the left is the hundreds, etc. The fractions are placed on the right where the first place to the right is the tenths; the second to the right is the hundredths, etc.

EXAMPLES

$$12 \frac{3}{10} = 12.3 \qquad 4 \frac{17}{100} = 4.17 \qquad \frac{3}{100} = .03$$

Since a **rational number** is of the form a/b, $b \neq 0$, then all rational numbers can be expressed as decimals by dividing b into a. The result is either a **terminating decimal**, meaning that b divides a with a remainder of 0 after a certain point; or **repeating decimal**, meaning that b continues to divide a so that the decimal has a repeating pattern of integers.

EXAMPLES

(A) $\dfrac{1}{2} = .5$

(B) $\dfrac{1}{3} = .333...$

(C) $\dfrac{11}{16} = .6875$

(D) $\dfrac{2}{7} = .285714285714...$

(A) and (C) are terminating decimals; (B) and (D) are repeating decimals. This explanation allows us to define **irrational numbers** as numbers whose decimal form is non-terminating and non-repeating, e.g.,

$$\sqrt{2} = 1.414...$$
$$\sqrt{3} = 1.732...$$

PROBLEM

Express $- \dfrac{10}{20}$ as a decimal.

SOLUTION

$$-\frac{10}{20} = -\frac{50}{100} = -.5$$

PROBLEM

Write $\frac{2}{7}$ as a repeating decimal.

SOLUTION

To write a fraction as a repeating decimal divide the numerator by the denominator until a pattern of repeated digits appears.

$$2 \div 7 = .285714285714\ldots$$

Identify the entire portion of the decimal which is repeated. The repeating decimal can then be written in the shortened form:

$$\frac{2}{7} = .\overline{285714}$$

OPERATIONS WITH DECIMALS

A) **To add numbers containing decimals,** write the numbers in a column making sure the decimal points are lined up, one beneath the other. Add the numbers as usual, placing the decimal point in the sum so that it is still in line with the others. It is important not to mix the digits in the tenths place with the digits in the hundredths place, and so on.

EXAMPLES

$2.558 + 6.391$ $\qquad$ $57.51 + 6.2$

$$\begin{array}{r} 2.558 \\ + \ 6.391 \\ \hline 8.949 \end{array} \qquad \begin{array}{r} 57.51 \\ + \ \ 6.20 \\ \hline 63.71 \end{array}$$

Similarly with subtraction,

$78.54 - 21.33$ $\qquad$ $7.11 - 4.2$

$$\begin{array}{r} 78.54 \\ - \ 21.33 \\ \hline 57.21 \end{array} \qquad \begin{array}{r} 7.11 \\ - \ 4.20 \\ \hline 2.91 \end{array}$$

Note that if two numbers differ according to the number of digits to the right of the decimal point, zeros must be added.

.63 − .214   15.224 − 3.6891

$$
\begin{array}{r}
.630 \\
-\,.214 \\
\hline
.416
\end{array}
\qquad
\begin{array}{r}
15.2240 \\
-\,3.6891 \\
\hline
11.5349
\end{array}
$$

B) **To multiply numbers with decimals,** simply multiply as usual. Then, to figure out the number of decimal places that belong in the product, find the total number of decimal places in the numbers being multiplied.

EXAMPLES

$$
\begin{array}{r}
6.555 \text{ (3 decimal places)} \\
\times \quad 4.5 \text{ (1 decimal place)} \\
\hline
32775 \\
26220 \\
\hline
294975
\end{array}
\qquad
\begin{array}{r}
5.32 \text{ (2 decimal places)} \\
\times \quad .04 \text{ (2 decimal places)} \\
\hline
2128 \\
000 \\
\hline
2128
\end{array}
$$

29.4975 (4 decimal places)   .2128 (4 decimal places)

C) **To divide numbers with decimals,** you must first make the divisor a whole number by moving the decimal point the appropriate number of places to the right. The decimal point of the dividend should also be moved the same number of places. Place a decimal point in the quotient, directly in line with the decimal point in the dividend.

EXAMPLES

12.92 ÷ 3.4   40.376 ÷ 7.21

$$
\begin{array}{r}
3.8 \\
3.4.\overline{)12.9.2} \\
-102 \\
\hline
272 \\
-272 \\
\hline
0
\end{array}
\qquad
\begin{array}{r}
5.6 \\
7.21.\overline{)40.37.6} \\
-3605 \\
\hline
4326 \\
-4326 \\
\hline
0
\end{array}
$$

If the question asks you to find the correct answer to two decimal places, simply divide until you have three decimal places and then round off. If the third decimal place is a 5 or larger, the number in the second decimal place is increased by 1. If the third decimal place is less than 5, that number is simply dropped.

PROBLEM

Find the answer to the following to two decimal places:

(1) $44.3 \div 3$ (2) $56.99 \div 6$

SOLUTION

(1)
$$
\begin{array}{r}
14.766 \\
3\overline{)44.300} \\
-3 \\
\hline
14 \\
-12 \\
\hline
23 \\
-21 \\
\hline
20 \\
-18 \\
\hline
20 \\
-18 \\
\hline
2
\end{array}
$$

(2)
$$
\begin{array}{r}
9.498 \\
6\overline{)56.990} \\
-54 \\
\hline
29 \\
-24 \\
\hline
59 \\
-54 \\
\hline
50 \\
-48 \\
\hline
2
\end{array}
$$

14.766 can be rounded off to 14.77

9.498 can be rounded off to 9.50

D) When comparing two numbers with decimals to see which is the larger, first look at the tenths place. The larger digit in this place represents the larger number. If the two digits are the same, however, take a look at the digits in the hundredths place, and so on.

EXAMPLES

.518 and .216

5 is larger than 2, therefore .518 is larger than .216

.723 and .726

6 is larger than 3, therefore .726 is larger than .723

☞ Drill: Decimals

Addition

<u>DIRECTIONS</u>: Solve the following equations.

1. $1.032 + 0.987 + 3.07 =$

(A) 4.089   (B) 5.089   (C) 5.189   (D) 6.189   (E) 13.972

2. $132.03 + 97.1483 =$

(A) 98.4686 (B) 110.3513 (C) 209.1783
(D) 229.1486 (E) 229.1783

3. $7.1 + 0.62 + 4.03827 + 5.183 =$

(A) 0.2315127 (B) 16.45433 (C) 16.94127
(D) 18.561 (E) 40.4543

4. $8 + 17.43 + 9.2 =$

(A) 34.63 (B) 34.86 (C) 35.63 (D) 176.63 (E) 189.43

5. $1,036.173 + 289.04 =$

(A) 382.6573 (B) 392.6573 (C) 1,065.077
(D) 1,325.213 (E) 3,926.573

Subtraction

DIRECTIONS: Solve the following equations.

6. $3.972 - 2.04 =$

(A) 1.932 (B) 1.942 (C) 1.976 (D) 2.013 (E) 2.113

7. $16.047 - 13.06 =$

(A) 2.887 (B) 2.987 (C) 3.041 (D) 3.141 (E) 4.741

8. $87.4 - 56.27 =$

(A) 30.27 (B) 30.67 (C) 31.1 (D) 31.13 (E) 31.27

9. $1,046.8 - 639.14 =$

(A) 303.84 (B) 313.74 (C) 407.66 (D) 489.74 (E) 535.54

10. $10,000 - 842.91 =$

(A) 157.09 (B) 942.91 (C) 5,236.09
(D) 9,057.91 (E) 9,157.09

Multiplication

DIRECTIONS: Solve the following equations.

11. $1.03 \times 2.6 =$

(A) 2.18   (B) 2.678   (C) 2.78   (D) 3.38   (E) 3.63

12. $93 \times 4.2 =$

(A) 39.06   (B) 97.2   (C) 223.2   (D) 390.6   (E) 3,906

13. $0.04 \times 0.23 =$

(A) 0.0092   (B) 0.092   (C) 0.27   (D) 0.87   (E) 0.920

14. $0.0186 \times 0.03 =$

(A) 0.000348 (B) 0.000558 (C) 0.0548   (D) 0.0848   (E) 0.558

15. $51.2 \times 0.17 =$

(A) 5.29   (B) 8.534   (C) 8.704   (D) 36.352   (E) 36.991

Division

DIRECTIONS: Solve the following equations.

16. $123.39 \div 3 =$

(A) 31.12   (B) 41.13   (C) 401.13   (D) 411.3   (E) 4,113

17. $1,428.6 \div 6 =$

(A) 0.2381   (B) 2.381   (C) 23.81   (D) 238.1   (E) 2,381

18. $25.2 \div 0.3 =$

(A) 0.84   (B) 8.04   (C) 8.4   (D) 84   (E) 840

19. $14.95 \div 6.5 =$

(A) 2.3   (B) 20.3   (C) 23   (D) 230   (E) 2,300

20. $46.33 \div 1.13 =$

(A) 0.41   (B) 4.1   (C) 41   (D) 410   (E) 4,100

Comparing

DIRECTIONS: Solve the following equations.

21. Which is the **largest** number in this set—{0.8, 0.823, 0.089, 0.807, 0.852}?

(A) 0.8   (B) 0.823   (C) 0.089   (D) 0.807   (E) 0.852

22. Which is the **smallest** number in this set—{32.98, 32.099, 32.047, 32.5, 32.304}?

(A) 32.98   (B) 32.099   (C) 32.047   (D) 32.5   (E) 32.304

23. In which set below are the numbers arranged correctly from smallest to largest?

(A) {0.98, 0.9, 0.993}   (B) {0.113, 0.3, 0.31}

(C) {7.04, 7.26, 7.2}   (D) {0.006, 0.061, 0.06}

(E) {12.84, 12.801, 12.6}

24. In which set below are the numbers arranged correctly from largest to smallest?

(A) {1.018, 1.63, 1.368}   (B) {4.219, 4.29, 4.9}

(C) {0.62, 0.6043, 0.643}   (D) {16.34, 16.304, 16.3}

(E) {12.98, 12.601, 12.86}

25. Which is the **largest** number in this set—{0.87, 0.89, 0.889, 0.8, 0.987}?

(A) 0.87   (B) 0.89   (C) 0.889   (D) 0.8   (E) 0.987

Changing a Fraction to a Decimal

DIRECTIONS: Solve the following equations.

26. What is $\frac{1}{4}$ written as a decimal?

(A) 1.4   (B) 0.14   (C) 0.2   (D) 0.25   (E) 0.3

27. What is $\frac{3}{5}$ written as a decimal?

(A) 0.3   (B) 0.35   (C) 0.6   (D) 0.65   (E) 0.8

28. What is $\dfrac{7}{20}$ written as a decimal?

(A) 0.35   (B) 0.4   (C) 0.72   (D) 0.75   (E) 0.9

29. What is $\dfrac{2}{3}$ written as a decimal?

(A) 0.23   (B) 0.33   (C) 0.5   (D) 0.6   (E) $0.\overline{6}$

30. What is $\dfrac{11}{25}$ written as a decimal?

(A) 0.1125   (B) 0.25   (C) 0.4   (D) 0.44   (E) 0.5

PERCENTAGES

A **percent** is a way of expressing the relationship between part and whole, where whole is defined as 100%. A percent can be defined by a fraction with a denominator of 100. Decimals can also represent a percent. For instance,

$$56\% = 0.56 = \frac{56}{100}$$

PROBLEM

Compute the value of

(1) 90% of 400   (3) 50% of 500

(2) 180% of 400   (4) 200% of 4

SOLUTION

The symbol % means per hundred, therefore $5\% = {}^5/_{100}$.

(1) 90% of 400 = 90 ÷ 100 × 400 = 90 × 4 = 360

(2) 180% of 400 = 180 ÷ 100 × 400 = 180 × 4 = 720

(3) 50% of 500 = 50 ÷ 100 × 500 = 50 × 5 = 250

(4) 200% of 4 = 200 ÷ 100 × 4 = 2 × 4 = 8

PROBLEM

What percent of

(1) 100 is 99.5   (2) 200 is 4

SOLUTION

(1) $99.5 = x \times 100$

$99.5 = 100x$

$.995 = x$; but this is the value of x per hundred. Therefore,

$99.5\% = x$

(2) $4 = x \times 200$

$4 = 200x$

$.02 = x$. Again this must be changed to percent, so

$2\% = x$

EQUIVALENT FORMS OF A NUMBER

Some problems may call for converting numbers into an equivalent or simplified form in order to make the solution more convenient.

A) Converting a fraction to a decimal:

$$\frac{1}{2} = 0.50$$

Divide the numerator by the denominator:

$$
\begin{array}{r}
.50 \\
2\overline{)1.00} \\
\underline{-10} \\
00
\end{array}
$$

B) Converting a number to a percent:

$0.50 = 50\%$

Multiply by 100:

$0.50 = (0.50 \times 100)\% = 50\%$

C) Converting a percent to a decimal:

$30\% = 0.30$

Divide by 100:

$30\% = 30 \div 100 = 0.30$

D) Converting a decimal to a fraction:

$$0.500 = \frac{1}{2}$$

Convert .500 to $^{500}/_{1000}$ and then simplify the fraction by dividing the numerator and denominator by common factors:

$$\frac{2 \times 2 \times 5 \times 5 \times 5}{2 \times 2 \times 2 \times 5 \times 5 \times 5}$$

and then cancel out the common numbers to get $^1/_2$.

PROBLEM

Express

(1)   1.65 as a percent

(2)   0.7 as a fraction

(3) $-\dfrac{10}{20}$ as a decimal

(4) $\dfrac{4}{2}$ as an integer

SOLUTION

(1) $1.65 \times 100 = 165\%$

(2) $0.7 = \dfrac{7}{10}$

(3) $-\dfrac{10}{20} = -0.5$

(4) $\dfrac{4}{2} = 2$

☞ Drill: Percentages

Finding Percents

DIRECTIONS: Solve to find the correct percentages.

1.   Find 3% of 80.

(A) 0.24   (B) 2.4   (C) 24   (D) 240   (E) 2,400

2.   Find 50% of 182.

(A) 9   (B) 90   (C) 91   (D) 910   (E) 9,100

3.   Find 83% of 166.

(A) 0.137   (B) 1.377   (C) 13.778 (D) 137   (E) 137.78

4. Find 125% of 400.

(A) 425 (B) 500 (C) 525 (D) 600 (E) 825

5. Find 300% of 4.

(A) 12 (B) 120 (C) 1,200 (D) 12,000 (E) 120,000

6. Forty-eight percent of the 1,200 students at Central High are males. How many male students are there at Central High?

(A) 57 (B) 576 (C) 580 (D) 600 (E) 648

7. For 35% of the last 40 days, there has been measurable rainfall. How many days out of the last 40 days have had measurable rainfall?

(A) 14 (B) 20 (C) 25 (D) 35 (E) 40

8. Of every 1,000 people who take a certain medicine, 0.2% develop severe side effects. How many people out of every 1,000 who take the medicine develop the side effects?

(A) 0.2 (B) 2 (C) 20 (D) 22 (E) 200

9. Of 220 applicants for a job, 75% were offered an initial interview. How many people were offered an initial interview?

(A) 75 (B) 110 (C) 120 (D) 155 (E) 165

10. Find 0.05% of 4,000.

(A) 0.05 (B) 0.5 (C) 2 (D) 20 (E) 400

Changing Percents to Fractions

DIRECTIONS: Solve to find the correct fractions.

11. What is 25% written as a fraction?

(A) $\dfrac{1}{25}$ (B) $\dfrac{1}{5}$ (C) $\dfrac{1}{4}$ (D) $\dfrac{1}{3}$ (E) $\dfrac{1}{2}$

12. What is $33\dfrac{1}{3}\%$ written as a fraction?

(A) $\dfrac{1}{4}$ (B) $\dfrac{1}{3}$ (C) $\dfrac{1}{2}$ (D) $\dfrac{2}{3}$ (E) $\dfrac{5}{9}$

13. What is 200% written as a fraction?

(A) $\dfrac{1}{2}$ (B) $\dfrac{2}{1}$ (C) $\dfrac{20}{1}$ (D) $\dfrac{200}{1}$ (E) $\dfrac{2,000}{1}$

14. What is 84% written as a fraction?

(A) $\dfrac{1}{84}$ (B) $\dfrac{4}{8}$ (C) $\dfrac{17}{25}$ (D) $\dfrac{21}{25}$ (E) $\dfrac{44}{50}$

15. What is 2% written as a fraction?

(A) $\dfrac{1}{50}$ (B) $\dfrac{1}{25}$ (C) $\dfrac{1}{10}$ (D) $\dfrac{1}{4}$ (E) $\dfrac{1}{2}$

Changing Fractions to Percents

DIRECTIONS: Solve to find the following percentages.

16. What is $\dfrac{2}{3}$ written as a percent?

(A) 23%   (B) 32%   (C) $33\dfrac{1}{3}\%$ (D) $57\dfrac{1}{3}\%$ (E) $66\dfrac{2}{3}\%$

17. What is $\dfrac{3}{5}$ written as a percent?

(A) 30%   (B) 35%   (C) 53%   (D) 60%   (E) 65%

18. What is $\dfrac{17}{20}$ written as a percent?

(A) 17%   (B) 70%   (C) 75%   (D) 80%   (E) 85%

19. What is $\dfrac{45}{50}$ written as a percent?

(A) 45%   (B) 50%   (C) 90%   (D) 95%   (E) 97%

20. What is $1\dfrac{1}{4}$ written as a percent?

(A) 114%   (B) 120%   (C) 125%   (D) 127%   (E) 133%

Changing Percents to Decimals

DIRECTIONS: Convert the percentages to decimals.

21. What is 42% written as a decimal?

(A) 0.42　　(B) 4.2　　(C) 42　　(D) 420　　(E) 422

22. What is 0.3% written as a decimal?

(A) 0.0003　(B) 0.003　(C) 0.03　(D) 0.3　　(E) 3

23. What is 8% written as a decimal?

(A) 0.0008　(B) 0.008　(C) 0.08　(D) 0.80　(E) 8

24. What is 175% written as a decimal?

(A) 0.175　　(B) 1.75　　(C) 17.5　　(D) 175　　(E) 17,500

25. What is 34% written as a decimal?

(A) 0.00034　(B) 0.0034　(C) 0.034　(D) 0.34　(E) 3.4

Changing Decimals to Percents

DIRECTIONS: Convert the following decimals to percents.

26. What is 0.43 written as a percent?

(A) 0.0043%　(B) 0.043%　(C) 4.3%　(D) 43%　(E) 430%

27. What is 1 written as a percent?

(A) 1%　　(B) 10%　　(C) 100%　　(D) 111%　　(E) 150%

28. What is 0.08 written as a percent?

(A) 0.08%　(B) 8%　　(C) 8.8%　　(D) 80%　　(E) 800%

29. What is 3.4 written as a percent?

(A) 0.0034%　(B) 3.4%　　(C) 34%　　(D) 304%　　(E) 340%

30. What is 0.645 written as a percent?

(A) 64.5%　　(B) 65%　　(C) 69%　　(D) 70%　　(E) 645%

RADICALS

The **square root** of a number is a number that when multiplied by itself results in the original number. Thus, the square root of 81 is 9 since $9 \times 9 = 81$. However, -9 is also a root of 81 since $(-9)(-9) = 81$. Every positive number will have two roots. The principal root is the positive one. Zero has only one square root, while negative numbers do not have real numbers as their roots.

A **radical sign** indicates that the root of a number or expression will be taken. The **radicand** is the number of which the root will be taken. The **index** tells how many times the root needs to be multiplied by itself to equal the radicand, e.g.,

index, radical sign → radicand

(1) $\sqrt[3]{64}$;

   3 is the index and 64 is the radicand. Since $4 \times 4 \times 4 = 64$, then $\sqrt[3]{64} = 4$.

(2) $\sqrt[5]{32}$;

   5 is the index and 32 is the radicand. Since $2 \times 2 \times 2 \times 2 \times 2 = 32$, then $\sqrt[5]{32} = 2$.

OPERATIONS WITH RADICALS

A) **To multiply two or more radicals**, we utilize the law that states,

   $\sqrt{a} \times \sqrt{b} = \sqrt{ab}$.

Simply multiply the whole numbers as usual. Then, multiply the radicands and put the product under the radical sign and simplify, e.g.,

   (1) $\sqrt{12} \times \sqrt{5} = \sqrt{60} = 2\sqrt{15}$

   (2) $3\sqrt{2} \times 4\sqrt{8} = 12\sqrt{16} = 48$

   (3) $2\sqrt{10} \times 6\sqrt{5} = 12\sqrt{50} = 60\sqrt{2}$

B) **To divide radicals**, simplify both the numerator and the denominator. By multiplying the radical in the denominator by itself, you can make the denominator a rational number. The numerator, however, must also be multiplied by this radical so that the value of the expression does not change. You must choose as many factors as necessary to rationalize the denominator, e.g.,

(1) $\dfrac{\sqrt{128}}{\sqrt{2}} = \dfrac{\sqrt{64} \times \sqrt{2}}{\sqrt{2}} = \dfrac{8\sqrt{2}}{\sqrt{2}} = 8$

(2) $\dfrac{\sqrt{10}}{\sqrt{3}} = \dfrac{\sqrt{10} \times \sqrt{3}}{\sqrt{3} \times \sqrt{3}} = \dfrac{\sqrt{30}}{3}$

(3) $\dfrac{\sqrt{8}}{2\sqrt{3}} = \dfrac{\sqrt{8} \times \sqrt{3}}{2\sqrt{3} \times \sqrt{3}} = \dfrac{\sqrt{24}}{2 \times 3} = \dfrac{2\sqrt{6}}{6} = \dfrac{\sqrt{6}}{3}$

C) **To add two or more radicals**, the radicals must have the same index and the same radicand. Only where the radicals are simplified can these similarities be determined.

EXAMPLES

(1) $6\sqrt{2} + 2\sqrt{2} = (6+2)\sqrt{2} = 8\sqrt{2}$

(2) $\sqrt{27} + 5\sqrt{3} = \sqrt{9}\sqrt{3} + 5\sqrt{3} = 3\sqrt{3} + 5\sqrt{3} = 8\sqrt{3}$

(3) $7\sqrt{3} + 8\sqrt{2} + 5\sqrt{3} = 12\sqrt{3} + 8\sqrt{2}$

Similarly, to subtract,

(1) $12\sqrt{3} - 7\sqrt{3} = (12-7)\sqrt{3} = 5\sqrt{3}$

(2) $\sqrt{80} - \sqrt{20} = \sqrt{16}\sqrt{5} - \sqrt{4}\sqrt{5} = 4\sqrt{5} - 2\sqrt{5} = 2\sqrt{5}$

(3) $\sqrt{50} - \sqrt{3} = 5\sqrt{2} - \sqrt{3}$

☞ Drill: Radicals

Multiplication

DIRECTIONS: Multiply and simplify each answer.

1. $\sqrt{6} \times \sqrt{5} =$

(A) $\sqrt{11}$ (B) $\sqrt{30}$ (C) $2\sqrt{5}$ (D) $3\sqrt{10}$ (E) $2\sqrt{3}$

2. $\sqrt{3} \times \sqrt{12} =$

(A) 3   (B) $\sqrt{15}$ (C) $\sqrt{36}$ (D) 6   (E) 8

3. $\sqrt{7} \times \sqrt{7} =$

(A) 7   (B) 49   (C) $\sqrt{14}$ (D) $2\sqrt{7}$ (E) $2\sqrt{14}$

4. $3\sqrt{5} \times 2\sqrt{5} =$

(A) $5\sqrt{5}$ (B) 25   (C) 30   (D) $5\sqrt{25}$ (E) $6\sqrt{5}$

5. $4\sqrt{6} \times \sqrt{2} =$

(A) $4\sqrt{8}$ (B) $8\sqrt{2}$ (C) $5\sqrt{8}$ (D) $4\sqrt{12}$ (E) $8\sqrt{3}$

Division

DIRECTIONS: Divide and simplify the answer.

6. $\sqrt{10} \div \sqrt{2} =$

(A) $\sqrt{8}$ (B) $2\sqrt{2}$ (C) $\sqrt{5}$ (D) $2\sqrt{5}$ (E) $2\sqrt{3}$

7. $\sqrt{30} \div \sqrt{15} =$

(A) $\sqrt{2}$ (B) $\sqrt{45}$ (C) $3\sqrt{5}$ (D) $\sqrt{15}$ (E) $5\sqrt{3}$

8. $\sqrt{100} \div \sqrt{25} =$

(A) $\sqrt{4}$ (B) $5\sqrt{5}$ (C) $5\sqrt{3}$ (D) 2   (E) 4

9. $\sqrt{48} \div \sqrt{8} =$

(A) $4\sqrt{3}$ (B) $3\sqrt{2}$ (C) $\sqrt{6}$ (D) 6   (E) 12

10. $3\sqrt{12} \div \sqrt{3} =$

(A) $3\sqrt{15}$ (B) 6   (C) 9   (D) 12   (E) $3\sqrt{36}$

Addition

DIRECTIONS: Simplify each radical and add.

11. $\sqrt{7} + 3\sqrt{7} =$

(A) $3\sqrt{7}$ (B) $4\sqrt{7}$ (C) $3\sqrt{14}$ (D) $4\sqrt{14}$ (E) $3\sqrt{21}$

12. $\sqrt{5} + 6\sqrt{5} + 3\sqrt{5} =$

(A) $9\sqrt{5}$ (B) $9\sqrt{15}$ (C) $5\sqrt{10}$ (D) $10\sqrt{5}$ (E) $18\sqrt{15}$

13. $3\sqrt{32} + 2\sqrt{2} =$

(A) $5\sqrt{2}$ (B) $\sqrt{34}$ (C) $14\sqrt{2}$ (D) $5\sqrt{34}$ (E) $6\sqrt{64}$

14. $6\sqrt{15} + 8\sqrt{15} + 16\sqrt{15} =$

(A) $15\sqrt{30}$ (B) $30\sqrt{45}$ (C) $30\sqrt{30}$ (D) $15\sqrt{45}$ (E) $30\sqrt{15}$

15. $6\sqrt{5} + 2\sqrt{45} =$

(A) $12\sqrt{5}$ (B) $8\sqrt{50}$ (C) $40\sqrt{2}$ (D) $12\sqrt{50}$ (E) $8\sqrt{5}$

Subtraction

DIRECTIONS: Simplify each radical and subtract.

16. $8\sqrt{5} - 6\sqrt{5} =$

(A) $2\sqrt{5}$ (B) $3\sqrt{5}$ (C) $4\sqrt{5}$ (D) $14\sqrt{5}$ (E) $48\sqrt{5}$

17. $16\sqrt{33} - 5\sqrt{33} =$

(A) $3\sqrt{33}$ (B) $33\sqrt{11}$ (C) $11\sqrt{33}$ (D) $11\sqrt{0}$ (E) $\sqrt{33}$

18. $14\sqrt{2} - 19\sqrt{2} =$

(A) $5\sqrt{2}$ (B) $-5\sqrt{2}$ (C) $-33\sqrt{2}$ (D) $33\sqrt{2}$ (E) $-4\sqrt{2}$

19. $10\sqrt{2} - 3\sqrt{8} =$

(A) $6\sqrt{6}$ (B) $-2\sqrt{2}$ (C) $7\sqrt{6}$ (D) $4\sqrt{2}$ (E) $-6\sqrt{6}$

20. $4\sqrt{3} - 2\sqrt{12} =$

(A) $-2\sqrt{9}$ (B) $-6\sqrt{15}$ (C) 0 (D) $6\sqrt{15}$ (E) $2\sqrt{12}$

EXPONENTS

When a number is multiplied by itself a specific number of times, it is said to be **raised to a power**. The way this is written is $a^n = b$ where a is the number or **base**, n is the **exponent** or **power** that indicates the number of times the base is to be multiplied by itself, and b is the product of this multiplication.

In the expression 3^2, 3 is the base and 2 is the exponent. This means that 3 is multiplied by itself 2 times and the product is 9.

An exponent can be either positive or negative. A negative exponent implies a fraction such that if n is a negative integer

$$a^{-n} = \frac{1}{a^n}, \ a \neq 0. \ \text{So, } 2^{-4} = \frac{1}{2^4} = \frac{1}{16}.$$

An exponent that is 0 gives a result of 1, assuming that the base is not equal to 0.

$$a^0 = 1, \ a \neq 0.$$

An exponent can also be a fraction. If m and n are positive integers,

$$a^{\frac{m}{n}} = \sqrt[n]{a^m}$$

The numerator remains the exponent of a, but the denominator tells what root to take. For example,

(1) $4^{\frac{3}{2}} = \sqrt[2]{4^3} = \sqrt{64} = 8$

(2) $3^{\frac{4}{2}} = \sqrt[2]{3^4} = \sqrt{81} = 9$

If a fractional exponent were negative, the same operation would take place, but the result would be a fraction. For example,

(1) $27^{-\frac{3}{2}} = \frac{1}{27^{2/3}} = \frac{1}{\sqrt[3]{27^2}} = \frac{1}{\sqrt[3]{729}} = \frac{1}{9}$

PROBLEM

Simplify the following expressions:

(1) -3^{-2}

(3) $\frac{-3}{4^{-1}}$

(2) $(-3)^{-2}$

SOLUTION

(1) Here the exponent applies only to 3. Since

$$x^{-y} = \frac{1}{x^y}, \quad -3^{-2} = -(3)^{-2} = -\left(\frac{1}{3^2}\right) = -\frac{1}{9}$$

(2) In this case the exponent applies to the negative base. Thus,

$$(-3)^{-2} = \frac{1}{(-3)^2} = \frac{1}{(-3)(-3)} = \frac{1}{9}$$

(3) $\dfrac{-3}{4^{-1}} = \dfrac{-3}{\left(\dfrac{1}{4}\right)^1} = \dfrac{-3}{\dfrac{1^1}{4^1}} = \dfrac{-3}{\dfrac{1}{4}}$

Division by a fraction is equivalent to multiplication by that fraction's reciprocal, thus

$$\frac{-3}{\dfrac{1}{4}} = -3 \times \frac{4}{1} = -12 \text{ and } \frac{-3}{4^{-1}} = -12$$

General Laws of Exponents

A) $a^p a^q = a^{p+q}$

$4^2 4^3 = 4^{2+3} = 1{,}024$

B) $(a^p)^q = a^{pq}$

$(2^3)^2 = 2^6 = 64$

C) $\dfrac{a^p}{a^q} = a^{p-q}$

$\dfrac{3^6}{3^2} = 3^4 = 81$

D) $(ab)^p = a^p b^p$

$(3 \times 2)^2 = 3^2 \times 2^2 = (9)(4) = 36$

E) $\left(\dfrac{a}{b}\right)^p = \dfrac{a^p}{b^p}, b \neq 0$

$\left(\dfrac{4}{5}\right)^2 = \dfrac{4^2}{5^2} = \dfrac{16}{25}$

☞ Drill: Exponents

Multiplication

DIRECTIONS: Simplify.

1. $4^6 \times 4^2 =$

(A) 4^4　　　(B) 4^8　　　(C) 4^{12}　　　(D) 16^8　　　(E) 16^{12}

2. $2^2 \times 2^5 \times 2^3 =$

(A) 2^{10}　　　(B) 4^{10}　　　(C) 8^{10}　　　(D) 2^{30}　　　(E) 8^{30}

3. $6^6 \times 6^2 \times 6^4 =$

(A) 18^8　　　(B) 18^{12}　　　(C) 6^{12}　　　(D) 6^{48}　　　(E) 18^{48}

4. $a^4b^2 \times a^3b =$

(A) ab　　　(B) $2a^7b^2$　　　(C) $2a^{12}b$　　　(D) a^7b^3　　　(E) a^7b^2

5. $m^8n^3 \times m^2n \times m^4n^2 =$

(A) $3m^{16}n^6$　(B) $m^{14}n^6$　　(C) $3m^{14}n^5$　(D) $3m^{14}n^5$　(E) m^2

Division

DIRECTIONS: Simplify.

6. $6^5 \div 6^3 =$

(A) 0　　　(B) 1　　　(C) 6　　　(D) 12　　　(E) 36

7. $11^8 \div 11^5 =$

(A) 1^3　　　(B) 11^3　　　(C) 11^{13}　　　(D) 11^{40}　　　(E) 88^5

8. $x^{10}y^8 \div x^7y^3 =$

(A) x^2y^5　　　(B) x^3y^4　　　(C) x^3y^5　　　(D) x^2y^4　　　(E) x^5y^3

9. $a^{14} \div a^9 =$

(A) 1^5　　　(B) a^5　　　(C) $2a^5$　　　(D) a^{23}　　　(E) $2a^{23}$

10. $c^{17}d^{12}e^4 \div c^{12}d^8e =$

(A) $c^4d^5e^3$　(B) $c^4d^4e^3$　(C) $c^5d^8e^4$　(D) $c^5d^4e^3$　(E) $c^5d^4e^4$

Power to a Power

DIRECTIONS: Simplify.

11. $(3^6)^2 =$

(A) 3^4 (B) 3^8 (C) 3^{12} (D) 9^6 (E) 9^8

12. $(4^3)^5 =$

(A) 4^2 (B) 2^{15} (C) 4^8 (D) 20^3 (E) 4^{15}

13. $(a^4b^3)^2 =$

(A) $(ab)^9$ (B) a^8b^6 (C) $(ab)^{24}$ (D) a^6b^5 (E) $2a^4b^3$

14. $(r^3p^6)^3 =$

(A) r^9p^{18} (B) $(rp)^{12}$ (C) r^6p^9 (D) $3r^3p^6$ (E) $3r^9p^{18}$

15. $(m^6n^5q^3)^2 =$

(A) $2m^6n^5q^3$ (B) m^4n^3q (C) $m^8n^7q^5$

(D) $m^{12}n^{10}q^6$ (E) $2m^{12}n^{10}q^6$

MEAN, MEDIAN, MODE

MEAN

The mean is the arithmetic average. It is the sum of the variables divided by the total number of variables. For example, the mean of 4, 3, and 8 is

$$\frac{4+3+8}{3} = \frac{15}{3} = 5$$

PROBLEM

Find the mean salary for four company employees who make $5/hr., $8/hr., $12/hr., and $15/hr.

SOLUTION

The mean salary is the average.

$$\frac{\$5 + \$8 + \$12 + \$15}{4} = \frac{\$40}{4} = \$10/hr$$

PROBLEM

Find the mean length of five fish with lengths of 7.5 in., 7.75 in., 8.5 in., 8.5 in., and 8.25 in.

SOLUTION

The mean length is the average length.

$$\frac{7.5 + 7.75 + 8.5 + 8.5 + 8.25}{5} = \frac{40.5}{5} = 8.1 \text{ in}$$

MEDIAN

The median is the middle value in a set when there is an odd number of values. There is an equal number of values larger and smaller than the median. When the set is an even number of values, the average of the two middle values is the median. For example:

The median of (2, 3, 5, 8, 9) is 5.

The median of (2, 3, 5, 9, 10, 11) is $\frac{5+9}{2} = 7$.

MODE

The mode is the most frequently occurring value in the set of values. For example, the mode of 4, 5, 8, 3, 8, 2 would be 8, since it occurs twice while the other values occur only once.

PROBLEM

For this series of observations find the mean, median, and mode.

500, 600, 800, 800, 900, 900, 900, 900, 900, 1,000, 1,100

SOLUTION

The mean is the value obtained by adding all the measurements and dividing by the number of measurements.

$$\frac{500 + 600 + 800 + 800 + 900 + 900 + 900 + 900 + 900 + 1,000 + 1,100}{11}$$

$$= \frac{9,300}{11} = 845.45.$$

The median is the value appearing in the middle. We have 11 values, so here the sixth, 900, is the median.

The mode is the value that appears most frequently. That is also 900, which has five appearances.

All three of these numbers are measures of central tendency. They describe the "middle" or "center" of the data.

PROBLEM

Nine rats run through a maze. The time each rat took to traverse the maze is recorded and these times (in minutes) are listed below.

1 min, 2.5 min, 3 min, 1.5 min, 2 min, 1.25 min, 1 min, .9 min, 30 min

Which of the three measures of central tendency would be the most appropriate in this case?

SOLUTION

We will calculate the three measures of central tendency and then compare them to determine which would be the most appropriate in describing these data.

The mean is the sum of the values listed divided by the number of values. In this case

$$\frac{1 + 2.5 + 3 + 1.5 + 2 + 1.25 + 1 + .9 + 30}{9} = \frac{43.15}{9} = 4.79.$$

The median is the "middle number" in an array of the values from the lowest to the highest.

0.9, 1.0, 1.0, 1.25, 1.5, 2.0, 2.5, 3.0, 30.0

The median is the fifth value in this ordered array or 1.5. There are four values larger than 1.5 and four values smaller than 1.5.

The mode is the most frequently occurring value in the sample. In this data set the mode is 1.0.

mean = 4.79

median = 1.5

mode = 1.0

The mean is not appropriate here. Only one rat took more than 4.79 minutes to run the maze and this rat took 30 minutes. We see that the mean has been distorted by this one large value.

The median or mode seems to describe this data set better and would be more appropriate to use.

☞ Drill: Averages

Mean

DIRECTIONS: Find the mean of each set of numbers.

1. 18, 25, and 32

(A) 3   (B) 25   (C) 50   (D) 75   (E) 150

2. $\frac{4}{9}, \frac{2}{3}$, and $\frac{5}{6}$

(A) $\frac{11}{18}$ (B) $\frac{35}{54}$ (C) $\frac{41}{54}$ (D) $\frac{35}{18}$ (E) $\frac{54}{18}$

3. 97, 102, 116, and 137

(A) 40   (B) 102   (C) 109   (D) 113   (E) 116

4. 12, 15, 18, 24, and 31

(A) 18   (B) 19.3   (C) 20   (D) 25   (E) 100

5. 7, 4, 6, 3, 11, and 14

(A) 5   (B) 6.5   (C) 7   (D) 7.5   (E) 8

Median

DIRECTIONS: Find the median value of each set of numbers.

6. 3, 8, and 6

(A) 3   (B) 6   (C) 8   (D) 17   (E) 20

7. 19, 15, 21, 27, and 12

(A) 19   (B) 15   (C) 21   (D) 27   (E) 94

8. $1\frac{2}{3}, 1\frac{7}{8}, 1\frac{3}{4}$, and $1\frac{5}{6}$

(A) $1\dfrac{30}{48}$ (B) $1\dfrac{2}{3}$ (C) $1\dfrac{3}{4}$ (D) $1\dfrac{19}{24}$ (E) $1\dfrac{21}{24}$

9.   29, 18, 21, and 35

(A) 29   (B) 18   (C) 21   (D) 35   (E) 25

10. 8, 15, 7, 12, 31, 3, and 28

(A) 7   (B) 11.6   (C) 12   (D) 14.9   (E) 104

Mode

DIRECTIONS: Find the mode(s) of each set of numbers.

11. 1, 3, 7, 4, 3, and 8

(A) 1   (B) 3   (C) 7   (D) 4   (E) None

12. 12, 19, 25, and 42

(A) 12   (B) 19   (C) 25   (D) 42   (E) None

13. 16, 14, 12, 16, 30, and 28

(A) 6   (B) 14   (C) 16   (D) $19.\overline{3}$ (E) None

14. 4, 3, 9, 2, 4, 5, and 2

(A) 3 and 9   (B) 5 and 9   (C) 4 and 5   (D) 2 and 4   (E) None

15. 87, 42, 111, 116, 39, 111, 140, 116, 97, and 111

(A) 111   (B) 116   (C) 39   (D) 140   (E) None

ARITHMETIC DRILLS

ANSWER KEY

Drill: Integers and Real Numbers

1.	(A)	9.	(E)	17.	(D)	25.	(D)
2.	(C)	10.	(B)	18.	(D)	26.	(D)
3.	(D)	11.	(B)	19.	(C)	27.	(B)
4.	(C)	12.	(E)	20.	(E)	28.	(C)
5.	(B)	13.	(C)	21.	(B)	29.	(A)
6.	(B)	14.	(A)	22.	(E)	30.	(C)
7.	(A)	15.	(B)	23.	(D)		
8.	(C)	16.	(B)	24.	(A)		

Drill: Fractions

1.	(D)	14.	(A)	27.	(D)	40.	(B)
2.	(A)	15.	(C)	28.	(B)	41.	(C)
3.	(D)	16.	(B)	29.	(A)	42.	(A)
4.	(E)	17.	(C)	30.	(C)	43.	(B)
5.	(C)	18.	(A)	31.	(D)	44.	(C)
6.	(D)	19.	(B)	32.	(C)	45.	(D)
7.	(D)	20.	(A)	33.	(B)	46.	(B)
8.	(B)	21.	(B)	34.	(E)	47.	(C)
9.	(A)	22.	(D)	35.	(A)	48.	(D)
10.	(E)	23.	(E)	36.	(A)	49.	(E)
11.	(D)	24.	(D)	37.	(D)	50.	(A)
12.	(E)	25.	(B)	38.	(E)		
13.	(C)	26.	(B)	39.	(C)		

Drill: Decimals

1.	(B)	9.	(C)	17.	(D)	25.	(E)
2.	(E)	10.	(E)	18.	(D)	26.	(D)
3.	(C)	11.	(B)	19.	(A)	27.	(C)
4.	(A)	12.	(D)	20.	(C)	28.	(A)
5.	(D)	13.	(A)	21.	(E)	29.	(E)
6.	(A)	14.	(B)	22.	(C)	30.	(D)
7.	(B)	15.	(C)	23.	(B)		
8.	(D)	16.	(B)	24.	(D)		

Drill: Percentages

1.	(B)	9.	(E)	17.	(D)	25.	(D)
2.	(C)	10.	(C)	18.	(E)	26.	(D)
3.	(E)	11.	(C)	19.	(C)	27.	(C)
4.	(B)	12.	(B)	20.	(C)	28.	(B)
5.	(A)	13.	(B)	21.	(A)	29.	(E)
6.	(B)	14.	(D)	22.	(B)	30.	(A)
7.	(A)	15.	(A)	23.	(C)		
8.	(B)	16.	(E)	24.	(B)		

Drill: Radicals

1.	(B)	6.	(C)	11.	(B)	16.	(A)
2.	(D)	7.	(A)	12.	(D)	17.	(C)
3.	(A)	8.	(D)	13.	(C)	18.	(B)
4.	(C)	9.	(C)	14.	(E)	19.	(D)
5.	(E)	10.	(B)	15.	(A)	20.	(C)

Drill: Exponents

1.	(B)	9.	(B)
2.	(A)	10.	(D)
3.	(C)	11.	(C)
4.	(D)	12.	(E)
5.	(B)	13.	(B)
6.	(E)	14.	(A)
7.	(B)	15.	(D)
8.	(C)		

Drill: Averages

1.	(B)	9.	(E)
2.	(B)	10.	(C)
3.	(D)	11.	(B)
4.	(C)	12.	(E)
5.	(D)	13.	(C)
6.	(B)	14.	(D)
7.	(A)	15.	(A)
8.	(D)		

II. ALGEBRA

In algebra, letters or variables are used to represent numbers. A **variable** is defined as a placeholder, which can take on any of several values at a given time. A **constant**, on the other hand, is a symbol which takes on only one value at a given time. A **term** is a constant, a variable, or a combination of constants and variables. For example: 7.76, $3x$, xyz, $5z/x$, $(0.99)x^2$ are terms. If a term is a combination of constants and variables, the constant part of the term is referred to as the **coefficient** of the variable. If a variable is written without a coefficient, the coefficient is assumed to be 1.

EXAMPLES

$3x^2$

coefficient: 3

variable: x

y^3

coefficient: 1

variable: y

An **expression** is a collection of one or more terms. If the number of terms is greater than 1, the expression is said to be the sum of the terms.

EXAMPLES

$$9, 9xy, 6x + \frac{x}{3}, 8yz - 2x$$

An algebraic expression consisting of only one term is called a **monomial**; of two terms is called a **binomial**; of three terms is called a **trinomial**. In general, an algebraic expression consisting of two or more terms is called a **polynomial**.

OPERATIONS WITH POLYNOMIALS

A) **Addition of polynomials** is achieved by combining like terms, terms which differ only in their numerical coefficients, e.g.,

$$P(x) = (x^2 - 3x + 5) + (4x^2 + 6x - 3)$$

Note that the parentheses are used to distinguish the polynomials.

By using the commutative and associative laws, we can rewrite $P(x)$ as:

$$P(x) = (x^2 + 4x^2) + (6x - 3x) + (5 - 3)$$

Using the distributive law, $ab + ac = a(b + c)$, yields:

$(1 + 4)x^2 + (6 - 3)x + (5 - 3)$

$= 5x^2 + 3x + 2$

B) **Subtraction of two polynomials** is achieved by first changing the sign of all terms in the expression which are being subtracted and then adding this result to the other expression, e.g.,

$(5x^2 + 4y^2 + 3z^2) - (4xy + 7y^2 - 3z^2 + 1)$

$= 5x^2 + 4y^2 + 3z^2 - 4xy - 7y^2 + 3z^2 - 1$

$= 5x^2 + (4y^2 - 7y^2) + (3z^2 + 3z^2) - 4xy - 1$

$= 5x^2 + (-3y^2) + 6z^2 - 4xy - 1$

C) **Multiplication of two or more polynomials** is achieved by using the laws of exponents, the rules of signs, and the commutative and associative laws of multiplication. Begin by multiplying the coefficients and then multiply the variables according to the laws of exponents, e.g.,

$(y^2) (5) (6y^2) (yz) (2z^2)$

$= (1) (5) (6) (1) (2) (y^2) (y^2) (yz) (z^2)$

$= 60[(y^2) (y^2) (y)] [(z) (z^2)]$

$= 60(y^5) (z^3)$

$= 60y^5z^3$

D) **Multiplication of a polynomial by a monomial** is achieved by multiplying each term of the polynomial by the monomial and combining the results, e.g.,

$(4x^2 + 3y) (6xz^2)$

$= (4x^2) (6xz^2) + (3y) (6xz^2)$

$= 24x^3z^2 + 18xyz^2$

E) **Multiplication of a polynomial by a polynomial** is achieved by multiplying each of the terms of one polynomial by each of the terms of the other polynomial and combining the result, e.g.,

$(5y + z + 1) (y^2 + 2y)$

$[(5y) (y^2) + (5y) (2y)] + [(z) (y^2) + (z) (2y)] + [(1) (y^2) + (1) (2y)]$

$$= (5y^3 + 10y^2) + (y^2z + 2yz) + (y^2 + 2y)$$
$$= (5y^3) + (10y^2 + y^2) + (y^2z) + (2yz) + (2y)$$
$$= 5y^3 + 11y^2 + y^2z + 2yz + 2y$$

F) **Division of a monomial by a monomial** is achieved by first dividing the constant coefficients and the variable factors separately, and then multiplying these quotients, e.g.,

$$6xyz^2 \div 2y^2z$$

$$= \left(\frac{6}{2}\right)\left(\frac{x}{1}\right)\left(\frac{y}{y^2}\right)\left(\frac{z^2}{z}\right)$$

$$= 3xy^{-1}z$$

$$= \frac{3xz}{y}$$

G) **Division of a polynomial by a polynomial** is achieved by following the given procedure, called long division.

Step 1: The terms of both the polynomials are arranged in order of ascending or descending powers of one variable.

Step 2: The first term of the dividend is divided by the first term of the divisor which gives the first term of the quotient.

Step 3: This first term of the quotient is multiplied by the entire divisor and the result is subtracted from the dividend.

Step 4: Using the remainder obtained from Step 3 as the new dividend, Steps 2 and 3 are repeated until the remainder is zero or the degree of the remainder is less than the degree of the divisor.

Step 5: The result is written as follows:

$$\frac{\text{dividend}}{\text{divisor}} = \text{quotient} + \frac{\text{remainder}}{\text{divisor}}$$

divisor $\neq 0$

e.g., $(2x^2 + x + 6) \div (x + 1)$

$$
\require{enclose}
\begin{array}{r}
2x - 1 \\
(x+1)\enclose{longdiv}{2x^2 + x + 6} \\
\underline{-(2x^2 + 2x)} \\
-x + 6 \\
\underline{-(-x - 1)} \\
7
\end{array}
$$

The result is $(2x^2 + x + 6) \div (x + 1) = 2x - 1 + \dfrac{7}{x+1}$

☞ Drill: Operations with Polynomials

Addition

DIRECTIONS: Add the following polynomials.

1.　$9a^2b + 3c + 2a^2b + 5c =$

(A) $19a^2bc$ 　　　　(B) $11a^2b + 8c$ 　　　　(C) $11a^4b^2 + 8c^2$

(D) $19a^4b^2c^2$ 　　　　(E) $12a^2b + 8c^2$

2.　$14m^2n^3 + 6m^2n^3 + 3m^2n^3 =$

(A) $20m^2n^3$ 　　　　(B) $23m^6n^9$ 　　　　(C) $23m^2n^3$

(D) $32m^6n^9$ 　　　　(E) $23m^8n^{27}$

3.　$3x + 2y + 16x + 3z + 6y =$

(A) $19x + 8y$ 　　　　(B) $19x + 11yz$ 　　　　(C) $19x + 8y + 3z$

(D) $11xy + 19xz$ 　　　　(E) $30xyz$

4.　$(4d^2 + 7e^3 + 12f) + (3d^2 + 6e^3 + 2f) =$

(A) $23d^2e^3f$ 　　　　(B) $33d^2e^2f$ 　　　　(C) $33d^4e^6f^2$

(D) $7d^2 + 13e^3 + 14f$ 　　　　(E) $23d^2 + 11e^3f$

5.　$3ac^2 + 2b^2c + 7ac^2 + 2ac^2 + b^2c =$

(A) $12ac^2 + 3b^2c$ 　　　　(B) $14ab^2c^2$ 　　　　(C) $11ac^2 + 4ab^2c$

(D) $15ab^2c^2$ 　　　　(E) $15a^2b^4c^4$

Subtraction

DIRECTIONS: Subtract the following polynomials.

6.　$14m^2n - 6m^2n =$

(A) $20m^2n$ 　　(B) $8m^2n$ 　　(C) $8m$ 　　(D) 8 　　(E) $8m^4n^2$

7. $3x^3y^2 - 4xz - 6x^3y^2 =$

(A) $-7x^2y^2z$ (B) $3x^3y^2 - 10x^4y^2z$ (C) $-3x^3y^2 - 4xz$

(D) $-x^2y^2z - 6x^3y^2$ (E) $-7xyz$

8. $9g^2 + 6h - 2g^2 - 5h =$

(A) $15g^2h - 7g^2h$ (B) $7g^4h^2$ (C) $11g^2 + 7h$

(D) $11g^2 - 7h^2$ (E) $7g^2 + h$

9. $7b^3 - 4c^2 - 6b^3 + 3c^2 =$

(A) $b^3 - c^2$ (B) $-11b^2 - 3c^2$ (C) $13b^3 - c$

(D) $7b - c$ (E) 0

10. $11q^2r - 4q^2r - 8q^2r =$

(A) $22q^2r$ (B) q^2r (C) $-2q^2r$

(D) $-q^2r$ (E) $2q^2r$

Multiplication

<u>**DIRECTIONS**</u>: Multiply the following polynomials.

11. $5p^2t \times 3p^2t =$

(A) $15p^2t$ (B) $15p^4t$ (C) $15p^4t^2$

(D) $8p^2t$ (E) $8p^4t^2$

12. $(2r + s)\,14r =$

(A) $28rs$ (B) $28r^2 + 14sr$ (C) $16r^2 + 14rs$

(D) $28r + 14sr$ (E) $17r^2s$

13. $(4m + p)\,(3m - 2p) =$

(A) $12m^2 + 5mp + 2p^2$ (B) $12m^2 - 2mp + 2p^2$ (C) $7m - p$

(D) $12m - 2p$ (E) $12m^2 - 5mp - 2p^2$

14. $(2a + b)\,(3a^2 + ab + b^2) =$

(A) $6a^3 + 5a^2b + 3ab^2 + b^3$ (B) $5a^3 + 3ab + b^3$

(C) $6a^3 + 2a^2b + 2ab^2$ (D) $3a^2 + 2a + ab + b + b^2$

(E) $6a^3 + 3a^2b + 5ab^2 + b^3$

15. $(6t^2 + 2t + 1) \, 3t =$

(A) $9t^2 + 5t + 3$ (B) $18t^2 + 6t + 3$ (C) $9t^3 + 6t^2 + 3t$

(D) $18t^3 + 6t^2 + 3t$ (E) $12t^3 + 6t^2 + 3t$

Division

DIRECTIONS: Divide the following polynomials.

16. $(x^2 + x - 6) \div (x - 2) =$

(A) $x - 3$ (B) $x + 2$ (C) $x + 3$ (D) $x - 2$ (E) $2x + 2$

17. $24b^4c^3 \div 6b^2c =$

(A) $3b^2c^2$ (B) $4b^4c^3$ (C) $4b^3c^2$ (D) $4b^2c^2$ (E) $3b^4c^3$

18. $(3p^2 + pq - 2q^2) \div (p + q) =$

(A) $3p + 2q$ (B) $2q - 3p$ (C) $3p - q$

(D) $2q + 3p$ (E) $3p - 2q$

19. $(y^3 - 2y^2 - y + 2) \div (y - 2) =$

(A) $(y - 1)^2$ (B) $y^2 - 1$ (C) $(y + 2)(y - 1)$

(D) $(y + 1)^2$ (E) $(y + 1)(y - 2)$

20. $(m^2 + m - 14) \div (m + 4) =$

(A) $m - 2$ (B) $m - 3 + \dfrac{-2}{m + 4}$ (C) $m - 3 + \dfrac{4}{m + 4}$

(D) $m - 3$ (E) $m - 2 + \dfrac{-3}{m + 4}$

FACTORING ALGEBRAIC EXPRESSIONS

To factor a polynomial completely is to find the prime factors of the polynomial with respect to a specified set of numbers.

The following concepts are important while factoring or simplifying expressions.

A) The factors of an algebraic expression consist of two or more algebraic expressions which, when multiplied together, produce the given algebraic expression.

B) A **prime factor** is a polynomial with no factors other than itself and 1. The **least common multiple (LCM)** for a set of numbers is the smallest quantity divisible by every number of the set. For algebraic expressions the least common numerical coefficients for each of the given expressions will be a factor.

C) The **greatest common factor (GCF)** for a set of numbers is the largest factor that is common to all members of the set.

D) For algebraic expressions, the greatest common factor is the polynomial of highest degree and the largest numerical coefficient which is a factor of all the given expressions.

Some important formulas, useful for the factoring of polynomials, are listed below.

$$a(c + d) = ac + ad$$

$$(a + b)(a - b) = a^2 - b^2$$

$$(a + b)(a + b) = (a + b)^2 = a^2 + 2ab + b^2$$

$$(a - b)(a - b) = (a - b)^2 = a^2 - 2ab + b^2$$

$$(x + a)(x + b) = x^2 + (a + b)x + ab$$

$$(ax + b)(cx + d) = acx^2 + (ad + bc)x + bd$$

$$(a + b)(c + d) = ac + bc + ad + bd$$

$$(a + b)(a + b)(a + b) = (a + b)^3 = a^3 + 3a^2b + 3ab^2 + b^3$$

$$(a - b)(a - b)(a - b) = (a - b)^3 = a^3 - 3a^2b + 3ab^2 - b^3$$

$$(a - b)(a^2 + ab + b^2) = a^3 - b^3$$

$$(a + b)(a^2 - ab + b^2) = a^3 + b^3$$

$$(a + b + c)^2 = a^2 + b^2 + c^2 + 2ab + 2ac + 2bc$$

$$(a - b)(a^3 + a^2b + ab^2 + b^3) = a^4 - b^4$$

$$(a - b)(a^4 + a^3b + a^2b^2 + ab^3 + b^4) = a^5 - b^5$$

$$(a - b)(a^5 + a^4b + a^3b^2 + a^2b^3 + ab^4 + b^5) = a^6 - b^6$$

$$(a - b)(a^{n-1} + a^{n-2}b + a^{n-3}b^2 + \ldots + ab^{n-2} + b^{n-1}) = a^n - b^n$$

where n is any positive integer (1, 2, 3, 4, ...).

$$(a + b)(a^{n-1} - a^{n-2}b + a^{n-3}b^2 - \ldots - ab^{n-2} + b^{n-1}) = a^n + b^n$$

where n is any positive odd integer $(1, 3, 5, 7, \ldots)$.

The procedure for factoring an algebraic expression completely is as follows:

Step 1: First find the greatest common factor if there is any. Then examine each factor remaining for greatest common factors.

Step 2: Continue factoring the factors obtained in Step 1 until all factors other than monomial factors are prime.

EXAMPLE

Factoring $4 - 16x^2$,

$$4 - 16x^2 = 4(1 - 4x^2) = 4(1 + 2x)(1 - 2x)$$

PROBLEM

Express each of the following as a single term.

(1) $3x^2 + 2x^2 - 4x^2$ (2) $5axy^2 - 7axy^2 - 3xy^2$

SOLUTION

(1)   Factor x^2 in the expression.

$$3x^2 + 2x^2 - 4x^2 = (3 + 2 - 4)x^2 = 1x^2 = x^2$$

(2)   Factor xy^2 in the expression and then factor a.

$$5axy^2 - 7axy^2 - 3xy^2 = (5a - 7a - 3)xy^2$$
$$= [(5 - 7)a - 3]xy^2$$
$$= (-2a - 3)xy^2$$

PROBLEM

Simplify $\dfrac{\frac{1}{x-1} - \frac{1}{x-2}}{\frac{1}{x-2} - \frac{1}{x-3}}$.

SOLUTION

Simplify the expression in the numerator by using the addition rule:

$$\frac{a}{b} + \frac{c}{d} = \frac{ad + bc}{bd}$$

Notice bd is the Least Common Denominator, LCD. We obtain

$$\frac{x-2-(x-1)}{(x-1)(x-2)} = \frac{-1}{(x-1)(x-2)}$$

in the numerator.

Repeat this procedure for the expression in the denominator:

$$\frac{x-3-(x-2)}{(x-2)(x-3)} = \frac{-1}{(x-2)(x-3)}$$

We now have

$$\frac{\frac{-1}{(x-1)(x-2)}}{\frac{-1}{(x-2)(x-3)}}$$

which is simplified by inverting the fraction in the denominator and multiplying it by the numerator and cancelling like terms

$$\frac{-1}{(x-1)(x-2)} \times \frac{(x-2)(x-3)}{-1} = \frac{x-3}{x-1}.$$

☞ Drill: Simplifying Algebraic Expressions

DIRECTIONS: Simplify the following expressions.

1. $16b^2 - 25z^2 =$

(A) $(4b - 5z)^2$ (B) $(4b + 5z)^2$ (C) $(4b - 5z)(4b + 5z)$

(D) $(16b - 25z)^2$ (E) $(5z - 4b)(5z + 4b)$

2. $x^2 - 2x - 8 =$

(A) $(x - 4)^2$ (B) $(x - 6)(x - 2)$ (C) $(x + 4)(x - 2)$

(D) $(x - 4)(x + 2)$ (E) $(x - 4)(x - 2)$

3. $2c^2 + 5cd - 3d^2 =$

(A) $(c - 3d)(c + 2d)$ (B) $(2c - d)(c + 3d)$ (C) $(c - d)(2c + 3d)$

(D) $(2c + d)(c + 3d)$ (E) $(2d + c)(c + 3d)$

4. $4t^3 - 20t =$

(A) $4t(t^2 - 5)$ (B) $4t^2(t - 20)$ (C) $4t(t + 4)(t - 5)$

(D) $2t(2t^2 - 10)$ (E) $12t(t - 20)$

5. $x^2 + xy - 2y^2 =$

(A) $(x - 2y)(x + y)$ (B) $(x - 2y)(x - y)$ (C) $(x + 2y)(x + y)$

(D) $(x + 2y)(x - y)$ (E) $(x - y)(2y - x)$

6. $5b^2 + 17bd + 6d^2 =$

(A) $(5b + d)(b + 6d)$ (B) $(5b + 2d)(b + 3d)$ (C) $(5b - 2d)(b - 3d)$

(D) $(5b - 2d)(b + 3d)$ (E) $(b + 3d)(5b - 2d)$

7. $x^2 + 2x + 1 =$

(A) $(x + 1)^2$ (B) $(x + 2)(x - 1)$ (C) $(x - 2)(x + 1)$

(D) $(x + 1)(x - 1)$ (E) $(x - 1)(x + 1)$

8. $3z^3 + 6z^2 =$

(A) $3(z^3 + 2z^2)$ (B) $3z^2(z + 2)$ (C) $3z(z^2 + 2z)$

(D) $z^2(3z + 6)$ (E) $3z^2(1 + 2z)$

9. $m^2p^2 + mpq - 6q^2 =$

(A) $(mp - 2q)(mp + 3q)$ (B) $mp(mp - 2q)(mp + 3q)$

(C) $mpq(1 - 6q)$ (D) $(mp + 2q)(mp + 3q)$

(E) $(mp + 2q)(1 - 6q)$

10. $2h^3 + 2h^2t - 4ht^2 =$

(A) $2(h^3 - t)(h + t)$ (B) $2h(h - 2t)^2$ (C) $4h(ht - t^2)$

(D) $2h(h + t) - 4ht^2$ (E) $2h(h + 2t)(h - t)$

EQUATIONS

An **equation** is defined as a statement that two separate expressions are equal.

A **solution** to an equation containing a single variable is a number that makes the equation true when it is substituted for the variable. For example, in the equation $3x = 18$, 6 is the solution since $3(6) = 18$. Depending on the equation, there can be more than one solution. Equations with the same solutions are said to be **equivalent equations**. An equation without a solution is said to have a solution set that is the **empty** or **null** set and is represented by ϕ.

Replacing an expression within an equation by an equivalent expression will result in a new equation with solutions equivalent to the original equation. Suppose we are given the equation

$$3x + y + x + 2y = 15.$$

By combining like terms we get

$$3x + y + x + 2y = 4x + 3y.$$

Since these two expressions are equivalent, we can substitute the simpler form into the equation to get

$$4x + 3y = 15$$

Performing the same operation to both sides of an equation by the same expression will result in a new equation that is equivalent to the original equation.

A) **Addition or subtraction**

$$y + 6 = 10$$

We can add (-6) to both sides

$$y + 6 + (-6) = 10 + (-6)$$

to get $y + 0 = 10 - 6 \rightarrow y = 4$

B) **Multiplication or division**

$$3x = 6$$

$$\frac{3x}{3} = \frac{6}{3}$$

$$x = 2$$

$3x = 6$ is equivalent to $x = 2$.

C) **Raising to a power**

$$a = x^2y$$

$$a^2 = (x^2y)^2$$

$$a^2 = x^4y^2$$

This can be applied to negative and fractional powers as well, e.g.,

$$x^2 = 3y^4$$

If we raise both sides to the -2 power, we get

$$(x^2)^{-2} = (3y^4)^{-2}$$
$$\frac{1}{(x^2)^2} = \frac{1}{(3y^4)^2}$$
$$\frac{1}{x^4} = \frac{1}{9y^8}$$

If we raise both sides to the $\frac{1}{2}$ power, which is the same as taking the square root, we get

$$(x^2)^{1/2} = (3y^4)^{1/2}$$
$$x = \pm\sqrt{3}y^2$$

D) The **reciprocal** of both sides of an equation are equivalent to the original equation. Note: The reciprocal of zero is undefined.

$$\frac{2x+y}{z} = \frac{5}{2} \qquad \frac{z}{2x+y} = \frac{2}{5}$$

PROBLEM

Solve for x, justifying each step.

$$3x - 8 = 7x + 8$$

SOLUTION

$$3x - 8 = 7x + 8$$

Add 8 to both sides: $\qquad\qquad 3x - 8 + 8 = 7x + 8 + 8$

Additive inverse property: $\qquad\qquad 3x + 0 = 7x + 16$

Additive identity property: $\qquad\qquad 3x = 7x + 16$

Add $(-7x)$ to both sides: $\qquad\qquad 3x - 7x = 7x + 16 - 7x$

Commute: $\qquad\qquad -4x = 7x - 7x + 16$

Additive inverse property: $\qquad\qquad -4x = 0 + 16$

Additive identity property: $\qquad\qquad -4x = 16$

Divide both sides by -4: $\qquad\qquad x = {}^{16}/_{-4}$

$$x = -4$$

Check: Replacing x with -4 in the original equation:

$$3x - 8 = 7x + 8$$

$$3(-4) - 8 = 7(-4) + 8$$

$$-12 - 8 = -28 + 8$$

$$-20 = -20$$

LINEAR EQUATIONS

A linear equation with one unknown is one that can be put into the form $ax + b = 0$, where a and b are constants, $a \neq 0$.

To solve a linear equation means to transform it in the form $x = {}^{-b}/_a$.

A) If the equation has unknowns on both sides of the equality, it is convenient to put similar terms on the same sides. Refer to the following example.

$$4x + 3 = 2x + 9$$

$$4x + 3 - 2x = 2x + 9 - 2x$$

$$(4x - 2x) + 3 = (2x - 2x) + 9$$

$$2x + 3 = 0 + 9$$

$$2x + 3 - 3 = 0 + 9 - 3$$

$$2x = 6$$

$$\frac{2x}{2} = \frac{6}{2}$$

$$x = 3$$

B) If the equation appears in fractional form, it is necessary to transform it, using cross-multiplication, and then repeating the same procedure as in A), we obtain:

$$\frac{3x + 4}{3} \diagup\hspace{-1em}\diagdown \frac{7x + 2}{5}$$

By using cross-multiplication we would obtain:

$$3(7x + 2) = 5(3x + 4).$$

This is equivalent to:

$$21x + 6 = 15x + 20,$$

which can be solved as in A).

$$21x + 6 = 15x + 20$$

$$21x - 15x + 6 = 15x - 15x + 20$$

$$6x + 6 - 6 = 20 - 6$$

$$6x = 14$$

$$x = \frac{14}{6}$$

$$x = \frac{7}{3}$$

C) If there are radicals in the equation, it is necessary to square both sides and then apply A).

$$\sqrt{3x + 1} = 5$$

$$(\sqrt{3x + 1})^2 = 5^2$$

$$3x + 1 = 25$$

$$3x + 1 - 1 = 25 - 1$$

$$3x = 24$$

$$x = \frac{24}{3}$$

$$x = 8$$

PROBLEM

Solve the equation $2(x + 3) = (3x + 5) - (x - 5)$.

SOLUTION

We transform the given equation to an equivalent equation in which we can easily recognize the solution set.

$$2(x + 3) = 3x + 5 - (x - 5)$$

Distribute: $\quad\quad\quad\quad\quad\quad 2x + 6 = 3x + 5 - x + 5$

Combine terms: $\quad\quad\quad\quad 2x + 6 = 2x + 10$

Subtract $2x$ from both sides: $\quad 6 = 10$

Since $6 = 10$ is not a true statement, there is no real number x which will make the original equation true. The equation is inconsistent and the solution set is ϕ, the empty set.

PROBLEM

Solve the equation $2(^2/_3 \, y + 5) + 2(y + 5) = 130$.

SOLUTION

The procedure for solving this equation is as follows:

Distribute: $\dfrac{4}{3}y + 10 + 2y + 10 = 130$

Combine like terms: $\dfrac{4}{3}y + 2y + 20 = 130$

Subtract 20 from both sides: $\dfrac{4}{3}y + 2y = 110$

Convert $2y$ into a fraction with denominator 3: $\dfrac{4}{3}y + \dfrac{6}{3}y = 110$

Combine like terms: $\dfrac{10}{3}y = 110$

Divide by $^{10}/_3$: $y = 110 \times \dfrac{3}{10} = 33$

Check: Replace y with 33 in the original equation.

$$2(\dfrac{2}{3}(33) + 5) + 2(33 + 5) = 130$$

$$2(22 + 5) + 2(38) = 130$$

$$2(27) + 76 = 130$$

$$54 + 76 = 130$$

$$130 = 130$$

Therefore, the solution to the given equation is $y = 33$.

☞ Drill: Linear Equations

DIRECTIONS: Solve for *x*.

1. $4x - 2 = 10$

(A) -1 (B) 2 (C) 3 (D) 4 (E) 6

2. $7z + 1 - z = 2z - 7$

(A) -2 (B) 0 (C) 1 (D) 2 (E) 3

3. $\frac{1}{3}b + 3 = \frac{1}{2}b$

(A) $\frac{1}{2}$ (B) 2   (C) $3\frac{3}{5}$ (D) 6   (E) 18

4. $0.4p + 1 = 0.7p - 2$

(A) 0.1   (B) 2   (C) 5   (D) 10   (E) 12

5. $4(3x + 2) - 11 = 3(3x - 2)$

(A) −3   (B) −1   (C) 2   (D) 3   (E) 7

TWO LINEAR EQUATIONS

Equations of the form $ax + by = c$, where a, b, c are constants and a, b $\neq 0$ are called **linear equations** with two unknown variables.

There are several ways to solve systems of linear equations with two variables.

Method 1: **Addition or subtraction**—if necessary, multiply the equations by numbers that will make the coefficients of one unknown in the resulting equations numerically equal. If the signs of equal coefficients are the same, subtract the equation, otherwise add.

The result is one equation with one unknown; we solve it and substitute the value into the other equations to find the unknown that we first eliminated.

Method 2: **Substitution**—find the value of one unknown in terms of the other. Substitute this value in the other equation and solve.

Method 3: **Graph**—graph both equations. The point of intersection of the drawn lines is a simultaneous solution for the equations and its coordinates correspond to the answer that would be found analytically.

If the lines are parallel they have no simultaneous solution.

Dependent equations are equations that represent the same line; therefore, every point on the line of a dependent equation represents a solution. Since there is an infinite number of points on a line there is an infinite number of simultaneous solutions, for example,

$$\begin{cases} 2x + y = 8 \\ 4x + 2y = 16 \end{cases}$$

The equations on the previous page are dependent. Since they represent the same line, all points that satisfy either of the equations are solutions of the system.

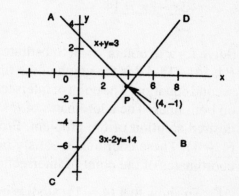

A system of linear equations is consistent if there is only one solution for the system.

A system of linear equations is inconsistent if it does not have any solutions.

EXAMPLE

Find the point of intersection of the graphs of the equations as shown in the previous figure.

$$x + y = 3$$

$$3x - 2y = 14$$

To solve these linear equations, solve for y in terms of x. The equations will be in the form $y = mx + b$, where m is the slope and b is the intercept on the y-axis.

Subtract x from both sides:

$$x + y = 3$$
$$y = 3 - x$$

Subtract $3x$ from both sides:

$$3x - 2y = 14$$

Divide by -2:

$$-2y = 14 - 3x$$

$$y = -7 + \frac{3}{2}x$$

The graphs of the linear functions, $y = 3 - x$ and $y = 7 + \frac{3}{2}x$ can be determined by plotting only two points. For example, for $y = 3 - x$, let $x = 0$, then $y = 3$. Let $x = 1$, then $y = 2$. The two points on this first line are $(0, 3)$ and $(1, 2)$. For $y = -7 + \frac{3}{2}x$, let $x = 0$, then $y = -7$. Let $x = 1$, then $y = -5\frac{1}{2}$. The two points on this second line are $(0, -7)$ and $(1, -5\frac{1}{2})$.

To find the point of intersection P of

$$x + y = 3 \quad \text{and} \quad 3x - 2y = 14,$$

solve them algebraically. Multiply the first equation by 2. Add these two equations to eliminate the variable y.

$$2x + 2y = 6$$
$$3x - 2y = 14$$
$$5x \qquad = 20$$

Solve for x to obtain $x = 4$. Substitute this into $y = 3 - x$ to get $y = 3 - 4 = -1$. P is $(4, -1)$. AB is the graph of the first equation, and CD is the graph of the second equation. The point of intersection P of the two graphs is the only point on both lines. The coordinates of P satisfy both equations and represent the desired solution of the problem. From the graph, P seems to be the point $(4, -1)$. These coordinates satisfy both equations, and hence are the exact coordinates of the point of intersection of the two lines.

To show that $(4, -1)$ satisfies both equations, substitute this point into both equations.

$$x + y = 3 \qquad\qquad\qquad 3x - 2y = 14$$
$$4 + (-1) = 3 \qquad\qquad 3(4) - 2(-1) = 14$$
$$4 - 1 = 3 \qquad\qquad\qquad 12 + 2 = 14$$
$$3 = 3 \qquad\qquad\qquad\qquad 14 = 14$$

EXAMPLE

Solve the equations $2x + 3y = 6$ and $4x + 6y = 7$ simultaneously.

We have 2 equations and 2 unknowns,

$$2x + 3y = 6 \quad (1)$$

and

$$4x + 6y = 7 \quad (2)$$

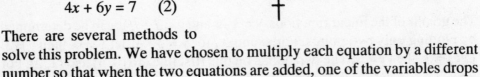

There are several methods to solve this problem. We have chosen to multiply each equation by a different number so that when the two equations are added, one of the variables drops out. Thus,

Multiply equation (1) by 2: $\qquad 4x + 6y = 12 \qquad\qquad\qquad (3)$

Multiply equation (2) by -1: $\qquad \underline{-4x - 6y = -7} \qquad\qquad (4)$

Add equations (3) and (4): $\qquad\qquad\qquad 0 = 5$

We obtain a peculiar result!

Actually, what we have shown in this case is that if there were a simultaneous solution to the given equations, then 0 would equal 5. But the conclusion is impossible; therefore there can be no simultaneous solution to these two equations, hence no point satisfying both.

The straight lines which are the graphs of these equations must be parallel if they never intersect, but not identical, which can be seen from the graph of these equations (see the accompanying diagram).

EXAMPLE

Solve the equations $2x + 3y = 6$ and $y = -\left(\frac{2x}{3}\right) + 2$ simultaneously.

We have 2 equations and 2 unknowns.

$$2x + 3y = 6 \tag{1}$$

and

$$y = -\left(\frac{2x}{3}\right) + 2 \tag{2}$$

There are several methods of solution for this problem. Since equation (2) already gives us an expression for y, we use the method of substitution. Substitute: $-\left(\frac{2x}{3}\right) + 2$ for y in the first equation:

$$2x + 3\left(-\frac{2x}{3} + 2\right) = 6$$

Distribute:
$$2x - 2x + 6 = 6$$

$$6 = 6$$

Apparently we have gotten nowhere! The result $6 = 6$ is true, but indicates no solution. Actually, our work shows that no matter what real number x is, if y is determined by the second equation, then the first equation will always be satisfied.

The reason for this peculiarity may be seen if we take a closer look at the equation $y = -\left(\frac{2x}{3}\right) + 2$. It is equivalent to $3y = -2x + 6$, or $2x + 3y = 6$.

In other words, the two equations are equivalent. Any pair of values of x and y which satisfies one satisfies the other.

It is hardly necessary to verify that in this case the graphs of the given equations are identical lines, and that there are an infinite number of simultaneous solutions of these equations.

A system of three linear equations in three unknowns is solved by

eliminating one unknown from any two of the three equations and solving them. After finding two unknowns substitute them in any of the equations to find the third unknown.

PROBLEM

Solve the system

$$2x + 3y - 4z = -8 \tag{1}$$

$$x + y - 2z = -5 \tag{2}$$

$$7x - 2y + 5z = 4 \tag{3}$$

SOLUTION

We cannot eliminate any variable from two pairs of equations by a single multiplication. However, both x and z may be eliminated from equations 1 and 2 by multiplying equation (2) by -2. Then

$$2x + 3y - 4z = -8 \tag{1}$$

$$-2x - 2y + 4z = 10 \tag{4}$$

By addition, we have $y = 2$. Although we may now eliminate either x or z from another pair of equations, we can more conveniently substitute $y = 2$ in equations (2) and (3) to get two equations with two variables. Thus, making the substitution $y = 2$ in equations (2) and (3), we have

$$x - 2z = -7 \tag{5}$$

$$7x + 5z = 8 \tag{6}$$

Multiply equation (5) by 5 and multiply (6) by 2. Then add the two new equations. Then $x = -1$. Substitute x in either equation (5) or (6) to find z.

The solution of the system is $x = -1$, $y = 2$, and $z = 3$. Check by substitution.

A system of equations, as shown below, that has all constant terms b_1, b_2, ..., b_n equal to zero is said to be a homogeneous system.

$$\begin{cases} a_{11}x_1 + a_{12}x_2 + \ldots + a_{1n}x_m = b_1 \\ a_{21}x_1 + a_{22}x_2 + \ldots + a_{2n}x_m = b_2 \\ \vdots \qquad \vdots \qquad\qquad \vdots \qquad \vdots \\ a_{n1}x_1 + a_{n2}x_2 + \ldots + a_{nn}x_m = b_n \end{cases}$$

A homogeneous system (one in which each variable can be replaced by

a constant and the constant can be factored out) always has at least one solution which is called the trivial solution that is $x_1 = 0$, $x_2 = 0$, ..., $x_m = 0$.

For any given homogeneous system of equations, in which the number of variables is greater than or equal to the number of equations, there are non-trivial solutions.

Two systems of linear equations are said to be equivalent if and only if they have the same solution set.

PROBLEM

Solve for x and y.

$$x + 2y = 8 \tag{1}$$

$$3x + 4y = 20 \tag{2}$$

SOLUTION

Solve equation (1) for x in terms of y: $x = 8 - 2y$ (3)

Substitute $(8 - 2y)$ for x in (2): $3(8 - 2y) + 4y = 20$ (4)

Solve equation (4) for y as follows:

Distribute: $24 - 6y + 4y = 20$

Combine like terms and then subtract 24 from both sides:

$$24 - 2y = 20$$

$$24 - 24 - 2y = 20 - 24$$

$$-2y = -4$$

Divide both sides by -2: $y = 2$

Substitute 2 for y in equation (1): $x + 2(2) = 8$

$$x = 4$$

Thus, our solution is $x = 4$, $y = 2$.

Check: Substitute $x = 4$, $y = 2$ in equations (1) and (2):

$$4 + 2(2) = 8$$

$$8 = 8$$

$$3(4) + 4(2) = 20$$

$$20 = 20$$

PROBLEM

Solve algebraically.

$$4x + 2y = -1 \qquad (1)$$
$$5x - 3y = 7 \qquad (2)$$

SOLUTION

We arbitrarily choose to eliminate x first.

Multiply (1) by 5: $\qquad 20x + 10y = -5 \qquad\qquad$ (3)

Multiply (2) by 4: $\qquad 20x - 12y = 28 \qquad\qquad$ (4)

Subtract (3) from (4): $\qquad 22y = -33 \qquad\qquad$ (5)

Divide (5) by 22: $\qquad y = \dfrac{33}{22} = -\dfrac{3}{2}$

To find x, substitute $y = -^3/_2$ in either of the original equations. If we use equation (1), we obtain $4x + 2(-^3/_2) = -1$, $4x - 3 = -1$, $4x = 2$, $x = ^1/_2$.

The solution $(^1/_2, -^3/_2)$ should be checked in both equations of the given system.

Replacing $(^1/_2, -^3/_2)$ in equation (1):

$$4x + 2y = -1$$

$$4(\frac{1}{2}) + 2(-\frac{3}{2}) = -1$$

$$\frac{4}{2} - 3 = -1$$

$$2 - 3 = -1$$

$$-1 = -1$$

Replacing $(^1/_2, -^3/_2)$ in equation (2):

$$5x - 3y = 7$$

$$5(\frac{1}{2}) - 3(-\frac{3}{2}) = 7$$

$$\frac{5}{2} + \frac{9}{2} = 7$$

$$\frac{14}{2} = 7$$

$$7 = 7$$

(Instead of eliminating x from the two given equations, we could have eliminated y by multiplying equation (1) by 3, multiplying equation (2) by 2, and then adding the two derived equations.)

☞ Drill: Two Linear Equations

DIRECTIONS: Find the solution set for each pair of equations.

1. $3x + 4y = -2$
    $x - 6y = -8$

(A) $(2, -1)$ (B) $(1, -2)$ (C) $(-2, -1)$

(D) $(1, 2)$ (E) $(-2, 1)$

2. $2x + y = -10$
    $-2x - 4y = 4$

(A) $(6, -2)$ (B) $(-6, 2)$ (C) $(-2, 6)$

(D) $(2, 6)$ (E) $(-6, -2)$

3. $6x + 5y = -4$
    $3x - 3y = 9$

(A) $(1, -2)$ (B) $(1, 2)$ (C) $(2, -1)$

(D) $(-2, 1)$ (E) $(-1, 2)$

4. $4x + 3y = 9$
    $2x - 2y = 8$

(A) $(-3, 1)$ (B) $(1, -3)$ (C) $(3, 1)$

(D) $(3, -1)$ (E) $(-1, 3)$

5. $x + y = 7$
    $x = y - 3$

(A) $(5, 2)$ (B) $(-5, 2)$ (C) $(2, 5)$

(D) $(-2, 5)$ (E) $(2, -5)$

6. $5x + 6y = 4$
    $3x - 2y = 1$

(A) $(3, 6)$ (B) $\left(\dfrac{1}{2}, \dfrac{1}{4}\right)$ (C) $(-3, 6)$

(D) $(2, 4)$ (E) $\left(\dfrac{1}{3}, \dfrac{3}{2}\right)$

7. $x - 2y = 7$
    $x + y = -2$

(A) $(-2, 7)$ (B) $(3, -1)$ (C) $(-7, 2)$

(D) $(1, -3)$ (E) $(1, -2)$

8. $4x + 3y = 3$
    $-2x + 6y = 3$

(A) $\left(\dfrac{1}{2}, \dfrac{2}{3}\right)$ (B) $(-0.3, 0.6)$ (C) $(\dfrac{2}{3}, -1)$

(D) $(-0.2, 0.5)$ (E) $(0.3, 0.6)$

9. $4x - 2y = -14$
    $8x + y = 7$

(A) $(0, 7)$ (B) $(2, -7)$ (C) $(7, 0)$

(D) $(-7, 2)$ (E) $(0, 2)$

10. $6x - 3y = 1$
    $-9x + 5y = -1$

(A) $(1, -1)$ (B) $(\dfrac{2}{3}, 1)$ (C) $(1, \dfrac{2}{3})$

(D) $(-1, 1)$ (E) $(\dfrac{2}{3}, -1)$

QUADRATIC EQUATIONS

A second degree equation in x of the type $ax^2 + bx + c = 0$, $a \neq 0$, a, b and c are real numbers, is called a **quadratic equation.**

To solve a quadratic equation is to find values of x which satisfy $ax^2 + bx + c = 0$. These values of x are called **solutions**, or **roots**, of the equation.

A quadratic equation has a maximum of two roots. Methods of solving quadratic equations:

A) **Direct solution**: Given $x^2 - 9 = 0$.

We can solve directly by isolating the variable x.

$$x^2 = 9$$

$$x = \pm 3$$

B) **Factoring**: Given a quadratic equation $ax^2 + bx + c = 0$, a, b, $c \neq 0$, to factor means to express it as the product $a(x - r_1)(x - r_2) = 0$, where r_1 and r_2 are the two roots.

Some helpful hints to remember are

a) $r_1 + r_2 = -\dfrac{b}{a}$.

b) $r_1 r_2 = \dfrac{c}{a}$.

Given $x^2 - 5x + 4 = 0$.

Since

$$r_1 + r_2 = -\frac{b}{a} = -\frac{(-5)}{1} = 5,$$

the possible solutions are $(3, 2)$, $(4, 1)$, and $(5, 0)$. Also

$$r_1 r_2 = \frac{c}{a} = \frac{4}{1} = 4;$$

this equation is satisfied only by the second pair, so $r_1 = 4$, $r_2 = 1$, and the factored form is $(x - 4)(x - 1) = 0$.

If the coefficient of x^2 is not 1, it is necessary to divide the equation by this coefficient and then factor.

Given $2x^2 - 12x + 16 = 0$.

Dividing by 2, we obtain

$$x^2 - 6x + 8 = 0.$$

Since

$$r_1 + r_2 = -\frac{b}{a} = 6,$$

the possible solutions are (6, 0), (5, 1), (4, 2), and (3, 3). Also $r_1 r_2 = 8$, so the only possible answer is (4, 2) and the expression $x^2 - 6x + 8 = 0$ can be factored as $(x - 4)(x - 2)$.

C) **Completing the squares**: If it is difficult to factor the quadratic equation using the previous method, we can complete the squares.

Given $x^2 - 12x + 8 = 0$.

We know that the two roots added up should be 12 because

$$r_1 + r_2 = -\frac{b}{a} = \frac{-(-12)}{1} = 12.$$

The possible roots are (12, 0), (11, 1), (10, 2), (9, 3), (8, 4), (7, 5), and (6, 6).

But none of these satisfy $r_1 r_2 = 8$, so we cannot use (B).

To complete the square, it is necessary to isolate the constant term,

$$x^2 - 12x = -8.$$

Then take $^1/_2$ the coefficient of x, square it and add to both sides.

$$x^2 - 12x + \left(\frac{-12}{2}\right)^2 = -8 + \left(\frac{-12}{2}\right)^2$$

$$x^2 - 12x + 36 = -8 + 36 = 28$$

Now we can use the previous method to factor the left side.

$$r_1 + r_2 = 12, \; r_1 r_2 = 36$$

is satisfied by the pair (6, 6), so we have

$$(x - 6)^2 = 28.$$

Now extract the root of both sides and solve for x.

$$(x - 6) = \pm \sqrt{28} = \pm 2\sqrt{7}$$
$$x = \pm 2\sqrt{7} + 6$$

So the roots are

$$x = 2\sqrt{7} + 6, \; x = -2\sqrt{7} + 6.$$

PROBLEM

Solve the equation $x^2 + 8x + 15 = 0$.

SOLUTION

Since

$$(x + a)(x + b) = x^2 + bx + ax + ab$$
$$= x^2 + (a + b)x + ab,$$

we may factor the given equation,

$$0 = x^2 + 8x + 15,$$

replacing $a + b$ by 8 and ab by 15. Thus,

$$a + b = 8, \quad \text{and} \quad ab = 15.$$

We want the two numbers a and b whose sum is 8 and whose product is 15. We check all pairs of numbers whose product is 15.

(a) $1 \times 15 = 15$; thus, $a = 1$, $b = 15$, and $ab = 15$.

$1 + 15 = 16$; therefore, we reject these values because $a + b \neq 8$.

(b) $3 \times 5 = 15$; thus, $a = 3$, $b = 5$, and $ab = 15$.

$3 + 5 = 8$; therefore, $a + b = 8$, and we accept these values.

Hence, $x^2 + 8x + 15 = 0$ is equivalent to

$$0 = x^2 + (3 + 5)x + 3 \times 5 = (x + 3)(x + 5)$$

Hence, $x + 5 = 0$ or $x + 3 = 0$

since the product of these two numbers is zero, one of the numbers must be zero. Hence, $x = -5$, or $x = -3$, and the solution set is $x = \{-5, -3\}$.

The student should note that $x = -5$ or $x = -3$. We are certainly not making the statement that $x = -5$ and $x = -3$. Also, the student should check that both these numbers do actually satisfy the given equations and hence are solutions.

Check: Replacing x by (-5) in the original equation:

$$x^2 + 8x + 15 = 0$$
$$(-5)^2 + 8(-5) + 15 = 0$$
$$25 - 40 + 15 = 0$$

$$-15 + 15 = 0$$

$$0 = 0$$

Replacing x by (-3) in the original equation:

$$x^2 + 8x + 15 = 0$$

$$(-3)^2 + 8(-3) + 15 = 0$$

$$9 - 24 + 15 = 0$$

$$-15 + 15 = 0$$

$$0 = 0$$

PROBLEM

Solve the following equations by factoring.

(1) $2x^2 + 3x = 0$ (3) $z^2 - 2z - 3 = 0$

(2) $y^2 - 2y - 3 = y - 3$ (4) $2m^2 - 11m - 6 = 0$

SOLUTION

(1) $2x^2 + 3x = 0$. Factor out the common factor of x from the left side of the given equation.

$$x(2x + 3) = 0$$

Whenever a product $ab = 0$, where a and b are any two numbers, either $a = 0$ or $b = 0$. Then, either

$$x = 0 \quad \text{or} \quad 2x + 3 = 0$$

$$2x = -3$$

$$x = -\frac{3}{2}$$

Hence, the solution set to the original equation $2x^2 + 3x = 0$ is $\{-3/2, 0\}$

(2) $y^2 - 2y - 3 = y - 3$. Subtract $(y - 3)$ from both sides of the given equation:

$$y^2 - 2y - 3 - (y - 3) = y - 3 - (y - 3)$$

$$y^2 - 2y - 3 - y + 3 = y - 3 - y + 3$$

$$y^2 - 2y - 3 - y + 3 = y - 3 - y + 3$$

$$y^2 - 3y = 0$$

Factor out a common factor of y from the left side of this equation:

$$y(y-3) = 0$$

Thus, $y = 0$ or $y - 3 = 0$, $y = 3$.

Therefore, the solution set to the original equation $y^2 - 2y - 3 = y - 3$ is $\{0, 3\}$.

(3) $z^2 - 2z - 3 = 0$. Factor the original equation into a product of two polynomials.

$$z^2 - 2z - 3 = (z - 3)(z + 1) = 0$$

Hence,

$$(z - 3)(z + 1) = 0; \text{ and } z - 3 = 0 \quad \text{or } z + 1 = 0$$

$$z = 3 \qquad z = -1$$

Therefore, the solution set to the original equation $z^2 - 2z - 3 = 0$ is $\{-1, 3\}$.

(4) $2m^2 - 11m - 6 = 0$. Factor the original equation into a product of two polynomials.

$$2m^2 - 11m - 6 = (2m + 1)(m - 6) = 0$$

Thus,

$$2m + 1 = 0 \qquad \text{or } m - 6 = 0$$

$$2m = -1 \qquad\qquad m = 6$$

$$m = -\frac{1}{2}$$

Therefore, the solution set to the original equation $2m^2 - 11m - 6 = 0$ is $\{-\frac{1}{2}, 6\}$.

☞ Drill: Quadratic Equations

DIRECTIONS: Solve for all values of x.

1. $x^2 - 2x - 8 = 0$

(A) 4 and –2   (B) 4 and 8   (C) 4

(D) –2 and 8   (E) –2

2. $x^2 + 2x - 3 = 0$

(A) -3 and 2 (B) 2 and 1 (C) 3 and 1

(D) -3 and 1 (E) -3

3. $x^2 - 7x = -10$

(A) -3 and 5 (B) 2 and 5 (C) 2

(D) -2 and -5 (E) 5

4. $x^2 - 8x + 16 = 0$

(A) 8 and 2 (B) 1 and 16 (C) 4

(D) -2 and 4 (E) 4 and -4

5. $3x^2 + 3x = 6$

(A) 3 and -6 (B) 2 and 3 (C) -3 and 2

(D) 1 and -3 (E) 1 and -2

6. $x^2 + 7x = 0$

(A) 7 (B) 0 and -7 (C) -7

(D) 0 and 7 (E) 0

7. $x^2 - 25 = 0$

(A) 5 (B) 5 and -5 (C) 15 and 10

(D) -5 and 10 (E) -5

8. $2x^2 + 4x = 16$

(A) 2 and -2 (B) 8 and -2 (C) 4 and 8

(D) 2 and -4 (E) 2 and 4

9. $6x^2 - x - 2 = 0$

(A) 2 and 3 (B) $\dfrac{1}{2}$ and $\dfrac{1}{3}$ (C) $-\dfrac{1}{2}$ and $\dfrac{2}{3}$

(D) $\dfrac{2}{3}$ and 3 (E) 2 and $-\dfrac{1}{3}$

10. $12x^2 + 5x = 3$

(A) $\dfrac{1}{3}$ and $-\dfrac{1}{4}$ (B) 4 and -3 (C) 4 and $\dfrac{1}{6}$

(D) $\dfrac{1}{3}$ and -4 (E) $-\dfrac{3}{4}$ and $\dfrac{1}{3}$

ABSOLUTE VALUE EQUATIONS

The absolute value of a, $|\,a\,|$, is defined as

$|\,a\,| = a$ when $a > 0$,

$|\,a\,| = -a$ when $a < 0$,

$|\,a\,| = 0$ when $a = 0$.

When the definition of absolute value is applied to an equation, the quantity within the absolute value symbol is considered to have two values. This value can be either positive or negative before the absolute value is taken. As a result, each absolute value equation actually contains two separate equations.

When evaluating equations containing absolute values, proceed as follows:

EXAMPLE

$|\,5 - 3x\,| = 7$ is valid if either

$5 - 3x = 7$ or $5 - 3x = -7$

$-3x = 2$ $-3x = -12$

$x = -\dfrac{2}{3}$ $x = 4$

The solution set is therefore $x = (-^2/_3, 4)$.

Remember, the absolute value of a number cannot be negative. So, for the equation $|\,5x + 4\,| = -3$, there would be no solution.

EXAMPLE

Solve for x in $|\,2x - 6\,| = |\,4 - 5x\,|$.

There are four possibilities here. $2x - 6$ and $4 - 5x$ can be either positive or negative. Therefore,

$$2x - 6 = 4 - 5x \tag{1}$$

$$-(2x-6) = 4-5x \qquad\qquad (2)$$

$$2x-6 = -(4-5x) \qquad\qquad (3)$$

$$-(2x-6) = -(4-5x) \qquad\qquad (4)$$

Equations (2) and (3) result in the same solution, as do equations (1) and (4). Therefore, it is necessary to solve only for equations (1) and (2). This gives

$$2x-6 = 4-5x \qquad \text{or} \qquad -(2x-6) = 4-5x$$
$$7x = 10 \qquad\qquad\qquad -2x+6 = 4-5x$$
$$x = \frac{10}{7} \qquad\qquad\qquad x = -\frac{2}{3}$$

The solution set is $(^{10}/_7, -^2/_3)$.

☞ Drill: Absolute Value Equations

DIRECTIONS: Find the appropriate solutions.

1. $|4x-2| = 6$

(A) -2 and -1 (B) -1 and 2   (C) 2

(D) $\dfrac{1}{2}$ and -2 (E) No solution

2. $\left|3-\dfrac{1}{2}y\right| = -7$

(A) -8 and 20   (B) 8 and -20 (C) 2 and -5

(D) 4 and -2 (E) No solution

3. $2|x+7| = 12$

(A) -13 and -1 (B) -6 and 6   (C) -1 and 13

(D) 6 and -13 (E) No solution

4. $|5x| - 7 = 3$

(A) 2 and 4   (B) $\dfrac{4}{5}$ and 3   (C) -2 and 2

(D) 2   (E) No solution

5. $\left|\dfrac{3}{4}m\right| = 9$

(A) 24 and -16 (B) $\dfrac{4}{27}$ and $-\dfrac{4}{3}$ (C) $\dfrac{4}{3}$ and 12

(D) -12 and 12   (E) No solution

INEQUALITIES

An inequality is a statement where the value of one quantity or expression is greater than ($>$), less than ($<$), greater than or equal to ($\geq$), less than or equal to ($\leq$), or not equal to ($\neq$) that of another.

EXAMPLE

$5 > 4$

The expression above means that the value of 5 is greater than the value of 4.

A **conditional inequality** is an inequality whose validity depends on the values of the variables in the sentence. That is, certain values of the variables will make the sentence true, and others will make it false.

$3 - y > 3 + y$

is a conditional inequality for the set of real numbers, since it is true for any replacement less than zero and false for all others.

$x + 5 > x + 2$

is an **absolute inequality** for the set of real numbers, meaning that for any real value x, the expression on the left is greater than the expression on the right.

$5y < 2y + y$

is inconsistent for the set of non-negative real numbers. For any y greater than 0 the sentence is always false. A sentence is inconsistent if it is always false when its variables assume allowable values.

The solution of a given inequality in one variable x consists of all values of x for which the inequality is true.

The graph of an inequality in one variable is represented by either a ray or a line segment on the real number line.

The endpoint is not a solution if the variable is strictly less than or greater than a particular value.

EXAMPLE

$x > 2$

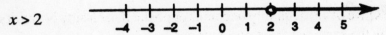

2 is not a solution and should be represented as shown.

The endpoint is a solution if the variable is either (1) less than or equal to or (2) greater than or equal to a particular value.

EXAMPLE

$5 > x \geq 2$

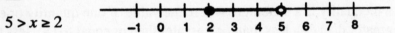

In this case 2 is the solution and should be represented as shown.

PROPERTIES OF INEQUALITIES

If x and y are real numbers, then one and only one of the following statements is true.

$x > y, x = y,$ or $x < y$.

This is the order property of real numbers.

If $a, b,$ and c are real numbers, the following are true:

A)   If $a < b$ and $b < c$, then $a < c$.

B)   If $a > b$ and $b > c$, then $a > c$.

This is the transitive property of inequalities.

If $a, b,$ and c are real numbers and $a > b$, then $a + c > b + c$ and $a - c > b - c$. This is the **addition property of inequality**.

Two inequalities are said to have the same **sense** if their signs of inequality point in the same direction.

The sense of an inequality remains the same if both sides are multiplied or divided by the same positive real number.

EXAMPLE

$4 > 3$

If we multiply both sides by 5, we will obtain

$4 \times 5 > 3 \times 5$

$20 > 15$

The sense of the inequality does not change.

The sense of an inequality becomes opposite if each side is multiplied or divided by the same negative real number.

EXAMPLE

$4 > 3$

If we multiply both sides by -5, we would obtain

$4 \times -5 < 3 \times -5$

$-20 < -15$

The sense of the inequality becomes opposite.

If $a > b$ and a, b, and n are positive real numbers, then

$a^n > b^n$ and $a^{-n} < b^{-n}$

If $x > y$ and $q > p$, then $x + q > y + p$.

If $x > y > 0$ and $q > p > 0$, then $xq > yp$.

Inequalities that have the same solution set are called **equivalent inequalities**.

PROBLEM

Solve the inequality $2x + 5 > 9$.

SOLUTION

Add -5 to both sides: $\quad 2x + 5 + (-5) > 9 + (-5)$

Additive inverse property: $\quad 2x + 0 > 9 + (-5)$

Additive identity property: $\quad 2x > 9 + (-5)$

Combine terms: $\quad 2x > 4$

Multiply both sides by $\dfrac{1}{2}$: $\quad \dfrac{1}{2}(2x) > \dfrac{1}{2} \times 4$

$x > 2$

The solution set is

$X = \{x \mid 2x + 5 > 9\}$

$= \{x \mid x > 2\}$

(that is all x, such that x is greater than 2).

PROBLEM

Solve the inequality $4x + 3 < 6x + 8$.

SOLUTION

In order to solve the inequality $4x + 3 < 6x + 8$, we must find all values of x which make it true. Thus, we wish to obtain x alone on one side of the inequality.

Add -3 to both sides:

$$
\begin{array}{r}
4x + 3 < 6x + 8 \\
-3 \qquad -3 \\
\hline
4x < 6x + 5
\end{array}
$$

Add $-6x$ to both sides:

$$
\begin{array}{r}
4x < \quad 6x + 5 \\
-6x \quad -6x \\
\hline
-2x < \quad 5
\end{array}
$$

In order to obtain x alone we must divide both sides by (-2). Recall that dividing an inequality by a negative number reverses the inequality sign, hence

$$\frac{-2x}{-2} > \frac{5}{-2}$$

Cancelling $^{-2}/_{-2}$ we obtain, $x > -^5/_2$.

Thus, our solution is $\{x : x > -^5/_2\}$ (the set of all x such that x is greater than $-^5/_2$).

☞ Drill: Inequalities

<u>DIRECTIONS</u>: Find the solution set for each inequality.

1. $3m + 2 < 7$

(A) $m \geq \dfrac{5}{3}$ (B) $m \leq 2$ (C) $m < 2$

(D) $m > 2$ (E) $m < \dfrac{5}{3}$

2. $\frac{1}{2}x - 3 \le 1$

(A) $-4 \le x \le 8$ (B) $x \ge -8$ (C) $x \le 8$

(D) $2 \le x \le 8$ (E) $x \ge 8$

3. $-3p + 1 \ge 16$

(A) $p \ge -5$ (B) $p \ge \frac{-17}{3}$ (C) $p \le \frac{-17}{3}$

(D) $p \le -5$ (E) $p \ge 5$

4. $-6 < \frac{2}{3}r + 6 \le 2$

(A) $-6 < r \le -3$ (B) $-18 < r \le -6$ (C) $r \ge -6$

(D) $-2 < r \le -\frac{4}{3}$ (E) $r \le -6$

5. $0 < 2 - y < 6$

(A) $-4 < y < 2$ (B) $-4 < y < 0$ (C) $-4 < y < -2$

(D) $-2 < y < 4$ (E) $0 < y < 4$

RATIOS AND PROPORTIONS

The ratio of two numbers x and y written $x : y$ is the fraction x/y where $y \ne 0$. A ratio compares x to y by dividing one by the other. Therefore, in order to compare ratios, simply compare the fractions.

A proportion is an equality of two ratios. The laws of proportion are listed below.

If $\frac{a}{b} = \frac{c}{d}$, then

(A) $ad = bc$

(B) $\frac{b}{a} = \frac{d}{c}$

(C) $\frac{a}{c} = \frac{b}{d}$

(D) $\dfrac{a+b}{b} = \dfrac{c+d}{d}$

(E) $\dfrac{a-b}{b} = \dfrac{c-d}{d}$

Given a proportion $a : b = c : d$, then a and d are called extremes, b and c are called the means, and d is called the fourth proportion to a, b, and c.

PROBLEM

Solve the proportion $\dfrac{x+1}{4} = \dfrac{15}{12}$.

SOLUTION

Cross-multiply to determine x; that is, multiply the numerator of the first fraction by the denominator of the second, and equate this to the product of the numerator of the second and the denominator of the first.

$$(x + 1)\,12 = 4 \times 15$$

$$12x + 12 = 60$$

$$x = 4$$

PROBLEM

Find the ratios of $x : y : z$ from the equations

$$7x = 4y + 8z, \quad 3z = 12x + 11y.$$

SOLUTION

By transposition we have

$$7x - 4y - 8z = 0$$

$$12x + 11y - 3z = 0$$

To obtain the ratio of $x : y$, we convert the given system into an equation in terms of just x and y. We may eliminate z as follows: Multiply each term of the first equation by 3 and each term of the second equation by 8 (because they are both z variables which we wish to eliminate), and then subtract the second equation from the first. We thus obtain

$$21x - 12y - 24z = 0$$
$$\underline{-(96x + 88y - 24z = 0)}$$
$$-75x - 100y \qquad = 0$$

Dividing each term of the last equation by 25, we obtain

$$-3x - 4y = 0$$

or,
$$-3x = 4y$$

Dividing both sides of this equation by 4 and by -3, we have the proportion

$$\frac{x}{4} = \frac{y}{-3}$$

We are now interested in obtaining the ratio of $y : z$. To do this we convert the given system of equations into an equation in terms of just y and z, by eliminating x as follows: Multiply each term of the first equation by 12, and each term of the second equation by 7, and then subtract the second equation from the first. We thus obtain

$$84x - 48y - 96z = 0$$
$$\underline{-(84x + 77y - 21z = 0)}$$
$$-125y - 75z = 0$$

Dividing each term of the last equation by 25, we obtain

$$-5y - 3z = 0$$

or,
$$-3z = 5y$$

Dividing both sides of this equation by 5 and by -3, we have the proportion

$$\frac{z}{5} = \frac{y}{-3}.$$

From this result and our previous result we obtain

$$\frac{x}{4} = \frac{y}{-3} = \frac{z}{5}$$

as the desired ratios.

☞ Drill: Ratios and Proportions

DIRECTIONS: Find the appropriate solutions.

1. Solve for *n:* $\dfrac{4}{n} = \dfrac{8}{5}$.

(A) 10   (B) 8   (C) 6   (D) 2.5   (E) 2

2. Solve for *n:* $\dfrac{2}{3} = \dfrac{n}{72}$.

(A) 12   (B) 48   (C) 64   (D) 56   (E) 24

3. Solve for *n:* $n : 12 = 3 : 4$.

(A) 8   (B) 1   (C) 9   (D) 4   (E) 10

4. Four out of every five students at West High take a mathematics course. If the enrollment at West is 785, how many students take mathematics?

(A) 628   (B) 157   (C) 705   (D) 655   (E) 247

5. At a factory, three out of every 1,000 parts produced are defective. In a day, the factory can produce 25,000 parts. How many of these parts would be defective?

(A) 7   (B) 75   (C) 750   (D) 7,500   (E) 75,000

6. A summer league softball team won 28 out of the 32 games they played. What is the ratio of games won to games played?

(A) 4 : 5   (B) 3 : 4   (C) 7 : 8   (D) 2 : 3   (E) 1 : 8

7. A class of 24 students contains 16 males. What is the ratio of females to males?

(A) 1 : 2   (B) 2 : 1   (C) 2 : 3   (D) 3 : 1   (E) 3 : 2

8. A family has a monthly income of $1,250, but they spend $450 a month on rent. What is the ratio of the amount of income to the amount paid for rent?

(A) 16 : 25   (B) 25 : 9   (C) 25 : 16   (D) 9 : 25   (E) 36 : 100

9. A student attends classes 7.5 hours a day and works a part-time job for 3.5 hours a day. She knows she must get 7 hours of sleep a night. Write the ratio of the number of free hours in this student's day to the total number of hours in a day.

(A) 1 : 3   (B) 4 : 3   (C) 8 : 24   (D) 1 : 4   (E) 5 : 12

10. In a survey by mail, 30 out of 750 questionnaires were returned. Write the ratio of questionnaires returned to questionnaires mailed (write in simplest form).

(A) 30 : 750 (B) 24 : 25   (C) 3 : 75   (D) 1 : 4   (E) 1 : 25

ALGEBRA DRILLS

ANSWER KEY

Drill: Operations with Polynomials

1.	(B)	6.	(B)	11.	(C)	16.	(C)
2.	(C)	7.	(C)	12.	(B)	17.	(D)
3.	(C)	8.	(E)	13.	(E)	18.	(E)
4.	(D)	9.	(A)	14.	(A)	19.	(B)
5.	(A)	10.	(D)	15.	(D)	20.	(B)

Drill: Simplifying Algebraic Expressions

1.	(C)	6.	(B)
2.	(D)	7.	(A)
3.	(B)	8.	(B)
4.	(A)	9.	(A)
5.	(D)	10.	(E)

Drill: Linear Equations

1.	(C)
2.	(A)
3.	(E)
4.	(D)
5.	(B)

Drill: Two Linear Equations

1.	(E)	6.	(B)
2.	(B)	7.	(D)
3.	(A)	8.	(E)
4.	(D)	9.	(A)
5.	(C)	10.	(B)

Drill: Quadratic Equations

1.	(A)	6.	(B)
2.	(D)	7.	(B)
3.	(B)	8.	(D)
4.	(C)	9.	(C)
5.	(E)	10.	(E)

Drill: Absolute Value Equations

1.	(B)	4.	(C)
2.	(E)	5.	(D)
3.	(A)		

Drill: Inequalities

1.	(E)	4.	(B)
2.	(C)	5.	(A)
3.	(D)		

Drill: Ratios and Proportions

1.	(D)	4.	(A)	7.	(A)	10.	(E)
2.	(B)	5.	(B)	8.	(B)		
3.	(C)	6.	(C)	9.	(D)		

III. GEOMETRY

POINTS, LINES, AND ANGLES

Geometry is built upon a series of undefined terms. These terms are those which we accept as known in order to define other undefined terms.

A) **Point**: Although we represent points on paper with small dots, a point has no size, thickness, or width.

B) **Line**: A line is a series of adjacent points which extends indefinitely. A line can be either curved or straight; however, unless otherwise stated, the term "line" refers to a straight line.

C) **Plane**: A plane is a collection of points lying on a flat surface, which extends indefinitely in all directions.

If A and B are two points on a line, then the **line segment** $\overline{AB}$ is the set of points on that line between A and B and including A and B, which are endpoints. The line segment is referred to as $\overline{AB}$.

A **ray** is a series of points that lie to one side of a single endpoint.

PROBLEM

How many lines can be found that contain (a) one given point, (b) two given points, and (c) three given points?

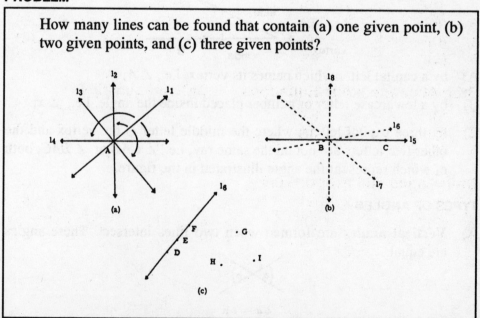

(a)

(b)

(c)

SOLUTION

(a) *Given one point A*, there are an infinite number of distinct lines that contain the given point. To see this, consider line l_1 passing through point A. By rotating l_1 around A like the hands of a clock, we obtain different lines l_2, l_3, etc. Since we can rotate l_1 in infinitely many ways, there are infinitely many lines containing A.

(b) *Given two distinct points B and C*, there is one and only one straight line passing through both. To see this, consider all the lines containing point B: l_5, l_6, l_7, and l_8. Only l_5 contains both points B and C. Thus, there is only one line containing both points B and C. Since there is always at least one line containing two distinct points and never more than one, the line passing through the two points is said to be determined by the two points.

(c) *Given three distinct points*, there may be one line or none. If a line exists that contains the three points, such as D, E, and F, then the points are said to be **colinear**. If no such line exists (as in the case of points G, H, and I), then the points are said to be **noncolinear**.

INTERSECTION LINES AND ANGLES

An **angle** is a collection of points which is the union of two rays having the same endpoint. An angle such as the one illustrated below can be referred to in any of the following ways:

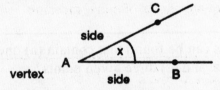

A) by a capital letter which names its vertex, i.e., $\angle A$;

B) by a lowercase letter or number placed inside the angle, i.e., $\angle x$;

C) by three capital letters, where the middle letter is the vertex and the other two letters are not on the same ray, i.e., $\angle CAB$ or $\angle BAC$, both of which represent the angle illustrated in the figure.

TYPES OF ANGLES

A) **Vertical angles** are formed when two lines intersect. These angles are equal.

$$\angle a = \angle b$$

B)   **Adjacent angles** are two angles with a common vertex and a common side, but no common interior points. In the following figure, $\angle DAC$ and $\angle BAC$ are adjacent angles. $\angle DAB$ and $\angle BAC$ are not.

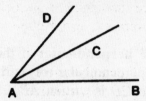

C)   A **right angle** is an angle whose measure is 90°.

D)   An **acute angle** is an angle whose measure is larger than 0°, but less than 90°.

E)   An **obtuse angle** is an angle whose measure is larger than 90° but less than 180°.

F)   A **straight angle** is an angle whose measure is 180°. Such an angle is, in fact, a straight line.

G)   A **reflex angle** is an angle whose measure is greater than 180° but less than 360°.

H)   **Complimentary angles** are two angles whose measures total 90°.

I)   **Supplementary angles** are two angles whose measures total 180°.

J)   **Congruent angles** are angles of equal measure.

PROBLEM

In the figure, we are given $\overline{AB}$ and triangle ABC. We are told that the measure of $\angle 1$ is five times the measure of $\angle 2$. Determine the measures of $\angle 1$ and $\angle 2$.

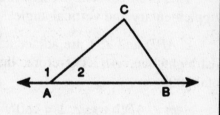

SOLUTION

Since $\angle 1$ and $\angle 2$ are adjacent angles whose non-common sides lie on a straight line, they are, by definition, supplementary. As supplements, their measures must total 180°.

If we let x = the measure of $\angle 2$, then $5x$ = the measure of $\angle 1$.

To determine the respective angle measures, set $x + 5x = 180$ and solve for x. $6x = 180$. Therefore, $x = 30$ and $5x = 150$.

Therefore, the measure of $\angle 1 = 150$ and the measure of $\angle 2 = 30$.

PERPENDICULAR LINES

Two lines are said to be **perpendicular** if they intersect and form right angles. The symbol for perpendicular (or, is therefore perpendicular to) is $\perp$; $\overline{AB}$ is perpendicular to $\overline{CD}$ is written $\overline{AB} \perp \overline{CD}$.

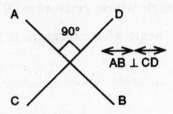

PROBLEM

We are given straight lines $\overline{AB}$ and $\overline{CD}$ intersecting at point P. $\overline{PR} \perp \overline{AB}$ and the measure of $\angle APD$ is 170°. Find the measures of $\angle 1$, $\angle 2$, $\angle 3$, and $\angle 4$.

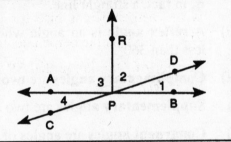

SOLUTION

This problem will involve making use of several of the properties of supplementary and vertical angles, as well as perpendicular lines.

$\angle APD$ and $\angle 1$ are adjacent angles whose non-common sides lie on a straight line, $\overline{AB}$. Therefore, they are supplements and their measures total 180°.

$$m \angle APD + m \angle 1 = 180°.$$

We know $m \angle APD = 170°$. Therefore, by substitution, $170° + m \angle 1 = 180°$. This implies $m \angle 1 = 10°$.

$\angle 1$ and $\angle 4$ are vertical angles because they are formed by the intersection of two straight lines, $\overline{CD}$ and $\overline{AB}$, and their sides form two pairs of opposite rays. As vertical angles, they are, by theorem, of equal measure. Since $m \angle 1 = 10°$, then $m \angle 4 = 10°$.

Since $\overline{PR} \perp \overline{AB}$, at their intersection the angles formed must be right angles. Therefore, $\angle 3$ is a right angle and its measure is 90°. $m \angle 3 = 90°$.

The figure shows us that $\angle APD$ is composed of $\angle 3$ and $\angle 2$. Since the measure of the whole must be equal to the sum of the measures of its parts, $m \angle APD = m \angle 3 + m \angle 2$. We know the $m \angle APD = 170°$ and $m \angle 3 = 90°$; therefore, by substitution, we can solve for $m \angle 2$, our last unknown.

$$170° = 90° + m \angle 2$$

$$80° = m \angle 2$$

Therefore, $m \angle 1 = 10°$, $m \angle 2 = 80°$,

          $m \angle 3 = 90°$, $m \angle 4 = 10°$.

PROBLEM

In the accompanying figure $\overline{SM}$ is the perpendicular bisector of $\overline{QR}$, and $\overline{SN}$ is the perpendicular bisector of $\overline{QP}$. Prove that $SR = SP$.

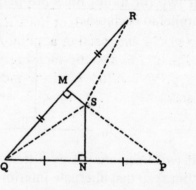

SOLUTION

Every point on the perpendicular bisector of a segment is equidistant from the endpoints of the segment.

Since point S is on the perpendicular bisector of $\overline{QR}$,

$SR = SQ$ \hfill (1)

Also, since point S is on the perpendicular bisector of $\overline{QP}$,

$SQ = SP$ \hfill (2)

By the transitive property (quantities equal to the same quantity are equal), we have

$SR = SP$. \hfill (3)

PARALLEL LINES

Two lines are called **parallel lines** if, and only if, they are in the same plane (coplanar) and do not intersect. The symbol for parallel, or is parallel to, is $\|$; $\overline{AB}$ is parallel to $\overline{CD}$ is written $\overline{AB} \parallel \overline{CD}$.

The distance between two parallel lines is the length of the perpendicular segment from any point on one line to the other line.

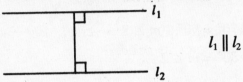

$l_1 \parallel l_2$

Given a line l and a point P not on line l, there is one and only one line through point P that is parallel to line l.

Two coplanar lines are either intersecting lines or parallel lines.

If two (or more) lines are perpendicular to the same line, then they are parallel to each other.

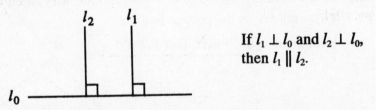

If $l_1 \perp l_0$ and $l_2 \perp l_0$, then $l_1 \parallel l_2$.

If two lines are cut by a transversal (a line intersecting two or more other lines) so that alternate interior angles are equal, the lines are parallel.

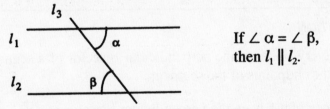

If $\angle \alpha = \angle \beta$, then $l_1 \parallel l_2$.

If two lines are parallel to the same line, then they are parallel to each other.

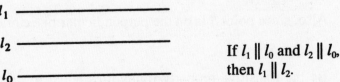

If $l_1 \parallel l_0$ and $l_2 \parallel l_0$, then $l_1 \parallel l_2$.

If a line is perpendicular to one of two parallel lines, then it is perpendicular to the other line, too.

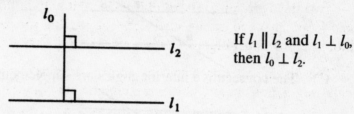

If $l_1 \parallel l_2$ and $l_1 \perp l_0$, then $l_0 \perp l_2$.

If two lines being cut by a transversal form congruent corresponding angles, then the two lines are parallel.

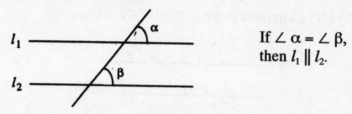

If $\angle \alpha = \angle \beta$, then $l_1 \parallel l_2$.

If two lines being cut by a transversal form interior angles on the same side of the transversal that are supplementary, then the two lines are parallel.

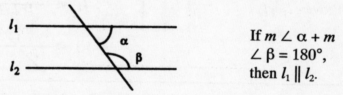

If $m \angle \alpha + m \angle \beta = 180°$, then $l_1 \parallel l_2$.

If a line is parallel to one of two parallel lines, it is also parallel to the other line.

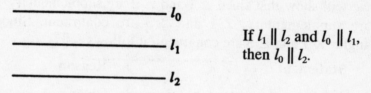

If $l_1 \parallel l_2$ and $l_0 \parallel l_1$, then $l_0 \parallel l_2$.

If two parallel lines are cut by a transversal, then:

A)   The alternate interior angles are congruent.

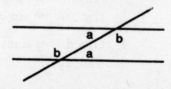

B) The corresponding angles are congruent.

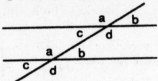

C) The consecutive interior angles are supplementary.

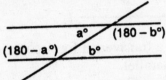

D) The alternate exterior angles are congruent.

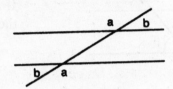

PROBLEM

Given: $\angle 2$ is supplementary to $\angle 3$.

Prove: $l_1 \parallel l_2$.

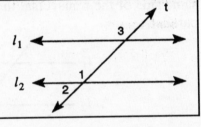

SOLUTION

Given two lines intercepted by a transversal, if a pair of corresponding angles are congruent, then the two lines are parallel. In this problem, we will show that since $\angle 1$ and $\angle 2$ are supplementary and $\angle 2$ and $\angle 3$ are supplementary, $\angle 1$ and $\angle 3$ are congruent. Since corresponding angles $\angle 1$ and $\angle 3$ are congruent, it follows $l_1 \parallel l_2$.

Statement	**Reason**
1. $\angle 2$ is supplementary to $\angle 3$.	1. Given.
2. $\angle 1$ is supplementary to $\angle 2$.	2. Two angles that form a linear pair are supplementary.
3. $\angle 1 \cong \angle 3$.	3. Angles supplementary to the same angle are congruent.
4. $l_1 \parallel l_2$.	4. Given two lines intercepted by a transversal, if a pair of corre-

sponding angles are congruent, then the two lines are parallel.

PROBLEM

If line $\overline{AB}$ is parallel to line $\overline{CD}$ and line $\overline{EF}$ is parallel to line $\overline{GH}$, prove that $m \angle 1 = m \angle 2$.

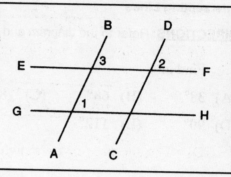

SOLUTION

To show $\angle 1 = \angle 2$, we relate both to $\angle 3$. Because $\overline{EF} \parallel \overline{GH}$, corresponding angles 1 and 3 are congruent. Since $\overline{AB} \parallel \overline{CD}$, corresponding angles 3 and 2 are congruent. Because both $\angle 1$ and $\angle 2$ are congruent to the same angle, it follows that $\angle 1 = \angle 2$.

Statement	**Reason**
1. $\overline{EF} \parallel \overline{GH}$	1. Given.
2. $m \angle 1 = m \angle 3$	2. If two parallel lines are cut by a transversal, corresponding angles are of equal measure.
3. $\overline{AB} \parallel \overline{CD}$	3. Given.
4. $m \angle 2 = m \angle 3$	4. If two parallel lines are cut by a transversal, corresponding angles are equal in measure.
5. $m \angle 1 = m \angle 2$	5. If two quantities are equal to the same quantity, they are equal to each other.

☞ Drill: Lines and Angles

Intersecting Lines

<u>**DIRECTIONS**</u>: Refer to the diagram and find the appropriate solution.

1. Find *a*.

(A) 38°   (B) 68°   (C) 78°

(D) 90°   (E) 112°

2. Find *c*.

(A) 32°   (B) 48°   (C) 58°

(D) 82°   (E) 148°

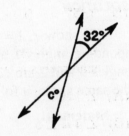

3. Determine *x*.

(A) 21°   (B) 23°   (C) 51°

(D) 102°   (E) 153°

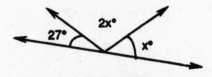

4. Find *x*.

(A) 8   (B) 11.75   (C) 21

(D) 23   (E) 32

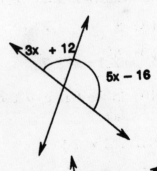

5. Find *z*.

(A) 29°   (B) 54°   (C) 61°

(D) 88°   (E) 92°

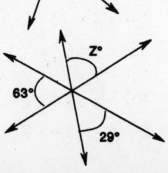

Perpendicular Lines

DIRECTIONS: Refer to the diagram and find the appropriate solution.

6. $\overrightarrow{BA} \perp \overrightarrow{BC}$ and $m \angle DBC = 53°$. Find $m \angle ABD$.

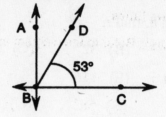

(A) 27°   (B) 33°   (C) 37°

(D) 53°   (E) 90°

7. $m \angle 1 = 90°$. Find $m \angle 2$.

(A) 80°   (B) 90°   (C) 100°

(D) 135°   (E) 180°

8. If $n \perp p$, which of the following statements is true?

(A) $\angle 1 \cong \angle 2$

(B) $\angle 4 \cong \angle 5$

(C) $m \angle 4 + m \angle 5 > m \angle 1 + m \angle 2$

(D) $m \angle 3 > m \angle 2$

(E) $m \angle 4 = 90°$

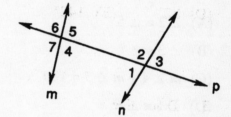

9. $\overline{CD} \perp \overline{EF}$. If $m \angle 1 = 2x$, $m \angle 2 = 30°$ and $m \angle 3 = x$, find x.

(A) 5°   (B) 10°   (C) 12°

(D) 20°   (E) 25°

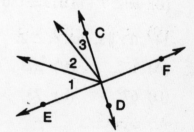

10. In the figure, $p \perp t$ and $q \perp t$. Which of the following statements is false?

(A) $\angle 1 \cong \angle 4$

(B) $\angle 2 \cong \angle 3$

(C) $m \angle 2 + m \angle 3 = m \angle 4 + m \angle 6$

(D) $m \angle 5 + m \angle 6 = 180°$

(E) $m \angle 2 > m \angle 5$

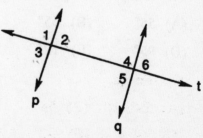

Parallel Lines

DIRECTIONS: Refer to the diagram and find the appropriate solution.

11. If $a \parallel b$, find z.

(A) 26°   (B) 32°   (C) 64°

(D) 86°   (E) 116°

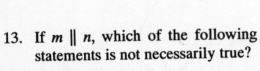

12. In the figure, $p \parallel q \parallel r$. Find $m \angle 7$.

(A) 27°   (B) 33°   (C) 47°

(D) 57°   (E) 64°

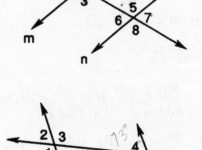

13. If $m \parallel n$, which of the following statements is not necessarily true?

(A) $\angle 2 \cong \angle 5$

(B) $\angle 3 \cong \angle 6$

(C) $m \angle 4 + m \angle 5 = 180°$

(D) $\angle 1 \cong \angle 6$

(E) $m \angle 7 + m \angle 3 = 180°$

14. If $r \parallel s$, find $m \angle 2$.

(A) 17°   (B) 27°   (C) 43°

(D) 67°   (E) 73°

15. If $a \parallel b$ and $c \parallel d$, find $m \angle 5$.

(A) 55°   (B) 65°   (C) 75°

(D) 95°   (E) 125°

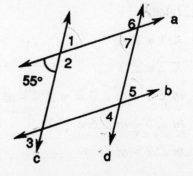

POLYGONS (CONVEX)

A **polygon** is a figure with the same number of sides as angles.

An **equilateral polygon** is a polygon all of whose sides are of equal measure.

An **equiangular polygon** is a polygon all of whose angles are of equal measure.

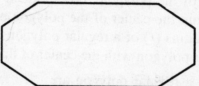

A **regular polygon** is a polygon that is both equilateral and equiangular.

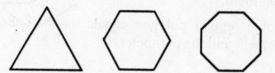

PROBLEM

Each interior angle of a regular polygon contains 120°. How many sides does the polygon have?

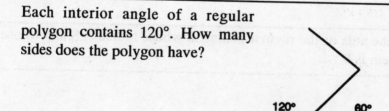

120°   60°

SOLUTION

At each vertex of a polygon, the exterior angle is supplementary to the interior angle, as shown in the diagram.

Since we are told that the interior angles measure 120°, we can deduce that the exterior angle measures 60°.

Each exterior angle of a regular polygon of *n* sides measures $^{360°}/_n$ degrees. We know that each exterior angle measures 60°, and, therefore,

by setting $360°/_n$ equal to $60°$, we can determine the number of sides in the polygon. The calculation is as follows:

$$\frac{360°}{n} = 60°$$

$$60°n = 360°$$

$$n = 6$$

Therefore, the regular polygon, with interior angles of $120°$, has six sides and is called a hexagon.

The area of a regular polygon can be determined by using the **apothem** and **radius** of the polygon. The apothem (a) of a regular polygon is the segment from the center of the polygon perpendicular to a side of the polygon. The radius (r) of a regular polygon is the segment joining any vertex of a regular polygon with the center of that polygon.

(1) All radii of a regular polygon are congruent.

(2) All apothems of a regular polygon are congruent.

The **area** of a regular polygon equals one-half the product of the length of the apothem and the perimeter.

$$\text{Area} = \frac{1}{2} a \times p$$

PROBLEM

Find the area of the regular pentagon whose radius is 8 and whose apothem is 6.

SOLUTION

If the radius is 8, the length of a side is also 8. Therefore, the perimeter of the polygon is 40.

$$A = \frac{1}{2} a \times p$$

$$A = \frac{1}{2} (6)(40)$$

$$A = 120$$

PROBLEM

Find the area of a regular hexagon if one side has length 6.

SOLUTION

Since the length of a side equals 6, the radius also equals 6 and the perimeter equals 36. The base of the right triangle, formed by the radius and apothem, is half the length of a side, or 3. You can find the length of the apothem by using what is known as the Pythagorean Theorem (discussed further in the next section).

$$a^2 + b^2 = c^2$$

$$a^2 + (3)^2 = (6)^2$$

$$a^2 = 36 - 9$$

$$a^2 = 27$$

$$a = 3\sqrt{3}$$

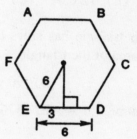

The apothem equals $3\sqrt{3}$. Therefore, the area of the hexagon

$$= \frac{1}{2} a \times p$$

$$= \frac{1}{2} (3\sqrt{3}) (36)$$

$$= 54\sqrt{3}$$

☞ Drill: Regular Polygons

Angle Measures

<u>DIRECTIONS</u>: Find the appropriate solution.

1. Find the measure of an interior angle of a regular pentagon.

(A) 55°   (B) 72°   (C) 90°   (D) 108°   (E) 540°

2. Find the measure of an exterior angle of a regular octagon.

(A) 40°   (B) 45°   (C) 135°   (D) 540°   (E) 1,080°

3. Find the sum of the measures of the exterior angles of a regular triangle.

(A) 90°   (B) 115°   (C) 180°   (D) 250°   (E) 360°

Area(s) and Perimeter(s)

<u>DIRECTIONS</u>: Find the appropriate solution.

4. Find the area of a square with a perimeter of 12 cm.

(A) 9 cm²   (B) 12 cm²   (C) 48 cm²   (D) 96 cm²   (E) 144 cm²

5. A regular triangle has sides of 24 mm. If the apothem is $4\sqrt{3}$ mm, find the area of the triangle.

(A) 72 mm²   (B) $96\sqrt{3}$ mm²   (C) 144 mm²

(D) $144\sqrt{3}$ mm²   (E) 576 mm²

6. Find the area of a regular hexagon with sides of 4 cm.

(A) $12\sqrt{3}$ cm²   (B) 24 cm²   (C) $24\sqrt{3}$ cm²

(D) 48 cm²   (E) $48\sqrt{3}$ cm²

7. Find the area of a regular decagon with sides of length 6 cm and an apothem of length 9.2 cm.

(A) 55.2 cm²   (B) 60 cm²   (C) 138 cm²

(D) 138.3 cm²   (E) 276 cm²

8. The perimeter of a regular heptagon (7-gon) is 36.4 cm. Find the length of each side.

(A) 4.8 cm   (B) 5.2 cm   (C) 6.7 cm   (D) 7 cm   (E) 10.4 cm

9. The apothem of a regular quadrilateral is 4 in. Find the perimeter.

(A) 12 in.   (B) 16 in.   (C) 24 in.   (D) 32 in.   (E) 64 in.

10. A regular triangle has a perimeter of 18 cm; a regular pentagon has a perimeter of 30 cm; a regular hexagon has a perimeter of 33 cm. Which figure (or figures) have sides with the longest measure?

(A) Regular triangle

(B) Regular triangle and regular pentagon

(C) Regular pentagon

(D) Regular pentagon and regular hexagon

(E) Regular hexagon

TRIANGLES

A closed three-sided geometric figure is called a **triangle**. The points of the intersection of the sides of a triangle are called the **vertices** of the triangle.

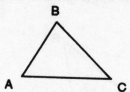

The **perimeter** of a triangle is the sum of the measures of the sides of the triangle.

A triangle with no equal sides is called a **scalene triangle**.

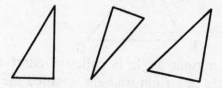

A triangle having at least two equal sides is called an **isosceles triangle**. The third side is called the **base** of the triangle.

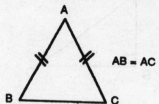

A side of a triangle is a line segment whose endpoints are the vertices of two angles of the triangle.

An **interior angle** of a triangle is an angle formed by two sides and includes the third side within its collection of points.

An **equilateral triangle** is a triangle having three equal sides. $\overline{AB}$ = $\overline{AC}$ = $\overline{BC}$.

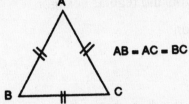

The sum of the measures of the interior angles of a triangle is 180°.

A triangle with one obtuse angle greater than 90° is called an **obtuse triangle**.

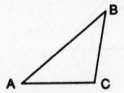

An **acute triangle** is a triangle with three acute angles (less than 90°).

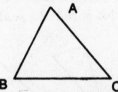

A triangle with a right angle is called a **right triangle**. The side opposite the right angle in a right triangle is called the hypotenuse of the right triangle. The other two sides are called arms or legs of the right triangle.

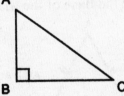

An **altitude** of a triangle is a line segment from a vertex of the triangle perpendicular to the opposite side.

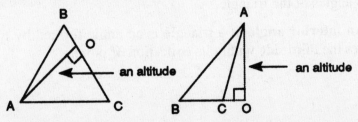

A line segment connecting a vertex of a triangle and the midpoint of the opposite side is called a **median** of the triangle.

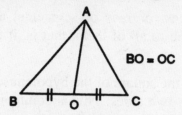

BO = OC

A line that bisects and is perpendicular to a side of a triangle is called a **perpendicular bisector** of that side.

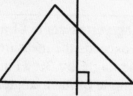

An **angle bisector** of a triangle is a line that bisects an angle and extends to the opposite side of the triangle.

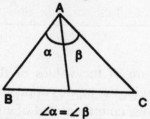

$\angle\alpha = \angle\beta$

The line segment that joins the midpoints of two sides of a triangle is called a **midline** of the triangle.

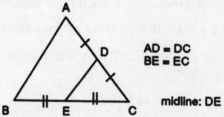

AD = DC
BE = EC

midline: DE

An **exterior angle** of a triangle is an angle formed outside a triangle by one side of the triangle and the extension of an adjacent side.

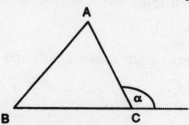

A triangle whose three interior angles have equal measure (60° each) is said to be **equiangular**.

Three or more lines (or rays or segments) are concurrent if there exists one point common to all of them, that is, if they all intersect at the same point.

In a right triangle, the square of the hypotenuse is equal to the sum of the squares of the other two sides. This is commonly known as the theorem of Pythagoras or the Pythagorean theorem.

PROBLEM

The measure of the vertex angle of an isosceles triangle exceeds the measurement of each base angle by 30°. Find the value of each angle of the triangle.

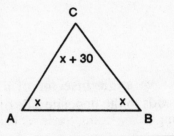

SOLUTION

We know that the sum of the values of the angles of a triangle is 180°. In an isosceles triangle, the angles opposite the congruent sides (the base angles) are, themselves, congruent and of equal value.

Therefore,

(1)   Let x = the measure of each base angle.

(2)   Then $x + 30$ = the measure of the vertex angle.

We can solve for x algebraically by keeping in mind the sum of all the measures will be 180°.

$$x + x + (x + 30) = 180$$
$$3x + 30 = 180$$
$$3x = 150$$
$$x = 50$$

Therefore, the base angles each measure 50°, and the vertex angle measures 80°.

PROBLEM

Prove that the base angles of an isosceles right triangle measure 45° each.

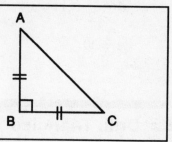

SOLUTION

As drawn in the figure, $\triangle ABC$ is an isosceles right triangle with base angles *BAC* and *BCA*. The sum of the measures of the angles of any triangle is 180°. For $\triangle ABC$, this means

$$m \angle BAC + m \angle BCA + m \angle ABC = 180° \qquad (1)$$

But $m \angle ABC = 90°$ because *ABC* is a right triangle. Furthermore, $m \angle BCA = m \angle BAC$, since the base angles of an isosceles triangle are congruent. Using these facts in equation (1)

$$m \angle BAC + m \angle BCA + 90° = 180°$$

or $\quad 2m \angle BAC = 2m \angle BCA = 90°$

or $\quad m \angle BAC = m \angle BCA = 45°.$

Therefore, the base angles of an isosceles right triangle measure 45° each.

The area of a triangle is given by the formula $A = \frac{1}{2}bh$, where *b* is the length of a base, which can be any side of the triangle, and *h* is the corresponding height of the triangle, which is the perpendicular line segment that is drawn from the vertex opposite the base to the base itself.

$$A = \frac{1}{2}\, bh$$

$$A = \frac{1}{2}\,(10)\,(3)$$

$$A = 15$$

The area of a right triangle is found by taking $\frac{1}{2}$ the product of the lengths of its two arms.

$$A = \frac{1}{2} (5) (12)$$

$$A = 30$$

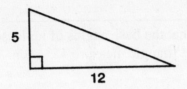

☞ Drill: Triangles

Angle Measures

DIRECTIONS: Refer to the diagram and find the appropriate solution.

1. In $\triangle PQR$, $\angle Q$ is a right angle. Find $m \angle R$.

(A) 27°   (B) 33°   (C) 54°

(D) 67°   (E) 157°

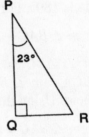

2. $\triangle MNO$ is isosceles. If the vertex angle, $\angle N$, has a measure of 96°, find the measure of $\angle M$.

(A) 21°   (B) 42°   (C) 64°

(D) 84°   (E) 96°

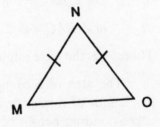

3. Find x.

(A) 15°   (B) 25°   (C) 30°

(D) 45°   (E) 90°

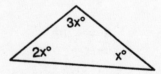

4. Find $m \angle 1$.

(A) 40°   (B) 66°   (C) 74°

(D) 114°   (E) 140°

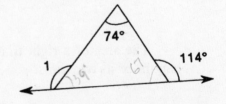

5. Δ *ABC* is a right triangle with a right
    angle at *B*. Δ *BDC* is a right triangle
    with right angle ∠ *BDC*. If *m* ∠ *C* =
    36°. Find *m* ∠ *A*.

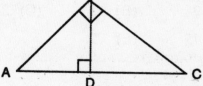

(A) 18°   (B) 36°   (C) 54°

(D) 72°   (E) 180°

Similar Triangles

<u>**DIRECTIONS**</u>: Refer to the diagram and find the appropriate solution.

6. The two triangles shown are similar. Find *b*.

(A) $2\frac{2}{3}$ (B) 3   (C) 4

(D) 16   (E) 24

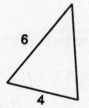

7. The two triangles shown are similar.
    Find *m* ∠ 1.

(A) 48°   (B) 53°   (C) 74°

(D) 127°   (E) 180°

8. The two triangles shown are similar.
    Find *a* and *b*.

(A) 5 and 10   (B) 4 and 8

(C) $4\frac{2}{3}$ and $7\frac{1}{3}$ (D) 5 and 8

 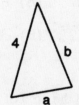

(E) $5\frac{1}{3}$ and 8

9. The perimeter of △ *LXR* is 45 and the perimeter of △ *ABC* is 27. If $\overline{LX}$ = 15, find the length of $\overline{AB}$.

(A) 9   (B) 15   (C) 27

(D) 45   (E) 72

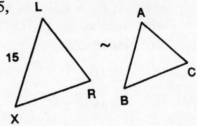

10. Find *b*.

(A) 9   (B) 15   (C) 20

(D) 45   (E) 60

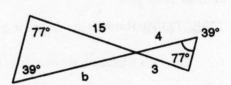

Area

DIRECTIONS: Refer to the diagram and find the appropriate solution.

11. Find the area of △ *MNO*.

(A) 22   (B) 49   (C) 56

(D) 84   (E) 112

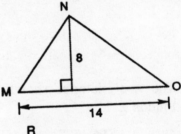

12. Find the area of △ *PQR*.

(A) 31.5   (B) 38.5   (C) 53

(D) 77   (E) 82.5

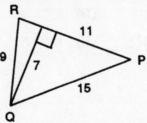

13. Find the area of △ *STU*.

(A) $4\sqrt{2}$ (B) $8\sqrt{2}$ (C) $12\sqrt{2}$

(D) $16\sqrt{2}$ (E) $32\sqrt{2}$

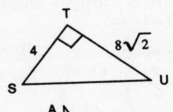

 14. Find the area of △ *ABC*.

(A) 54 cm²   (B) 81 cm²   (C) 108 cm²

(D) 135 cm²   (E) 180 cm²

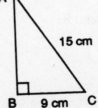

15. Find the area of Δ *XYZ*.

(A) 20 cm²   (B) 50 cm²   (C) 50√2 cm²

(D) 100 cm²   (E) 200 cm²

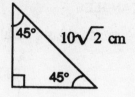

QUADRILATERALS

A **quadrilateral** is a polygon with four sides.

PARALLELOGRAMS

A **parallelogram** is a quadrilateral whose opposite sides are parallel.

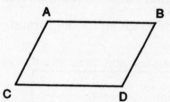

Two angles that have their vertices at the endpoints of the same side of a parallelogram are called **consecutive angles**.

The perpendicular segment connecting any point of a line containing one side of the parallelogram to the line containing the opposite side of the parallelogram is called the **altitude** of the parallelogram.

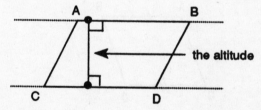

A diagonal of a polygon is a line segment joining any two non-consecutive vertices.

The area of a parallelogram is given by the formula $A = bh$, where b is the base and h is the height drawn perpendicular to that base. Note that the height equals the altitude of the parallelogram.

$A = bh$

$A = (10)(3)$

$A = 30$

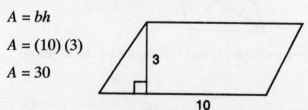

RECTANGLES

A rectangle is a parallelogram with right angles.

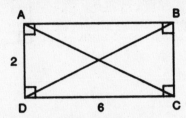

The diagonals of a rectangle are equal.

If the diagonals of a parallelogram are equal, the parallelogram is a rectangle.

If a quadrilateral has four right angles, then it is a rectangle.

The area of a rectangle is given by the formula $A = lw$, where l is the length and w is the width.

$A = lw$

$A = (3)(10)$

$A = 30$

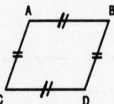

RHOMBI

A rhombus is a parallelogram which has two adjacent sides that are equal.

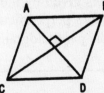

All sides of a rhombus are equal.

The diagonals of a rhombus are perpendicular to each other.

The diagonals of a rhombus bisect the angles of the rhombus.

If the diagonals of a parallelogram are perpendicular, the parallelogram is a rhombus.

If a quadrilateral has four equal sides, then it is a rhombus.

A parallelogram is a rhombus if either diagonal of the parallelogram bisects the angles of the vertices it joins.

SQUARES

A square is a rhombus with a right angle.

A square is an equilateral quadrilateral.

A square has all the properties of parallelograms and rectangles.

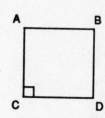

A rhombus is a square if one of its interior angles is a right angle.

In a square, the measure of either diagonal can be calculated by multiplying the length of any side by the square root of 2.

The area of a square is given by the formula $A = s^2$, where s is the side of the square. Since all sides of a square are equal, it does not matter which side is used.

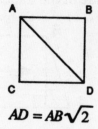

$$AD = AB\sqrt{2}$$

$A = s^2$

$A = 6^2$

$A = 36$

6

The area of a square can also be found by taking $\frac{1}{2}$ the product of the length of the diagonal squared.

$A = \frac{1}{2}d^2$

$A = \frac{1}{2}(8)^2$

8

$A = 32$

TRAPEZOIDS

A **trapezoid** is a quadrilateral with two and only two sides parallel. The parallel sides of a trapezoid are called **bases**.

The **median** of a trapezoid is the line joining the midpoints of the non-parallel sides.

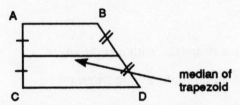

The perpendicular segment connecting any point in the line containing one base of the trapezoid to the line containing the other base is the **altitude** of the trapezoid.

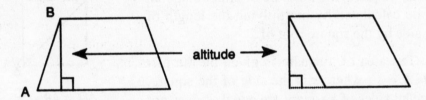

An **isosceles trapezoid** is a trapezoid whose non-parallel sides are equal. A pair of angles including only one of the parallel sides is called **a pair of base angles**.

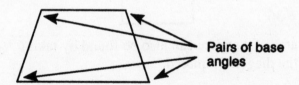

The median of a trapezoid is parallel to the bases and equal to one-half their sum.

The base angles of an isosceles trapezoid are equal.

The diagonals of an isosceles trapezoid are equal.

The opposite angles of an isosceles trapezoid are supplementary.

PROBLEM

Prove that all pairs of consecutive angles of a parallelogram are supplementary.

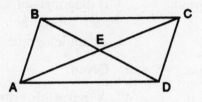

SOLUTION

We must prove that the pairs of angles ∠ *BAD* and ∠ *ADC*, ∠ *ADC* and ∠ *DCB*, ∠ *DCB* and ∠ *CBA*, and ∠ *CBA* and ∠ *BAD* are supplementary. (This means that the sum of their measures is 180°.)

Because *ABCD* is a parallelogram, $\overline{AB} \parallel \overline{CD}$. Angles *BAD* and *ADC* are consecutive interior angles, as are ∠ *CBA* and ∠ *DCB*. Since the consecutive interior angles formed by two parallel lines and a transversal are supplementary, ∠ *BAD* and ∠ *ADC* are supplementary, as are ∠ *CBA* and ∠ *DCB*.

Similarly, $\overline{AD} \parallel \overline{BC}$. Angles *ADC* and *DCB* are consecutive interior angles, as are ∠ *CBA* and ∠ *BAD*. Since the consecutive interior angles formed by two parallel lines and a transversal are supplementary, ∠ *CBA* and ∠ *BAD* are supplementary, as are ∠ *ADC* and ∠ *DCB*.

PROBLEM

In the accompanying figure, Δ *ABC* is given to be an isosceles right triangle with ∠ *ABC* a right angle and $\overline{AB} \cong \overline{BC}$. Line segment $\overline{BD}$, which bisects $\overline{CA}$, is extended to *E*, so that $\overline{BD} \cong \overline{DE}$. Prove *BAEC* is a square.

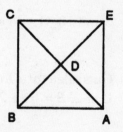

SOLUTION

A square is a rectangle in which two consecutive sides are congruent. This definition will provide the framework for the proof in this problem. We will prove that *BAEC* is a parallelogram that is specifically a rectangle with consecutive sides congruent, namely a square.

Statement	**Reason**
1. $\overline{BD} \cong \overline{DE}$ and $\overline{AD} \cong \overline{DC}$.	1. Given ($\overline{BD}$ bisects $\overline{CA}$).
2. *BAEC* is a parallelogram.	2. If diagonals of a quadrilateral bisect each other, then the quadrilateral is a parallelogram.
3. $\angle ABC$ is a right angle.	3. Given.
4. *BAEC* is a rectangle.	4. A parallelogram, one of whose angles is a right angle, is a rectangle.
5. $\overline{AB} \cong \overline{BC}$.	5. Given.
6. *BAEC* is a square.	6. If a rectangle has two congruent consecutive sides, then the rectangle is a square.

☞ Drill: Quadrilaterals

Parallelograms, Rectangles, Rhombi, Squares, Trapezoids

DIRECTIONS: Refer to the diagram and find the appropriate solution.

1. In parallelogram *WXYZ*, $\overline{WX}$ = 14, $\overline{WZ}$ = 6, $\overline{ZY}$ = 3x + 5, and $\overline{XY}$ = 2y − 4. Find *x* and *y*.

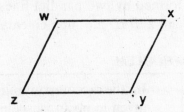

    (A) 3 and 5   (B) 4 and 5   (C) 4 and 6

    (D) 6 and 10 (E) 6 and 14

2. Quadrilateral *ABCD* is a parallelogram. If $m \angle B = 6x + 2$ and $m \angle D = 98$, find *x*.

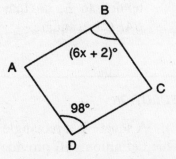

    (A) 12   (B) 16   (C) $16\frac{2}{3}$

    (D) 18   (E) 20

3. Find the area of parallelogram *STUV*.

(A) 56   (B) 90   (C) 108

(D) 162   (E) 180

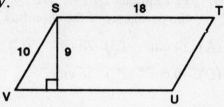

4. Find the area of parallelogram *MNOP*.

(A) 19   (B) 32   (C) $32\sqrt{3}$

(D) 44   (E) $44\sqrt{3}$

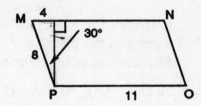

5. If the perimeter of rectangle *PQRS* is 40, find *x*.

(A) 31 in.   (B) 38 in.   (C) 2 in.

(D) 44 in.   (E) 121 in.

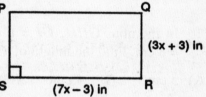

6. In rectangle *ABCD*, $\overline{AD}$ = 6 cm and $\overline{DC}$ = 8 cm. Find the length of the diagonal $\overline{AC}$.

(A) 10 cm   (B) 12 cm   (C) 20 cm

(D) 28 cm   (E) 48 cm

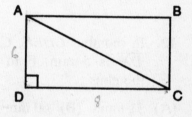

7. Find the area of rectangle *UVXY*.

(A) 17 cm²   (B) 34 cm²   (C) 35 cm²

(D) 70 cm²   (E) 140 cm²

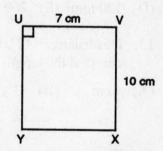

8. Find the length of $\overline{BO}$ in rectangle *BCDE* if the diagonal $\overline{EC}$ is 17 mm.

(A) 6.55 mm   (B) 8 mm   (C) 8.5 mm

(D) 17 mm   (E) 34 mm

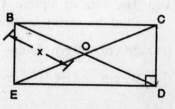

9. In rhombus *DEFG*, $\overline{DE}$ = 7 cm. Find the perimeter of the rhombus.

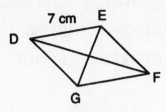

(A) 14 cm   (B) 28 cm   (C) 42 cm

(D) 49 cm   (E) 56 cm

10. In rhombus *RHOM*, the diagonal $\overline{RO}$ is 8 cm and the diagonal $\overline{HM}$ is 12 cm. Find the area of the rhombus.

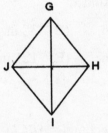

(A) 20 cm²   (B) 40 cm²   (C) 48 cm²

(D) 68 cm²   (E) 96 cm²

11. In rhombus *GHIJ*, $\overline{GI}$ = 6 cm and $\overline{HJ}$ = 8 cm. Find the length of $\overline{GH}$.

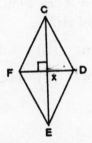

(A) 3 cm   (B) 4 cm   (C) 5 cm

(D) $4\sqrt{3}$ cm   (E) 14 cm

12. In rhombus *CDEF*, $\overline{CD}$ is 13 mm and $\overline{DX}$ is 5 mm. Find the area of the rhombus.

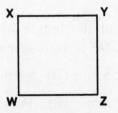

(A) 31 mm²   (B) 60 mm²   (C) 78 mm²

(D) 120 mm²   (E) 260 mm²

13. Quadrilateral *ATUV* is a square. If the perimeter of the square is 44 cm, find the length of $\overline{AT}$.

(A) 4 cm   (B) 11 cm   (C) 22 cm   (D) 30 cm   (E) 40 cm

14. The area of square *XYZW* is 196 cm². Find the perimeter of the square.

(A) 28 cm   (B) 42 cm   (C) 56 cm

(D) 98 cm   (E) 196 cm

15. In square *MNOP*, $\overline{MN}$ is 6 cm. Find the length of diagonal $\overline{MO}$.

(A) 6 cm (B) $6\sqrt{2}$ cm (C) $6\sqrt{3}$ cm
(D) $6\sqrt{6}$ cm (E) 12 cm

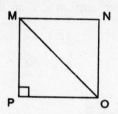

16. In square *ABCD*, $\overline{AB} = 3$ cm. Find the area of the square.

(A) 9 cm² (B) 12 cm² (C) 15 cm²
(D) 18 cm² (E) 21 cm²

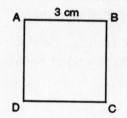

17. Find the area of trapezoid *RSTU*.

(A) 80 cm² (B) 87.5 cm² (C) 140 cm²
(D) 147 cm² (E) 175 cm²

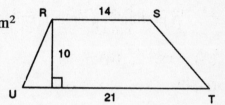

18. *ABCD* is an isosceles trapezoid. Find the perimeter.

(A) 21 cm (B) 27 cm (C) 30 cm
(D) 50 cm (E) 54 cm

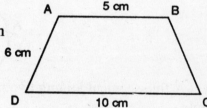

19. Find the area of trapezoid *MNOP*.

(A) $(17 + 3\sqrt{3})$ mm²

(B) $\dfrac{33}{2}$ mm²

(C) $\dfrac{33\sqrt{3}}{2}$ mm²

(D) 33 mm²

(E) $33\sqrt{3}$ mm²

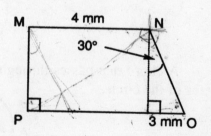

20. Trapezoid *XYZW* is isosceles. If *m* ∠ *W* = 58° and *m* ∠ *Z* = (4*x* – 6), find *x*°.

(A) 8°   (B) 12°   (C) 13°

(D) 16°   (E) 58°

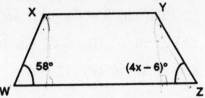

CIRCLES

A **circle** is a set of points in the same plane equidistant from a fixed point, called its center.

A **radius** of a circle is a line segment drawn from the center of the circle to any point on the circle.

A portion of a circle is called an **arc** of the circle.

A line that intersects a circle in two points is called a **secant.**

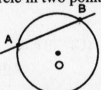

A line segment joining two points on a circle is called a **chord** of the circle.

A chord that passes through the center of the circle is called a **diameter** of the circle.

The line passing through the centers of two (or more) circles is called the **line of centers**.

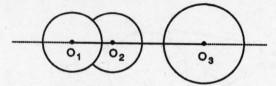

An angle whose vertex is on the circle and whose sides are chords of the circle is called an **inscribed angle**.

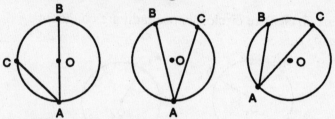

An angle whose vertex is at the center of a circle and whose sides are radii is called a **central angle**.

The measure of a minor arc is the measure of the central angle that intercepts that arc.

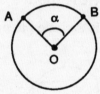

$$m \overset{\frown}{AB} = \alpha = m \ \angle AOB$$

The distance from a point P to a given circle is the distance from that point to the point where the circle intersects with a line segment with endpoints at the center of the circle and point P.

The distance of point P to the diagrammed circle with center O is the line segment $\overline{PB}$ of line segment $\overline{PO}$.

A line that has one and only one point of intersection with a circle is called a tangent to that circle, while their common point is called a **point of tangency**.

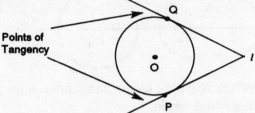

Congruent circles are circles whose radii are congruent.

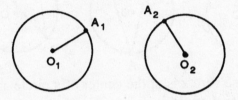

If $O_1A_1 \cong O_2A_2$, then $O_1 \cong O_2$.

The measure of a semicircle is 180°.

A **circumscribed circle** is a circle passing through all the vertices of a polygon.

Circles that have the same center and unequal radii are called **concentric circles**.

Concentric Circles

PROBLEM

A and *B* are points on circle *Q* such that △ *AQB* is equilateral. If the length of side $\overline{AB}$ = 12, find the length of arc *AB*.

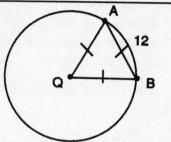

SOLUTION

To find the arc length of arc *AB*, we must find the measure of the central angle ∠ *AQB* and the measure of the radius $\overline{QA}$. ∠ *AQB* is an interior angle of the equilateral triangle △ *AQB*. Therefore,

$$m \angle AQB = 60°.$$

Similarly, in the equilateral △ *AQB*,

$$\overline{AQ} = \overline{AB} = \overline{QB} = 12.$$

Given the radius, *r*, and the central angle, *n*, the arc length is given by

$$\frac{n}{360} \times 2\pi r.$$

Therefore, by substitution,

$$\angle AQB = \frac{60}{360} \times 2\pi \times 12 = \frac{1}{6} \times 2\pi \times 12 = 4\pi.$$

Therefore, the length of arc *AB* = 4π.

PROBLEM

In circle *O*, the measure of arc *AB* is 80°. Find the measure of ∠ *A*.

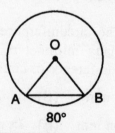

SOLUTION

The accompanying figure shows that arc *AB* is intercepted by central angle *AOB*. By definition, we know that the measure of the central angle is the measure of its intercepted arc. In this case,

arc $mAB = m \angle AOB = 80°$.

Radius $\overline{OA}$ and radius $\overline{OB}$ are congruent and form two sides of $\triangle OAB$. By a theorem, the angles opposite these two congruent sides must, themselves, be congruent. Therefore, $m \angle A = m \angle B$.

The sum of the measures of the angles of a triangle is 180°. Therefore,

$$m \angle A + m \angle B + m \angle AOB = 180°.$$

Since $m \angle A = m \angle B$, we can write

$$m \angle A + m \angle A + 80° = 180°$$

or $\quad 2m \angle A = 100°$

or $\quad m \angle A = 50°$.

Therefore, the measure of $\angle A$ is 50°.

☞ Drill: Circles

Circumference, Area, Concentric Circles

DIRECTIONS: Determine the accurate measure.

1. Find the circumference of circle A if its radius is 3 mm.

    (A) 3π mm   (B) 6π mm   (C) 9π mm   (D) 12π mm   (E) 15π mm

2. The circumference of circle H is 20π cm. Find the length of the radius.

    (A) 10 cm   (B) 20 cm   (C) 10π cm   (D) 15π cm   (E) 20π cm

3. The circumference of circle A is how many millimeters larger than the circumference of circle B?

    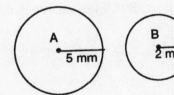

    (A) 3 mm   (B) 6 mm   (C) 3π mm

    (D) 6π mm   (E) 7π mm

4. If the diameter of circle X is 9 cm and if $\pi = 3.14$, find the circumference of the circle to the nearest tenth.

    (A) 9 cm   (B) 14.1 cm   (C) 21.1 cm   (D) 24.6 cm   (E) 28.3 cm

5. Find the area of circle *I*.

(A) 22 mm²   (B) 121 mm²

(C) 121π mm²   (D) 132 mm²

(E) 132π mm²

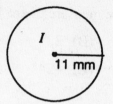

6. The diameter of circle *Z* is 27 mm. Find the area of the circle.

(A) 91.125 mm²   (B) 182.25 mm²   (C) 191.5π mm²

(D) 182.25π mm²   (E) 729 mm²

7. The area of circle *B* is 225π cm². Find the length of the diameter of the circle.

(A) 15 cm   (B) 20 cm   (C) 30 cm   (D) 20π cm   (E) 25π cm

8. The area of circle *X* is 144π mm² while the area of circle *Y* is 81π mm². Write the ratio of the radius of circle *X* to that of circle *Y*.

(A) 3 : 4   (B) 4 : 3   (C) 9 : 12   (D) 27 : 12   (E) 18 : 24

9. The circumference of circle *M* is 18π cm. Find the area of the circle.

(A) 18π cm² (B) 81 cm²   (C) 36 cm²   (D) 36π cm² (E) 81π cm²

10. In two concentric circles, the smaller circle has a radius of 3 mm while the larger circle has a radius of 5 mm. Find the area of the shaded region.

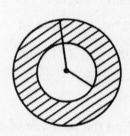

(A) 2π mm²   (B) 8π mm²

(C) 13π mm²   (D) 16π mm²

(E) 26π mm²

11. The radius of the smaller of two concentric circles is 5 cm while the radius of the larger circle is 7 cm. Determine the area of the shaded region.

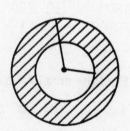

(A) 7π cm²   (B) 24π cm²

(C) 25π cm²   (D) 36π cm²

(E) 49π cm²

12. Find the measure of arc *MN* if *m* ∠ *MON* = 62°.

(A) 16°   (B) 32°   (C) 59°

(D) 62°   (E) 124°

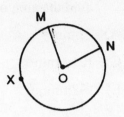

13. Find the measure of arc *AXC*.

(A) 150°   (B) 160°   (C) 180°

(D) 270°   (E) 360°

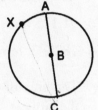

14. If arc *MXP* = 236°, find the measure of arc *MP*.

(A) 62°   (B) 124°   (C) 236°

(D) 270°   (E) 360°

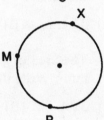

15. In circle *S*, major arc *PQR* has a measure of 298°. Find the measure of the central angle ∠ *PSR*.

(A) 62°   (B) 124°   (C) 149°

(D) 298°   (E) 360°

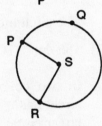

16. Find the measure of arc *XY* in circle *W*.

(A) 40°   (B) 120°   (C) 140°

(D) 180°   (E) 220°

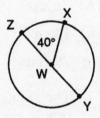

17. Find the area of the sector shown.

(A) 4 cm²   (B) 2π cm²   (C) 16 cm²

(D) 8π cm²   (E) 16π cm²

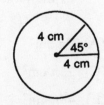

18. Find the area of the shaded region.

(A) 10   (B) 5π   (C) 25

(D) 20π   (E) 25π

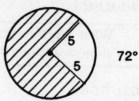

19. Find the area of the shaded sector shown

(A) $\dfrac{9\pi \text{ mm}^2}{4}$ (B) $\dfrac{9\pi \text{ mm}^2}{2}$ (C) 18 mm²

(D) 6π mm² (E) 9π mm²

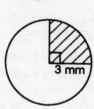

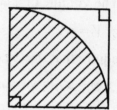

20. If the area of the square is 100 cm², find the area of the shaded sector.

(A) 10π cm² (B) 25 cm² (C) 25π cm²

(D) 100 cm² (E) 100π cm²

SOLIDS

Solid geometry is the study of figures which consist of points not all in the same plane.

RECTANGULAR SOLIDS

A solid with lateral faces and bases that are rectangles is called a **rectangular solid**.

The surface area of a rectangular solid is the sum of the areas of all the faces.

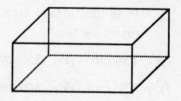

The volume of a rectangular solid is equal to the product of its length, width, and height.

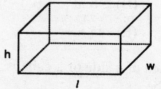

$V = lwh$

PROBLEM

What are the dimensions of a solid cube whose surface area is numerically equal to its volume?

SOLUTION

The surface area of a cube of edge length a is equal to the sum of the areas of its six faces. Since a cube is a regular polygon, all six faces are congruent. Each face of a cube is a square of edge length a. Hence, the surface area of a cube of edge length a is

$S = 6a^2$.

The volume of a cube of edge length a is

$V = a^3$.

We require that $A = V$, or that

$6a^2 = a^3$ or $a = 6$

Hence, if a cube has edge length 6, its surface area will be numerically equal to its volume.

☞ Drill: Solids

Area and Volume

DIRECTIONS: Refer to the diagram and find the appropriate solution.

1. Find the surface area of the rectangular prism shown.

    (A) 138 cm² (B) 336 cm² (C) 381 cm²

    (D) 426 cm² (E) 540 cm²

    12 cm

    5 cm

    9 cm

2. Find the volume of the rectangular storage tank shown.

    (A) 24 m³ (B) 36 m³ (C) 38 m³

    (D) 42 m³ (E) 45 m³

    1.5 m

    4 m

    6 m

3. The area of a side of a cube is 100 cm². Find the length of an edge of the cube.

    (A) 4 cm (B) 5 cm (C) 10 cm (D) 12 cm (E) 15 cm

COORDINATE GEOMETRY

Coordinate geometry refers to the study of geometric figures using algebraic principles.

The graph shown is called the Cartesian coordinate plane. The graph consists of a pair of perpendicular lines called **coordinate axes**. The **vertical axis** is the y-axis and the **horizontal axis** is the x-axis. The point of intersection of these two axes is called the **origin**; it is the

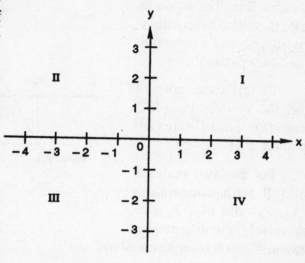

zero point of both axes. Furthermore, points to the right of the origin on the x-axis and above the origin on the y-axis represent positive real numbers. Points to the left of the origin on the x-axis or below the origin on the y-axis represent negative real numbers.

The four regions cut off by the coordinate axes are, in counterclockwise direction from the top right, called the first, second, third, and fourth quadrant, respectively. The first quadrant contains all points with two positive coordinates.

In the graph shown, two points are identified by the ordered pair (x, y) of numbers. The x-coordinate is the first number and the y-coordinate is the second number.

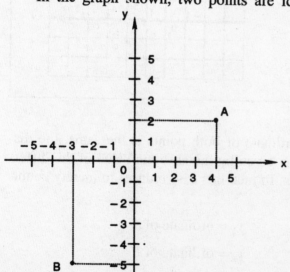

To plot a point on the graph when given the coordinates, draw perpendicular lines from the number-line coordinates to the point where the two lines intersect.

To find the coordinates of a given point on the graph, draw perpen-

dicular lines from the point to the coordinates on the number line. The x-coordinate is written before the y-coordinate and a comma is used to separate the two.

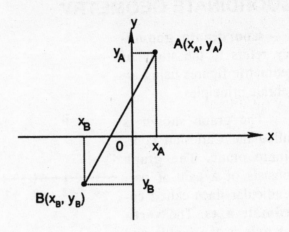

In this case, point A has the coordinates $(4, 2)$ and the coordinates of point B are $(-3, -5)$.

For any two points A and B with coordinates (X_A, Y_A) and (X_B, Y_B), respectively, the distance between A and B is represented by:

$$AB = \sqrt{(X_A - X_B)^2 + (Y_A - Y_B)^2}$$

This is commonly known as the distance formula.

PROBLEM

Find the distance between the point $A(1, 3)$ and $B(5, 3)$.

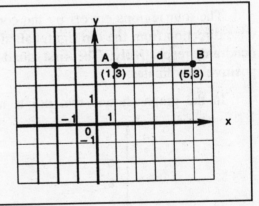

SOLUTION

In this case, where the ordinate of both points is the same, the distance between the two points is given by the absolute value of the difference between the two abscissas. In fact, this case reduces to merely counting boxes as the figure shows.

Let, $\quad x_1 =$ abscissa of A $\qquad y_1 =$ ordinate of A

$\qquad\quad x_2 =$ abscissa of B $\qquad y_2 =$ ordinate of B

$\qquad\quad d =$ the distance

Therefore, $d = |\,x_1 - x_2\,|$. By substitution, $d = |\,1 - 5\,| = |\,-4\,| = 4$. This answer can also be obtained by applying the general formula for distance between any two points.

$$d = \sqrt{(x_1 - x_2)^2 + (y_1 - y_2)^2}$$

By substitution,

$$
\begin{aligned}
d &= \sqrt{(1-5)^2 + (3-3)^2} \\
&= \sqrt{(-4)^2 + (0)^2} \\
&= \sqrt{16} \\
&= 4
\end{aligned}
$$

The distance is 4.

To find the midpoint of a segment between the two given endpoints, use the formula

$$MP = \left(\frac{x_1 + x_2}{2}, \frac{y_1 + y_2}{2} \right)$$

where x_1 and y_1 are the coordinates of one point; x_2 and y_2 are the coordinates of the other point.

☞ Drill: Coordinate Geometry

Coordinates

<u>DIRECTIONS</u>: Refer to the diagram and find the appropriate solution.

1.   Which point shown has the coordinates $(-3, 2)$?

(A) A   (B) B   (C) C

(D) D   (E) E

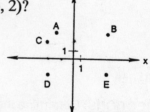

2.   Name the coordinates of point A.

(A) $(4, 3)$ (B) $(3, -4)$ (C) $(3, 4)$

(D) $(-4, 3)$ (E) $(4, -3)$

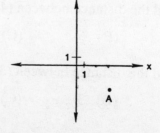

245

3. Which point shown has the coordinates $(2.5, -1)$?

(A) M   (B) N   (C) P

(D) Q   (E) R

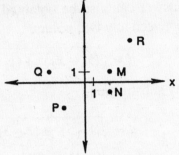

4. The correct x-coordinate for point H is what number?

(A) 3   (B) 4   (C) -3

(D) -4 (E) -5

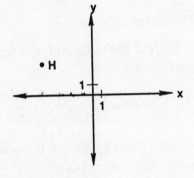

5. The correct y-coordinate for point R is what number?

(A) -7 (B) 2   (C) -2

(D) 7   (E) 8

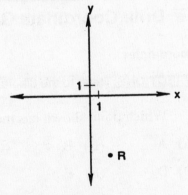

Distance

DIRECTIONS: Determine the distance or value as appropriate.

6. Find the distance between $(4, -7)$ and $(-2, -7)$.

(A) 4   (B) 6   (C) 7   (D) 14   (E) 15

7. Find the distance between $(3, 8)$ and $(5, 11)$.

(A) 2   (B) 3   (C) $\sqrt{13}$ (D) $\sqrt{15}$ (E) $3\sqrt{3}$

8. How far from the origin is the point (3, 4)?

(A) 3   (B) 4   (C) 5   (D) $5\sqrt{3}$ (E) $4\sqrt{5}$

9. Find the distance between the point (− 4, 2) and (3, − 5).

(A) 3   (B) $3\sqrt{3}$ (C) 7   (D) $7\sqrt{2}$ (E) $7\sqrt{3}$

10. The distance between points A and B is 10 units. If A has coordinates (4, − 6) and B has coordinates (− 2, y), determine the value of y.

(A) − 6   (B) − 2   (C) 0   (D) 1   (E) 2

Midpoints and Endpoints

<u>DIRECTIONS</u>: Determine the coordinates or value as appropriate.

11. Find the midpoint between the points (− 2, 6) and (4, 8).

(A) (3, 7)   (B) (1, 7)   (C) (3, 1)   (D) (1, 1)   (E) (− 3, 7)

12. Find the coordinates of the midpoint between the points (− 5, 7) and (3, − 1).

(A) (− 4, 4)   (B) (3, − 1)   (C) (1, − 3)   (D) (− 1, 3)   (E) (4, − 4)

13. The y-coordinate of the midpoint of segment $\overline{AB}$ if A has coordinates (− 3, 7) and B has coordinates (− 3, − 2) is what value?

(A) $\dfrac{5}{2}$ (B) 3   (C) $\dfrac{7}{2}$ (D) 5   (E) $\dfrac{15}{2}$

14. One endpoint of a line segment is (5, − 3). The midpoint is (− 1, 6). What is the other endpoint?

(A) (7, 3)   (B) (2, 1.5)   (C) (− 7, 15)

(D) (− 2, 1.5)   (E) (− 7, 12)

15. The point (− 2, 6) is the midpoint for which of the following pair of points?

(A) (1, 4) and (− 3, 8)   (B) (− 1, − 3) and (5, 9)

(C) (1, 4) and (5, 9)   (D) (− 1, 4) and (3, − 8)

(E) (1, 3) and (− 5, 9)

GEOMETRY DRILLS

ANSWER KEY

Drill: Lines and Angles

1.	(B)	5.	(D)	9.	(D)	13.	(B)
2.	(A)	6.	(C)	10.	(E)	14.	(E)
3.	(C)	7.	(B)	11.	(C)	15.	(A)
4.	(D)	8.	(A)	12.	(D)		

Drill: Regular Polygons

1.	(D)	4.	(A)	7.	(E)	10.	(B)
2.	(B)	5.	(D)	8.	(B)		
3.	(E)	6.	(C)	9.	(D)		

Drill: Triangles

1.	(D)	5.	(C)	9.	(A)	13.	(D)
2.	(B)	6.	(A)	10.	(C)	14.	(A)
3.	(C)	7.	(B)	11.	(C)	15.	(B)
4.	(E)	8.	(E)	12.	(B)		

Drill: Quadrilaterals

1.	(A)	6.	(A)	11.	(C)	16.	(A)
2.	(B)	7.	(D)	12.	(D)	17.	(E)
3.	(D)	8.	(C)	13.	(B)	18.	(B)
4.	(E)	9.	(B)	14.	(C)	19.	(C)
5.	(C)	10.	(C)	15.	(B)	20.	(D)

Drill: Circles

1.	(B)	6.	(D)	11.	(B)	16.	(C)
2.	(A)	7.	(C)	12.	(D)	17.	(B)
3.	(D)	8.	(B)	13.	(C)	18.	(D)
4.	(E)	9.	(E)	14.	(B)	19.	(A)
5.	(C)	10.	(D)	15.	(A)	20.	(C)

Drill: Solids

1. (D)　　　2. (B)　　　3. (C)

Drill: Coordinate Geometry

1.	(C)	5.	(A)	9.	(D)	13.	(A)
2.	(E)	6.	(B)	10.	(E)	14.	(C)
3.	(B)	7.	(C)	11.	(B)	15.	(E)
4.	(D)	8.	(C)	12.	(D)		

IV. WORD PROBLEMS

One of the main problems students have in mathematics involves solving word problems. The secret to solving these problems is being able to convert words into numbers and variables in the form of an algebraic equation.

The easiest way to approach a word problem is to read the question and ask yourself what you are trying to find. This unknown quantity can be represented by a variable.

Next, determine how the variable relates to the other quantities in the problem. More than likely, these quantities can be explained in terms of the original variable. If not, a separate variable may have to be used to represent a quantity.

Using these variables and the relationships determined among them, an equation can be written. Solve for a particular variable and then plug this number in for each relationship that involves this variable in order to find any unknown quantities.

Lastly, re-read the problem to be sure that you have answered the questions correctly and fully.

ALGEBRAIC

The following illustrates how to formulate an equation and solve the problem.

EXAMPLE

Find two consecutive odd integers whose sum is 36.

Let x = the first odd integer

Let $x + 2$ = the second odd integer

The sum of the two numbers is 36. Therefore,

$$x + (x + 2) = 36$$

Simplifying,

$$2x + 2 = 36$$
$$2x + 2 + (-2) = 36 + (-2)$$

$$2x = 34$$

$$x = 17$$

Plugging 17 in for x, we find the second odd integer = $(x + 2) = (17 + 2) =$ 19. Therefore, we find that the two consecutive odd integers whose sum is 36 are 17 and 19, respectively.

☞ Drill: Algebraic

Algebraic Word Problems

DIRECTIONS: Solve the following word problems algebraically.

1. The sum of two numbers is 41. One number is one less than twice the other. Find the larger of the two numbers.

(A) 13   (B) 14   (C) 21   (D) 27   (E) 41

2. The sum of two consecutive integers is 111. Three times the larger integer less two times the smaller integer is 58. Find the value of the smaller integer.

(A) 55   (B) 56   (C) 58   (D) 111   (E) 112

3. The difference between two integers is 12. The sum of the two integers is 2. Find both integers.

(A) 7 and 5   (B) 7 and – 5   (C) – 7 and 5

(D) 2 and 12   (E) – 2 and 12

RATE

One of the formulas you will use for rate problems will be

Rate × Time = Distance

PROBLEM

If a plane travels five hours from New York to California at a speed of 600 miles per hour, how many miles does the plane travel?

SOLUTION

Using the formula rate × time = distance, multiply 600 mph × 5 hours

= 3,000 miles.

The average rate at which an object travels can be solved by dividing the total distance traveled by the total amount of time.

PROBLEM

On a 40-mile bicycle trip, Cathy rode half the distance at 20 mph and the other half at 10 mph. What was Cathy's average speed on the bike trip?

SOLUTION

First you need to break down the problem. On half of the trip which would be 20 miles, Cathy rode 20 mph. Using the rate formula,

$$\frac{\text{distance}}{\text{rate}} = \text{time},$$

you would compute,

$$\frac{20 \text{ miles}}{20 \text{ miles per hour}} = 1 \text{ hour}$$

to travel the first 20 miles. During the second 20 miles, Cathy traveled at 10 miles per hour, which would be

$$\frac{20 \text{ miles}}{10 \text{ miles per hour}} = 2 \text{ hours}$$

Thus, the average speed Cathy traveled would be $^{40}/_3 = 13.3$ miles per hour.

In solving for some rate problems you can use cross multiplication involving ratios to solve for x.

PROBLEM

If 2 pairs of shoes cost $52, then what is the cost of 10 pairs of shoes at this rate?

SOLUTION

$$\frac{2}{52} = \frac{10}{x}, \; 2x = 52 \times 10, \; x = \frac{520}{2}, \; x = \$260$$

☞ Drill: Rate

Rate Word Problems

<u>DIRECTIONS</u>: Solve to find the rate.

1. Two towns are 420 miles apart. A car leaves the first town traveling toward the second town at 55 mph. At the same time, a second car leaves the other town and heads toward the first town at 65 mph. How long will it take for the two cars to meet?

(A) 2 hr   (B) 3 hr   (C) 3.5 hr   (D) 4 hr   (E) 4.25 hr

2. A camper leaves the campsite walking due east at a rate of 3.5 mph. Another camper leaves the campsite at the same time but travels due west. In two hours the two campers will be 15 miles apart. What is the walking rate of the second camper?

(A) 2.5 mph   (B) 3 mph   (C) 3.25 mph

(D) 3.5 mph   (E) 4 mph

3. A bicycle racer covers a 75 mile training route to prepare for an upcoming race. If the racer could increase his speed by 5 mph, he could complete the same course in $3/4$ of the time. Find his average rate of speed.

(A) 15 mph   (B) 15.5 mph   (C) 16 mph

(D) 18 mph   (E) 20 mph

WORK

In work problems, one of the basic formulas is

$$\frac{1}{x} + \frac{1}{y} = \frac{1}{z}$$

where x and y represent the number of hours it takes two objects or people to complete the work and z is the total number of hours working together.

PROBLEM

> Otis can seal and stamp 400 envelopes in 2 hours while Elizabeth seals and stamps 400 envelopes in 1 hour. In how many hours can Otis and Elizabeth, working together, complete a 400-piece mailing at these rates?

SOLUTION

$$\frac{1}{2} + \frac{1}{1} = \frac{1}{z}$$

$$\frac{1}{2} + \frac{2}{2} = \frac{3}{2}$$

$$\frac{3}{2} = \frac{1}{z}$$

$$3z = 2$$

$z = {}^2/_3$ of an hour or 40 minutes. Working together, Otis and Elizabeth can seal and stamp 400 envelopes in 40 minutes.

☞ Drill: Work

Work Word Problems

<u>DIRECTIONS</u>: Solve to find amount of work.

1. It takes Marty 3 hours to type the address labels for his club's newsletter. It only takes Pat $2^1/_4$ hours to type the same amount of labels. How long would it take them working together to complete the address labels?

(A) $\frac{7}{9}$ hr

(B) $1\frac{2}{7}$ hr

(C) $1\frac{4}{5}$ hour

(D) $2\frac{5}{8}$ hr

(E) $5\frac{1}{4}$ hr

2. It takes Troy 3 hours to mow his family's large lawn. With his little brother's help, he can finish the job in only 2 hours. How long would it take the little brother to mow the entire lawn alone?

) 4 hr   (B) 5 hr   (C) 5.5 hr   (D) 6 hr   (E) 6.75 hr

3. A tank can be filled by one inlet pipe in 15 minutes. It takes an outlet pipe 75 minutes to drain the tank. If the outlet pipe is left open by accident, how long would it take to fill the tank?

(A) 15.5 min   (B) 15.9 min   (C) 16.8 min

(D) 18.75 min   (E) 19.3 min

MIXTURE

Mixture problems present the combination of different products and ask you to solve for different parts of the mixture.

PROBLEM

A chemist has an 18% solution and a 45% solution of a disinfectant. How many ounces of each should be used to make 12 ounces of a 36% solution?

SOLUTION

Let x = Number of ounces from the 18% solution, and

y = Number of ounces from the 45% solution.

$$x + y = 12 \tag{1}$$

$$.18x + .45y = .36(12) \tag{2}$$

Note that .18 of the first solution is pure disinfectant and that .45 of the second solution is pure disinfectant. When the proper quantities are drawn from each mixture the result is 12 ounces of mixture which is .36 pure disinfectant.

The second equation cannot be solved with two unknowns. Therefore, write one variable in terms of the other and plug it into the second equation.

$$x = 12 - y \tag{1}$$

$$.18(12 - y) + .45y = .36(12) \tag{2}$$

Simplifying,

$$2.16 - .18y + .45y = 4.32$$

$$.27y = 4.32 - 2.16$$

$$.27y = 2.16$$

$$y = 8$$

Plugging in for *y* in the first equation,

$$x + 8 = 12$$

$$x = 4$$

Therefore, 4 ounces of the first and 8 ounces of the second solution should be used.

PROBLEM

> Clark pays $2.00 per pound for 3 pounds of peanut butter chocolates and then decides to buy 2 pounds of chocolate covered raisins at $2.50 per pound. If Clark mixes both together, what is the cost per pound of the mixture?

SOLUTION

The total mixture is 5 pounds and the total value of the chocolates is

$$3(\$2.00) + 2(\$2.50) = \$11.00$$

The price per pound of the chocolates is

$$\frac{\$11.00}{5 \text{ pounds}} = \$2.20.$$

☞ Drill: Mixture

Mixture Word Problems

<u>DIRECTIONS</u>: Find the appropriate solution.

1. How many liters of a 20% alcohol solution must be added to 80 liters of a 50% alcohol solution to form a 45% solution?

(A) 4   (B) 8   (C) 16   (D) 20   (E) 32

2. How many kilograms of water must be evaporated from 50 kg of a 10% salt solution to obtain a 15% salt solution?

(A) 15   (B) 15.75   (C) 16   (D) $16.\overline{66}$ (E) 16.75

3. How many pounds of coffee *A* at $3.00 a pound should be mixed with 2.5 pounds of coffee *B* at $4.20 a pound to form a mixture selling for $3.75 a pound?

(A) 1   (B) 1.5   (C) 1.75   (D) 2   (E) 2.25

INTEREST

If the problem calls for computing simple interest, the interest is computed on the principal alone. If the problem involves compounded interest, then the interest on the principal is taken into account in addition to the interest earned before.

PROBLEM

> How much interest will Jerry pay on his loan of $400 for 60 days at 6% per year?

SOLUTION

Use the formula:

Interest = Principal × Rate × Time ($I = P \times R \times T$).

$$\$400 \times 6\%/\text{year} \times 60 \text{ days} = \$400 \times .06 \times \frac{60}{365}$$

$$= \$400 \times 0.00986 = \$3.94$$

Jerry will pay $4.00.

PROBLEM

> Mr. Smith wishes to find out how much interest he will receive on $300 if the rate is 3% compounded annually for three years.

SOLUTION

Compound interest is interest computed on both the principal and the interest it has previously earned. The interest is added to the principal at the end of every year. The interest on the first year is found by multiplying the rate by the principal. Hence, the interest for the first year is

$$3\% \times \$300 = .03 \times \$300 = \$9.00.$$

The principal for the second year is now $309, the old principal ($300) plus the interest ($9). The interest for the second year is found by multiplying the rate by the new principal. Hence, the interest for the second year is

$$3\% \times \$309 = .03 \times \$309 = \$9.27.$$

The principal now becomes $309 + $9.27 = $318.27.

The interest for the third year is found using this new principal. It is

$$3\% \times \$318.27 = .03 \times \$318.27 = \$9.55.$$

At the end of the third year his principal is $318.27 + 9.55 = $327.82. To find how much interest was earned, we subtract his starting principal ($300) from his ending principal ($327.82) to obtain

$$327.82 - $300.00 = $27.82.$$

☞ Drill: Interest

Interest Word Problems

DIRECTIONS: Determine the amount of money invested or possible amount earned as appropriate.

1. A man invests $3,000, part in a 12-month certificate of deposit paying 8% and the rest in municipal bonds that pay 7% a year. If the yearly return from both investments is $220, how much was invested in bonds?

(A) $80   (B) $140   (C) $220   (D) $1,000   (E) $2,000

2. A sum of money was invested at 11% a year. Four times that amount was invested at 7.5%. How much was invested at 11% if the total annual return was $1,025?

(A) $112.75   (B) $1,025   (C) $2,500

(D) $3,400   (E) $10,000

3. One bank pays 6.5% a year simple interest on a savings account while a credit union pays 7.2% a year. If you had $1,500 to invest for three years, how much more would you earn by putting the money in the credit union?

(A) $10.50   (B) $31.50   (C) $97.50   (D) $108   (E) $1,500

DISCOUNT

If the discount problem asks to find the final price after the discount, first multiply the original price by the percent of discount. Then subtract this result from the original price.

If the problem asks to find the original price when only the percent of discount and the discounted price are given, simply subtract the percent of discount from 100% and divide this percent into the sale price. This will give you the original price.

PROBLEM

> A popular bookstore gives 10% discount to students. What does a student actually pay for a book costing $24.00?

SOLUTION

10% of $24 is $2.40 and hence the student pays

$24 – $2.40 = $21.60.

PROBLEM

> Eugene paid $100 for a business suit. The suit's price included a 25% discount. What was the original price of the suit?

SOLUTION

Let x represent the original price of the suit and take the complement of .25 (discount price) which is .75.

$.75x = 100 or $x = 133.34.$

So, the original price of the suit is $133.34.

☞ Drill: Discount

Discount Word Problems

DIRECTIONS: Find cost, price, or discount as appropriate.

1. A man bought a coat marked 20% off for $156. How much had the coat cost originally?

(A) $136   (B) $156   (C) $175   (D) $195   (E) $205

2. A woman saved $225 on the new sofa which was on sale for 30% off. What was the original price of the sofa?

(A) $25   (B) $200   (C) $225   (D) $525   (E) $750

3. At an office supply store, customers are given a discount if they pay in cash. If a customer is given a discount of $9.66 on a total order of $276, what is the percent of discount?

(A) 2%   (B) 3.5%   (C) 4.5%   (D) 9.66%   (E) 276%

PROFIT

The formula used for the profit problems is

Profit = Revenue – Cost

or Profit = Selling Price – Expenses.

PROBLEM

Four high school and college friends started a business of remodeling and selling old automobiles during the summer. For this purpose they paid $600 to rent an empty barn for the summer. They obtained the cars from a dealer for $250 each, and it takes an average of $410 in materials to remodel each car. How many automobiles must the students sell at $1,440 each to obtain a gross profit of $7,000?

SOLUTION

Total Revenues – Total Cost = Gross Profit

Revenue – [Variable Cost + Fixed Cost] = Gross Profit

Let a = number of cars

Revenue = $1,440$a$

Variable Cost = ($250 + 410)$a$

Fixed Cost = $600

The desired gross profit is $7,000.

Using the equation for the gross profit,

$$1,440a - [660a + 600] = 7,000$$

$$1,440a - 660a - 600 = 7,000$$

$$780a = 7,000 + 600$$

$$780a = 7,600$$

$$a = 9.74$$

or to the nearest car, $a = 10$.

PROBLEM

A glass vase sells for $25.00. The net profit is 7%, and the operating expenses are 39%. Find the gross profit on the vase.

SOLUTION

The gross profit is equal to the net profit plus the operating expenses. The net profit is 7% of the selling cost; thus, it is equal to

$$7\% \times \$25.00 = .07 \times \$25 = \$1.75.$$

The operating expenses are 39% of the selling price, thus equal to

$$39\% \times \$25 = .39 \times \$25 = \$9.75.$$

$$
\begin{array}{rl}
\$1.75 & \text{net profit} \\
+\ \$9.75 & \text{operating expenses} \\
\hline
\$11.50 & \text{gross profit}
\end{array}
$$

☞ Drill: Profit

Profit Word Problems

DIRECTIONS: Determine profit or stock worth as appropriate.

1. An item cost a store owner $50. She marked it up 40% and advertised it at that price. How much profit did she make if she later sold it at 15% off the advertised price?

(A) $7.50   (B) $9.50   (C) $10.50   (D) $39.50   (E) $50

2. An antique dealer makes a profit of 115% on the sale of an oak desk. If the desk cost her $200, how much profit did she make on the sale?

(A) $230   (B) $315   (C) $430   (D) $445   (E) $475

3. As a graduation gift, a young man was given 100 shares of stock worth $27.50 apiece. Within a year the price of the stock had risen by 8%. How much more were the stocks worth at the end of the first year than when they were given to the young man?

(A) $110   (B) $220   (C) $1,220   (D) $2,750   (E) $2,970

SETS

A **set** is any collection of well defined objects called elements.

A set which contains only a finite number of elements is called a **finite set**; a set which contains an infinite number of elements is called an **infinite set**. Often the sets are designated by listing their elements. For example:

{*a, b, c, d*} is the set which contains elements *a, b, c,* and *d.*

The set of positive integers is {1, 2, 3, 4, ...}.

Venn diagrams can represent sets. These diagrams are circles which help to visualize the relationship between members or objects of a set.

PROBLEM

In a certain Broadway show audition, it was asked of 30 performers if they knew how to either sing or dance, or both. If 20 auditioners said they could dance and 14 said they could sing, how many could sing and dance?

SOLUTION

Divide the 30 people into 3 sets: those who dance, those who sing, and those who dance and sing. S is the number of people who both sing and dance. So $20 - S$ represents the number of people who dance and $14 - S$ represents the number of people who sing.

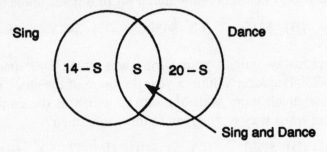

The equation for this problem is as follows:

$$(20 - S) + S + (14 - S) = 30$$
$$20 + 14 - 30 = S$$
$$34 - 30 = S$$
$$4 = S$$

So, 4 people in the audition both sing and dance.

☞ Drill: Sets

Set Word Problems

DIRECTIONS: Determine the appropriate set.

1. In a small school there are 147 sophomores. Sophomores are required to take either Chemistry, Biology or both. Ninety-six take Biology and 83 take Chemistry. How many students take both courses?

    (A) 32   (B) 51   (C) 64   (D) 83   (E) 96

2. In a survey of 100 people, 73 owned only stocks. Six of the people invested in both stocks and bonds. How many people owned bonds only?

    (A) 6   (B) 21   (C) 73   (D) 94   (E) 100

3. On a field trip, the teachers counted the orders for a snack and sent the information in with a few people. The orders were for 77 colas only and 39 fries only. If there were 133 orders, how many were for colas and fries?

    (A) 17   (B) 56   (C) 77   (D) 95   (E) 150

GEOMETRY

PROBLEM

A boy knows that his height is 6 ft. and his shadow is 4 ft. long. At the same time of day, a tree's shadow is 24 ft. long. How high is the tree? (See the figure.)

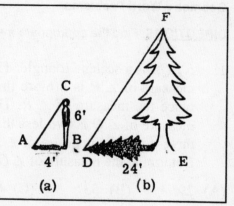

SOLUTION

Show that $\triangle ABC \approx \triangle DEF$, and then set up a proportion between the known sides $\overline{AB}$ and $\overline{DE}$, and the sides $\overline{BC}$ and $\overline{EF}$.

First, assume that both the boy and the tree are $\perp$ to the earth. Then, $\overline{BC} \perp \overline{BA}$ and $\overline{EF} \perp \overline{ED}$. Hence,

$$\angle ABC \cong \angle DEF.$$

Since it is the same time of day, the rays of light from the sun are incident on both the tree and the boy at the same angle, relative to the earth's surface. Therefore,

$$\angle BAC \cong \angle EDF.$$

We have shown, so far, that two pairs of corresponding angles are congruent. Since the sum of the angles of any triangle is 180°, the third pair of corresponding angles is congruent (i.e., $\angle ACB \cong \angle DFE$). By the Angle-Angle-Angle Theorem

$$\angle ABC \approx \angle DEF.$$

By definition of similarity,

$$\frac{\overline{FE}}{\overline{CB}} = \frac{\overline{ED}}{\overline{BA}}$$

$\overline{CB} = 6'$, $\overline{ED} = 24'$, and $\overline{BA} = 4'$. Therefore,

$$FE = (6') \left(\frac{24'}{4'} \right) = 36'.$$

☞ Drill: Geometry

Geometry Word Problems

<u>DIRECTIONS</u>: Find the appropriate measurements.

1. $\triangle PQR$ is a scalene triangle. The measure of $\angle P$ is 8 more than twice the measure of $\angle R$. The measure of $\angle Q$ is two less than three times the measure of $\angle R$. Determine the measure of $\angle Q$.

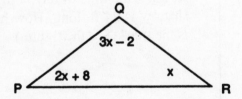

(A) 29° (B) 53° (C) 60°

(D) 85° (E) 174°

2.   Angle A and angle B are supplementary. The measure of angle B is 5 more than four times the measure of angle A. Find the measure of angle B.

(A) 35°   (B) 125°   (C) 140°   (D) 145°   (E) 155°

3.   Triangle *RUS* is isosceles with base $\overline{SU}$. Each leg is 3 less than 5 times the length of the base. If the perimeter of the triangle is 60 cm, find the length of a leg.

(A) 6 cm   (B) 12 cm   (C) 27 cm   (D) 30 cm   (E) 33 cm

MEASUREMENT

When measurement problems are presented in either metric or English units which involve conversion of units, the appropriate data will be given in the problem.

PROBLEM

The Eiffel Tower is 984 feet high. Express this height in meters, in kilometers, in centimeters, and in millimeters.

SOLUTION

A meter is equivalent to 39.370 inches. In this problem, the height of the tower in feet must be converted to inches and then the inches can be converted to meters. There are 12 inches in 1 foot. Therefore, feet can be converted to inches by using the factor 12 inches/1 foot.

$$984 \text{ feet} \times 12\text{in}/1 \text{ ft} = 118 \times 10^2 \text{ inches.}$$

Once the height is found in inches, this can be converted to meters by the factor 1 meter/39.370 inches.

$$11{,}808 \text{ in} \times 1 \text{ m}/39.370 \text{ inches} = 300 \text{ m.}$$

Therefore, the height in meters is 300 m.

There are 1,000 meters in one kilometer. Meters can be converted to kilometers by using the factor 1 km/1,000 m.

$$300 \text{ m} \times 1 \text{ km}/1{,}000 \text{ m} = .300 \text{ km.}$$

As such, there are .300 kilometers in 300 m.

There are 100 centimeters in 1 meter, thus meters can be converted to centimeters by multiplying by the factor 100 cm/1 m.

300 m × 100 cm/1 m = 300 × 10^2 cm.

There are 30,000 centimeters in 300 m.

There are 1,000 millimeters in 1 meter; therefore, meters can be converted to millimeters by the factor 1,000 mm/1 m.

300 m × 1,000 mm/1 m = 300 × 10^3 mm.

There are 300,000 millimeters in 300 meters.

PROBLEM

> The unaided eye can perceive objects which have a diameter of 0.1 mm. What is the diameter in inches?

SOLUTION

From a standard table of conversion factors, one can find that 1 inch = 2.54 cm. Thus, cm can be converted to inches by multiplying by 1 inch/2.54 cm. Here, one is given the diameter in mm, which is .1 cm. Millimeters are converted to cm by multiplying the number of mm by .1 cm/1 mm. Solving for cm, you obtain

0.1 mm × .1 cm/1 mm = .01 cm.

Solving for inches:

$$0.01 \text{ cm} \times \frac{1 \text{ inch}}{2.54 \text{ cm}} = 3.94 = 10^{-3} \text{ inches.}$$

☞ Drill: Measurement

Measurement Word Problems

<u>DIRECTIONS</u>: Determine the appropriate solution from the information provided.

1. A brick walkway measuring 3 feet by 11 feet is to be built. The bricks measure 4 inches by 6 inches. How many bricks will it take to complete the walkway?

(A) 132   (B) 198   (C) 330   (D) 1,927   (E) 4,752

2. A wall to be papered is three times as long as it is wide. The total area to be covered is 192 ft^2. Wallpaper comes in rolls that are 2 feet wide by 8 feet long. How many rolls will it take to cover the wall?

(A) 8   (B) 12   (C) 16   (D) 24   (E) 32

3.   A bottle of medicine containing 2 kg is to be poured into smaller containers that hold 8 grams each. How many of these smaller containers can be filled from the 2 kg bottle?

(A) 0.5   (B) 1   (C) 5   (D) 50   (E) 250

DATA INTERPRETATION

Some of the problems test ability to apply information given in graphs and tables.

PROBLEM

> In which year was the least number of bushels of wheat produced? (See figure below.)

SOLUTION

By inspection of the graph, we find that the shortest bar representing wheat production is the one representing the wheat production for 1976. Thus, the least number of bushels of wheat was produced in 1976.

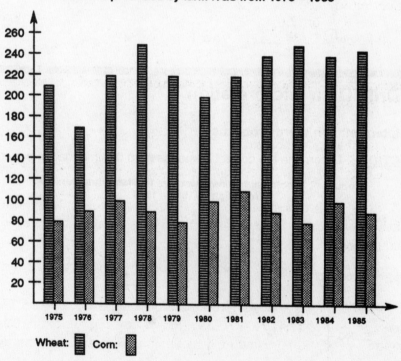

Number of bushels (to the nearest 5 bushels) of wheat and corn produced by farm RQS from 1975 – 1985

PROBLEM

What was the ratio of wheat production in 1985 to that of 1975?

SOLUTION

From the graph representing wheat production, the number of bushels of wheat produced in 1975 is equal to 210 bushels. This number can be found by locating the bar on the graph representing wheat production in 1975 and then drawing a horizontal line from the top of that bar to the vertical axis. The point where this horizontal line meets the vertical axis represents the number of bushels of wheat produced in 1975. This number on the vertical axis is 210. Similarly, the graph indicates that the number of bushels of wheat produced in 1985 is equal to 245 bushels.

Thus, the ratio of wheat production in 1985 to that of 1975 is 245 to 210, which can be written as $^{245}/_{210}$. Simplifying this ratio to its simplest form yields

$$\frac{245}{210} = \frac{5 \times 7 \times 7}{2 \times 3 \times 5 \times 7}$$

$$= \frac{7}{2 \times 3}$$

$$= \frac{7}{6} \text{ or } 7:6$$

☞ Drill: Data Interpretation

Date Interpretation Word Problems

DIRECTIONS: Determine the correct response from the information provided.

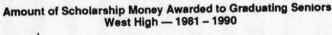

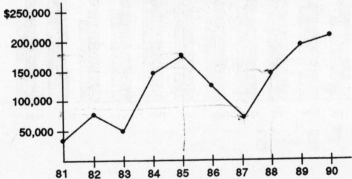

Amount of Scholarship Money Awarded to Graduating Seniors
West High — 1981 – 1990

1. What was the approximate amount of scholarship money awarded in 1985?

(A) $150,000   (B) $155,000   (C) $165,000

(D) $175,000   (E) $190,000

2. By how much did the scholarship money increase between 1987 and 1988?

(A) $25,000   (B) $30,000   (C) $50,000

(D) $55,000   (E) $75,000

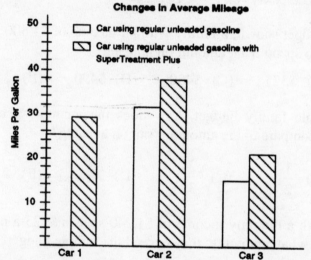

Changes in Average Mileage

3. By how much did the mileage increase for Car 2 when the new product was used?

(A) 5 mpg   (B) 6 mpg   (C) 7 mpg   (D) 10 mpg   (E) 12 mpg

4. Which car's mileage increased the most in this test?

(A) Car 1   (B) Car 2   (C) Car 3

(D) Cars 1 and 2   (E) Cars 2 and 3

5. According to the bar graph, if your car averages 25 mpg, what mileage might you expect with the new product?

(A) 21 mpg   (B) 30 mpg   (C) 31 mpg   (D) 35 mpg   (E) 37 mpg

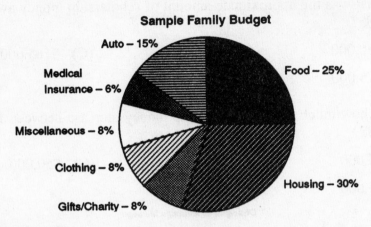

Sample Family Budget

Auto – 15%
Medical Insurance – 6%
Miscellaneous – 8%
Clothing – 8%
Gifts/Charity – 8%
Food – 25%
Housing – 30%

6. Using the budget shown, a family with an income of $1,500 a month would plan to spend what amount on housing?

(A) $300   (B) $375   (C) $450   (D) $490   (E) $520

7. In this sample family budget, how does the amount spent on an automobile compare to the amount spent on housing?

(A) $\frac{1}{3}$ (B) $\frac{1}{2}$ (C) $\frac{2}{3}$ (D) $1\frac{1}{2}$ (E) 2

8. A family with a monthly income of $1,240 spends $125 a month on clothing. By what amount do they exceed the sample budget?

(A) $1.00   (B) $5.20   (C) $10.00   (D) $25.80   (E) $31.75

CALORIE CHART — BREADS

Bread	Amount	Calories
French Bread	2 oz	140
Bran Bread	1 oz	95
Whole Wheat Bread	1 oz	115
Oatmeal Bread	0.5 oz	55
Raisin Bread	1 oz	125

9. One dieter eats two ounces of french bread. A second dieter eats two ounces of bran bread. The second dieter has consumed how many more calories than the first dieter?

(A) 40   (B) 45   (C) 50   (D) 55   (E) 65

10. One ounce of whole wheat bread has how many more calories than an ounce of oatmeal bread?

(A) 5   (B) 15   (C) 60   (D) 75   (E) 125

WORD PROBLEM DRILLS

ANSWER KEY

Drill: Algebraic

1. (D)   2. (A)   3. (B)

Drill: Rate

1. (C)   2. (E)   3. (A)

Drill: Work

1. (B)   2. (D)   3. (D)

Drill: Mixture

1. (C)   2. (D)   3. (B)

Drill: Interest

1. (E)   2. (C)   3. (B)

Drill: Discount

1. (D)   2. (E)   3. (B)

Drill: Profit

1. (B)   2. (A)   3. (B)

Drill: Sets

1. (A)   2. (B)   3. (A)

Drill: Geometry

1. (D)   2. (D)   3. (C)

Drill: Measurement

1. (B)   2. (B)   3. (E)

Drill: Data Interpretation

1. (D)	4. (E)	7. (B)	10. (A)
2. (E)	5. (B)	8. (D)	
3. (B)	6. (C)	9. (C)	

PPST
Pre-Professional Skills Tests

Chapter 4
Writing Skills
Review

Chapter 4

WRITING SKILLS REVIEW

The requirements for informal spoken English are much more relaxed than the rigid rules for "standard written English." While slang, colloquialisms, and other informal expressions are acceptable and sometimes very appropriate in casual speech, they are inappropriate in academic and business writing. More often than not, writers, especially student writers, do not make a distinction between the two: they use the same words, grammar, and sentence structure from their everyday speech in their college papers, albeit unsuccessfully.

The PPST does not require you to know grammatical terms such as *gerund, subject complement,* or *dependent clause,* although general familiarity with such terms may be helpful to you in determining whether a sentence or part of a sentence is correct or incorrect. You should watch for errors in grammar, spelling, punctuation, capitalization, sentence structure, and word choice. Remember: this is a test of written language skills; therefore, your responses should be based on what you know to be correct for written work, not what you know to be appropriate for a casual conversation. For instance, in informal speech, you might say "Who are you going to choose?" But in formal academic writing, you would write "Whom are you going to choose?" Your choices, then, should be dictated by requirements for *written,* not *conversational* English.

WORD CHOICE SKILLS

Connotative and Denotative Meanings

The denotative meaning of a word is its *literal,* dictionary definition: what the word denotes or "means." The connotative meaning of a word is what the word connotes or "suggests"; it is a meaning apart from what the word literally means. A writer should choose a word based on the tone and

context of the sentence; this ensures that a word bears the appropriate connotation while still conveying some exactness in denotation. For example, a gift might be described as "cheap," but the directness of this word has a negative connotation—something cheap is something of little or no value. The word "inexpensive" has a more positive connotation, though "cheap" is a synonym for "inexpensive." Questions of this type require you to make a decision regarding the appropriateness of words and phrases for the context of a sentence.

Wordiness and Conciseness

Effective writing is concise. Wordiness, on the other hand, decreases the clarity of expression by cluttering sentences with unnecessary words.

Wordiness questions test your ability to detect redundancies (unnecessary repetitions), circumlocution (failure to get to the point), and padding with loose synonyms. Wordiness questions require you to choose sentences that use as few words as possible to convey a message clearly, economically, and effectively.

Notice the difference in impact between the first and second sentences in the following pairs:

INCORRECT: The medical exam that he gave me was entirely complete.

CORRECT: The medical exam he gave me was complete.

INCORRECT: Larry asked his friend John, who was a good, old friend, if he would join him and go along with him to see the foreign film made in Japan.

CORRECT: Larry asked his good, old friend John if he would join him in seeing the Japanese film.

INCORRECT: I was absolutely, totally happy with the present that my parents gave to me at 7 a.m. on the morning of my birthday.

CORRECT: I was happy with the present my parents gave me on the morning of my birthday.

☞ Drill: Word Choice Skills

> **DIRECTIONS:** Choose the correct option.

1. His <u>principal</u> reasons for resigning were his <u>principles</u> of right and wrong.

   (A) principal . . . principals   (C) principle . . . principles

   (B) principle . . . principals   (D) No change is necessary.

2. The book tells about Alzheimer's disease—how it <u>affects</u> the patient and what <u>effect</u> it has on the patient's family.

   (A) effects . . . affect   (C) effects . . . effects

   (B) affects . . . affect   (D) No change is necessary.

3. The <u>amount</u> of homeless children we can help depends on the <u>number</u> of available shelters.

   (A) number . . . number   (C) number . . . amount

   (B) amount . . . amount   (D) No change is necessary.

4. All students are <u>suppose to</u> pass the test before <u>achieving</u> upper-division status.

   (A) suppose to . . . acheiving

   (B) suppose to . . . being achieved

   (C) supposed to . . . achieving

   (D) No change is necessary.

5. The reason he <u>succeeded</u> is <u>because</u> he worked hard.

   (A) succeeded . . . that   (C) succede . . . because of

   (B) seceded . . . that   (D) No change is necessary.

DIRECTIONS: Select the sentence that clearly and effectively states the idea and has no structural errors.

6. (A) South of Richmond, the two roads converge together to form a single highway.

   (B) South of Richmond, the two roads converge together to form an interstate highway.

   (C) South of Richmond, the two roads converge to form an interstate highway.

   (D) South of Richmond, the two roads converge to form a single interstate highway.

7. (A) The student depended on his parents for financial support.

   (B) The student lacked the ways and means to pay for his room and board, so he depended on his parents for this kind of money and support.

   (C) The student lacked the ways and means or the wherewithal to support himself, so his parents provided him with the financial support he needed.

   (D) The student lacked the means to pay for his room and board, so he depended on his parents for financial support.

8. (A) Vincent van Gogh and Paul Gaugin were close personal friends and companions who enjoyed each other's company and frequently worked together on their artwork.

   (B) Vincent van Gogh and Paul Gaugin were friends who frequently painted together.

   (C) Vincent van Gogh was a close personal friend of Paul Gaugin's, and the two of them often worked together on their artwork because they enjoyed each other's company.

   (D) Vincent van Gogh, a close personal friend of Paul Gaugin's, often worked with him on their artwork.

9. (A) A college education often involves putting away childish thoughts, which are characteristic of youngsters, and concentrating on the future, which lies ahead.

(B) A college education involves putting away childish thoughts, which are characteristic of youngsters, and concentrating on the future.

(C) A college education involves putting away childish thoughts and concentrating on the future.

(D) A college education involves putting away childish thoughts and concentrating on the future which lies ahead.

10. (A) I had the occasion to visit an Oriental pagoda while I was a tourist on vacation and visiting in Kyoto, Japan.

(B) I visited a Japanese pagoda in Kyoto.

(C) I had occasion to visit a pagoda when I was vacationing in Kyoto, Japan.

(D) On my vacation, I visited a Japanese pagoda in Kyoto.

SENTENCE STRUCTURE SKILLS

Parallelism

Parallel structure is used to express matching ideas. It refers to the grammatical balance of a series of any of the following:

Phrases:

The squirrel ran *along the fence, up the tree,* and *into his burrow* with a mouthful of acorns.

Adjectives:

The job market is flooded with *very talented, highly motivated,* and *well-educated* young people.

Nouns:

You will need a *notebook, pencil,* and *dictionary* for the test.

Clauses:

The children were told to decide *which toy they would keep* and *which toy they would give away.*

Verbs:

The farmer *plowed, planted,* and *harvested* his corn in record time.

Verbals:

Reading, writing, and *calculating* are fundamental skills that all of us should possess.

Correlative conjunctions:

Either you will do your homework *or* you will fail.

Repetition of structural signals:

(such as articles, auxiliaries, prepositions, and conjunctions)

INCORRECT: I have quit my job, enrolled in school, and am looking for a reliable babysitter.

CORRECT: I *have quit* my job, *have enrolled* in school, and *am looking* for a reliable babysitter.

Note: Repetition of prepositions is considered formal and is not necessary.

You can travel *by car, by plane, or by train;* it's all up to you.

OR

You can travel *by car, plane, or train;* it's all up to you.

When a sentence contains items in a series, check for both punctuation and sentence balance. When you check for punctuation, make sure the commas are used correctly. When you check for parallelism, make sure that the conjunctions connect similar grammatical constructions, such as all adjectives or all clauses.

Misplaced and Dangling Modifiers

A misplaced modifier is one that is in the wrong place in the sentence. Misplaced modifiers come in all forms—words, phrases, and clauses. Sentences containing misplaced modifiers are often very comical: *Mom made me eat the spinach instead of my brother.* Misplaced modifiers, like the one in this sentence, are usually too far away from the word or words they modify. This sentence should read: *Mom made me, instead of my brother, eat the spinach.*

Modifiers like *only*, *nearly*, and *almost* should be placed next to the word they modify and not in front of some other word, especially a verb, that they are not intended to modify.

A modifier is misplaced if it appears to modify the wrong part of the sentence or if we cannot be certain what part of the sentence the writer intended it to modify. To correct a misplaced modifier, move the modifier next to the word it describes.

> INCORRECT: She served hamburgers to the men on paper plates.

> CORRECT: She served hamburgers on paper plates to the men.

Split infinitives also result in misplaced modifiers. Infinitives consist of the marker *to* plus the plain form of the verb. The two parts of the infinitive make up a grammatical unit that should not be split. Splitting an infinitive is placing an adverb between the *to* and the verb.

> INCORRECT: The weather service expects temperatures to not rise.

> CORRECT: The weather service expects temperatures not to rise.

Sometimes a split infinitive may be natural and preferable, though it may still bother some readers.

> EX: Several U.S. industries expect *to* more than *triple* their use of robots within the next decade.

A squinting modifier is one that may refer to either a preceding or a following word, leaving the reader uncertain about what it is intended to modify. Correct a squinting modifier by moving it next to the word it is intended to modify.

> INCORRECT: Snipers who fired on the soldiers often escaped capture.

> CORRECT: Snipers who often fired on the soldiers escaped capture.

> OR Snipers who fired on the soldiers escaped capture often.

A dangling modifier is a modifier or verb in search of a subject: the modifying phrase (usually an *-ing* word group, an *-ed* or *-en* word group, or a *to + a verb* word group—participle phrase or infinitive phrase respectively) either appears to modify the wrong word or has nothing to modify. It is literally dangling at the beginning or the end of a sentence. The sentences often look and sound correct: *To be a student government officer, your grades must be above average.* (However, the verbal modifier has nothing to describe. Who is *to be a student government officer*? Your

grades?) Questions of this type require you to determine whether a modifier has a headword or whether it is dangling at the beginning or the end of the sentence.

To correct a dangling modifier, reword the sentence by either: 1) changing the modifying phrase to a clause with a subject, or 2) changing the subject of the sentence to the word that should be modified. The following are examples of a dangling gerund, a dangling infinitive, and a dangling participle:

INCORRECT: Shortly after leaving home, the accident occurred.

Who is <u>leaving home</u>, the accident?

CORRECT: Shortly after we left home, the accident occurred.

INCORRECT: To get up on time, a great effort was needed.

<u>To get up</u> needs a subject.

CORRECT: To get up on time, I made a great effort.

Fragments

A fragment is an incomplete construction which may or may not have a subject and a verb. Specifically, a fragment is a group of words pretending to be a sentence. Not all fragments appear as separate sentences, however. Often, fragments are separated by semicolons.

INCORRECT: Traffic was stalled for ten miles on the freeway. Because repairs were being made on potholes.

CORRECT: Traffic was stalled for ten miles on the freeway because repairs were being made on potholes.

INCORRECT: It was a funny story; one that I had never heard before.

CORRECT: It was a funny story, one that I had never heard before.

Run-on/Fused Sentences

A run-on/fused sentence is not necessarily a long sentence or a sentence that the reader considers too long; in fact, a run-on may be two short sentences: *Dry ice does not melt it evaporates.* A run-on results when the writer fuses or runs together two separate sentences without any correct mark of punctuation separating them.

INCORRECT: Knowing how to use a dictionary is no problem each dictionary has a section in the front of the book telling how to use it.

CORRECT: Knowing how to use a dictionary is no problem. Each dictionary has a section in the front of the book telling how to use it.

Even if one or both of the fused sentences contains internal punctuation, the sentence is still a run-on.

INCORRECT: Bob bought dress shoes, a suit, and a nice shirt he needed them for his sister's wedding.

CORRECT: Bob bought dress shoes, a suit, and a nice shirt. He needed them for his sister's wedding.

Comma Splices

A comma splice is the unjustifiable use of only a comma to combine what really is two separate sentences.

INCORRECT: One common error in writing is incorrect spelling, the other is the occasional use of faulty diction.

CORRECT: One common error in writing is incorrect spelling; the other is the occasional use of faulty diction.

Both run-on sentences and comma splices may be corrected in one of the following ways:

RUN-ON: Neal won the award he had the highest score.

COMMA SPLICE: Neal won the award, he had the highest score.

Separate the sentences with a period:

Neal won the award. He had the highest score.

Separate the sentences with a comma and a coordinating conjunction *(and, but, or, nor, for, yet, so)*:

Neal won the award for he had the highest score.

Separate the sentences with a semicolon:

Neal won the award; he had the highest score.

Separate the sentences with a subordinating conjunction such as *although, because, since, if*:

Neal won the award because he had the highest score.

Subordination, Coordination, and Predication

Suppose, for the sake of clarity, you wanted to combine the information in these two sentences to create one statement:

I studied a foreign language. I found English quite easy.

How you decide to combine this information should be determined by the relationship you'd like to show between the two facts. *I studied a foreign language, and I found English quite easy* seems rather illogical. The **coordination** of the two ideas (connecting them with the coordinating conjunction *and*) is ineffective. Using **subordination** instead (connecting the sentences with a subordinating conjunction) clearly shows the degree of relative importance between the expressed ideas:

After I studied a foreign language, I found English quite easy.

When using a conjunction, be sure that the sentence parts you are joining are in agreement.

INCORRECT: She loved him dearly but not his dog.

CORRECT: She loved him dearly but she did not love his dog.

A common mistake that is made is to forget that each member of the pair must be followed by the same kind of construction.

INCORRECT: They complimented them for their bravery and they thanked them for their being kind.

CORRECT: They complimented them for their bravery and thanked them for their kindness.

While refers to time and should not be used as a substitute for *although, and,* or *but.*

INCORRECT: While I'm usually interested in Fellini movies, I'd rather not go tonight.

CORRECT: Although I'm usually interested in Fellini movies, I'd rather not go tonight.

Where refers to time and should not be used as a substitute for *that.*

INCORRECT: We read in the paper where they are making great strides in DNA research.

CORRECT: We read in the paper that they are making great strides in DNA research.

After words like reason and explanation, use *that*, not *because*.

INCORRECT: His explanation for his tardiness was because his alarm did not go off.

CORRECT: His explanation for his tardiness was that his alarm did not go off.

☞ Drill: Sentence Structure Skills

DIRECTIONS: Choose the sentence that expresses the thought most clearly and that has no error in structure.

1. (A) Many gases are invisible, odorless, and they have no taste.

   (B) Many gases are invisible, odorless, and have no taste.

   (C) Many gases are invisible, odorless, and tasteless.

2. (A) Everyone agreed that she had neither the voice or the skill to be a speaker.

   (B) Everyone agreed that she had neither the voice nor the skill to be a speaker.

   (C) Everyone agreed that she had either the voice nor the skill to be a speaker.

3. (A) The mayor will be remembered because he kept his campaign promises and because of his refusal to accept political favors.

   (B) The mayor will be remembered because he kept his campaign promises and because he refused to accept political favors.

   (C) The mayor will be remembered because of his refusal to accept political favors and he kept his campaign promises.

4. (A) While taking a shower, the doorbell rang.

   (B) While I was taking a shower, the doorbell rang.

   (C) While taking a shower, someone rang the doorbell.

5. (A) He swung the bat, while the runner stole second base.

   (B) The runner stole second base while he swung the bat.

   (C) While he was swinging the bat, the runner stole second base.

DIRECTIONS: Choose the correct option.

---

6. Nothing grows as well in Mississippi as <u>cotton. Cotton</u> being the state's principal crop.

    (A) cotton, cotton   (C) cotton cotton

    (B) cotton; cotton   (D) No change is necessary.

7. It was a heartwrenching <u>movie; one</u> that I had never seen before.

    (A) movie and   (C) movie. One

    (B) movie, one   (D) No change is necessary.

8. Traffic was stalled for three miles on the <u>bridge. Because</u> repairs were being made.

    (A) bridge because   (C) bridge, because

    (B) bridge; because   (D) No change is necessary.

9. The ability to write complete sentences comes with <u>practice writing</u> run-on sentences seems to occur naturally.

    (A) practice, writing   (C) practice and

    (B) practice. Writing   (D) No change is necessary.

10. Even though she had taken French classes, she could not understand native French <u>speakers they</u> all spoke too fast.

    (A) speakers, they   (C) speaking

    (B) speakers. They   (D) No change is necessary.

VERBS

Verb Forms

This section covers the principal parts of some irregular verbs including troublesome verbs like *lie* and *lay*. The use of regular verbs like *look* and *receive* poses no real problem to most writers since the past and past participle forms end in *-ed*; it is the irregular forms which pose the most serious problems—for example, *seen*, *written*, and *begun*.

Verb Tenses

Tense sequence indicates a logical time sequence.

Use present tense

in statements of universal truth:

> I learned that the sun *is* 90 million miles from the earth.

in statements about the contents of literature and other published works:

> In this book, Sandy *becomes* a nun and *writes* a book on psychology.

Use past tense

in statements concerning writing or publication of a book:

> He *wrote* his first book in 1949, and it *was published* in 1952.

Use present perfect tense

for an action that began in the past but continues into the future:

> I *have lived* here all my life.

Use past perfect tense

for an earlier action that is mentioned in a later action:

> Cindy ate the apple that she *had picked*.

(First she picked it, then she ate it.)

Use future perfect tense

for an action that will have been completed at a specific future time:

> By May, I *shall have graduated*.

Use a present participle

for action that occurs at the same time as the verb:

> *Speeding* down the interstate, I saw a cop's flashing lights.

Use a perfect participle

for action that occurred before the main verb:

> *Having read* the directions, I started the test.

Use the subjunctive mood

to express a wish or state a condition contrary to fact:

> *If it were not raining,* we could have a picnic.

in *that* clauses after verbs like *request, recommend, suggest, ask, require,* and *insist*; and after such expressions as *it is important* and *it is necessary*:

> It is necessary that all papers *be* submitted on time.

Subject-Verb Agreement

Agreement is the grammatical correspondence between the subject and the verb of a sentence: *I do; we do; they do; he, she, it does.*

Every English verb has five forms, two of which are the bare form (plural) and the *-s* form (singular). Simply put, singular verb forms end in *-s;* plural forms do not.

Study these rules governing subject-verb agreement:

A verb must agree with its subject, not with any additive phrase in the sentence such as a prepositional or verbal phrase. Ignore such phrases.

> Your *copy* of the rules *is* on the desk.

> Ms. Craig's *record* of community service and outstanding teaching *qualifies* her for a promotion.

In an inverted sentence beginning with a prepositional phrase, the verb still agrees with its subject.

> At the end of the summer *come* the best *sales.*

> Under the house *are* some old Mason *jars.*

Prepositional phrases beginning with compound prepositions such as *along with, together with, in addition to,* and *as well as* should be ignored, for they do not affect subject-verb agreement.

> *Gladys Knight,* as well as the Pips, *is* riding the midnight train to Georgia.

A verb must agree with its subject, not its subject complement.

> *Taxes are* a problem.

> A *problem is* taxes.

When a sentence begins with an expletive such as *there, here,* or *it,* the verb agrees with the subject, not the expletive.

> Surely, there *are* several *alumni* who would be interested in forming a group.

> There *are* 50 *students* in my English class.

> There *is* a horrifying *study* on child abuse in *Psychology Today.*

Indefinite pronouns such as *each, either, one, everyone, everybody,* and *everything* are singular.

> *Somebody* in Detroit *loves* me.

> *Does either* [one] of you have a pencil?

> *Neither* of my brothers *has* a car.

Indefinite pronouns such as *several, few, both,* and *many* are plural.

> *Both* of my sorority sisters *have* decided to live off campus.

> *Few seek* the enlightenment of transcendental meditation.

Indefinite pronouns such as *all, some, most,* and *none* may be singular or plural depending on their referents.

> *Some* of the food *is* cold.

> *Some* of the vegetables *are* cold.

> I can think of some retorts, but *none seem* appropriate.

> *None* of the children *is* as sweet as Sally.

Fractions such as *one-half* and *one-third* may be singular or plural depending on the referent.

> *Half* of the mail *has* been delivered.

> *Half* of the letters *have* been read.

Subjects joined by *and* take a plural verb unless the subjects are thought to be one item or unit.

> *Jim* and *Tammy were* televangelists.

> *Earth, Wind, and Fire is* my favorite group.

In cases when the subjects are joined by *or, nor, either . . . or,* or *neither . . . nor,* the verb must agree with the subject closer to it.

> Either the teacher or the *students are* responsible.

> Neither the students nor the *teacher is* responsible.

Relative pronouns, such as *who, which,* or *that,* which refer to plural antecedents require plural verbs. However, when the relative pronoun refers to a singular subject, the pronoun takes a singular verb.

> She is one of the girls *who cheer* on Friday nights.

> She is the only cheerleader *who has* a broken leg.

Subjects preceded by *every, each,* and *many a* are singular.

> *Every* man, woman, and child *was* given a life preserver.

> *Each* undergraduate *is* required to pass a proficiency exam.

> *Many a* tear *has* to fall before one matures.

A collective noun, such as *audience, faculty, jury,* etc., requires a singular verb when the group is regarded as a whole, and a plural verb when the members of the group are regarded as individuals.

> The *jury has* made its decision.

> The *faculty are* preparing their grade rosters.

Subjects preceded by *the number of* or *the percentage of* are singular, while subjects preceded by *a number of* or *a percentage of* are plural.

> The *number of* vacationers in Florida *increases* every year.

> *A number of* vacationers *are* young couples.

Titles of books, companies, name brands, and groups are singular or plural depending on their meaning.

> *Great Expectations is* my favorite novel.

> The *Rolling Stones are* performing in the Super Dome.

Certain nouns of Latin and Greek origin have unusual singular and plural forms.

Singular	Plural
criterion	criteria
alumnus	alumni
datum	data
medium	media

> The *data are* available for inspection.

> The only *criterion* for membership *is* a high GPA.

Some nouns such as *deer, shrimp,* and *sheep* have the same spellings for both their singular and plural forms. In these cases, the meaning of the

sentence will determine whether they are singular or plural.

>   *Deer are* beautiful animals.

>   The spotted *deer is* licking the sugar cube.

Some nouns like *scissors, jeans,* and *wages* have plural forms but no singular counterparts. These nouns almost always take plural verbs.

>   The *scissors are* on the table.

>   My new *jeans fit* me like a glove.

Words used as examples, not as grammatical parts of the sentence, require singular verbs.

>   *Can't is* the contraction for "cannot."

>   *Cats is* the plural form of "cat."

Mathematical expressions of subtraction and division require singular verbs, while expressions of addition and multiplication take either singular or plural verbs.

>   Ten *divided* by two *equals* five.

>   Five *times* two *equals* ten.

>   OR   Five *times* two *equal* ten.

Nouns expressing time, distance, weight, and measurement are singular when they refer to a unit and plural when they refer to separate items.

>   *Fifty yards is* a short distance.

>   *Ten years have* passed since I finished college.

Expressions of quantity are usually plural.

>   *Nine out of ten* dentists *recommend* that their patients floss.

Some nouns ending in *-ics,* such as *economics* and *ethics,* take singular verbs when they refer to principles or a field of study; however, when they refer to individual practices, they usually take plural verbs.

>   *Ethics is* being taught in the spring.

>   His unusual business *ethics are* what got him into trouble.

Some nouns like *measles, news,* and *calculus* appear to be plural but are actually singular in number. These nouns require singular verbs.

>   *Measles is* a very contagious disease.

>   *Calculus requires* great skill in algebra.

A verbal noun (infinitive or gerund) serving as a subject is treated as singular, even if the object of the verbal phrase is plural.

>*Hiding* your mistakes *does* not make them go away.

>*To run* five miles *is* my goal.

A noun phrase or clause acting as the subject of a sentence requires a singular verb.

>What I need is to be loved.

>Whether there is any connection between them is unknown.

Clauses beginning with *what* may be singular or plural depending on the meaning, that is, whether *what* means "the thing" or "the things."

>What I want for Christmas is a new motorcycle.

>What matters are Clinton's ideas.

A plural subject followed by a singular appositive requires a plural verb; similarly, a singular subject followed by a plural appositive requires a singular verb.

>When the girls throw a party, *they* each bring a *gift*.

>The *board*, all ten members, *is* meeting today.

☞ Drill: Verbs

> **DIRECTIONS:** Choose the correct option.

1. If you <u>had been concerned</u> about Marilyn, you <u>would have went</u> to greater lengths to ensure her safety.

    (A) had been concern . . . would have gone

    (B) was concerned . . . would have gone

    (C) had been concerned . . . would have gone

    (D) No change is necessary.

2. Susan <u>laid</u> in bed too long and missed her class.

    (A) lays   (C) lied

    (B) lay   (D) No change is necessary.

3. The Great Wall of China <u>is</u> fifteen hundred miles long; it <u>was built</u> in the third century B.C.

   (A) was . . . was built

   (B) is . . . is built

   (C) has been . . . was built

   (D) No change is necessary.

4. Joe stated that the class <u>began</u> at 10:30 a.m.

   (A) begins

   (B) had begun

   (C) was beginning

   (D) No change is necessary.

5. The ceiling of the Sistine Chapel <u>was</u> painted by Michelangelo; it <u>depicted</u> scenes from the Creation in the Old Testament.

   (A) was . . . depicts

   (B) is . . . depicts

   (C) has been . . . depicting

   (D) No change is necessary.

6. After Christmas <u>comes</u> the best sales.

   (A) has come

   (B) come

   (C) is coming

   (D) No change is necessary.

7. The bakery's specialty <u>are</u> wedding cakes.

   (A) is

   (B) were

   (C) be

   (D) No change is necessary.

8. Every man, woman, and child <u>were given</u> a life preserver.

   (A) have been given

   (B) had gave

   (C) was given

   (D) No change is necessary.

9. Hiding your mistakes <u>don't</u> make them go away.

   (A) doesn't

   (B) do not

   (C) have not

   (D) No change is necessary.

10. The Board of Regents <u>has recommended</u> a tuition increase.

   (A) have recommended

   (B) has recommend

   (C) had recommended

   (D) No change is necessary.

PRONOUNS

Pronoun Case

Pronoun case questions test your knowledge of the use of nominative and objective case pronouns:

Nominative Case	Objective Case
I	me
he	him
she	her
we	us
they	them
who	whom

This review section answers the most frequently asked grammar questions: when to use *I* and when to use *me*; when to use *who* and when to use *whom*. Some writers avoid *whom* altogether, and instead of distinguishing between *I* and *me*, many writers incorrectly use *myself*.

Use the nominative case (subject pronouns)

for the subject of a sentence:

We students studied until early morning for the final.

Alan and *I* "burned the midnight oil," too.

for pronouns in apposition to the subject:

Only two students, Alex and *I*, were asked to report on the meeting.

for the predicate nominative/subject complement:

The actors nominated for the award were *she* and *I*.

for the subject of an elliptical clause:

Molly is more experienced than *he*.

for the subject of a subordinate clause:

Robert is the driver *who* reported the accident.

for the complement of an infinitive with no expressed subject:

I would not want to be *he*.

Use the objective case (object pronouns)

for the direct object of a sentence:

Mary invited *us* to her party.

for the object of a preposition:

The books that were torn belonged to *her*.

Just between you and *me*, I'm bored.

for the indirect object of a sentence:

Walter gave a dozen red roses to *her*.

for the appositive of a direct object:

The committee elected two delegates, Barbara and *me*.

for the object of an infinitive:

The young boy wanted to help *us* paint the fence.

for the object of a gerund:

Enlisting *him* was surprisingly easy.

for the object of a past participle:

Having called the other students and *us*, the secretary went home for the day.

for a pronoun that precedes an infinitive (the subject of an infinitive):

The supervisor told *him* to work late.

for the complement of an infinitive with an expressed subject:

The fans thought the best player to be *him*.

for the object of an elliptical clause:

Bill tackled Joe harder than *me*.

for the object of a verb in apposition:

Charles invited two extra people, Carmen and *me*, to the party.

When a conjunction connects two pronouns or a pronoun and a noun, remove the "and" and the other pronoun or noun to determine what the correct pronoun form should be:

Mom gave ~~Tom and~~ myself a piece of cake.

Mom gave ~~Tom and~~ I a piece of cake

Mom gave ~~Tom and~~ me a piece of cake.

Removal of these words reveals what the correct pronoun should be:

Mom gave *me* a piece of cake.

The only pronouns that are acceptable after *between* and other prepositions are: *me, her, him, them,* and *whom*. When deciding between *who* and *whom,* try substituting *he* for *who* and *him* for *whom;* then follow these easy transformation steps:

1. Isolate the *who* clause or the *whom* clause:

    whom we can trust

2. Invert the word order, if necessary. Place the words in the clause in the natural order of an English sentence, subject followed by the verb:

    we can trust whom

3. Read the final form with the *he* or *him* inserted:

    We can trust ~~whom~~ him.

When a pronoun follows a comparative conjunction like *than* or *as,* complete the elliptical construction to help you determine which pronoun is correct.

EX: She has more credit hours than me [do].

She has more credit hours than I [do].

Pronoun-Antecedent Agreement

These kinds of questions test your knowledge of using an appropriate pronoun to agree with its antecedent in number (singular or plural form) and gender (masculine, feminine, or neuter). An antecedent is a noun or pronoun to which another noun or pronoun refers.

Here are the two basic rules for pronoun reference-antecedent agreement:

1. Every pronoun must have a conspicuous antecedent.

2. Every pronoun must agree with its antecedent in number, gender, and person.

When an antecedent is one of dual gender like *student, singer, artist, person, citizen,* etc., use *his* or *her*. Some careful writers change the antecedent to a plural noun to avoid using the sexist, singular masculine pronoun *his*:

INCORRECT: Everyone hopes that he will win the lottery.

CORRECT: Most people hope that they will win the lottery.

Ordinarily, the relative pronoun *who* is used to refer to people, *which* to refer to things and places, *where* to refer to places, and *that* to refer to places or things. The distinction between *that* and *which* is a grammatical distinction (see the section on Word Choice Skills).

Many writers prefer to use *that* to refer to collective nouns.

EX: A family *that* traces its lineage is usually proud of its roots.

Many writers, especially students, are not sure when to use the reflexive case pronoun and when to use the possessive case pronoun. The rules governing the usage of the reflexive case and the possessive case are quite simple.

Use the possessive case

before a noun in a sentence:

Our friend moved during the semester break.

My dog has fleas, but *her* dog doesn't.

before a gerund in a sentence:

Her running helps to relieve stress.

His driving terrified her.

as a noun in a sentence:

Mine was the last test graded that day.

to indicate possession:

Karen never allows anyone else to drive *her* car.

Brad thought the book was *his,* but it was someone else's.

Use the reflexive case

as a direct object to rename the subject:

I kicked *myself.*

as an indirect object to rename the subject:

Henry bought *himself* a tie.

as an object of a prepositional phrase:

Tom and Lillie baked the pie for *themselves.*

as a predicate pronoun:

> She hasn't been *herself* lately.

Do not use the reflexive in place of the nominative pronoun:

INCORRECT: Both Randy and *myself* plan to go.

CORRECT: Both Randy and *I* plan to go.

INCORRECT: *Yourself* will take on the challenges of college.

CORRECT: *You* will take on the challenges of college.

INCORRECT: Either James or *yourself* will paint the mural.

CORRECT: Either James or *you* will paint the mural.

Watch out for careless use of the pronoun form:

INCORRECT: George *hisself* told me it was true.

CORRECT: George *himself* told me it was true.

INCORRECT: They washed the car *theirselves*.

CORRECT: They washed the car *themselves*.

Notice that reflexive pronouns are not set off by commas:

INCORRECT: Mary, *herself*, gave him the diploma.

CORRECT: Mary *herself* gave him the diploma.

INCORRECT: I will do it, *myself*.

CORRECT: I will do it *myself*.

Pronoun Reference

Pronoun reference questions require you to determine whether the antecedent is conspicuously written in the sentence or whether it is remote, implied, ambiguous, or vague, none of which results in clear writing. Make sure that every italicized pronoun has a conspicuous antecedent and that one pronoun substitutes only for another noun or pronoun, not for an idea or a sentence.

Pronoun reference problems occur

when a pronoun refers to either of two antecedents:

INCORRECT: Joanna told Tim that *she* was getting fat.

CORRECT: Joanna told Tim, "I'm getting fat."

when a pronoun refers to a remote antecedent:

INCORRECT: A strange car followed us closely, and *he* kept blinking his lights at us.

CORRECT: A strange car followed us closely, and its driver kept blinking his lights at us.

when *this, that,* and *which* refer to the general idea of the preceding clause or sentence rather than the preceding word:

INCORRECT: The students could not understand the pronoun reference handout, which annoyed them very much.

CORRECT: The students could not understand the pronoun reference handout, a fact which annoyed them very much.

OR The students were annoyed because they could not understand the pronoun reference handout.

when a pronoun refers to an unexpressed but implied noun:

INCORRECT: My husband wants me to knit a blanket, but I'm not interested in it.

CORRECT: My husband wants me to knit a blanket, but I'm not interested in knitting.

when *it* is used as something other than an expletive to postpone a subject:

INCORRECT: It says in today's paper that the newest shipment of cars from Detroit, Michigan, seems to include outright imitations of European models.

CORRECT: Today's paper says that the newest shipment of cars from Detroit, Michigan, seems to include outright imitations of European models.

INCORRECT: The football game was canceled because it was bad weather.

CORRECT: The football game was canceled because the weather was bad.

when *they* or *it* is used to refer to something or someone indefinitely, and there is no definite antecedent:

INCORRECT: At the job placement office, they told me to stop wearing ripped jeans to my interviews.

CORRECT: At the job placement office, I was told to stop wearing ripped jeans to my interviews.

when the pronoun does not agree with its antecedent in number, gender, or person:

INCORRECT: Any graduate student, if they are interested, may attend the lecture.

CORRECT: Any graduate student, if he or she is interested, may attend the lecture.

OR All graduate students, if they are interested, may attend the lecture.

INCORRECT: Many Americans are concerned that the overuse of slang and colloquialisms is corrupting the language.

CORRECT: Many Americans are concerned that the overuse of slang and colloquialisms is corrupting their language.

INCORRECT: The Board of Regents will not make a decision about tuition increase until their March meeting.

CORRECT: The Board of Regents will not make a decision about tuition increase until its March meeting.

when a noun or pronoun has no expressed antecedent:

INCORRECT: In the President's address to the union, he promised no more taxes.

CORRECT: In his address to the union, the President promised no more taxes.

☞ Drill: Pronouns

DIRECTIONS: Choose the correct option.

1. My friend and <u>myself</u> bought tickets for *Cats*.

   (A) I

   (B) me

   (C) us

   (D) No change is necessary.

2. Alcohol and tobacco are harmful to <u>whomever</u> consumes them.

   (A) whom

   (B) who

   (C) whoever

   (D) No change is necessary.

3. Everyone is wondering <u>whom</u> her successor will be.

   (A) who

   (B) whose

   (C) who'll

   (D) No change is necessary.

4. Rosa Lee's parents discovered that it was <u>her who</u> wrecked the family car.

   (A) she who

   (B) she whom

   (C) her whom

   (D) No change is necessary.

5. A student <u>who</u> wishes to protest <u>his or her</u> grades must file a formal grievance in the Dean's office.

   (A) that . . . their

   (B) which . . . his

   (C) whom . . . their

   (D) No change is necessary.

6. One of the best things about working for this company is that <u>they pay</u> big bonuses.

   (A) it pays

   (B) they always pay

   (C) they paid

   (D) No change is necessary.

7. Every car owner should be sure that <u>their</u> automobile insurance is adequate.

   (A) your

   (B) his or her

   (C) its

   (D) No change is necessary.

8. My mother wants me to become a teacher, but I'm not interested in <u>it</u>.

    (A) this   (C) that

    (B) teaching   (D) No change is necessary.

9. Since I had not paid my electric bill, <u>they</u> sent me a delinquent notice.

    (A) the power company (C) it

    (B) he   (D) No change is necessary.

10. Margaret seldom wrote to her sister when <u>she</u> was away at college.

    (A) who   (C) her sister

    (B) her   (D) No change is necessary.

ADJECTIVES AND ADVERBS

Correct Usage

Adjectives are words that modify nouns or pronouns by defining, describing, limiting, or qualifying those nouns or pronouns.

Adverbs are words that modify verbs, adjectives, or other adverbs and that express such ideas as time, place, manner, cause, and degree. Use adjectives as subject complements with linking verbs; use adverbs with action verbs.

EX:	The old man's speech was *eloquent*.	ADJECTIVE
	Mr. Brown speaks *eloquently*.	ADVERB
	Please be *careful*.	ADJECTIVE
	Please drive *carefully*.	ADVERB

Good or well

Good is an adjective; its use as an adverb is colloquial and nonstandard.

INCORRECT:	He plays *good*.
CORRECT:	He looks *good* to be an octogenarian.
	The quiche tastes very *good*.

Well may be either an adverb or an adjective. As an adjective, *well* means "in good health."

CORRECT:	He plays *well*.	ADVERB
	My mother is not *well*.	ADJECTIVE

Bad or badly

Bad is an adjective used after sense verbs such as *look, smell, taste, feel,* or *sound,* or after linking verbs (*is, am, are, was, were*).

> INCORRECT: I feel *badly* about the delay.

> CORRECT: I feel *bad* about the delay.

Badly is an adverb used after all other verbs.

> INCORRECT: It doesn't hurt very *bad*.

> CORRECT: It doesn't hurt very *badly*.

Real or really

Real is an adjective; its use as an adverb is colloquial and nonstandard. It means "genuine."

> INCORRECT: He writes *real* well.

> CORRECT: This is *real* leather.

Really is an adverb meaning "very."

> INCORRECT: This is *really* diamond.

> CORRECT: Have a *really* nice day.

EX:	This is *real* amethyst.	ADJECTIVE
	This is *really* difficult.	ADVERB
	This is a *real* crisis.	ADJECTIVE
	This is *really* important.	ADVERB

Sort of and kind of

Sort of and *kind of* are often misused in written English by writers who actually mean *rather* or *somewhat*.

> INCORRECT: Jan was *kind of* saddened by the results of the test.

> CORRECT: Jan was *somewhat* saddened by the results of the test.

Faulty Comparisons

Sentences containing a faulty comparison often sound correct because their problem is not one of grammar but of logic. Read these sen-

tences closely to make sure that like things are being compared, that the comparisons are complete, and that the comparisons are logical.

When comparing two persons or things, use the comparative, not the superlative form, of an adjective or an adverb. Use the superlative form for comparison of more than two persons or things. Use *any*, *other*, or *else* when comparing one thing or person with a group of which it/he or she is a part.

Most one- and two-syllable words form their comparative and super-lative degrees with *-er* and *-est* suffixes. Adjectives and adverbs of more than two syllables form their comparative and superlative degrees with the addition of *more* and *most*.

Positive	Comparative	Superlative
good	better	best
old	older	oldest
friendly	friendlier	friendliest
lonely	lonelier	loneliest
talented	more talented	most talented
beautiful	more beautiful	most beautiful

A double comparison occurs when the degree of the modifier is changed incorrectly by adding both *-er* and *more* or *-est* and *most* to the adjective or adverb.

INCORRECT: He is the *most nicest* brother.

CORRECT: He is the *nicest* brother.

INCORRECT: She is the *more meaner* of the sisters.

CORRECT: She is the *meaner* sister.

Illogical comparisons occur when there is an implied comparison between two things that are not actually being compared or that cannot be logically compared.

INCORRECT: The interest at a loan company is higher *than* a bank.

CORRECT: The interest at a loan company is higher *than* that *at* a bank.

OR The interest at a loan company is higher *than at* a bank.

Ambiguous comparisons occur when elliptical words (those omitted) create for the reader more than one interpretation of the sentence.

INCORRECT: I like Mary better than you. (than you *what?*)

CORRECT: I like Mary better than I like you.

OR I like Mary better than you do.

Incomplete comparisons occur when the basis of the comparison (the two categories being compared) is not explicitly stated.

INCORRECT: Skywriting is *more* spectacular.

CORRECT: Skywriting is *more* spectacular *than* billboard advertising.

Do not omit the words *other, any,* or *else* when comparing one thing or person with a group of which it/he or she is a part.

INCORRECT: Joan writes better *than any* student in her class.

CORRECT: Joan writes better *than any other* student in her class.

Do not omit the second *as* of *as . . . as* when making a point of equal or superior comparison.

INCORRECT: The University of West Florida is *as large* or larger than the University of North Florida.

CORRECT: The University of West Florida is *as large as* or larger than the University of Northern Florida.

Do not omit the first category of the comparison, even if the two categories are the same.

INCORRECT: This is one of the best, if not the best, college in the country.

CORRECT: This is one of the best colleges in the country, if not the best.

The problem with the incorrect sentence is that *one of the best* requires the plural word *colleges,* not *college.*

☞ Drill: Adjectives and Adverbs

DIRECTIONS: Choose the correct option.

1. Although the band performed <u>badly,</u> I feel <u>real bad</u> about missing the concert.

    (A) badly . . . real badly

    (B) bad . . . badly

    (C) badly . . . very bad

    (D) No change is necessary.

2. These reports are <u>relative simple</u> to prepare.

   (A) relatively simple   (C) relatively simply

   (B) relative simply   (D) No change is necessary.

3. He did <u>very well</u> on the test although his writing skills are not <u>good</u>.

   (A) real well . . . good   (C) good . . . great

   (B) very good . . . good   (D) No change is necessary.

4. Shake the medicine bottle <u>good</u> before you open it.

   (A) very good   (C) well

   (B) real good   (D) No change is necessary.

5. Though she speaks <u>fluently</u>, she writes <u>poorly</u> because she doesn't observe <u>closely</u> or think <u>clear</u>.

   (A) fluently . . . poorly . . . closely . . . clearly

   (B) fluent . . . poor . . . close . . . clear

   (C) fluently . . . poor . . . closely . . . clear

   (D) No change is necessary.

DIRECTIONS: Select the sentence that clearly and effectively states the idea and has no structural errors.

---

6. (A) Los Angeles is larger than any city in California.

   (B) Los Angeles is larger than all the cities in California.

   (C) Los Angeles is larger than any other city in California.

7. (A) Art history is as interesting as, if not more interesting than, music appreciation.

   (B) Art history is as interesting, if not more interesting than, music appreciation.

   (C) Art history is as interesting as, if not more interesting, music appreciation.

8. (A) The baseball team here is as good as any other university.

   (B) The baseball team here is as good as all the other universities.

   (C) The baseball team here is as good as any other university's.

9.   (A) I like him better than you.

     (B) I like him better than I like you.

     (C) I like him better.

10.   (A) You are the most stingiest person I know.

     (B) You are the most stingier person I know.

     (C) You are the stingiest person I know.

PUNCTUATION

Commas

Commas should be placed according to standard rules of punctuation for purpose, clarity, and effect. The proper use of commas is explained in the following rules and examples:

In a series:

When more than one adjective describes a noun, use a comma to separate and emphasize each adjective. The comma takes the place of the word *and* in the series.

> the long, dark passageway
>
> another confusing, sleepless night
>
> an elaborate, complex, brilliant plan
>
> the old, grey, crumpled hat

Some adjective-noun combinations are thought of as one word. In these cases, the adjective in front of the adjective-noun combination needs no comma. If you inserted *and* between the adjective-noun combination, it would not make sense.

> a stately oak tree
>
> an exceptional wine glass
>
> my worst report card
>
> a china dinner plate

The comma is also used to separate words, phrases, and whole ideas (clauses); it still takes the place of *and* when used this way.

an apple, a pear, a fig, and a banana

a lovely lady, an elegant dress, and many admirers

She lowered the shade, closed the curtain, turned off the light, and went to bed.

The only question that exists about the use of commas in a series is whether or not one should be used before the final item. It is standard usage to do so, although many newspapers and magazines have stopped using the final comma. Occasionally, the omission of the comma can be confusing.

INCORRECT: He got on his horse, tracked a rabbit and a deer and rode on to Canton.

We planned the trip with Mary and Harold, Susan, Dick and Joan, Gregory and Jean and Charles.

With a long introductory phrase:

Usually if a phrase of more than five or six words or a dependent clause precedes the subject at the beginning of a sentence, a comma is used to set it off.

After last night's fiasco at the disco, she couldn't bear the thought of looking at him again.

Whenever I try to talk about politics, my wife leaves the room.

Provided you have said nothing, they will never guess who you are.

It is not necessary to use a comma with a short sentence.

In January she will go to Switzerland.

After I rest I'll feel better.

During the day no one is home.

If an introductory phrase includes a verb form that is being used as another part of speech (a *verbal*), it must be followed by a comma.

INCORRECT: When eating Mary never looked up from her plate.

CORRECT: When eating, Mary never looked up from her plate.

INCORRECT: Because of her desire to follow her faith in James wavered.

CORRECT: Because of her desire to follow, her faith in James wavered.

INCORRECT: Having decided to leave Mary James wrote her a letter.

CORRECT: Having decided to leave Mary, James wrote her a letter.

To separate sentences with two main ideas:

To understand this use of the comma, you need to be able to recognize compound sentences. When a sentence contains more than two subjects and verbs (clauses), and the two clauses are joined by a conjunction (*and, but, or, nor, for, yet*), use a comma before the conjunction to show that another clause is coming.

> I thought I knew the poem by heart, but he showed me three lines I had forgotten.

> Are we really interested in helping the children, or are we more concerned with protecting our good names?

> He is supposed to leave tomorrow, but he is not ready to go.

> Jim knows you are disappointed, and he has known it for a long time.

If the two parts of the sentence are short and closely related, it is not necessary to use a comma.

> He threw the ball and the dog ran after it.

> Jane played the piano and Michael danced.

Be careful not to confuse a sentence that has a compound verb and a single subject with a compound sentence. If the subject is the same for both verbs, there is no need for a comma.

INCORRECT: Charles sent some flowers, and wrote a long letter explaining why he had not been able to attend.

CORRECT: Charles sent some flowers and wrote a long letter explaining why he had not been able to attend.

INCORRECT: Last Thursday we went to the concert with Julia, and afterwards dined at an old Italian restaurant.

CORRECT: Last Thursday we went to the concert with Julia and afterwards dined at an old Italian restaurant.

INCORRECT: For the third time, the teacher explained that the literacy level for high school students was much lower than it had been in previous years, and, this time, wrote the statistics on the board for everyone to see.

CORRECT: For the third time, the teacher explained that the literacy level for high school students was much lower than it had been in previous years and this time wrote the statistics on the board for everyone to see.

In general, words and phrases that stop the flow of the sentence or are unnecessary for the main idea are set off by commas.

Abbreviations after names:

Did you invite John Paul, Jr., and his sister?

Martha Harris, Ph.D., will be the speaker tonight.

Interjections (an exclamation without added grammatical connection):

Oh, I'm so glad to see you.

I tried so hard, alas, to do it.

Hey, let me out of here.

Direct address:

Roy, won't you open the door for the dog?

I can't understand, Mother, what you are trying to say.

May I ask, Mr. President, why you called us together?

Hey, lady, watch out for that car!

Tag questions:

You're really hungry, aren't you?

Jerry looks like his father, doesn't he?

Geographical names and addresses:

The concert will be held in Chicago, Illinois, on August 12.

The letter was addressed to Mrs. Marion Heartwell, 1881 Pine Lane, Palo Alto, CA 95824.

(Note: No comma is needed before the ZIP code, because it is already clearly set off from the state name.)

Transitional words and phrases:

On the other hand, I hope he gets better.

In addition, the phone rang constantly this afternoon.

I'm, nevertheless, going to the beach on Sunday.

You'll find, therefore, that no one is more loyal than I am.

Parenthetical words and phrases:

You will become, I believe, a great statesman.

We know, of course, that this is the only thing to do.

In fact, I planted corn last summer.

The Mannes affair was, to put it mildly, a surprise.

Unusual word order:

The dress, new and crisp, hung in the closet.

Intently, she stared out the window.

With nonrestrictive elements:

Parts of a sentence that modify other parts are sometimes essential to the meaning of the sentence and sometimes not. When a modifying word or group of words is not vital to the meaning of the sentence, it is set off by commas. Since it does not restrict the meaning of the words it modifies, it is called "nonrestrictive." Modifiers that are essential to the meaning of the sentence are called "restrictive" and are not set off by commas.

ESSENTIAL: The girl *who wrote the story* is my sister.

NONESSENTIAL: My sister, *the girl who wrote the story*, has always loved to write.

ESSENTIAL: John Milton's famous poem *Paradise Lost* tells a remarkable story.

NONESSENTIAL: Dante's greatest work, *The Divine Comedy,* marked the beginning of the Renaissance.

ESSENTIAL: The cup *that is on the piano* is the one I want.

NONESSENTIAL: The cup, *which my brother gave me last year*, is on the piano.

ESSENTIAL: The people *who arrived late* were not seated.

NONESSENTIAL: George, *who arrived late*, was not seated.

To set off direct quotations:

Most direct quotes or quoted materials are set off from the rest of the sentence by commas.

> "Please read your part more loudly," the director insisted.
>
> "I won't know what to do," said Michael, "if you leave me."
>
> The teacher said sternly, "I will not dismiss this class until I have silence."
>
> Who was it who said "Do not ask for whom the bell tolls; it tolls for thee"?

Note: Commas always go inside the closing quotation mark, even if the comma is not part of the material being quoted.

Be careful not to set off indirect quotes or quotes that are used as subjects or complements.

> "To be or not to be" is the famous beginning of a soliloquy in Shakespeare's *Hamlet*. (subject)
>
> She said she would never come back. (indirect quote)
>
> Back then my favorite poem was "Evangeline." (complement)

To set off contrasting elements:

> Her intelligence, not her beauty, got her the job.
>
> Your plan will take you a little further from, rather than closer to, your destination.
>
> It was a reasonable, though not appealing, idea.
>
> He wanted glory, but found happiness instead.

In dates:

Both forms of the date are acceptable.

> She will arrive on April 6, 1998.
>
> He left on 5 December 1980.
>
> In January 1967, he handed in his resignation.
>
> On October 22, 1992, Frank and Julie were married.

Usually, when a subordinate clause is at the end of a sentence, no comma is necessary preceding the clause. However, when a subordinate clause introduces a sentence, a comma should be used after the clause.

Some common subordinating conjunctions are:

after	so that
although	though
as	till
as if	unless
because	until
before	when
even though	whenever
if	while
inasmuch as	since

Semicolons

Questions testing semicolon usage require you to be able to distinguish between the semicolon and the comma, and the semicolon and the colon. This review section covers the basic uses of the semicolon: to separate independent clauses not joined by a coordinating conjunction, to separate independent clauses separated by a conjunctive adverb, and to separate items in a series with internal commas. It is important to be consistent; if you use a semicolon between *any* of the items in the series, you must use semicolons to separate *all* of the items in the series.

Usually, a comma follows the conjunctive adverb. Note also that a period can be used to separate two sentences joined by a conjunctive adverb. Some common conjunctive adverbs are:

accordingly	nevertheless
besides	next
consequently	nonetheless
finally	now
furthermore	on the other hand
however	otherwise
indeed	perhaps
in fact	still
moreover	therefore

Then is also used as a conjunctive adverb, but it is not usually followed by a comma.

Use the semicolon

to separate independent clauses which are not joined by a coordinating conjunction:

> I understand how to use commas; the semicolon I have not yet mastered.

to separate two independent clauses connected by a conjunctive adverb:

> He took great care with his work; *therefore*, he was very successful.

to combine two independent clauses connected by a coordinating conjunction if either or both of the clauses contain other internal punctuation:

> Success in college, some maintain, requires intelligence, industry, and perseverance; *but* others, fewer in number, assert that only personality is important.

to separate items in a series when each item has internal punctuation:

> I bought an old, dilapidated chair; an antique table which was in beautiful condition; and a new, ugly, blue and white rug.

> Call our customer service line for assistance: Arizona, 1-800-555-6020; New Mexico, 1-800-555-5050; California, 1-800-555-3140; or Nevada, 1-800-555-3214.

Do not use the semicolon

to separate a dependent and an independent clause:

> INCORRECT: You should not make such statements; even though they are correct.

> CORRECT: You should not make such statements even though they are correct.

to separate an appositive phrase or clause from a sentence:

> INCORRECT: His immediate aim in life is centered around two things; becoming an engineer and learning to fly an airplane.

> CORRECT: His immediate aim in life is centered around two things: becoming an engineer and learning to fly an airplane.

to precede an explanation or summary of the first clause:

Note: Although the sentence below is punctuated correctly, the use of the semicolon provides a miscue, suggesting that the second clause is merely

an extension, not an explanation, of the first clause. The colon provides a better clue.

> WEAK: The first week of camping was wonderful; we lived in cabins instead of tents.

> BETTER: The first week of camping was wonderful: we lived in cabins instead of tents.

to substitute for a comma:

> INCORRECT: My roommate also likes sports; particularly football, basketball, and baseball.

> CORRECT: My roommate also likes sports, particularly football, basketball, and baseball.

to set off other types of phrases or clauses from a sentence:

> INCORRECT: Being of a cynical mind; I should ask for a recount of the ballots.

> CORRECT: Being of a cynical mind, I should ask for a recount of the ballots.

> INCORRECT: The next meeting of the club has been postponed two weeks; inasmuch as both the president and vice-president are out of town.

> CORRECT: The next meeting of the club has been postponed two weeks, inasmuch as both the president and vice-president are out of town.

Note: The semicolon is not a terminal mark of punctuation; therefore, it should not be followed by a capital letter unless the first word in the second clause ordinarily requires capitalization.

Colons

While it is true that a colon is used to precede a list, one must also make sure that a complete sentence precedes the colon. The colon signals the reader that a list, explanation, or restatement of the preceding will follow. It is like an arrow, indicating that something is to follow. The difference between the colon and the semicolon and between the colon and the period is that the colon is an introductory mark, not a terminal mark. Look at the following examples:

> The Constitution provides for a separation of powers among the three branches of government.

government. The period signals a new sentence.

government; The semicolon signals an interrelated sentence.

government, The comma signals a coordinating conjunction followed by another independent clause.

government: The colon signals a list.

The Constitution provides for a separation of powers among the three branches of *government*: executive, legislative, and judicial.

Ensuring that a complete sentence precedes a colon means following these rules:

Use the colon to introduce a list (one item may constitute a list):

I hate this one course: English.

Three plays by William Shakespeare will be presented in repertory this summer at the University of Michigan: *Hamlet, Macbeth,* and *Othello.*

To introduce a list preceded by *as follows* or *the following*:

The reasons he cited for his success are as follows: integrity, honesty, industry, and a pleasant disposition.

To separate two independent clauses, when the second clause is a restatement or explanation of the first:

All of my high school teachers said one thing in particular: college is going to be difficult.

To introduce a word or word group which is a restatement, explanation, or summary of the first sentence:

These two things he loved: an honest man and a beautiful woman.

To introduce a formal appositive:

I am positive there is one appeal which you can't overlook: money.

To separate the introductory words from a quotation which follows, if the quotation is formal, long, or paragraphed separately:

The actor then stated: "I would rather be able to adequately play the part of Hamlet than to perform a miraculous operation, deliver a great lecture, or build a magnificent skyscraper."

The colon should only be used after statements that are grammatically complete.

Do *not* use a colon after a verb:

INCORRECT: My favorite holidays are: Christmas, New Year's Eve, and Halloween.

CORRECT: My favorite holidays are Christmas, New Year's Eve, and Halloween.

Do *not* use a colon after a preposition:

INCORRECT: I enjoy different ethnic foods such as: Greek, Chinese, and Italian.

CORRECT: I enjoy different ethnic foods such as Greek, Chinese, and Italian.

Do *not* use a colon interchangeably with the dash:

INCORRECT: Mathematics, German, English: These gave me the greatest difficulty of all my studies.

CORRECT: Mathematics, German, English—these gave me the greatest difficulty of all my studies.

Information preceding the colon should be a complete sentence regardless of the explanatory information following the clause.

Do *not* use the colon before the words *for example, namely, that is,* or *for instance* even though these words may be introducing a list.

INCORRECT: We agreed to it: namely, to give him a surprise party.

CORRECT: There are a number of well-known American women writers: for example, Nikki Giovanni, Phillis Wheatley, Emily Dickinson, and Maya Angelou.

Colon usage questions test your knowledge of the colon preceding a list, restatement, or explanation. These questions also require you to be able to distinguish between the colon and the period, the colon and the comma, and the colon and the semicolon.

Apostrophes

Apostrophe questions require you to know when an apostrophe has been used appropriately to make a noun possessive, not plural. Remember the following rules when considering how to show possession.

Add *'s* to singular nouns and indefinite pronouns:

>Tiffany's flowers
>
>a dog's bark
>
>everybody's computer
>
>at the owner's expense
>
>today's paper

Add *'s* to singular nouns ending in *s,* unless this distorts the pronunciation:

>Delores's paper
>
>the boss's pen
>
>Dr. Yots' class
>
>for righteousness' sake
>
>Dr. Evans's office OR Dr. Evans' office

Add *an apostrophe* to plural nouns ending in *s* or *es*:

>two cents' worth
>
>ladies' night
>
>thirteen years' experience
>
>two weeks' pay

Add *'s* to plural nouns not ending in *s:*

>men's room
>
>children's toys

Add *'s* to the last word in compound words or groups:

>brother-in-law's car
>
>someone else's paper

Add *'s* to the last name when indicating joint ownership:

>Joe and Edna's home
>
>Julie and Kathy's party
>
>women and children's clinic

Add *'s* to both names if you intend to show ownership by each person:

>Joe's and Edna's trucks
>
>Julie's and Kathy's pies

Ted's and Jane's marriage vows

Possessive pronouns change their forms *without* the addition of an apostrophe:

her, his, hers

your, yours

their, theirs

it, its

Use the possessive form of a noun preceding a gerund:

His driving annoys me.

My bowling a strike irritated him.

Do you mind our stopping by?

We appreciate your coming.

Add *'s* to words and initials to show that they are plural:

no if's, and's, or but's

the do's and don't's of dating

three A's

IRA's are available at the bank.

Add *s* to numbers, symbols, and letters to show that they are plural:

TVs

VCRs

the 1800s

the returning POWs

Quotation Marks and Italics

These kinds of questions test your knowledge of the proper use of quotation marks with other marks of punctuation, with titles, and with dialogue. These kinds of questions also test your knowledge of the correct use of italics and underlining with titles and words used as sample words (for example, *the word is is a common verb*).

The most common use of double quotation marks (") is to set off quoted words, phrases, and sentences.

"If everybody minded their own business," said the Duchess in a hoarse growl, "the world would go round a great deal faster than it does."

> "Then you would say what you mean," the March Hare went on.
>
> "I do," Alice hastily replied: "at least—at least I mean what I say— that's the same thing, you know."
>
> —from Lewis Carroll's *Alice in Wonderland*

Single quotation marks are used to set off quoted material within a quote.

> "Shall I bring 'Rime of the Ancient Mariner' along with us?" she asked her brother.
>
> Mrs. Green said, "The doctor told me, 'Go immediately to bed when you get home!'"
>
> "If she said that to me," Katherine insisted, "I would tell her, 'I never intend to speak to you again! Goodbye, Susan!'"

When writing dialogue, begin a new paragraph each time the speaker changes.

> "Do you know what time it is?" asked Jane.
>
> "Can't you see I'm busy?" snapped Mary.
>
> "It's easy to see that you're in a bad mood today!" replied Jane.

Use quotation marks to enclose words used as words (sometimes italics are used for this purpose).

> "Judgment" has always been a difficult word for me to spell.
>
> Do you know what "abstruse" means?
>
> "Horse and buggy" and "bread and butter" can be used either as adjectives or as nouns.

If slang is used within more formal writing, the slang words or phrases should be set off with quotation marks.

> Harrison's decision to leave the conference and to "stick his neck out" by flying to Jamaica was applauded by the rest of the conference attendees.

When words are meant to have an unusual or specific significance to the reader, for instance irony or humor, they are sometimes placed in quotation marks.

> For years, women were not allowed to buy real estate in order to "protect" them from unscrupulous dealers.
>
> The "conversation" resulted in one black eye and a broken nose.

To set off titles of TV shows, poems, stories, and book chapters, use quotation marks. (Book, motion picture, newspaper, and magazine titles are underlined when handwritten and italicized when printed.)

> The article "Moving South in the Southern Rain," by Jergen Smith in the *Southern News*, attracted the attention of our editor.

> The assignment is "Childhood Development," Chapter 18 of *Human Behavior.*

> My favorite essay by Montaigne is "On Silence."

> "Happy Days" led the TV ratings for years, didn't it?

> You will find Keats' "Ode to a Grecian Urn" in Chapter 3, "The Romantic Era," in Lastly's *Selections from Great English Poets.*

Errors to avoid:

Be sure to remember that quotation marks always come in pairs. Do not make the mistake of using only one set.

> INCORRECT: "You'll never convince me to move to the city, said Thurman. I consider it an insane asylum."

> CORRECT: "You'll never convince me to move to the city," said Thurman. "I consider it an insane asylum."

> INCORRECT: "Idleness and pride tax with a heavier hand than kings and parliaments," Benjamin Franklin is supposed to have said. If we can get rid of the former, we may easily bear the latter."

> CORRECT: "Idleness and pride tax with a heavier hand than kings and parliaments," Benjamin Franklin is supposed to have said. "If we can get rid of the former, we may easily bear the latter."

When a quote consists of several sentences, do not put the quotation marks at the beginning and end of each sentence; put them at the beginning and end of the entire quotation.

> INCORRECT: "It was during his student days in Bonn that Beethoven fastened upon Schiller's poem." "The heady sense of liberation in the verses must have appealed to him." "They appealed to every German." —John Burke

> CORRECT: "It was during his student days in Bonn that Beethoven fastened upon Schiller's poem. The heady sense of liberation in the verses must have appealed to him. They appealed to every German." —John Burke

Instead of setting off a long quote with quotation marks, if it is longer than five or six lines you may want to indent and single space it. If you do indent, do not use quotation marks.

> In his *First Inaugural Address,* Abraham Lincoln appeals to the war-torn American people:

>> We are not enemies, but friends. We must not be enemies. Though passion may have strained, it must not break, our bonds of affection. The mystic chords of memory, stretching from every battlefield and patriot grave to every living heart and hearthstone all over this broad land, will yet swell the chorus of the Union when again touched, as surely they will be, by the better angels of our nature.

Be careful not to use quotation marks with indirect quotations.

> INCORRECT: Mary wondered "if she would get over it."

> CORRECT: Mary wondered if she would get over it.

> ---

> INCORRECT: The nurse asked "how long it had been since we had visited the doctor's office."

> CORRECT: The nurse asked how long it had been since we had visited the doctor's office.

When you quote several paragraphs, it is not sufficient to place quotation marks at the beginning and end of the entire quote. Place quotation marks at the *beginning of each paragraph,* but only at the *end of the last paragraph.* Here is an abbreviated quotation for an example:

> "Here begins an odyssey through the world of classical mythology, starting with the creation of the world . . .

> "It is true that themes similar to the classical may be found in any corpus of mythology . . . Even technology is not immune to the influence of Greece and Rome . . .

> "We need hardly mention the extent to which painters and sculptors . . . have used and adapted classical mythology to illustrate the past, to reveal the human body, to express romantic or antiromantic ideals, or to symbolize any particular point of view."

Remember that commas and periods are *always* placed inside the quotation marks even if they are not actually part of the quote.

> INCORRECT: "Life always gets colder near the summit", Nietzsche is purported to have said, "—the cold increases, responsibility grows".

CORRECT: "Life always gets colder near the summit," Nietzsche is purported to have said, "—the cold increases, responsibility grows."

INCORRECT: "Get down here right away", John cried. "You'll miss the sunset if you don't."

CORRECT: "Get down here right away," John cried. "You'll miss the sunset if you don't."

INCORRECT: "If my dog could talk", Mary mused, "I'll bet he would say, 'Take me for a walk right this minute'".

CORRECT: "If my dog could talk," Mary mused, "I'll bet he would say, 'Take me for a walk right this minute'."

Other marks of punctuation, such as question marks, exclamation points, colons, and semicolons, go inside the quotation marks if they are part of the quoted material. If they are not part of the quotation, however, they go outside the quotation marks. Be careful to distinguish between the guidelines for the comma and period, which always go inside the quotation marks, and those for other marks of punctuation.

INCORRECT: "I'll always love you"! he exclaimed happily.

CORRECT: "I'll always love you!" he exclaimed happily.

INCORRECT: Did you hear her say, "He'll be there early?"

CORRECT: Did you hear her say, "He'll be there early"?

INCORRECT: She called down the stairs, "When are you going"?

CORRECT: She called down the stairs, "When are you going?"

INCORRECT: "Let me out"! he cried. "Don't you have any pity"?

CORRECT: "Let me out!" he cried. "Don't you have any pity?"

Remember to use only one mark of punctuation at the end of a sentence ending with a quotation mark.

INCORRECT: She thought out loud, "Will I ever finish this paper in time for that class?".

CORRECT: She thought out loud, "Will I ever finish this paper in time for that class?"

INCORRECT: "Not the same thing a bit!", said the Hatter. "Why, you might just as well say that 'I see what I eat' is the same thing as 'I eat what I see'!".

CORRECT: "Not the same thing a bit!" said the Hatter. "Why, you might just as well say that 'I see what I eat' is the same thing as 'I eat what I see'!"

☞ Drill: Punctuation

DIRECTIONS: Choose the correct option.

1. Indianola, <u>Mississippi, where B.B. King and my father grew up,</u> has a population of less than 50,000 people.

    (A) Mississippi where, B.B. King and my father grew up,

    (B) Mississippi where B.B. King and my father grew up,

    (C) Mississippi; where B.B. King and my father grew up,

    (D) No change is necessary.

2. John Steinbeck's best known novel *The Grapes of Wrath* is the story of the <u>Joads an Oklahoma family</u> who were driven from their dustbowl farm and forced to become migrant workers in California.

    (A) Joads, an Oklahoma family

    (B) Joads, an Oklahoma family,

    (C) Joads; an Oklahoma family

    (D) No change is necessary.

3. All students who are interested in student teaching next <u>semester, must submit an application to the Teacher Education Office.</u>

    (A) semester must submit an application to the Teacher Education Office.

    (B) semester, must submit an application, to the Teacher Education Office.

    (C)   semester: must submit an application to the Teacher Education Office.

    (D)   No change is necessary.

4.   Whenever you travel by <u>car, or plane, you</u> must wear a seatbelt.

    (A)   car or plane you   (C)   car or plane, you

    (B)   car, or plane you   (D)   No change is necessary.

5.   Wearing a seatbelt is not just a good <u>idea, it's</u> the law.

    (A)   idea; it's   (C)   idea. It's

    (B)   idea it's   (D)   No change is necessary.

6.   Senators and representatives can be reelected <u>indefinitely; a</u> president can only serve two terms.

    (A)   indefinitely but a   (C)   indefinitely a

    (B)   indefinitely, a   (D)   No change is necessary.

7.   Students must pay a penalty for overdue library <u>books, however, there</u> is a grace period.

    (A)   books; however, there   (C)   books: however, there

    (B)   books however, there   (D)   No change is necessary.

8.   Among the states that seceded from the Union to join the Confederacy in 1860-1861 <u>were:</u> Mississippi, Florida, and Alabama.

    (A)   were   (C)   were.

    (B)   were;   (D)   No change is necessary.

9.   The art exhibit displayed works by many famous <u>artists such as:</u> Dali, Picasso, and Michelangelo.

    (A)   artists such as;   (C)   artists. Such as

    (B)   artists such as   (D)   No change is necessary.

10.   The National Shakespeare Company will perform <u>the following plays:</u> *Othello, Macbeth, Hamlet,* and *As You Like It.*

    (A)   the following plays,   (C)   the following plays

    (B)   the following plays;   (D)   No change is necessary.

CAPITALIZATION

When a word is capitalized, it calls attention to itself. This attention should be for a good reason. There are standard uses for capital letters. In general, capitalize (1) all proper nouns, (2) the first word of a sentence, and (3) the first word of a direct quotation.

You should also capitalize

Names of ships, aircraft, spacecraft, and trains:

Apollo 13	*Mariner IV*
DC-10	S.S. *United States*
Sputnik II	Boeing 707

Names of deities:

God	Jupiter
Allah	Holy Ghost
Buddha	Venus
Jehovah	Shiva

Geological periods:

Neolithic age	Cenozoic era
late Pleistocene times	Ice Age

Names of astronomical bodies:

Mercury	Big Dipper
the Milky Way	Halley's comet
Ursa Major	North Star

Personifications:

Reliable Nature brought her promised Spring.

Bring on Melancholy in his sad might.

She believed that Love was the answer to all her problems.

Historical periods:

the Middle Ages	World War I
Reign of Terror	Great Depression
Christian Era	Roaring Twenties
Age of Louis XIV	Renaissance

Organizations, associations, and institutions:

Girl Scouts	North Atlantic Treaty Organization
Kiwanis Club	League of Women Voters
New York Yankees	Unitarian Church
Smithsonian Institution	Common Market
Library of Congress	Franklin Glen High School
New York Philharmonic	Harvard University

Government and judicial groups:

United States Court of Appeals	Senate
Committee on Foreign Affairs	Parliament
New Jersey City Council	Peace Corps
Arkansas Supreme Court	Census Bureau
House of Representatives	Department of State

A general term that accompanies a specific name is capitalized only if it follows the specific name. If it stands alone or comes before the specific name, it is put in lowercase:

Washington State	the state of Washington
Senator Dixon	the senator from Illinois
Central Park	the park
Golden Gate Bridge	the bridge
President Clinton	the president of the United States
Pope John XXIII	the pope
Queen Elizabeth I	the queen of England
Tropic of Capricorn	the tropics
Monroe Doctrine	the doctrine of expansion
the Mississippi River	the river
Easter Day	the day
Treaty of Versailles	the treaty
Webster's Dictionary	the dictionary
Equatorial Current	the equator

Use a capital to start a sentence:

> Our car would not start.
>
> When will you leave? I need to know right away.
>
> Never!
>
> Let me in! Please!

When a sentence appears within a sentence, start it with a capital letter:

> We had only one concern: When would we eat?
>
> My sister said, "I'll find the Monopoly game."
>
> He answered, "We can only stay a few minutes."

The most important words of titles are capitalized. Those words not capitalized are conjunctions (*and, or, but*) and short prepositions (*of, on, by, for*). The first and last word of a title must always be capitalized:

A Man for All Seasons	*Crime and Punishment*
Of Mice and Men	*Rise of the West*
Strange Life of Ivan Osokin	"Sonata in G Minor"
"Let Me In"	"Ode to Billy Joe"
"Rubaiyat of Omar Khayyam"	"All in the Family"

Capitalize newspaper and magazine titles:

> *U.S. News & World Report*
>
> *National Geographic*
>
> the *New York Times*
>
> the *Washington Post*

Capitalize radio and TV station call letters:

ABC	NBC
WNEW	WBOP
CNN	HBO

Do not capitalize compass directions or seasons:

west	north
east	south
spring	winter
autumn	summer

Capitalize regions:

the South	the Northeast
the West	Eastern Europe

BUT: the south of France

the east part of town

Capitalize specific military units:

the U.S. Army

the 7th Fleet

the German Navy

the 1st Infantry Division

Capitalize political groups and philosophies:

Democrat	Communist
Marxist	Nazism
Whig	Federalist
Existentialism	Transcendentalism

BUT do not capitalize systems of government or individual adherents to a philosophy:

democracy	communism
fascist	agnostic

☞ Drill: Capitalization

DIRECTIONS: Choose the correct option.

1. Mexico is the southernmost country in <u>North America</u>. It borders the United States on the north; it is bordered on the <u>south</u> by Belize and Guatemala.

   (A) north America . . . South

   (B) North America . . . South

   (C) North america . . . south

   (D) No change is necessary.

2. (A) Until 1989, Tom Landry was the only Coach the Dallas cow-boys ever had.

   (B) Until 1989, Tom Landry was the only coach the Dallas Cow-boys ever had.

   (C) Until 1989, Tom Landry was the only Coach the Dallas Cow-boys ever had.

3. The <u>Northern Hemisphere</u> is the half of the <u>earth</u> that lies north of the <u>Equator.</u>

   (A) Northern hemisphere . . . earth . . . equator

   (B) Northern hemisphere . . . Earth . . . Equator

   (C) Northern Hemisphere . . . earth . . . equator

   (D) No change is necessary.

4. (A) My favorite works by Ernest Hemingway are "The Snows of Kilamanjaro," *The Sun Also Rises,* and *For Whom the Bell Tolls.*

   (B) My favorite works by Ernest Hemingway are "The Snows Of Kilamanjaro," *The Sun Also Rises,* and *For Whom The Bell Tolls.*

   (C) My favorite works by Ernest Hemingway are "The Snows of Kilamanjaro," *The Sun also Rises,* and *For whom the Bell Tolls.*

5. Aphrodite (<u>Venus in Roman Mythology</u>) was the <u>Greek</u> goddess of love.

   (A) Venus in Roman mythology . . . greek

   (B) venus in roman mythology . . . Greek

   (C) Venus in Roman mythology . . . Greek

   (D) No change is necessary.

6. The <u>Koran</u> is considered by <u>Muslims</u> to be the holy word.

   (A) koran . . . muslims   (C) Koran . . . muslims

   (B) koran . . . Muslims   (D) No change is necessary.

7.   (A)   The freshman curriculum at the community college includes english, a foreign language, Algebra I, and history.

     (B)   The freshman curriculum at the community college includes English, a foreign language, Algebra I, and history.

     (C)   The Freshman curriculum at the Community College includes English, a foreign language, Algebra I, and History.

8.   At the <u>spring</u> graduation ceremonies, the university awarded over 2,000 <u>bachelor's</u> degrees.

     (A)   Spring . . . Bachelor's   (C)   Spring . . . bachelor's

     (B)   spring . . . Bachelor's   (D)   No change is necessary.

9.   The fall of the <u>Berlin wall</u> was an important symbol of the collapse of <u>Communism</u>.

     (A)   berlin Wall . . . communism

     (B)   Berlin Wall . . . communism

     (C)   berlin wall . . . Communism

     (D)   No change is necessary.

10. A photograph of <u>mars</u> was printed in <u>the *New York Times*</u>.

     (A)   Mars . . . *The New York Times*

     (B)   mars . . . *The New York times*

     (C)   mars . . . *The New York Time*s

     (D)   No change is necessary.

SPELLING

Spelling questions test your ability to recognize misspelled words. This section reviews spelling tips and rules to help you spot incorrect spellings. Problems such as the distinction between *to* and *too* and *lead* and *led* are covered under the Word Choice Skills section of this review.

* Remember, *i* before *e* except after *c*, or when sounded as "a" as in *neighbor* and *weigh*.

* There are only three words in the English language that end in *-ceed*:

proceed, succeed, exceed

- There are several words that end in *-cede*:

    secede, recede, concede, precede

- There is only one word in the English language that ends in *-sede*:

    supersede

Many people learn to read English phonetically; that is, by sounding out the letters of the words. However, many English words are not pronounced the way they are spelled, and those who try to spell English words phonetically often make spelling *errors*. It is better to memorize the correct spelling of English words rather than relying on phonetics to spell correctly.

Frequently Misspelled Words

The following list of words are frequently misspelled words. Study the spelling of each word by having a friend or teacher drill you on the words. Then mark down the words that you misspelled and study those select ones again. (The words appear in their most popular spellings.)

a lot	across	all right
ability	address	almost
absence	addressed	already
absent	adequate	although
abundance	advantage	altogether
accept	advantageous	always
acceptable	advertise	amateur
accident	advertisement	American
accommodate	advice	among
accompanied	advisable	amount
accomplish	advise	analysis
accumulation	advisor	analyze
accuse	aerial	angel
accustomed	affect	angle
ache	affectionate	annual
achieve	again	another
achievement	against	answer
acknowledge	aggravate	antiseptic
acquaintance	aggressive	anxious
acquainted	agree	apologize
acquire	aisle	apparatus

apparent	bargain	carriage
appear	basic	carrying
appearance	beautiful	category
appetite	because	ceiling
application	become	cemetery
apply	before	cereal
appreciate	beginning	certain
appreciation	being	changeable
approach	believe	characteristic
appropriate	benefit	charity
approval	benefited	chief
approve	between	choose
approximate	bicycle	chose
argue	board	cigarette
arguing	bored	circumstance
argument	borrow	citizen
arouse	bottle	clothes
arrange	bottom	clothing
arrangement	boundary	coarse
article	brake	coffee
artificial	breadth	collect
ascend	breath	college
assistance	breathe	column
assistant	brilliant	comedy
associate	building	comfortable
association	bulletin	commitment
attempt	bureau	committed
attendance	burial	committee
attention	buried	communicate
audience	bury	company
August	bushes	comparative
author	business	compel
automobile	cafeteria	competent
autumn	calculator	competition
auxiliary	calendar	compliment
available	campaign	conceal
avenue	capital	conceit
awful	capitol	conceivable
awkward	captain	conceive
bachelor	career	concentration
balance	careful	conception
balloon	careless	condition

conference
confident
congratulate
conquer
conscience
conscientious
conscious
consequence
consequently
considerable
consistency
consistent
continual
continuous
controlled
controversy
convenience
convenient
conversation
corporal
corroborate
council
counsel
counselor
courage
courageous
course
courteous
courtesy
criticism
criticize
crystal
curiosity
cylinder
daily
daughter
daybreak
death
deceive
December
deception
decide

decision
decisive
deed
definite
delicious
dependent
deposit
derelict
descend
descent
describe
description
desert
desirable
despair
desperate
dessert
destruction
determine
develop
development
device
dictator
died
difference
different
dilemma
dinner
direction
disappear
disappoint
disappointment
disapproval
disapprove
disastrous
discipline
discover
discriminate
disease
dissatisfied
dissection
dissipate

distance
distinction
division
doctor
dollar
doubt
dozen
earnest
easy
ecstasy
ecstatic
education
effect
efficiency
efficient
eight
either
eligibility
eligible
eliminate
embarrass
embarrassment
emergency
emphasis
emphasize
enclosure
encouraging
endeavor
engineer
English
enormous
enough
entrance
envelope
environment
equipment
equipped
especially
essential
evening
evident
exaggerate

exaggeration	gardener	independent
examine	general	indispensable
exceed	genius	inevitable
excellent	government	influence
except	governor	influential
exceptional	grammar	initiate
exercise	grateful	innocence
exhausted	great	inoculate
exhaustion	grievance	inquiry
exhilaration	grievous	insistent
existence	grocery	instead
exorbitant	guarantee	instinct
expense	guess	integrity
experience	guidance	intellectual
experiment	half	intelligence
explanation	hammer	intercede
extreme	handkerchief	interest
facility	happiness	interfere
factory	healthy	interference
familiar	heard	interpreted
fascinate	heavy	interrupt
fascinating	height	invitation
fatigue	heroes	irrelevant
February	heroine	irresistible
financial	hideous	irritable
financier	himself	island
flourish	hoarse	its
forcibly	holiday	it's
forehead	hopeless	itself
foreign	hospital	January
formal	humorous	jealous
former	hurried	journal
fortunate	hurrying	judgment
fourteen	ignorance	kindergarten
fourth	imaginary	kitchen
frequent	imbecile	knew
friend	imitation	knock
frightening	immediately	know
fundamental	immigrant	knowledge
further	incidental	labor
gallon	increase	laboratory
garden	independence	laid

language
later
latter
laugh
leisure
length
lesson
library
license
light
lightning
likelihood
likely
literal
literature
livelihood
loaf
loneliness
loose
lose
losing
loyal
loyalty
magazine
maintenance
maneuver
marriage
married
marry
match
material
mathematics
measure
medicine
million
miniature
minimum
miracle
miscellaneous
mischief
mischievous
misspelled

mistake
momentous
monkey
monotonous
moral
morale
mortgage
mountain
mournful
muscle
mysterious
mystery
narrative
natural
necessary
needle
negligence
neighbor
neither
newspaper
newsstand
niece
noticeable
o'clock
obedient
obstacle
occasion
occasional
occur
occurred
occurrence
ocean
offer
often
omission
omit
once
operate
opinion
opportune
opportunity
optimist

optimistic
origin
original
oscillate
ought
ounce
overcoat
paid
pamphlet
panicky
parallel
parallelism
particular
partner
pastime
patience
peace
peaceable
pear
peculiar
pencil
people
perceive
perception
perfect
perform
performance
perhaps
period
permanence
permanent
perpendicular
perseverance
persevere
persistent
personal
personality
personnel
persuade
persuasion
pertain
picture

piece
plain
playwright
pleasant
please
pleasure
pocket
poison
policeman
political
population
portrayal
positive
possess
possession
possessive
possible
post office
potatoes
practical
prairie
precede
preceding
precise
predictable
prefer
preference
preferential
preferred
prejudice
preparation
prepare
prescription
presence
president
prevalent
primitive
principal
principle
privilege
probably
procedure

proceed
produce
professional
professor
profitable
prominent
promise
pronounce
pronunciation
propeller
prophet
prospect
psychology
pursue
pursuit
quality
quantity
quarreling
quart
quarter
quiet
quite
raise
realistic
realize
reason
rebellion
recede
receipt
receive
recipe
recognize
recommend
recuperate
referred
rehearsal
reign
relevant
relieve
remedy
renovate
repeat

repetition
representative
requirements
resemblance
resistance
resource
respectability
responsibility
restaurant
rhythm
rhythmical
ridiculous
right
role
roll
roommate
sandwich
Saturday
scarcely
scene
schedule
science
scientific
scissors
season
secretary
seize
seminar
sense
separate
service
several
severely
shepherd
sheriff
shining
shoulder
shriek
siege
sight
signal
significance

significant
similar
similarity
sincerely
site
soldier
solemn
sophomore
soul
source
souvenir
special
specified
specimen
speech
stationary
stationery
statue
stockings
stomach
straight
strength
strenuous
stretch
striking
studying
substantial
succeed
successful
sudden
superintendent
suppress
surely
surprise
suspense

sweat
sweet
syllable
symmetrical
sympathy
synonym
technical
telegram
telephone
temperament
temperature
tenant
tendency
tenement
therefore
thorough
through
title
together
tomorrow
tongue
toward
tragedy
transferred
treasury
tremendous
tries
truly
twelfth
twelve
tyranny
undoubtedly
United States
university
unnecessary

unusual
useful
usual
vacuum
valley
valuable
variety
vegetable
vein
vengeance
versatile
vicinity
vicious
view
village
villain
visitor
voice
volume
waist
weak
wear
weather
Wednesday
week
weigh
weird
whether
which
while
whole
wholly
whose
wretched

☞ Drill: Spelling

> **DIRECTIONS:** Identify the misspelled word in each set.

1. (A) probly
   (B) accommodate
   (C) acquaintance

2. (A) auxiliary
   (B) atheletic
   (C) beginning

3. (A) environment
   (B) existence
   (C) Febuary

4. (A) ocassion
   (B) occurrence
   (C) omitted

5. (A) perspiration
   (B) referring
   (C) priviledge

> **DIRECTIONS:** Choose the correct option.

6. <u>Preceding</u> the <u>business</u> session, lunch will be served in a <u>separate</u> room.

   (A) preceeding . . . business . . . seperate
   (B) proceeding . . . bussiness . . . seperate
   (C) proceeding . . . business . . . seperite
   (D) No change is necessary.

7. Monte <u>inadvertently</u> left <u>several</u> of his <u>libary</u> books in the cafeteria.

   (A) inadverdently . . . serveral . . . libery

   (B) inadvertently . . . several . . . library

   (C) inadvertentely . . . several . . . librery

   (D) No change is necessary.

8. Sam wished he had more <u>liesure</u> time so he could <u>persue</u> his favorite hobbies.

   (A) leisure . . . pursue   (B) Liesure . . . pursue

   (C) leisure . . . persue   (D) No change is necessary.

9. One of my <u>favrite charecters</u> in <u>litrature</u> is Bilbo from *The Hobbit.*

   (A) favrite . . . characters . . . literature

   (B) favorite . . . characters . . . literature

   (C) favourite . . . characters . . . literature

   (D) No change is necessary.

10. Even <u>tho</u> Joe was badly hurt in the <u>accidant</u>, the company said they were not <u>lible</u> for damages.

    (A) though . . . accidant . . . libel

    (B) though . . . accident . . . liable

    (C) though . . . acident . . . liable

    (D) No change is necessary.

ESSAY WRITING REVIEW

The PPST contains one writing exercise. You will have 30 minutes to plan and write an essay on a given topic. You must write on only that topic. Since you will have only 30 minutes to complete the essay, efficient use of your time is essential.

Writing under pressure can be frustrating, but if you study this review, practice and polish your essay skills, and have a realistic sense of what to expect, you can turn problems into possibilities. The following

review will show you how to plan and write a logical, coherent, and interesting essay.

PRE-WRITING/PLANNING

Before you begin to actually write, there are certain preliminary steps you need to take. A few minutes spent planning pays off—your final essay will be more focused, well-developed, and clearer. For a 20-minute essay, you should spend about five minutes on the pre-writing process.

Understand the Question

Read the essay question very carefully and ask yourself the following questions:

- What is the meaning of the topic statement?

- Is the question asking me to persuade the reader of the validity of a certain opinion?

- Do I agree or disagree with the statement? What will be my thesis (main idea)?

- What kinds of examples can I use to support my thesis? Explore personal experiences, historical evidence, current events, and literary subjects.

Consider Your Audience

Essays would be pointless without an audience. Why write an essay if no one wants or needs to read it? Why add evidence, organize your ideas, or correct bad grammar? The reason to do any of these things is because someone out there needs to understand what you mean or say.

What does the audience need to know to believe you or to come over to your position? Imagine someone you know listening to you declare your position or opinion and then saying, "Oh, yeah? Prove it!" This is your audience—write to them. Ask yourself the following questions so that you will not be confronted with a person who says, "Prove it!"

- What evidence do I need to prove my idea to this skeptic?

- What would s/he disagree with me about?

- What does he or she share with me as common knowledge? What do I need to tell the reader?

WRITING YOUR ESSAY

Once you have considered your position on the topic and thought of several examples to support it, you are ready to begin writing.

Organizing Your Essay

Decide how many paragraphs you will write. In a 30-minute exercise, you will probably have time for no more than four or five paragraphs. In such a format, the first paragraph will be the introduction, the next two or three will develop your thesis with specific examples, and the final paragraph should be a strong conclusion.

The Introduction

The focus of your introduction should be the thesis statement. This statement allows your reader to understand the point and direction of your essay. The statement identifies the central idea of your essay and should clearly state your attitude about the subject. It will also dictate the basic content and organization of your essay. If you do not state your thesis clearly, your essay will suffer.

The thesis is the heart of the essay. Without it, readers won't know what your major message or central idea is in the essay.

The thesis must be something that can be argued or needs to be proven, not just an accepted fact. For example, "Animals are used every day in cosmetic and medical testing," is a fact—it needs no proof. But if the writer says, "Using animals for cosmetic and medical testing is cruel and should be stopped," we have a point that must be supported and defended by the writer.

The thesis can be placed in any paragraph of the essay, but in a short essay, especially one written for evaluative exam purposes, the thesis is most effective when placed in the last sentence of the opening paragraph.

Consider the following sample question:

ESSAY TOPIC:

"That government is best which governs least."

ASSIGNMENT: Do you agree or disagree with this statement? Choose a specific example from current events, personal experience, or your reading to support your position.

After reading the topic statement, decide if you agree or disagree. If you agree with this statement, your thesis statement could be the following:

> "Government has the right to protect individuals from interference but no right to extend its powers and activities beyond this function."

This statement clearly states the writer's opinion in a direct manner. It also serves as a blueprint for the essay. The remainder of the introduction should give two or three brief examples that support your thesis.

Supporting Paragraphs

The next two or three paragraphs of your essay will elaborate on the supporting examples you gave in your introduction. Each paragraph should discuss only one idea. Like the introduction, each paragraph should be coherently organized, with a topic sentence and supporting details.

The topic sentence is to each paragraph what the thesis statement is to the essay as a whole. It tells the reader what you plan to discuss in that paragraph. It has a specific subject and is neither too broad nor too narrow. It also establishes the author's attitude and gives the reader a sense of the direction in which the writer is going. An effective topic sentence also arouses the reader's interest.

Although it may occur in the middle or at the end of the paragraph, the topic sentence usually appears at the beginning of the paragraph. Placing it at the beginning is advantageous because it helps you stay focused on the main idea.

The remainder of each paragraph should support the topic sentence with examples and illustrations. Each sentence should progress logically from the previous one and be centrally connected to your topic sentence. Do not include any extraneous material that does not serve to develop your thesis.

Conclusion

Your conclusion should briefly restate your thesis and explain how you have shown it to be true. Since you want to end your essay on a strong note, your conclusion should be concise and effective.

Do not introduce any new topics that you cannot support. If you were watching a movie that suddenly shifted plot and characters at the end, you would be disappointed or even angry. Similarly, conclusions must not drift away from the major focus and message of the essay. Make sure your

conclusion is clearly on the topic and represents your perspective without any confusion about what you really mean and believe. The reader will respect you for staying true to your intentions.

The conclusion is your last chance to grab and impress the reader. You can even use humor, if appropriate, but a dramatic close will remind the reader you are serious, even passionate, about what you believe.

EFFECTIVE USE OF LANGUAGE

Clear organization, while vitally important, is not the only factor the graders of your essay consider. You must also demonstrate that you can express your ideas clearly, using correct grammar, diction, usage, spelling, and punctuation. For rules on grammar, usage, and mechanics, consult the English Language Skills Review in this book.

Point-of-View

Depending on the audience, essays may be written from one of three points of view:

1. *Subjective/Personal* Point of View:

   "I think . . ."

   "I believe cars are more trouble than they are worth."

   "I feel . . ."

2. *Second Person* Point of View (We . . . You; I . . . You):

   "If *you* own a car, *you* will soon find out that it is more trouble than it is worth."

3. *Third Person* Point of View (focuses on the idea, not what "I" think of it):

   "*Cars* are more trouble than *they* are worth."

It is very important to maintain a consistent point of view throughout your essay. If you begin writing in the first-person ("I"), do not shift to the second- or third-person in the middle of the essay. Such inconsistency is confusing to your reader and will be penalized by the graders of your essay.

Tone

A writer's tone results from his or her attitude towards the subject and the reader. If the essay question requires you to take a strong stand, the tone of your essay should reflect this.

Your tone should also be appropriate for the subject matter. A serious topic demands a serious tone. For a more light-hearted topic, you may wish to inject some humor into your essay.

Whatever tone you choose, be consistent. Do not make any abrupt shifts in tone in the middle of your essay.

Verb Tense

Make sure to remain in the same verb tense in which you began your essay. If you start in the past, make sure all verbs are past tense. Staying in the same verb tense improves the continuity and flow of ideas. Avoid phrases such as "now was," a confusing blend of present and past. Consistency of time is essential to the reader's understanding.

Transitions

Transitions are like the links of a bracelet, holding the beads or major points of your essay together. They help the reader follow the smooth flow of your ideas and show a connection between major and minor ideas. Transitions are used either at the beginning of a paragraph, or to show the connections among ideas within a single paragraph. Without transitions, you will jar the reader and distract him from your true ideas.

Here are some typical transitional words and phrases:

Linking similar ideas

again	for example	likewise
also	for instance	moreover
and	further	nor
another	furthermore	of course
besides	in addition	similarly
equally important	in like manner	too

Linking dissimilar/contradictory ideas

although	however	on the other hand
and yet	in spite of	otherwise
as if	instead	provided that
but	nevertheless	still
conversely	on the contrary	yet

Indicating cause, purpose, or result

as	for	so
as a result	for this reason	then
because	hence	therefore
consequently	since	thus

Indicating time or position

above	before	meanwhile
across	beyond	next
afterwards	eventually	presently
around	finally	second
at once	first	thereafter
at the present time	here	thereupon

Indicating an example or summary

as a result	in any event	in other words
as I have said	in brief	in short
for example	in conclusion	on the whole
for instance	in fact	to sum up

Common Writing Errors

The four writing errors most often made by beginning writers are run-ons (also known as fused sentences), fragments, lack of subject-verb agreement, and incorrect use of the object:

1. **Run-ons**: "She swept the floor it was dirty" is a run-on, because the pronoun "it" stands as a noun subject and starts a new sentence. A period or semicolon is needed after "floor."

2. **Fragments**: "Before Jimmy learned how to play baseball" is a fragment, even though it has a subject and verb (Jimmy learned). The word "before" fragmentizes the clause, and the reader needs to know what happened before Jimmy learned how to play baseball.

3. **Problems with subject-verb agreement**: "Either Maria or Robert are going to the game" is incorrect because either Maria is going or Robert is going, but not both. The sentence should say, "Either Maria or Robert is going to the game."

4. **Incorrect object**: Probably the most common offender in this area is saying "between you and I," which sounds correct, but isn't. "Between" is a preposition that takes the objective case "me." The correct usage is "between you and me."

The PPST test graders also cite lack of thought and development, misspellings, incorrect pronouns or antecedents, and lack of development as frequently occurring problems. Finally, keep in mind that clear, coherent handwriting always works to your advantage. Readers will appreciate an essay they can read with ease.

Five Words Weak Writers Overuse

Weak and beginning writers overuse the vague pronouns "you, we, they, this, and it" often without telling exactly who or what is represented by the pronoun.

1. Beginning writers often shift to second person **"you,"** when the writer means "a person." This shift confuses readers and weakens the flow of the essay. Although "you" is commonly accepted in creative writing, journalism, and other arenas, in a short, formal essay, it is best to avoid "you" altogether.

2. **"We"** is another pronoun that should be avoided. If by "we" the writer means "Americans," "society," or some other group, then he or she should say so.

3. **"They"** is often misused in essay writing, because it is overused in conversation: "I went to the doctor, and they told me to take some medicine." Tell the reader who "they" are.

4. **"This"** is usually used incorrectly without a referent: "She told me she received a present. This sounded good to me." This what? This idea? This news? This present? Be clear—don't make your readers guess what you mean. The word "this" should be followed by a noun or referent.

5. **"It"** is a common problem among weak writers. To what does "it" refer? Your readers don't appreciate vagueness, so take the time to be clear and complete in your expression of ideas.

Use Your Own Vocabulary

Is it a good idea to use big words that sound good in the dictionary or thesaurus, but that you don't really use or understand? No. So whose vocabulary should you use? Your own. You will be most comfortable with your own level of vocabulary.

This "comfort zone" doesn't give you license to be informal in a formal setting or to violate the rules of standard written English, but if you try to write in a style that is not yours, your writing will be awkward and lack a true voice.

You should certainly improve and build your vocabulary at every opportunity, but remember: you should not attempt to change your vocabulary level at this point.

Avoid the Passive Voice

In writing, the active voice is preferable because it is emphatic and direct. A weak passive verb leaves the doer unknown or seemingly unimportant. However, the passive voice is essential when the action of the verb is more important than the doer, when the doer is unknown, or when the writer wishes to place the emphasis on the receiver of the action rather than on the doer.

PROOFREADING

Make sure to leave yourself enough time at the end to read over your essay for errors such as misspellings, omitted words, or incorrect punctuation. You will not have enough time to make large-scale revisions, but take this chance to make any small changes that will make your essay stronger. Consider the following when proofreading your work:

- Are all your sentences really sentences? Have you written any fragments or run-on sentences?

- Are you using vocabulary correctly?

- Did you leave out any punctuation? Did you capitalize correctly?

- Are there any misspellings, especially of difficult words?

If you have time, read your essay backwards from end to beginning. By doing so, you may catch errors that you missed reading forward only.

☞ Drill: Essay Writing

DIRECTIONS: You have 30 minutes to plan and write an essay on the topic below. You may write only on the assigned topic.

Make sure to give specific examples to support your thesis. Proofread your essay carefully and take care to express your ideas clearly and effectively.

ESSAY TOPIC:

In the last 20 years, the deterioration of the environment has become a growing concern among both scientists and ordinary citizens.

ASSIGNMENT: Choose one pressing environmental problem, explain its negative impact, and discuss possible solutions.

WRITING SECTION DRILLS

ANSWER KEY

Drill: Word Choice Skills

1.	(D)	4.	(C)	7.	(A)	10.	(B)
2.	(D)	5.	(A)	8.	(B)		
3.	(A)	6.	(C)	9.	(C)		

Drill: Sentence Structure Skills

1.	(C)	4.	(B)	7.	(B)	10.	(B)
2.	(B)	5.	(A)	8.	(C)		
3.	(B)	6.	(A)	9.	(B)		

Drill: Verbs

1.	(C)	4.	(A)	7.	(A)	10.	(D)
2.	(D)	5.	(A)	8.	(C)		
3.	(D)	6.	(B)	9.	(A)		

Drill: Pronouns

1.	(A)	4.	(A)	7.	(B)	10.	(C)
2.	(C)	5.	(D)	8.	(B)		
3.	(A)	6.	(A)	9.	(A)		

Drill: Adjectives and Adverbs

1.	(C)	4.	(C)	7.	(A)	10.	(C)
2.	(A)	5.	(A)	8.	(C)		
3.	(D)	6.	(C)	9.	(B)		

Drill: Punctuation

1.	(D)	4.	(C)	7.	(A)	10.	(D)
2.	(A)	5.	(A)	8.	(A)		
3.	(A)	6.	(D)	9.	(B)		

Drill: Capitalization

1.	(D)	4.	(A)	7.	(B)	10.	(A)
2.	(B)	5.	(C)	8.	(D)		
3.	(C)	6.	(D)	9.	(B)		

Drill: Spelling

1.	(A)	4.	(A)	7.	(B)	10.	(B)
2.	(B)	5.	(C)	8.	(A)		
3.	(C)	6.	(D)	9.	(B)		

DETAILED EXPLANATIONS OF ANSWERS

Drill: Word Choice Skills

1.   **(D)**   Choice (D) is correct. No change is necessary. *Principal* as a noun means "head of a school." *Principle* is a noun meaning "axiom" or "rule of conduct."

2.   **(D)**   Choice (D) is correct. No change is necessary. *Affect* is a verb meaning "to influence" or "to change." *Effect* as a noun meaning "result."

3.   **(A)**   Choice (A) is correct. Use *amount* with noncountable, mass nouns (*amount* of food, help, money); use *number* with countable, plural nouns (*number* of children, classes, bills).

4.   **(C)**   Choice (C) is correct. *Supposed to* and *used to* should be spelled with a final *d*. *Achieving* follows the standard spelling rule—*i* before *e*.

5.   **(A)**   Choice (A) is correct. Use *that*, not *because*, to introduce clauses after the word *reason*. Choice (A) is also the only choice that contains the correct spelling of "succeeded."

6.   **(C)**   Choice (C) is correct. *Converge together* is redundant, and *single* is not needed to convey the meaning of *a highway*.

7.   **(A)**   Choice (A) is correct. It is economical and concise. The other choices contain unnecessary repetition.

8.   **(B)**   Choice (B) is correct. Choices (A) and (C) pad the sentences with loose synonyms that are redundant. Choice (D), although a short sentence, does not convey the meaning as clearly as choice (B).

9.   **(C)**   Choice (C) is correct. The other choices all contain unnecessary repetition.

10.   **(B)**   Choice (B) is correct. Choices (A) and (C) contain circumlocution; they fail to get to the point. Choice (D) does not express the meaning of the sentence as concisely as choice (B).

Drill: Sentence Structure Skills

1. **(C)** Choice (C) is correct. Each response contains items in a series. In choices (A) and (B), the word group after the conjunction is not an adjective like the first words in the series. Choice (C) contains three adjectives.

2. **(B)** Choice (B) is correct. Choices (A), (C), and (D) combine conjunctions incorrectly.

3. **(B)** Choice (B) is correct. Choices (A) and (C) appear to be parallel because the conjunction *and* connects two word groups that both begin with *because*, but the structure on both sides of the conjunction are very different. *Because he kept his campaign promises* is a clause; *because of his refusal to accept political favors* is a prepositional phrase. Choice (B) connects two dependent clauses.

4. **(B)** Choice (B) is correct. Choices (A) and (C) contain the elliptical clause *While . . . taking a shower*. It appears that the missing subject in the elliptical clause is the same as that in the independent clause—the *doorbell* in choice (A) and *someone* in choice (C), neither of which is a logical subject for the verbal *taking a shower*. Choice (B) removes the elliptical clause and provides the logical subject.

5. **(A)** Choice (A) is correct. Who swung the bat? Choices (B) and (C) both imply that it is the runner who swung the bat. Only choice (A) makes it clear that as *he* swung the bat, someone else (the *runner*) stole second base.

6. **(A)** Choice (A) is correct. The punctuation in the original sentence and in choice (B) creates a fragment. *Cotton being the state's principal crop* is not an independent thought because it lacks a complete verb—*being* is not a complete verb.

7. **(B)** Choice (B) is correct. The punctuation in the original sentence and in choice (A) creates a fragment. Both the semicolon and the period should be used to separate two independent clauses. The word group *one that I have never seen before* does not express a complete thought and therefore is not an independent clause.

8. **(C)** Choice (C) is correct. The dependent clause *because repairs were being made* in choices (B) and (D) is punctuated as if it were a sentence. The result is a fragment.

9. **(B)** Choice (B) is correct. Choices (A) and (C) do not separate the complete thoughts in the independent clauses with the correct punctuation.

10. **(B)** Choice (B) is correct. Choices (A) and (C) do not separate the independent clauses with the correct punctuation.

Drill: Verbs

1. **(C)** Choice (C) is correct. The past participle form of each verb is required because of the auxiliaries (helping verbs) *had been* (concerned) and *would have* (gone).

2. **(D)** Choice (D) is correct. The forms of the irregular verb meaning *to rest* are *lie (rest), lies (rests), lay (rested),* and *has lain (has rested)*. The forms of the verb meaning *to put* are *lay (put), lays (puts), laying (putting), laid (put),* and *have laid (have put)*.

3. **(D)** Choice (D) is correct. The present tense is used for universal truths and the past tense is used for historical truths.

4. **(A)** Choice (A) is correct. The present tense is used for customary happenings. Choice (B), *had begun,* is not a standard verb form. Choice (C), *was beginning,* indicates that 10:30 a.m. is not the regular class time.

5. **(A)** Choice (A) is correct. The past tense is used for historical statements, and the present tense is used for statements about works of art.

6. **(B)** Choice (B) is correct. The subject of the sentence is the plural noun *sales,* not the singular noun *Christmas,* which is the object of the prepositional phrase.

7. **(A)** Choice (A) is correct. The subject *specialty* is singular.

8. **(C)** Choice (C) is correct. Subjects preceded by *every* are considered singular and therefore require a singular verb form.

9. **(A)** Choice (A) is correct. The subject of the sentence is the gerund *hiding,* not the object of the gerund phrase *mistakes. Hiding* is singular; therefore, the singular verb form *does* should be used.

10. **(D)** Choice (D) is correct. Though the form of the subject *Board of Regents* is plural, it is singular in meaning.

Drill: Pronouns

1. **(A)** Choice (A) is correct. Do not use the reflexive pronoun *myself* as a substitute for *I*.

2. **(C)** Choice (C) is correct. In the clause *whoever consumes them*, *whoever* is the subject. *Whomever* is the objective case pronoun and should be used only as the object of a sentence, never as the subject.

3. **(A)** Choice (A) is correct. Use the nominative case pronoun *who* as the subject complement after the verb *is*.

4. **(A)** Choice (A) is correct. In this sentence use the nominative case/subject pronouns *she who* as the subject complement after the *be* verb *was*.

5. **(D)** Choice (D) is correct. *Student* is an indefinite, genderless noun that requires a singular personal pronoun. While *his* is a singular personal pronoun, a genderless noun includes both the masculine and feminine forms and requires *his or her* as the singular personal pronoun.

6. **(A)** Choice (A) is correct. The antecedent *company* is singular, requiring the singular pronoun *it*, not the plural *they*.

7. **(B)** Choice (B) is correct. Choice (A) contains a person shift: *Your* is a second person pronoun, and *his* and *her* are third person pronouns. The original sentence uses the third person plural pronoun *their* to refer to the singular antecedent *every car owner*. Choice (B) correctly provides the masculine and feminine forms *his or her* required by the indefinite, genderless *every car owner*.

8. **(B)** Choice (B) is correct. The implied antecedent is *teaching*. Choices (A) and (C) each contain a pronoun with no antecedent. Neither *it* nor *this* are suitable substitutions for *teacher*.

9. **(A)** Choice (A) is correct. The pronoun *they* in the original sentence has no conspicuous antecedent. Since the doer of the action is obviously unknown (and therefore genderless), choice (B), *he*, is not the correct choice.

10. **(C)** Choice (C) is correct. The original sentence is ambiguous: the pronoun *she* has two possible antecedents; we don't know whether it is Margaret or her sister who is away at college.

Drill: Adjectives and Adverbs

1. **(C)** Choice (C) is correct. *Bad* is an adjective; *badly* is an adverb. *Real* is an adjective meaning *genuine* (*a real problem, real leather*). To qualify an adverb of degree to express how bad, how excited, how boring, etc., choose *very*.

2. **(A)** Choice (A) is correct. Use an adverb as a qualifier for an adjective. *How simple? Relatively simple.*

3. **(D)** Choice (D) is correct. *Good* is an adjective; *well* is both an adjective and an adverb. As an adjective, *well* refers to health; it means "not ill."

4. **(C)** Choice (C) is correct. All the other choices use *good* incorrectly as an adverb. *Shake* is an action verb that requires an adverb, not an adjective.

5. **(A)** Choice (A) is correct. The action verbs *speaks*, *writes*, *observe*, and *think* each require adverbs as modifiers.

6. **(C)** Choice (C) is correct. The comparisons in choices (A) and (B) are illogical: these sentences suggest that Los Angeles is not in California because it *is larger than any city in California.*

7. **(A)** Choice (A) is correct. Do not omit the second *as* of the correlative pair *as . . . as* when making a point of equal or superior comparison, as in choice (B). Choice (C) omits *than* from "if not more interesting [than]."

8. **(C)** Choice (C) is correct. Choice (A) illogically compares *baseball team* to a *university*, and choice (B) illogically compares *baseball team* to *all the other universities*. Choice (C) logically compares the baseball team here to the one at any other university, as implied by the possessive ending on university—*university's.*

9. **(B)** Choice (B) is correct. Choices (A) and (C) are ambiguous; because these sentences are too elliptical, the reader does not know where to place the missing information.

10. **(C)** Choice (C) is correct. Choice (A) is redundant; there is no need to use *most* with *stingiest*. Choice (B) incorrectly combines the comparative word *more* with the superlative form *stingiest*.

Drill: Punctuation

1. **(D)** Choice (D) is correct. Nonrestrictive clauses, like other nonrestrictive elements, should be set off from the rest of the sentence with commas.

2. **(A)** Choice (A) is correct. Use a comma to separate a nonrestrictive appositive from the word it modifies. "An Oklahoma family" is a nonrestrictive appositive.

3. **(A)** Choice (A) is correct. Do not use unnecessary commas to separate a subject and verb from their complement. Both choices (B) and (C) use superfluous punctuation.

4. **(C)** Choice (C) is correct. Do not separate two items in a compound with commas. The original sentence incorrectly separates "car or plane." Choice (A) omits the comma after the introductory clause.

5. **(A)** Choice (A) is correct. Use a semicolon to separate two independent clauses/sentences that are not joined by a coordinating conjunction, especially when the ideas in the sentences are interrelated.

6. **(D)** Choice (D) is correct. Use a semicolon to separate two sentences not joined by a coordinating conjunction.

7. **(A)** Choice (A) is correct. Use a semicolon to separate two sentences joined by a conjunctive adverb.

8. **(A)** Choice (A) is correct. Do not use a colon after a verb or a preposition. Remember that a complete sentence must precede a colon.

9. **(B)** Choice (B) is correct. Do not use a colon after a preposition, and do not use a colon to separate a preposition from its objects.

10. **(D)** Choice (D) is correct. Use a colon preceding a list that is introduced by words such as *the following* and *as follows*.

Drill: Capitalization

1. **(D)** Choice (D) is correct. *North America*, like other proper names, is capitalized. *North, south, east,* and *west* are only capitalized when they refer to geographic regions (*the Southwest, Eastern Europe);* as compass directions, they are not capitalized.

2.   **(B)**   Choice (B) is correct. Although persons' names are capitalized, a person's title is not (*coach*, not *Coach*). Capitalize the complete name of a team, school, river, etc. (Dallas Cowboys).

3.   **(C)**   Choice (C) is correct. Capitalize all geographic units, and capitalize *earth* only when it is mentioned with other planets. *Equator* is not capitalized.

4.   **(A)**   Choice (A) is correct. Capitalize the first word in a title and all other words in a title except articles, prepositions with fewer than five letters, and conjunctions.

5.   **(C)**   Choice (C) is correct. Capitalize proper adjectives (proper nouns used as adjectives): *Greek* goddess, *Roman* mythology.

6.   **(D)**   Choice (D) is correct. Capitalize all religious groups, books, and names referring to religious deities.

7.   **(B)**   Choice (B) is correct. Do not capitalize courses unless they are languages (English) or course titles followed by a number (Algebra I).

8.   **(D)**   Choice (D) is correct. Do not capitalize seasons unless they accompany the name of an event such as *Spring Break*. Do not capitalize types of degrees (*bachelor's degrees*); capitalize only the name of the degree (*Bachelor of Arts degree*).

9.   **(B)**   Choice (B) is correct. As a landmark, *Berlin Wall* is capitalized; however, do not capitalize systems of government or individual adherents to a philosophy, such as *communism*.

10. **(A)**   Choice (A) is correct. The names of planets, as well as the complete names of newspapers and other periodicals, are capitalized.

Drill: Spelling

1.   **(A)**   The correct spelling of choice (A) is "probably."

2.   **(B)**   The correct spelling is "athletic."

3.   **(C)**   Choice (C) should be spelled "February."

4.   **(A)**   The correct spelling of this word is "occasion."

5. **(C)** Choice (C) should be spelled "privilege."

6. **(D)** Choice (D) is the best response. *Business* has only three *-s's*. Separate has an *-e* at the beginning and the end, not in the middle.

7. **(B)** Choice (B) is the best response. *Library* has two *r's*.

8. **(A)** Choice (A) is the best response. *Leisure* is one of the few English words that does not follow the *i* before *e* except after *c* rule. *Pursue* has two *u's* and only one *e*.

9. **(B)** Choice (B) is the best response. "Favorite," "characters," and "literature" are commonly mispronounced, and when someone who mispronounces them tries to spell them phonetically, he or she often misspells them.

10. **(B)** Choice (B) is the best response. Advertisements often misspell words to catch the consumer's eye (*lite* for light, *tho* for though, etc.), and these misspellings are becoming more common in student writing. "Accident" and "liable" are examples of words that are not pronounced the way they are spelled.

Drill: Essay Writing

This Answer Key provides three sample essays which represent possible responses to the essay topic. Compare your own response to those given on the next few pages. Allow the strengths and weaknesses of the sample essays help you to critique your own essay and improve your writing skills.

ESSAY I (Score: 5–6)

There are many pressing environmental problems facing both this country and the world today. Pollution, the misuse and squandering of resources, and the cavalier attitude many people express all contribute to the problem. But one of the most pressing problems this country faces is the apathetic attitude many Americans have towards recycling.

Why is recycling so imperative? There are two major reasons. First, recycling previously used materials conserves precious national resources. Many people never stop to think that reserves of metal ores are not unlimited. There is only so much gold, silver, tin, and other metals in the ground. Once it has all been mined, there will never be any more unless we recycle what has already been used.

Second, the United States daily generates more solid waste than any

other country on earth. Our disposable consumer culture consumes fast food meals in paper or styrofoam containers, uses disposable diapers with plastic liners that do not biodegrade, receives pounds, if not tons, of unsolicited junk mail every year, and relies more and more on prepackaged rather than fresh food.

No matter how it is accomplished, increased recycling is essential. We have to stop covering our land with garbage, and the best ways to do this are to reduce our dependence on prepackaged goods and to minimize the amount of solid waste disposed of in landfills. The best way to reduce solid waste is to recycle it. Americans need to band together to recycle, to preserve our irreplaceable natural resources, reduce pollution, and preserve our precious environment.

Analysis

This essay presents a clearly defined thesis, and the writer elaborates on this thesis in a thoughtful and sophisticated manner. Various aspects of the problem under consideration are presented and explored, along with possible solutions. The support provided for the writer's argument is convincing and logical. There are few usage or mechanical errors to interfere with the writer's ability to communicate effectively. This writer demonstrates a comprehensive understanding of the rules of written English.

ESSAY II (Score: 3–4)

A pressing environmental problem today is the way we are cutting down too many trees and not planting any replacements for them. Trees are beneficial in many ways, and without them, many environmental problems would be much worse.

One of the ways trees are beneficial is that, like all plants, they take in carbon dioxide and produce oxygen. They can actually help clean the air this way. When too many trees are cut down in a small area, the air in that area is not as good and can be unhealthy to breath.

Another way trees are beneficial is that they provide homes for many types of birds, insects, and animals. When all the trees in an area are cut down, these animals lose their homes and sometimes they can die out and become extinct that way. Like the spotted owls in Oregon, that the loggers wanted to cut down the trees they lived in. If the loggers did cut down all the old timber stands that the spotted owls lived in, the owls would have become extinct.

But the loggers say that if they can't cut the trees down then they will be out of work, and that peoples' jobs are more important than birds. The

loggers can do two things—they can either get training so they can do other jobs, or they can do what they should have done all along, and start replanting trees. For every mature tree they cut down, they should have to plant at least one tree seedling.

Cutting down the trees that we need for life, and that lots of other species depend on, is a big environmental problem that has a lot of long term consaquences. Trees are too important for all of us to cut them down without thinking about the future.

Analysis

This essay has a clear thesis, which the author does support with good examples. But the writer shifts between the chosen topic, which is that indiscriminate tree-cutting is a pressing environmental problem, and a list of the ways in which trees are beneficial and a discussion about the logging profession. Also, while there are few mistakes in usage and mechanics, the writer does have some problems with sentence structure. The writing is pedestrian and the writer does not elaborate on the topic as much as he or she could have. The writer failed to provide the kind of critical analysis that the topic required.

ESSAY III (Score: 1–2)

The most pressing environmental problem today is that lots of people and companies don't care about the environment, and they do lots of things that hurt the environment.

People throw littur out car windows and don't use trash cans, even if their all over a park, soda cans and fast food wrappers are all over the place. Cigarette butts are the worst cause the filters never rot. Newspapers and junk mail get left to blow all over the neighborhood, and beer bottles too.

Companies pollute the air and the water. Sometimes the ground around a company has lots of tocsins in it. Now companies can buy credits from other companies that let them pollute the air even more. They dump all kinds of chemacals into lakes and rivers that kills off the fish and causes acid rain and kills off more fish and some trees and small animuls and insects and then noone can go swimming or fishing in the lake.

People need to respect the environment because we only have one planet, and if we keep polluting it pretty soon nothing will grow and then even the people will die.

Analysis

The writer of this essay does not define his or her thesis for this

essay. Because of this lack of a clear thesis, the reader is left to infer the topic from the body of the essay. It is possible to perceive the writer's intended thesis; however, the support for this thesis is very superficial. The writer presents a list of common complaints about polluters, without any critical discussion of the problems and possible solutions. Many sentences are run-ons and the writer has made several spelling errors. While the author manages to communicate his or her position on the issue, he or she does so on such a superficial level and with so many errors in usage and mechanics that the writer fails to demonstrate an ability to effectively communicate.

PPST

Pre-Professional Skills Tests

Practice
PPST I

PPST Test I

Section I: Reading Comprehension

TIME: 60 Minutes
40 Questions

DIRECTIONS: A number of questions follow each of the passages in the reading section. Answer the questions by choosing the best answer from the five choices given.

Questions 1 and 2 refer to the following passage:

America's national bird, the mighty bald eagle, is being threatened by a new menace. Once decimated by hunters and loss of habitat, this newest danger is suspected to be from the intentional poisoning by livestock ranchers. Authorities have found animal carcasses injected with restricted pesticides. These carcasses are suspected to have been placed to attract and kill predators such as the bald eagle in an effort to preserve young grazing animals. It appears that the eagle is being threatened again by the consummate predator, humans.

1. One can conclude from this passage that

   (A) the pesticides used are detrimental to the environment.

   (B) the killing of eagles will protect the rancher's rangeland.

   (C) ranchers must obtain licenses to use the pesticides.

   (D) the poisoning could result in the extinction of the bald eagle.

   (E) pesticides have been obtained illegally.

2. The author's attitude is one of

   (A) detached observation.

   (D) suspicion.

   (B) concerned interest.

   (E) unbridled anger.

   (C) informed acceptance.

Questions 3 and 4 refer to the graph below.

Number of Boys and Girls in Scouting in 1989 (in millions)

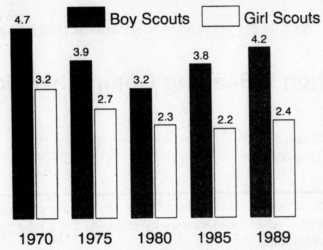

Source: 1991 Census Bureau's Statistical Abstract of the U.S.

3. In what year was the involvement in scouting closest to being equal between girls and boys?

   (A) 1970   (D) 1985

   (B) 1975   (E) 1989

   (C) 1980

4. How much difference between the number of boys and the number of girls involved in scouting was there (in millions) in 1970?

   (A) 1.6 million   (D) 2.4 million

   (B) .9 million   (E) 1 million

   (C) 1.5 million

5. The disparaging remarks about her performance on the job made Alice uncomfortable.

   The word "disparaging" is closest in meaning to

   (A) complimentary.   (D) technical.

   (B) evil.   (E) insulting.

   (C) funny.

Questions 6 to 8 refer to the following passage:

INSTRUCTIONS FOR ABSENTEE VOTING

These instructions describe conditions under which voters may register for or request absentee ballots to vote in the November 5, 1991, election.

(1) If you moved on or prior to October 7, 1991, and did not register to vote at your new address, you are not eligible to vote in this election.

(2) If you move after this date, you may vote via absentee ballot or at your polling place, using your previous address as your address of registration for this election.

(3) You must register at your new address to vote in future elections.

(4) The last day to request an absentee ballot is October 29, 1991.

(5) You must be a registered voter in the county.

(6) You must sign your request in your own handwriting.

(7) You must make a separate request for each election.

(8) The absentee ballot shall be issued to the requesting voter in person or by mail.

6. A voter will be able to participate in the November 5, 1991, election as an absentee if he or she

(A) planned to register for the next election in 1992.

(B) requested an absentee ballot on November 1, 1991.

(C) voted absentee in the last election.

(D) moved as a registered voter on October 13, 1991.

(E) moved on October 7, 1991.

7. On October 15, 1991, Mr. Applebee requested an absentee ballot for his daughter, a registered voting college student, to enable her to participate in the election process. Mr. Applebee will most likely need clarification on which of the following instructions?

(A) 2

(B) 3

(C) 4

(D) 5

(E) 6

8. Which of the following best describes the most important piece of information for potential voters who want to participate in the election process, either in person or by absentee ballot?

   (A) Do not change precincts.

   (B) Do register to vote in the appropriate precinct.

   (C) You may vote at your nearest polling place.

   (D) The last day to register is always October 29.

   (E) Your absentee ballot can be used for any election when you have to be out of town.

Questions 9 and 10 refer to the following statement:

The atrophy and incapacity which occur when a broken bone is encased in plaster and immobilized clearly demonstrate what a sedentary life-style can do to the human body.

9. In the passage above, "atrophy and incapacity" refer to

   (A) a strengthened condition brought about by rest.

   (B) a decrease in size and strength.

   (C) a type of exercise.

   (D) rest and recuperation.

   (E) the effects of body building.

10. Which of the following statements does NOT reflect the author's view of sedentary living?

   (A) If you don't use it, you lose it.

   (B) Mobility is affected by life-style.

   (C) A sedentary life-style is a healthy life-style.

   (D) A body is as a body does.

   (E) Exercise increases mobility.

Questions 11 to 15 refer to the following passage:

Frederick Douglass was born Frederick Augustus Washington Bailey in 1817 to a white father and a slave mother. Frederick was raised by his grandmother on a Maryland plantation until he was eight. It was then that he was sent to Baltimore by his owner to be a servant to the Auld family. Mrs. Auld recognized Frederick's intellectual acumen and defied the law of the state by teaching him to read and write. When Mr. Auld warned that education would make the boy unfit for slavery, Frederick sought to continue his education in the streets. When his master died, Frederick was returned to the plantation to work in the fields at age 16. Later, he was hired out to work in the shipyards in Baltimore as a ship caulker. He plotted an escape but was discovered before he could get away. It took five years before he made his way to New York City and then to New Bedford, Massachusetts, eluding slave hunters by changing his name to Douglass.

At an 1841 anti-slavery meeting in Massachusetts, Douglass was invited to give a talk about his experiences under slavery. His impromptu speech was so powerful and so eloquent that it thrust him into a career as an agent for the Massachusetts Anti-Slavery Society.

Douglass wrote his autobiography in 1845 primarily to counter those who doubted his authenticity as a former slave. This work became a classic in American literature and a primary source about slavery from the point of view of a slave. Douglass went on a two-year speaking tour abroad to avoid recapture by his former owner and to win new friends for the abolition movement. He returned with funds to purchase his freedom and to start his own anti-slavery newspaper. He became a consultant to Abraham Lincoln and throughout Reconstruction fought doggedly for full civil rights for freedmen; he also supported the women's rights movement.

11. According to the passage, Douglass's autobiography was motivated by

   (A) the desire to make money for his anti-slavery movement.

   (B) the desire to start a newspaper.

   (C) his interest in authenticating his life as a slave.

   (D) his desire to educate people about slavery.

   (E) his desire to promote the Civil War.

12. The central idea of the passage is that Frederick Douglass

    (A) was influential in changing the laws regarding the education of slaves.

    (B) was one of the most eminent human rights leaders of the century.

    (C) was a personal friend and confidant to a president.

    (D) wrote a classic in American literature.

    (E) supported women's rights.

13. According to the author of this passage, Mrs. Auld taught Frederick to read because

    (A) Frederick wanted to learn like the other boys.

    (B) she recognized his natural ability.

    (C) she wanted to comply with the laws of the state.

    (D) he needed to read to work in the home.

    (E) she obeyed her husband's wishes in the matter.

14. The title that best expresses the ideas of this passage is

    (A) The History of the Anti-Slavery Movement.

    (B) The Dogged Determination of Frederick Douglass.

    (C) Reading: Window to the World.

    (D) Frederick Douglass's Contributions to Freedom.

    (E) The Oratorical and Literary Brilliance of Frederick Douglass.

15. In the context of the passage, "impromptu" is closest in meaning to

    (A) unprepared.   (D) loud and excited.

    (B) a quiet manner.   (E) elaborate.

    (C) forceful.

Question 16 refers to the following passage:

Acupuncture practitioners, those who use the placement of needles at strategic locations under the skin to block pain, have been tolerated by American physicians since the 1930s. This form of Chinese treatment has been used for about 3,000 years and until recently has been viewed suspiciously by the West. New research indicates that acupuncture might provide relief for sufferers of chronic back pain, arthritis, and recently pain experienced by alcoholics and drug users as they kick the habit.

16. According to the passage, acupuncture has been found to help people suffering from all of the following EXCEPT

    (A) arthritis.

    (B) recurring back pain.

    (C) alcoholics in withdrawal.

    (D) liver disease.

    (E) drug addicts in withdrawal.

Question 17 refers to the following passage:

Each time a person opens his or her mouth to eat, he or she makes a nutritional decision. These selections make a definitive difference in how an individual looks, feels, and performs at work or play. When a good assortment of food in appropriate amounts is selected and eaten, the consequences are likely to be desirable levels of health and energy to allow one to be as active as needed. Conversely, when choices are less than desirable, the consequences can be poor health or limited energy or both. Studies of American diets, particularly the diets of the very young, reveal unsatisfactory dietary habits as evidenced by the numbers of overweight and out-of-shape young children.

17. The author's attitude toward American's dietary habits may be characterized as

    (A) lacking in interest.   (D) angry.

    (B) concerned.   (E) amused.

    (C) informational.

Question 18 refers to the following passage:

Commercial enterprises frequently provide the backdrop for the birth of a new language. When members of different language communities need to communicate or wish to bargain with each other, they may develop a new language through a process called "pidginization." A pidgin language, or pidgin, never becomes a native language; rather, its use is limited to business transactions with members of other language communities. Pidgins consist of very simple grammatical structures and small vocabularies. They have tended to develop around coastal areas where seafarers first made contact with speakers of other languages.

18. The passage suggests which of the following about pidgins?

(A) We could expect to hear pidgins along the west coast of Africa and in the Pacific islands.

(B) Pidgins are a complicated combination of two languages.

(C) Pidgins are located in inland mountain regions.

(D) Pidgins become the main language after several generations of use.

(E) Pidgins are the languages of seafarers.

Question 19 refers to the following passage:

There are two ways of measuring mass. One method to determine the mass of a body is to use a beam-balance. By this method, an unknown mass is placed on one pan at the end of a beam. The known masses are added to the pan at the other end of the beam until the pans are balanced. Since the force of gravity is the same on each pan, the masses must also be the same on each pan. When the mass of a body is measured by comparison with known masses on a beam-balance, it is called the gravitational mass of the body.

The second method to determine the mass of a body is distinctly different; this method uses the property of inertia. To determine mass in this way, a mass is placed on a frictionless horizontal surface. When a known force is applied to it, the magnitude of the mass is measured by the amount of acceleration produced upon it by the known force. Mass measured in this way is said to be the inertial mass of the body in question. This method is seldom used because it involves both a frictionless surface and a difficult measurement of acceleration.

19. Which of the following statements can best be supported from the passage?

    (A) The gravitational and inertia mass methods measure different properties of the object.

    (B) The masses are equal when the weights are equal and cause the beam to be balanced.

    (C) Gravitational and inertial measurements do not give the same numerical value for mass.

    (D) The same result for a beam-balance method cannot be obtained at higher altitudes.

    (E) The mass of a body depends on where it is located in the universe.

Question 20 refers to the following statement:

Her introductory remarks provided a segue into the body of the speech.

20. In this context the word "segue" means

    (A) delivery.   (D) credential.

    (B) a pause.   (E) critique.

    (C) direction.

Questions 21 to 23 refer to the following passage:

One of the many tragedies of the Civil War was the housing and care of prisoners. The Andersonville prison, built by the Confederates in 1864 to accommodate 10,000 Union prisoners, was not completed when prisoners started arriving. Five months later the total number of men incarcerated there had risen to 31,678.

The sounds of death and dying were not diminished by surrender of weapons to a captor. Chances of survival for prisoners in Andersonville were not much better than in the throes of combat. Next to overcrowding, inadequate shelter caused unimaginable suffering. The Confederates were not equipped with the manpower, tools, or supplies necessary to house such a population of captives; prisoners themselves gathered lumber, logs, anything they could find to construct some sort of protection from the elements. Some prisoners dug holes in the ground, risking suffocation from cave-ins, but many hundreds were left exposed to the wind, rain, cold, and heat.

Daily food rations were exhausted by the sheer numbers they had to serve, resulting in severe dietary deficiencies. The overcrowding, meager rations, and deplorable unsanitary conditions resulted in rampant disease and a high mortality rate. The consequences of a small scratch or wound could result in death in Andersonville. During the prison's 13-month existence, more than 12,000 prisoners died and were buried in the Andersonville cemetery. Most of the deaths were caused by diarrhea, dysentery, gangrene, and scurvy that could not be treated due to inadequate staff and supplies.

21. What is the central idea of the passage?

    (A) The major problem for the Confederates was finding burial spaces in the cemetery.

    (B) The prison was never fully completed.

    (C) Prison doctors were ill-equipped to handle emergencies.

    (D) Andersonville prison was not adequate to care for three times as many prisoners as it could hold.

    (E) Many prisoners died as a result of shelter cave-ins.

22. From this passage the author's attitude toward the Confederates is one of

    (A) approval.   (D) indifference.

    (B) impartiality.   (E) denial.

    (C) contempt.

23. The first sentence of the second paragraph of this passage can best be described as

    (A) a tribute.   (D) an exposé.

    (B) a digression.   (E) an irony.

    (C) a hypothesis.

Question 24 refers to the following statement:

Maria commented to Joe, "Ted's nose is out of joint because he wasn't invited to the reception."

24. Someone hearing the conversation would most likely conclude that Ted

    (A) had a swollen nose.

    (B) does not have a large nose.

    (C) was upset about not being asked to the reception.

    (D) was not invited to the reception because his nose was hurt.

    (E) had a bandage on his nose at the reception.

Questions 25 to 27 refer to the following passage:

To the Shakers, perfection was found in the creation of an object that was both useful and simple. Their Society was founded in 1774 by Ann Lee, an Englishwoman from the working classes who brought eight followers to New York with her. "Mother Ann" established her religious community on the belief that worldly interests were evil.

To gain entrance into the Society, believers had to remain celibate, have no private possessions, and avoid contact with outsiders. The order came to be called "Shakers" because of the feverish dance the group performed. Another characteristic of the group was the desire to seek perfection in their work.

Shaker furniture was created to exemplify specific characteristics: simplicity of design, quality of craftsmanship, harmony of proportion, and usefulness. While Shakers did not create any innovations in furniture designs, they were known for fine craftsmanship. The major emphasis was on function, and not on excessive or elaborate decorations that contributed nothing to the product's usefulness.

25. The passage indicates that members of the religious order were called the Shakers because

    (A) they shook hands at their meetings.

    (B) they did a shaking dance at their meetings.

    (C) they took their name from the founder.

    (D) they were named after the township where they originated.

    (E) they developed a shaking disorder.

26. Which of the following is the most appropriate substitute for the use of the term "innovations" in the third paragraph?

    (A) Corrections

    (B) Colors

    (C) Changes

    (D) Functions

    (E) Brocades

27. The passage suggests which of the following about the Shakers?

    (A) Shaker furniture is well-proportioned and ornate in design.

    (B) Shakers believed in form over function in their designs.

    (C) Shaker furniture has seen a surge in popularity.

    (D) Shakers appeared to believe that form follows function.

    (E) Shaker furniture is noted for the use of brass hardware.

Questions 28 and 29 refer to the following passage:

James Dean began his career as a stage actor, but in motion pictures he symbolized the confused, restless, and idealistic youth of the 1950s. He excelled at film parts that called for brooding, impulsive characterizations, the personification of frustrated youthful passion. Dean made three such movies: *East of Eden, Rebel Without a Cause*, and *Giant*, and established himself as a cult hero. Tragically, his career was cut short in an automobile crash before the release of *Giant*.

28. One conclusion that could be drawn from this passage is that

    (A) James Dean was not well regarded because of the kind of characters he portrayed.

    (B) James Dean had to be replaced by another actor in *Giant* due to his death.

    (C) James Dean was adept at portraying sensitive, youthful characters.

    (D) James Dean had a long and distinguished career.

    (E) James Dean was a promising stage actor.

29. The author's attitude is one of

    (A) regret.

    (B) anger.

    (C) humor.

    (D) pessimism.

    (E) indifference.

Questions 30 to 32 refer to the following passage:

Benjamin Franklin began writing his autobiography in 1771, but he set it aside to assist the colonies in gaining independence from England. After a hiatus of 13 years, he returned to chronicle his life, addressing his message to the younger generation. In this significant literary work of early United States, Franklin portrays himself as benign, kindhearted, practical, and hardworking. He established a list of ethical conduct and recorded his transgressions when he was unsuccessful in overcoming temptation. Franklin wrote that he was unable to arrive at perfection, "yet I was, by the endeavor, a better and happier man than I otherwise should have been if I had not attempted it."

30. Which of the following is the LEAST appropriate substitute for the use of the term "ethical" near the end of the passage?

    (A) Moral

    (B) Depraved

    (C) Virtuous

    (D) Honorable

    (E) Qualifiable

31. The passage suggests which of the following about Franklin's autobiography?

    (A) It was representative of early American literature.

    (B) It fell short of being a major work of literary quality.

    (C) It personified Franklin as a major political figure.

    (D) It was a notable work of early American literature.

    (E) It was directed toward his enemies.

32. Which of the following slogans best describes Franklin's assessment of the usefulness of attempting to achieve perfection?

    (A) Cleanliness is next to Godliness.

    (B) Nothing ventured, nothing gained.

(C) Ambition is its own reward.

(D) Time is money.

(E) Humility is everything.

Questions 33 to 35 refer to the graph below:

How the Average Consumer Spent Money in 1988
Total: $25,892

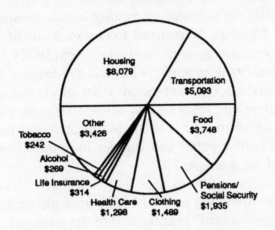

Source: 1991 Census Bureau's Statistical Abstract of the U.S.

33. According to the graph, the average consumer spent approximately 50 percent of her/his earnings on

(A) housing and health care costs.

(B) transportation and housing.

(C) leisure pursuits and food.

(D) transportation and pensions.

(E) none of the above.

34. After transportation, the next greatest amount of money was spent on

(A) clothing.   (D) health care.

(B) other.   (E) pensions/social security.

(C) food.

35. According to the graph, expenditure on health care was approximately equal to

    (A) clothing.

    (B) life insurance.

    (C) pensions.

    (D) food.

    (E) other.

Questions 36 to 38 refer to the following passage:

The scarlet flamingo is practically a symbol of Florida. Once the West Indian flamingo population wintered in Florida Bay and as far north as St. John's River and Tampa Bay, but the brilliantly colored birds abandoned these grounds around 1885 due to the decimation of their numbers by feather hunters. The flock at Hialeah Race Track is descended from a handful of birds imported from Cuba in the 1930s. It took seven years before the first flamingo was born in captivity, but several thousand have since been hatched.

Flamingo raisers found that the birds require a highly specialized diet of shrimps and mollusks to maintain their attractive coloring. It is speculated that hunters as well as the birds' selective breeding habits perhaps caused the disappearance of these beautiful birds from the wild in North America.

36. The central idea of the passage is that the flamingos of Florida

    (A) are a symbol of Florida.

    (B) are hard to raise in captivity.

    (C) are no longer found in the wild in North America.

    (D) came from Cuba.

    (E) eat shrimps and mollusks.

37. The word "decimation" is closest in meaning to

    (A) destination.

    (B) desecration.

    (C) restoration.

    (D) eradication.

    (E) appeasement.

38. According to the passage, which of the following is responsible for the flamingo's brilliant plumage?

   (A) Warm waters off the coast of Florida

   (B) Selective breeding

   (C) Their diet of marine organisms

   (D) Shallow water plants

   (E) Fish and water snakes

Questions 39 and 40 refer to the following passage:

Teachers should be cognizant of the responsibility they have for the development of children's competencies in basic concepts and principles of free speech. Freedom of speech is not merely the utterance of sounds into the air, rather, it is couched in a set of values and legislative processes that have developed over time. These values and processes are a part of our political conscience as Americans. Teachers must provide ample opportunities for children to express themselves effectively in an environment where their opinions are valued. Children should have ownership in the decision-making process in the classroom and should be engaged in activities where alternative resolutions to problems can be explored. Because teachers have such tremendous power to influence in the classroom, they must be careful to refrain from presenting their own values and biases that could "color" their students' belief systems. If we want children to develop their own voices in a free society, then teachers must support participatory democratic experiences in the daily workings of the classroom.

39. The title that best expresses the ideas in the passage is

   (A) The Nature of the Authoritarian Classroom.

   (B) Concepts and Principles of Free Speech.

   (C) Management Practices that Work.

   (D) Exploring Freedom in American Classrooms.

   (E) Developing Children's Citizenship Competencies.

40. It can be inferred from the passage that instructional strategies that assist children in the development of citizenship competencies include all of the following EXCEPT

    (A) children participation in rule making.

    (B) fostering self-esteem.

    (C) indoctrination in principles of society.

    (D) consideration of cultural and gender differences.

    (E) conflict management skills taught.

Section II: Mathematics

(Answer sheets appear in the back of this book.)

TIME: 60 Minutes
40 Questions

DIRECTIONS: Each of the questions or incomplete statements below is followed by five suggested answers or completions. Select the one that is best in each case.

---

1. Simplify the following expression: $6 + 2(x - 4)$.

   (A) $4x - 16$ (D) $-24x$

   (B) $2x - 14$ (E) $4x$

   (C) $2x - 2$

2. Referring to the following figure, if the measure of $\angle C$ is 20° and the measure of $\angle CBD$ is 36°, then what is the measure of $\angle A$?

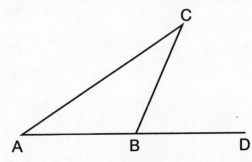

   (A) 16°   (D) 56°

   (B) 20°   (E) 144°

   (C) 36°

3. If six cans of beans cost $1.50, what is the price of eight cans of beans?

   (A) $.90   (D) $2.00

   (B) $1.00   (E) $9.60

   (C) $1.60

4. Bonnie's average score on three tests is 71. Her first two test scores are 64 and 87. What is her score on test three?

    (A) 62

    (D) 151

    (B) 71

    (E) 222

    (C) 74

5. In the figure below, what is the perimeter of square *ABCD* if diagonal $AC = 8$?

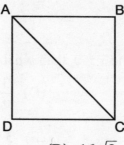

    (A) 32

    (D) $16\sqrt{2}$

    (B) 64

    (E) $8\sqrt{3}$

    (C) $4\sqrt{2}$

6. Three small circles, all the same size, lie inside a large circle as shown below. The diameter *AB* of the large circle passes through the centers of the three small circles. If each of the smaller circles has an area of 9π, what is the circumference of the large circle?

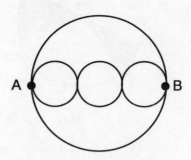

    (A) 9

    (D) 27π

    (B) 18

    (E) 54π

    (C) 18π

7. A jar contains 20 balls. These balls are labeled 1 through 20. What is the probability that a ball chosen from the jar has a number on it which is divisible by 4?

(A) $\dfrac{1}{20}$ (D) 4

(B) $\dfrac{1}{5}$ (E) 5

(C) $\dfrac{1}{4}$

8. If $2x^2 + 5x - 3 = 0$ and $x > 0$, then what is the value of x?

(A) $-\dfrac{1}{2}$ (D) $\dfrac{3}{2}$

(B) $\dfrac{1}{2}$ (E) 3

(C) 1

9. The center of the following circle is the point O. What percentage of the circle is shaded if the measure of arc AB is 65° and the measure of arc CD is 21.4°?

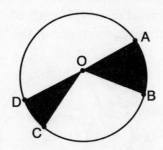

(A) 86.4% (D) 27.4%

(B) 50% (E) 24%

(C) 43.6%

10. According to the following chart, in what year was the total sales of Brand X televisions the greatest?

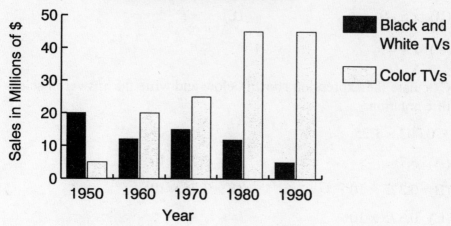

Sales of Brand X Televisions

(A) 1950   (D) 1980

(B) 1960   (E) 1990

(C) 1970

11. How many odd prime numbers are there between 1 and 20?

(A) 7   (D) 10

(B) 8   (E) 11

(C) 9

12. Two concentric circles are shown in the figure below. The smaller circle has radius $OA = 4$ and the larger circle has radius $OB = 6$. Find the area of the shaded region.

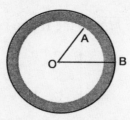

(A) 4π (D) 36π

(B) 16π (E) 100π

(C) 20π

13. Solve the following inequality for x: $8 - 2x \le 10$.

(A) $x \le 1$

(D) $x \ge -1$

(B) $x \ge -9$

(E) $x = \le \dfrac{5}{3}$

(C) $x \le -1$

14. Calculate the expression shown below and write the answer in scientific notation.

   0.003×1.25

(A) 3.75

(D) 3.75×10^{-3}

(B) 0.375×10^{-2}

(E) 3.75×10^3

(C) 0.375×10^2

15. In the figure below $l_1 \parallel l_2$, $\triangle RTS$ is an isosceles triangle, and the measure of $\angle T = 80°$. Find the measure of $\angle OPR$.

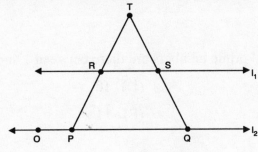

(A) $50°$

(D) $105°$

(B) $80°$

(E) $130°$

(C) $100°$

16. What is the midpoint of $\overline{MN}$ in the figure below?

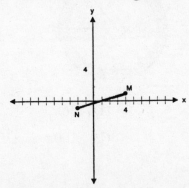

(A) (−4, 2)   (D) (1, 0)

(B) (0, 0)   (E) $\left(-\dfrac{1}{2}, 1\right)$

(C) $\left(-\dfrac{3}{2}, 1\right)$

17. The ratio of men to women at University X is 3:7. If there are 6,153 women at University X, how many men are at University X?

(A) 879   (D) 2,637

(B) 1,895   (E) 14,357

(C) 2,051

18. Find the slope of the line passing through the points W and Z in the following figure.

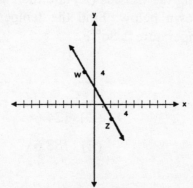

(A) $-\dfrac{1}{2}$ (D) −2

(B) $\dfrac{1}{2}$ (E) 2

(C) $\dfrac{1}{4}$

19. Linda bought a jacket on sale at a 25 percent discount. If she paid $54 for the jacket, what was the original price of the jacket?

(A) $72.00   (D) $40.50

(B) $67.50   (E) $36.00

(C) $54.00

20. Assume that △ABC below is an equilateral triangle. If CD⊥ AB and CD = 6, what is the area of △ABC?

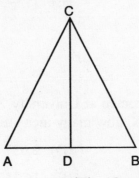

(A) $3\sqrt{3}$ (D) 18

(B) 12   (E) 36

(C) $12\sqrt{3}$

21. The formula relating the Celsius (C) and the Fahrenheit (F) scales of temperature is shown below. Find the temperature in the Celsius scale when the temperature is 86° F.

$$F = \frac{9}{5}C + 32$$

(A) 25°   (D) 124.6°

(B) 30°   (E) 188.6°

(C) 105°

22. In the number 72104.58, what is the place value of the 2?

(A) Thousands   (D) Tenths

(B) Millions   (E) Thousandths

(C) Ten thousands

23. Mrs. Wall has $300,000. She wishes to give each of her six children an equal amount of her money. Which of the following methods will result in the amount that each child is to receive?

(A) 6 × 300,000   (D) 6 – 300,000

(B) 6 ÷ 300,000   (E) 300,000 – 6

(C) 300,000 ÷ 6

24. Referring to the figure below, what is the length of $\overline{PQ}$?

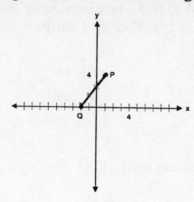

(A) $2\sqrt{5}$

(B) $5\sqrt{2}$

(C) 5

(D) 7

(E) 25

25. Bob wants to bake some cupcakes. His recipe uses $2^2/_3$ cups of flour to produce 36 cupcakes. How many cups of flour should Bob use to bake 12 cupcakes?

(A) $\dfrac{1}{3}$

(B) $\dfrac{8}{9}$

(C) 1

(D) $1\dfrac{2}{9}$

(E) $1\dfrac{2}{3}$

26. The area of rectangle *EFGH* below is 120 and $\overline{EF}$ is twice as long as $\overline{EH}$. Which of the following is the best approximation of the length of $\overline{EH}$?

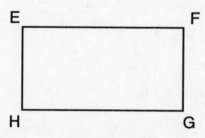

(A) 7

(B) 8

(C) 10

(D) 12

(E) 15

27. Ricky drove from Town A to Town B in 3 hours. His return trip from Town B to Town A took 5 hours because he drove 15 miles per hour slower on the return trip. How fast did Ricky drive on the trip from Town A to Town B?

(A) 25.5

(B) 32

(C) 37.5

(D) 45

(E) 52

28. Which of the following inequalities represents the shaded region in the figure below?

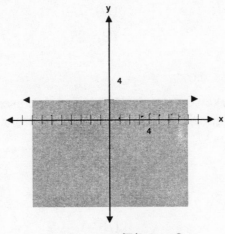

(A) $x \geq 2$

(B) $x \leq 2$

(C) $y \geq 2$

(D) $y \leq 2$

(E) $x + y \geq 2$

29. Given that x, y, and z are any real numbers, which of the following statements are true?

I.   If $x > y$, then $x^2 > y^2$.

II. If $x > y$, then $x + z > y + z$.

III. If $x > y$, then $x - y > 0$.

IV. If $x > y$, then $xz > yz$.

(A) I and II only

(B) II and III only

(C) II and IV only

(D) I, II, and III only

(E) II, III, and IV only

30. Round the following number to the nearest hundredths place: 287.416.

(A) 300

(D) 287.41

(B) 290

(E) 287.42

(C) 287.4

31. Simplify the following expression.

$$\frac{x^2 \times x^7}{x}$$

(A) x^6

(D) x^{10}

(B) x^7

(E) x^{13}

(C) x^8

32. List the fractions shown below from least to greatest.

$$\frac{1}{9}, \frac{2}{15}, \frac{3}{21}$$

(A) $\frac{1}{9}, \frac{2}{15}, \frac{3}{21}$

(D) $\frac{1}{9}, \frac{3}{21}, \frac{2}{15}$

(B) $\frac{2}{15}, \frac{3}{21}, \frac{1}{9}$

(E) $\frac{2}{15}, \frac{1}{9}, \frac{3}{21}$

(C) $\frac{3}{21}, \frac{1}{9}, \frac{2}{15}$

33. A rectangular box with a square base is shown below. If the volume of the box is 256 cubic feet and the height of the box is one-half the length of a side of the base, find the height of the box.

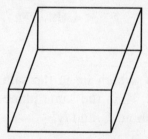

(A) 4 feet

(D) 10 feet

(B) 6 feet

(E) 12 feet

(C) 8 feet

34. If $x = -3$, then find the value of $-x^2 + 2x$.

    (A) -15 (D) 6

    (B) -3 (E) 15

    (C) 3

35. If $a = b^3$ and $a = \dfrac{1}{8}$, what is the value of b?

    (A) $\dfrac{1}{512}$ (D) $\dfrac{1}{2}$

    (B) $\dfrac{1}{8}$ (E) $\dfrac{3}{2}$

    (C) $\dfrac{3}{8}$

36. In a barn there were cows and people. If we counted 30 heads and 104 legs in the barn, how many cows and how many people were in the barn?

    (A) 10 cows and 20 people   (D) 22 cows and 8 people

    (B) 16 cows and 14 people   (E) 24 cows and 4 people

    (C) 18 cows and 16 people

37. Solve for x in the following proportion.

    $$\frac{12}{x-1} = \frac{5}{6}$$

    (A) 14.6 (D) 16.6

    (B) 15.4 (E) 16.8

    (C) 16

38. If two lines, l_1 and l_2, which lie in the same plane, are both perpendicular to a third line, l_3, in the same plane as the first two, what do you definitely know about l_1 and l_2?

    (A) l_1 and l_2 are perpendicular.   (D) l_1 and l_2 are skew.

    (B) l_1 and l_2 are parallel.   (E) l_1 and l_2 are the same line.

    (C) l_1 and l_2 intersect.

39. What is $\dfrac{1}{2} + \dfrac{1}{3}$?

   (A) $\dfrac{1}{5}$ (D) $\dfrac{2}{6}$

   (B) $\dfrac{2}{5}$ (E) $\dfrac{5}{6}$

   (C) $\dfrac{1}{6}$

40. Given that $\overline{BC} \parallel \overline{DE}$ in the following figure, write down the pair of similar (~) triangles.

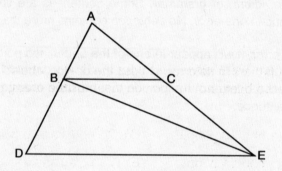

   (A) $\triangle ABC \sim \triangle ADE$ (D) $\triangle BCE \sim \triangle BAC$

   (B) $\triangle ABC \sim \triangle ABE$ (E) $\triangle ADE \sim \triangle CBE$

   (C) $\triangle ABC \sim \triangle AED$

Section III: Writing

(Answer sheets appear in the back of this book.)

TIME: 30 Minutes
45 Questions

Part A: Usage

> **DIRECTIONS**: Each of the following sentences may contain an error in diction, usage, idiom, or grammar. Some sentences are correct. Some sentences contain one error. No sentence contains more than one error.
>
> If there is an error, it will appear in one of the underlined portions labeled A, B, C, or D. If there is no error, choose the portion labeled E. If there is an error, select the letter of the portion that must be changed in order to correct the sentence.
>
> <u>**EXAMPLE:**</u>
>
> He drove <u>slowly</u> and <u>cautiously</u> in order to <u>hopefully</u> avoid having an
>   A   B   C
>
> <u>accident</u>. <u>No error</u>.
>   D   E
>
>

1. In 1877 Chief Joseph of the Nez Perces, <u>together with</u> 250 warriors
                                              A

    and 500 women and children, <u>were praised</u> by newspaper reporters
                                      B

    for <u>bravery</u> during the 115-day fight <u>for</u> freedom. <u>No error</u>.
        C   D   E

2. The ideals <u>upon which</u> American society <u>is based</u> <u>are</u> primarily those
                  A   B   C

    of Europe and not ones <u>derived from</u> the native Indian culture.
                                 D

    <u>No error</u>.
      E

3. $\underline{\text{An astute and powerful}}$ woman, Frances Nadel $\underline{\text{was}}$ a beauty contest
            A   **B**
    winner before she $\underline{\text{became}}$ president of the company $\underline{\text{upon the death}}$
                    C   **D**
    of her husband. $\underline{\text{No error}}$.
                  E

4. Representative Wilson $\underline{\text{pointed out}}$, however, that the legislature
                              A
    $\underline{\text{had not finalized}}$ the state budget and salary increases $\underline{\text{had depended}}$
         B   **C**
    on decisions $\underline{\text{to be made}}$ in a special session. $\underline{\text{No error}}$.
               D   **E**

5. Now the $\underline{\text{city}}$ librarian, doing more than checking out books, must
            A
    help $\underline{\text{to plan}}$ puppet shows and movies for children, garage sales for
         B
    $\underline{\text{used}}$ books, and $\underline{\text{arranging for}}$ guest lecturers and exhibits for adults.
     C   **D**
    $\underline{\text{No error}}$.
      E

6. In order $\underline{\text{to completely understand}}$ the psychological $\underline{\text{effects}}$ of the
                  A   **B**
    bubonic plague, $\underline{\text{one must}}$ realize that one-fourth to one-third of the
                     C
    population in an $\underline{\text{affected}}$ area died. $\underline{\text{No error}}$.
                 D   **E**

7. Rural roads, $\underline{\text{known}}$ in the United States as farm to market roads,
              A
    have always been a vital $\underline{\text{link in}}$ the economy of $\underline{\text{more advanced}}$
                        B   **C**
    nations because transportation of goods to markets $\underline{\text{is}}$ essential.
                                          D
    $\underline{\text{No error}}$.
      E

8. $\underline{\text{Many a}}$ graduate $\underline{\text{wishes}}$ to return to college and $\underline{\text{abide in}}$ the pro-
     A   **B**   **C**

tected environment of a university, particularly if <u>someone else</u> pays
                                                                              D

the bills. <u>No error</u>.
            E

9. <u>Confronted with</u> a choice of either <u>cleaning up</u> his room or <u>cleaning</u>
        A   B   C

    <u>out</u> the garage, the teenager became very <u>aggravated</u> with his parents.
                                                    D

    <u>No error</u>.
        E

10. My brother and <u>I</u> dressed as <u>quickly</u> as we could, but we missed the
                    A   B

    school bus, <u>which</u> made <u>us</u> late for class today. <u>No error</u>.
                C   D   E

11. <u>Among</u> the activities <u>offered at</u> the local high school <u>through</u> the
        A   B   C

    community education program <u>are</u> singing in the couples' chorus,
                                D

    ballroom dancing, and Chinese cooking. <u>No error</u>.
                                            E

12. If you are <u>disappointed by</u> an <u>inexpensive</u> bicycle, then an option you
                    A   B

    might consider is to work this summer and <u>save</u> your money for a
                                               C

    <u>more expensive</u> model. <u>No error</u>.
        D   E

13. Also being presented to the city council this morning <u>is</u> the mayor's
                                                          A

    city budget for next year and plans <u>to renovate</u> the <u>existing</u> music
                                          B   C

    theater, so the session <u>will focus</u> on financial matters. <u>No error</u>.
                             D   E

14. Even a movement <u>so delicate</u> as a <u>fly's walking</u> triggers the Venus
                        A   B

flytrap <u>to grow</u> extra cells on the outside of <u>its</u> hinge, immediately
        C   D

closing the petals of the trap. <u>No error</u>.
                              E

15. Although <u>outwardly</u> Thomas Hardy seemed quite <u>the picture</u> of
               A   B

    <u>respectability</u> and contentment, his works, especially the prose,
    C

    <u>deals with</u> the theme of man's inevitable suffering. <u>No error</u>.
    D   E

16. Though <u>unequal in</u> social standing, the everyday lives of ancient
            A

    Egyptian kings and commoners <u>alike</u> are visible in the pictures of
                                     B

    <u>them</u> found <u>inside of</u> tombs and temples. <u>No error</u>.
    C   D   E

17. Sometimes considered <u>unsafe for</u> crops, land around river <u>deltas</u>
                           A   B

    <u>can be</u> excellent land for farming because periodic flooding deposits
    C

    silt rich <u>in</u> nutrients. <u>No error</u>.
           D   E

18. For years <u>people</u> concerned with the environment <u>have compiled</u> in-
            A   B

    formation which <u>show</u> many species are extinct and others <u>are either</u>
                    C   D

    endangered or bordering on becoming endangered. <u>No error</u>.
                                             E

19. Little is known about Shakespeare's boyhood or his early career as an

    actor and playwright, but he <u>appears to have been</u> a financial success
                                     A

    <u>because he bought</u> many properties, including <u>one of the finest</u> homes
           B   C

    in Stratford, the town he <u>was born in</u>. <u>No error</u>.
                          D   E

20. *Scared Straight*, a program designed <u>to inhibit</u> criminal <u>behavior in</u>
                                              A   B
    juvenile offenders <u>who</u> seemed bound for prison as adults, had a
                        C
    significant <u>affect</u> on the youngsters. <u>No error</u>.
                 D   E

21. The <u>average</u> American tourist feels <u>quite</u> at home in a Japanese sta-
            A   B
    dium filled <u>at capacity</u> with sports fans watching Japan's <u>most</u> popu-
                 C   D
    lar sport, baseball. <u>No error</u>.
                          E

22. My brother is <u>engaged</u> to a woman <u>who</u> my parents <u>have</u> not met
                   A   B   C
    because she has not yet <u>emigrated from</u> her native country of Ecua-
                             D
    dor. <u>No error</u>.
          E

23. Colonel Jones <u>denies that</u> he <u>illegally</u> delivered funds to a foreign
                   A   B
    government agent or that <u>he</u> was involved in <u>any other</u> covert activ-
                              C   D
    ity. <u>No error</u>.
          E

24. In the United States, <u>testing for</u> toxicity, determining the <u>proper</u>
                           A   B
    dose and timing between doses, and evaluating the vaccine for
    <u>effectiveness</u> <u>is</u> the method used in researching new drugs. <u>No error</u>.
     C   D   E

25. George wants <u>to know if</u> <u>it is her</u> driving that expensive red sports car
                  A   B
    <u>at a rate of speed</u> <u>obviously exceeding</u> the posted speed limit.
     C   D
    <u>No error</u>.
     E

Part B: Sentence Correction

DIRECTIONS: In each of the following sentences, some portion of the sentence is underlined. Under each sentence are five choices. The first choice has the same wording as the original. The other four choices are reworded. Sometimes the first choice containing the original wording is the best; sometimes one of the other choices is the best. Choose the letter of the best choice. Your choice should produce a sentence which is not ambiguous or awkward and which is correct, clear, and precise.

This is a test of correct and effective English expression. Keep in mind the standards of English usage, punctuation, grammar, word choice, and construction.

EXAMPLE:

When you listen to opera, <u>a person may not appreciate it.</u>

(A)   a person may not appreciate it.

(B)   it may not be appreciated by a person.

(C)   which may not be appreciated by one.

(D)   you may not appreciate it.

(E)   appreciating it may be a problem for you.

26. <u>Being that you bring home more money than I do</u>, it is only fitting you should pay proportionately more rent.

  (A) Being that you bring home more money than I do

  (B) Bringing home the more money of the two of us

  (C) When more money is made by you than by me

  (D) Because you bring home more money than I do

  (E) If your bringing home more money than me

27. So tenacious is their grip on life, that sponge cells will regroup and form a new sponge even <u>when they are</u> squeezed through silk.

  (A) when they are

  (B) since they have been

  (C) as they will be

(D) after they have been

(E) because they should be

28. <u>Seeing as how the plane is late</u>, wouldn't you prefer to wait for a while on the observation deck?

(A) Seeing as how the plane is late

(B) When the plane comes in

(C) Since the plane is late

(D) Being as the plane is late

(E) While the plane is landing

29. Only with careful environmental planning can we protect the <u>world we live in</u>.

(A) world we live in

(B) world in which we live in

(C) living in this world

(D) world's living

(E) world in which we live

30. In the last three years we have added more varieties of vegetables to our garden <u>than those you suggested in the beginning</u>.

(A) than those you suggested in the beginning

(B) than the ones we began with

(C) beginning with your suggestion

(D) than what you suggested to us

(E) which you suggested in the beginning

31. As you know, I am not easily fooled by flattery, and while <u>nice words please you,</u> they don't get the job done.

(A) nice words please you

(B) nice words are pleasing

(C) nice words please a person

(D) flattering words please people

(E) flattering words are pleasing to some

32. Some pieces of the puzzle, in spite of Jane's search, <u>are still missing and probably will never be found</u>.

(A) are still missing and probably will never be found

(B) is missing still but never found probably

(C) probably will be missing and never found

(D) are still probably missing and to never be found

(E) probably are missing and will not be found

33. *Gone With the Wind* <u>is the kind of a movie</u> producers would like to release because it would bring them fame.

(A) is the kind of a movie

(B) is the sort of movie

(C) is the kind of movie

(D) is the type of a movie

(E) is the category of movie

34. Eighteenth century architecture, with its columns and balanced lines, <u>was characteristic of those of previous times in Greece and Rome</u>.

(A) was characteristic of those of previous times in Greece and Rome

(B) is similar to characteristics of Greece and Rome

(C) is similar to Greek and Roman building styles

(D) is characteristic with earlier Greek and Roman architecture

(E) was similar to architecture of Greece and Rome

35. Plato, one of the famous Greek philosophers, won many wrestling prizes when he was a young man, thus <u>exemplifying the Greek ideal of balance between the necessity for physical activity and using one's mind</u>.

(A) exemplifying the Greek ideal of balance between the necessity for physical activity and using one's mind

(B) serving as an example of the Greek ideal of balance between physical and mental activities

(C) an example of balancing Greek mental and athletic games

(D) this as an example of the Greek's balance between mental physical pursuits

(E) shown to be exemplifying the balancing of two aspects of Greek life, the physical and the mental

36. Allied control of the Philippine Islands during World War II proved to be <u>another obstacle as the Japanese scattered resistance</u> until the end of the war.

(A) another obstacle as the Japanese scattered resistance

(B) difficult because of the Japanese giving resistance

(C) continuing scattered Japanese resistance as obstacles

(D) as another scattered obstacle due to Japanese resistance

(E) difficult because the Japanese gave scattered resistance

37. Flooding abated and the river waters receded as the <u>rainfall finally let up</u>.

(A) rainfall finally let up

(B) rain having let up

(C) letting up of the rainfall

(D) rainfall, when it finally let up

(E) raining finally letting up

38. Unless China slows its population growth to zero, that country <u>would still have</u> a problem feeding its people.

(A) would still have

(B) will have still had

(C) might have had still

(D) will still have

(E) would have still

39. In *The Music Man* Robert Preston portrays a fast-talking salesman who comes to a small town in Iowa <u>inadvertently falling in love with</u> the librarian.

    (A) inadvertently falling in love with

    (B) and inadvertently falls in love with

    (C) afterwards he inadvertently falls in love with

    (D) after falling inadvertently in love with

    (E) when he inadvertently falls in love with

40. Many naturalists have a reverence for the woods and wildlife <u>which exhibits itself through their</u> writings or paintings.

    (A) which exhibits itself through their

    (B) this exhibits itself through their

    (C) showing up in

    (D) and exhibiting itself in

    (E) when they produce

41. The art <u>of any region</u> is influenced by the cultural and physical environment of that region.

    (A) of any region

    (B) of any other region

    (C) of the region

    (D) from that region

    (E) for regions

42. <u>Ringing loudly, Doug's girlfriend called him on the telephone to insist</u> he come over right away.

    (A) Ringing loudly, Doug's girlfriend called him on the telephone to insist

    (B) Doug's loud girlfriend rang him on the telephone to insist

    (C) Loudly ringing, the telephone was the insisting girlfriend of Doug

(D) When the telephone rang loudly, Doug's girlfriend insisting

(E) The telephone rang loudly, and Doug's girlfriend was calling to insist

43. Women live longer and have fewer illnesses than men, <u>which proves that women are the strongest sex</u>.

(A) which proves that women are the strongest sex.

(B) which proves that women are the stronger sex.

(C) facts which prove that women are the stronger sex.

(D) proving that women are the strongest sex.

(E) a proof that women are the stronger sex.

44. The word "boycott" was originally the last name of an English land agent in Ireland who was ostracized in <u>1880 because he refused to reduce rents</u>.

(A) 1880 because he refused to reduce rents.

(B) 1880 for refusing to reduce the prevailing rent at the time.

(C) 1880 being that he refused to reduce rents.

(D) 1880 being that he refused to reduce the current prevailing rents.

(E) 1880 because of his refusal to reduce rents.

45. <u>In Virginia Woolf's essay titled "The Death of the Moth," it</u> says that nothing and nobody have a chance against death.

(A) In Virginia Woolf's essay titled "The Death of the Moth," it

(B) In the essay by Virginia Woolf titled "The Death of the Moth," it

(C) Virginia wrote an essay titled "The Death of the Moth," it

(D) In "The Death of the Moth," an essay by Virginia Woolf, it

(E) Virginia Woolf's essay, "The Death of the Moth"

Part C: Essay

TIME: 30 Minutes

DIRECTIONS: You have 30 minutes to plan and write an essay on the topic below. You may write only on the assigned topic.

Make sure to give specific examples to support your thesis. Proofread your essay carefully and take care to express your ideas clearly and effectively.

<u>**ESSAY TOPIC**</u>:

In the twentieth century, the concept of heroism is dead.

<u>**ASSIGNMENT**</u>: Do you agree or disagree with the statement? Support your opinion with specific examples from history, current events, literature, or personal experience.

PPST TEST I

ANSWER KEY

Section I — Reading Comprehension

1. (D)	11. (C)	21. (D)	31. (D)
2. (B)	12. (B)	22. (B)	32. (B)
3. (C)	13. (B)	23. (E)	33. (B)
4. (C)	14. (D)	24. (C)	34. (C)
5. (E)	15. (A)	25. (B)	35. (A)
6. (D)	16. (D)	26. (C)	36. (C)
7. (E)	17. (B)	27. (D)	37. (D)
8. (B)	18. (A)	28. (C)	38. (C)
9. (B)	19. (B)	29. (A)	39. (E)
10. (C)	20. (C)	30. (B)	40. (C)

Section II — Mathematics

1. (C)	11. (A)	21. (B)	31. (C)
2. (A)	12. (C)	22. (A)	32. (A)
3. (D)	13. (D)	23. (C)	33. (A)
4. (A)	14. (D)	24. (C)	34. (A)
5. (D)	15. (E)	25. (B)	35. (D)
6. (C)	16. (D)	26. (B)	36. (D)
7. (C)	17. (D)	27. (C)	37. (B)
8. (B)	18. (D)	28. (D)	38. (B)
9. (E)	19. (A)	29. (B)	39. (E)
10. (D)	20. (C)	30. (E)	40. (A)

Section III — Writing

1. (B)	13. (A)	25. (B)	37. (A)
2. (E)	14. (A)	26. (D)	38. (D)
3. (B)	15. (D)	27. (D)	39. (B)
4. (C)	16. (D)	28. (C)	40. (A)
5. (D)	17. (E)	29. (E)	41. (A)
6. (A)	18. (C)	30. (A)	42. (E)
7. (C)	19. (D)	31. (B)	43. (C)
8. (E)	20. (D)	32. (A)	44. (A)
9. (D)	21. (C)	33. (C)	45. (E)
10. (C)	22. (B)	34. (E)	
11. (E)	23. (C)	35. (B)	
12. (A)	24. (E)	36. (E)	

DETAILED EXPLANATIONS OF ANSWERS

Section I: Reading Comprehension

1. **(D)**   It is implied that the poisoning of animal carcasses in the habitat of bald eagles presents a new danger of extinction for America's symbol. Choices (A), (C), and (E) are not mentioned in the passage. Choice (B) suggests a reason for the poisoning; however, the overall focus of the passage does not support this.

2. **(B)**   The author's use of words such as "mighty bald eagle" and "threatened by a new menace" supports concern for the topic. Therefore, choices (A) and (C) are not applicable. The author appears for the most part, to be objective. Answers (D) and (E) are too strong to be correct.

3. **(C)**   In 1980, the difference between the numbers of boys and girls in scouting was .9 million. This represents the closest margin, the largest being 1.6 in 1985.

4. **(C)**   In 1970, the difference between the numbers of boys and girls in scouting was 1.5 million.

5. **(E)**   If Alice is uncomfortable with remarks about her performance on the job, it could mean either that the remarks were unkind or that compliments might lead to embarrassment. However, the prefix "dis" means to take away or not. In this instance then, we can assume that the remarks were not complimentary or funny, choices (A) and (C). Nothing in the text indicates that the remarks were technical or menacing, responses (B) and (D).

6. **(D)**   Answer (D) fulfills requirements stated in rules 2 and 4 of the instructions for absentee voting. All other choices do not.

7. **(E)**   Mr. Applebee's daughter must sign her own request for an absentee ballot. Since the passage indicates that she is registered, the most important instruction for her is number 6 (E).

8. **(B)** Choices (A), (D), and (E) are not stated in the passage. Choice (C) is not true unless voters have registered, answer (B).

9. **(B)** Atrophy and incapacity mean to experience a decrease in size and strength.

10. **(C)** The passage associates loss of mobility with a sedentary life-style.

11. **(C)** Douglass was interested in raising social consciousness about slavery. The passage stresses his interest in refuting those who doubted his claim to have been a slave.

12. **(B)** Choice (A) is not supported by the text. All other choices, while true, are irrelevant to the question.

13. **(B)** This choice is supported by the statement, "Mrs. Auld recognized Frederick's intellectual acumen." Choices (C) and (E) contradict information in the passage. The passage does not support choices (A) and (D).

14. **(D)** Choices (A), (B), and (C) are either too broad or too general. Choice (E) is too specific and limited to cover the information in the passage.

15. **(A)** An "impromptu" speech is one given suddenly without preparation.

16. **(D)** All other choices are mentioned as providing relief from pain.

17. **(B)** Use of terms "good," "consequences," and "desirable" indicate a concern for a healthy diet. Choices (A) and (C) contradict the author's attitude. Choices (D) and (E) are not supported by the text.

18. **(A)** Choices (B), (C), and (D) are contradicted in the passage, and choice (E) is not relevant.

19. **(B)** All other choices are not supported in the text.

20. **(C)** A "segue" provides a direction or lead into the speech.

21. **(D)**   The passage states that housing of prisoners was "one of many tragedies of the Civil .War," and that "overcrowding, meager rations . . . resulted in rampant disease and a high mortality rate," implying that the prison facility was inadequate for the number of prisoners. All other choices are discussed, but the main issue was overcrowded conditions.

22. **(B)**   The author emphasizes a lack of supplies and manpower to care for the prisoners, not a lack of interest in doing so by the Confederates. Hence, choices (C), (D), and (E) are not appropriate. Choice (A) is not suggested by the text.

23. **(E)**   An irony is a result that is the opposite of what might be expected or appropriate. The passage implies that being captured was not a guarantee of survival in Andersonville. This choice is supported by the second sentence of the second paragraph.

24. **(C)**   The figure of speech "his or her nose is out of joint" is an expression used to indicate that someone feels slighted. It has nothing to do with the condition of someone's nose.

25. **(B)**   This choice is supported by the first paragraph of the passage. All other choices are irrelevant to information in the passage.

26. **(C)**   Innovative means to introduce something new or make changes.

27. **(D)**   The passage discusses the importance of usefulness as well as simplicity to the Shakers; therefore, the function of the piece of furniture would be more important than the particular form. Choices (A), (B), and (E) are contradictory to the information given, while choice (C) is beyond information given in the text.

28. **(C)**   The passage states that Dean "symbolized the confused, restless, and idealistic youth," which implies that he was adept at portraying sensitive youthful characters. Choices (A), (B), and (D) are contradictory to information in the text. Choice (E) is a conclusion not supported by the text.

29. **(A)**   The author's use of the word "tragically" in reference to Dean's death indicates a feeling of regret.

30. **(B)** Depraved means corrupted or perverted. All other choices have to do with accepted standards of conduct.

31. **(D)** The author states that Franklin's work was a "significant work of early United States." Each of the other choices is not supported by the text.

32. **(B)** The final sentence of the paragraph supports this choice. Choice (C) might apply, but choice (B) is closest to the overall mood of the passage. Choices (A), (D), and (E) are not relevant to the question.

33. **(B)** Transportation and housing total about half of the $25,892.

34. **(C)** According to the graph, food is next after transportation in amount of expense paid by the consumer.

35. **(A)** According to the graph, health care was closest to clothing in total amount spent.

36. **(C)** The author's use of the word "decimation" as well as the last sentence in the second paragraph supports this choice. All other choices are secondary to the central idea of the passage.

37. **(D)** To decimate is to eradicate or destroy a large part of something.

38. **(C)** This choice is supported by the first sentence of the second paragraph. All other choices are irrelevant to the discussion of the flamingo's plumage.

39. **(E)** The first and last sentences of the passage support this choice. Choice (A) contradicts information in the passage, and choices (B), (C), and (D) are too broad in nature and go beyond the scope of the passage.

40. **(C)** Reviewing the author's discussion of developing children's citizenship competencies, we may conclude that indoctrination is contradictory to information given in the passage.

Section II: Mathematics

NOTATION: $m\angle PQR$ will represent "the measure of angle PQR."

1.   **(C)**   When simplifying algebraic expressions, always work from left to right. First perform all multiplications and divisions then once this is done, start again from the left and do all additions and subtractions.

SUGGESTION: It can be helpful to translate the algebraic statement to English. For example, $6 + 2(x - 4)$ is "six plus two *times* the quantity x minus 4." The word *times* indicates multiplication, so we must first perform $2(x - 4)$ by using the *distributive property* $a(b - c) = ab - ac$:

$$6 + 2(x - 4) = 6 + 2 \times x - 2 \times 4 = 6 + 2x - 8.$$

Then we perform the subtraction to combine the terms 6 and 8:

$$6 + 2x - 8 = 2x + (6 - 8) = 2x - 2.$$

Note that we did not combine the $2x$ term with the other terms. This is because they are not *like terms*. Like terms are terms which have the same variables (with the same exponents). Since the terms 6 and 8 have no variable x, they are not like terms with $2x$.

2.   **(A)**   The sum of the measures of the interior angles of a triangle is 180°, therefore;

$$\angle A + m\angle ABC + m\angle C = 180°.$$

We also know that $m\angle C = 20°$, so if we substitute this into the previous equation we have

$$m\angle A + m\angle ABC + 20° = 180°.$$

Subtracting 20° from both sides of this equation gives us

$$m\angle A + m\angle ABC = 160°$$

or $m\angle A = 160° - m\angle ABC.$

Therefore, if we know $m\angle ABC$, we are done! To find $m\angle ABC$, notice that $\angle ABD$ is a straight angle and, thus, $m\angle ABD = 180°$. But

$$m\angle ABC + m\angle CBD = m\angle ABD.$$

So, using the facts that

$$m\angle CBD = 36° \text{ and } m\angle ABD = 180°,$$

and substituting, we have

$$m\angle ABC + 36° = 180°$$

or $\qquad m\angle ABC = 180° - 36° = 144°.$

Hence, $m\angle A = 160° - m\angle ABC = 160° - 144° = 16°.$

3. **(D)** Let x be the cost of one can of beans. Then $6x$ is the cost of six cans of beans. So $6x = \$1.50$. Dividing both sides of the equation by 6, we get $x = \$.25$ and, hence, since $8x$ is the cost of eight cans of beans, we have

$$8x = 8 \times \$.25 = \$2.00.$$

4. **(A)** Let t_1, t_2, and t_3 represent Bonnie's scores on tests one, two, and three, respectively. Then the equation representing Bonnie's average score is

$$\frac{t_1 + t_2 + t_3}{3} = 71.$$

We know that $t_1 = 64$ and $t_2 = 87$. Substitute this information into the equation above:

$$\frac{64 + 87 + t_3}{3} = 71$$

Combining 64 and 87 and then multiplying both sides of the equation by 3 gives us

$$3 \times \frac{151 + t_3}{3} = 3 \times 71$$

or $\qquad 151 + t_3 = 213.$

Now subtract 151 from both sides of the equation so that

$$t_3 = 213 - 151 = 62.$$

5. **(D)** Let s be the length of each side of square $ABCD$. Since triangle ADC is a right triangle, we can use the Pythagorean Theorem to solve for s. We have

$$AD^2 + DC^2 = AC^2$$

or $s^2 + s^2 = 8^2$.

Simplifying the equation, we get: $2s^2 = 64$. Now divide both sides of the equation by two:

$$s^2 = 32 \text{ so } s = \sqrt{32} = \sqrt{16} \times \sqrt{2} = 4\sqrt{2}.$$

Therefore, the perimeter of square *ABCD* is

$$P = 4s = 4 \times 4\sqrt{2} = 16\sqrt{2}.$$

6.   **(C)**   Let *r* be the length of the radius of each of the small circles and let *R* be the length of the radius of the large circle. Then, $R = 3r$. The area of each of the small circles is $\pi r^2 = 9\pi$. Now divide both sides of the equation by π:

$$r^2 = 9 \rightarrow r = 3.$$

Then, $R = 3r = 3 \times 3 = 9$.

Therefore, the circumference of the large circle is

$$C = 2\pi R = 2\pi \times 9 = 18\pi.$$

7.   **(C)**   Note that the numbers 4, 8, 12, 16, and 20 are the only numbers from 1 through 20 that are divisible by 4. The probability that a ball chosen from the jar has a number on it which is divisible by 4 is given by

$$\frac{\text{total number of balls with numbers that are divisible by 4}}{\text{total number of possible outcomes}} = \frac{5}{20} = \frac{1}{4}$$

8.   **(B)**   To solve the equation

$$2x^2 + 5x - 3 = 0,$$

we can factor the left side of the equation to get

$$(2x - 1)(x + 3) = 0.$$

Then use the following rule (this rule is sometimes called the Zero Product Property): If $a \times b = 0$, then either $a = 0$ or $b = 0$. Applying this to our problem gives us

$$2x - 1 = 0 \text{ or } x + 3 = 0.$$

Solve these two equations:

$$2x - 1 = 0 \rightarrow 2x = 1 \rightarrow x = \frac{1}{2} \text{ or } x + 3 = 0 \rightarrow x = -3.$$

But $x > 0$, so $x = \frac{1}{2}$.

9. **(E)** $\angle AOB$ and $\angle COD$ are central angles, meaning that their vertices are at the center of a circle. The measure of a central angle is equal to the measure of its intercepted arc. Hence, since arc AB and arc CD are the intercepted arcs of $\angle AOB$ and $\angle COD$, respectively, $m\angle AOB = 65°$ and $m\angle COD = 21.4°$. So,

$$m\angle AOB + m\angle COD = 86.4°.$$

Therefore, since one revolution of a circle is 360°, the shaded portion of the circle is represented by the following:

$$\frac{86.4}{360} = 0.24 = 24\%.$$

10. **(D)** First find the total sales for each year by reading the graph for the sales of (i) black and white televisions and (ii) color televisions. Then combine these numbers:

1950 $20,000,000 + $5,000,000 = $25,000,000

1960 $10,000,000 + $20,000,000 = $30,000,000

1970 $15,000,000 + $25,000,000 = $40,000,000

1980 $10,000,000 + $45,000,000 = $55,000,000

1990 $5,000,000 + $45,000,000 = $50,000,000

The greatest total sales occurred in 1980.

11. **(A)** A prime number is an integer which is greater than one and which has no integer divisors other than 1 and itself. So, the prime numbers between 1 and 20 (not including 1 and 20) are: 2, 3, 5, 7, 11, 13, 17, 19. But 2 is not an odd number, so the odd primes between 1 and 20 are: 3, 5, 7, 11, 13, 17, 19. Hence, there are seven odd primes between 1 and 20.

12. **(C)** The area of the shaded region is equal to the area of the large circle (which has $\overline{OB}$ as a radius), minus the area of the smaller circle

(which has $\overline{OA}$ as a radius). Since the area of a circle with radius r is $A = \pi r^2$, the area of the shaded region is:

$$\pi (OB)^2 - \pi (OA)^2 = 36\pi - 16\pi = 20\pi.$$

13. **(D)** To solve this inequality, we shall use the following rules:

    (i)   If $a \le b$ and c is any number, then $a + c \le b + c$.

    (ii) If $a \le b$ and $c < 0$, then $ca \ge cb$.

The goal in solving inequalities, as in solving equalities, is to change the inequality so that the variable is isolated (i.e., by itself on one side). So, in the equation $8 - 2x \le 10$, we want the term $-2x$ by itself. To achieve this, use rule (i) above and add -8 to both sides obtaining

$$8 - 2x + (-8) \le 10 + (-8)$$

or $-2x \le 2$.

Now we use rule (ii) and multiply both sides of the inequality by $-\frac{1}{2}$ as follows:

$$-\frac{1}{2} \times 2x \ge -\frac{1}{2} \times 2$$

or $x \ge -1$.

14. **(D)** Since 0.003 has three numbers to the right of the decimal point and 1.25 has two numbers to the right of the decimal point, our answer will have (three plus two) or five numbers to the right of the decimal point. Multiplying 0.003 and 1.25, we get 0.00375, since 3 times 125 is 375. Numbers of the form $A \times 10^n$, where A is a number between 0 and 1 inclusive, and n is an integer, are in scientific notation. Thus, 0.00375 in scientific notation is 3.75×10^{-3}. Notice that when the exponent $n < 0$, the original number is smaller than A.

15. **(E)** Since $\angle OPQ$ is a straight angle, $m\angle OPQ = 180°$. But

$$m\angle OPQ = m\angle OPR + m\angle RPQ,$$

so $m\angle OPR + m\angle RPQ = 180°$

or $m\angle OPR = 180° - m\angle RPQ.$

Thus, we need to find $m\angle RPQ$. Now, $l_1 \parallel l_2$, therefore, $m\angle RPQ = m\angle TRS$ since $\angle RPQ$ and $\angle TRS$ are corresponding angles. Recall that corresponding angles are two angles which lie on the same side of the transversal

(i.e., a line intersecting other lines, in this case line TP is a transversal since it intersects both line l_1 and l_2) are not adjacent, and one is interior ($\angle RPQ$ in this problem) while the other is exterior ($\angle TRS$). Also, we know that the sum of the measures of the interior angles of a triangle is 180° and

$$m\angle T = 80°, \text{ so } m\angle TRS + m\angle RST = 180° - m\angle T = 100°.$$

But $m\angle TRS = m\angle RST$

since $\triangle RTS$ is isosceles. Thus, $m\angle TRS = 50°$. Thus,

$$m\angle RPQ = 50°$$

and $m\angle OPR = 180° - m\angle RPQ = 180° - 50° = 130°.$

16. **(D)**   The midpoint of a segment with endpoints (x_1, y_1) and (x_2, y_2) is

$$\left(\frac{x_1 + x_2}{2}, \frac{y_1 + y_2}{2}\right).$$

Endpoints are $M = (4, 1)$ and $N = (-2, -1)$, so the midpoint of $\overline{MN}$ is

$$\left(\frac{4 + (-2)}{2}, \frac{1 + (-1)}{2}\right) = (1, 0).$$

17. **(D)**   Let m = the number of men at University X. Then we have the following proportion:

$$\frac{3}{7} = \frac{m}{6,153}$$

To solve this equation, we isolate the variable (i.e., get m by itself) by multiplying both sides of the equation by 6,153 to get

$$\left(\frac{3}{7}\right) 6,153 = \left(\frac{m}{6,153}\right) 6,153 \text{ or } m = 2,637.$$

18. **(D)**   Note that the line passing through W and Z slants downward as we look at it from left to right. This means our slope should be a negative number! To find the slope of the line passing through the points (x_1, y_1), and (x_2, y_2) we use the following formula:

$$slope = \frac{y_2 - y_1}{x_2 - x_1}.$$

Our points are $W = (-1, 4)$ and $Z = (2, -2)$ and so our slope is

$$\frac{(-2) - 4}{2 - (-1)} = \frac{-6}{3} = -2.$$

19. **(A)** Let p be the original price of the jacket. Linda received a 25 percent discount so she paid 75 percent of the original price. Thus, 75 percent of p equals 54. Writing this in an equation, we get

$$0.75p = 54 \text{ or } \frac{3}{4}p = 54.$$

To solve this equation, multiply both sides of the equation by the reciprocal of $3/4$ which is $4/3$. This will isolate the variable p.

$$\frac{4}{3}\left(\frac{3}{4}p\right) = \left(\frac{4}{3}\right) 54 \text{ or } p = \frac{216}{3} = 72$$

20. **(C)** The area of

$$\triangle ABC = \frac{1}{2}(\text{base})(\text{height}) = \frac{1}{2}(AB)(CD) = \frac{1}{2}(AB)(6) = 3(AB).$$

So we need to find AB. Let $s = AB$. Then since $\triangle ABC$ is equilateral (i.e., all the sides have the same length), $BC = s$. Also, since $\triangle ABC$ is equilateral, D is the midpoint of AB, so $DB = s/2$ Now $CD \perp AB$ so $\triangle CDB$ is a right triangle and we can use the Pythagorean Theorem:

$$(CD)^2 + (DB)^2 = (BC)^2.$$

As $CD = 6$, this equation becomes

$$6^2 + \left(\frac{s}{2}\right)^2 = s^2,$$

or $\quad 36 + \frac{s^2}{4} = s^2.$

To solve for s, subtract $\frac{s^2}{4}$ from both sides:

$$36 = s^2 - \frac{s^2}{4} = \frac{3}{4}s^2.$$

Now multiply both sides of the equation by the reciprocal of $^3/_4$ which is $^4/_3$:

$$\frac{4}{3}(36) = s^2$$

or $s^2 = 48.$

Hence, $s = \sqrt{48} = \sqrt{16} = \sqrt{3} = 4\sqrt{3}$

The area of $\triangle ABC =$

$$3s = 3(4\sqrt{3}) = 12\sqrt{3}$$

21. **(B)**   Substituting $F = 86$ into the formula

$$F = \frac{9}{5}C + 32$$

we get

$$86 = \frac{9}{5}C + 32.$$

To solve for C, first subtract 32 from both sides:

$$86 - 32 = \frac{9}{5}C + 32 - 32$$

or $54 = \frac{9}{5}C.$

Now multiply both sides of this equation by the reciprocal of $^9/_5$ which is $^5/_9$:

$$\left(\frac{5}{9}\right)54 = \left(\frac{5}{9}\right)\frac{9}{5}C \text{ or } \frac{270}{9} = C \text{ or } C = 30$$

22. **(A)**   72104.58 is read "seventy-**two thousand,** one hundred four and fifty-eight hundredths."

23. **(C)** Another way to phrase the second sentence is: She wants to divide her money equally among her six children. Therefore, each child is to receive $300,000 \div 6$.

24. **(C)** To find the distance between two points (x_1, y_1) and (x_2, y_2), we may use the following formula:

$$d = \sqrt{(x_2 - x_1)^2 + (y_2 - y_1)^2}$$

For our two points, $P = (1, 4)$ and $Q = (-2, 0)$, the above formula gives us the length of segment PQ:

$$d = \sqrt{(-2-1)^2 + (0-4)^2} = \sqrt{(-3)^2 + (4)^2} = \sqrt{9+16} = \sqrt{25} = 5.$$

25. **(B)** Bob wants to bake 12 cupcakes. The recipe is for 36 cupcakes. Therefore, Bob wants to make $12/36$ or $1/3$ of the usual amount of cupcakes. Thus, Bob should use $1/3$ of the recipe's flour or

$$\left(\frac{1}{3}\right)\left(\frac{8}{3}\right) = \frac{8}{9}.$$

Note we used $8/3$ since $2\frac{2}{3} = 8/3$.

26. **(B)** Let x be the length of EH, then the length of EF is $2x$. The area of a rectangle is length (EF) times width (EH). So we have

$$(2x)(x) = 120 \text{ or } 2x^2 = 120.$$

To solve for x divide both sides of the equation by 2 to get $x^2 = 60$. Note that $49 < x^2 < 64$, so

$$\sqrt{49} < \sqrt{x^2} < \sqrt{64} \text{ or } 7 < x < 8.$$

But 60 is closer to 64 than it is to 49, so 8 is the best approximation of x which represents the length of EH.

27. **(C)** Let s_1 and s_2 be Ricky's speed (rate) on the trip from A to B and the return trip from B to A, respectively. Then, since he drove 15 miles per hour slower on the return trip, $s_2 = s_1 - 15$. Recall that rate times time equals distance. So the distance from A to B is $(s_1)3 = 3s_1$ and the distance from B to A is

$$(s_2)5 = 5s_2 = 5(s_1 - 15) = 5s_1 - 75.$$

But the distance from Town A to Town B is the same as the distance from Town B to Town A, so we have the following equation:

$$3s_1 = 5s_1 - 75.$$

To solve this equation, first add 75 to both sides of the equation:

$$3s_1 + 75 = 5s_1 - 75 + 75 \text{ or } 3s_1 + 75 = 5s_1.$$

Now to isolate the variable, subtract $3s_1$ from both sides:

$$3s_1 + 75 - 3s_1 = 5s_1 - 3s_1 \text{ or } 75 = 2s_1.$$

To finish the problem, divide both sides of the equation by 2:

$$s_1 = \frac{75}{2} = 37.5.$$

Thus, Ricky drove 37.5 miles per hour on his trip from Town A to Town B.

28. **(D)**   The shaded region consists of all the points on the horizontal line passing through the point (0, 2) and those below the line. All of these points have $y =$ coordinate less than or equal to 2. Thus, our answer is $y \le 2$.

29. **(B)**   Statement I is not always true. For example, let $x = 2$ and $y = -3$. Then $x > y$, but $x^2 = 4$ and $y^2 = 9$ so $x^2 < y^2$. Statement IV is not always true. For example, let $x = 5$, $y = 1$, and $z = -2$. Then $xz = -10$ and $yz = -2$ so that $xz < yz$. Statements II and III are true.

30. **(E)**   The 1 is in the hundredths place. If the number to the immediate right of the 1 (i.e., the number in the thousandths place) is greater than or equal to 5, we increase 1 to 2, otherwise do not change the 1. Then we leave off all numbers to the right of the 1. In our problem a 6 is in the thousandths place so we change the 1 to a 2 to get 287.42 as our answer.

31. **(C)**   Recall the following Laws of Exponents:

$$x^p \times x^q = x^{p+q} \text{ and } \frac{x^p}{x^q} = x^{p-q}.$$

So, $x^2 \times x^7 = x^{2+7} = x^9$. Hence,

$$\frac{x^2 \times x^7}{x} = \frac{x^9}{x^1} = x^{9-1} = x^8.$$

32. **(A)**   We need to write the three fractions with the same denominator. So, find the least common multiple (LCM) of 9, 15, and 21.

$$9 = 3^2, 15 = 3 \times 5, \text{ and } 21 = 3 \times 7$$

Therefore, the LCM is

$$3^2 \times 5 \times 7 = 315.$$

Then $\dfrac{1}{9} = \dfrac{5 \times 7}{5 \times 7} \times \dfrac{1}{9} = \dfrac{35}{315},$

$$\dfrac{2}{15} = \dfrac{3 \times 7}{3 \times 7} \times \dfrac{2}{15} = \dfrac{42}{315},$$

and $\dfrac{3}{21} = \dfrac{3 \times 5}{3 \times 5} \times \dfrac{3}{21} = \dfrac{45}{315}.$

Clearly,

$$\dfrac{35}{315} < \dfrac{42}{315} < \dfrac{45}{315}$$

and hence, in order, from least to greatest, we have:

$$\dfrac{1}{9}, \dfrac{2}{15}, \dfrac{3}{21}.$$

33. **(A)**   The volume of a rectangular box is the area of the base times the height. So if we let s be the length of each side of the base (it is a square), the area of the base is s^2. The height of the box is one-half the length of a side of the base, thus, the height is $^1/_2$ The volume is then

$$V = s^2 \times \frac{1}{2}s = \frac{1}{2}s^3.$$

But the volume is given as 256. Substituting this into the equation

$$V = \frac{1}{2}s^3 V$$

gives us:

$$256 = \frac{1}{2}s^3.$$

Now multiply both sides of the equation by 2 to get

$$2 \times 256 = 2\frac{1}{2}s^3 \text{ or } 512 = s^3.$$

But, $512 = 8^3$ so that we have $8^3 = s^3$ or $s^3 = 8$. The height of the box is

$$\frac{1}{2}s = \frac{1}{2} \times 8 = 4 \text{ feet.}$$

34. **(A)** If $x = -3$ then

$$-x^2 + 2x = -(-3)^2 + 2(-3) = -(9) + (-6) = -15.$$

35. **(D)** If $a = b^3$ and $a = \frac{1}{8}$, then substituting into the first equation we have

$$\frac{1}{8} = b^3 \text{ or } \left(\frac{1}{2}\right)^3 = b^3 \text{ so } b = \frac{1}{2}.$$

36. **(D)** Let x be the number of people in the barn. Then, since each person and cow has only one head, the number of cows must be $30 - x$. Since people have two legs, the number of human legs totals $2x$. Similarly, since the number of legs each cow has is 4, the total number of cow legs in the barn is $4(30 - x)$. Thus, we have this equation:

$$2x + 4(30 - x) = 104.$$

To solve this equation, use the distributive property:

$$a(b - c) = ab - ac.$$

We get

$$4(30 - x) = (4 \times 30) - (4 \times x) = 120 - 4x.$$

Our equation reduces to:

$$2x + 120 - 4x = 104 \text{ or } 120 - 2x = 104.$$

Now subtract 120 from both sides or the equation to get

$$-2x = 104 - 120 = -16.$$

Dividing both sides of the equation by -2: $x = 8$. Therefore, there were 8 people and $30 - 8 = 22$ cows in the barn.

37. **(B)** To solve the proportion

$$\frac{12}{x-1} = \frac{5}{6}$$

multiply both sides of the equation by 6 and by $(x-1)$ so that we have

$$6(x-1) \times \frac{12}{x-1} = 6(x-1) \times \frac{5}{6} \text{ or } 72 = 5(x-1).$$

Now, use the distributive property:

$$a(b-c) = ab - ac$$

to get $72 = 5x - 5$. Add 5 to both sides of the equation:

$$77 = 5x$$

and then divide both sides by 5:

$$x = \frac{77}{5} = 15.4.$$

38. **(B)** If two lines, l_1 and l_2, which lie in the same plane, are both perpendicular to a third line, l_3, l_1 and l_2 are parallel.

39. **(E)** First of all the least common multiple (LCM) of 2 and 3 is 2 × 3 = 6, so let's rewrite the expression so that both fractions have 6 as a common denominator:

$$\frac{1}{2} + \frac{1}{3} = \frac{3}{3} \times \frac{1}{2} + \frac{2}{2} \times \frac{1}{3} = \frac{3}{6} + \frac{2}{6} = \frac{5}{6}.$$

40. **(A)** Two triangles are similar if we can find two pairs of angles, one in each triangle, that are congruent. Given that $BC \parallel DE$ we know that $(\angle ABC, \angle BDE)$ and $(\angle ACB, \angle CED)$ are two pairs of corresponding and hence congruent angles. Thus, taking care in the order that we write the angles so that we match the correct angles, $\triangle ABC \sim \triangle ADE$.

Section III: Writing

1. **(B)** "Were praised" is a plural verb; since the subject is Chief Joseph, a singular proper noun, the verb should be "was praised." The intervening phrase of choice (A), "*together with* 250 warriors and 500 women and children," does not change the singular subject. Choice (C), "bravery," is the correct noun form, and choice (D), "for," is idiomatically correct in that phrase.

2. **(E)** Choice (A), "upon which," is a correct prepositional phrase. Choice (B), "is based," agrees with its subject, "society." In choice (C), "are" agrees with its subject, "ideals." "Derived from" in choice (D) is correct idiomatic usage.

3. **(B)** Two past actions are mentioned. The earlier of two past actions should be indicated by past perfect tense, so the answer is "had been." Choice (C) is correct. Choice (A) contains two adjectives as part of an appositive phrase modifying the subject, and choice (D), "upon the death," is idiomatically correct.

4. **(C)** Choice (C) should be "depend," not "had depended" because that use of past perfect would indicate prior past action. There is a series of events in this sentence: first, the legislature "had not finalized" the budget (B); then, Representative Wilson "pointed out" this failure (A). Choice (C) needs to be present tense as this situation still exists, and (D) is future action.

5. **(D)** In order to complete the parallelism, choice (D) should be "arrangements." Choice (A) is a noun used as an adjective. "To plan" (B) is an infinitive phrase followed by noun objects: "puppet shows and movies" and "garage sales." Choice (C), "used," is a participate modifying books.

6. **(A)** An infinitive, "to understand," should never be split by any adverbial modifier, "completely." Choice (B), "effects," is the noun form, and choice (D), "affected," is the adjective form. "One must," choice (C), is used in standard English.

7. **(C)** "More" is used to compare two things. Since the number of nations is not specified, "more" cannot be used in this sentence. Choice

(A), "known," modifies "roads"; choice (B) is idiomatically correct; choice (D), "is," agrees in number with its subject, "transportation."

8. **(E)** Choice (A), "many a," should always be followed by the singular verb, "wishes," of choice (B). Choice (C) is idiomatically correct. In "someone else," (D), "else" is needed to indicate a person other than the student would pay the bills.

9. **(D)** Choice (D) should read, "became very irritated." "To aggravate" means "to make worse"; "to irritate" means "to excite to impatience or anger." A situation is "aggravated" and becomes worse, but one does not become "aggravated" with people. Choices (A), (B), and (C) are correctly used idioms.

10. **(C)** The reference in choice (C) is vague because it sounds as if the bus made the two students late. Choice (A) is a correct subject pronoun; choice (B) is the correct adverb form to modify "dressed"; choice (D) is a correct object pronoun.

11. **(E)** Choice (A), "among," indicates choice involving more than two things. The prepositions in (B) and (C) are correct. "Are," (D), is a plural verb, agreeing in number with the compound subject "singing . . . dancing . . . cooking."

12. **(A)** One is "disappointed by" a person or action but "disappointed in" what is not satisfactory. "Inexpensive," (B), is the adjective form. Parallel with "to work," choice (C), "save," had the word "to" omitted. Choice (D) compares the two models, one "inexpensive" and one "more expensive."

13. **(A)** The verb should be plural, "are," in order to agree with the compound subject, "budget . . . plans." Choice (B) begins an infinitive phrase which includes a participle, "existing," (C). Choice (D) is idiomatically correct.

14. **(A)** The expression should be phrased "as delicate as." Choice (B) uses a possessive before a gerund; choice (C) is correctly used; and choice (D) is a possessive pronoun of neuter gender which is appropriate to use in referring to a plant.

15. **(D)** The verb "deal" must agree with the subject, "works," and not

a word in the intervening phrase. "Outwardly," choice (A), is an adverb modifying "seemed." Choices (B) and (C), "the picture of respectability," describe the subject; (D) is idiomatically correct.

16. **(D)**   The word "of" in "inside of" is redundant and should not be used. Choice (A) is idiomatically correct and signals two classes of people once considered unequal in merit, and choice (B), "alike," is appropriate when comparing the two. Choice (C), "them," is correct pronoun usage.

17. **(E)**   Choice (A), "unsafe for," is idiomatically correct; choice (B), "deltas," is a plural noun. Choice (C), "can be," is grammatically correct. The preposition "in," choice (D), is correct.

18. **(C)**   The verb in this subordinate clause is incorrect; the clause begins with, "which," and this word refers to "information." Therefore, the clause, in order to agree with the antecedent, must read, "which shows." The verb "shows" should not be made to agree with "species" and "others." Choices (A), "people," and (B), "have compiled," agree in number. "Either" in choice (D) is correctly placed after the verb to show a choice of "endangered" or "becoming endangered."

19. **(D)**   Do not end a sentence with a preposition; the phrase should read, "in which he was born." The verbs show proper time sequence in (A) and (B); choice (C) is correct pronoun usage and correct superlative degree of adjective.

20. **(D)**   The noun form "effect" is the correct one to use. Choice (A), "to inhibit," is an infinitive; choice (B) is correctly worded; in choice (C), the nominative case "who" is the correct subject of "seemed."

21. **(C)**   The idiom should be "filled to capacity." The adjective in choice (A), "average," is correct, as is the adverb in choice (B). Choice (D), "most," is appropriate for the superlative degree.

22. **(B)**   The subordinate clause, "who my parents have not met," has as its subject "parents," which agrees with choice (C), "have . . . met." Therefore, the pronoun is a direct object of the verb and should be in the objective case, "whom." Both choice (A) and choice (D) are idiomatically correct.

23. **(C)**   The pronoun reference is unclear. The meaning of the sentence

indicated that Colonel Jones denies involvement in any other covert activity. The agent from a foreign country may or may not have been involved in other covert activities, but that is not the issue here. The verb tense of choice (A) is correct. Choice (B) is the correct adverb form, and "other" in choice (D) is necessary to the meaning of the sentence.

24. **(E)**   Choice (A), "testing," is parallel to "determining" and "evaluating." "Proper" in choice (B) and "effectiveness" in choice (C) are correct. In choice (D) "is" must be singular because all three steps mentioned comprise the one process.

25. **(B)**   Choice (A) is correct. Choice (B) should read, "it is she"; nominative case pronoun is required following a linking verb. Choice (C) is proper English, and the correct form of the modifiers appears in choice (D).

26. **(D)**   "Because" is the correct word to use in the cause-and-effect relationship in this sentence. Choice (A), "being that"; choice (E), "than me"; and choice (B), "the more," are not grammatically correct. Choice (C), "is made by you," is in the passive voice and not as direct as (D).

27. **(D)**   "After they have been" completes the proper time sequence. Choice (A), "when"; choice (B), "have been"; and choice (C), "will be," are the wrong time sequences. Choice (E), "should be," is an idea not contained in the original sentence.

28. **(C)**   "Since the plane is late" shows correct time sequence and good reasoning. Choice (A), "seeing as how," and choice (D), "being as," are poor wording. Choices (B), "when," and (E), "while," are the wrong time, logically, to be on the observation deck.

29. **(E)**   Since a sentence should not end with a preposition, choices (A) and (B) are eliminated. Choices (C), "living in this world," and (D), "world's living," introduce new concepts.

30. **(A)**   The construction, "than those," clarifies the fact that more vegetables have been added. Choice (C), "your suggestion"; choice (D), "than what"; and choice (E), "which," do not contain the idea of adding more varieties of vegetables. Choice (B) ends with a preposition.

31. **(B)**   The voice must be consistent with "I," so (B) is the only pos-

sible correct answer. All other choices have a noun or pronoun that is not consistent with "I"; choice (A), "you"; choice (C), "a person"; choice (D), "people"; and choice (E), "some."

32. **(A)** The correct answer has two concepts—pieces are missing and pieces will probably never be found. Choice (B) has a singular verb, "is." Choice (C) indicates the pieces "probably will be" missing, which is not the problem. Choice (D) and choice (E) both indicate the pieces are "probably" missing, which is illogical because the pieces either are or are not missing.

33. **(C)** Choice (A), "the kind of a," and choice (D), "the type of a," are incorrect grammatical structures. Choice (E) introduces the new concept of "category." Choice (B), "sort of," is poor wording.

34. **(E)** Choice (E) is clear and concise and shows the correct comparison of architecture. The antecedent of "those" in choice (A) is not clear. Choice (B) is comparing "characteristics," not just architecture. Choice (C) is awkward, and choice (D) incorrectly uses an idiom, "characteristic with."

35. **(B)** Choice (B) is clear and direct. Choices (A) and (E) are too wordy. Choice (C) has the wrong concept, "balancing games." Choice (D) "this as an example" is poorly worded.

36. **(E)** An opposing force "gives" scattered resistance; therefore, choice (A) is incorrect. Choices (B), (C), and (D) are poorly worded and do not have the correct meaning.

37. **(A)** Choice (A) produces a complete sentence: "rainfall" is the subject and "let up" is the verb. None of the other choices produces a complete sentence.

38. **(D)** This choice uses the correct tense, "will have," showing action in the future. All the other verbs listed do not show correct future verb construction.

39. **(B)** The correct choice has a compound verb: "comes" and "falls in love." The salesman comes to town first, then he meets and falls in love with the librarian. Choice (A), with its misplaced participial phrase, sounds as if either the town or Iowa is in love with the librarian. Choice (C) would produce a run-on sentence. Choices (D) and (E) have unclear tense.

40. **(A)**   Choice (A) has clear reference. Choice (B) will produce a run-on sentence. Choices (C) and (D) do not indicate whose writings or paintings. Choice (E) sounds as if the only time naturalists feel reverence is when they write or paint.

41. **(A)**   This choice is correct when used in conjunction with "of that region." Choices (B), (C), and (D) imply the mention of a specific region; in addition, (D) would be repetitious. Choice (E) does not agree in number, "regions."

42. **(E)**   This choice indicates that the telephone has a loud ring and that it is Doug's girlfriend who is calling. Choice (A) is a misplaced participial phrase. Choice (B) has an error, "Doug's loud girlfriend"; choice (C) has an error, "the telephone was the insisting girlfriend"; and choice (D) is missing a verb to make it a complete sentence.

43. **(C)**   General reference should be avoided. The pronoun "which" does not have a clear reference in choices (A) or (B). In (C) "which" clearly refers to "facts." The reference "proving" in choice (D) is too general. In choice (E) "a proof" is an incorrect number to refer to the two strengths of women.

44. **(A)**   You should find the original acceptable from the start; and if you look at the alternates, it is the briefest one. Choices (C) and (D) incorrectly use "being that" (and choice (D) is wordy). Choice (B) is repetitious ("prevailing rent at the time"). Choice (E) looks like a good possibility, but it does convert the verb to a noun, unnecessarily adding a word.

45. **(E)**   Simple awkward wordiness or even repetition mars all the choices except (E) and (C). In choice (A), (B), and (D), there is no need for the "in [a work] it" phrasing. (C) incorrectly splices independent clauses together with a comma. Therefore, choice (E) is the best answer.

PPST ESSAY SCORING GUIDE

The PPST essay sections are scored by two writing experts on the basis of the criteria outlined below. In addition to comparing your essay to those included in our practice tests, you may use these guidelines to estimate your score on this section. Remember that your score is the sum of the scores of two writing experts, so provided you respond to the assigned topic, your score will fall somewhere between two and twelve. Scores will be assigned based on the following guidelines:

6 An essay receiving a score of 6 may contain one or two spelling or punctuation errors, but overall it exhibits a high degree of proficiency and thought on the assigned topic.

An essay scoring a 6

- is both well organized and well developed
- engages important concepts and explains them clearly
- varies expression and language
- demonstrates deft use of language
- is virtually free from errors involving syntax and structure

5 An essay receiving a score of 5 exhibits a high degree of proficiency and thought on the assigned topic, however it contains a number of minor mistakes.

An essay scoring a 5

- is both well organized and well developed
- engages important concepts and explains them
- varies expression and language somewhat
- demonstrates deft use of language
- is virtually free from errors involving syntax and structure

4 An essay receiving a score of 4 responds to the assignment and exhibits some degree of deeper understanding.

An essay scoring a 4

- demonstrates adequate organization and development
- engages and explains some important concepts, but not all that are necessary to demonstrate full understanding

- exhibits adequate use of language
- contains some syntactical and structural errors, without excessive repetition of those errors

3 An essay receiving a score of 3 exhibits some degree of understanding, but its response to the topic is obviously deficient.

An essay scoring a 3 is deficient in one or more of the following areas:

- insufficient organization or development
- insufficient engagement or explanation of important concepts
- consistent repetition of syntactical or structural errors
- redundant or unsuitable word choice

2 An essay receiving a score of 2 exhibits limited understanding and its response to the topic is seriously deficient.

An essay scoring a 2 is deficient in one or more of the following areas:

- weak organization or development
- very few pertinent details
- consistent and serious errors in syntax, structure
- consistent and serious errors in word choice

1 An essay receiving a score of 1 exhibits a lack of basic writing skills.

An essay scoring a 1 is disorganized, undeveloped, contains consistent repetition of errors, or is incomprehensible.

Sample Essays with Commentary

ESSAY I (Score: 5–6)

A poll was recently conducted to determine American heroes. Sadly, most of the heroes listed in the top ten are cartoon characters or actors who portray heroic roles. What does this say about American ideals? Perhaps we do not know enough, or perhaps we know too much in order to have heroes. Having access to instant information about a variety of military, political and religious figures, citizens of modern society have outgrown the innocence of previous centuries.

The ancient hero possessed many idealized virtues, such as physical strength, honesty, courage, and intelligence. Oedipus saved his people from pestilence by solving the riddle of the Sphinx. As leader, he was sworn to find the murderer of the previous king; Oedipus' brave pursuit of justice was conducted with honesty and integrity. Beowulf, another famous ancient hero, existed at a time when life was wild, dangerous, unpredictable.

Modern society is missing several of the ingredients necessary to produce a hero of this calibre. For one thing, there are no mythical monsters such as the Sphinx or Grendel. War is left as the stuff of heroic confrontation, but modern wars only add to our confusion. Men have been decorated for killing their brothers and friends in the Civil War; America fought the Germans in World War I and the Germans and Japanese in World War II, but our former enemies are our current allies. As for honesty, modern role models too often let us down. The media exposes politicians who are involved in scandal, sports figures who do drugs, and religious leaders who make multi-million dollar incomes.

No wonder Americans name Superman and actors John Wayne and Clint Eastwood to the list of modern heroes. These heroes are larger than life on the theatre screen, and their vices are at least predictable and reasonably innocuous. Wisely, we have chosen those who will not surprise us with ugly or mundane reality.

ANALYSIS

Essay I has a score range of 5–6. It is the strongest of the four essays. Although it is not perfect, it shows a good command of the English language and depth of thought. The writer employs a traditional essay structure: the first paragraph is the introduction and ends with the thesis statement; the second and third paragraphs discuss traditional and contemporary heroes,

as stated in the last sentence of the thesis paragraph; the fourth paragraph concludes. Each of the two body paragraphs has a clear topic sentence. The writer gives several distinct examples to support his ideas. Vocabulary is effective, and sentence structure is varied.

ESSAY II (Score: 4–5)

Heroes are people who perform the extraordinary and who are highly regarded by society. These outstanding people have characteristics that are desirable to everyone, but the ways in which heroes use their talents glorify them even more. A true hero will do anything in his power to help others.

Two heroes from modern literature exhibit the quality of self-sacrifice. In Remarque's novel *All Quiet on the Western Front,* Paul Baumer is a German ground soldier who endures many disappointments and difficulties while fighting for his country. Paul does not shirk his duties as a soldier of the German people. Moreover, Paul goes out of his way to train the raw recruits and to care for a soldier suffering from shell shock. Another hero, Willy Loman in *Death of a Salesman* makes all the everyday sacrifices a father makes for children and a husband makes for his wife. Willy drives long distances in order to make a living. When Willy feels he is hindering his family, he makes the ultimate sacrifice of suicide to get out of the way.

The true heroes of today are the common people, not unlike Willy and Paul. Stories regularly appear in the newspapers of everyday heroes. The woman with knowledge of CPR saves a drowning child from certain death. A neighbor saves two children from an apartment fire. Teachers take the extra time to listen to a student's personal problem. Parents stand tough against their child's unreasonable demands. Adults who stop to help a stranded motorist are all heroic in their own way.

Every day they stand behind their ideals, living up to their moral standards, in order to help others. It is the day-to-day dedication that makes these twentieth-century heroes extraordinary.

ANALYSIS

Essay II has a score range of 4–5. It still has the traditional essay organization, but the thesis paragraph and conclusion are a bit less focused and less interesting than in Essay I. The paper is supported by examples, but the sentence structure is not varied enough. The last sentence of the third paragraph is weak.

ESSAY III (Score: 3-4)

I would say that there are some heroes still left in modern society. Although we don't have heroes like we used to, our heroes are different now.

When I was a child, I thought that Superman was a real person. He was my hero. He was strong and always won the fights he got into. Villains didn't stand a chance with him. My parents thought I should watch *Sesame Street,* but I wanted to go to the moves to see Luke Skywalker. Even though I later knew it was not real, I still enjoy going to the movies. I want to see a good conflict between the forces of good and the forces of evil, especially when justice rules.

Now I am more realistic. My heroes are good people or successful people. My uncle, for example. He owns his own business and lets me work there part time to earn money. That's what I want to be, someone who is successful and independent but will still help out a young person. When a person is brave, that's heroism too. My friend's brother has a medal for being a hero in Viet Nam. You have different ways to be brave now. The innocent days of childhood are gone, but there are still people to be admired.

ANALYSIS

Essay III has a score range of 3–4. There is a thesis in the opening paragraph, and the remaining two paragraphs are organized so as to support that thesis. However, this paper is not as strong as the previous two. The conclusion is not well defined. Also, the writer uses mixed voice, slang, and contractions. His use of the first person pronoun becomes intrusive, and all examples are drawn from his personal experience. The sentence structure could be better, and there is even a fragment.

ESSAY IV (Score: 1–2)

It is not true that there are no heroes nowadays. Everywhere you look, a person see heroes to believe in.

When you go to the movie theatre, many movies are about good guys versus bad buys. Not just Westerns. Sometimes the good cop gets killed. But he usually kills a few criminals for himself before he dies. In many movies, justice wins when the villain is defeated. No matter who wins, people in the audience know what is right and what is wrong because the heroes kill because he needs to defend themselves or because the guy needed to be killed. Rambo would not kill anyone except the enemy. This

teaches good values about heroes and their motives since people like to go to the movies, they see a lot of heroes.

ANALYSIS

Essay IV has a score range of 1–2. It is the weakest of the four essays. The ideas are inexact, and the sentences are ill-formed. This essay uses mixed voice and slang. There is an agreement error and a fragment. The most serious faults of this essay are the lack of specific examples and the use of sweeping generalizations. The concluding two sentences are exceptionally poor in clarity of thought and wording.

PPST
Pre-Professional Skills Tests

Practice
PPST II

PPST Test II

Section I: Reading Comprehension

TIME: 60 Minutes
40 Questions

DIRECTIONS: A number of questions follow each of the passages in the reading section. Answer the questions by choosing the best answer from the five choices given.

Questions 1 to 5 refer to the following passage:

Spa water quality is maintained through a filter to ensure cleanliness and clarity. Wastes such as perspiration, hairspray, and lotions which cannot be removed by the spa filter can be controlled by shock treatment or super chlorination every other week. Although the filter traps most of the solid material to control bacteria and algae and to oxidize any organic material, the addition of disinfectants such as bromine or chlorine is necessary.

As all water solutions have a pH which controls corrosion, proper pH balance is also necessary. A pH measurement determines if the water is acid or alkaline. Based on a 14-point scale, a pH reading of 7.0 is considered neutral while a lower reading is considered acidic, and a higher reading indicates alkalinity or basic. High pH (above 7.6) reduces sanitizer efficiency, clouds water, promotes scale formation on surfaces and equipment, and interferes with filter operation. When pH is high, add a pH decrease such as sodium bisulphate (e.g., Spa Down). Because the spa water is hot, scale is deposited more rapidly. A weekly dose of a stain and scale fighter also will help to control this problem. Low pH (below 7.2) is equally damaging, causing equipment corrosion, water which is irritating, and rapid sanitizer dissipation. To increase pH add sodium bicarbonate (e.g., Spa Up).

The recommended operating temperature of a spa (98° – 104°) is a fertile environment for the growth of bacteria and viruses. This growth is prevented when appropriate sanitizer levels are continuously monitored.

Bacteria can also be controlled by maintaining a proper bromine level of 3.0 to 5.0 parts per million (ppm) or a chlorine level of 1.0 – 2.0 ppm. As bromine tablets should not be added directly to the water, a bromine floater will properly dispense the tablets. Should chlorine be the chosen sanitizer, a granular form is recommended, as liquid chlorine or tablets are too harsh for the spa.

1. Although proper chemical and temperature maintenance of spa water is necessary, the most important condition to monitor is

   (A) preventing growth of bacteria and virus.

   (B) preventing equipment corrosion.

   (C) preventing soap build up.

   (D) preventing scale formation.

   (E) preventing cloudy water.

2. Of the chemical and temperature conditions in a spa, the condition most dangerous to one's health is

   (A) spa water temperature above 104°.

   (B) bromine level between 3.0 and 5.0.

   (C) pH level below 7.2.

   (D) spa water temperature between 90° and 104°.

   (E) cloudy and dirty water.

3. The primary purpose of the passage is to

   (A) relate that maintenance of a spa can negate the full enjoyment of the spa experience.

   (B) provide evidence that spas are not a viable alternative to swimming pools.

   (C) convey that the maintenance of a spa is expensive and time consuming.

   (D) explain the importance of proper spa maintenance.

   (E) detail proper spa maintenance.

4. The spa filter can be relied upon to

   (A) control algae and bacteria.

   (B) trap most solid material.

   (C) oxidize organic material.

   (D) assure an adequate level of sanitation.

   (E) maintain clear spa water.

5. Which chemical should one avoid when maintaining a spa?

   (A) Liquid chlorine   (D) Baking soda

   (B) Bromine   (E) All forms of chlorine

   (C) Sodium bisulfate

Questions 6 to 10 refer to the following passage:

The relationship of story elements found in children's generated stories to reading achievement was analyzed. Correlations ranged from .61101 (p = .64) at the beginning of first grade to .83546 (p = .24) at the end of first grade, to .85126 (p = .21) at the end of second grade, and to .82588 (p=.26) for fifth/sixth grades. Overall, the correlation of the story elements to reading achievement appeared to indicate a high positive correlation trend even though it was not statistically significant.

Multiple regression equation analyses dealt with the relative contribution of the story elements to reading achievement. The contribution of certain story elements was substantial. At the beginning of first grade, story conventions added 40 percent to the total variance while the other increments were not significant. At the end of first grade, story plot contributed 44 percent to the total variance, story conventions contributed 20 percent, and story sources contributed 17 percent. At the end of second grade, the story elements contributed more equal percentages to the total partial correlation of .8513. Although none of the percentages were substantial, story plot (.2200), clausal connectors (.1858), and T-units (.1590) contributed the most to the total partial correlation. By the fifth and sixth grades three other story elements—T-units (.2241), story characters (.3214), and clausal connectors (.1212)—contributed most to the total partial correlation. None of these percentages were substantial.

6. Which of the following is the most complete and accurate definition of the term "statistically significant" as used in the passage?

(A) Consists of important numerical data

(B) Is educationally significant

(C) Departs greatly from chance expectations

(D) Permits prediction of reading achievement by knowing the story elements

(E) Indicates two measures (reading achievement and story elements) give the same information

7. The passage suggests which of the following conclusions about the correlation of story elements to reading achievement?

(A) That there are other more important story elements that should also be included in the analyses

(B) That children's inclusion of story elements in their stories causes them to achieve higher levels in reading

(C) That these story elements are important variables to consider in reading achievement

(D) That correlations of more than 1.0 are needed for this study to be statistically significant

(E) That this correlation was not statistically significant because there was little variance between story elements and reading achievement,

8. The relative contribution of story conventions and story plot in first grade suggests that

(A) children may have spontaneously picked up these story elements as a result of their exposure to stories.

(B) children have been explicitly taught these story elements.

(C) these story elements were not important because in fifth/sixth grades other story elements contributed more to the total partial correlation.

(D) other story elements were more substantial.

(E) children's use of story conventions and plots were not taken from story models.

9. The content of the passage suggests that the passage would most likely appear in which of the following?

   (A) *Psychology Today*   (D) *Language Arts*

   (B) *The Creative Writer*   (E) *Reading Research Quarterly*

   (C) *Educational Leadership*

10. "None of these percentages were substantial" is the last statement in the passage. It refers to

   (A) the story elements for fifth/sixth grades.

   (B) the story elements for second grade.

   (C) the story elements at the end of first grade.

   (D) the story elements at the beginning of first grade.

   (E) the story elements for all of the grades, i.e., first grade, second grade, and fifth/sixth grade.

Questions 11 to 13 refer to the following passage:

There is an importance of learning communication and meaning in language. Yet the use of notions such as communication and meaning as the basic criteria for instruction, experiences, and materials in classrooms may misguide a child in several respects. Communication in the classroom is vital. The teacher should use communication to help students develop the capacity to make their private responses become public responses. Otherwise, one's use of language would be in danger of being what the younger generation refers to as mere words, mere thoughts, and mere feelings.

Learning theorists emphasize specific components of learning: behaviorists stress behavior in learning; humanists stress the affective in learning; and cognitivists stress cognition in learning. All three of these components occur simultaneously and cannot be separated from each other in the learning process. In 1957, Festinger referred to dissonance as the lack of harmony between what one does (behavior) and what one believes (attitude). Attempts to separate the components of learning either knowingly or unknowingly create dissonances wherein language, thought, feeling, and behavior become diminished of authenticity. As a result, ideas and concepts lose their content and vitality, and the manipulation and politics of communication assume prominence.

11. Which of the following best describes the author's attitude toward the subject discussed?

   (A) A flippant disregard   (D) A passive resignation

   (B) A mild frustration   (E) An informed concern

   (C) A moral indignation

12. The primary purpose of the passage is to

   (A) explain the criteria for providing authentic communication in classroom learning.

   (B) discuss the relationships between learning and communication.

   (C) assure teachers that communication and meaning are the basic criteria for learning in classrooms.

   (D) stress the importance of providing authentic communication in classroom learning.

   (E) address the role of communication and meaning in classrooms.

13. Which of the following is the most complete and accurate definition of the term "mere" as used in the passage?

   (A) Small   (D) Poor

   (B) Minor   (E) Insignificant

   (C) Little

Questions 14 to 16 refer to the following passage:

In 1975, Sinclair observed that it had often been supposed that the main factor in learning to talk is being able to imitate. Schlesinger (1975) noted that at certain stages of learning to speak, a child tends to imitate everything an adult says to him or her, and it therefore seems reasonable to accord to such imitation an important role in the acquisition of language.

Moreover, various investigators have attempted to explain the role of imitation in language. In his discussion of the development of imitation and cognition of adult speech sounds, Nakazema (1975) stated that although the parent's talking stimulates and accelerates the infant's articulatory activity, the parent's phoneme system does not influence the child's articulatory mechanisms. Slobin and Welsh (1973) suggested that imitation is the reconstruction of the adult's utterance and that the child does so by employing the grammatical rules that he has developed at a

specific time. Schlesinger proposed that by imitating the adult the child practices new grammatical constructions. Brown and Bellugi (1964) noted that a child's imitations resemble spontaneous speech in that they drop inflections, most function words, and sometimes other words. However, the word order of imitated sentences usually was preserved. Brown and Bellugi assumed that imitation is a function of what the child attended to or remembered. Shipley et al. (1969) suggested that repeating an adult's utterance assists the child's comprehension. Ervin (1964) and Braine (1971) found that a child's imitations do not contain more advanced structures than his or her spontaneous utterances; thus, imitation can no longer be regarded as the simple behavioristic act that earlier scholars assumed it to be.

14. The author of the passage would tend to agree with which of the following statements?

    (A) Apparently, children are physiologically unable to imitate a parent's phoneme system.

    (B) Apparently, children require practice with more advanced structures before they are able to imitate.

    (C) Apparently, children only imitate what they already do, using whatever is in their repertoire.

    (D) Apparently, the main factor in learning to talk remains being able to imitate.

    (E) Apparently, children cannot respond meaningfully to a speech situation until they have reached a stage where they can make symbol-orientation responses.

15. The primary purpose of the passage is to

    (A) explain language acquisition.

    (B) explain the role of imitation in language acquisition.

    (C) assure parents of their role in assisting imitation in language acquisition.

    (D) relate the history of imitation in language acquisition.

    (E) discuss relationships between psychological and physiological processes in language acquisition.

16. An inference that parents may make from the passage is that they should

    (A) be concerned when a child imitates their language.

    (B) focus on developing imitation in their child's language.

    (C) realize that their child's imitations may reflect several aspects of language acquisition.

    (D) realize that their talking may over-stimulate their child's articulatory activity.

    (E) not be concerned as imitation is too complex for anyone to understand.

Questions 17 and 18 refer to the following passage:

A major problem with reading/language arts instruction is that practice assignments from workbooks often provide short, segmented activities that do not really resemble the true act of reading. Perhaps more than any computer application, word processing is capable of addressing these issues.

17. The author would tend to agree that a major benefit of computers in reading/language arts instruction is

    (A) that the reading act may be more closely resembled.

    (B) that short segmented assignments will be eliminated.

    (C) that the issues in reading/language arts instruction will be addressed.

    (D) that computer application will be limited to word processing.

    (E) that reading practice will be eliminated.

18. The appropriate use of a word processor to assist in making practice resemble a reading act is

    (A) detailed.   (D) alluded.

    (B) desirable.   (E) costly.

    (C) unstated.

Questions 19 to 21 refer to the following passage:

In view of the current emphasis on literature-based reading instruction, a greater understanding by teachers of variance in cultural, language, and story components should assist in narrowing the gap between reader and text and improve reading comprehension. Classroom teachers should begin with students' meaning and intentions about stories before moving students to the commonalities of story meaning based on common background and culture. With teacher guidance, students should develop a fuller understanding of how complex narratives are when they are generating stories as well as when they are reading stories.

19. Which of the following is the intended audience for the passage?

    (A) Students in a reading class

    (B) Teachers using literature-based curriculum

    (C) Professors teaching a literature course

    (D) Parents concerned about their child's comprehension of books

    (E) Teacher educators teaching reading methods courses

20. Which of the following is the most complete and accurate definition of the term "variance" as used in the passage?

    (A) Change   (D) Deviation

    (B) Fluctuations   (E) Incongruity

    (C) Diversity

21. The passage supports a concept of meaning primarily residing in

    (A) culture, language, and story components.

    (B) comprehension.

    (C) student's stories only.

    (D) students only.

    (E) students and narratives.

Questions 22 to 25 refer to the following passage:

As noted by Favat in 1977, the study of children's stories has been an ongoing concern of linguists, anthropologists, and psychologists. The past decade has witnessed a surge of interest in children's stories from researchers in these and other disciplines. The use of narratives for reading

and reading instruction has been commonly accepted by the educational community. The notion that narrative is highly structured and that children's sense of narrative structure is more highly developed than expository structure has been proposed by some researchers.

Early studies of children's stories followed two approaches for story analysis: the analysis of story content or the analysis of story structure. Story content analysis has centered primarily on examining motivational and psychodynamic aspects of story characters as noted in the works of Erikson and Pitcher and Prelinger in 1963 and Ames in 1966. These studies have noted that themes or topics predominate and that themes change with age.

Early research on story structure focused on formal models of structure, such as story grammar and story schemata. These models specified basic story elements and formed sets of rules similar to sentence grammar for ordering the elements.

The importance or centrality of narrative in a child's development of communicative ability has been proposed by Halliday (1976) and Hymes (1975). Thus, the importance of narrative for language communicative ability and for reading and reading instruction has been well documented. However, the question still remains about how these literacy abilities interact and lead to conventional reading.

22. This passage is most probably directed at which of the following audience?

(A) Reading educators   (D) Reading researchers

(B) Linguists   (E) Anthropologists

(C) Psychologists

23. According to the passage, future research should address

(A) how story structure and story schema interact with comprehension.

(B) how children's use and understanding of narrative interacts and leads to conventional reading.

(C) how basal texts and literature texts differ from children's story structure.

(D) how story content interacts with story comprehension.

(E) how narrative text structure differs from expository text structure.

24. The major distinction between story content and story structure is that

    (A) story content focuses on motivational aspects whereas story structure focuses on rules similar to sentence grammar.

    (B) story content focuses on psychodynamic aspects whereas story structure focuses on formal structural models.

    (C) story content and story structure essentially refer to the same concepts.

    (D) story content focuses on themes and topics whereas story structure focuses on specific basic story elements.

    (E) story content focuses primarily on characters whereas story structure focuses on story grammar and schemata.

25. Which of the following is the most complete and accurate definition of the term "surge" as used in the following sentence? The past decade has witnessed a surge of interest in children's stories from researchers in these and other disciplines.

    (A) A heavy swell   (D) A sudden increase

    (B) A slight flood   (E) A sudden rush

    (C) A sudden rise

Questions 26 to 29 refer to the following passage:

Seldom has the American school system not been the target of demands for change to meet the social priorities of the times. This theme has been traced through the following significant occurrences in education: Benjamin Franklin's advocacy in 1749 for a more useful type of education; Horace Mann's zealous proposals in the 1830s espousing the tax-supported public school; John Dewey's early twentieth century attack on traditional schools for not developing the child effectively for his or her role in society; the post-Sputnik pressure for academic rigor; the prolific criticism and accountability pressures of the 1970s, and the ensuing disillusionment and continued criticism of schools until this last decade of the twentieth century. Indeed, the waves of criticism about American education have reflected currents of social dissatisfaction for any given period of this country's history.

As dynamics for change in the social order result in demands for change in the American educational system, so in turn insistence has developed for revision of teacher education (witness the more recent Holmes report (1986)). Historically, the education of American teachers has re-

flected evolving attitudes about public education. With slight modifications, the teacher education pattern established following the demise of the normal school during the early 1900s has persisted in most teacher preparation programs. The pattern has been one requiring certain academic and professional (educational) courses often resulting in teachers prone to teach as they had been taught.

26. The author of this passage would probably agree with which of the following statements?

    (A) Teacher education courses tend to be of no value.

    (B) Social dissatisfaction should drive change in the American school systems.

    (C) Teacher education programs have changed greatly since normal schools were eliminated.

    (D) Critics of American education reflect vested interests.

    (E) Teachers teaching methods tend to reflect what they have learned in their academic and professional courses.

27. The evolving attitudes about public education are

    (A) stated.   (D) unchanged.

    (B) unstated.   (E) unwarranted.

    (C) alluded.

28. One possible sequence of significant occurrences in education noted in the passage is

    (A) Mann's tax-supported public schools, post-Sputnik pressures for academic rigor, and the Holmes' report.

    (B) Franklin's more useful type of education, Dewey's educating children for their role in society, and Mann's tax-supported public schools.

    (C) Mann's tax-supported public schools, the Holmes' report, and post-Sputnik pressures for academic rigor.

    (D) Franklin's more useful type of education, the Holmes' report, and accountability pressures of the 1970s.

    (E) Mann's tax-supported public schools, accountability pressures of the 1970s, and the post-Sputnik pressures for academic rigor.

29. Which of the following statements most obviously implies dissatisfaction with preparation of teachers in the United States?

(A) Demands for change in the American education system lead to insistence for revision of teacher education programs.

(B) The pattern of teacher education requires certain academic and professional education courses.

(C) The education of U.S. teachers has reflected evolving attitudes about public education.

(D) Teachers tend to teach as they were taught.

(E) Teacher education has changed very little since the decline of the normal school.

Questions 30 to 33 refer to the following passage:

HAWK ON A FRESHLY PLOWED FIELD
My Lord of the Field, proudly perched on the sod,
You eye with disdain
And mutter with wings
As steadily each furrow I tractor-plod.
"Intruder!" you glare, firmly standing your ground,
Proclaim this fief yours
By Nature so willed—
Yet bound to the air on my very next round.
You hover and soar, skimming close by the earth,
Distract me from work
To brood there with you
Of changes that Man wrought your land—for his worth.
In medieval days, lords were god over all:
Their word was the law.
Yet here is this hawk
A ruler displaced—Man and Season forestall.
My Lord of the Field, from sight you have flown
For purpose untold,
When brave, you return
And perch once again, still liege-lord—but Alone.

Jacqueline K. Hultquist (1952)

30. Which of the following is the most complete and accurate definition of the term "liege-lord" as used in the passage?

    (A) Monarch   (D) Sovereign

    (B) King   (E) Master

    (C) Owner

31. Which of the following best describes the author's attitude toward the hawk?

    (A) Whimsical   (D) Intimidating

    (B) Romantic   (E) Fearful

    (C) Pensive

32. Which of the following groups of words about the hawk carry human qualities?

    (A) Mutter, brood, and ruler

    (B) Brave, disdain, and perch

    (C) Mutter, disdain, and perch

    (D) Brave, brood, and distract

    (E) Mutter, disdain, and skimming

33. Which of the following is the most complete and accurate definition of the term "medieval" as used in the passage?

    (A) Antiquated   (D) Antebellum

    (B) Feudal   (E) Antediluvian

    (C) Old

Questions 34 to 37 refer to the following passage:

Reduced to its simplest form, a political system is really no more than a device enabling groups of people to live together in a more or less orderly society. As they have developed, political systems generally have fallen into the broad categories of those which do not offer direct subject participation in the decision-making process, and those which allow citizen participation—in form, if not in actual effectiveness.

Let us consider, however, the type of political system that is classified as the modern democracy in a complex society. Such a democracy is

defined by Lipset (1963) as "a political system which supplies regular constitutional opportunities for changing the governing officials, and a social mechanism which permits the largest possible part of the population to influence major decisions by choosing among alternative contenders for political office."

Proceeding from another concept (that of Easton and Dennis), a political system is one of inputs, conversion, and outputs by which the wants of a society are transformed into binding decisions. Easton and Dennis (1967) observed: "To sustain a conversion process of this sort, a society must provide a relatively stable context for political interaction, set of general rules for participating in all parts of the political process." As a rule, this interaction evolves around the settling of differences (satisfying wants or demands) involving the elements of a "political regime," which consists of minimal general goal constraints, norms governing behavior, and structures of authority for the input-output function.

In order to persist, a political system would seem to need a minimal support for the political regime. To insure the maintenance of such a support is the function of political socialization, a process varying according to political systems but toward the end of indoctrinating the members to the respective political system. "To the extent that the maturing members absorb and become attached to the overarching goals of the system and its basic norms and come to approve its structure of authority as legitimate, we can say that they are learning to contribute support to the regime." The desired political norm (an expectation about the way people will behave) is that referred to as political efficacy—a feeling that one's action can have an impact on government.

Adapted from Easton, B. and J. Dennis, "The Child's Acquisition of Regime Norms: Political Efficacy" *American Political Science Review*, March 1967.

34. Political efficacy according to the passage is

    (A) most likely to be found where citizen participation is encouraged.

    (B) most likely to be found where little direct citizen participation is offered.

    (C) in an expanding concept of political efficiency.

    (D) in a diminishing concept of political efficiency.

    (E) in a figurehead political system.

35. Political socialization is a process which

    (A) occurs only in democracies.

    (B) occurs only in totalitarian regimes.

    (C) occurs in any type of political system.

    (D) occurs less frequently in recent years.

    (E) occurs when members reject the goals of the system.

36. As used in the passage, which of the following is the most complete and accurate definition of the term "conversion"?

    (A) Transformation   (D) Resolution

    (B) Changeover   (E) Passing

    (C) Growth

37. The major distinction between the concepts of Easton and Dennis as opposed to the concepts of Lipset is

    (A) that the concepts of Easton and Dennis are based on the wants of a society, whereas Lipset's concepts are based on change of governing officials.

    (B) that Easton and Dennis' concepts are based on arbitrary decisions, whereas Lipset's concepts are based on influencing major decisions.

    (C) that Easton and Dennis' concepts must have a set of general rules, whereas Lipset's concepts provide for irregular constitutional opportunities.

    (D) that Easton and Dennis' concepts have no inputs, conversion, and outputs, whereas Lipset's concepts allow for no regular constitutional opportunities.

    (E) that Easton and Dennis' concepts evolve around the settling of differences, whereas Lipset's concepts permit the largest conflict possible.

Questions 38 to 40 refer to the following passage:

Assignment: Research for a White Paper Proposing U.S. Foreign Policy

Imagine you are in charge (or assigned to) a foreign policy desk in the U.S. Department of State. Select one of the following regions (descriptors are merely suggestions):

Western Europe—A Changing Alliance

Eastern Europe—Out from Behind the Iron Curtain

The U.S.S.R.—Still an Enigma

The Middle East—History and Emotions

Africa—Rising Expectations in the Postwar Continent

South and Southeast Asia—Unrest in Far Away Places

The Far East—Alienation and Alliance

The Western Hemisphere—Neighbors; Pro and Con

Through research, prepare a White Paper for that area which will indicate:

1. a General Policy Statement toward the nations of that region;

2. a statement as to how World War II set the stage for that policy;

3. a summary of the major events since 1945 in that region which have affected U.S. foreign policy;

4. a list of suggested problems and/or possibilities for near-future interactions of that region and the U.S.

38. In order to complete this assignment, research into which of the following disciplines (areas of study) would be most appropriate?

   (A) History, Economics, Political Science, and Language

   (B) History, Political Science, Education, Economics

   (C) Political Science, Economics, Geography, and Religion

   (D) Geography, Education, History, and Political Science

   (E) History, Political Science, Economics, and Culture

39. Which of the following is the most complete and accurate definition of the term "Enigma" as used in the passage?

   (A) Problem   (D) Secret

   (B) Riddle   (E) Mystery

   (C) Puzzle

40. Which of the following is the most appropriate secondary school audience for the assignment?

   (A) Students in a World Geography class

   (B) Students in a World History class

   (C) Students in a Content Area Reading class

   (D) Students in an Economics class

   (E) Students in an American Government class

Section II: Mathematics

(Answer sheets appear in the back of this book.)

TIME: 60 Minutes
40 Questions

DIRECTIONS: Each of the questions or incomplete statements below is followed by five suggested answers or completions. Select the one that is best in each case.

---

1. If 406.725 is rounded off to the nearest tenth, the number is

   (A) 406.3.
   (D) 406.8.

   (B) 406.5.
   (E) 407.0.

   (C) 406.7.

2. The mean IQ score for 1,500 students is 100, with a standard deviation of 15. Assuming normal curve distribution, how many students have an IQ between 85 and 115? Refer to the figure shown below.

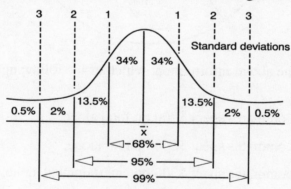

   (A) 510
   (D) 1,275

   (B) 750
   (E) 1,425

   (C) 1,020

3. The sum of 12 and twice a number is 24. Find the number.

   (A) 6
   (B) 8

(C) 10   (D) 11

(E) 12

4.   Twice the sum of 10 and a number is 28. Find the number.

(A) 4   (D) 14

(B) 8   (E) 24

(C) 12

5.   Two college roommates spent $2,000 for their total monthly expenses. A pie graph below indicates a record of their expenses.

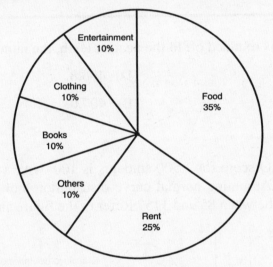

Based on the above information, which of the following statements is accurate?

(A) The roommates spent $700 on food alone.

(B) The roommates spent $550 on rent alone.

(C) The roommates spent $300 on entertainment alone.

(D) The roommates spent $300 on clothing alone.

(E) The roommates spent $300 on books alone.

6.   You can buy a telephone for $24. If you are charged $3 per month for renting a telephone from the telephone company, how long will it take you to recover the cost of the phone if you buy one?

(A) 6 months   (B) 7 months

(C) 8 months   (D) 9 months

(E) 10 months

7. What would be the measure of the third angle in the following triangle?

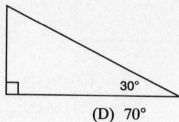

(A) 45°   (D) 70°

(B) 50°   (E) 240°

(C) 60°

8. What is the perimeter of this figure?

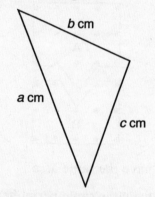

(A) abc cm   (D) $(a + b + c)$ cm^2

(B) abc cm^2 (E) abc cm^3

(C) $(a + b + c)$ cm

9. What is the perimeter of the given triangle?

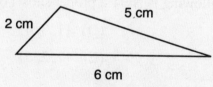

(A) 6 cm   (D) 13 cm

(B) 11 cm   (E) 15 cm

(C) 12 cm

10. Assuming that the quadrilateral in the following figure is a parallelogram, what would be its area?

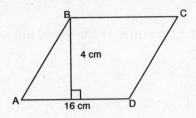

(A) 32 cm

(B) 40 cm

(C) 40 cm²

(D) 64 cm

(E) 64 cm²

11. Refer to the figure below to determine which of the following statements is correct.

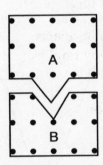

I.   Figures A and B have the same area.

II. Figures A and B have the same perimeter.

(A) Only I

(B) Only II

(C) Both I and II

(D) Neither I nor II

(E) Can't be determined.

12. Which of the following is NOT a proper subset of {1, 2, 3, 4}?

(A) {1, 2}

(B) {1, 2, 3}

(C) {1, 2, 4}

(D) {1, 3, 4}

(E) {1, 2, 5}

13. Which of the following is an example of a rational number?

   (A) $\sqrt{17}$

   (B) $6\sqrt[3]{7}$

   (C) $4\sqrt{11}$

   (D) $7 + \sqrt{9}$

   (E) $2 - \sqrt{15}$

14. Which of the following statements includes a cardinal number?

   (A) There are 15 volumes in the set of periodicals.

   (B) I received my 14th volume recently.

   (C) The students meet at Room 304.

   (D) My phone number is 213-617-8442.

   (E) James lives on 3448 Lucky Avenue.

15. In a group of 30 students, 12 are studying mathematics, 18 are studying English, 8 are studying science, 7 are studying both mathematics and English, 6 are studying English and science, 5 are studying mathematics and science, and 4 are studying all three subjects. How many of these students are taking only English? How many of these students are not taking any of these subjects?

   (A) 9 students take only English; 6 students take none of these subjects.

   (B) 10 students take only English; 5 students take none of these subjects.

   (C) 11 students take only English; 5 students take none of these subjects.

   (D) 12 students take only English; 6 students take none of these subjects.

   (E) 13 students take only English; 4 students take none of these subjects.

16. For the given Venn diagram, find n(A ∩ B ∩ C):

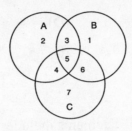

(A) 3

(D) 6

(B) 4

(E) 7

(C) 5

17. Find the next three terms in this sequence: 1, 4, 9, 16, ...

(A) 19, 24, 31

(D) 25, 36, 49

(B) 20, 25, 31

(E) 25, 34, 43

(C) 21, 28, 36

18. Assume that one pig eats 4 pounds of food each week. There are 52 weeks in a year. How much food do 10 pigs eat in a week?

(A) 40 lb.

(D) 20 lb.

(B) 520 lb.

(E) 60 lb.

(C) 208 lb.

19. Suppose that a pair of pants and a shirt cost $65 and the pants cost $25 more than the shirt. What did they each cost?

(A) The pants cost $35 and the shirt costs $30.

(B) The pants cost $40 and the shirt costs $25.

(C) The pants cost $43 and the shirt costs $22.

(D) The pants cost $45 and the shirt costs $20.

(E) The pants cost $50 and the shirt costs $15.

20. There are five members in a basketball team. Supposing each member shakes hands with every other member of the team before the game starts, how many handshakes will there be in all?

(A) 6   (D) 10

(B) 8   (E) 12

(C) 9

21. Which figure can be obtained from figure Y by translation?

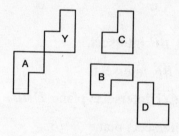

(A) A   (D) D

(B) B   (E) None of the above

(C) C

22. Which of the polygons below is a triangular pyramid?

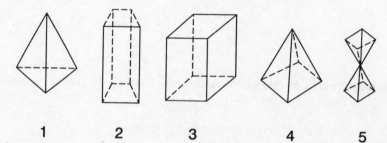

(A) 1   (D) 4

(B) 2   (E) 5

(C) 3

23. The figure below represents a portion of a square pyramid viewed from above. Which of the following statements is true?

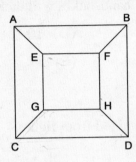

(A) Edges $\overline{AE}$ and $\overline{BF}$ intersect.

(B) Lines $\overline{AE}$ and $\overline{BF}$ intersect.

(C) Line segment $\overline{CG}$ intersects plane $\overline{DHB}$.

(D) Face $\overline{CGEA}$ intersects plane $\overline{DHB}$.

(E) Line $\overline{CG}$ intersects line $\overline{AB}$.

24. Below is a rectangular pyramid ABCDE.

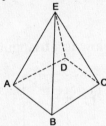

How many vertices does it have?

(A) 3   (D) 6

(B) 4   (E) 7

(C) 5

25. Tom bought a piece of land selling for $20,000. If he had to pay 20 percent of the price as a down payment, how much was the down payment?

(A) $2,500   (D) $4,500

(B) $3,000   (E) $5,000

(C) $4,000

26. A Macintosh LC computer sells for $3,200 to the general public. If you purchase one in the university, the price is reduced by 20 percent. What is the sale price of the computer?

    (A) $640

    (B) $2,000

    (C) $2,410

    (D) $2,560

    (E) $3,180

27. In order for Sue to receive a final grade of C, she must have an average greater than or equal to 70% but less than 80% on five tests. Suppose her grades on the first four tests were 65%, 85%, 60%, and 90%. What range of grades on the fifth test would give her a C in the course?

    (A) 40 up to but excluding 95

    (B) 45 up to but excluding 95

    (C) 47 up to but excluding 90

    (D) 49 up to but excluding 98

    (E) 50 up to but excluding 100

28. A certain company produces two types of lawnmowers. Type A is self-propelled while type B is not. The company can produce a maximum of 18 mowers per week. It can make a profit of $15 on mower A and a profit of $20 on mower B. The company wants to make at least 2 mowers of type A but not more than 5. They also plan to make at least 2 mowers of type B. Let x be the number of type A produced, and let y be the number of type B produced.

    From the above, which of the following is NOT one of the listed constraints?

    (A) $x \geq 2$

    (B) $x \leq 5$

    (C) $x + y \leq 18$

    (D) $y < 5$

    (E) $y \geq 2$

29. Mr. Smith died and left an estate to be divided among his wife, two children, and a foundation of his choosing in the ratio of 8:6:6:1. How much did his wife receive if the estate was valued at $300,000?

    (A) $114,285.71

    (B) $120,421.91

(C) $85,714.29   (D) $14,285.71

(E) $125,461.71

30. There were 19 hamburgers for nine people on a picnic. How many whole hamburgers were there for each person if they were divided equally?

(A) 1   (D) 4

(B) 2   (E) 5

(C) 3

31. George has four ways to get from his house to the park. He has seven ways to get from the park to the school. How many ways can George get from his house to school by way of the park?

(A) 4   (D) 3

(B) 7   (E) 11

(C) 28

32. If it takes one minute per cut, how long will it take to cut a 15-foot long timber into 15 equal pieces?

(A) 5   (D) 20

(B) 10   (E) 15

(C) 14

33. Ed has six new shirts and four new pairs of pants. How many combinations of new shirts and pants does he have?

(A) 10   (D) 20

(B) 14   (E) 24

(C) 18

34. The property tax rate of the town of Grandview is $32 per $1,000 of assessed value. What is the tax if the property is assessed at $50,000?

(A) $32   (D) $1,600

(B) $1,000   (E) $2,000

(C) $1,562

35. Ralph kept track of his work time in gardening. Refer to the broken-line graph below:

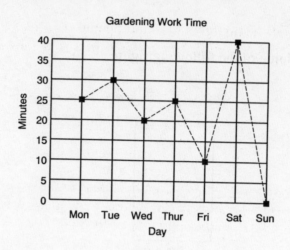

Gardening Work Time

How many minutes did he average per day?

(A) 10 min.

(B) 20 min.

(C) 21.43 min.

(D) 23.05 min.

(E) 25 min.

36. Mary had been selling printed shirts in her neighborhood. She made this pictograph to show how much money she made each week.

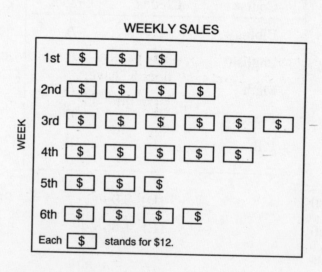

WEEKLY SALES

Each $ stands for $12.

How many weeks were sales more than $55?

(A) 1 week

(B) 2 weeks

(C) 3 weeks

(D) 4 weeks

(E) 5 weeks

37. Find the volume of the following figure.

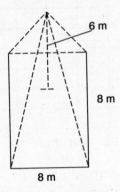

(A) 48 m²

(B) 64 m²

(C) 128 m³

(D) 192 m³

(E) 384 m³

38. The result of Mary's spring semester grades follow. Find her grade point average for the term (A = 4, B = 3, C = 2, D = 1, F = 0).

Course	Credits	Grades
Biology	5	A
English	3	C
Math	3	A
French	3	D
P.E.	2	B

(A) 3.80

(B) 3.50

(C) 2.94

(D) 2.00

(E) 1.86

39. In a biology class at International University, the grades on the final examination were as follows:

91	81	65	81
50	70	81	93
36	90	43	87
96	81	75	81

Find the mode.

(A) 36

(B) 70

(C) 81

(D) 87

(E) 96

40. One commonly used standard score is a z-score. A z-score gives the number of standard deviations by which the score differs from the mean, as shown in the following example.

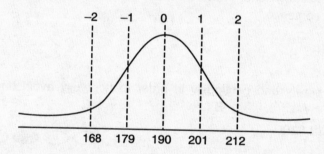

The mean (x) is 190 and the standard deviation(s) is 11. The score of 201 has a z-score of 1 and the score of 168 has a z-score of –2. Consider the mean height of a certain group of people as 190 cm with a standard deviation of 11 cm. Suppose Glenn's height has a z-score of 1.6, what is his height? (Note $z = x - x.$)

(A) 207.60 cm

(B) 190 cm

(C) 201 cm

(D) 179 cm

(E) 212 cm

Section III: Writing

(Answer sheets appear in the back of this book.)

TIME: 30 Minutes
45 Questions

Part A: Usage

> **DIRECTIONS**: Each of the following sentences may contain an error in diction, usage, idiom, or grammar. Some sentences are correct. Some sentences contain one error. No sentence contains more than one error.
>
> If there is an error, it will appear in one of the underlined portions labeled A, B, C, or D. If there is no error, choose the portion labeled E. If there is an error, select the letter of the portion that must be changed in order to correct the sentence.
>
> **EXAMPLE:**
>
> He drove <u>slowly</u> and <u>cautiously</u> in order to <u>hopefully</u> avoid having an
>   **A**   **B**   **C**
>
> <u>accident</u>. <u>No error.</u>   Ⓐ Ⓑ ⬤ Ⓓ Ⓔ
>   **D**   **E**

1. *Huckleberry Finn*, by <u>general consensus agreement</u> Mark Twain's
                            A

   <u>greatest</u> work, is <u>supremely</u> the American <u>Classic</u>; it is also one of the
    B   **C**   **D**

   great books of the world. <u>No error</u>.
                      E

2. The U.S. <u>Constitution</u> <u>supposes</u> what the history of all governments
              A   **B**

   <u>demonstrate</u>, that the executive is the branch <u>most</u> interested in war
     C   **D**

   and most prone to it. <u>No error</u>.
                   E

3. Mama, the <u>narrator</u> of Alice Walker's short story "Everyday Use,"
           A

<u>speaks</u> fondly of her daughter upon her return home after a long
  B

absence <u>like</u> Mama is <u>proud</u> of her. <u>No error</u>.
      C   D   E

4. <u>Nearly</u> one <u>hundred</u> years after the impoverished Vincent Van Gogh
  A   B

died, his paintings <u>had sold</u> for more than a <u>million dollars</u>. <u>No error</u>.
           C   D   E

5. Many athletes <u>recruited</u> for football by college coaches <u>expect</u> that
          A   B

they will, <u>in fact</u>, receive an education when they <u>accept</u> a scholar-
        C   D

ship. <u>No error</u>.
     E

6. <u>Hopefully</u>, by the end of the <u>Twentieth Century</u>, computer scientists
  A   B

will invent machines with <u>enough</u> intelligence to work without break-
                    C

ing down <u>continually</u>. <u>No error</u>.
       D   E

7. Studies <u>showing</u> that the earth includes a <u>vast series</u> of sedimentary
       A   B

rocks, some with <u>embedded</u> fossils <u>that</u> prove the existence of ancient
            C   D

organisms. <u>No error</u>.
      E

8. When Martin Luther King, <u>Jr.</u>, wrote his famous letter from the Bir-
                A

mingham jail, he advocated neither evading <u>or</u> defying the law; <u>but</u>
                       B   C

he accepted the idea that a penalty <u>results from</u> breaking a law, even
                      D

an unjust one. <u>No error</u>.
      E

9. The Eighteenth Century philosopher Adam Smith asserted that a na-
        A   B

    tion achieves the best economic results when individuals work both
         C

    for their own interests and to gain more goods. No error.
                             D   E

10. According to Niccolo Machiavelli, wise rulers cannot and should not
                                           A   B

    keep their word when such integrity would be to their disadvantage
                                                     C

    and when the reasons for the promise no longer exist. No error.
                                                 D   E

11. The Milky Way galaxy, which comprises millions of stars, has both
                                        A

    thin and congested spots, but shines their brightest in the constella-
          B   C   D

    tion Sagittarius. No error.
                         E

12. To learn an ancient language like Latin or Greek is one way to dis-
        A   B

    cover the roots of Western Culture; studying Judaeo-Christian reli-

    gious beliefs is another. No error.
          C D   E

13. Many political conservatives contribute the problems of modern
                                        A

    American society to the twin evils of the New Deal and secular
                                                        B

    humanism, both of which are presumed to stem from Marxism.
                        C   D

    No error.
     E

14. Having minimal exposure to poetry when they attended school, most
              A   B

    Americans chose to watch television or to read popular magazines for
              C   D

entertainment. <u>No error</u>.
　　　　　　　　　　E

15. What makes <u>we</u> humans <u>different from</u> other animals <u>can be defined</u>
　　　　　　　A　　　　　　　B　　　　　　　　　　　　C
at least <u>partly</u> by our powerful and efficient intelligence. <u>No error</u>.
　　　　　D　　　　　　　　　　　　　　　　　　　　　　　E

16. When one contrasts the ideas of the Romantic William Wordsworth

<u>with</u> <u>those</u> of Neoclassicist John Dryden, <u>one finds</u> that neither of the
　A　　B　　　　　　　　　　　　　　　　　　　C
poets <u>differ</u> as much as one would expect. <u>No error</u>.
　　　　D　　　　　　　　　　　　　　　　　E

17. Carl Jung's hypothesis of the collective unconscious <u>suggests</u> that we
　　　　　　　　　　　　　　　　　　　　　　　　　　　　A
inherit <u>cultural-experimental</u> memory in the form of mythological
　　　　　　B
archetype, <u>which arise</u> from repeated <u>patterns</u> of human behavior.
　　　　　　　C　　　　　　　　　　　　　D
<u>No error</u>.
　E

18. Bertrand Russell believed that a free <u>person's</u> liberation is <u>effected</u> by
　　　　　　　　　　　　　　　　　　A　　　　　　　　B
a contemplation of <u>Fate</u>; one achieves emancipation through passion-
　　　　　　　　　　C
ate pursuit of eternal things, <u>not through</u> the pursuit of private happi-
　　　　　　　　　　　　　　　　D
ness. <u>No error</u>.
　　　　E

19. <u>Latin American</u> literature <u>includes</u> the works of Gabriel Garcia
　　　A　　　　　　　　　　　　B
Marquez, Pablo Neruda, and Jorge Luis Borges; each of these

<u>acclaimed</u> artists has won <u>their</u> share of prizes. <u>No error</u>.
　　C　　　　　　　　　　　　D　　　　　　　　　E

20. The reason <u>a large percentage</u> of American college students <u>located</u>
                   A   **B**

    Moscow in California is <u>because</u> they <u>were not required</u> to learn the
                         C   **D**

    facts of geography. <u>No error</u>.
                        E

21. Astronomers and physicists <u>tell</u> us that the universe is <u>constant</u> ex-
                            A   **B**

    panding <u>and that</u> it <u>comprises</u> numerous galaxies like ours. <u>No error</u>.
            C   **D**   **E**

22. <u>Less</u> students chose liberal arts and <u>sciences</u> majors in the 1980s
    A   **B**

    than in the 1960s <u>because of</u> the contemporary view that a college
                         C

    education <u>is</u> a ticket to enter the job market. <u>No error</u>.
            D   **E**

23. Span of control is the term <u>that</u> refers to the <u>limits</u> of a leader's <u>ability</u>
                            A   **B**   **C**

    <u>for managing</u> those employees <u>under</u> his/her supervision. <u>No error</u>.
    D   **D**   **E**

24. <u>Because some</u> people believe <u>strongly</u> that channelling, the <u>process</u>
          A   **B**   **C**

    <u>by which</u> an individual goes into a trance-like state and communi-

    cates the thoughts of an ancient warrior or guru to an audience, helps

    them cope with modern problems, but others condemn the whole

    ideas <u>as</u> mere superstition. <u>No error</u>.
          D   **E**

25. The reed on a woodwind instrument is <u>essential</u> <u>being that</u> it <u>controls</u>
                                           A   **B**   **C**

    <u>the quality</u> of <u>tone and sound</u>. <u>No error</u>.
            D   **E**

Part B: Sentence Correction

DIRECTIONS: In each of the following sentences, some portion of the sentence is underlined. Under each sentence are five choices. The first choice has the same wording as the original. The other four choices are reworded. Sometimes the first choice containing the original wording is the best; sometimes one of the other choices is the best. Choose the letter of the best choice. Your choice should produce a sentence which is not ambiguous or awkward and which is correct, clear, and precise.

This is a test of correct and effective English expression. Keep in mind the standards of English usage, punctuation, grammar, word choice, and construction.

EXAMPLE:

When you listen to opera, <u>a person may not appreciate it.</u>

(A)   a person may not appreciate it.

(B)   it may not be appreciated by a person.

(C)   which may not be appreciated by one.

(D)   you may not appreciate it.

(E)   appreciating it may be a problem for you.

26.   Two-thirds of American 17-year-olds do not know that the Civil War <u>takes place</u> between 1850–1900.

(A) takes place   (D) have taken place

(B) took place   (E) is taking place

(C) had taken place

27.   Both professional and amateur ornithologists, <u>people that study birds,</u> recognize the Latin or scientific names of bird species.

(A) people that study birds

(B) people which study birds

(C) the study of birds

(D) people who study birds

(E) in which people study birds

28. Many of the oil-producing states spent their huge surplus tax revenues during the oil boom of the 1970s and early 1980s <u>in spite of the fact that</u> oil production from new wells began to flood the world market as early as 1985.

    (A) in spite of the fact that

    (B) even in view of the fact that

    (C) however clearly it was known that

    (D) even though

    (E) when it was clear that

29. The president of the community college reported <u>as to the expectability of the tuition increase as well as the actual amount</u>.

    (A) as to the expectability of the tuition increase as well as the actual amount

    (B) that the tuition will likely increase by a specific amount

    (C) as to the expectability that tuition will increase by a specific amount

    (D) about the expected tuition increase of five percent

    (E) regarding the expectation of a tuition increase expected to be five percent

30. Although Carmen developed an interest in classical music, <u>she did not read notes and had never played an instrument</u>.

    (A) she did not read notes and had never played an instrument

    (B) she does not read notes and has never played an instrument

    (C) it is without being able to read notes or having played an instrument

    (D) she did not read notes nor had she ever played them

    (E) it is without reading notes nor having played an instrument

31. Political candidates must campaign on issues and ideas that strike a chord within their constituency but <u>with their goal to sway</u> undecided voters to support their candidacy.

    (A) with their goal to sway

(B) need also to sway

(C) aiming at the same time to sway

(D) also trying to sway

(E) its goal should also be in swaying

32. The major reason students give for failing courses in college <u>is that</u> <u>they have demanding professors and work at</u> full- or part-time jobs.

(A) is that they have demanding professors and work at

(B) are demanding professors and they work at

(C) is having demanding professors and having

(D) are demanding professors, in addition to working at

(E) are that they have demanding professors and that they have

33. <u>Having command of color, symbolism, as well as technique</u>, Georgia O'Keeffe is considered to be a great American painter.

(A) Having command of color, symbolism, as well as technique

(B) Having command of color, symbolism, and her technical ability

(C) Because of her command of color, symbolism, and technique

(D) With her command of color and symbolism and being technical

(E) By being in command of both color and symbolism and also technique

34. <u>Whether the ancient ancestors of American Indians actually migrated</u> <u>or did not</u> across a land bridge now covered by the Bering Strait remains uncertain, but that they could have has not been refuted by other theories.

(A) Whether the ancient ancestors of American Indians actually migrated or did not

(B) That the ancient ancestors of American Indians actually did migrate

(C) The actuality of whether the ancient ancestors of American Indians migrated

(D) Whether in actuality the ancient ancestors of American Indians migrated or not

(E) That the ancient ancestors of American Indians may actually have migrated

35. Caution in scientific experimentation can <u>sometimes be related more to integrity than to lack of knowledge</u>.

(A) sometimes be related more to integrity than to lack of knowledge

(B) sometimes be related more to integrity as well as lack of knowledge

(C) often be related to integrity as to lack of knowledge

(D) be related more to integrity rather than lack of knowledge

(E) be related often to integrity, not only to lack of knowledge

36. Separated by their successful rebellion against England from any existing form of government, the citizens of the United States <u>have developed a unique constitutional political system</u>.

(A) have developed a unique constitutional political system

(B) had developed a very unique constitutional political system

(C) had developed their constitutional political system uniquely

(D) have developed their political system into a very unique constitutional one

(E) have a unique political system, based on a constitution

37. <u>Returning to the ancestral home after 12 years, the house itself seemed much smaller to Joe</u> than it had been when he visited it as a child.

(A) Returning to the ancestral home after 12 years, the house itself seemed much smaller to Joe

(B) When Joe returned to the ancestral home after 12 years, he thought the house itself much smaller

(C) Joe returned to the ancestral home after 12 years, and then he thought the house itself much smaller

(D) After Joe returned to the ancestral home in 12 years, the house itself seemed much smaller

(E) Having returned to the ancestral home after 12 years, it seemed a much smaller house to Joe

38. Historians say that the New River of North Carolina, Virginia, and West Virginia, which is 2,700 feet above sea level and 2,000 feet above the surrounding foothills, is the oldest river in the United States.

(A) which is 2,700 feet above sea level and 2,000 feet above

(B) with a height of 2,700 feet above sea level as well as 2,000 feet above that of

(C) 2,700 feet higher than sea level and ascending 2,000 feet above

(D) being 2,700 feet above sea level and 2,000 feet high measure from that of

(E) located 2,700 feet high above sea level while measuring 2,000 feet above

39. The age of 36 having been reached, the Ukrainian-born Polish sailor Teodor Josef Konrad Korzeniowski changed his name to Joseph Conrad and began a new and successful career as a British novelist and short story writer.

(A) The age of 36 having been reached

(B) When having reached the age of 36

(C) When he reached the age of 36

(D) The age of 36 being reached

(E) At 36, when he reached that age

40. During the strike, Black South African miners threw a cordon around the gold mine, and they thereby blocked it to all white workers.

(A) gold mine, and they thereby blocked it to all white workers

(B) gold mine, by which all white workers were therefore blocked

(C) gold mine, and therefore this had all white workers blocked

(D) gold mine and therefore blocking it to all white workers

(E) gold mine, thereby blocking it to all white workers

41. Because of the long half-life of low-level nuclear <u>wastes, this means that waste depositories could emit dangerous doses of radiation thousands of years into the future</u>.

    (A) wastes, this means that waste depositories could emit dangerous doses of radiation thousands of years into the future

    (B) wastes is the reason why waste depositories could emit dangerous doses of radiation thousands of years into the future

    (C) wastes, this is the reason why waste depositories could emit dangerous doses of radiation thousands of years into the future

    (D) wastes, depositories for these wastes could still emit dangerous doses of radiation thousands of years into the future

    (E) wastes, the future means that waste depositories could emit dangerous doses of radiation for thousands of years

42. <u>The more you listen to and understand classical music</u>, the more our ears will prefer music for the mind to music for the body.

    (A) The more you listen to and understand classical music

    (B) The more we listen to and understand classical music

    (C) The more classical music is listened to and understood

    (D) As understanding and listening to classical music increases

    (E) As people listen to and understand classical music

43. As modern archaeologists discover new fossils, biologists are amending Darwin's theory of evolution <u>that once served as the standard</u>.

    (A) that once served as the standard

    (B) by which all others were measured

    (C) having served as the standard for over a hundred years

    (D) thereby changing the standard

    (E) and creating a new standard

44. <u>The fewer mistakes one makes in life</u>, the fewer opportunities you have to learn from your mistakes.

    (A) The fewer mistakes one makes in life

    (B) The fewer mistakes you make in life

(C) The fewer mistakes he or she makes in life

(D) The fewer mistakes there are in one's life

(E) The fewer mistakes in life

45. Although the word *millipede* means one thousand feet, millipedes have no more than 115 pairs of legs <u>that are attached to the segments of their bodies.</u>

(A) that are attached to the segments of their bodies.

(B) each of which are attached to a segment of their bodies.

(C) attaching themselves to segments of their bodies.

(D) whose attachment is to the segments of their bodies.

(E) the attachment of which is to the segments of their bodies.

Part C: Essay

TIME: 30 Minutes

DIRECTIONS: You have 30 minutes to plan and write an essay on the topic below. You may write only on the assigned topic.

Make sure to give specific examples to support your thesis. Proofread your essay carefully and take care to express your ideas clearly and effectively.

ESSAY TOPIC:

Many leaders have suggested over the last few years that instead of a military draft we should require all young people to serve the public in some way for a period of time. The service could be military or any other reasonable form of public service.

ASSIGNMENT: Do you agree or disagree with the statement? Support your opinion with specific examples from history, current events, literature, or personal experience.

PPST TEST II

ANSWER KEY

Section I — Reading Comprehension

1.	(A)	11.	(E)	21.	(E)	31.	(C)
2.	(A)	12.	(D)	22.	(D)	32.	(A)
3.	(D)	13.	(E)	23.	(B)	33.	(B)
4.	(B)	14.	(C)	24.	(B)	34.	(A)
5.	(A)	15.	(B)	25.	(D)	35.	(C)
6.	(D)	16.	(C)	26.	(E)	36.	(A)
7.	(C)	17.	(A)	27.	(B)	37.	(A)
8.	(A)	18.	(C)	28.	(A)	38.	(E)
9.	(E)	19.	(B)	29.	(E)	39.	(C)
10.	(A)	20.	(C)	30.	(E)	40.	(E)

Section II — Mathematics

1.	(C)	11.	(B)	21.	(C)	31.	(C)
2.	(C)	12.	(E)	22.	(A)	32.	(C)
3.	(A)	13.	(D)	23.	(B)	33.	(E)
4.	(A)	14.	(A)	24.	(C)	34.	(D)
5.	(A)	15.	(A)	25.	(C)	35.	(C)
6.	(C)	16.	(C)	26.	(D)	36.	(B)
7.	(C)	17.	(D)	27.	(E)	37.	(C)
8.	(C)	18.	(A)	28.	(D)	38.	(C)
9.	(D)	19.	(D)	29.	(A)	39.	(C)
10.	(E)	20.	(D)	30.	(B)	40.	(A)

Section III — Writing

1.	(A)	13.	(A)	25.	(B)	37.	(B)
2.	(C)	14.	(C)	26.	(B)	38.	(A)
3.	(C)	15.	(A)	27.	(D)	39.	(C)
4.	(C)	16.	(D)	28.	(D)	40.	(E)
5.	(B)	17.	(E)	29.	(B)	41.	(D)
6.	(A)	18.	(E)	30.	(A)	42.	(B)
7.	(A)	19.	(D)	31.	(B)	43.	(A)
8.	(B)	20.	(C)	32.	(E)	44.	(B)
9.	(D)	21.	(B)	33.	(C)	45.	(A)
10.	(E)	22.	(A)	34.	(B)		
11.	(C)	23.	(C)	35.	(A)		
12.	(A)	24.	(A)	36.	(A)		

DETAILED EXPLANATIONS OF ANSWERS

Section I: Reading Comprehension

1. **(A)** Choices (B), (D), and (E) present minor problems in spa maintenance, whereas choice (C) cannot be prevented. As bacteria and virus are controlled by both temperature and chemicals, it becomes a possible source of health problems if ignored.

2. **(A)** Choices (B), (C), and (D) are correct levels or degrees. Although choice (E) is important, it is not as dangerous as choice (A) where temperatures in excess of 104° can cause dizziness, nausea, fainting, drowsiness, and reduced awareness.

3. **(D)** Choices (A), (B), and (C) represent an inference that goes beyond the scope of the passage and would indicate biases of the reader. Although the passage explains spa maintenance, choice (E), the information is not adequate to serve as a detailed guide.

4. **(B)** The other choices (A), (C), and (D) refer to chemical or temperature maintenance. Although choice (E) helps to ensure clarity, choice (B) is explicitly stated in the passage.

5. **(A)** Choices (B), (C), and (D) are appropriate chemicals. Although chlorine is an alternative to bromine, this passage indicates it should be granular as indicated in choice (A); liquid and tablet chlorines are too harsh for spas, thus all forms are not acceptable as indicated by choice (E).

6. **(D)** Choices (A) and (B) appear to be acceptable, whereas choice (E) indicates a perfect correlation. Although choice (C) is a definition of statistical significance, choice (D) is correct as the passage is about correlational statistical significance which permits prediction.

7. **(C)** Choice (A) goes beyond the information provided in the passage. Choice (B) is incorrect as correlation cannot indicate causality, and choice (E) states incorrectly there was no variance. Choice (D) is not

statistically possible. The high positive correlation trend indicates that these variables are important to consider for future research, thus choice (C).

8. **(A)** Choices (B), (C), (D), and (E) represent inferences that are based on inadequate information which go beyond the scope of the passage. As these story elements are not taught explicitly in the first grade or prior to entering school, children apparently have picked up these elements from their exposures to stories as indicated by choice (A).

9. **(E)** Although the content might be appropriate for each of the journals, choices (A), (B), (C), and (D), the style of writing suggests that it would be most appropriate for choice (E), *Reading Research Quarterly,* as this passage reports research results.

10. **(A)** The passage provides information for the grade level and mentions if it was significant or substantial. As this statement follows information provided for fifth/sixth grades, it refers to that level, thus choice (A).

11. **(E)** Choices (A), (B), (C), and (D) all connote extreme or inappropriate attitudes not expressed in the passage. The author presents an informed concern—choice (E).

12. **(D)** For the other choices, (A), (B), (C), and (E), the criteria, the role, the discussion, and the assurance for communication or learning are not provided in the passage. The passage stresses the importance of authenticity in communication—choice (D)

13. **(E)** Each of the choices is a possible definition, but the passage overall suggests that communication needs to be developed so that students' responses may become more significant and authentic—choice (E).

14. **(C)** Choices (A), (B), and (E) are not supported by the passage. Choice (D) represents an incorrect conclusion. Choice (C) is supported by the various investigators' explanations.

15. **(B)** As stated explicitly in the passage, the various investigators have attempted to explain the role of imitation in language—choice (B). The other choices go beyond the scope of the passage.

16. **(C)** As the investigators studied different aspects of language while

attempting to explain the role of imitation in language, choice (C) is correct. The other choices go beyond the scope of the passage.

17. **(A)** The passage explicitly states that computers are capable of addressing the issues of practice and the true act of reading, choice (A). The other choices represent inferences that are not supported by the passage.

18. **(C)** Although the reader might make inferences to select choices (A), (B), (D), and (E), ways to use a word processor to make practice resemble the true reading act are not stated in the passage, thus choice (C).

19. **(B)** Although audiences in choices (A), (C), (D), and (E) may benefit from the information provided in the passage, the passage explicitly states that a greater understanding of the information in the passage should assist teachers—choice (B).

20. **(C)** Each of the choices is a definition of variance. However, for this passage, choice (C) is the most appropriate.

21. **(E)** Although meaning is found in the components of each choice, the passage states that we should begin with students' meaning before moving to the commonalities of story meaning—choice (E).

22. **(D)** As the passage presents information by various researchers on children's stories, the passage ends with an unanswered question that still needs to be addressed by reading researchers as provided in choice (D).

23. **(B)** Although more information may be needed about story content and story structure as indicated in choices (A), (C), (D), and (E), the main question that remains to be answered is choice (B).

24. **(B)** Each choice provides partially correct information about story content and story structure; choice (B) provides the most complete response.

25. **(D)** Each choice is a possible definition. However, choice (D) is most appropriate as there was an increased interest by researchers in these and other areas even though it has been an ongoing concern of some researchers.

26. **(E)** Choices (A) and (C) are not supported by the passage. Choices

(B) and (D) go beyond the passage. The last sentence states "The pattern . . . resulting in teachers prone to teach as they had been taught"— thus choice (E).

27. **(B)** The other choices (A), (C), (D), and (E) are not supported by the passage. Although the passage mentions that teacher education has reflected evolving attitudes about education, the attitudes are not spelled out—choice (B).

28. **(A)** Only choice (A) has the correct sequence; the other sequences are incorrect.

29. **(E)** Choices (A), (B), (C), and (D) are statements about education, teacher education, and teachers. Choice (E)'s statement that teacher education has changed very little implies that this lack of change could be a source of dissatisfaction.

30. **(E)** Choices (A), (B), and (D) suggest rights either by heredity or supreme authority, whereas choice (C) indicates rights just by possession. The hyphenated term "liege-lord" connotes both entitled rights and power to command respect. Thus choice (E), "master" (one who assumes authority and property rights through ability and power to control), best represents the hawk.

31. **(C)** Choices (A), (D), and (E) are not supported by the passage. Choice (B) represents a possible conclusion, but choice (C) suggests real thought about the hawk.

32. **(A)** Each of the other choices contains a term which does not refer to human qualities. The other qualities may refer to the hawk, e.g., perch or to the author of the passage, e.g., disdain.

33. **(B)** Choices (D) and (E) are incorrect because of definitions. Choices (A) and (C) are possible definitions, but feudal most clearly denotes an association to the Middle Ages.

34. **(A)** The passage explicitly states that political efficacy is a feeling that one's actions can have an impact on government—choice (A). Choices (C), (D), and (E) are not supported by the passage. Choice (B) is incorrect.

35. **(C)** Choices (A), (B), (D), and (E) are not supported by the pas-

sage. The passage states "...political socialization, a process varying according to political systems but toward the end of indoctrinating the members to the respective political system"— choice (C).

36. **(A)** Although the other choices (B), (C), (D), and (E) are possible definitions, the passage explicitly states that "a political system is one of inputs, conversions, and outputs by which the wants of a society are transformed into binding decisions"—thus choice (A).

37. **(A)** Choices (B), (C), (D), and (E) contain an incorrect concept of either Easton and Dennis or Lipset. Only choice (A) has the correct concepts for both Easton and Dennis and Lipset.

38. **(E)** Choices (A), (B), (C), and (D) each contain an area which is considered a component of culture, such as religion, education, and language. Thus, choice (E) is the most appropriate response.

39. **(C)** Although each definition appears appropriate, choices (B), (D), and (E) assume that a solution is known, or has been known at one time, and could be solved. Although choice (A) suggests difficulty in solving, choice (C) suggests a situation that is intricate enough to perplex the mind. Choice (C) is most appropriate for this passage as a definition of enigma is an inexplicable situation.

40. **(E)** Although choices (A), (B), (C), and (D) may touch on such a topic, the roles and functions of governmental offices and departments are generally addressed in an American Government class, thus choice (E).

Section II: Mathematics

1. **(C)** 7 is in the tenth's place. Since the next digit (2) is below 5, drop this digit and retain the 7. The answer, therefore, is 406.7.

2. **(C)** The mean IQ score of 100 is given. One standard deviation above the mean is 34% of the cases, with an IQ score up to 115. One standard deviation below the mean is another 34% of the cases, with an IQ score till 85. So, a total of 68% of the students have an IQ between 85 and 115. Therefore, $1,500 \times .68 = 1,020$.

3. **(A)**

$$12 + 2x = 24$$
$$2x = 24 - 12$$
$$2x = 12$$
$$x = \frac{12}{2}$$
$$x = 6$$

4. **(A)**

$$(10 + x)2 = 28$$
$$20 + 2x = 28$$
$$2x = 28 - 20$$
$$2x = 8$$
$$x = \frac{8}{2}$$
$$x = 4$$

5. **(A)**

$$\$2,000 \times .35 = \$700.$$

The rest have wrong computations.

6. **(C)** Let x = length of time (# of mos) to recover cost.

$$3x = 24$$

$$x = \frac{24}{3}$$

$$x = 8 \text{ mos.}$$

7. **(C)** With one right angle (90°) and a given 30° angle, the missing angle, therefore, is a 60° angle.

$$90° + 30° = 120°; 180° - 120° = 60°$$

8. **(C)** The perimeter is the distance around the triangle which is, therefore,

$$(a + b + c) \text{ cm.}$$

9. **(D)** The perimeter is the distance around the triangle. Therefore,

$$2 \text{ cm} + 6 \text{ cm} + 5 \text{ cm} = 13 \text{ cm.}$$

10. **(E)** The area of a parallelogram is base × height. Therefore,

$$A = bh = (16 \text{ cm}) \times (4 \text{ cm}) = 64 \text{ cm}^2.$$

11. **(B)** Figure A has an area of about 9 square units while Figure B has an area of about 7 square units. Both Figures A and B have the same perimeter of about 12 units.

12. **(E)** Only (E) has an element (which is 5) not present in the given set of {1, 2, 3, 4}.

13. **(D)** Nine is the square of an integer. 17, 11, and 15 are not squares of an integer, therefore, they are irrational numbers. 7 is not the cube of an integer, hence, it is an irrational number as well.

14. **(A)** 15 is used as a cardinal number. The rest are either ordinal (B) or nominal, (C), (D), (E), numbers.

15. **(A)** Use the Venn diagram (as shown below) with three circles to represent the set of students in each of the listed subject matter areas. Start with four students taking all three subjects. We write the number 4 in the

region that is the intersection of all these circles. Then we work backward: Since seven are taking math and English, and four of these have already been identified as also taking English, math, and science, there must be exactly three taking only math and English. That is, there must be three in the region representing math and English, but not science. Continuing in this manner, we enter the given data in the diagram.

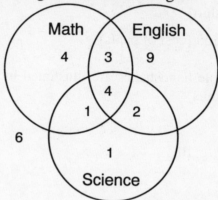

16. **(C)**   There is one element in the intersection of all three sets. Thus,

$n(A \cap B \cap C) = 5$.

17. **(D)**   The sequence 1, 4, 9, 16 is the sum of the odd numbers.

1. 1

2. $1 + 3 = 4$

3. $1 + 3 + 5 = 9$

4. $1 + 3 + 5 + 7 = 16$

18. **(A)**   Here one must use only the needed information. Do not be distracted by superfluous data. Simple multiplication will do. If one pig eats four pounds of food per week, how much will 10 pigs eat in one week? $10 \times 4 = 40$ pounds. The problem intentionally contains superfluous data (52 weeks), which should not distract the reader from its easy solution. Ratio and proportion will also work here

$$\frac{1}{10} = \frac{4}{x}, \ x = 40 \text{ pounds/week.}$$

19. **(D)**   Let the variable S stand for the cost of the shirt. Then the cost of the pair of pants is $S + 25$ and

$$S + (S + 25) = 65$$
$$2S = 65 - 25$$
$$2S = 40$$
$$S = 20$$

$20 (cost of shirt)

$20 + $25 = $45 (cost of pants)

20. **(D)**   The possible handshakes are illustrated by listing all the possible pairs of letters, thus

AB   AC   AD   AE

BC   BD   BE

CD   CE

DE

(a total of 10 handshakes)

21. **(C)**   Only (C) involves a change by only translation.

22. **(A)**   (B) is a rectangular prism. (C) is a square prism. (D) is a square pyramid. (E) is neither a prism nor a pyramid.

23. **(B)**   If one continues lines $\overline{AE}$ and $\overline{BF}$, they intersect at a common vertex. The rest do not.

24. **(C)**   Points ABCDE are the vertices, thus 5.

25. **(C)**   Let

D = down payment

$D = \$20,000 \times .20$

$D = \$4,000$

26. **(D)**

20% of $3,200 = $640 (amount price reduced)

$3,200 - $640 = $2,560 (sale price)

27. **(E)** Let x = 5th grade

$$\text{Average} = \frac{65 + 85 + 60 + 90 + x}{5}$$

For Sue to obtain a C, her average must be greater than or equal to 70 but less than 80.

$$70 \le \frac{65 + 85 + 60 + 90 + x}{5}$$

$$70 \le \frac{300 + x < 80}{5}$$

$$5(70) \le 5(300 + x \div 5) < 5(80)$$

$$350 \le 300 + x < 400$$

$$350 - 300 \le x < 400 - 300$$

$$50 \le x < 100$$

Thus, a grade of 50 up to but not including a grade of 100 will result in a C.

28. **(D)** All but (E) are constraints. The constraint for y is to at least make two mowers.

29. **(A)** The ratio 8:6:6:1 implies that for each \$8 the wife received, each child received \$6 and the foundation \$1. The estate is divided into 8 + 6 + 6 + 1, or 21 equal shares. The wife received $8/21$ of \$300,000 or \$114,285.71, each child received $6/21$ of \$300,000, or \$85,714.29, and the foundation received $1/21$ of \$300,000 or \$14,285.71. As a check,

\$114,285.71 + \$85,714.29 + \$85,714.29 + \$14,285.71 = \$300,000.

30. **(B)** Simple division: $19/9$ = 2 whole hamburgers with one left over.

31. **(C)** Simple multiplication: $7 \times 4 = 28$.

32. **(C)** For a 15 ft. log, it will take 14 cuts to make 15 equal pieces. Therefore, 14 minutes for 14 cuts.

33. **(E)** Simple multiplication.

$6 \times 4 = 24.$

34. **(D)**   First find out how many shares of $1,000 there are in $50,000

$50,000 \div 1,000 = 50$

Then multiply the shares by the cost ($50 \times $32) and the answer is $1,600.

35. **(C)**   Find the sum of the seven days. Thus:

M = 25;

T = 30;

W = 20;

Th = 25;

F = 10;

Sat = 40;

Sun = 0,

or a total of 150 minutes. Find the average by dividing 150 by 7 = 21.43 minutes.

36. **(B)**   If each $\boxed{\$}$ stands for $12, only weeks 3 and 4 had a sale of $72 and $60, respectively. The rest are below $55.

37. **(C)**   The volume of a pyramid is

$$V = \frac{1}{3} Bh,$$

where B is the area of the base and h is the height of the pyramid. Thus,

$$V = \frac{1}{3} (64) (6)$$

$$= \frac{1}{3} (384) = 128 \text{ m}^3.$$

38. **(C)**   Total the number of credits earned (in this case = 16 credits). Multiply the credit and the weight for the earned grade per subject (e.g., biology = 5 × 4 = 20). Then add the total of the products of the credits and

corresponding weights (in this case = 47). Then divide 47 by 16 to get the grade point average of 2.94. See table below.

$$\text{Biology} = 5 \times 4 = 20$$

$$\text{English} = 3 \times 2 = 6$$

$$\text{Math} = 3 \times 4 = 12$$

$$\text{French} = 3 \times 1 = 3$$

$$\text{GPA} = \frac{\text{total cr} \times \text{wt}}{\text{total cr}} = \frac{47}{16} = 2.94$$

$$\text{P.E.} = \frac{2}{16 \text{ cr}} \times 3 = \frac{6}{47 \text{ cr} \times \text{gr wt}}$$

39. **(C)**   Mode is the most frequent score. 81 appeared five times and is therefore the mode.

40. **(A)**   Following the formula

$$z = \frac{x - \bar{x}}{\text{s.d.}}$$

thus, $$1.6 = x - \frac{190}{11}$$

$$17.60 = x - 190$$

$$x = 190 + 17.60$$

$$x = 207.60 \text{ cm (Glenn's height)}$$

Section III: Writing

1. **(A)** Choice (A) is obviously wordy, "consensus" meaning the same as "general agreement," so it is the best choice. None of the others has a usage error. Choice (B) is acceptable in that it implies a well-known fact that Twain wrote many other works. Choice (C) underscores the claim made in the whole sentence by establishing the book as the "best" American work. Finally, choice (D) is acceptable because of commas in other parts of the sentence. Choice (E) clearly does not apply.

2. **(C)** This question has several potential errors. Choice (A) requires that you know to capitalize important historical documents, so it is correct. Choice (B) calls to question the attribution of human rationality to an inanimate object, but since the Constitution actually does have logical premises, we can correctly say that the document can posit the premise stated. Choice (D) is acceptable because the superlative is referenced within the sentence; one should know that the U.S. government has three branches. That leaves choices (C) and (E). Choice (C) is the verb in the clause beginning with the word "what"; it is plural, and therefore, incorrect because it does not agree with its subject "history," a singular noun. Do not be fooled by the intervening plural word "governments." Since choice (C) is the error, choice (E) would no longer be considered.

3. **(C)** Even though people use "like" as a conjunction in conversation and public speaking, it is a preposition, and formal written English requires "as," "as if," or "as though" when what follows is a clause. No other choice is even suspect.

4. **(C)** One could question the use of "nearly" (A), but it is correct. One might argue also that "million dollars" (D) should be written "$1 million," but choice (C) is so clearly an incorrect use of the past perfect tense that the other possibilities, remote at best, pale by comparison. The simple past tense ("sold"), the present progressive tense ("are selling"), or the present perfect progressive tense ("have been selling") could each be used correctly depending on the meaning intended.

5. **(B)** This choice is not as obvious, but authorities agree that the use of "expect" to mean "suppose" or "believe" (the usage here) is either informal or colloquial, but again not formal written English. The next most likely choice, (E), would suggest that informal or colloquial usage is

appropriate. The third most likely choice, (D), brings to mind the distinction between "accept" and "except," a word pair often confused. However, "accept" is correct here.

6. **(A)** Regardless of its popular usage "hopefully" is an adverb trying to be a clause ("it is hoped" or "I hope"). However, instances still exist that require a distinction between the two uses. To be clear, use "hopefully" when you mean "in a hopeful manner." ["He wished hopefully that she would accept his proposal of marriage."] Choice (D) appears suspicious. "Continually" means recurrence at intervals over a period of time, so it is correctly used to imply that machines do break down often. (B) Capitalizing "Twentieth Century" is also appropriate as it is here used as the specific historical period (like the "Middle Ages"). We would not capitalize the phrase if it were used simply to count, as in "The twentieth century from now will surely find enormous changes in the world." It is incorrect to hyphenate a number-noun phrase like this one when it stands alone as a noun phrase. Choice (C), "enough," is correct as used.

7. **(A)** The two most suspicious choices are (A) and (D) because the item is a sentence fragment. No reasonable substitute for (D) would solve both the logic problem (incomplete thought) and the punctuation problem (comma splice if you omit "that"). Changing "showing" to "show" would, however, make the clause into a complete sentence with correct punctuation. Neither (B) or (C) provoke suspicion.

8. **(B)** Again, the two most questionable choices, (B) and (C), compete for our attention. The use of "but" makes sense because it shows contrast to the previous idea. ("Don't evade or defy the law, *but* if caught breaking a law, accept the penalty.") The use of "or," however, is clearly not parallel to the immediately preceding use of "neither." The proper phrase is "neither . . . nor" for negative alternate choices. Neither choice (A) nor choice (D) demands a second look.

9. **(D)** This choice involves parallel construction, or the lack of it. The word "both" introduces a pair of phrases, one a prepositional phrase ("for their own interests"), the other an infinitive phrase ("to gain more goods"). Aside from being inelegant, "to gain more goods" is also not the same structure and should be changed to "their own gain" to make the two phrases perfectly parallel. Choices (B) and (C) are not problematic. Choice (A) is another candidate because of the capitalization and the lack of a hyphen between "Eighteenth" and "Century." The capitalization is correct

and no hyphen is needed when the phrase becomes an adjective that has meaning as a single phrase, which the capitalization suggests, or if the first word forms a familiar pair with the following word and if there is no danger of confusion. [The sentence clearly does not mean that Smith is the eighteenth (small "e") philosopher, but *the* Eighteenth Century philosopher.]

10. **(E)** The other choices all fail to exhibit inappropriate usage. Choice (A), "cannot," is spelled as one word; choice (B), "should not," is parallel to "cannot" and adds meaning necessary to the thought. Choice (C) is a correct plural possessive pronoun, the antecedent of which is "rulers." Finally, choice (D) is a third-person plural verb agreeing with its subject, "reasons."

11. **(C)** "Milky Way galaxy" is the singular antecedent, for which the pronoun referent should be "its" (inanimate object). Do not be confused by the intervening words ("stars" and "spots"); it is the galaxy which shines in this sentence, not the stars or the spots. Choice (A) is the correct usage of "comprises." Choice (B) is an appropriate pair of adjectives with no apparent problem. Choice (D) is appropriate because the sentence has an internally supplied superlative sense; it does not need a "brightest of" phrase.

12. **(A)** Again, non-parallel structure is the key of this and many other test items. Because of the overwhelming importance of understanding balance in sentence structure, tests like this one emphasize parallel sentence structures. "To learn" clashes with "studying" in the parallel clause. You cannot choose "studying." "Learning" substituted for "To learn" would make the clauses parallel. Choice (B) is a correct use of "like" as a preposition (objects: "Latin," "Greek"). Choice (D) is correctly singular as the verb of the noun phrase "studying . . . beliefs." Nothing is incorrect about choice (C).

13. **(A)** This is a colloquial, nonstandard substitution for the correct word, "attribute." Choice (B) is correctly lowercase, not capitalized. Choice (C) is a correct, if a bit stiff, phrase. Choice (D) is a correct plural verb the subject of which is "both," also plural.

14. **(C)** This is an incorrect simple past verb tense. You have to spot the context clue "most Americans" "attended" school (B) in the past, which suggests they no longer do so now. They must then "choose" their

entertainment. Choice (A) is questionable, but the present participial phrase suggests coincidence with the time "most Americans" "attended school." It is, therefore, correct. Choice (D) is correctly an infinitive that is parallel to "to watch."

15. **(A)** The two most questionable choices are (A) and (B). Choice (A) is incorrectly a subjective case pronoun when it should be objective (object of verb "makes," subject "What"). If you know the difference between "different from" (correctly used in this sentence) and "difference than" (correctly used only to introduce a clause), then choice (B) is no longer viable. Besides being a passive construction, choice (C) has no objectionable qualities; it is grammatically correct. So is choice (D) correctly an adverb that has meaning in context.

16. **(D)** This is a case of subject-verb disagreement related to the definition of the word "neither" (subject) as singular. Its verb must also be singular, and "differ" is plural. Choice (A) correctly uses English idiom ("compare to"—"contrast with"). Choice (B) refers clearly to "ideas," its antecedent, and agrees with it (both plural). Choice (C) is a singular verb agreeing with its subject, "one."

17. **(E)** Everything in the sentence is acceptable or correct usage, even though some of it may be a bit stuffy and pedantic, i.e., choice (B). You might question choice (A) in that instead of suggesting, perhaps asserting or stating would be more appropriate. Even though these terms clearly differ, there is nothing wrong with using "suggests" (correct subject-verb agreement with "hypothesis") because a hypothesis can suggest as well as theorize, assert, etc. Choice (C) correctly agrees with its subject "which" (plural, antecedent "archetypes"). Choice (D) might be considered redundant ("repeated" and "patterns"), but that is not apparent from the context.

18. **(E)** You are likely to have chosen either (B) or (C) here. The affect/effect word pair often confuses students, and this instance is one in which "effected" is correctly used as a verb meaning "brought about" or "caused to happen." The question in choice (C) is whether or not to capitalize the word "Fate." When it refers to the collective term for the Greek concept of destiny (actually gods, the Fates), as it does here, it is appropriately capitalized. Choices (A) and (D) do not seem questionable.

19. **(D)** Again, the problem here is pronoun-antecedent agreement. "Their" does not refer to the three writers collectively; its antecedent is

"each," which is always singular, not plural ("each one"). There is nothing wrong with choices (A), (B), and (C).

20. **(C)**   The error here is known as faulty predication ("reason . . . is because"). The usage rule is that "because" is redundant for "reason." Choice (A) is appropriate, if a bit general (not 30 or 70 percent, for example). The verb in choice (B) is correct and in the past tense, as is the verb phrase in choice (D).

21. **(B)**   Choice (A) is a verb correctly in agreement with its compound subject. Choice (C) is an appropriate parallel structure requiring no punctuation. Choice (D) correctly uses the word "comprises" and makes it agree with its subject. Only (B) seems incorrect. The structure requires the adverb form "constantly," since it describes an adjective, "expanding."

22. **(A)**   This is the classic confusion of "less" for the correct "fewer." "Few(er)" refers to countable things or persons; "little (less)" refers to things that can be measured or estimated but not itemized. The only other choice to examine is (D), but it is the appropriate tense referring to the "contemporary" (now) view.

23. **(C)**   Choice (A) is a correct use of the relative pronoun. Nothing is unusual about (B). (C) is the culprit here: it should be the infinitive form to adhere to the idiom, "ability to (verb)." (D) is an appropriate reference to hierarchy and responsibility.

24. **(A)**   The sentence as it stands is illogical. Removing "Because" will make it sensible. (B) is an appropriate adverb modifying "believe"; (C) is a clear and effective subordination of an explanation of a term. (D) uses "as" properly as a preposition.

25. **(B)**   "Being that" is colloquial for "because," which is better for at least the reason that it is shorter, but also that it is more formal. No other choices seem out of bounds.

26. **(B)**   This question of appropriate verb tense requires the simple past tense verb "took" because the Civil War happened in a finite time period in the past. The other choices all fail that test. The original and choice (E) are present tense, and do not logically fit the facts. Choice (D) is the present perfect tense, which suggests a continuous action from the past to the present. Choice (C) is the past perfect tense, which suggests a continu-

ing action from one time in the past to another in the more recent past.

27. **(D)**   We can eliminate fairly quickly choices (C) and (E) as either inappropriate or awkward appositives to "ornithology," instead of "ornithologists." Neither is (A) the best choice even though some may consider it acceptable. Likewise, choice (B) tends to be limited to nonrestrictive clauses, unlike this one. Choice (D) then correctly uses a "personal" relative pronoun.

28. **(D)**   Choices (A), (D), and (E) are the best candidates because they are more concise than the other two choices. Each does express the same idea, but (E) does not as strongly indicate the contrast between the two clauses in the sentence as do choices (A) and (D). Choice (D) clearly makes its point in fewer words and is the better choice.

29. **(B)**   The phrase "as to" often is overblown and unclear, so it is best to eliminate it when there are other choices. Likewise, "expectability" does not exactly roll off your tongue. That leaves choices (B) and (D). Choice (D) adds a definite figure, unwarranted by the original sentence. It also is duller than (B), which does change the wording for the better and also indicates that the "actual amount" is to be announced, rather than that it is already known.

30. **(A)**   Choices (C) and (E) introduce unnecessary absolute phrases beginning with "it," which makes the sentences wordy. They can be eliminated immediately. Choice (D) has an illogical comparison suggesting notes = instrument, so it, too, is not the best choice. Between (A) and (B) the difference boils down to the present tense vs. the past tense. Choice (A) uses past tenses, which seem better in sequence to follow the past tense verb "developed."

31. **(B)**   Choices (A), (C), and (D) can be disqualified quickly because they are not parallel to the structure of the main clause. Choice (E) is ungainly and introduces a vague pronoun "its" (unclear antecedent). Choice (B) reads well and has the virtue of brevity.

32. **(E)**   The choices are easy to discern in this sentence. The original verb does not agree with its subject, nor is the structure parallel. The former reason also eliminates choice (C). Choice (B) does not have parallel structure (phrase and clause). Choice (D) does not logically agree with the subject ("reasons") since it names one ("demanding professors") but

relegates the other reason to an afterthought. Choice (D) has both parallel structure and subject-verb agreement; it also names two reasons.

33. **(C)**   The original suffers from inadequate causal relationship and non-parallel structure. Choices (D) and (E) are both unnecessarily wordy; (D) is still not parallel, and (E) is internally illogical ("both" with three things). Choice (B) switches its structure at the end. Although it is technically parallel, it is still awkward because of the addition of the possessive pronoun "her." Choice (C) solves both problems by clearly showing cause and by being parallel (three nouns in series).

34. **(B)**   This sentence presents an incomplete comparison and a redundancy ("Whether"/"or did not"/"remains uncertain"). Choice (B) eliminates both problems clearly. Choice (C) tries to undo the damage, but it remains inelegant in syntax and leaves partial redundancy ("whether"/ "remains uncertain"). Choice (D) is worse in both respects. Choice (E) clears up the syntax but leaves some redundancy ("may actually have"/ "remains uncertain"). Choice (B) eliminates both problems clearly.

35. **(A)**   The sentence as is reads well; it is perfectly balanced. Choice (B) introduces an incomplete comparison ("more" but no "than"). Choice (C) awkwardly uses "as to." Choices (D) and (E) make a scrambled mess by introducing illogical structures.

36. **(A)**   "Unique" means just that; it should not have qualifiers like "very" or "nearly." That eliminates choices (B) and (D). Choice (C) changes the meaning by making the development unique, instead of the system. Choice (E) uses an inappropriate verb tense because the first of the sentence suggests the Revolutionary War period, definitely in the past.

37. **(B)**   The original sentence (A) has a dangling modifier (participial phrase); it remains that way in choice (E). The house cannot return to itself, nor can "it" (pronoun for house). Choice (D) seems to leave something out: "returned to . . . home in 12 years." Choice (C) solves the original problem but is unnecessarily wordy. Choice (B) properly solves the dangling modifier problem by subordinating the return in an adverbial clause.

38. **(A)**   Choice (A) is the only response that makes sense. Each of the others introduces illogical comparisons or structures (non-parallel); (B), (D), and (E) are also verbose. Choice (C) is concise but not parallel.

39. **(C)** This sentence suggests causal relationships between the parts of the sentence that do not belong there. Choices (B) and (D) echo the original (A) in that regard. Choice (E) has garbled syntax. (C) shows clearly that the cause-effect relationship is, rather, a time relationship.

40. **(E)** This is essentially a problem of wordiness. (E) is the shortest and most clear of all the choices. The punctuation is weak in (C), and the syntax of (B) complicates the idea unnecessarily. (D) does not use the appropriate conjunctive adverb; "thereby" is more precise than "therefore" when referring to an event.

41. **(D)** All the other responses repeat the cause-effect relationship stated in the phrase "Because of." (D) is the only choice which does not do so.

42. **(B)** Choice (B) would solve the problem of needless pronoun voice shift from second person to first person ("you" to "our"). It correctly substitutes first person "we" for "you." (C) uses the passive voice awkwardly. (D) introduces non-parallel structure (and incomplete comparison). (E) is a similar voice shift from third to first person.

43. **(A)** This is the best response from the choices. The sentence implies a change of the standard. For that reason, (B) is an incorrect choice. (C) is unnecessarily awkward and wordy. (D) is redundant and (E) states more than the sentence implies.

44. **(B)** The problem in this sentence involves the need for consistent pronoun use and for parallel construction. Because the portion of the sentence not underlined uses the pronouns "you" and "your," the first part of the sentence must also use the second person pronoun. Choice (B) alone accomplishes that consistency and yet retains parallel construction.

45. **(A)** This sentence contains no error in standard written English. Each of the possible revisions makes no real improvement, and choice (B) adds an error in subject-verb agreement. Choice (C) creates confusion in pronoun reference with the addition of "themselves," and choices (D) and (E) are not idiomatic.

PPST ESSAY SCORING GUIDE

The PPST essay sections are scored by two writing experts on the basis of the criteria outlined below. In addition to comparing your essay to those included in our practice tests, you may use these guidelines to estimate your score on this section. Remember that your score is the sum of the scores of two writing experts, so provided you respond to the assigned topic, your score will fall somewhere between two and twelve. Scores will be assigned based on the following guidelines:

6 An essay receiving a score of 6 may contain one or two spelling or punctuation errors, but overall it exhibits a high degree of proficiency and thought on the assigned topic.

An essay scoring a 6

- is both well organized and well developed
- engages important concepts and explains them clearly
- varies expression and language
- demonstrates deft use of language
- is virtually free from errors involving syntax and structure

5 An essay receiving a score of 5 exhibits a high degree of proficiency and thought on the assigned topic, however it contains a number of minor mistakes.

An essay scoring a 5

- is both well organized and well developed
- engages important concepts and explains them
- varies expression and language somewhat
- demonstrates deft use of language
- is virtually free from errors involving syntax and structure

4 An essay receiving a score of 4 responds to the assignment and exhibits some degree of deeper understanding.

An essay scoring a 4

- demonstrates adequate organization and development
- engages and explains some important concepts, but not all that are necessary to demonstrate full understanding

- exhibits adequate use of language
- contains some syntactical and structural errors, without excessive repetition of those errors

3 An essay receiving a score of 3 exhibits some degree of understanding, but its response to the topic is obviously deficient.

An essay scoring a 3 is deficient in one or more of the following areas:

- insufficient organization or development
- insufficient engagement or explanation of important concepts
- consistent repetition of syntactical or structural errors
- redundant or unsuitable word choice

2 An essay receiving a score of 2 exhibits limited understanding and its response to the topic is seriously deficient.

An essay scoring a 2 is deficient in one or more of the following areas:

- weak organization or development
- very few pertinent details
- consistent and serious errors in syntax, structure
- consistent and serious errors in word choice

1 An essay receiving a score of 1 exhibits a lack of basic writing skills.

An essay scoring a 1 is disorganized, undeveloped, contains consistent repetition of errors, or is incomprehensible.

Sample Essays with Commentary

ESSAY I (Score: 5-6)

The cynic in me wants to react to the idea of universal public service for the young with a reminder about previous complaints aimed at the military draft. These complaints suggest that wars might never be fought if the first people drafted were the adult leaders and lawmakers. Still the idea of universal public service sounds good to this concerned citizen who sees everywhere—not just in youth—the effects of a selfish and self-indulgent culture.

One reads and hears constantly about young people who do not care about the problems of our society. These youngsters seem interested in money and the luxuries money can buy. They do not want to work from the minimum wage up, but want instead to land a high paying job without "paying their dues." An informal television news survey of high school students a few years ago suggested that students had the well entrenched fantasy that with no skills or higher education they would not accept a job paying less than $20 an hour. Perhaps universal service helping out in an urban soup kitchen for six months would instill a sense of selflessness rather than selfishness.

The shiny gleam of a new expensive sports sedan bought on credit by a recent accounting student reflects self indulgence that might be toned down by universal service. That self indulgence may reflect merely a lack of discipline, but it also may reflect a lack of purpose in life. Philosophers, theologians and leaders of all types suggest throughout the ages that money and objects do not ultimately satisfy. Helping others—service to our fellow human beings—often does. Universal public service for that accounting student might require a year helping low income or senior citizens prepare income tax forms. This type of service would dim that self indulgence, give the person some experience in the real world, and also give satisfaction that one's life is not lived only to acquire things.

Universal service might also help young people restore faith in their nation and what it means to them. Yes, this is the land of opportunity, but it is also a land of forgotten people, and it is a land that faces outside threats. Part of the requisite public service should remind young people of their past and of their responsibility to the future.

ANALYSIS

Essay I has a score range of 5-6. It uses a traditional structure: the first

paragraph states the topic, the second and third present development with specific examples from personal observation. The fourth ends the essay, but it is not as strong a conclusion as it could be. The writer probably ran out of time. The essay as a whole is unified and uses pertinent examples to support the opinion stated. The sentence structure varies, and the vocabulary is effective. Generally, it is well done within the 30-minute time limit.

ESSAY II (Score: 4-5)

In the U.S. today, when a boy turns 18 he is obligated, by law, to register for the military draft. This is done so that in case of a war or something catastrophic these boys and men can be called on for active duty in the military. It is good to know that we will have the manpower in case of a war but my opinion on the military draft is negative. I don't like the idea of forcing someone to sign up at a certain age for something that they don't want to happen. Of course, I know that we need some sort of military manpower on hand just in case, but it would be so much better if it was left to the individual to decide what area to serve in and what time.

When a boy turns 18, he's a rebel of sorts. He doesn't want someone telling him what to do and when to do it; he's just beginning to live. In Switzerland, when a boy turns 18, he goes into some branch of the military for a time of training. He is given his gun, uniform and badge number. Then, once a year for about two weeks he suits up for retraining. He does this until he is about 65 years old. Now in a way this is like a draft but the men love it and feel that it is honorable. I think that they like it because it does not discriminate and their jobs pay them for the time away. Switzerland seems to give the 18 year old somewhat of a choice what division to go in and whether or not to join. They're not as strict on joining as we are so it's more of an honorable thing to do.

Of course, I'd love to see it as strictly up to the individual but it can't be that way. We have too many enemies that we might go to war with and we would need a strong military. Switzerland has nothing to worry about as long as they have their banks.

ANALYSIS

Essay II has a score range of 4-5. It displays competence in overall thought. It does not state its topic quite as well as Essay I. The extended example of Swiss military conscription is the main strength of the essay. The writer hedges a bit but manages to convey an opinion. Sentences have some variety, and the vocabulary is competent. Some spelling and grammatical errors interfere with the communication.

ESSAY III (Score: 3-4)

I agree with the many leaders who suggest we require young people to serve the public in some way, rather than the military draft.

There are several reasons this could benefit our country. The first being giving the young people, perhaps just out of high school, with no job experience, an opportunity to give something to his community. In return for this, he gains self-respect and pride.

Whether it be taking flowers to shut-ins or just stopping for a chat in a rest home, a young person would have gained something and certainly given, perhaps hope, to that elder person. I can tell from my own experience, not quite old enough for the military draft, how enriched I feel when visiting the elderly. They find joy in the simplest things, which in turn, teaches me I should do the same.

Another thing gained by doing voluntary type work, is a sense of caring about doing the job right—quality! If you can't do it for your country, what else matters?

ANALYSIS

Essay III has a score range of 3-4. It has major faults, not the least of them the lack of a clear sense of overall organization. The thoughts do have some coherence, but they don't seem to have a plan, except to express agreement with the statement. Examples from personal observation do help, but the paragraphs are not well developed. Several severe grammatical problems interfere with the communication.

ESSAY IV (Score: 1-2)

Feeling strongly against the draft, as I do. I could not agree with the idea of requiring young people to serve in the military. I feel this would say something about the world situation. I believe the leaders and people would have to give up the idea of peace totally. Which would eventually lead to our own destruction.

Although I do believe young people should serve their country in a peaceful more useful way. They should be more politically aware of what the government is trying to do. They should work in a peaceful way to try and make changes that work for the good of all people of the world.

There has never in the history of the world been a military state that survived.

ANALYSIS

Essay IV has a score range of 1-2. It has many problems. Not only does it fail to present a coherent argument, it also shows a fundamental lack of understanding of sentence structure. The concluding statement seems to come out of nowhere. The writer also confuses the topic with that of required military service, which would be only part of universal service.

PPST

Pre-Professional Skills Tests

Practice
PPST III

PPST Test III

(Answer sheets appear in the back of this book.)

Section I: Reading Comprehension

TIME: 60 Minutes
        40 Questions

DIRECTIONS: A number of questions follow each of the passages in the reading section. Answer the questions by choosing the best answer from the five choices given.

Questions 1 to 3 refer to the following passage:

Representatives of the world's seven richest and most industrialized nations held a three-day economic summit in London on July 14-16, 1991. On the second day of the summit, Mikhail Gorbachev, who appealed for help, was offered support by the seven leaders for his economic reforms and his "new' thinking" regarding political reforms. However, because the allies were split on giving a big aid package to Gorbachev, the seven leaders decided to provide help in the form of technical assistance in fields such as banking and energy, rather than in hard cash.

1.   Which of the following statements best synthesizes what the passage is about?

(A) A seven-nation economic summit was held in London in July 1991.

(B) An economic summit of the world's richest nations was held in London in July.

(C) Mikhail Gorbachev appealed for help and the seven leaders agreed to support his economic reforms.

(D) At a three-day economic summit held in London in July 1991, leaders of the world's seven richest and most industrialized nations agreed to provide technical assistance to Gorbachev.

(E) Representatives of the world's seven most industrialized nations, at a summit conference in London, were split on giving Gorbachev assistance in the form of hard cash.

2. The passage implies

(A) that, under the leadership of Gorbachev, the Soviet Union is faced with a financial crisis.

(B) that Gorbachev's "new thinking" on democratic reforms needs support from the seven nations meeting in London.

(C) that the seven leaders meeting in London were split on giving Gorbachev economic and political support.

(D) that with only technical assistance from the seven nations that met in London, the Soviet Union under the leadership of Gorbachev is heading for economic disaster.

(E) that with the support of political and economic reforms along with provisions for technical assistance from the seven nations that met in London, the Soviet Union under the leadership of Gorbachev can achieve political and economic stability.

3. The passage suggests that technical assistance will be provided to the Soviet Union

(A) only in the fields of banking and energy.

(B) in the fields of banking and energy and possibly other fields also.

(C) by the U.S. in the fields of banking and energy.

(D) by any of the seven nations that met at a summit in London.

(E) by all seven nations—U.S., Great Britain, France, Germany, Italy, Canada, and Japan.

Questions 4 to 6 refer to the following passage:

A follow-up survey of the 1990 census showed an estimated undercount of 5.2 million people nationwide. This "undercount" was greatest in California where approximately 1.1 million people were not recorded. This estimated undercount was based on a post-census survey of 171,390 households nationwide. Failure to achieve an accurate count would affect federal funding and political representation. If the higher numbers were used, California would gain eight congressional seats instead of seven and

about $1 billion in federal funds. Last July 14, 1991, however, Commerce Secretary Robert Mosbacher decided to stick to the original figures of the 1990 census.

4. Which of the following statements gives the main idea of the passage you just read?

(A) California will gain an additional congressional seat and more federal money if the 1.1 million people undercounted in the census are included.

(B) The population in a state is the basis for determining the political representation for that state.

(C) An undercount in the census, if not considered, will be a disadvantage to any state.

(D) A post-census survey is necessary in getting to a more accurate population figure for the states.

(E) California will suffer the most because of the 1.1 million undercount in the 1990 census.

5. If the 1.1 million undercount was considered for California

(A) it would settle any political dispute arising from the undercount.

(B) it would give California eight congressional seats and $1 billion in federal funds.

(C) it would discourage the practice of a post-census survey.

(D) it would create political unrest for other states.

(E) it would reverse the decision made by Commerce Secretary Mosbacher.

6. What would it mean for California if the original figures of the 1990 census were to remain the same?

(A) No additional federal funding will be given.

(B) There will be no additional political representation.

(C) The amount of federal funding and number of congressional seats will remain the same.

(D) The census undercount will not make a difference.

(E) The results of the follow-up survey of the 1990 census will be meaningless.

Questions 7 to 10 refer to the following passage:

A big toxic spill took place on the upper Sacramento River in California on July 13, 1991 about 10 P.M. when a slow moving Southern Pacific train derailed north of the town of Dansmuir. A tank car containing 19,500 gallons of pesticide broke open and spilled into the river. This pesticide is used to kill soil pests. Since the spill, thousands of trout and other fish were poisoned along a 45-mile stretch of river. In addition, 190 people were treated at a local hospital for respiratory and related illnesses. Residents along the river have been warned to stay away from the tainted water. Once this water reaches Lake Shasta, a source of water for millions of Californians, samples will be taken to assess the quality of the water.

7. Which of the following statements conveys the message in the passage?

(A) Pesticides intended to kill soil pests can be dangerous to all living things.

(B) Water uncontaminated by pesticides is safe to drink.

(C) Take every precaution not to come in contact with the pesticide infected water.

(D) Pesticides that killed thousands of trout and other fish will not necessarily kill human beings.

(E) Only residents along the tainted river need worry.

8. The Southern Pacific train that derailed was

(A) a passenger train.

(B) a cargo train.

(C) a commuter train.

(D) a cargo and passenger train.

(E) a special train.

9. The most serious problem that can come about as a result of the toxic spill is

   (A) possible movement of residents in Dansmuir to another place of residence.

   (B) reduction in tourism attraction for Dansmuir and other nearby areas.

   (C) the negative effects on those whose livelihood depends on the fishing industry.

   (D) when the tainted water reaches Lake Shasta, which is a source of water supply for millions of Californians.

   (E) the uncertain length of time it will take to make the tainted water safe and healthy again.

10. This unfortunate incident of toxic spill resulting from train derailment implies

    (A) the need for more environmental protection.

    (B) other means for transporting pesticides need to be considered.

    (C) that there should be more precaution for trains running by night-time.

    (D) that there should be an investigation as to the cause of the train derailment and effective measures to prevent its occurrence again should be applied.

    (E) that there should be research on how to expedite making in-fected water safe and healthy again.

Questions 11 to 13 refer to the following passage:

Labor Day, a national holiday observed in the United States, is really a day we should remember to give thanks to the labor unions. In the days before the unions became effective, a holiday meant a day off, but the loss of a day's pay to working people. It was not until World War II that unions succeeded, through negotiations with the federal government, in making paid holidays a common practice.

11. The main idea in the passage you just read is

    (A) the role labor unions played in employer-employee relations.

    (B) Labor Day as a national holiday in the U.S.

(C) the role labor unions played in effecting paid holidays.

(D) the dispute between paid and unpaid holidays.

(E) Labor Day before World War II.

12. The passage implies that before World War II

(A) a holiday gave working people a chance to rest from work.

(B) Labor Day meant losing a day's pay.

(C) a holiday was a day to make up for upon returning to work.

(D) labor unions were ineffective.

(E) taking off from work set a worker one day behind in his or her work.

13. As a national holiday, Labor Day should really be a day to remember and be thankful for

(A) working people.

(B) help from the federal government.

(C) paid holidays.

(D) labor unions.

(E) a free day.

Question 14 refers to the following passage:

President Bush's proposed educational "program of choice" will give parents more say in choosing schools for their children. This will encourage states and local districts to change their laws so that parents can apply their tax dollars toward the public or private school to which they choose to send their children, rather than be forced to send their child to the public school in their district or pay for private school tuition.

14. President Bush's proposed educational program implies

(A) the freedom to choose.

(B) competition among schools.

(C) school standards need to be raised.

(D) more money is needed.

(E) curricula should be improved.

Questions 15 to refer to the following passage:

Ash from Mt. Pinatubo in the Philippines has been found to contain gold and other precious metals. However, officials warned against any hopes of a new "gold rush." They found gold content of only 20 parts per billion, which is far below commercial levels. Other metals found were chromium, copper, and lithium.

15. The passage indicates

   (A) the possibility of existing gold mines beneath Mt. Pinatubo.

   (B) the need for further exploration of what else lies beneath the volcano.

   (C) that there is a new resource for boosting the economy of the Philippines.

   (D) other active volcanoes might be worth exploring as possible gold resources.

   (E) that the gold content of the ash from Mt. Pinatubo does not warrant a commercial level.

16. Which of the following makes a good title for the passage you just read?

   (A) A New Gold Rush

   (B) Mt. Pinatubo's Gold Mine

   (C) Ash Content from Mt. Pinatubo

   (D) A Philippine Discovery

   (E) Precious Metals

17. What might be a possible research project resulting from the ash content finding of Mt. Pinatubo?

   (A) Research on the ash content from the eruption of Mt. Fujiyama in Japan

   (B) Potential market value of the gold and other metals content in the volcanic ash from Mt. Pinatubo

   (C) Further excavation into possible gold underneath Mt. Pinatubo

   (D) Research on what lies underneath active volcanoes

   (E) Compare volcanic ash content with what lies underneath the same volcano when it is inactive

Questions 18 to 20 refer to the following passage:

Gary Harris, a farmer from Conrad, Montana, has invented and patented a motorcycle helmet. It provides a brake light which can signal traffic intentions to other drivers behind. In the U.S., all cars sold are now required to carry a third, high-mounted brake light. Harris' helmet will meet this requirement for motorcyclists.

18. The passage tells about

    (A) a new invention for motorcyclists.

    (B) a requirement for all cars in the U.S.

    (C) a brake light for motorcyclists.

    (D) Harris' helmet.

    (E) Gary Harris, inventor.

19. An implication regarding the new invention is

    (A) any farmer can come up with a similar traffic invention.

    (B) the new brake light requirement for cars should likewise apply to motorcycles.

    (C) the new brake light requirement for cars cannot apply to motorcycles.

    (D) if you buy a car from outside of the U.S., you are exempted from the brake light requirement.

    (E) as an inventor, Gary Harris can make more money if he leaves farming.

20. Because of the new brake light requirement for cars

    (A) drivers can readily see the traffic signals of car drivers ahead of them.

    (B) less accidents can happen on the road.

    (C) car prices will go up and will be less affordable to buy.

    (D) more lights on the road can be hazardous.

    (E) more traffic policemen will be needed.

Questions 21 to 24 refer to the following passage:

Lead poisoning is considered by health authorities to be the most common and devastating environmental disease of young children. According to studies made, it affects 15% to 20% of urban children and from 50% to 75% of inner-city, poor children. As a result of a legal settlement in July 1991, all of California's medical eligible children, ages one through five, will now be routinely screened annually for lead poisoning. Experts estimate that more than 50,000 cases will be detected in California because of the newly mandated tests. This will halt at an early stage a disease that leads to learning disabilities and life-threatening disorders.

21. Lead poisoning among young children, if not detected early, can lead to

    (A) physical disabilities.   (D) heart disease.

    (B) mental disabilities.   (E) death.

    (C) learning disabilities.

22. The new mandate to screen all young children for lead poisoning is required of

    (A) all young children in California.

    (B) all children with learning disabilities.

    (C) all medical-eligible children, ages one through five, in California.

    (D) all minority children in California.

    (E) all school-age children in California.

23. According to findings, more cases of lead poisoning are found among

    (A) urban children.   (D) children in rural areas.

    (B) inner-city poor children. (E) middle-class children.

    (C) immigrant children.

24. The implication of this new mandate in California regarding lead poisoning is

    (A) non-eligible children will not be screened.

    (B) children older than five years will not be screened.

(C) middle-class children will not be screened.

(D) new immigrant children will not be screened.

(E) thousands of young children in California will remain at risk for lead poisoning.

Question 25 refers to the following passage:

As millions of children returned to school in the year 1991-1992, teachers in California had to face the reality of what many consider as the worst fiscal crisis to hit the schools in more than a decade. This crisis caused reductions in teaching positions, increases in class sizes, cuts in teacher paychecks in some school districts, reductions in special programs, reductions in school supplies, etc.

25. Those who will be most affected by the effects of the financial crisis in California schools are

(A) the teachers.   (D) the paraprofessionals.

(B) the parents.   (E) the students.

(C) the school administrators.

Questions 26 to 28 refer to the following passage:

The U.S. Postal Service issued a 50-cent stamp in Anchorage, Alaska on October 12, 1991 to commemorate the 500th anniversary of the arrival of the Italian explorer Christopher Columbus in the New World. The stamp depicts how Americans may have appeared to Asians crossing the Bering Strait. The stamp series will show the pre-Columbian voyages of discovery.

26. Which of the following makes an appropriate title for the passage?

(A) The Discovery of the Americas

(B) 500th Anniversary of the Discovery of America

(C) The Significance of the Bering Strait

(D) A Commemorative New U.S. Postal Stamp

(E) A Tribute to Asians

27. The passage implies that

    (A) historical facts need to be verified.

    (B) Christopher Columbus was not the first to arrive in the New World.

    (C) Asians discovered America.

    (D) Native Americans came from Asia.

    (E) history books need to be rewritten.

28. Which of the following would you consider as the most historically significant?

    (A) Asians crossed over the Bering Strait to the New World before Columbus came.

    (B) It has been 500 years since Christopher Columbus arrived in the New World.

    (C) A tribute to Christopher Columbus was held on October 12, 1991.

    (D) Native Americans are of Asian origin.

    (E) There were other voyages undertaken before Christopher Columbus'.

Questions 29 and 30 refer to the following passage:

A 150 million-year-old allosaurus skeleton which appears to be intact was found on September 9, 1991, by a Swiss team in north-central Wyoming. This Zurich-based company sells fossils to museums. They were digging on private property, but the fossil actually showed up on federal land.

Immediately, the federal government sealed off the site along the foot of Big Horn Mountains in Wyoming and deployed rangers from the Bureau of Land Management to prevent vandalism. Paleontologists believe that this discovery could lead them to a vast dinosaur graveyard.

29. The passage you just read can best be utilized by a classroom teacher in

    (A) reading.   (D) zoology.

    (B) mathematics.   (E) history.

    (C) biology.

30. A teaching strategy that the classroom teacher can use appropriately with the students regarding the allosaurus fossil discovery is

   (A) the problem-solving approach.

   (B) the survey approach.

   (C) the deductive approach.

   (D) the comparative study approach.

   (E) the historical approach.

Questions 31 to 33 refer to the following passage:

Popular U.S. attractions such as Disneyland, the Golden Gate Bridge, Las Vegas, and the Statue of Liberty have attracted millions of foreign tourists whose spending helped the U.S. post a $31.7 billion service trade surplus in 1990 compared with a $101 billion merchandise trade deficit in the same year. The heavy-spending Japanese tourists accounted for the biggest portion of the tourism trade surplus, spending $5.5 billion more touring the U.S than U.S. tourists spent visiting Japan. Canadians also outspent American tourists to Canada by $2.2 billion.

31. The main idea in the passage is

   (A) foreign tourists in the U.S. spend more than American tourists spend abroad.

   (B) there are more tourist attractions in the U.S. than any foreign country.

   (C) Japanese tourists are the biggest spenders among tourists to the U.S.

   (D) Canadians rank second to Japan in tourism spending in the U.S.

   (E) tourism is very important to the economy of the U.S.

32. A significant implication of the passage is

   (A) that Japan will have to reduce its tourist spending in the U.S.

   (B) that the U.S. should increase its tourist spending in Japan.

   (C) that tourist spending in the U.S. reduces its trade deficit.

   (D) that Canada needs to improve its tourism attractions.

   (E) that Japan has more money on which to spend on tourism than any other country.

33. Based on the passage, which of the following would be an appropriate topic of discussion with students?

    (A) International relations

    (B) Global relations

    (C) Balance in global tourism industry

    (D) Interdependency of nations

    (E) Global competition

Questions 34 and 35 refer to the following passage:

San Francisco was named the world's favorite travel destination in the prestigious 1991 *Conde Nast Traveler* magazine poll. It was considered the best city in the world that year, beating out Florence, Italy (No. 2), and London and Vienna which tied for No. 3. A red-carpet gala in the City Hall rotunda is planned in which Mayor Agnos will laud the city's 60,000 tourism industry workers including hotel maids, taxi drivers, bellhops, and others in the local hospitality industry.

34. An appropriate title for the passage is

    (A) San Francisco: World's Favorite Travel Destination.

    (B) A Gala for San Francisco's Tourism Workers.

    (C) San Francisco: Top in Ranking.

    (D) Best City in the World.

    (E) Top City in 1991.

35. The prestigious citation for the city of San Francisco could mean in practical terms

    (A) increasing tourism attractions for city runner-ups in the poll.

    (B) more openings for tourism industry workers.

    (C) higher pay demands from hotel maids, bellhops, and other workers.

    (D) more tourists will come to the city.

    (E) more money coming to the city from its tourism industry.

Questions 36 to 38 refer to the following passage:

Results of a study released by the College Board and the Western Interstate Commission for Higher Education shows that by 1994, the majority of California's high school graduates will be non-white and that by 1995, one-third of all the nation's students will be from minority groups. It is also predicted that, nationally, the total non-white and Hispanic student population for all grade levels will increase from 10.4 million in 1985-1986 to 13.7 million in 1994-1995. The figures suggest that now, more than ever, equal educational opportunity for all students must be our nation's number one priority.

36. The foregoing passage suggests

    (A) that this nation is, educationally, at risk.

    (B) that something needs to be done to reduce the growing numbers of minority students in the school system.

    (C) that urgent educational reforms are needed to provide equal opportunity for all students.

    (D) that a Spanish bilingual system be endorsed.

    (E) that immigration laws be strictly enforced to balance the numbers of white and non-white student populations.

37. Because of changes in demographics, what preparation is needed in California in the area of teacher preparation?

    (A) Recruitment of more minority teachers

    (B) Increase budget appropriation for schools

    (C) Enforce school desegregation

    (D) Encourage non-Hispanic, white students to enroll in private schools

    (E) Revise teacher preparation programs to reflect appropriate preparation for multicultural classrooms

38. What problem could result from the increasing minority population in the nation?

    (A) Strong resentment from mainstream whites towards the school system

(B) Increase in enrollment in private and parochial schools

(C) "White flight" to the suburbs where minorities are not yet the majority

(D) School budget crisis

(E) Inappropriate and inadequate school curriculum and teacher preparation to meet the needs in multicultural classrooms

Questions 39 and 40 refer to the following passage:

The United States' final offer on a lease agreement for the Subic Bay Naval Base in the Philippines was rejected by the Philippine Senate. Hence, for the first time in nearly a century, U.S. military strategy for the Asia-Pacific region will no longer be centered on the Philippines, and the nation's economic survival and development will no longer rely on U.S. dependency. Somehow, this dependency on the U.S. has served as an impediment to the Philippines' ability to join East Asia's economic boom.

39. Which of the following best summarizes what the passage is about?

(A) Philippine-U.S. military relations have come to an end.

(B) The Philippines' economic dependency on the U.S. ended with its Senate's rejection of the U.S. lease offer.

(C) The U.S. lease offer for the Subic Bay Naval Base was rejected by the Philippine Senate, hence the U.S. will no longer have its military base in the Asia-Pacific region.

(D) The Philippines is now on its own in its economic survival and development.

(E) The U.S. military strategy for the Asia-Pacific region will no longer be on the Philippines following the Philippine Senate's rejection of the U.S. lease offer.

40. The U.S. military's pullout from Subic Bay would mean

(A) less jobs for Filipinos.

(B) less Americans in the Philippines.

(C) a chance for the Philippines to survive on its own.

(D) weakening of U.S.-Philippine relations.

(E) less protection for the Philippines.

Section II: Mathematics

(Answer sheets appear in the back of this book.)

TIME: 60 Minutes
40 Questions

DIRECTIONS: Each of the questions or incomplete statements below is followed by five suggested answers or completions. Select the one that is best in each case.

1. What is the least common denominator of $\frac{2}{15}, \frac{1}{21}$, and $\frac{4}{35}$?

(A) 105

(D) 735

(B) 35

(E) 175

(C) 415

2. On July 19, a Friday, Dick received a letter to have a class reunion exactly four years from that day. On what day of the week is his reunion?

(A) Monday

(D) Thursday

(B) Tuesday

(E) Friday

(C) Wednesday

3. John and Mary are working on a job together. If John does it alone, it will take him seven days, while Mary can do it alone in five days. How long will it take them to do it together?

(A) 12 days

(D) 3 and $\frac{1}{2}$ days

(B) 2 days

(E) 6 days

(C) 2 and $\frac{11}{12}$ days

4. How much water is needed to add to a half-pint of syrup with 60 percent sugar to obtain a drink with 5 percent sugar?

   (A) 3 pints

   (B) 2.5 pints

   (C) 4 pints

   (D) 5.5 pints

   (E) 7 pints

5. Which of the following is true about triangle *ABC*?

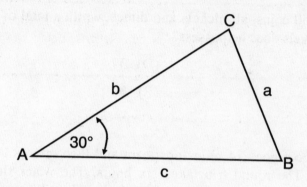

   (A) Sides *b* and *c* are equal in measurement. ✗

   (B) Angle *a* is the smallest angle. ✓

   (C) Side *a* is not the longest side. ✓

   (D) Angle *b* or *c* must be a right angle. ✗

   (E) Side *b* must be greater than side *a* in measurement. ✓

6. If the diameter of circle *A* is twice that of circle *B*, what is the ratio of the area of circle *A* to the area of circle *B*?

   (A) 2 to 1

   (B) 3 to 1

   (C) 4 to 1

   (D) π to 1

   (E) 8 to 1

7. A solid cube has a volume of 8. What is the volume of the cube whose sides are twice that of this cube?

   (A) 16

   (B) 28

   (C) 32

   (D) 36

   (E) 64

8. Jack flies from New York to Los Angeles. His plane leaves New York at 2:15 p.m. The flying time is 5 hours and 45 minutes. Since New York is three hours ahead of Los Angeles, what time does he arrive in Los Angeles?

   (A) 11:00 p.m.   (D) 5:00 p.m.

   (B) 8:00 p.m.   (E) 4:45 p.m.

   (C) 7:45 p.m.

9. Bob has 50 coins, all nickels and dimes, worth a total of $4.85. How many nickels does he possess?

   (A) 30   (D) 37

   (B) 15   (E) 3

   (C) 7

10. A steamboat goes 24 miles upstream and then returns to its original position. The round trip takes six hours. The water flows at three miles per hour. What is the speed of the boat in still water?

    (A) 10 miles/hour   (D) 7 miles/hour

    (B) 9 miles/hour   (E) 6 miles/hour

    (C) 8 miles/hour

11. If ten babies drink a total of ten gallons of milk in ten days, how many gallons of milk will 20 babies drink in 20 days?

    (A) 20   (D) 35

    (B) 25   (E) 40

    (C) 30

12. Jane has three kinds of coins, quarters, dimes, and nickels, totalling 24 in number and worth $3.00. How many coins of each kind does she have?

    (A) Jane has 12 nickels, 4 dimes, and 8 quarters.

    (B) Jane has 9 nickels, 8 dimes, and 7 quarters.

    (C) Jane has 6 nickels, 12 dimes, and 6 quarters.

    (D) Jane has 3 nickels, 16 dimes, and 5 quarters.

    (E) There is no unique answer; further information is needed.

13. A parallelogram *ABCD* has all its sides measure 4, one of the diagonals $\overline{AC}$ also measures 4. What is its area?

(A) Its area is 16.

(B) Its area is 32.

(C) Its area is $4\sqrt{3}$.

(D) Its area is $8\sqrt{3}$.

(E) Its area cannot be found; further information is needed.

14. Jack gave one-third of his money to his daughter and one-quarter of his money to his son. He then had $150,000 left. How much money did he have before he gave away some?

(A) $225,000

(B) $250,000

(C) $300,000

(D) $360,000

(E) $400,000

15. The fraction $\dfrac{1}{\left(\sqrt{3}-\sqrt{2}\right)}$ is equivalent to

(A) $\sqrt{3}+\sqrt{2}$.

(B) $\sqrt{3}-\sqrt{2}$.

(C) $\dfrac{1}{\left(\sqrt{3}+\sqrt{2}\right)}$.

(D) 1.

(E) None of the above.

16. If Don and Ron can paint a house in five days, and Ron can paint it alone in seven days, how long will it take Don to paint it alone?

(A) 2 days

(B) 7 days

(C) 17.5 days

(D) 9.75 days

(E) 11.25 days

17. If the volume of a cube is 8, how long is its main diagonal (the line segment joining the two farthest corners)?

(A) $2\sqrt{2}$

(B) $3\sqrt{2}$

(C) $2\sqrt{3}$

(D) $3\sqrt{3}$

(E) The length of the main diagonal cannot be found for lack of information.

18. Norman lives six blocks north and six blocks east of Bob. The town is made up of all square blocks. How many ways can Bob walk to Norman's house walking only 12 blocks?

(A) 2 ways

(D) 4,096 ways

(B) 924 ways

(E) Infinitely many ways

(C) 36 ways

19. If the area of a right isosceles triangle is 4, how long are its sides?

(A) $2\sqrt{2}, 2\sqrt{2}, 4$

(B) $2, 2, 2\sqrt{2}$

(C) $3, 3, 3\sqrt{2}$

(D) $3\sqrt{2}, 3\sqrt{2}, 6$

(E) The lengths of the triangle cannot be found for lack of information.

20. Donald gave Louie a number of marbles to share with Dewey and Huey. Making sure that he got his share, Louie took one-third of the marbles and hid them. Dewey, after hearing from Donald that he is entitled to one-third of the marbles as well, went and hid one-third of the remaining marbles. Not knowing what was going on, Daisy took two marbles from the pile. When Huey came, there were only 10 marbles left. How many marbles did Donald give to Louie in the beginning?

(A) 18

(B) 21

(C) 24

(D) 27

(E) That number cannot be found for lack of information.

21. A steamboat left Hong Kong on May 25, at 6 a.m., New York time. It sailed 400 hours and arrived in New York. When did it arrive?

   (A) 10 p.m., June 9

   (B) 10 p.m., June 10

   (C) 10 p.m., June 11

   (D) 4 p.m., June 10

   (E) 4 p.m., June 11

22. Joan is eight years older than Georgette. Joan was twice as old as Georgette eight years ago. How old are they now?

   (A) Joan is 30 and Georgette is 22.

   (B) Joan is 28 and Georgette is 20.

   (C) Joan is 26 and Georgette is 18.

   (D) Joan is 24 and Georgette is 16.

   (E) Further information is needed to figure their ages.

23. A river flows at a speed of five miles per hour. A steamboat went upstream for five hours and stopped at a point 20 miles from where it started. What is the speed of the steamboat in still waters?

   (A) 9 miles per hour

   (B) 12 miles per hour

   (C) 14 miles per hour

   (D) 18 miles per hour

   (E) The speed of the boat cannot be found for lack of information.

24. Sarah bought 10 pounds of apples and nuts. Apples are 89 cents a pound, and nuts are $1.29 a pound. She spent a total of $10.10. How many pounds of nuts did she buy?

   (A) 1

   (B) 2

   (C) 3

   (D) 4

   (E) 5

25. Jim and Joe were running together. Jim's average speed was 400 meters per minute. Jim started running four minutes before Joe. Ten minutes after Joe started, he caught up with Jim. What was Joe's average speed?

(A) 440 meters per minute

(D) 500 meters per minute

(B) 450 meters per minute

(E) 560 meters per minute

(C) 480 meters per minute

26. If 96 chickens and rabbits are put together, they have a total of 312 legs. How many chickens are there?

(A) 36

(D) 24

(B) 60

(E) 42

(C) 72

27. Harold decided to cut down his sugar consumption in coffee, tea, and other drinks. He had been consuming 120 grams of sugar a day. He was determined to cut down two grams per week until he no longer used sugar in his drinks. Starting from the first day that he began cutting down his sugar, how much sugar would he have consumed before he arrived at his goal?

(A) 92,160 grams

(D) 8,200 grams

(B) 10,900 grams

(E) 24,780 grams

(C) 72,000 grams

28. John and Kevin have a total of $97. John has $9 more than Kevin. How much money does Kevin have?

(A) $40

(D) $46

(B) $42

(E) $48

(C) $44

29. Three circles of equal radii with centers *A*, *B*, and *C* are lying on a straight line and tangent to each other as in the figure shown below. A tangent line to circle *C* is drawn from *A*, meeting circle *B* at *S* and *T*, and tangent to circle *C* at *D*. What is the ratio of the line segment $\overline{ST}$ to the radii?

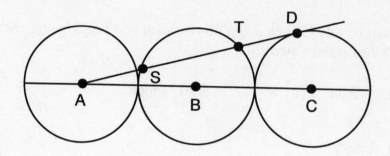

(A) $\dfrac{\sqrt{3}}{2}$ (D) 1

(B) $\dfrac{3}{2}$ (E) $\sqrt{2}$

(C) $\sqrt{3}$

30. If a number times itself is added to five times itself, the result is 24. What could this number possibly be?

(A) 3 or 8   (D) –3 or –8

(B) –3 or 8   (E) –4 or 6

(C) 3 or –8

31. Concerning the number π, which statement is the most accurate?

(A) π = 3.14.

(B) π = 3.1416.

(C) $\pi = \dfrac{22}{7}$

(D) π cannot be calculated.

(E) π is an irrational number.

32. What is the measurement of an angle of a regular pentagon?

(A) 72°

(D) 84°

(B) 108°

(E) 104°

(C) 100°

33. A boat travels 15 mph going downstream and 8 mph going upstream. How fast is the waterflow?

(A) $\frac{7}{2}$ mph

(D) 4 mph

(B) 3 mph

(E) $\frac{5}{2}$ mph

(C) $\frac{9}{2}$ mph

34. The longest side of a triangle measures 2 and the shortest side measures 1. What cannot be the measurement of the angle between them?

(A) 30°

(D) 20°

(B) 60°

(E) 90°

(C) 70°

35. Which of the following is closest to the graph of the equation $y = x^2$?

(A)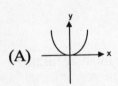

(D)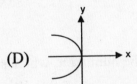

(B)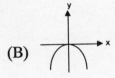

(E)

(C)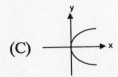

36. Roger took off at 8:00 a.m. driving 45 mph. Bill went after him two hours later and caught up with him at 4:00 p.m. How fast did Bill drive?

(A) 70 mph

(B) 65 mph

(C) 60 mph

(D) 55 mph

(E) 50 mph

37. The expression $\dfrac{x+1}{x-1} - \dfrac{x-1}{x+1}$ simplifies to

(A) −1.

(B) 1.

(C) $\dfrac{2x}{x^2-1}$.

(D) $\dfrac{4x}{x^2-1}$.

(E) $\dfrac{x}{x^2-1}$.

38. If an equilateral triangle has an area of $\sqrt{3}$, what are the lengths of its sides?

(A) 1

(B) $\dfrac{3}{2}$

(C) 2

(D) $\dfrac{5}{2}$

(E) 3

39. Jane went shopping. On her first trip, she bought six pairs of shoes, all at the same price, and three pairs of socks, also at the same price (shoes and socks are not necessarily of the same price), and she spent $96. On her second trip, she went to the same shop and bought four more pairs of the same socks and returned a pair of shoes; she spent $2. How much does a pair of her shoes cost?

(A) $10

(B) $12

(C) $14

(D) $16

(E) $18

40. Triangle *ABC* is inscribed in a circle with center *O* at the midpoint of the side *BC*. If angle *B* measures 47°, what is the measurement of angle *C*?

(A) 43°

(B) 47°

(C) 53°

(D) 37°

(E) Insufficient information

Section III: Writing

(Answer sheets appear in the back of this book.)

TIME: 30 Minutes
45 Questions

Part A: Usage

DIRECTIONS: Each of the following sentences may contain an error in diction, usage, idiom, or grammar. Some sentences are correct. Some sentences contain one error. No sentence contains more than one error.

If there is an error, it will appear in one of the underlined portions labeled A, B, C, or D. If there is no error, choose the portion labeled E. If there is an error, select the letter of the portion that must be changed in order to correct the sentence.

EXAMPLE:

He drove <u>slowly</u> and <u>cautiously</u> in order to <u>hopefully</u> avoid having an
　　　　　　A　　　　　　B　　　　　　　　　　C
<u>accident</u>. <u>No error</u>.
　D　　　　E

1.　<u>Which</u> suspension bridge <u>is</u> the <u>longest</u>, the Verrazano-Narrows
　　　A　　　　　　　　　　　B　　　　C
Bridge in New York City <u>or</u> the Golden Gate Bridge in San Fran-
　　　　　　　　　　　　　　D
cisco? <u>No error</u>.
　　　　　E

2.　A main function <u>of proteins</u>, whether <u>they come</u> from <u>plant or animal</u>
　　　　　　　　　A　　　　　　　　B　　　　　　C
<u>sources, is</u> the building of body tissue. <u>No error</u>.
　D　　　　　　　　　　　　　　　　E

3. <u>Recognizing</u> that we <u>had worked</u> very hard to complete our project,
    A   B

the teacher told Janice and <u>I</u> that we could give it to her <u>tomorrow</u>.
                     C   D

<u>No error</u>.
E

4. <u>According to</u> the United States Constitution, the legislative branch of
    A

the government <u>has</u> powers <u>different than</u> <u>those</u> of the executive
             B   C   D

branch. <u>No error</u>.
        E

5. After <u>being studied</u> for the <u>preceding ten years</u> by the National Heart,
        A   B

Lung, and Blood Institute, the relationship of high levels of

cholesterol in the blood to the possibility of <u>having</u> heart attacks
                                                C

<u>was reported</u> in 1984. <u>No error</u>.
   D   E

6. The book *Cheaper By the Dozen* <u>demonstrates</u> that each of the chil-
                                    A

dren of Frank and Lillian Gilbreth <u>was expected</u> <u>to use</u> <u>his or her</u> time
                                     B   C   D

efficiently. <u>No error</u>.
          E

7. His aversion <u>with</u> snakes made camping an unpleasant activity
            A

<u>for him</u> and <u>one</u> <u>that</u> he tried diligently to avoid. <u>No error</u>.
  B   C D   E

8. The story of the American pioneers, <u>those</u> who willingly left the
                                 A

safety of <u>their</u> homes to move into unsettled territory, <u>show</u> <u>us</u> great
        B   C D

courage in the face of danger. <u>No error</u>.
                           E

9. <u>Because of</u> the long, cold winters <u>and</u> short summers, farming in high
      A   B

    latitudes is <u>more difficult</u> <u>than low latitudes</u>. <u>No error</u>.
                    C   D   E

10. When my sister and <u>I</u> <u>were</u> in Los Angeles, <u>we</u> hoped that both of us
                          A B   C

    could be <u>a contestant</u> on a quiz show. <u>No error</u>.
               D   E

11. After he <u>had broke</u> the vase <u>that</u> his mother <u>had purchased</u> in Europe,
                A   B   C

    he tried to buy a new one for his father and <u>her</u>. <u>No error</u>.
                                            D   E

12. Some of the people <u>with whom</u> the witness <u>worked</u> <u>were engaged</u> in
                        A   B   C

    covert activities <u>on behalf of</u> the United States government. <u>No error</u>.
                     D   E

13. <u>Because of</u> their cold personalities and hot tempers, <u>neither</u> John
       A   B

    Adams <u>nor</u> his son John Quincy Adams <u>were</u> especially successful in
           C   D

    politics. <u>No error</u>.
            E

14. <u>Among</u> the reasons <u>for United States participation</u> in World War II
      A   B

    <u>were</u> the Japanese attack on the <u>naval base</u> at Pearl Harbor on De-
    C   D

    cember 7, 1941. <u>No error</u>.
                    E

15. Some parents make a <u>greater</u> attempt to frighten <u>their</u> children about
                       A   B

    the dangers of driving <u>than</u> <u>teaching</u> them safe driving habits.
                           C   D

    <u>No error</u>.
     E

16. The high standard <u>of living</u> in Sweden <u>is shown</u> by <u>their</u> statistics
                      A   **B**   **C**

    <u>of life expectancy</u> and per capita income. <u>No error</u>.
      D   **E**

17. The snow leopard <u>is</u> a wild mammal in Central Asia <u>that has</u> large
                A   **B**

    eyes, a four-foot body, <u>and</u> <u>white and bluish gray in color</u>. <u>No error</u>.
                      C   **D**   **E**

18. Selecting a lifetime vocation, <u>a young person</u> may have to choose
                                A

    either a vocation that he enjoys <u>and</u> a vocation that will make <u>him</u>
                              B   **C**

    rich; that choice is perhaps the <u>most important</u> one he will ever make.
                               D

    <u>No error</u>.
    E

19. Failing a test because the student <u>is</u> nervous <u>is</u> understandable; <u>to fail</u>
                               A   **B**   **C**

    because <u>he or she</u> did not study is quite another matter. <u>No error</u>.
           D   **E**

20. Although she <u>had grown up</u> in the North and <u>had been</u> neither a slave
                  A   **B**

    <u>or</u> a slave owner, Harriet Beecher Stowe <u>vividly</u> portrayed life on a
    C   **D**

    slave-holding plantation in her famous book. <u>No error</u>.
                                    E

21. The reason Jason failed <u>his</u> speech was <u>because</u> he suffered <u>such</u>
                        A   **B**   **C**

    <u>stage fright</u> <u>that he refused</u> to give his final speech. <u>No error</u>.
                D   **E**

22. <u>After completing the typing course</u>, he made <u>less</u> errors and typed
                A   **B**

    <u>more rapidly</u> than <u>anyone else</u> in his office. <u>No error</u>.
    C   **D**   **E**

23. Learning the basic <u>components of good nutrition</u> is <u>important for</u> the
                              A   B
    young adult <u>who want</u> <u>to gain independence</u> by living in his or her
                    C   D
    own apartment. <u>No error</u>.
                        E

24. Because condominiums offer the advantages of property ownership

    <u>along with</u> <u>those</u> of apartment rental, <u>this</u> <u>has made</u> condominiums
        A   B   C   D
    popular since the 1970s. <u>No error</u>.
                                  E

25. Students <u>who</u> eat every day in the college cafeteria <u>generally</u> tire of
                 A   B
    the <u>frequent</u> repetitious menu <u>that is provided</u>. <u>No error</u>.
            C   D   E

Part B: Sentence Correction

DIRECTIONS: In each of the following sentences, some portion of the sentence is underlined. Under each sentence are five choices. The first choice has the same wording as the original. The other four choices are reworded. Sometimes the first choice containing the original wording is the best; sometimes one of the other choices is the best. Choose the letter of the best choice. Your choice should produce a sentence which is not ambiguous or awkward and which is correct, clear, and precise.

This is a test of correct and effective English expression. Keep in mind the standards of English usage, punctuation, grammar, word choice, and construction.

EXAMPLE:

When you listen to opera, <u>a person may not appreciate it.</u>

(A)   a person may not appreciate it.

(B)   it may not be appreciated by a person.

(C)   which may not be appreciated by one.

(D)   you may not appreciate it.

(E)   appreciating it may be a problem for you.

26. Wealthy citizens often protest <u>about the building of</u> low-cost housing in the affluent communities where they reside.

   (A) about the building of

   (B) whether they should build

   (C) if builders should build

   (D) the building of

   (E) whether or not they should build

27. Siblings growing up in a family do not necessarily have equal opportunities to achieve, <u>the difference being their placement in the family, their innate abilities, and their personalities.</u>

   (A) the difference being their placement in the family, their innate abilities, and their personalities.

(B) because of their placement in the family, their innate abilities, and their personalities.

(C) and the difference is their placement in the family, their innate abilities, and their personalities.

(D) they have different placements in the family, different innate abilities, and different personalities.

(E) their placement in the family, their innate abilities, and their personalities being different.

28. Two major provisions of the United States Bill of Rights <u>is freedom of speech and that citizens are guaranteed a trial by jury</u>.

(A) is freedom of speech and that citizens are guaranteed a trial by jury.

(B) is that citizens have freedom of speech and a guaranteed trial by jury.

(C) is freedom of speech and the guarantee of a trial by jury.

(D) are freedom of speech and that citizens are guaranteed a trial by jury.

(E) are freedom of speech and the guarantee of a trial by jury.

29. Poets of the nineteenth century tried <u>to entertain their readers but also with the attempt of teaching them</u> lessons about life.

(A) to entertain their readers but also with the attempt of teaching them

(B) to entertain their readers but also to attempt to teach them

(C) to both entertain their readers and to teach them

(D) entertainment of their readers and the attempt to teach them

(E) both to entertain and to teach their readers

30. The city council decided to remove parking meters <u>so as to encourage</u> people to shop in Centerville.

(A) so as to encourage

(B) to encourage

(C) thus encouraging

(D) with the desire

(E) thereby encouraging

31. Visiting New York City for the first time, <u>the sites most interesting to Megan were</u> the Statue of Liberty, the Empire State Building, and the Brooklyn Bridge.

(A) the sites most interesting to Megan were

(B) the sites that Megan found most interesting were

(C) Megan found that the sites most interesting to her were

(D) Megan was most interested in

(E) Megan was most interested in the sites of

32. Although most college professors have expertise in their areas of specialty, <u>some are more interested in continuing their research than in teaching undergraduate students.</u>

(A) some are more interested in continuing their research than in teaching undergraduate students.

(B) some are most interested in continuing their research rather than in teaching undergraduate students.

(C) some prefer continuing their research rather than to teach undergraduate students.

(D) continuing their research, not teaching undergraduate students, is more interesting to some.

(E) some are more interested in continuing their research than to teach undergraduate students.

33. <u>Whether adult adoptees should be allowed to see their original birth certificates or not</u> is controversial, but many adoptive parents feel strongly that records should remain closed.

(A) Whether adult adoptees should be allowed to see their original birth certificates or not

(B) Whether or not adult adoptees should be allowed to see their original birth certificates or not

(C) The fact of whether adult adoptees should be allowed to see their original birth certificates

(D) Allowing the seeing of their original birth certificates by adult adoptees

(E) That adult adoptees should be allowed to see their original birth certificates

34. Having studied theology, music, along with medicine, Albert Schweitzer became a medical missionary in Africa.

(A) Having studied theology, music, along with medicine

(B) Having studied theology, music, as well as medicine

(C) Having studied theology and music, and, also, medicine

(D) With a study of theology, music, and medicine

(E) After he had studied theology, music, and medicine

35. When the Mississippi River threatens to flood, sandbags are piled along its banks, and they do this to keep its waters from overflowing.

(A) and they do this to keep its waters from overflowing.

(B) to keep its waters from overflowing.

(C) and then its waters won't overflow.

(D) and, therefore, keeping its waters from overflowing.

(E) and they keep its waters from overflowing.

36. Because of the popularity of his light verse, Edward Lear is seldom recognized today for his travel books and detailed illustrations of birds.

(A) Because of the popularity of his light verse

(B) Owing to the fact that his light verse was popular

(C) Because of his light verse, that was very popular

(D) Having written light verse that was popular

(E) Being the author of popular light verse

37. Lincoln's Gettysburg Address, <u>despite its having been very short and delivered after a two-hour oration by Edward Everett,</u> is one of the greatest speeches ever delivered.

    (A) despite its having been very short and delivered after a two-hour oration by Edward Everett

    (B) which was very short and delivered after a two-hour oration by Edward Everett

    (C) although it was very short and delivered after a two-hour oration by Edward Everett

    (D) despite the fact that it was very short and delivered after a two-hour oration by Edward Everett

    (E) was very short and delivered after a two-hour oration by Edward Everett

38. China, <u>which ranks third in area and first in population among the world's countries,</u> also has one of the longest histories.

    (A) which ranks third in area and first in population among the world's countries

    (B) which ranks third in area and has the largest population among the world's countries

    (C) which is the third largest in area and ranks first in population among the world's countries

    (D) in area ranking third and in population ranking first among the world's countries

    (E) third in area and first in the number of people among the world's countries

39. <u>Leonardo Da Vinci was a man who</u> was a scientist, an architect, an engineer, and a sculptor.

    (A) Leonardo Da Vinci was a man who

    (B) The man Leonardo Da Vinci

    (C) Being a man, Leonardo Da Vinci

    (D) Leonardo Da Vinci

    (E) Leonardo Da Vinci, a man who

40. <u>The age of 35 having been reached</u>, a natural-born United States citizen is eligible to be elected President of the United States.

    (A) The age of 35 having been reached

    (B) The age of 35 being reached

    (C) At 35, when that age is reached

    (D) When having reached the age of 35

    (E) When he or she is 35 years old

41. <u>It was my roommate who caught the thief stealing my wallet, which is the reason</u> I gave him a reward.

    (A) It was my roommate who caught the thief stealing my wallet, which is the reason

    (B) My roommate caught the thief stealing my wallet, which is the reason

    (C) Because my roommate caught the thief stealing my wallet,

    (D) That my roommate caught the thief stealing my wallet is the reason why

    (E) My roommate having caught the thief stealing my wallet,

42. <u>The fewer mistakes one makes in life</u>, the fewer opportunities you have to learn from your mistakes.

    (A) The fewer mistakes one makes in life

    (B) The fewer mistakes you make in life

    (C) The fewer mistakes he or she makes in life

    (D) The fewer mistakes there are in one's life

    (E) The fewer mistakes in life

43. Although the word "millipede" means one thousand feet, millipedes have no more than 115 pairs of legs <u>that are attached to the segments of their bodies.</u>

    (A) that are attached to the segments of their bodies.

    (B) each of which are attached to a segment of their bodies.

    (C) attaching themselves to segments of their bodies.

(D) whose attachment is to the segments of their bodies.

(E) the attachment of which is to the segments of their bodies.

44. Father Junipero Sera, who was a Franciscan missionary sent from Spain to Mexico, <u>where he taught and worked among the Indians</u> and then founded many missions in California that later became cities.

(A) where he taught and worked among the Indians

(B) there he taught and worked among the Indians

(C) he taught and worked among the Indians

(D) taught and worked among the Indians

(E) teaching and working among the Indians

45. He went to the meeting eager to explain his point of view <u>but with some fear of public speaking</u>.

(A) but with some fear of public speaking.

(B) but afraid to speak in public.

(C) but having fear that he would have to speak in public.

(D) fearing public speaking.

(E) but fearing public speaking.

Part C: Essay

TIME: 30 Minutes

DIRECTIONS: You have 30 minutes to plan and write an essay on the topic below. You may write only on the assigned topic.

Make sure to give specific examples to support your thesis. Proofread your essay carefully and take care to express your ideas clearly and effectively.

ESSAY TOPIC:

"There is a wonderful, mystical law of nature that the three things we crave most in life—happiness, freedom, and peace of mind—are always attained by giving them to someone else."

ASSIGNMENT: Do you agree or disagree with the statement? Support your opinion with specific examples from history, current events, literature, or personal experience.

PPST TEST III

ANSWER KEY

Section I — Reading Comprehension

1.	(D)	11.	(C)	21.	(E)	31.	(A)
2.	(E)	12.	(B)	22.	(C)	32.	(C)
3.	(B)	13.	(D)	23.	(B)	33.	(C)
4.	(A)	14.	(B)	24.	(E)	34.	(A)
5.	(B)	15.	(E)	25.	(E)	35.	(E)
6.	(C)	16.	(C)	26.	(D)	36.	(C)
7.	(C)	17.	(B)	27.	(B)	37.	(E)
8.	(B)	18.	(A)	28.	(A)	38.	(E)
9.	(D)	19.	(B)	29.	(D)	39.	(E)
10.	(D)	20.	(A)	30.	(E)	40.	(C)

Section II — Mathematics

1.	(A)	11.	(E)	21.	(B)	31.	(E)
2.	(C)	12.	(E)	22.	(D)	32.	(B)
3.	(C)	13.	(D)	23.	(A)	33.	(A)
4.	(D)	14.	(D)	24.	(C)	34.	(E)
5.	(C)	15.	(A)	25.	(E)	35.	(A)
6.	(C)	16.	(C)	26.	(A)	36.	(C)
7.	(E)	17.	(C)	27.	(E)	37.	(D)
8.	(D)	18.	(B)	28.	(C)	38.	(C)
9.	(E)	19.	(A)	29.	(C)	39.	(C)
10.	(B)	20.	(D)	30.	(C)	40.	(A)

Section III — Writing

1.	(C)	13.	(D)	25.	(C)	37.	(C)
2.	(E)	14.	(C)	26.	(D)	38.	(A)
3.	(C)	15.	(D)	27.	(B)	39.	(D)
4.	(C)	16.	(C)	28.	(E)	40.	(E)
5.	(A)	17.	(D)	29.	(E)	41.	(C)
6.	(E)	18.	(B)	30.	(B)	42.	(B)
7.	(A)	19.	(C)	31.	(D)	43.	(A)
8.	(C)	20.	(C)	32.	(A)	44.	(D)
9.	(D)	21.	(B)	33.	(E)	45.	(B)
10.	(D)	22.	(B)	34.	(E)		
11.	(A)	23.	(C)	35.	(B)		
12.	(E)	24.	(C)	36.	(A)		

DETAILED EXPLANATIONS OF ANSWERS

Section I: Reading Comprehension

1. **(D)** The question asks for the best synthesis of the passage and (D) is the best and most complete answer. Choices (A), (B), (C), and (E) are not as complete. For example, (A) left out the duration of the conference, (B) left out the number of the nations represented at the summit, (C) left out both the duration of the conference and the number of the nations represented at the summit, and (E) left out the number of nations represented and support for Gorbachev's "new thinking."

2. **(E)** Of the choices provided, (E) gives the most logical and sound implication of the passage. (A) falls short of the capabilities of Gorbachev's leadership; in (B) the "new thinking" referred to already has the support of the seven leaders at the summit; (C) is a rather sweeping, unfair statement; and (D) left out support for economic and political reforms.

3. **(B)** The mention of banking and energy did not rule out technical assistance in other fields, hence, (B) is the correct answer. Choice (A) limited the assistance to only the fields of banking and energy; in (C) the statement is only partly true—the U.S. is not alone in providing support; in (D) the statement implies that there is no consensus among the seven nations; and in (E) technical assistance can likewise come from other nations outside of the seven.

4. **(A)** The question asks for the main idea in the passage and (A) gives the best and complete main idea. Choices (B), (C), and (D) are generalizations derived from the passage and (E), while it is true and specific to the passage, is stated in the negative.

5. **(B)** (B) gives the most specific consequence for California. The other choices, while all plausible or possible answers, do not get to the "root" of the issue specific to California.

6. **(C)** Based on the passage read, the answer to this question is (C)—two things are mentioned that could affect California and these are federal funding and the number of congressional seats. While (A) and (B) are correct, they are incomplete. Choices (D) and (E) are consequential generalizations which are both correct but lack the preciseness of (C).

7. **(C)** The question asks for the "message" conveyed in the passage. Choice (C) is the correct answer, as it gives a warning. In choice (A), pesticides cannot necessarily be dangerous to all living things—some are good for the protection of plants, for example; in (B), water can be contaminated by something other than pesticides; the statement in choice (D) may be true, but it is certainly not the best answer.

8. **(B)** The train is definitely a cargo train, hence, (B) is the correct answer. In (A), if it were a passenger train, hundreds would have been killed; in (C) and (D), according to the clues, the choices here don't apply; and in (E) the answer used "special train" but could have appropriately used "cargo train" instead.

9. **(D)** The question here asks for the most "serious problem" that can come about; so, of all the choices, (D) provides the most serious problem resulting from the pesticide spill for Californians. Choices (A), (B), (C), and (E) are not life-threatening as is (D)

10. **(D)** (D) is the most logical and straightforward answer. (D) prioritizes which action should be first taken, and is therefore the correct answer. While the choices in (A), (B), (C), and (E) are sound answers, they don't list the most urgent thing to do.

11. **(C)** The correct answer here is (C) because this choice synthesizes the key or main idea in the passage. The other choices, while partly true, don't give the main idea.

12. **(B)** Before World War II, which were the depression years, one can easily presume that people were more practical or money minded, hence, Labor Day as celebrated then could mean the loss of a day's pay for working people. Hence, (B) is the correct answer. While choices (A), (C), (D), and (E) are also possible answers they don't get to the "root" of the issue.

13. **(D)**   Explicitly given in the passage is (D), the correct answer. Choices (A), (B), (C), and (E), while they may all be true and correct, are not what is precisely given in the passage.

14. **(B)**   The question asks for implication. The most straight forward implication of the choices provided has got to be (B). Choice (A) is too general and is actually given in the passage. Choice (C) is an eventual consequence of the proposed program and the same can be said of (D) and (E).

15. **(E)**   The gold content found in the volcanic ash from Mt. Pinatubo could easily stir or trigger a "gold rush." However, people are warned that the gold content found is not at a "commercial level." Hence, (E) is the correct answer. The other choices provided are all mere speculations.

16. **(C)**   Choice (C) is the most appropriate answer—it also synthesizes the content of the reading passage; hence, it is the correct answer. Choices (A) and (B) are both incorrect. Choices (D) and (E) are somewhat applicable as titles but do not really synthesize the main idea of the passage as choice (C).

17. **(B)**   If priorities will have to be established, to determine the most immediate research needed on the ash content from Mt. Pinatubo, choice (B) will have to be the most logical choice because there is already some data with which to work. Other research possibilities such as those in choice (A), (C), (D), and (E) will have to come later.

18. **(A)**   The best and correct answer here is (A)—it's the main idea of the passage. Choice (B) is incorrect. Choice (C) is partially correct—if it has to be specific, it should refer to the brake lights on the helmet. Choice (D) is incomplete as a key or main idea of the passage and the same could be said of choice (E).

19. **(B)**   It would follow that the rationale behind the new brake light requirement for cars in California is the same for all other vehicles on the road. Hence, choice (B) is the correct answer. The implication provided in (A) is not necessarily true; (C) is illogical; in (D) any car driven in California, wherever its been bought, cannot be exempted from the requirement; and in (E) Harris can go on inventing while remaining a farmer—he'll make more money doing both.

20. **(A)** Choice (A) is the most logical and appropriate answer, hence, it is the correct answer. Choice (B) can be, but is not necessarily true; (C) is a logical possibility but will not drastically raise car prices beyond affordability; (D) may be true, but not as road hazards; and (E), the contrary may also be true.

21. **(E)** All the choices in this question are possible answer; however, since the question asks for what lead poisoning, if not detected early "can lead to," it calls for the ultimate consequence. Hence, (E) is the correct answer inasmuch as the passage states "life-threatening disorders" as among the possible consequences.

22. **(C)** The correct answer to this question is choice (C)—it gives the complete and precise category. Other choices are incomplete—(A) left out the age group and the medical eligibility; (B) is narrowed down and all inclusive of "children with learning disabilities" and choices (D) and (E) are incorrect.

23. **(B)** As indicated by figures in the passage, the correct answer is (B). Other choices (A), (C), (D), and (E) are obviously incorrect. This is an example of a question in which the incorrect choices are not possible answers. The correct answer is derived from the figures provided in the passage.

24. **(E)** The implications provided in choices (A) through (E) are correct. However, each of the implications for (A) through (D) are narrowed down to only one specific category of children—not any one is inclusive of all that needs to be addressed. Hence, (E) is the best and appropriate answer because it addresses the thousands who will not be screened which include those in choices to (A) through (D).

25. **(E)** If schools exist to serve the best interest of students, then the correct answer for this question is (E). Choices (A) through (D) are also correct; however, the group that will be most affected by the financial crisis in California would have to be the "students." The fact remains that schools exist to serve the best interest of students.

26. **(D)** A title is supposed to synthesize the main idea and (D) does. Choice (A) left out the main idea of a commemorative stamp; choice (B) is incorrect because it implies Columbus discovered the Americas; choice

(C) is not the main idea of the passage; and choice (E), while it may be implied in the passage, does not synthesize its focus.

27. **(B)** The underlying fact behind the passage is explicitly implied; therefore, (B) is the correct answer. Choice (A), while true, is a generalized implication, not addressing the specific issue; choice (C) is debatable and so is choice (D); choice (E) like (A) is also a generalized implication.

28. **(A)** Of the choices given (A) is the most historically significant, and, therefore, the correct answer. Choice (B) is significant but left out the fact that Columbus was not the first to arrive in the New World, the main point in the passage; choice (C) is a mere commemoration day; choice (D) remains a debatable assumption; and choice (E) is not specific enough as an historically significant fact.

29. **(D)** Since zoology is the study of animals (D) is the correct and appropriate answer. The other choices which are other subject areas, as in (A), (B), (C), and (E), while they may be used by the classroom teacher, they are not quite the most appropriate subject areas.

30. **(E)** A study of a 150 million-year-old fossil will require digging up into history; hence, (E) is the correct answer. Choice (A) could be used if there is a problem focus in the passage; choices (B), (C), and (D) are poor and incorrect choices. Survey applies to a descriptive study; deductive is an approach that proceeds from a generalization or theory, and comparative requires two things to compare which is not addressed in the passage.

31. **(A)** (A) clearly synthesizes the main idea in the passage; hence, it is the correct answer. Choice (B) is more of an implication, hence, the wrong answer; choice (C) is merely stating a fact which does not speak of the main idea; the same can be said of choice (D); and choice (E), while it may be true, is not really the passage's main idea.

32. **(C)** The most sound and significant implication of the passage is stated in (C); hence, this is the correct answer. Choices (A) and (B) are not sound, they reflect a rather immature reasoning; choice (D) merely states some degree of competitiveness which is not the issue's focus; and (E) is a "so what" kind of statement and not a sound implication.

33. **(C)** The passage is really on global tourism providing comparisons and implying some inter-nation balance in tourism trade; hence, (C) is the

appropriate and correct answer. Choices (A), (B), (D), and (E) are stated in general terms, missing out on the specific focus or topic of the passage, hence, not the logical and immediate topics to discuss.

34. **(A)** The most appropriate and complete title is expressed in (A); hence this is the correct answer. Choice (B) merely states a planned activity and does not address the main idea; choice (C) is incomplete—it does not specify basis for ranking; the same can be said for choices (D) and (E), likewise, incomplete titles.

35. **(E)** The best answer in considering "practical terms" will have to be (E) which is the correct answer. Choice (A) is an implication that does not apply to San Francisco; choice (C) is a possible consequence but an undesirable one; and choice (D) is a true implication but the "practicality" is merely implied. (E) says this explicitly.

36. **(C)** The suggestion in (C) is the most sound and logical if equal opportunity for all students is to be our nation's priority; hence, this is the correct answer. Choice (A) is a mere statement of concern and does not provide a plan for action; choice (B) is illogical—you cannot cut down the number of minority students who are already in the system; choice (D) disregards other languages existing in the school system and in the community at large; and (E) is only secondary to the major issue.

37. **(E)** Since the passage points out the fact that there will soon be more minority students in the classroom, priority should be in providing the appropriate teacher preparation; hence, the correct answer is (E). Choice (A) is a need but secondary to those who are already in the system; choice (B) has always been an issue even before the rapid changes in the demographics; choice (C) is something that has triggered legislations since the 1950s—the natural composition of the classroom today is already desegregated. While the other choices are a need, the one that needs immediate action is (E).

38. **(E)** The answer to this question has to tie in with the foregoing answer; hence, the correct choice should be (E). Choices (A), (B), (C), and (D), while also problems arising from the changes in demographics, are secondary to (E).

39. **(E)** The most complete summary of the passage is stated in (E); hence, this is the correct answer. Choice (A) is not true, therefore, is

incorrect; choice (B) is rather put in general terms—the U.S. pullout is not the only issue related to the Philippine economy. The interdependence of nations will remain no matter what, i.e., trade relations will continue; choice (C) is incorrect. The U.S. military strategy will have to be relocated elsewhere in the Asia-Pacific region, the same can be said for choice (D)—the Philippines will not be completely on its own—it continues to maintain its trade relations with the U.S. and other trading partners.

40. **(C)**   The passage is quite explicit in stating that the U.S. presence on the Philippines has been an impediment to the nation's capability in joining East Asia's "economic boom"; hence, the correct answer is (C). Choices (A), (B), (D), and (E) are all possible consequences but are all quite debatable.

Section II: Mathematics

1. **(A)** The least common denominator of the fractions is the least common multiple of their denominators: 15, 21, and 35. Since

$$15 = 3 \times 5,$$

$$21 = 3 \times 7,$$

and $\quad 35 = 5 \times 7,$

we see that their least common multiple is $3 \times 5 \times 7 = 105$.

2. **(C)** Since his reunion will be $365 \times 4 + 1 = 1,461$ days from a Friday, dividing 1,461 by 7 yields a remainder of 5. Therefore, his reunion is 5 days from a Friday, which makes it on a Wednesday.

3. **(C)** In one day, John can do $^1/_7$ of the work, and Mary can do $^1/_5$; together, they can do

$$\frac{1}{5} + \frac{1}{7} = \frac{12}{35}$$

of the job. To finish the whole job, it takes

$$\frac{35}{12} = 2 \text{ and } \frac{11}{12} \text{ days.}$$

4. **(D)** Since the sugar content is 60 percent of $^1/_2$ pint and will not be changed after the water is added, we obtain an equation by equating the sugar content before and after adding in x pints of water. The equation is then

$$\left(\frac{1}{2}\right) \times 60\% = \left(\frac{1}{2} + x\right) \times 5\%$$

or $\qquad 30 = \dfrac{5}{2} + 5x$

$$60 = 5 + 10x$$

$$55 = 10x$$

$$5.5 = x$$

5.   **(C)**   Since the only information we have concerning the triangle is that angle A measures $30°$, we know that in a triangle, the largest angle faces the longest side, the sum of the three angles of a triangle is $180°$, and a $30°$ angle is not the largest angle. Therefore, a is not the longest side.

6.   **(C)**   The diameter of circle A is twice that of circle B, so if the radius of B is r, then the radius of A is $2r$. Since the area of a circle with radius r is πr^2, the area of B is πr^2; while the area of A is

$$\pi(2r)^2 = 4\pi r^2,$$

therefore the ratio is 4:1.

7.   **(E)**   Since the cube has a volume of 8, its sides have length 2. The cube whose sides are twice that would be of length 4, so the volume of the other cube is

$$4 \times 4 \times 4 = 64.$$

8.   **(D)** $2:15 + 5:45 = 8:00$ means he arrives in Los Angeles at 8 p.m. New York time. But New York is 3 hours ahead of Los Angeles, so the Los Angeles time of arrival is 5 p.m.

9.   **(E)**   We set up two equations. Let n be the number of nickels, and let d be the number of dimes. We have

$$n + d = 50.$$

Since each nickel is worth 5 cents and each dime is worth 10 cents, we have

$$5n + 10d = 485.$$

Multiplying the first equation by 10, we obtain

$$10n + 10d = 500.$$

Subtracting the second equation from it, we obtain $5n = 15$, or $n = 3$.

10. **(B)**   Let s be the speed of the boat in still water. Then the speed of the boat upstream is $(s - 3)$ miles per hour, and the speed of the boat downstream is $(s + 3)$ miles per hour. Therefore, the time going upstream,

$$\frac{24}{s - 3}$$

hours plus the time going downstream,

$$\frac{24}{s+3}$$

hours, equals 6 hours. Solving for s gives $s = 9$ miles/hour.

$$\frac{24}{s-3} + \frac{24}{s+3} = 6$$

$$\frac{(s+3)}{(s+3)(s-3)} + \frac{(s+3)}{(s-3)(s+3)} = \frac{6}{24} = \frac{1}{4}$$

$$\frac{2s}{(s+3)(s-3)} = \frac{1}{4}$$

$$8s = (s+3)(s-3)$$

$$= s^2 - 9$$

$$s^2 - 8s - 9 = 0;$$

$$(s-9)(s+1) = 0;$$

$$s = 9 \text{ or } -1,$$

but we require $s > 0$. Thus $s = 9$ miles per hour.

11. **(E)**   Since 10 babies drink 10 gallons of milk in 10 days, each baby drinks; $^1/_{10}$ gallon of milk per day. Each baby drinks 2 gallons of milk in 20 days, so 20 babies will drink $2 \times 20 = 40$ gallons of milk in 20 days.

12. **(E)**   Let x be the number of nickels, y be the number of dimes, and z be the number of quarters. We have two equations:

$$x + y + z = 24$$

and $5x + 10y + 25z = 300$

and three unknowns. Therefore, no unique answer can be found without one more equation.

13. **(D)**   Draw both diagonals to divide the parallelogram into four equal parts. Each part is a right triangle with hypotenuse measuring 4 and one side measuring 2. Therefore, the other side must measure $2\sqrt{3}$ by the Pythagorean Theorem. The area of this triangle is

$$\left(\frac{1}{2}\right) \times (2 \times 2\sqrt{3}) = 2\sqrt{3},$$

and the area of the parallelogram is four times that, which is $8\sqrt{3}$.

14. **(D)** Let the amount of money he had before be x. We have

$$x - \left(\frac{1}{3}\right)x - \left(\frac{1}{4}\right)x = 150,000.$$

Or, $\left(\frac{5}{12}\right)x = 150,000$.

Therefore, $x = 360,000$.

15. **(A)** If we multiply both the numerator and denominator by the conjugate of the expression $\sqrt{3} - \sqrt{2}$, namely, $\sqrt{3} + \sqrt{2}$, the numerator becomes $\sqrt{3} + \sqrt{2}$, and the denominator becomes $3 - 2 = 1$.

16. **(C)** Since Don and Ron can paint the house in 7 days, they finish $\frac{1}{5}$ of the job in a day. Now Ron's contribution in a day is $\frac{1}{7}$ of the job, so

$$\frac{1}{5} - \frac{1}{7}$$

is Don's contribution in a day, which amounts to $\frac{2}{35}$ Therefore, if Don is to do it alone, it will take him

$$\frac{35}{2} = 17.5 \text{ days.}$$

17. **(C)** Since the volume of the cube is 8, each side has a measure of 2, and the main diagonal is found with the Pythagorean Theorem.

18. **(B)** Each way for Bob to walk to Norman's consists of six blocks northward and six blocks eastward in different orders. The total number of ways of walking is then the same as the number of ways to choose 6 out of 12 things, and the number is

$$12 \times 11 \times 10 \times 9 \times 8 \times 7 \text{ divided by } 6 \times 5 \times 4 \times 3 \times 2, \text{ or } 924.$$

19. **(A)** For a right isosceles triangle, the area is half of the product of the two equal sides. Therefore, each of the equal sides measure $\sqrt{8}$, or $2\sqrt{2}$, and the hypotenuse must be 4.

20. **(D)** Let the number of marbles in the beginning be x. We have

$$x - \left(\frac{1}{3}\right)x - \left(\frac{1}{3}\right)\left(\frac{2}{3}\right)x - 2 = 10.$$

Solving the equation, $x = 27$.

21. **(B)** We divide 400 by 24 (number of hours in a day); we obtain a partial quotient of 16 and a remainder of 16. This means that it takes 16 days and 16 hours for the trip. With 31 days in May, the boat must arrive on June 10. And 16 hours from 6 a.m. is 10 p.m.

22. **(D)** If we let Joan's age be x, then Georgette's age is $(x - 8)$. Solving the equation

$$(x - 8) = 2[(x - 8) - 8] = 2x - 32,$$

we obtain $x = 24$.

23. **(A)** Since the boat took five hours to go 20 miles, its speed upstream was four miles per hour. But the water effect was five miles per hour. If that effect had been taken away, the boat would have been five miles faster; therefore, the boat in still waters goes $4 + 5 = 9$ miles per hour.

24. **(C)** Suppose Sarah bought x pounds of apples and y pounds of nuts. We have the following equations to solve:

$$x + y = 10$$

$$89x + 129y = 1,010$$

Solving these equations give $x = 7$, $y = 3$.

25. **(E)** When Joe caught Jim, Jim had been running for $(10 + 4) = 14$ minutes, at the rate of 400 meters per minute. So the total distance covered was $(14 \times 400) = 5,600$ meters. But Joe covered this distance in 10 minutes. Thus, his average speed was

$$\frac{5,600}{10} = 560 \text{ meters per minute.}$$

26. **(A)** Since a chicken has two legs and a rabbit has four legs, letting x be the number of chickens and y be the number of rabbits, we have the following equations to solve:

$$x + y = 96$$

$$2x + 4y = 312$$

$$x = 96 - y$$

$$\frac{2x + 4y}{2} = 312$$

$$x + 2y = 156$$

$$96 - y + 2y = 156$$

$$96 + y = 156$$

$$y = 60$$

$$x + 60 = 96$$

$$x = 36$$

27. **(E)** In the first week, he consumed 118 grams of sugar daily; in the second week, he consumed 116 grams of sugar daily, etc. We are then to add

$$118 + 116 + 114 + \ldots + 2$$

and since there are seven days in a week, the result must be multiplied by 7. Observing that

$$118 + 116 + 114 + \ldots + 2 = 2 \times (1 + 2 + 3 + \ldots + 59)$$

$$= 2 \times (1 + 59)\left(\frac{59}{2}\right) = 3{,}540$$

And $3{,}540 \times 7 = 24{,}780.$

28. **(C)** Let x be the amount of money Kevin has, and let y be the amount of money John has. Then $y + x = 97$, and $y - x = 9$. Subtracting the two equations, we have

$$2x = 88, \text{ or } x = 44.$$

29. **(C)** If we draw a perpendicular line from B to the tangent line, say BE, then the right-angled triangles ABE and ACD are similar, so BE equals half of CD, the radius. BET is also a right-angled triangle, and BT is a radius. Using the Pythagorean Theorem, ET measures

$$\frac{\sqrt{3}}{2}$$

of the radius. Thus, ST measures $\sqrt{3}$ of the radius.

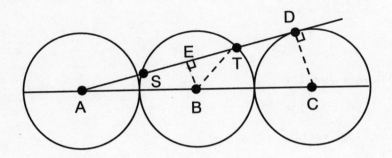

30. **(C)** Letting this number be x, we have

$$x^2 + 5x = 24, \text{ or } x^2 + 5x - 24 = 0,$$

or $(x + 8)(x - 3) = 0,$

so $x = 3$ or $x = -8$.

31. **(E)** π is an irrational number, while (A), (B), and (C) are all approximate rational values of π, and the statement (D) is vague.

32. **(B)** We do not need to memorize any formula. If we inscribe the regular pentagon in a circle, the angle with the vertex at the center facing each side is

$$\frac{360°}{5} = 72°,$$

and each of the other angles of that triangle must be

$$\frac{(180° - 72°)}{2} = 54°.$$

Thus, each of the angles is $108°$.

33. **(A)** Let x be the speed of the boat in still waters, and let y be the speed of the waterflow. Then $x + y = 15$ mph, and $x - y = 8$ mph. Subtracting the equations, we get $2y = 7$, or

$$y = \frac{7}{2}.$$

34. **(E)**   Since a 90° angle must be the largest in a triangle, it must face the longest side, and the angle between the longest side and the shortest side is not facing the longest side.

35. **(A)** $y = x^2$ has a graph like (A). (B) is the graph of $y = -x^2$; (C) is the graph of $x = y^2$; (D) is the graph of $x = -y^2$; and (E) is not even the graph of a second degree equation.

36. **(C)**   Since Bill took six hours to catch up, and Roger has gone 90 miles, Bill was

$$\frac{90}{6} = 15$$

miles closer each hour. Thus, he was driving 60 miles per hour.

37. **(D)**   The common denominator is $x^2 - 1$, and the numerator is

$$(x + 1)^2 - (x - 1)^2 = 4x.$$

38. **(C)**   Using the Pythagorean Theorem and the formula for the area of a triangle,

$$b = a \text{ and } h = \sqrt{a^2 - \left(\frac{1}{2}a\right)^2}$$

where a is the length of the sides.

$$\frac{1}{2}bh = \text{area}$$

$$\frac{1}{2}a\sqrt{a^2 - \frac{1}{4}a^2} = \sqrt{3}$$

$$\frac{1}{2}a\sqrt{\frac{3}{4}a^2} = \sqrt{3}$$

$$\frac{1}{4}a^2\left(\frac{3}{4}a^2\right) = 3$$

$$a^2 = (3)\left(\frac{16}{3}\right)$$

$$a^2 = 2$$

39. **(C)**   Let the price for a pair of shoes be x, and let the price for a pair of socks be y. Then,

$$6x + 3y = 96,$$

and $4y - x = 2.$

Solving these equations, we have $x = 14$.

40. **(A)**   Since $\overline{BC}$ is the diameter of the circle, angle A is a right angle. Therefore, angle C is complementary to angle B, i.e.,

$$90° - 47° = 43°.$$

Section III: Writing

1. **(C)** As you read the sentence, you should recognize that choice (C) presents an error in comparison. The comparison of two bridges requires the comparative form "longer." All of the other choices are acceptable in standard written English. Choice (A), the interrogative adjective "Which," introduces the question; choice (B), "is," agrees with its singular subject "bridge"; and choice (D), "or," is a coordinating conjunction joining the names of the two bridges.

2. **(E)** The correct response to this question is choice (E). All labeled elements are choices acceptable in standard written English. Choice (A), "of proteins," is a prepositional phrase that modifies the word "function"; in choice (B), the pronoun "they " is plural to agree with its antecedent, "proteins," and the verb "come" is also plural to agree with its subject, "they"; choice (C), "plant or animal sources," is idiomatic; and choice (D), "is," is singular to agree with its singular subject, "function."

3. **(C)** The error is choice (C), "I," which is in the nominative case. Because the words "Janice" and "I" serve as indirect objects in the sentence, the correct pronoun is the first person objective form, "me." Choice (A), "Recognizing," is a participle introducing an introductory participial phrase modifying "teacher;" choice (B), "had worked," is a verb in the past perfect tense because the action in the phrase was completed before the action in the main clause occurred; and choice (D), "tomorrow," is an adverb modifying the verb "could give."

4. **(C)** The error occurs at choice (C), where the preposition "from" is idiomatic after the word "different." Although some experts insist upon the use of "from" after the adjective "different," others accept the use of "different than" in order to save words. An example would be "different than you thought"; the use of "from" would require the addition of the word "what." Choice (A), "According to," is a preposition correctly introducing a prepositional phrase; choice (B), "has," is third person singular to agree with its subject "branch"; and choice (D), "those," is a plural pronoun to agree with its antecedent "powers."

5. **(A)** Choice (A) should be a gerund in the present perfect form (having "been studied") to indicate that the action expressed by the gerund occurred before the relationship was reported. Choice (B), "preceding ten

years," is idiomatic. Choice (C), "having," is a gerund introducing the phrase "having heart attacks" which is the object of the preposition "of"; and choice (D), the past tense passive verb "was reported," is singular to agree with its subject, "relationship."

6. **(E)** Your answer should be choice (E), indicating that this sentence contains no error in standard written English. Choice (A), "demonstrates," is present tense third person singular to agree with its subject, "book"; choice (B), "was expected," uses the third person singular form of "to be" to agree with its subject "each;" choice (C), the infinitive "to use," is idiomatic after the passive verb "was expected"; and choice (D), "his or her," is singular to agree with its antecedent, the indefinite pronoun "each," and provides gender neutrality.

7. **(A)** You should recognize in choice (A) that the idiomatically acceptable preposition to follow "aversion" is "to." The other choices in the sentence are acceptable in standard written English. Choice (B), "for him," is a prepositional phrase modifying "activity"; choice (C), "one," is a pronoun appropriate to refer to its antecedent "activity"; and choice (D), "that," is a relative pronoun introducing a restrictive adjective subordinate clause modifying "one."

8. **(C)** Choice (C) contains the error because the subject of the verb "show" is "story," a singular noun that calls for the third person singular verb, "shows." The rest of the sentence represents correct usage. Choices (A) and (B), "those" and "their," are plural pronouns that agree with the antecedent "pioneers"; and choice (D), "us," is in the objective case because it is the indirect object in the sentence.

9. **(D)** Choice (D) presents an error in comparison, appearing to compare "farming" with "low latitudes" when what is intended is a comparison of "farming in high latitudes" with "farming in low latitudes." The corrected sentence reads: "Because of the long, cold winters and short summer growing season, farming in high latitudes is more difficult than farming in low latitudes." The other choices all represent appropriate usage in standard written English. Choice (A), "Because of," is idiomatically correct as a preposition; choice (B), "and," is a coordinating conjunction joining the nouns "winters" and "summers." Choice (C), "more difficult," is the comparative form appropriate to compare two items.

10. **(D)** The error is in choice (D). The word "contestant" is a predicate

nominative in the subordinate noun clause, and it must agree in number with the plural subject of the clause, the pronoun "both," to which it refers. The noun clause should, therefore, read: "that both of us could be contestants on a quiz show." Choice (A), "I," is part of the compound subject of the introductory adverb clause and is, correctly, in the nominative case. Choice (B), "were," is plural to agree with its compound subject. Choice (C), "we," is plural to agree with its compound antecedent, "sister and I," and is in the nominative case because it is the subject of the verb "hoped."

11. **(A)**   The error is in choice (A). The auxiliary verb "had" calls for the past participle form of the verb "break," which is "broken." All of the other choices are acceptable in standard written English. Choice (B), "that," is the correct relative pronoun to follow "vase" and introduce the subordinate adjective clause; choice (C), "had purchased," is the past perfect form of the verb to indicate action completed in the past before the action of the verb in the main clause; and choice (D), "her," is the object of the preposition "for."

12. **(E)**   This sentence contains no error in standard written English. Choice (A), the prepositional phrase "with whom," introduces an adjective clause modifying the word "people." The relative pronoun "whom" is in the objective case because it serves as the object of the preposition "with." The simple past tense "worked" is appropriate for choice (B); choice (C), "were engaged," is plural to agree with its subject "some"; and choice (D) is an idiomatic expression replacing the preposition "for."

13. **(D)**   Your reading of the sentence should indicate that choice (D), "were," presents an error in subject-verb agreement. A compound subject joined by "or" or "neither . . . nor" calls for a verb that agrees in number with the second part of the compound subject, which is, in this case, singular. The correct choice is the verb "was." The other choices represent correct usage. Choice (A), "Because of," is idiomatic; and choices (B) and (C) are correlative conjunctions.

14. **(C)**   Again the error is one of agreement of the subject and verb. Choice (C), "were," is plural; because its subject is "attack," not "reasons," which is the object of the preposition "among" and therefore cannot be the subject of the sentence, the verb should be the singular "was." Choice (A), "Among," introduces a prepositional phrase; choice (B) is an idiomatically acceptable prepositional phrase to modify the noun "reasons;" choice (D), "naval base," poses no error in usage.

15. **(D)** Your analysis of this sentence should disclose an error in parallelism in choice (D). "Teaching" should be replaced by "to teach," an infinitive parallel with "to frighten." Both infinitives modify the noun "attempt." The other choices all represent standard usage in written English. Choice (A), "greater," is the comparative form of the adjective, correctly used to compare two items; choice (B), "their," is a plural possessive pronoun agreeing in number with its plural antecedent, "parents"; and choice (C), "than," is idiomatic to introduce the second part of the comparison.

16. **(C)** You should recognize that the possessive pronoun in choice (C), "their," is not the appropriate pronoun to use in referring to a country. Choice (A), "of living," and choice (D), "of life expectancy," are both idiomatically acceptable prepositional phrases; choice (B), "is shown," is passive and agrees in number with its singular subject, "standard."

17. **(D)** Choice (D), "white and bluish gray in color," is the third in a series of objects of the verb "has." The error lies in its lack of parallelism with the other two objects, "eyes" and "body." Corrected, the sentence reads: "The snow leopard is a wild mammal in Central Asia that has large eyes, a four-foot body, and a white and bluish gray color." The other choices are all acceptable in standard written English. Choice (A), "is," is singular to agree with its subject "leopard." Choice (B), "that has," is composed of the relative pronoun "that" referring to the noun "mammal," and the verb "has," that agrees with its subject in number. Choice (C), "and," is a coordinating conjunction correctly used to join the three objects of the verb.

18. **(B)** You should recognize that choice (B), "and," is not the correct correlative conjunction to follow "either." The correct word is "or." The other choices all represent acceptable choices in standard written English. Choice (A), "a young person," is correctly placed immediately after the introductory participial phrase that modifies it; choice (C), "him," is singular to agree with its antecedent "person" and objective because it is the object of the verb "make." Choice (D), "most important," is in the superlative form because the comparison involves more than two choices.

19. **(C)** Choice (C), "to fail," is incorrect in standard written English. The sentence contains two parallel ideas that should be expressed with the same grammatical form. Because "Failing" is a gerund, the "infinitive" to "fail" should be replaced with "failing" to make the construction parallel.

Choice (A), "is," agrees in number with its subject, "student"; choice (B), "is," agrees in number with its subject, "Failing"; and choice (D) is singular to agree with its antecedent, "student," and indicates no sexual preference.

20. **(C)**   You should recognize that choice (C), "or," is in error because the correlative conjunction that should follow "neither" is "nor." All other choices are correct. Choice (A), "had grown up," is idiomatically acceptable and it and choice (B), "had been," are in the past perfect tense to indicate that the actions occurred before the action mentioned in the main clause; choice (D), "vividly," is an adverb correctly modifying the verb "portrayed."

21. **(B)**   As you read the sentence, you should recognize that choice (B) is incorrect because "that" is the relative pronoun that should introduce a noun clause following "reason"; another option would be to revise the sentence by omitting the words "The reason," but that is not an option provided on this test. Choice (A), "his," is the correct possessive pronoun to refer to "Jason." Choice (C), "such stage fright," is idiomatic, and choice (D) is the relative pronoun, subject, and verb of an adjective clause modifying "fright."

22. **(B)**   Your recognition that the word "less" is used with a singular noun and the word "fewer" is appropriate before a plural noun will lead you to locate the error in choice (B). Choice (A) is an introductory participial phrase, correctly followed by the pronoun it modifies. Choice (C) is the comparative adverb, the correct choice to compare two people ("anyone else" is singular), and choice (D) is idiomatic as a singular indefinite pronoun.

23. **(C)**   You should recognize that the verb "want" in choice (C) does not agree with its subject "who," a pronoun that is singular to agree with its antecedent, "adult." The word ordering used in choices (A), (B), and (D) are all idiomatic in standard written English.

24. **(C)**   As you read the sentence, you should recognize that the pronoun "this" in choice (C) does not have a clear antecedent in the sentence. The other choices are all correct in standard written English. Choice (A), "along with," is idiomatic and serves as one preposition. Choice (B), "those," has as its antecedent "advantages," and choice (D), "has made," is in the

present perfect tense because the action began in the past and continues into the present.

25. **(C)** You should find the error at choice (C), where the adverb "frequently" is needed to modify the adjective "repetitious"; "frequent" is an adjective and does not correctly modify another adjective. Choice (A), the pronoun "who," correctly refers to its antecedent "Students"; choice (B), the adverb "generally," modifies the verb; and choice (D) is a relative pronoun "that" and its verb, "is provided," that comprise the adjective clause modifying "menu."

26. **(D)** Because the verb "protest" can be transitive and have a direct object, choice (D) avoids awkward wordiness and use of the unnecessary preposition "about." Choices (B) and (E) include unnecessary words and uses the pronoun "they" that has no clear antecedent; choice (C) is also unnecessarily wordy and contains the repetitious words, "builders should build."

27. **(B)** Choice (B) best shows the causal relationship between sibling opportunities and their placement in the family, their abilities, and their personalities, and retains the subordination of the original sentence. Choices (A) and (E) provide dangling phrases. Choice (C) with its use of the coordinating conjunction "and" treats the lack of opportunity and its cause as if they are equal ideas and does not show the causal relationship between them, and choice (D) results in a run-on sentence.

28. **(E)** Only choice (E) corrects the two major problems in the sentence, the lack of subject-verb agreement and the lack of parallelism. In choices (A), (B), and (C), the verb "is" does not agree with its plural subject, "provisions." Choices (A) and (D) have unlike constructions serving as predicate nominatives, the noun "freedom" and the clause "that citizens are guaranteed a trial by jury." Choice (E) correctly uses the plural verb "are" to agree with the plural subject, and the predicate nominative is composed of two parallel nouns, "freedom" and "guarantee."

29. **(E)** The errors found in the original sentence, choice (A), involve parallelism and redundancy. Choice (E) uses the parallel infinitives "to entertain" and "to teach" as direct objects and eliminates the repetition created in the use of both "tried" and "attempt" in the original sentence. Choices (B) and (C) provide parallel construction, but choice (B) retains the redundancy and choice (C) incorrectly splits the infinitive "to enter-

tain"; although choice (D) provides parallelism of the nouns "entertainment" and "attempt," the redundancy still remains, and the word order is not idiomatic.

30. **(B)**   Choice (B) adequately conveys the reason for removal of the parking meters with the least wordiness. Choices (A) and (D) contain unnecessary words; choices (C) and (E) have dangling participial phrases.

31. **(D)**   Choice (D), in which "Megan" correctly follows the phrase, conveys the meaning with the least wordiness. The problem with choice (A) is the introductory participial phrase; it must be eliminated or followed immediately by the word modified. Choice (B) does not solve the problem of the dangling phrase; choices (C) and (E) add words unnecessary to the meaning of the sentence.

32. **(A)**   The given sentence is acceptable in standard written English. Each of the alternate choices introduces a problem. Choice (B) uses the superlative form of the adjective, "most interested," when the comparative form "more interested" is correct for the comparison of two options; choices (C) and (E) introduce a lack of parallelism; and choice (D) is not idiomatic.

33. **(E)**   The noun clause in choice (E) is idiomatically acceptable. The use of "Whether" in choices (A) and (B) leads the writer to add "or not," words that contribute nothing to the meaning and result in awkwardness of construction. In choice (C), "the fact of whether," is not idiomatic, and choice (D) with its awkward gerund phrase is also not idiomatic.

34. **(E)**   This sentence presents two problems, namely use of a preposition instead of a coordinating conjunction to join the objects of the participle "having studied" and failure to show a time relationship. Choice (E) corrects both problems. Choice (B) simply replaces the preposition "along with" by "as well as"; choice (C) unnecessarily repeats the conjunction "and" rather than using the quite appropriate series construction. None of the choices (A), (B), (C), or (D) correctly shows the time relationship.

35. **(B)**   This sentence contains the ambiguous pronoun "they," for which there is no antecedent and fails to show the relationship of the ideas expressed. Choice (B) eliminates the clause with the ambiguous pronoun and correctly expresses the reason for the sandbag placement. Choice (C) suggests that the two clauses joined by "and" are equal and does not show

the subordinate relationship of the second to the first. Choice (D) introduces a dangling phrase with a coordinating conjunction, "and," that suggests the joining of equals; and choice (E) retains both errors from the original sentence.

36. **(A)** This sentence is correct in standard written English. Choices (B) and (C) introduce unnecessary words that add nothing to the meaning and make the sentence awkward and wordy; choices (D) and (E) do not correctly show relationship.

37. **(C)** Choice (C) shows the relationship accurately and eliminates the awkward gerund construction as the object of the preposition "despite." The adjective clause in choice (B) fails to show the relationship of the original sentence; choice (D) introduces the superfluous words "the fact that." Choice (E) inappropriately places the qualifying information in equal and parallel construction to the main idea of the sentence.

38. **(A)** This sentence is correct in standard written English. Choices (B) and (C) lose the strength of the parallelism in choice (A). Choice (D), although containing parallel construction, is idiomatically awkward with its participial phrases. Choices (B), (C), and (E) all exhibit wordiness.

39. **(D)** The original sentence, choice (A), contains the obvious and redundant words "was a man who." Choices (B), (C), and (E) are also unnecessarily verbose. Choice (D) makes the statement in the most direct way possible and represents correct standard usage.

40. **(E)** Choice (E) eliminates the awkward participial phrase with its passive verb, and, in direct fashion, clearly shows the desired relationship. Choices (A), (B), and (D) retain the awkward construction; choice (C) is repetitious, wordy, and not idiomatic.

41. **(C)** The error in this sentence involves the use of the pronoun "which," that refers not to a single antecedent but to the entire main clause in the sentence. A pronoun should have a single noun or pronoun as its antecedent. Choice (C) most economically shows the causal relationship of the original sentence and effectively eliminates the pronoun altogether. Although choice (B) eliminates unnecessary words, the basic problem remains; choice (D) is also wordy and repetitive; and choice (E) is not idiomatic.

42. **(B)** The problem in this sentence involves the need for consistent pronoun use and for parallel construction. Because the portion of the sentence not underlined uses the pronouns "you" and "your," the first part of the sentence must also use the second person pronoun. Choice (B) alone accomplishes that consistency and yet retains parallel construction.

43. **(A)** This sentence contains no error in standard written English. Each of the possible revisions makes no real improvement, and choice (B) adds an error in subject-verb agreement. Choice (C) creates confusion in pronoun reference with the addition of "themselves," and choices (D) and (E) are not idiomatic.

44. **(D)** This exercise is a sentence fragment, not a complete sentence. The subject has no verb but is followed by two subordinate clauses. To correct this sentence, eliminate the subordinating conjunction, "where," and the subject of the subordinate clause, "he," to provide a predicate for the subject, "Father Junipero Serra." Choice (D) accompishes what is necessary. Choices (B) and (C) result in run-on sentences; and choice (E) substitutes a verbal phrase for the necessary predicate and does not solve the problem of the fragment.

45. **(B)** The given sentence does not provide parallelism in construction. The conjunction "but" joins the adjective "eager" with a prepositional phrase. Choice (B) correctly provides the adjective "afraid" followed by an infinitive phrase parallel with "eager to explain his point of view." The verbal phrases in the other choices do not result in parallel construction; in addition, choice (C) is a dangling phrase.

PPST ESSAY SCORING GUIDE

The PPST essay sections are scored by two writing experts on the basis of the criteria outlined below. In addition to comparing your essay to those included in our practice tests, you may use these guidelines to estimate your score on this section. Remember that your score is the sum of the scores of two writing experts, so provided you respond to the assigned topic, your score will fall somewhere between two and twelve. Scores will be assigned based on the following guidelines:

6 An essay receiving a score of 6 may contain one or two spelling or punctuation errors, but overall it exhibits a high degree of proficiency and thought on the assigned topic.

An essay scoring a 6

- is both well organized and well developed
- engages important concepts and explains them clearly
- varies expression and language
- demonstrates deft use of language
- is virtually free from errors involving syntax and structure

5 An essay receiving a score of 5 exhibits a high degree of proficiency and thought on the assigned topic, however it contains a number of minor mistakes.

An essay scoring a 5

- is both well organized and well developed
- engages important concepts and explains them
- varies expression and language somewhat
- demonstrates deft use of language
- is virtually free from errors involving syntax and structure

4 An essay receiving a score of 4 responds to the assignment and exhibits some degree of deeper understanding.

An essay scoring a 4

- demonstrates adequate organization and development
- engages and explains some important concepts, but not all that are necessary to demonstrate full understanding

- exhibits adequate use of language
- contains some syntax and structure errors, without excessive repetition of those errors

3 An essay receiving a score of 3 exhibits some degree of understanding, but its response to the topic is obviously deficient.

An essay scoring a 3 is deficient in one or more of the following areas:

- insufficient organization or development
- insufficient engagement or explanation of important concepts
- consistent repitition of syntactical or structural errors
- redundant or unsuitable word choice

2 An essay receiving a score of 2 exhibits limited understanding and its response to the topic is seriously deficient.

An essay scoring a 2 is deficient in one or more of the following areas:

- weak organization or development
- very few pertinent details
- consistent and serious errors in syntax, structure
- consistent and serious errors in word choice

1 An essay receiving a score of 1 exhibits a lack of basic writing skills.

An essay scoring a 1 is disorganized, undeveloped, contains consistent repetition of errors, or is incomprehensible.

Sample Essays with Commentary

ESSAY I (Score: 5–6)

Happiness, freedom, and peace of mind are goals that everyone wants in life. Yet they are very abstract and difficult to measure. Happiness is a frame of mind that means we enjoy what we do. Freedom is the ability to do what we want, although it is limited to not doing anything that takes away freedom from other people. Peace of mind is a feeling that we are all right and that the world is a good place. How does one achieve these important goals? They can best be acquired when we try to give them to other people rather than when we try to get them ourselves.

The people who feel happiest, experience freedom, and enjoy peace of mind are most often people who are concentrating on helping others. Mother Theresa of Calcutta is an example. Because she takes care of homeless people and is so busy, she probably doesn't have time to worry about whether she is happy, free, and peaceful. She always looks cheerful in her pictures.

There are other people in history who seem to have attained the goals we all want by helping others. Jane Addams established Hull House in the slums of Chicago to help other people, and her life must have brought her great joy and peace of mind. She gave to the mothers in the neighborhood freedom to work and know that their children were being taken care of; and Jane Addams apparently had the freedom to do what she wanted to help them.

On the other hand, there are people in literature who directly tried to find happiness, freedom, and peace of mind; and they were often miserable. The two people who come to mind are Scrooge and Silas Marner. Scrooge had been selfish in the past, and he wouldn't give anything for the poor. He wasn't a bit happy even at Christmas. Later, when he began helping others, he became happy. Silas Marner was very selfish, hoarding his money and thinking it would make him happy. Only when he tried to make little Eppie happy was he able to be happy, too, even without his stolen money.

If we want to achieve happiness, freedom, and peace of mind, we should get involved in helping others so much that we forget ourselves and find joy from the people we are helping. When we try to give away the qualities we want, we find them ourselves.

ANALYSIS

Essay I has a score range of 5-6. It is well organized, with the opening paragraph serving as the introduction and stating the thesis of the paper in its last sentence. Defining the terms serves as an effective way to introduce the paper. The last paragraph concludes the essay, restating the thesis. The three middle paragraphs support the thesis with specific examples that are adequately explained and have a single focus. Transitions effectively relate the ideas. The sentence structure varies, and the vocabulary is effective. There are no major errors in sentence construction, usage, or mechanics. Although the essay would benefit from some minor revisions, it is well done considering the 30 minute time limit imposed upon the writer.

ESSAY II (Score: 4–5)

I think there is a basic problem in this quotation. I do not think that anyone can give happiness, freedom, or peace of mind to anybody. Those things have to come from inside the person, not from someone else, no matter how hard they try to give them to him. That means that the person trying to make someone else happy, free, and peacefull will be frusterated because he really can't do what he wants to do. And if he is frustrated, he won't be happy, free, and peacefull himself.

I think an example of this in history is when the missionaries went to Oregon in early United States history and tried to help the Indians, and the Indians got smallpox and then killed the missionaries. So no one was happy, free, or had a peacefull mind. That's happened with other missionaries in China and other places, too. It just wasn't possible to give happiness, freedom, and peace of mind to anyone else, and the people giving it often lost it themselves.

I know an example from my own life. My parents have tried very hard to make my little sister happy. They have done everything for her and, I'll tell you, she's so spoiled that nothing makes her happy. When they gave her a new bicycle, she was unhappy because she didn't like the color. I'd think she'd be glad just to have a nice bike. I know they never gave me one as nice as they gave her.

So I really think that whoever said the quotation was not right at all. You can't give happiness, freedom, and peace of mind to someone else at all, so you can't get those qualities by giving them.

ANALYSIS

Essay II has a score range of 4-5. It is organized clearly, with an introduction in the first paragraph, a clear statement of thesis, and a

conclusion in the last paragraph. Although a few sentences are not relevant to the topic being discussed, the writer attempts to maintain one focus and to support his position with specific details. Paragraphing is good. The use of "I think" and "I know" weakens the essay, and pronouns without clear antecedents occur throughout the essay. Sentence patterns and vocabulary lack variety, and there are some errors in spelling, usage, and sentence construction. Transitions are also lacking.

ESSAY III (Score: 3–4)

I agree with the idea that you don't get happiness without trying to make other people happy. But I'm not sure that you *always* get happiness when you give it to someone else, you may try to make someone else happy and you're miserable even though you do it.

For instance, I've tried many times to make my grandmother happy. No matter what I do, she complains about me and tells my mother I should do everything different. She didn't even act like she liked my Christmas present last year, and she sure didn't make me happy either. Its just the opposite when you let someone else be free he takes away from your freedom and you don't feel free at all.

So, all in all, I think maybe sometimes you get happiness and freedom when you give it to others but most of the time things just get worse.

ANALYSIS

Essay III has a score range of 3-4. The writer attempts to introduce his topic in the first paragraph, but the thesis is not stated precisely. Although the last paragraph serves as a conclusion, it, too, lacks clarity and singleness of purpose. Paragraph 2 gives a specific illustration to develop the theme, but paragraph 3 lacks specific detail. Although there are some transitional words, the essay rambles with words and ideas repeated. In addition, the essay contains errors in usage, sentence construction, and mechanics.

ESSAY IV (Score: 1–2)

I don't think you can give happiness or piece of mind to anyone maybe you can give freedom. My folks are giving me more freedom now that I useta have, so you can give that to someone else. But nobody knows what makes me happy so I can be happy only if I decide what it is I want and go out and get it for myself. And then I'll have piece of mind, too.

Happiness don't come much but I'm happyest when I'm with a bunch of friends and we are having fun together. That's what friends like being

together with other people. but nobody gives me that kind of happiness I have to find a bunch of friends I like and than be with them. And thats real freedom, too, but nobody gave it to any of us. My folks think they can make me happy by giving me gifts but usually I don't like what they give me, and there idea of going for a ride or eating together isn't my idea of being happy.

ANALYSIS

Essay IV has a score range of 1-2. The writer states the thesis in the first sentence and maintains a consistent position, but fails to have an introductory paragraph; and there is no conclusion at all. The writer does give some specific details but rambles, failing to use the details effectively to support his thesis. In addition, there are serious errors in sentence construction like the run-on sentence in the beginning of the paper. There are also major problems with spelling, usage, and mechanics.

PPST

Pre-Professional Skills Tests

Practice
PPST IV

PPST Test IV

(Answer sheets appear in the back of this book.)

Section I: Reading Comprehension

TIME: 60 Minutes
40 Questions

DIRECTIONS: A number of questions follow each of the passages in the reading section. Answer the questions by choosing the best answer from the five choices given.

Question 1 refers to the following statement:

The funnel cloud appeared capricious with its destruction, darting from one street to another, obliterating any object in its path.

1. In this context the word "capricious" means

   (A) unpredictable.

   (B) intense.

   (C) threatening.

   (D) adaptable.

   (E) belligerent.

Questions 2 and 3 refer to the following passage:

Many times different animal species can inhabit the same environment and share a common food supply without conflict, because each species occupies a separate niche defined by its specific physical adaptations and habits. For example, the little green heron, equipped with legs too short to do much wading, fishes from shore for its food. The Louisiana heron wades out a little further into the shallows during the daytime hours, while the yellow-crowned night heron stalks the same shallows after dark. Diet also varies in size and amount, according to the size of the bird.

2. According to the passage, which one of the following basic assumptions can be made about how a bird's diet varies according to size?

   (A) Small birds can eat twice their weight.

(B) The larger birds can swallow larger fish and water snakes.

(C) Birds have to adapt their diets according to what is available within their environment.

(D) Fishing from shore is difficult for smaller birds.

(E) The type of bill is an adaptation for the type of food the animal eats.

3. The title that best expresses the ideas of this passage is

(A) The Heron Family.

(B) Diet Variations of Birds.

(C) A Separate Niche at the Same Pond.

(D) Long-Legged Fishing.

(E) Fishing Habits of the Heron.

Questions 4 and 5 refer to the following passage:

Most Americans assume that English is the language of the United States, but they are naive to imagine that every American speaks it fluently. According to the 1980 U.S. census, 11 percent of Americans come from non-English-speaking homes. Over one percent of the U.S. population speaks English not well or not at all.

Non-English speakers reside in all 50 states. In some 23 states, the non-English speaking minority makes up 10 percent or more of the total population. All of American history is characterized by this language phenomenon. For those misguided Americans who believe that their country is and always has been a monolingual country, the facts just do not support their claim.

4. This selection implies that the author's attitude toward a belief that America is a monolingual country is one of

(A) impartiality.　　　　(D) anger.

(B) indifference.　　　　(E) optimism.

(C) criticism.

5. Which of the following statements can best be inferred from the information given?

    (A) Non-English languages are found primarily along the East and West Coast areas.

    (B) No indicators suggest that the percentages of non-English speaking populations will decrease.

    (C) This language situation is relatively new to the United States.

    (D) In the next decade the United States should become primarily monolingual.

    (E) The United States is comparable to Great Britain in percentage of non-English speakers.

Questions 6 to 8 refer to the following passage:

The Indians of California had five varieties of acorn which they used as their principle source of food. This was a noteworthy accomplishment in technology since they first had to make the acorn edible. A process had to be developed for leaching out the poisonous tannic acid. They ground the acorns into a meal and then filtered it many times with water. This had to be done through sand or through tightly woven baskets. Early Indian campsites reveal the evidence of the acorn-processing labor necessary to provide enough food for their subsistence. The women patiently ground acorns into meal with stone pestles. The result, a pinkish flour that was cooked into a mush or thin soup, formed the bulk of their diet.

6. The central idea of the passage is the early Indians of California

    (A) had ample food sources.

    (B) left evidence of their meal processing at ancient campsites.

    (C) differed from other Indians in their use of natural resources.

    (D) contributed distinctive talents and technological expertise in providing food sources.

    (E) produced finely crafted woven baskets.

7. According to the passage, which of the following was a technological innovation developed by the early California Indians in the production of food?

    (A) Irrigation of crops   (B) Grinding meal

(C) Filtration system   (D) Dams

(E) Removal of tannic acid

8. It can be inferred from the passage that the early Indians faced a major problem in their production of food. What was it?

(A) They needed many pounds of acorns to produce enough meal.

(B) Acorns had to be carried a great distance to their campsites for grinding.

(C) The acorn grinding took many hours of hard labor.

(D) Acorns were scarce.

(E) It was difficult to filter the meal without losing it.

Question 9 refers to the following statement:

There was a vestige of the original manuscript for us to review.

9. In the context of the passage, "vestige" means

(A) reproduction.   (D) engraving.

(B) cartoon.   (E) trace.

(C) counterfeit.

Questions 10 to 12 refer to the following passage:

Beginning readers, and those who are experiencing difficulty with reading, benefit from assisted reading. During assisted reading the teacher orally reads a passage with a student or students. The teacher fades in and out of the reading act. For example, the teacher lets his or her voice drop to a whisper when students are reading on their own at an acceptable rate and lets his/her voice rise to say the words clearly when the students are having difficulty.

Students who are threatened by print, read word-by-word, or rely on grapho-phonemic cues will be helped by assisted reading. These students are stuck on individual language units which can be as small as a single letter or as large as phrases or sentences. As Frank Smith (1977) and other reading educators have noted, speeding up reading, not slowing it down, helps the reader make sense of a passage: This strategy allows students to concentrate on meaning as the short-term memory is not overload by focusing on small language units. As the name implies, assisted reading

lets the reader move along without being responsible for every language unit; the pressure is taken off the student. Consequently, when the reading act is sped up, it sounds more like language, and students can begin to integrate the cueing systems of semantics and syntax along with grapho-phonemics.

10. As a strategy, assisted reading is best for

(A) beginning readers who are relying on grapho-phonemic cues.

(B) learning disabled readers who are experiencing neurological deficits.

(C) beginning readers who are relying on phono-graphic cues.

(D) remedial readers who are experiencing difficulty with silent reading.

(E) beginning readers who are experiencing difficulty with silent reading.

11. Language units as presented in the passage refer to

(A) individual letters, syllables, or phrases.

(B) individual letters, syllables, or sentences.

(C) individual letters, phrases, or paragraphs.

(D) individual letters, phrases, or sentences.

(E) individual letters, sentences, or paragraphs.

12. According to the passage, to make sense of a passage a reader must

(A) focus on small language units.

(B) overload short-term memory.

(C) slow down when reading.

(D) read word-by-word.

(E) speed up the reading act.

Questions 13 to 16 refer to the following passage:

The information about the comparison of the technology (duplex versus one-way video and two-way audio) and the comparison of site classes versus regular classes tends to indicate that although there was not much

of an apparent difference between classes and technology, student participation and student involvement were viewed as important components in any teaching/learning setting. For the future, perhaps revisiting what learning is might be helpful so that this component of distance learning can be more adequately addressed. The question remains whether or not student participation can be equated with learning. Participation per se does not demonstrate learning. A more rigorous instrument which assesses and determines learning may need to be addressed with future distance learning studies.

13. Duplex, as used in the passage, suggests which of the following when comparing distance learning technology?

(A) One-way video and two-way audio

(B) One-way video and one-way audio

(C) Two-way video and two-way audio

(D) Two-way video and one-way audio

(E) Two-way video

14. Which of the following is the most complete and accurate definition of the term "rigorous" as used in the passage?

(A) Harsh

(D) Dogmatic

(B) Austere

(E) Precise

(C) Uncompromising

15. The author of the passage would tend to agree with which of the following statements?

(A) Learning consists of more than student participation.

(B) Duplex technology is better than one-way video and two-way audio.

(C) Student participation and student involvement are not important in learning.

(D) An instrument which assesses and demonstrates learning is not currently available.

(E) A review of learning is not important as the topic has been thoroughly researched.

16. The primary purpose of the passage is to

    (A) delineate the issues in distance learning

    (B) note student participation in distance learning and question this role in learning.

    (C) detail the comparison of site classes versus regular classes.

    (D) share information about duplex technology versus one-way video and two-way audio.

    (E) request an assessment instrument which includes a learning component.

Questions 17 and 18 refer to the following passage:

Eyes are. There is no doubt about it—they are certainly in existence. Eyes have many purposes in this world. Eyes are to see with, to be seen, to be heard, and even to be felt. I suppose they could be tasted, and in some cases could be smelled. Now anything that can satisfy all five of the body's senses must have a great deal of value.

To begin with, I shall start with the thing that enables us to see the other kinds of eyes, and that is the eye—e-y-e. It is a very delicate and effeminate mechanism, as any optician or optometrist will tell you. However, if one of these is not close at hand, just consult a hygiene, psychology, or physics textbook. It (the eye) is also very intricate; the cornea, iris, retina, and crystalline lens are a few of its main members. Each is arranged very neatly in its proper place, where it helps form a part of a very necessary whole.

17. Which of the following is the most complete and accurate definition of the term "effeminate" as used in the passage?

    (A) Womanish   (D) Soft, delicate

    (B) Unmanly   (E) Female

    (C) Emasculate

18. The author's attitude about the subject discussed is best described as

    (A) flippant disregard.   (D) imaginative.

    (B) moral indignation.   (E) humorous.

    (C) critical.

Questions 19 to 21 refer to the following passage:

The Matsushita Electric Industrial Co. in Japan has developed a computer program that can use photographs of faces to predict the aging process and, also, how an unborn child will look. The system can show how a couple will look after 40 years of marriage and how newlyweds' future children will look. The computer analyzes facial characteristics from a photograph based on shading and color differences, and then creates a three-dimensional model in its memory. The system consists of a personal computer with a program and circuit board and will be marketed by the Matsushita Company soon.

19. The main idea in the passage you just read is about

    (A) a computer that shows the aging process.

    (B) a computer that chooses the right mate.

    (C) a computer that predicts the number of children for newlyweds.

    (D) a computer that predicts the looks of future children as well as their parents.

    (E) a computer that analyzes photographs.

20. The new computer program developed in Japan uses

    (A) a three-dimensional face model.

    (B) photographs of faces to predict the aging process and looks of an unborn child.

    (C) shading and color differences in photographs.

    (D) a personal computer and circuit board.

    (E) facial characteristics from a photograph.

21. What might result from their new computer system developed in Japan?

    (A) The U.S. will develop an even more sophisticated computer system.

    (B) Competition among trading partners of Japan will be keener.

    (C) Japan's economy will skyrocket.

    (D) The trade imbalance between Japan and the U.S. will increase.

(E) The next computer system Japan will develop will be even more refined and sophisticated.

Questions 22 and 23 refers to the following passage:

On September 17, 1991, a communications power failure brought New York's three big airports to a virtual stop for several hours. Air traffic control centers communicate with planes through a network of radio towers linked to them by phone. Due to this power failure, local air traffic centers could not communicate properly amongst themselves or with other U.S. airports.

22. What could have happened to airplanes en route to New York when the power failure took place?

   (A) They could have turned back from where they came.

   (B) They could have encircled New York until the control towers were able to communicate with the pilots.

   (C) They could have been diverted to other airports by other air control centers.

   (D) They could have slowed down their speed while waiting for the power failure to be corrected.

   (E) They could have landed, as usual, at the New York airports.

23. What can air travelers learn from this power failure incident?

   (A) Expect delays or being diverted to other airports for landing.

   (B) Take the train instead.

   (C) Prepare for the unexpected each time you fly.

   (D) A power failure in New York can happen again.

   (E) Flight delays are due to failure in communications systems.

Questions 24 to 27 refer to the following passage:

New health research shows that regular vigorous exercise during the middle and late years of life not only keeps the heart healthy, but also may protect against colon cancer, one of the major killers in the U.S. The researchers in the study compared the rate of colon cancer among those who were physically inactive with those who were either active or highly active. Seventeen thousand one hundred forty eight men, ages 30 to 79,

were covered in the study. Among men judged to be inactive there were 55 cases of colon cancer; among those moderately active, there were 11; and only 10 cases of colon cancer were found among the very active ones.

24. Which of the following makes an appropriate title for the passage?

    (A) New Health Research on Colon Cancer

    (B) Colon Cancer: A Major Killer in the U.S.

    (C) Regular Vigorous Exercise May Prevent Colon Cancer

    (D) Results of Research on Colon Cancer

    (E) A Prescription for Preventing Colon Cancer

25. Based on the result of the research, can one make a generalization regarding colon cancer for men and women?

    (A) Yes   (D) It depends

    (B) No   (E) Not applicable

    (C) Maybe

26. What important message did you get from the passage?

    (A) Regular exercise is good for the health.

    (B) Only middle-aged men get colon cancer.

    (C) Women need not worry about colon cancer.

    (D) Regular exercise is needed only by older people.

    (E) Children are too young to exercise.

27. What is the major limitation of the study?

    (A) It did not explain "vigorous exercise."

    (B) It did not include children.

    (C) It did not include men below 30.

    (D) It did not include women of the same age group.

    (E) None of the above.

Questions 28 to 33 are based on the following passage.

A submarine was first used as an offensive weapon during the American Revolutionary War. The Turtle, a one-man submersible designed by an American inventor named David Bushnell and hand-operated by a screw propeller, attempted to sink a British man-of-war in New York Harbor. The plan was to attach a charge of gunpowder to the ship's bottom with screws and explode it with a time fuse. After repeated failures to force the screws through the copper sheathing of the hull of the *H.M.S. Eagle,* the submarine gave up and withdrew, exploding its powder a short distance from the *Eagle.* Although the attack was unsuccessful, it caused the British to move their blockading ships from the harbor to the outer bay.

On 17 February 1864, a Confederate craft, a hand-propelled submersible, carrying a crew of eight men, sank a federal corvette that was blockading Charleston Harbor. The hit was accomplished by a torpedo suspended ahead of the Confederate *Hunley* as she rammed the Union frigate *Housatonic* and is the first recorded instance of a submarine sinking a warship.

The submarine first became a major component in naval warfare during World War I, when Germany demonstrated its full potential. Wholesale sinking of Allied shipping by the German U-boats almost swung the war in favor of the Central Powers. Then, as now, the submarine's greatest advantage was that it could operate beneath the ocean surface where detection was difficult. Sinking a submarine was comparatively easy, once it was found—but finding it before it could attack was another matter.

During the closing months of World War I, the Allied Submarine Devices Investigation Committee was found to obtain from science and technology more effective underwater detection equipment. The committee developed a reasonably accurate device for locating a submerged submarine. This device was a trainable hydrophone, which was attached to the bottom of the ASW ship, and used to detect screw noises and other sounds that came from a submarine. Although the committee disbanded after World War I, the British made improvements on the locating device during the interval between then and World War II, and named it ASDIC after the committee.

American scientists further improved on the device, calling it SONAR, a name derived from the underlined initials of the words <u>so</u>und <u>n</u>avigation and <u>r</u>anging.

At the end of World War II, the United States improved the snorkel (a device for bringing air to the crew and engines when operating submerged on diesels) and developed the Guppy (short for greater underwater propulsion power), a conversion of the fleet-type submarine of World War II fame. The superstructure was changed by reducing the surface area,

streamlining every protruding object, and enclosing the periscope shears in a streamlined metal fairing. Performance increased greatly with improved electronic equipment, additional battery capacity, and the addition of the snorkel.

28. The thematic emphasis of the passage lies in

    (A) the Americans' improvements in the design of the submarine.

    (B) the discussion of the submarine in nonmilitary contexts.

    (C) the technical explanation of the snorkel as a device.

    (D) the history of submarine development as an effective weapon.

    (E) submarine advancements specific to the Second World War.

29. World War I has particular import for the submarine because

    (A) of the antidetection devices that were developed.

    (B) German use of the submarine exploited its offensive power.

    (C) the sinking of the vessel became comparatively simple.

    (D) the obsolescence of land-craft was made increasingly obvious.

    (E) increasing government subsidies of science and technology aided the War Department.

30. We can infer from the British removal of their ships from New York Harbor

    (A) that the British interests lay in the outer bay.

    (B) that the British were confident their men-of-war could withstand assault.

    (C) that submarine warfare had proved of some tactical advantage.

    (D) that they indicated their need to overhaul the *H.M.S. Eagle.*

    (E) that they insured that the importation of American gunpowder would be limited.

31. The word "trainable" (line 28) means

    (A) having domestic, not military use.

    (B) relating to transportation.

(C) capable of being adapted to various sea transports.

(D) capable of being focused on a specific target.

(E) easily dismantled and reassembled onboard ship.

32. The function of the final paragraph is

   (A) to review the contributions to warfare the submarine had made until World War II.

   (B) to develop the operational use of SONAR.

   (C) to discuss the function of the snorkel.

   (D) to telescope several developments in the design of submarine offensive capability.

   (E) to compare SONAR with the use of the Guppy.

33. Lines 30–33 attribute improvements in submarine technology to

   (A) the British exclusively, who worked on the location device.

   (B) the Allied Submarine Devices Investigation Committee.

   (C) the desire to end the World War as quickly as possible.

   (D) a desire to develop antidetection devices to protect the submarine crew.

   (E) the British, who advanced work already performed by ASDIC.

Questions 34 to 40 are based on the following passage.

We cannot walk alone, and as we walk, we must make the pledge that we shall always march ahead. We cannot turn back. There are those who are asking the devotees of civil rights: "When will you be satisfied?" We can never be satisfied as long as the Negro is the victim of unspeakable horrors of police brutality. We can never be satisfied as long as our bodies, heavy with the fatigue of travel, cannot gain lodging in the motels of the highways and the hotels of the cities. We can never be satisfied as long as the Negro's basic mobility is from a smaller ghetto to a larger one. We can never be satisfied as long as our children are stripped of their selfhood and robbed of their dignity by signs stating "For Whites Only."

We cannot be satisfied so long as the Negro in Mississippi cannot vote and the Negro in New York believes he has nothing for which to vote. No, no, we will not be satisfied until justice rolls down like water and righteousness like a mighty stream.

I am not unmindful that some of you have come here out of great trials and tribulations. Some of you have come from narrow jail cells. Some of you have come from areas where your quest for freedom left you battered by the storms of persecution and staggered by the winds of police brutality. You have been the veterans of creative suffering. Continue to work with the faith that unearned suffering is redemptive.

Go back to Mississippi. Go back to Alabama; go back to South Carolina; go back to Georgia; go back to Louisiana; go back to the slums and ghettoes of our northern cities knowing that somehow this situation can and will be changed. Let us not wallow in the valley of despair.

I say to you today, my friends, even though we face the difficulties of today and tomorrow, I still have a dream. It is a dream deeply rooted in the American dream. I have a dream that one day this Nation will rise up and live out the true meaning of its creeds—"we hold these truths to be self-evident that all men are created equal."

I have a dream that one day on the red hills of Georgia the sons of slaves and the sons of former slaveowners will be able to sit down together at the table of brotherhood. I have a dream that one day even the state of Mississippi, sweltering with the heat of injustice, sweltering with the heat of oppression, will be transformed into an oasis of freedom and justice.

I have a dream that my four little children will one day live in a Nation where they will not be judged by the color of their skins, but by the content of their character.

I have a dream that one day in Alabama, with this vicious racist, its Governor, having his lips dripping the words of interposition and nullification—one day right there in Alabama, little black boys and black girls will be able to join hands with little white boys and little white girls as brothers and sisters.

I have a dream that one day every valley shall be exalted: every hill and mountain shall be made low, the rough places will be made plane, the crooked places will be made straight and the glory of the Lord shall be revealed and all flesh shall see it together.

This is our hope. This is the faith that I go back to the South with. With this faith, we will be able to hew out of the mountains of despair a stone of hope. With this faith, we will be able to transform the jangling discord of our Nation into a beautiful symphony of brotherhood. With this faith, we will be able to work together; to play together; to struggle together; to go to jail together; to stand up for freedom together knowing that we will be free one day. . . .

34. In line 40 the word "interposition" most nearly means

    (A) a mixing, a conglomeration.

    (B) a lofty height or position.

    (C) a coming together, a union.

    (D) a uniting.

    (E) an intervention.

35. In lines 13–14 the words "justice rolls down like water and righteousness like a mighty stream" can best be described as

    (A) onomatopoeic words.

    (B) an alliterative expression.

    (C) an understatement.

    (D) an analogy.

    (E) a fantasy.

36. The Southern states, the slums, and the ghettos in the fourth paragraph were listed

    (A) in order to show that though the United States is large, racial inequality is limited to two main areas.

    (B) in order to name the areas from which most of the audience came.

    (C) in order to single out areas where political leaders were most biased.

    (D) to warn those areas of the violence planned.

    (E) to remind people in those areas that even though times may be rough, not to give up.

37. King reminded the audience that "unearned suffering is redemptive" in line 20. The best explanation for this statement is that

    (A) some suffering is earned; it is deserved.

    (B) some suffering is justified; it is purifying, as such.

    (C) unearned suffering is cruel and unforgivable.

(D) unearned suffering is desirable.

(E) some undeserved suffering is freeing and releasing.

38. The "old saying" which best fits lines 36–38 is

(A) "A soft answer turneth away wrath."

(B) "You can't judge a book by its cover."

(C) "Birds of a feather flock together."

(D) "Let sleeping dogs lie."

(E) "A good name is rather to be chosen than great riches."

39. King compares his audience to those who had fought in great battles by calling them

(A) veterans.

(B) battered.

(C) staggered.

(D) flesh.

(E) devotees.

40. King used the analogy of winds for police brutality because winds

(A) rise up and then die.

(B) turn first one way and then another.

(C) are easy to protect oneself against.

(D) can be harnessed and used as a windmill.

(E) when strong can be damaging and a fearful obstacle.

Section II: Mathematics

(Answer sheets appear in the back of this book.)

TIME: 60 Minutes
           40 Questions

DIRECTIONS: Each of the questions or incomplete statements below is followed by five suggested answers or completions. Select the one that is best in each case.

---

1.   The cost of gas for heating a house in Riverview, Florida is $1.83 per cubic foot. What is the monthly gas bill if the customer uses 145 cubic feet?

(A) $265.35   (D) $79.23

(B) $145.00   (E) $200.00

(C) $183.00

2.   Which of the following figures below represent simple closed curves?

(A) a and b   (D) d and e

(B) a, b, and c   (E) c, d, and e

(C) c and d

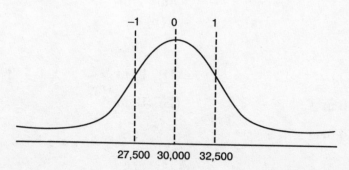

3. The wear-out mileage of a certain tire is normally distributed with a mean of 30,000 miles and a standard deviation of 2,500 miles, as shown above. What will be the percentage of tires that will last at least 30,000 miles?

    (A) 40%   (D) 55%

    (B) 45%   (E) 60%

    (C) 50%

4. How many lines of symmetry, if any, does the following figure have?

    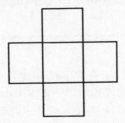

    (A) 1   (D) 4

    (B) 2   (E) 5

    (C) 3

5. Suppose a person 2 m tall casts a shadow 1 m long when a tree has an 8 m shadow. How high is the tree?

    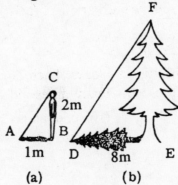

    (A) 8 m   (D) 16 m

    (B) 10 m   (E) 18 m

    (C) 14 m

6. How many 12 oz. cans of orange juice would it take to give 75 people an 8 oz. cup of orange juice?

(A) 112 cans

(D) 900 cans

(B) 75 cans

(E) 50 cans

(C) 600 cans

7. A car rental agency charges $139 per week plus $0.08 per mile for an average size car. How far can you travel to the nearest mile on a maximum budget of $350?

(A) 2,637 mi.

(D) 1,737 mi.

(B) 2,640 mi.

(E) 4,375 mi.

(C) 2,110 mi.

8. Suppose 4 people have to split 50 hours of overtime. Twice the number of hours must be assigned to one worker as to each of the other three. Find the number of hours of overtime that will be assigned to each worker.

(A) 10 hrs. for the first three workers; 20 hrs. for the 4th worker

(B) 8 hrs. for the first three workers; 16 hrs. for the 4th worker

(C) 9 hrs. for the first three workers; 18 hrs. for the 4th worker

(D) 11 hrs. for the first three workers; 22 hrs. for the 4th worker

(E) 12 hrs. for the first three workers; 24 hrs. for the 4th worker

9. Peter took a 1,500 mile trip in 5 days. Each day, he drove 30 miles more than the day before. How many miles did he cover on the first day?

(A) 375 mi.

(D) 240 mi.

(B) 294 mi.

(E) 250 mi.

(C) 230 mi.

10. Mr. Reagan needs 75 m to enclose his rectangular property. If the length of the property is 5 m more than the width, what are the dimensions of his property? Note the figure below.

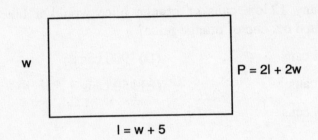

$P = 2l + 2w$

$l = w + 5$

(A) $w = 16.25$ m; $l = 21.25$ m

(B) $w = 18.25$ m; $l = 19.25$ m

(C) $w = 13.00$ m; $l = 24.50$ m

(D) $w = 17.50$ m; $l = 20.00$ m

(E) $w = 35.00$ m; $l = 40.00$ m

11. Which of the following sets is graphed below?

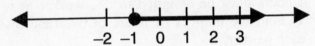

(A) $\{x \mid x \geq -1\}$ (D) $\{x \mid x < -1\}$

(B) $\{x \mid x > -1\}$ (E) $\{x \mid x \neq -1\}$

(C) $\{x \mid x \leq -1\}$

12. Sal has a set of blocks. If 8 percent of this collection is shown in the box below, how many blocks did Sal have?

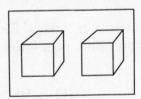

(A) 8   (D) 64

(B) 16   (E) 100

(C) 25

13. Solve the following problem: $|x - 3| < 2$

(A) $-5 < x < 5$ (B) $x = -5$ or 5

(C) $x < 5$ (D) $1 < x < 5$

(E) $x = 5$

14. In the following figure, a semicircle is attached to the top of rectangle ABCD. If $\overline{AB} = 4$ and $\overline{AC} = 6$, what is the total area enclosed by the following figure?

(A) 26p   (D) 24 + 16p

(B) 40p   (E) 24 + 2p

(C) 20 + 4p

15. The area of the circle below is 144p square feet. If $\overline{OB}$ is increased by 2 feet, what is the area of the new circle (in square feet)?

(A) 4p   (D) 169p

(B) 121p   (E) 196p

(C) 146p

16. On what interval is the following function positive?

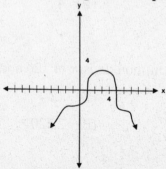

(A) [0, 2]   (D) [1, 5]

(B) (0, 2)   (E) (1, 5)

(C) (0, 2]

17. In the following figure, $\overline{AB} \perp \overline{BC}$, $\overline{AC} = 10$, and $\overline{AB} = 6$. What is the area of $\triangle ABC$?

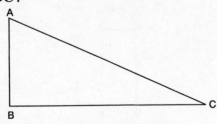

(A) 24   (D) 240

(B) 48   (E) 480

(C) 121

18. According to the graph below, during how many months was supply greater than demand?

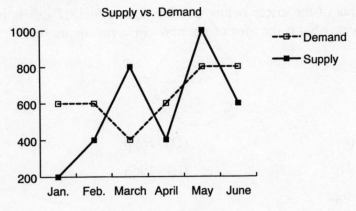

(A) 0   (D) 3

(B) 1   (E) 4

(C) 2

19. What is the greatest common divisor of 120 and 252?

(A) 2   (D) 12

(B) 3   (E) 2,520

(C) 6

20. How many negative integers are between −9 and 5?

    (A) 13   (D) 8

    (B) 10   (E) 6

    (C) 9

21. Dan flies north at a speed of 200 miles per hour, and Tom flies east at a speed of 150 miles per hour. Head wind and air resistance all having been taken into consideration, how far are they apart two hours later?

    (A) 300 miles   (D) 450 miles

    (B) 350 miles   (E) 500 miles

    (C) 400 miles

22. The sum of the base and altitude of a triangle is 12 and the area is 16. What are the base and altitude of the triangle?

    (A) 2 and 10   (D) 3 and 9

    (B) 6   (E) 5 and 7

    (C) 4 and 8

23. The repeating decimal 0.36363636...., when written as a fraction is

    (A) $\dfrac{9}{25}$

    (B) $\dfrac{4}{11}$

    (C) $\dfrac{63}{175}$

    (D) $\dfrac{8}{13}$

    (E) Not expressible as a fraction.

24. An isosceles triangle *ABC* is inscribed in a circle with center *O* in such a way that *OBC* forms an equilateral triangle. The measurement of angle *B* is

   (A) 80°.   (D) 65°.

   (B) 75°.   (E) 60°.

   (C) 70°.

25. If subtracting 13 from a number is the same as taking $3/4$ of the number, what is the number?

   (A) 52   (D) 76

   (B) 39   (E) 97

   (C) 48

26. Mr. Jones is nine times as old as his grandson. If they are 56 years apart, how old is his grandson?

   (A) 9   (D) 6

   (B) 8   (E) 5

   (C) 7

27. Bob is lending money at 6 percent simple interest. How much does he need to lend at the beginning of the year to yield $1,000 by the end of the year? (Figure to the nearest dollar.)

   (A) $850   (D) $943

   (B) $950   (E) $927

   (C) $894

28. The expression $x^n - y^n$

   (A) can be factored only when *n* is odd.

   (B) can never be factored.

   (C) can always be factored.

   (D) can be factored only when *n* is a power of 4.

   (E) can be factored only when *n* is twice an odd integer.

29. If one root of the equation $ax^2 + bx + c = 0$ is 2, the other root must be

(A) $\dfrac{c}{2}$.

(D) $\dfrac{b}{2c}$.

(B) $\dfrac{c}{2a}$.

(E) $\dfrac{a}{2c}$.

(C) $\dfrac{c}{2b}$.

30. If five gallons of 50% alcohol solution is mixed with three gallons of 20% alcohol solution, what is the resulting solution?

(A) 38.75%

(D) 42.25%

(B) 37.5%

(E) 32.25%

(C) 35%

31. Divide $3\dfrac{1}{5}$ by $1\dfrac{1}{3}$.

(A) $2\dfrac{2}{5}$

(D) $4\dfrac{4}{15}$

(B) $3\dfrac{1}{15}$

(E) 8

(C) $3\dfrac{3}{5}$

32. Change 125.937% to a decimal.

(A) 1.25937

(D) 1,259.37

(B) 12.5937

(E) 12,593.7

(C) 125.937

33. Evaluate $4(a + b) + 2[5 - (a^2 + b^2)]$, if $a = 2, b = 1$.

(A) 6

(D) 20

(B) 7

(E) 62

(C) 12

34. Find the mean of the following scores:

    5, 7, 9, 8, 5, 8, 9, 8, 7, 8, 7, 5, 9, 5, 8, 5, 9, 6, 5

    (A) 5   (D) 8

    (B) 6   (E) 9

    (C) 7

35. What percent is 260 of 13?

    (A) .05%   (D) .5%

    (B) 5%   (E) 20%

    (C) 50%

36. How many corners does a cube have?

    (A) 4   (D) 12

    (B) 6   (E) 24

    (C) 8

37. Subtract $4\frac{1}{3} - 1\frac{5}{6}$.

    (A) $3\frac{2}{3}$ (D) $2\frac{1}{6}$

    (B) $2\frac{1}{2}$ (E) None of these.

    (C) $3\frac{1}{2}$

38. In rhombus *ABCD*, which of the following are true?

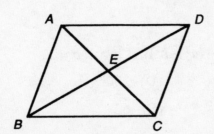

I.   ∠*BAE* and ∠*ECD* are congruent.

II. ∠*ADE* and ∠*CDE* are congruent.

III. ∠*ABE* and ∠*ADE* are congruent.

(A) I only.   (D) I and III only.

(B) II only.   (E) I, II, and III.

(C) I and II only.

39. The rates of a laundry are $6.25 for the first 15 pieces and $0.35 for each additional piece. If the laundry charge is $8.35, how many pieces were laundered?

(A) 5   (D) 21

(B) 6   (E) 25

(C) 15

40. The enrollment in Eastern High School is 1,050. If the attendance for a month was 94 percent, how many students were absent during the month?

(A) 50   (D) 987

(B) 63   (E) 1,044

(C) 420

Section III: Writing

(Answer sheets appear in the back of this book.)

TIME: 30 Minutes
45 Questions

Part A: Usage

DIRECTIONS: Each of the following sentences may contain an error in diction, usage, idiom, or grammar. Some sentences are correct. Some sentences contain one error. No sentence contains more than one error.

If there is an error, it will appear in one of the underlined portions labeled A, B, C, or D. If there is no error, choose the portion labeled E. If there is an error, select the letter of the portion that must be changed in order to correct the sentence.

EXAMPLE:

He drove <u>slowly</u> and <u>cautiously</u> in order to <u>hopefully</u> avoid having an
       A   **B**   **C**

<u>accident</u>. <u>No error</u>.
  D   **E**

1.   Each campus appointed <u>their</u> own committee to apply the <u>findings of</u>
                         A   **B**

    the city-wide survey concerning ways <u>in which</u> the school district <u>can</u>
                                        C   **D**

    save money. <u>No error</u>.
                E

2.   When <u>I</u> asked Gary and John what would be <u>good</u> for dinner, the
            A   **B**

    boys said they <u>could care less</u> <u>about eating</u> liver for the main dish
                    C   **D**

    with spinach for a vegetable. <u>No error</u>.
                              E

3. John will be <u>liable for</u> damages to Mrs. Simon's car because he was
   A
   <u>fascinated by</u> his new red truck and driving so <u>fast</u> that he failed to
   B   C
   <u>conform to</u> a law limiting the speed of any vehicle within the city
   D
   limits. <u>No error</u>.
   E

4. I <u>have seen</u>, <u>more than</u> anything <u>else</u>, that self-esteem is a <u>problem in</u>
   A   B   C   D
   many people of all ages and nationalities. <u>No error</u>.
                                               E

5. Mr. Burgess made sure the ten-year-olds were <u>accommodated with</u>
                                                 A
   quarters for a video games party; afterwards, he declined <u>to say how</u>
                                                             B
   much the event cost him but <u>allowed as how</u> it was more than he
                               C
   <u>had expected</u>. <u>No error</u>.
   D   E

6. This afternoon's boating accident <u>having</u> turned out <u>differently</u>
                                     A   B
   through the efforts of Jack Williams, a fellow vacationer <u>who</u> knows
                                                             C
   CPR, <u>so</u> the little girl has survived. <u>No error</u>.
        D   E

7. Three hundred <u>years ago</u> John Milton <u>protested against</u> laws which
                 A   B
   required a government official to <u>approve of</u> <u>any</u> manuscript before it
                                     C   D
   was published. <u>No error</u>.
                  E

8. Frequently <u>called</u> the "Fourth Estate," journalists have <u>rapidly</u>
              A   B
   <u>developed into</u> powerful people, influencing public opinion and gov-
   C
   ernment policy that <u>has</u> a bearing on the course of history. <u>No error</u>.
                       D   E

9. Totaling <u>more than expected</u>, the groom's wedding expenses
                   A

    <u>included</u> hiring a limousine for the trip to the airport after the wed-
    B

    ding, <u>buying gifts</u> for his groomsmen, and <u>a tuxedo</u> for the ceremony.
          C   **D**

    <u>No error.</u>
    E

10. <u>Our viewing</u> these photographs of Dad standing in front of the throne
     A

    at Macchu Pichu <u>brings</u> back pleasant memories for <u>we</u> children,
                B   **C**

    reminding us <u>of the need for</u> more family get-togethers. <u>No error.</u>
             D   **E**

11. Finally confessing to the <u>theft of</u> money collected for a class movie,
                        A

    Jules said <u>he only</u> stole money once in his life and <u>his</u> conscience
          B   **C**

    would not allow <u>him</u> to enjoy spending it. <u>No error.</u>
             D   **E**

12. If <u>a person</u> is a criminal, <u>he</u> should be punished for <u>it</u>; unfortunately,
      A   **B**   **C**

    many criminals are <u>never</u> caught. <u>No error.</u>
               D   **E**

13. An intriguing habit many hawks have <u>is bringing</u> a fresh green
                           A

    branch <u>daily</u> to line the nest <u>during the season</u> in which <u>they</u> are
        B   **C**   **D**

    mating and rearing their young. <u>No error.</u>
                     E

14. Hawks and owls can be seen <u>more frequent</u> in populated areas than
                      A

    <u>most people</u> <u>suppose</u>, and it is <u>possible</u> to hear screech owls at night
      B   **C**   **D**

    when the adult birds feed their chicks. <u>No error.</u>
                           E

15. The grass was <u>growing over</u> the curb and the oak tree had a branch
              A

    hanging almost <u>to</u> the ground, so we decided to trim <u>it</u> before the
            B   **C**

    neighbors became <u>annoyed with us</u>. <u>No error</u>.
                D   **E**

16. Charles Draper developed the <u>theory of</u> and invented the <u>technology</u>
                     A   **B**

    <u>for</u> inertial navigation, a guidance system <u>which</u> does not <u>rely on</u>
                            C   **D**

    external sources. <u>No error</u>.
                E

17. Inertial navigation is a system of navigation <u>employed</u> in submarines
                                   A

    when <u>they are</u> underwater, missiles used <u>for</u> defense purposes, air-
          B   **C**

    craft, and <u>to get</u> man to the moon in the Apollo exploration series.
            D

    <u>No error</u>.
     E

18. Much <u>to</u> <u>everyone's</u> surprise, the company president, <u>known for</u> his
         A   **B**   **C**

    intelligence and good business judgment, <u>and enjoying</u> a hobby of
                                     D

    sky diving. <u>No error</u>.
             E

19. <u>They</u> are very <u>grateful the city</u> has <u>set up</u> a special fund which <u>helps</u>
     A   **B**   **C**   **D**

    <u>pay</u> for electric bills of the elderly and the handicapped. <u>No error</u>.
                                            E

20. <u>In order to</u> stay cool during the summer months, Americans <u>not only</u>
      A   **B**

    are using ceiling fans, but they are also using devices <u>to add humidity</u>
                                               C

    to the air in <u>particularly</u> arid climates such as Arizona. <u>No error</u>.
                  D   **E**

21. <u>After seeing</u> the technique demonstrated on television, Janie baked
       A

    homemade bread for the first time yesterday, <u>and her</u> brother thought
                                                        B

    it tasted <u>good</u>, an opinion everyone <u>agreed with</u>. <u>No error</u>.
            C   **D**   **E**

22. Although not <u>so</u> prevalent as they once were, <u>hood</u> ornaments still
            A   **B**

    exist, <u>some of which</u> are quite distinctive, <u>such as</u> the symbol for
           C   **D**

    Mercedes-Benz and Jaguar. <u>No error</u>.
                             E

23. If I <u>were</u> that tourist, I would not <u>argue with</u> those two members of
          A   **B**

    the Guardia Civil because, although they are <u>speaking politely</u>, it is
                                            C

    obvious they are <u>becoming angry</u>. <u>No error</u>.
                  D   **E**

24. Mr. Burns is fully <u>aware of</u> statistics proving the <u>harmful</u> conse-
                  A   **B**

    quences of smoking; <u>irregardless</u>, he <u>persists</u> in his habit. <u>No error</u>.
                      C   **D**   **E**

25. David was not capable <u>to win</u> the singles tennis match because he
                      A

    <u>had been</u> injured <u>in</u> a game last week and the doctor prohibited him
      B   **C**

    <u>from</u> playing for two weeks. <u>No error</u>.
     D   **E**

Part B: Sentence Correction

DIRECTIONS: In each of the following sentences, some portion of the sentence is underlined. Under each sentence are five choices. The first choice has the same wording as the original. The other four choices are reworded. Sometimes the first choice containing the original wording is the best; sometimes one of the other choices is the best. Choose the letter of the best choice. Your choice should produce a sentence which is not ambiguous or awkward and which is correct, clear, and precise.

This is a test of correct and effective English expression. Keep in mind the standards of English usage, punctuation, grammar, word choice, and construction.

EXAMPLE:

When you listen to opera, <u>a person may not appreciate it.</u>

(A) a person may not appreciate it.

(B) it may not be appreciated by a person.

(C) which may not be appreciated by one.

(D) you may not appreciate it.

(E) appreciating it may be a problem for you.

26. The new secretary proved herself <u>to be not only capable and efficient but also a woman who was adept</u> at working under pressure and handling irate customers.

   (A) to be not only capable and efficient but also a woman who was adept

   (B) not only to be capable or efficient but also a woman who was adept

   (C) not only to be capable and efficient but also a woman who was adept

   (D) to be not only capable and efficient but also adept

   (E) to be not only capable and efficient but also an adept woman

27. <u>Hunting, if properly managed and carefully controlled,</u> can cull excess animals, thereby producing a healthier population of wild game.

    (A) Hunting, if properly managed and carefully controlled,

    (B) Managing it wisely, carefully controlled hunting

    (C) Managed properly hunting that is carefully controlled

    (D) Properly and wisely controlled, careful hunting

    (E) If properly managed, hunting, carefully controlled,

28. In spite of my reservations, <u>I agreed on the next day to help her put up new wallpaper.</u>

    (A) I agreed on the next day to help her put up new wallpaper.

    (B) I agreed on the next day to help put up her new wallpaper.

    (C) I agreed to help her put up new wallpaper on the next day.

    (D) I, on the next day, agreed to help her put up new wallpaper.

    (E) I agreed to, on the next day, help her put up new wallpaper.

29. <u>We saw many of, though not nearly all, the existing Roman ruins</u> along the Mediterranean coastline of Africa.

    (A) We saw many of, though not nearly all, the existing Roman ruins

    (B) We saw many, though not nearly all, of the existing Roman ruins

    (C) Seeing many, though not nearly all, of the existing Roman ruins

    (D) Having seen many of, though not nearly all, the existing Roman ruins

    (E) Many of, though not nearly all, the existing Roman ruins we saw

30. <u>The horned owl is a carnivore who hunts a diversity of creatures, like</u> hares, grouse, and ground squirrels.

    (A) The horned owl is a carnivore who hunts a diversity of creatures, like

    (B) The horned owl, a carnivore who hunts a diversity of creatures like

(C) A hunting carnivore, the horned owl likes a diversity of creatures

(D) The horned owl likes a diversity of carnivorous creatures, such as

(E) The horned owl is a carnivore who hunts a diversity of creatures, such as

31. In many of his works Tennessee Williams, <u>of whom much has been written</u>, has as main characters drifters, dreamers, and those who are crushed by having to deal with reality.

(A) of whom much has been written

(B) of who much has been written

(C) of whom much has been written about

(D) about him much having been written

(E) much having been written about him

32. The world history students wanted to know <u>where the Dead Sea was at and what it was famous for</u>.

(A) where the Dead Sea was at and what it was famous for.

(B) where the Dead Sea is at and for what it is famous.

(C) where the Dead Sea is located and why it is famous.

(D) at where the Dead Sea was located and what it was famous for.

(E) the location of the Dead Sea and what it is famous for.

33. Literary historians <u>cannot help but admit that they do not know</u> whether poetry or drama is the oldest form of literature.

(A) cannot help but admit that they do not know

(B) cannot admit that they do not admit to knowing

(C) cannot help admitting that they do not know

(D) cannot help but to admit that they do not know

(E) cannot know but admit that they do not

34. Getting to know a person's parents <u>will often provide an insight to</u> his personality and behavior.

    (A) will often provide an insight to

    (B) will often provide an insight into

    (C) will often provide an insight for

    (D) will provide often an insight for

    (E) often will provide an insight with

35. Upon leaving the nursery, Mr. Greene, together with his wife, <u>put the plants in the trunk of the car they had just bought</u>.

    (A) put the plants in the trunk of the car they had just bought.

    (B) put in the plants to the trunk of the car they had just bought.

    (C) put into the trunk of the car they had just bought the plants.

    (D) put the plants they had just bought in the trunk of the car.

    (E) put the plants into the trunk of the car.

36. The way tensions are increasing in the Middle East, some experts <u>are afraid we may end up with a nuclear war</u>.

    (A) are afraid we may end up with a nuclear war.

    (B) being afraid we may end up with a nuclear war.

    (C) afraid that a nuclear war may end up over there.

    (D) are afraid a nuclear war may end there.

    (E) are afraid a nuclear war may occur.

37. <u>Whether Leif Erickson was the first to discover America or not</u> is still a debatable issue, but there is general agreement that there probably were a number of "discoveries" through the years.

    (A) Whether Leif Erickson was the first to discover America or not

    (B) That Leif Erickson was the first to discover America

    (C) That Leif Erickson may have been the first to have discovered America

(D) Whether Leif Erickson is the first to discover America or he is not

(E) Whether or not Leif Erickson was or was not the first discoverer of America

38. <u>People who charge too much are likely to develop</u> a bad credit rating.

(A) People who charge too much are likely to develop

(B) People's charging too much are likely to develop

(C) When people charge too much, likely to develop

(D) That people charge too much is likely to develop

(E) Charging too much is likely to develop for people

39. The museum of natural science has a special exhibit of gems and minerals, <u>and the fifth graders went to see it on a field trip.</u>

(A) and the fifth graders went to see it on a field trip.

(B) and seeing it were the fifth graders on a field trip.

(C) when the fifth graders took a field trip to see it.

(D) which the fifth graders took a field trip to see.

(E) where the fifth graders took their field trip to see it.

40. <u>When the case is decided, he plans appealing</u> if the verdict is unfavorable.

(A) When the case is decided, he plans appealing

(B) When deciding the case, he plans appealing

(C) After the case is decided, he is appealing

(D) After deciding the case, he is planning to appeal

(E) When the case is decided, he plans to appeal

41. <u>We decided there was hardly any reason for his allowing us</u> to stay up later on weeknights.

(A) We decided there was hardly any reason for his allowing us

(B) We, deciding there was hardly any reason for his allowing us,

(C) Deciding there was hardly any reason, we allowed

(D) We decided there were none of the reasons for him to allow us

(E) For him to allow us there was hardly any reason we decided

42. At this time <u>it is difficult for me agreeing with your plan of having everyone</u> in the club working on the same project.

(A) it is difficult for me agreeing with your plan of having everyone

(B) I find it difficult to agree to your plan of having everyone

(C) for my agreement with your plan is difficult for everyone

(D) an agreement to your plan seems difficult for everyone

(E) finding it difficult for me to agree to your plan of having everyone

43. When the Whites hired a contractor to do remodeling on their home, he <u>promised to completely finish the work inside of three months</u>.

(A) promised to completely finish the work inside of three months.

(B) promised to complete the work within three months.

(C) completely promised to finish the work inside of three months' span.

(D) promising to completely finish the work in three months.

(E) completely finished the work within three months.

44. <u>The more we use machines,</u> the more human beings live at odds with their environment.

(A) The more we use machines

(B) The more they use machines

(C) The more machines are used by us

(D) As our use of machines is increased

(E) As we add to our use of machines

45. Many politicians believe in "ad hominem" arguments, <u>meaning that one attacks</u> the person, not the issue.

(A) meaning that one attacks

(B) meaning that they attack

(C) which attack

(D) the meaning of which is that one attacks

(E) attacking

Part C: Essay

TIME: 30 Minutes

DIRECTIONS: You have 30 minutes to plan and write an essay on the topic below. You may write only on the assigned topic.

Make sure to give specific examples to support your thesis. Proofread your essay carefully and take care to express your ideas clearly and effectively.

ESSAY TOPIC:

Television often causes the viewer to lose touch with reality and become completely passive and unaware. Like other addictions, television provides a pleasurable escape route from action to inaction.

ASSIGNMENT: Do you agree or disagree with the statement? Support your opinion with specific examples from history, current events, literature, or personal experience.

PPST TEST IV

ANSWER KEY

Section I — Reading Comprehension

1. (A)	11. (D)	21. (E)	31. (D)
2. (B)	12. (E)	22. (C)	32. (D)
3. (C)	13. (C)	23. (A)	33. (E)
4. (C)	14. (E)	24. (C)	34. (E)
5. (B)	15. (A)	25. (E)	35. (D)
6. (D)	16. (B)	26. (A)	36. (E)
7. (C)	17. (D)	27. (D)	37. (E)
8. (E)	18. (D)	28. (D)	38. (B)
9. (E)	19. (D)	29. (B)	39. (A)
10. (A)	20. (B)	30. (C)	40. (E)

Section II — Mathematics

1. (A)	11. (A)	21. (E)	31. (A)
2. (A)	12. (C)	22. (C)	32. (A)
3. (C)	13. (D)	23. (B)	33. (C)
4. (D)	14. (E)	24. (B)	34. (C)
5. (D)	15. (E)	25. (A)	35. (B)
6. (E)	16. (E)	26. (C)	36. (C)
7. (A)	17. (A)	27. (D)	37. (B)
8. (A)	18. (C)	28. (C)	38. (E)
9. (D)	19. (D)	29. (B)	39. (D)
10. (A)	20. (D)	30. (A)	40. (B)

Section III — Writing

1. (A)	13. (B)	25. (A)	37. (B)
2. (C)	14. (A)	26. (D)	38. (A)
3. (D)	15. (C)	27. (A)	39. (D)
4. (E)	16. (E)	28. (C)	40. (E)
5. (C)	17. (D)	29. (B)	41. (A)
6. (A)	18. (D)	30. (E)	42. (B)
7. (B)	19. (A)	31. (A)	43. (B)
8. (D)	20. (B)	32. (C)	44. (B)
9. (D)	21. (D)	33. (C)	45. (C)
10. (C)	22. (A)	34. (B)	
11. (B)	23. (E)	35. (D)	
12. (C)	24. (C)	36. (E)	

DETAILED EXPLANATIONS OF ANSWERS

Section I: Reading Comprehension

1. **(A)** Capricious means unpredictable.

2. **(B)** This choice is supported by the last sentence in the passage.

3. **(C)** The author discusses how the birds share the same food supply but occupy different areas of the pond. Each of the other choices is too broad and general.

4. **(C)** The author's terms "misguided" and "facts just do not support their claim" indicate more than impartiality, choice (A), or indifference, choice (B), for those who believe that America is or ever was a monolingual country. Nothing in the passage characterizes anger, choice (D), or an optimistic nature, choice (E).

5. **(B)** Choices (A), (D), and (E) generalize beyond information in the passage. Choice (C) contradicts information given in the passage.

6. **(D)** This choice is supported in the second sentence. All other choices are secondary to the central idea.

7. **(C)** The passage states that this was a "noteworthy accomplishment in technology."

8. **(E)** The passage emphasizes the complicated process of filtering the meal through sand or tightly woven baskets. Choices (A), (B), and (C), while true, are not the most difficult problem. Choice (D) is contradictory to information given in the text.

9. **(E)** In the context of the passage, vestige means a small remaining amount.

10. **(A)** Choices (D) and (E) are incorrect as the strategy is for oral reading, not silent reading. Choices (B) and (C) are not supported by the passage—thus choice (A) is correct.

11. **(D)** Choices (A), (B), (C), and (E) include syllable and paragraph elements which are not supported by the passage. The passage states " . . . individual language units which can be as small as a single letter or as large as phrases or sentences."

12. **(E)** Choices (A), (B), (C), and (D) are not supported by the passage. The passages states that "speeding up reading, not slowing it down, helps the reader make sense of a passage."

13. **(C)** The passage compares duplex versus one-way video and two-way audio. The reader must infer that duplex indicates two-way video and two-way audio since duplex refers to two. The other choices (A), (B), (D), and (E) are incorrect.

14. **(E)** Choices (A), (B), (C), and (D) are inappropriate for defining an instrument which assesses learning and demonstrates learning.

15. **(A)** Choices (B), (C), (D), and (E) are not supported by the passage.

16. **(B)** While choices (A), (C), (D), and (E) are mentioned briefly in the passage, the passage focuses on student participation and learning.

17. **(D)** Choices (A), (B), (C), and (E) appear to be definitions of effeminate. However, for this passage choice (D) is most appropriate since it relates to the eyes.

18. **(D)** Choices (A), (B), and (C) are not supported by the passage. The passage hints at choice (E), but the passage remains primarily imaginative, thus choice (D) is correct.

19. **(D)** Choice (D) states the most complete main idea in the passage, hence, it is the correct answer. Choice (A) addresses only one part of the correct answer; choices (B) and (C) are incorrect; and choice (E) is an incomplete answer.

20. **(B)** Of the choices provided, (B) provides the most complete answer—namely, the two things that the computer program does: predicts the aging process and predicts how an unborn child will look. The other choices, (A), (C), (D), and (E) while all true, are incomplete in providing the main capability of the new computer program developed in Japan.

21. **(E)** A logical answer to this question has got to be (E). With this new computer system it certainly will follow that Japan will do a more refined and sophisticated system next. Choices (A) and (B) are related—the answers are natural outgrowths of the competitive market among nations; and choices (C) and (D) have been an on-going trend anyway.

22. **(C)** In an emergency situation, the most sound and logical thing to do would have to be (C). Choice (A) is not the best thing to do in the situation; choice (B) is running a risk of consuming the fuel; the same could be said of choice (D); and choice (E) is too risky, hence, incorrect.

23. **(A)** For air travelers who are aware of possible communications breakdown due to a power failure, choice (A) is the best and correct answer. Choice (B) could be true only to certain people; choice (C) is a good answer but does not relate to the specific incident; choice (D) is besides the point; and choice (E) is an incorrect generalization—delays are caused by other reasons besides a power failure.

24. **(C)** A title is supposed to synthesize the main idea of a passage. In this passage the best synthesis is (C), hence, the correct answer. Choices (A), (B), (D), and (E) are possible titles but are all incomplete as titles.

25. **(E)** The question is inappropriate to the passage—it addresses men and women. However, the research addressed in the passage was done on men only. Hence, the correct answer is (E); all the rest of the answers, (A), (B), (C), and (D), are incorrect.

26. **(A)** The answer in (A) is sound and is the best and correct answer. Choice (B) is an incorrect answer; choice (C) is an incorrect implication; the same can be said of choices (D) and (E).

27. **(D)** The study covered only men, hence, a major limitation is the fact that it did not include women of the same age group. The correct answer, therefore, is (D). Choice (A) may not be an essential in the study, hence, definitely not a major limitation; choice (B), while a limitation,

cannot be considered "major." Besides, "children" could include babies through young adolescents—a rather wide age range. Choice (C) is also a limitation, but it does not state the precise age range.

28. **(D)** The passage traces the history of the submarine "as an offensive weapon" (line 1); the dates from 1864 negate the specific reference to WW II in (E). Both German and English advances discussed in lines 17–33 negate (A). The opening sentence specifies military contexts, negating (B). Innovations discussed extend beyond the snorkel (C).

29. **(B)** Germany exploited the full resources of the submarine; while (A) is a strong distractor, detection devices did not become refined until after WW I. (C) is ambiguous as to whether "the vessel" means the sub or its target—it is untrue in any case. (E) is a misreading corollary of British technological work; (D) is not discussed.

30. **(C)** The very attempt to sink a British man-of-war proved intimidating; (B) is the wrong conclusion based on the British fear of attack. (A) may be a rationalization of the British, and (E) merely correlates to that misreading. (D) is a distractor.

31. **(D)** The hydrophone could be "aimed" at a specific target. (B) is the only "reasonable" distractor.

32. **(D)** While (A) is a reasonable choice, the last paragraph, especially line 56, exceeds the chronology of WW II. (B) and (E) list specific technologies incidental to submarine history; (C) also deals with a specific element in the course of a list of technological innovations.

33. **(E)** Choice (E) is more correct than (A), since the early work on detection devices was done by a committee cited on lines 24–25. (B) ignores work by the later group; (C) is reasonable speculation. (D) is illogical.

34. **(E)** The word "interposition" means most nearly an intervention or a mediation. Answer (E) most nearly satisfies that definition. A conglomeration is not an intervention or a coming between but a mixing; (A) would not be the best choice. One who intervenes does not necessarily have to be in a lofty position; (B) is not, therefore, the best answer; perhaps the person who chose this answer selected it merely because both the word being considered and the answer contained the letters "position."

After an intervention there may be a coming together (C) or a uniting (D), but interposition does not necessarily ensure this result; (C) and (D) are not, therefore, the best answers.

35. **(D)** In lines 13–14 the words "justice rolls down like water and righteousness like a mighty stream" can best be described as a comparison, or an analogy (D). Since an onomatopoeic word is formed by making an imitation of the sound associated with the object or action, onomatopoeic (A) is not the best answer. An alliterative expression repeats the same sound; this has not been done in the phrase "justice rolls down like water and righteousness like a mighty stream"; (B) is incorrect. Using terms like "mighty stream" and "righteousness" are not understatements; (C) should not be selected. The words in question were not fanciful words but words which were capable of being fulfilled. (E) should not be selected since it expresses this quotation as being a fantasy.

36. **(E)** The Southern states, the slums, and the ghettos in the fourth paragraph were listed to inspire hope; even if those areas were desolate at this time, King had faith that in the future things would change. (E) is the best answer. Unfortunately, racial bias and inequality were not just evident in one area. (A), then, was an inadequate answer. The audience did not necessarily come from the areas listed above; (B) is not the best answer. Biased political leaders are not restricted to slums, ghettos, and Southern states; (C) is not the best choice. King did not plan violence, so choice (D) is not appropriate.

37. **(E)** King reminded the audience that "unearned suffering is redemptive" in line 20. The best explanation for this statement is that King was suggesting that some undeserved suffering may actually be freeing and releasing. (E) is the best choice. King makes no reference to the fact that some of the suffering endured was earned or deserved. (A) is not the best choice. King does not see suffering as being justified or purifying so (B) is incorrect. King does not view unearned suffering as unforgivable; (C) is incorrect. King does not advocate followers seeking to suffer for no reason; he does not see unearned suffering as something to be sought or desired. (D) is incorrect.

38. **(B)** The "old saying" which best fits lines 36–38 is (B), "You can't judge a book by its cover." King is looking forward to the day when people are judged by their character and not by their skin color. (B) is the answer to be chosen. Although (A) is an oft-repeated statement and even

though it does not fit at this point, it does fit some of King's speeches. (A) should not be chosen. Judging little children by their skin color does not relate to birds of a feather flocking together; (C) should not be chosen. Not disturbing the situation, or letting sleeping dogs lie, does not relate to the color of the children's skin; (D) does not fit. "A good name is rather to be chosen than great riches," but this has nothing to do with judging children by their skin color. (E) is not the best answer.

39. **(A)**   King best compared his audience to those who had fought in great battles by calling them (A) veterans. It is true that the audience may have been (B) battered, but that does not necessarily go along with war alone; victims of other situations may be battered. (B) should not be chosen. The audience may be opposed and may stagger, but this does not necessarily relate to war; staggered (C) is not a good choice. Flesh (D) does not necessarily relate to war; (D) should not be selected. A devotee (E) may or may not relate to war; (E) should not be chosen.

40. **(E)**   King used the analogy of winds for police brutality because winds when strong can be damaging and a fearful obstacle; (E) is the best choice. Winds do rise up and then die, but that analogy is not the best here; it does not seem to relate to the police. (A) is not the best answer. A reference to the police as turning first one way and then another (B) is not the best answer. Since winds are not always easy to protect one's self against, (C) is not the best choice. A wind which can be harnessed and used by a windmill does not seem to be a good analogy here; one does not usually think of harnessing police. (D) is not the best answer.

Section II: Mathematics

1. **(A)** Multiply $1.83 by 145 and the answer is $265.35.

2. **(A)** By definition, a simple curve is a curve that can be traced in such a way that no point is traced more than once with the exception that the tracing may stop where it started. A closed curve is a curve that can be traced so that the starting and stopping points are the same. Therefore, a and b are simple closed curves. The rest are not.

3. **(C)** In a normal distribution, half the data are always above the mean. Since 30,000 miles is the mean, half or 50 percent of the tires will last at least 30,000 miles.

4. **(D)** A line of symmetry for a figure is a line in which you can stand a mirror, so that the image you see in the mirror is just like the part of the figure that the mirror is hiding. In this case there are four lines.

5. **(D)** This can be solved using ratio and proportion, thus, 2 is to 1 as x is to 8.

$$\frac{2}{1} = \frac{x}{8}$$

so $x = 16$ m.

6. **(E)** First find how many ounces of orange juice is needed, so multiply 75×8 oz. = 600 oz. needed. Then divide 600 by 12 oz. = 50 12 oz. cans needed to serve 75 people with 8 oz. of juice each.

7. **(A)** m = number of miles you can travel

$0.08m = amount spent for m miles travelled at 8 cents per mile,

(rental fee + mileage charge = total amount spent)

$139 + $0.08m = $350

$139 - 139 + 0.08m = 350 - 139$

$$\frac{0.08m}{0.08} = \frac{211}{0.08}$$

$$m = 2,637.5$$

$$m = 2,637$$

Therefore, you can travel 2,637 miles (if you go 2,638 miles you have travelled too far).

8. **(A)**   Let x = number of hours of overtime for the 1st worker,

x = number of hours of overtime for the 2nd worker,

x = number of hours of overtime for the 3rd worker,

$2x$ = number of hours of overtime for the 4th worker.

$$x + x + x + 2x = 50$$

$$5x = 50$$

$$x = \frac{50}{5}$$

$x = 10$ hrs of overtime for the 1st three workers

$2x = 20$ hrs of overtime for the 4th worker

9. **(D)**   Let m = number of miles covered the 1st day.

$m + 30$ = number of miles covered the 2nd day,

$m + 30 + 30$ = number of miles covered the 3rd day,

$m + 30 + 30 + 30$ = number of miles covered the 4th day,

$m + 30 + 30 + 30 + 30$ = number of miles covered the 5th day.

$m + m + 30$ and so on... = 1,500

$$5m + 30 (10) = 1,500$$

$$5m + 300 = 1,500$$

$$5m = 1,500 - 300$$

$$5m = 1,200$$

$$m = \frac{1,200}{5}$$

$$m = 240 \text{ mi}$$

10. **(A)** Using the formula

$$P = 2w + 2l$$

$$75 = 2w + 2(w + 5)$$

$$75 = 2w + 2w + 10$$

$$75 = 4w + 10$$

$$65 = 4w$$

$$16.25 = w$$

The width is therefore 16.25 m and the length is $w + 5$ or $16.25 + 5 =$ 21.25 m.

11. **(A)** Note that there is a solid dot on -1 which means to include -1 in the set. The numbers to the right of -1 are shaded; this means to include these numbers also. Hence, this is the graph of all numbers greater than or equal to -1 ($\{x \mid x \geq -1\}$).

12. **(C)** Let 2 be the number of blocks that Sal has. Then, 8% of x is 2 according to the given figure. Thus, we have the equation:

$.08x = 2$ or, dividing both sides by .08,

$$x = \frac{2}{.08} = \frac{2}{.08} \times \frac{100}{100} = \frac{200}{8} = 25.$$

13. **(D)** $|x - 3| < 2$ is equivalent to $-2 < x - 3 < 2$. To solve this double inequality, we must add 3 to all three sides:

$$3 + -2 < x - 3 + 3 < 2 + 3 \text{ or } 1 < x < 5.$$

14. **(E)** We must find the area of the rectangle and of the semicircle. The area of the rectangle is length times width or $6 \times 4 = 24$. The area the semicircle is one-half the area of a circle with diameter $\overline{AB}$ or $1/2 \times \pi r^2$ where r is one-half the length of the diameter $\overline{AB}$. So $r = 2$ and the area of the semicircle is

$$\frac{1}{2}\pi(2)^2 = 2\pi$$

Thus, the total area is $24 + 2\pi$.

15. **(E)** The area of a circle is πr^2 where r is the radius. In the given circle, $\overline{OB}$ is the radius and $A = 144\pi$. So, $144\pi = \pi r^2$ so that $r = 12$. If we increased the radius by 2 feet so that now $r = 14$, the area of the new circle is

$$A = \pi (14)^2 = 196\pi.$$

16. **(E)** A function is positive when the points on its graph lie above the x-axis. In our graph this occurs when x is between 1 and 5 or (1, 5).

17. **(A)** Since $\overline{AB} \perp \overline{BC}$, we know that $\triangle ABC$ is a right triangle and thus we may use the Pythagorean Theorem to find the length of $\overline{BC}$ (let x be the length of $\overline{BC}$):

$$\overline{AC}^2 = \overline{AB}^2 + \overline{BC}^2$$
or $\quad (10)^2 = 6^2 + x^2$

or $\quad 100 = 36 + x^2$.

To solve this, subtract 36 from both sides of the equation to get: $64 = x^2$ so that $x = 8$. The area of $\triangle ABC =$

$$\frac{1}{2}(AB)(BC) = \frac{1}{2}(6)(8) = 24.$$

18. **(C)** According to the graph, the supply was greater than the demand in March and May only.

19. **(D)** The greatest common divisor (GCD) is the greatest integer which divides both 120 and 252. To find the GCD, factor both numbers and look for common factors.

$$120 = 2^3 \times 3 \times 5$$
and $\quad 252 = 2^2 \times 3^2 \times 7,$

so the GCD $= 2^2 \times 3 = 12$.

20. **(D)** The list of all the negative integers between −9 and 5 is:

−8, −7, −6, −5, −4, −3, −2, −1.

21. **(E)** Since they travel on the two sides of a right-angled triangle, the Pythagorean Theorem yields

$$400^2 + 300^2 = 500^2.$$

22. **(C)**   Let b be the base and a be the altitude of the triangle. We have the equations:

$$a + b = 12,$$

and $$\frac{ab}{2} = 16.$$

To solve these equations, substitute $b = 12 - a$ into the second equation, we have

$$a(12 - a) = 32,$$

or $$12a - a^2 = 32,$$

or $$a^2 - 12a + 32 = (a - 8)(a - 4) = 0;$$

thus, $a = 4$ or 8, and $b = 8$ or 4 respectively.

23. **(B)**   Since a two-digit repeating decimal is the two digits over 99, we have

$$\frac{36}{99} = \frac{4}{11}.$$

24. **(B)**   Since the angle BOC measures $60°$, angle BAC measures $30°$, angles B and C will be half of

$$\frac{(180° - 30°)}{2} = 75°.$$

25. **(A)**   Since

$$x - 13 = \frac{3x}{4},$$

or $$4x - 52 = 3x,$$

we have $x = 52$.

26. **(C)**   Letting Mr. Jones' age be x, and his grandson's be y, we have $x = 9y$ and $x - y = 56$. Substitute the first into the second equation,

$$9y - y = 56, \quad y = 7.$$

27. **(D)**   His principle and interest need to be 1,000, which is 1.06 times his principle. Thus, we divide 1,000 by 1.06 and it is close to 943.

28. **(C)**   In fact,

$$x^n - y^n = (x - y)(x^{n-1} + x^{n-2}y + x^{n-3}y^2 + \ldots + y^{n-1}).$$

29. **(B)**   The original equation is equivalent to

$$x^2 + \frac{bx}{a} + \frac{c}{a} = 0.$$

The product of the two roots must equal $\dfrac{c}{a}$.

30. **(A)**   The alcohol content is

$$5 \times 0.5 + 3 \times 0.2 = 3.1 \text{ gallons,}$$

and the total amount of solution is 8 gallons.

$$3.1 \div 8 = .3875 = 38.75\%.$$

31. **(A)**   In order to divide $3^1/_5$ by $1^1/_3$, we must first change both mixed numbers into improper fractions.

$$\frac{16}{5} \div \frac{4}{3} = \frac{16}{5} \times \frac{3}{4}$$

$$= \frac{4}{5} \times \frac{3}{1}$$

$$= \frac{12}{5}$$

Since the result is an improper fraction, we must convert it back into a mixed number.

$$\frac{12}{5} = \frac{10}{5} + \frac{2}{5}$$

$$= 2 + \frac{2}{5}$$

Therefore, the correct answer is $2^2/_5$.

32. **(A)** To change a percent to a decimal, drop the percent sign and move the decimal point two place values to the left. The correct answer is 1.25937.

33. **(C)** Substitute 2 for each a, 1 for each b, and simplify the expression.

$$4(2 + 1) + 2[5 - (2^2 + 1^2)] = 4(2 + 1) + 2[5 - (4 + 1)]$$
$$= 4(3) + 2[5 - (5)]$$
$$= 4(3) + 2[0]$$
$$= 12 + 0$$
$$= 12$$

34. **(C)** To find the mean, first add the individual scores together. The sum is 133. Next, count the number of scores which is 19 and divide 19 into 133, for a mean of 7.

35. **(B)** In order to find what percent of 260 is 13, one needs only to form the following equation:

$$x\%(260) = 13$$
$$\frac{x(260)}{100} = 13$$
$$260x = 13(100)$$
$$x = \frac{1,300}{260} = 5 \text{ percent} = 5\%$$

The other answer choices are incorrect, however. Response (A) is obtained by dividing 13 by 260 and attaching the percent symbol. Response (D) is obtained by again dividing 13 by 260, moving the decimal point one place to the right and attaching the percent symbol. Response (E) is obtained by dividing 260 by 13 and attaching the percent sign. Finally, response (C) is absurd because 50% of 260 is half of 260 which is 130 or 10 times 13.

36. **(C)** Referring to the figure shown below, it is easy to see that a cube has 8 corners. There are four in the front (points 1, 2, 3, and 4) and four in the back (points 5, 6, 7, and 8).

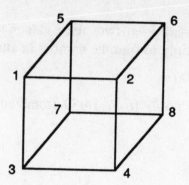

37. **(B)**

$$4\frac{1}{3} - 1\frac{5}{6} = 4\frac{2}{6} - 1\frac{5}{6}$$

$$= 3\frac{2+6}{6} - 1\frac{5}{6}$$

$$= 3\frac{8}{6} - \frac{5}{6}$$

$$= 2\frac{3}{6} = 2\frac{1}{2}$$

38. **(E)**   All three statements are true. Since a rhombus is a parallelogram, sides $\overline{BA}$ and $\overline{CD}$ are parallel. Using $\overline{AC}$ as a transversal, $\angle BAE$ and $\angle ECD$ are alternate interior angles and are therefore congruent making I true. The diagonals of a rhombus bisect the angles and so $\angle ADE$ and $\angle CDE$ are congruent making II true. In a rhombus, all four sides are congruent so triangle ABD is isosceles with congruent sides $\overline{AB}$ and $\overline{AD}$. The angles opposite those congruent sides are congruent, so $\angle ABE$ and $\angle ADE$ are congruent making III true. Therefore, the answer is choice (E).

39. **(D)**   The total cost is $8.35; subtract $6.25 for the cost of the first 15 pieces of laundry.

$$8.35 - 6.25 = \$2.10$$

Divide $2.10 by $0.35 to determine the number of pieces of laundry over 15.

$$.35\ \sqrt{2.10}$$

$$\frac{6}{35\ \sqrt{210}}$$

15 (cost of $6.25) + 6 (cost of $2.10) = 21 pieces of laundry.

40. **(B)** Move the decimal point two place values to the left and drop the percent sign, then multiply to find the number in attendance.

$$1,050 \times .94 = 987.00$$

Subtract 987 (attended school) from 1,050 (total enrolled) to find the number absent.

$$1,050 - 987 = 63$$

The correct answer is 63.

Section III: Writing

1. **(A)** "Campus" is a singular noun; therefore, the pronoun referring to "campus" should be "its" so that the pronoun will agree with its antecedent. Choices (B), "findings of," and (C), "in which," both have prepositions appropriately used. Choice (D), "can," is a helping verb in the correct tense.

2. **(C)** Choice (C) should read, "could not care less." A person using this expression is indicating his total lack of interest in something; to say, "I could care less" indicates some interest, so the correct expression is "I could not care less." Choice (A) is the correct subject pronoun; choice (B), "good," is the adjective form used to follow the linking verb "be" and choice (D) is a gerund used as the object of a preposition.

3. **(D)** The idiom is "conform with" a law; something or someone will "conform to" an environment. Choices (A) and (B) are correctly used idioms. Choice (C) is the proper form of the adjective.

4. **(E)** Choice (A), "have seen," is the present perfect tense, which is used to make a statement about something occurring in the past but continuing into the present. The speaker has observed the problem of lack of self-esteem, but this problem has not stopped in the present time. Choice (B) is a comparative form, and "else" of choice (C) is necessary when comparing one thing with the group of which it is a member or part. (The observation about self-esteem is but one of several observations the speaker has made.) Choice (D) has a preposition to indicate relationship between "problem" and "people."

5. **(C)** "Allowed as how" is used sometimes in speaking, but the proper expression should be "allowed that." "Accommodated with," choice (A), is an idiom used to indicate "to supply with." Choice (B) is an infinitive phrase followed by a subordinate clause as the direct object. Choice (D), "had expected," is the past perfect tense to indicate previous past action: Mr. Burgess's estimate of the cost was made before the actual event.

6. **(A)** As this sentence reads, it is a fragment. "Having" should be eliminated, leaving "turned out" as the main verb in the proper tense. Choice (D), "so," is a coordinating conjunction relating two events of cause-and-effect; therefore, both main clauses should be independent.

Choice (B) is the adverb form modifying the verb "turned out," and choice (C), "who," is the nominative form serving as the subject of "knows."

7. **(B)** "Protested against" is redundant; "protested" is sufficient. "Ago" in choice (A) is an adjective used following the noun "years" or as an adverb following "long." Choice (C) is a correct idiom. Choice (D), "any," is an adjective.

8. **(D)** Two subjects joined by "and" require a plural verb; "public opinion and government policy" should be completed by "have." Choice (A), "called," is a participle modifying "journalists." Choice (B), "rapidly," is an adverb modifying choice (C), which is a correct idiom.

9. **(D)** The expression should read, "renting (or buying) a tuxedo," in order to complete the parallelism following choice (B) "included": "hiring a limousine" and "buying gifts," choice (C). Choice (A) is a correct expression which can also be phrased, "more than he expected," if greater clarity is desired.

10. **(C)** The object pronoun "us" should follow the preposition "of." In choice (A), "viewing" is a gerund used as the subject and therefore requires the possessive adjective "our." Choice (B) is the verb. Choice (D) is a correct idiom.

11. **(B)** The modifier "only" is misplaced. To place this word before "stole" indicates that stealing is a minor problem; also, the meaning of the sentence clearly indicates Jules has stolen money one time, so the sentence should read, "stole money only once." Choice (A) is a correct preposition; choice (C) is a possessive pronoun modifying "conscience"; and choice (D) is an object pronoun as the object of "allow."

12. **(C)** There is no antecedent for "it." Choice (A), "a person," is the subject to which "he" in choice (B) refers. "Never" in choice (D) is a correctly placed adverb. The sentence should include a phrase such as "a crime" to serve as the antecedent of "it," or the phrase "for it" could be deleted.

13. **(B)** The adverb "daily" is misplaced and should be placed with "is bringing," choice (A), or with "habit." Choice (C) is a prepositional phrase, and choice (D) is a subject pronoun for the subordinate clause.

14. **(A)** The adverb form, "frequently," should be used to modify the verb. Choices (B) and (C) are a correct subject-verb combination. The adjective form, "possible," of choice (D) follows the linking verb "is."

15. **(C)** The antecedent for "it" is unclear because "it" can refer to the grass or to the branch. Choice (A), "growing over," and choice (B), "to," are correct pronouns. Choice (D) is a correct idiom because we become "annoyed with" people but "annoyed at" things or situations.

16. **(E)** The sentence is correct as written. Choices (A) and (B) are a compound structure and are in proper parallel form. Choice (C) has a clear reference to "system." Choice (D) is a correct idiom.

17. **(D)** The preposition "in" has three objects: "submarines," "missiles," and choice (D) which must be made parallel to the previous two nouns. Choice (A) is a participle modifying "navigation." Choice (B) is a part of a subordinate clause modifying "submarines." Choice (C) is a correct preposition.

18. **(D)** This sentence is a fragment made by the conjunction "and" linking "enjoying" with "known," the participial adjective of choice (B); "and" should be eliminated and "enjoying" changed to "enjoys" to be the subject of "president." Choice (A) is an idiom. Choice (B) is the correct possessive form to complete the idiom.

19. **(A)** There is no antecedent for this pronoun, although it is implied that the elderly and the handicapped are the logical ones to be grateful. Choice (B) and (D) are elliptical constructions, "grateful [that] the city" and "helps [to] pay." Choice (C) is a verb.

20. **(B)** This sentence is not parallel. Two actions are mentioned, connected by "not only" and "but also." The sentence should read, "not only are Americans . . . but also they are." Choices (A) and (C) contain properly used infinitives. Choice (D), "particularly," is the adverb form modifying the adjective, "arid."

21. **(D)** Sentences should not end with a preposition; the sentence should read, "an opinion with which everyone agreed." Choice (A) is a gerund as the object of a preposition. Choice (B) is an appropriate conjunction; and choice (C), "good," is the positive form of the adjective to follow the linking verb "tasted."

22. **(A)** The expression should read, "as prevalent as" for the proper comparison. Choice (B) is a noun used as an adjective. Choice (C), "some of which," has clear reference to "ornaments." Choice (D), "such as," is correct to mean, "for example."

23. **(E)** Choice (A) is subjunctive mood to indicate a condition contrary to fact. Choice (B) is a correct idiom. Choice (C) uses the adverb "politely" to modify "speaking," and choice (D) uses the adjective "angry" to follow the linking verb "becoming."

24. **(C)** "Irregardless," an incorrect expression, is a combination of "irrespective" and "regardless." (Taking into account the prefix and the suffix of "irregardless," the combination would mean, "not, not regarding," and so would be redundant.) Usually, "regardless" is used, although "irrespective" is also correct. The idioms in choices (A) and (D) are correct. Choice (B) is an adjective.

25. **(A)** The idiom should be "capable of winning." The verb in choice (B) indicates the prior action of two past actions; the prepositions in choices (C) and (D) are correct.

26. **(D)** The conjunction "not only . . . but also" must be properly placed to indicate which qualities are being discussed and to maintain proper parallelism. Choice (D) contains three adjectives to follow the verb "to be": "capable and efficient" and "adept." Choices (A), (B), (C), and (E) are not parallel. In addition, choices (B) and (C) have "to be" after the conjunction, and this construction would require another verb after the second conjunction, "but also."

27. **(A)** This sentence contains two concepts, proper management and careful control. In choice (A) these two concepts are concisely worded and appear in parallel form. Choice (B) has no noun for "Managing" to modify. Choice (C) would be acceptable with the addition of commas to set off the introductory phrase. Choice (D) mangles the concepts, and the wording in choice (E) is poor.

28. **(C)** Choice (A) is a "squinting" modifier: it is unclear if "on the next day" tells when "I agreed" or when "to put up." Choice (B) does not clarify this problem. Choice (D) unnecessarily splits the subject and the verb, and choice (E) unnecessarily splits an infinitive.

29. **(B)** The interrupter, "though not nearly all," should be placed so as not to split important parts of the sentence. Choices (A), (D), and (E) are incorrect because the interrupter splits a preposition and its object. Choices (C) and (D) will produce a fragment because the subject "we" is missing.

30. **(E)** To mean "for example," the expression "like" is incorrect; the correct usage is "such as." Therefore, choices (A) and (B) are incorrect. Choices (C) and (D) incorrectly use "likes" as a verb, thereby changing the intent of the sentence.

31. **(A)** Choice (A) correctly uses the object pronoun "whom" to follow the preposition "of." Choice (B) uses the wrong pronoun. Choice (C) inserts an extraneous preposition "about" that has no object. Choice (D) is awkward wording; choice (E) is also poor wording, especially with the pronoun "him" so far away from its antecedent.

32. **(C)** Choice (C) clearly and simply deals with the location and the fame of the Dead Sea. It is incorrect to use a preposition with no object in order to end a sentence. Choices (A), (D), and (E) are incorrect because they end with "famous for." Also, in the phrase, "where the Dead Sea is at," the word *at* is redundant; it is sufficient to write "where the Dead Sea is." Therefore, choices (A) and (B) are incorrect. Finally, since the Dead Sea still exists, the verbs must be in the present tense.

33. **(C)** The phrase "cannot help" should be followed by a gerund, not by "but." Choice (C) follows "cannot help" with the gerund "admitting." Choices (A) and (D) are incorrect because they follow "cannot help" with "but." The wording of choice (B), "cannot admit," and choice (E), "cannot know," twists the meaning of the sentence.

34. **(B)** The correct idiom is to have an insight into a situation or person. While "to" in choice (A) is close in meaning, it is not exact; "for" and "with" of choices (C), (D), and (E) are unacceptable. The location of "often" in choice (D) is poor, and the location of "often" in choice (E) makes no significant change in the meaning.

35. **(D)** It is obvious that the Greenes have just purchased plants: "Upon leaving the nursery." The location of the modifying phrase, "they had just bought," should be carefully placed in the sentence so it clearly modifies "plants" and not "car." Choice (D) has the modifying phrase immediately following "plants," and the meaning is clear. The wording of choices (A),

(B), and (C) makes the reader think the car has just been purchased. Choice (E) omits the concept "they had just bought."

36. **(E)**   Choice (E) retains the central idea while eliminating the wording problems of the other choices. There is no antecedent for "we" in choices (A) and (B). Also, the phrase "end up" is redundant; "up" should be eliminated. Therefore, choice (C) is incorrect. Choice (D) introduces a new concept of "war may end over there," an idea clearly not intended by the original.

37. **(B)**   Choice (B) clearly and precisely states the issue of debate. Choice (C) is eliminated because it is too wordy and not the precise issue under debate. The correlative conjunctions, "whether . . . or," should be followed by parallel structures. Choice (A) follows "Whether" with a subject-verb combination not seen after "not." Choice (D) is parallel but in the wrong tense. Choice (E) has "Whether or not" run together and uses poor wording in the rest of the sentence.

38. **(A)**   Choice (A) has both correct agreement and clear reference. Choice (B) has a subject-verb agreement problem, "charging . . . are." Choice (C) produces a fragment. It is unclear in choice (D) who will have the bad credit rating, and the wording of choice (E) has the obvious subject, "people," in a prepositional phrase.

39. **(D)**   Choice (D) correctly presents the fifth grade field trip in a subordinate clause modifying "exhibit." Choices (A) and (B) have the coordinating conjunction "and," but the first part of the sentence is not equal in meaning or importance to the second part of the sentence. Choice (C) introduces "when" with no antecedent. Choice (E) uses "where" as the subordinating conjunction, but it is too far from its antecedent and is not the important idea of the sentence.

40. **(E)**   In choice (E) the present infinitive is correctly used to express an action following another action: "plans to appeal." Choices (A) and (B) use the wrong form, "appealing." Choice (C) uses the wrong tense, "is appealing." Choice (D) sounds as if the same person is deciding the case and appealing the case.

41. **(A)**   Choice (A) has clear wording. Choice (B) is a fragment because it puts the verb in the nonessential phrase. Choices (C), (D), and (E) produce twisted wording. Choice (C) has no object for the verb "allowed"

and sounds as if the speakers were allowed to stay up later. Choice (E) needs commas and sounds as if the speakers decided to stay up later.

42. **(B)** Choice (B) plainly states the subject and the verb, "I find." Choices (A) and (E) have the subject in a prepositional phrase, "for me." Choice (E) produces a fragment. Choice (C), a fragment, has no subject because both potential subjects are in prepositional phases: "agreement" and "plan." Choices (C) and (D) imply "everyone" as the main subject.

43. **(B)** Choice (B) avoids the split infinitive and the incorrect expression, "inside of." Choices (A) and (D) split the infinitive "to finish" with the adverb "completely." Choice (C) uses "inside of," an expression that is incorrect to use because it is redundant ("of" should be deleted) and because it should not be used with measuring time. Choice (E) erroneously changes the idea and would employ two verbs in simple past tense: "hired" and "finished."

44. **(B)** The original involves a needless voice shift from first person to third person. Choice (B) correctly uses third person for both. Choices (C), (D), and (E) all retain the voice shift; each is awkwardly wordy as well.

45. **(C)** A fine line separates this choice from the others, except for (E). Choice (E) is more concise, but it also is a dangling modifier. Each of the other choices adds unnecessary words. Choice (C) is both clear and concise.

PPST ESSAY SCORING GUIDE

The PPST essay sections are scored by two writing experts on the basis of the criteria outlined below. In addition to comparing your essay to those included in our practice tests, you may use these guidelines to estimate your score on this section. Remember that your score is the sum of the scores of two writing experts, so provided you respond to the assigned topic, your score will fall somewhere between two and twelve. Scores will be assigned based on the following guidelines:

6 An essay receiving a score of 6 may contain one or two spelling or punctuation errors, but overall it exhibits a high degree of proficiency and thought on the assigned topic.

An essay scoring a 6

- is both well organized and well developed
- engages important concepts and explains them clearly
- varies expression and language
- demonstrates deft use of language
- is virtually free from errors involving syntax and structure

5 An essay receiving a score of 5 exhibits a high degree of proficiency and thought on the assigned topic, however it contains a number of minor mistakes.

An essay scoring a 5

- is both well organized and well developed
- engages important concepts and explains them
- varies expression and language somewhat
- demonstrates deft use of language
- is virtually free from errors involving syntax and structure

4 An essay receiving a score of 4 responds to the assignment and exhibits some degree of deeper understanding.

An essay scoring a 4

- demonstrates adequate organization and development
- engages and explains some important concepts, but not all that are necessary to demonstrate full understanding

- exhibits adequate use of language
- contains some syntactical and structural errors, without excessive repetition of those errors

3 An essay receiving a score of 3 exhibits some degree of understanding, but its response to the topic is obviously deficient.

An essay scoring a 3 is deficient in one or more of the following areas:

- insufficient organization or development
- insufficient engagement or explanation of important concepts
- consistent repetition of syntactical or structural errors
- redundant or unsuitable word choice

2 An essay receiving a score of 2 exhibits limited understanding and its response to the topic is seriously deficient.

An essay scoring a 2 is deficient in one or more of the following areas:

- weak organization or development
- very few pertinent details
- consistent and serious errors in syntax, structure
- consistent and serious errors in word choice

1 An essay receiving a score of 1 exhibits a lack of basic writing skills.

An essay scoring a 1 is disorganized, undeveloped, contains consistent repetition of errors, or is incomprehensible.

Sample Essays with Commentary

ESSAY I (Score: 5–6)

In the past thirty years, television has become a very popular pasttime for almost everyone. From the time the mother places the baby in his jumpseat in front of the television so that she can relax and have a second cup of coffee until the time the senior citizen in the retirement home watches Vanna White turn the letters on "Wheel of Fortune," Americans spend endless hours in front of the "boob tube." I believe that television can become an addiction that provides an escape from the problems of the world and from facing responsibility for your own life.

When my mother was a little girl, what did children do to entertain themselves? They played. Their games usually involved social interaction with other children as well as imaginatively creating entertainment for themselves. They also developed hobbies like woodworking and sewing. Today, few children really know how to play with each other or entertain themselves. Instead, they sit in front of the television, glued to cartoons that are senseless and often violent. Even if they watch educational programs like "Sesame Street," they don't really have to do anything but watch and listen to what the answer to the question is.

Teenagers, also, use television as a way of avoiding doing things that will help them mature. How many kids do much homework anymore? Why not? Because they come home from work tired and relax in front of the television. Even if they watch a controversial program about some problem in the world like AIDS or the war in the Middle East, they don't usually do anything about it.

In addition, young mothers use television to escape their problems. The terrible woes of the people on the soap operas make their problems seem less important. This means that they don't need to solve their own problems.

Although it may seem as if television is really great for older people, I think even my grandma would have more fun if she had more interests rather than just watching quiz shows. I know she has blotted out the "real world" when she expects us to act like the Cosby kids when she comes to visit.

In conclusion, I believe that television really can become an addiction that allows people of all ages to avoid facing their own problems and lose themselves in the problems of other people.

ANALYSIS

Essay I has a score range of 5–6. It has a traditional structure; the first paragraph introduces the topic, even suggesting the chronological organization of the essay. Each of the next four paragraphs has a clear topic sentence and details that develop it. The concluding paragraph, although only one sentence in length, restates the main idea. The essay is, therefore, clearly unified around the writer's opinion, which the writer tries to prove in a logical fashion. The writer effectively employs transitional words to relate the main ideas, varied sentence structure, and controlled vocabulary. Although the writer misspells *pastime,* uses the colloquial word *kids,* and has some problem with parallelism, repetition, and pronoun usage, the essay is well written considering the 30-minute time limit.

ESSAY II (Score: 4–5)

I do not agree with the given statement. I think that instead of being bad for people, television not only does not blot out the real world but, instead, gives the person watching it a chance to experience the real world, even places he can't possibly go and may never get a chance to go.

For instance, I've learned a lot about the Vietnam War by watching TV. For a while, I heard things about it, about how some of the veterans didn't feel as if they were welcomed right when they came back from that war. I didn't understand what was the matter. Then they built a special memorial in Washington for the veterans that didn't come back. Since then, I have seen a lot of programs that showed what went on in Vietnam, and I've heard Vietnam vets talk about what happened to them. I think that that war has become very real to me because of TV.

Television educates us about the dangers of growing up in America today. I've seen good programs about the dangers of using drugs, about teenage pregnancy and what happens if you try to keep the baby, about eating too much cholesterol (That doesn't matter to me yet, but my dad needs to watch that!), and also anorexia. These are things we all need to know about, and TV has told about them so we know what to do.

I really am convinced that television brings the real world into your house. I think us kids today know a lot more about the real world than our grandparents did who grew up without television.

ANALYSIS

Essay II has a score range of 4–5. It is competently written. The writer takes one position and develops it. The first paragraph provides a clear

introduction, and paragraphs two and three develop the thesis. Generalized examples are provided. The final paragraph concludes the essay. The essay contains some problems in correct usage, colloquial words like *kids,* and a lack of specific, concrete examples. (What, specifically, did the writer learn about the Vietnam War?) Sentences lack variety in length and construction, with many beginning with the pronoun "I." Ideas are not always clearly related to each other. The theme contains unnecessary repetition and errors in pronoun use.

ESSAY III (Score: 3–4)

On the one hand, I think television is bad, But it also does some good things for all of us. For instants, my little sister thought she wanted to be a policeman until she saw police shows on TV. Then she learned how dangerous it is and now she wants to be an astronaut. I guess she didn't watch the Challenger explode often enough to scare her out of that.

But the bad thing about television programs are the ideas it puts in kids heads. Like violent things happen on television, and little kids see it and don't know that other people hurt when they are hit, battered up, beat, shot, ect. Then the kids go out and try to knock their friends around and think if they are strong and handsome that they can get their own way whatever happens. Even parents sometimes have trouble controling their own kids because of too much TV. Of course that's partly because the parents watch too much too when they should of been taking care of the kids they necklected them watching television.

So I think that television has both it's good and it's bad points. I'd hate to see us get rid of it all together, but I wonder if I'll let my kids watch it when I have them. It sometimes puts bad ideas in their heads.

ANALYSIS

Essay III has a score range of 3–4. The failure of the writer of this essay, to take one opinion and clearly develop it, weakens the essay. The writer does try to give specific examples, but the details in the introductory paragraph would be more appropriate later in the essay. The apparent topic sentence of the second paragraph suggests a discussion of the results of children's watching television, but the writer discusses the parents' viewing in the same paragraph. The last sentence of the conclusion repeats the idea of the topic sentence of the second paragraph. The writer does not express his ideas in precise fashion ("Even parents sometimes have trouble controling (sic) their own kids because of too much TV.") or provide clear relationships between them. The essay also contains colloquialisms and errors in pronoun

use, spelling, use of the apostrophe, and sentence construction.

ESSAY IV (Score: 1–2)

I get really upset when someone says they don't think we should watch television. Us students learn a lot more from television than whats in a lot of our classes in school. I've even learned stuff from the comertials they show the best way to clean house or the best kinds of car to buy right now I wouldn't have no idea what to get my sister for her birthday if I hadn't of seen it on television and said to myself, "Sally'd love one of those!"

If no one watched television, can you just think about how much crime there would be because kids would be board and would have to get excitment somewheres else than in his own living room where the TV set is.

There's also educational television with shows that ask questions and see if you know any answers. That's where I learned a lot of stuff about the world and everything.

ANALYSIS

Essay IV has a score range of 1–2. The writer of this essay digresses from the emphasis of the assigned topic in his effort to defend the watching of television. Although he has a clearly stated opinion, he falls to develop it in a logical, unified fashion. There is no clear introduction; the second paragraph, only one sentence in length, is not properly developed; and the paper is lacking a conclusion. In addition, the language of this essay is not exact, and the ideas are not developed with specific examples. For example, what "stuff" has he learned from educational television? The essay contains serious problems in grammar and usage such as double negatives, run-on sentences, errors in pronoun reference and case, misspelled words, and errors in idiom.

PPST

Pre-Professional Skills Tests

Answer Sheets

Practice PPST I

Reading

Comprehension

1. Ⓐ Ⓑ Ⓒ Ⓓ Ⓔ

2. Ⓐ Ⓑ Ⓒ Ⓓ Ⓔ

3. Ⓐ Ⓑ Ⓒ Ⓓ Ⓔ

4. Ⓐ Ⓑ Ⓒ Ⓓ Ⓔ

5. Ⓐ Ⓑ Ⓒ Ⓓ Ⓔ

6. Ⓐ Ⓑ Ⓒ Ⓓ Ⓔ

7. Ⓐ Ⓑ Ⓒ Ⓓ Ⓔ

8. Ⓐ Ⓑ Ⓒ Ⓓ Ⓔ

9. Ⓐ Ⓑ Ⓒ Ⓓ Ⓔ

10. Ⓐ Ⓑ Ⓒ Ⓓ Ⓔ

11. Ⓐ Ⓑ Ⓒ Ⓓ Ⓔ

12. Ⓐ Ⓑ Ⓒ Ⓓ Ⓔ

13. Ⓐ Ⓑ Ⓒ Ⓓ Ⓔ

14. Ⓐ Ⓑ Ⓒ Ⓓ Ⓔ

15. Ⓐ Ⓑ Ⓒ Ⓓ Ⓔ

16. Ⓐ Ⓑ Ⓒ Ⓓ Ⓔ

17. Ⓐ Ⓑ Ⓒ Ⓓ Ⓔ

18. Ⓐ Ⓑ Ⓒ Ⓓ Ⓔ

19. Ⓐ Ⓑ Ⓒ Ⓓ Ⓔ

20. Ⓐ Ⓑ Ⓒ Ⓓ Ⓔ

21. Ⓐ Ⓑ Ⓒ Ⓓ Ⓔ

22. Ⓐ Ⓑ Ⓒ Ⓓ Ⓔ

23. Ⓐ Ⓑ Ⓒ Ⓓ Ⓔ

24. Ⓐ Ⓑ Ⓒ Ⓓ Ⓔ

25. Ⓐ Ⓑ Ⓒ Ⓓ Ⓔ

26. Ⓐ Ⓑ Ⓒ Ⓓ Ⓔ

27. Ⓐ Ⓑ Ⓒ Ⓓ Ⓔ

28. Ⓐ Ⓑ Ⓒ Ⓓ Ⓔ

29. Ⓐ Ⓑ Ⓒ Ⓓ Ⓔ

30. Ⓐ Ⓑ Ⓒ Ⓓ Ⓔ

31. Ⓐ Ⓑ Ⓒ Ⓓ Ⓔ

32. Ⓐ Ⓑ Ⓒ Ⓓ Ⓔ

33. Ⓐ Ⓑ Ⓒ Ⓓ Ⓔ

34. Ⓐ Ⓑ Ⓒ Ⓓ Ⓔ

35. Ⓐ Ⓑ Ⓒ Ⓓ Ⓔ

36. Ⓐ Ⓑ Ⓒ Ⓓ Ⓔ

37. Ⓐ Ⓑ Ⓒ Ⓓ Ⓔ

38. Ⓐ Ⓑ Ⓒ Ⓓ Ⓔ

39. Ⓐ Ⓑ Ⓒ Ⓓ Ⓔ

40. Ⓐ Ⓑ Ⓒ Ⓓ Ⓔ

Mathematics

1. Ⓐ Ⓑ Ⓒ Ⓓ Ⓔ

2. Ⓐ Ⓑ Ⓒ Ⓓ Ⓔ

3. Ⓐ Ⓑ Ⓒ Ⓓ Ⓔ

4. Ⓐ Ⓑ Ⓒ Ⓓ Ⓔ

5. Ⓐ Ⓑ Ⓒ Ⓓ Ⓔ

6. Ⓐ Ⓑ Ⓒ Ⓓ Ⓔ

7. Ⓐ Ⓑ Ⓒ Ⓓ Ⓔ

8. Ⓐ Ⓑ Ⓒ Ⓓ Ⓔ

9. Ⓐ Ⓑ Ⓒ Ⓓ Ⓔ

10. Ⓐ Ⓑ Ⓒ Ⓓ Ⓔ

11. Ⓐ Ⓑ Ⓒ Ⓓ Ⓔ

12. Ⓐ Ⓑ Ⓒ Ⓓ Ⓔ

13. Ⓐ Ⓑ Ⓒ Ⓓ Ⓔ

14. Ⓐ Ⓑ Ⓒ Ⓓ Ⓔ

15. Ⓐ Ⓑ Ⓒ Ⓓ Ⓔ

16. Ⓐ Ⓑ Ⓒ Ⓓ Ⓔ

17. Ⓐ Ⓑ Ⓒ Ⓓ Ⓔ

18. Ⓐ Ⓑ Ⓒ Ⓓ Ⓔ

19. Ⓐ Ⓑ Ⓒ Ⓓ Ⓔ

20. Ⓐ Ⓑ Ⓒ Ⓓ Ⓔ

21. Ⓐ Ⓑ Ⓒ Ⓓ Ⓔ

22. Ⓐ Ⓑ Ⓒ Ⓓ Ⓔ

23. Ⓐ Ⓑ Ⓒ Ⓓ Ⓔ

24. Ⓐ Ⓑ Ⓒ Ⓓ Ⓔ

25. Ⓐ Ⓑ Ⓒ Ⓓ Ⓔ

26. Ⓐ Ⓑ Ⓒ Ⓓ Ⓔ

27. Ⓐ Ⓑ Ⓒ Ⓓ Ⓔ

28. Ⓐ Ⓑ Ⓒ Ⓓ Ⓔ

29. Ⓐ Ⓑ Ⓒ Ⓓ Ⓔ

30. Ⓐ Ⓑ Ⓒ Ⓓ Ⓔ

31. Ⓐ Ⓑ Ⓒ Ⓓ Ⓔ

32. Ⓐ Ⓑ Ⓒ Ⓓ Ⓔ

33. Ⓐ Ⓑ Ⓒ Ⓓ Ⓔ

34. Ⓐ Ⓑ Ⓒ Ⓓ Ⓔ

35. Ⓐ Ⓑ Ⓒ Ⓓ Ⓔ

36. Ⓐ Ⓑ Ⓒ Ⓓ Ⓔ

37. Ⓐ Ⓑ Ⓒ Ⓓ Ⓔ

38. Ⓐ Ⓑ Ⓒ Ⓓ Ⓔ

39. Ⓐ Ⓑ Ⓒ Ⓓ Ⓔ

40. Ⓐ Ⓑ Ⓒ Ⓓ Ⓔ

Writing

1. Ⓐ Ⓑ Ⓒ Ⓓ Ⓔ

2. Ⓐ Ⓑ Ⓒ Ⓓ Ⓔ

3. Ⓐ Ⓑ Ⓒ Ⓓ Ⓔ

4. Ⓐ Ⓑ Ⓒ Ⓓ Ⓔ

5. Ⓐ Ⓑ Ⓒ Ⓓ Ⓔ

6. Ⓐ Ⓑ Ⓒ Ⓓ Ⓔ

7. Ⓐ Ⓑ Ⓒ Ⓓ Ⓔ

8. Ⓐ Ⓑ Ⓒ Ⓓ Ⓔ

9. Ⓐ Ⓑ Ⓒ Ⓓ Ⓔ

10. Ⓐ Ⓑ Ⓒ Ⓓ Ⓔ

11. Ⓐ Ⓑ Ⓒ Ⓓ Ⓔ

12. Ⓐ Ⓑ Ⓒ Ⓓ Ⓔ

13. Ⓐ Ⓑ Ⓒ Ⓓ Ⓔ

14. Ⓐ Ⓑ Ⓒ Ⓓ Ⓔ

15. Ⓐ Ⓑ Ⓒ Ⓓ Ⓔ

16. Ⓐ Ⓑ Ⓒ Ⓓ Ⓔ

17. Ⓐ Ⓑ Ⓒ Ⓓ Ⓔ

18. Ⓐ Ⓑ Ⓒ Ⓓ Ⓔ

19. Ⓐ Ⓑ Ⓒ Ⓓ Ⓔ

20. Ⓐ Ⓑ Ⓒ Ⓓ Ⓔ

21. Ⓐ Ⓑ Ⓒ Ⓓ Ⓔ

22. Ⓐ Ⓑ Ⓒ Ⓓ Ⓔ

23. Ⓐ Ⓑ Ⓒ Ⓓ Ⓔ

24. Ⓐ Ⓑ Ⓒ Ⓓ Ⓔ

25. Ⓐ Ⓑ Ⓒ Ⓓ Ⓔ

26. Ⓐ Ⓑ Ⓒ Ⓓ Ⓔ

27. Ⓐ Ⓑ Ⓒ Ⓓ Ⓔ

28. Ⓐ Ⓑ Ⓒ Ⓓ Ⓔ

29. Ⓐ Ⓑ Ⓒ Ⓓ Ⓔ

30. Ⓐ Ⓑ Ⓒ Ⓓ Ⓔ

31. Ⓐ Ⓑ Ⓒ Ⓓ Ⓔ

32. Ⓐ Ⓑ Ⓒ Ⓓ Ⓔ

33. Ⓐ Ⓑ Ⓒ Ⓓ Ⓔ

34. Ⓐ Ⓑ Ⓒ Ⓓ Ⓔ

35. Ⓐ Ⓑ Ⓒ Ⓓ Ⓔ

36. Ⓐ Ⓑ Ⓒ Ⓓ Ⓔ

37. Ⓐ Ⓑ Ⓒ Ⓓ Ⓔ

38. Ⓐ Ⓑ Ⓒ Ⓓ Ⓔ

39. Ⓐ Ⓑ Ⓒ Ⓓ Ⓔ

40. Ⓐ Ⓑ Ⓒ Ⓓ Ⓔ

41. Ⓐ Ⓑ Ⓒ Ⓓ Ⓔ

42. Ⓐ Ⓑ Ⓒ Ⓓ Ⓔ

43. Ⓐ Ⓑ Ⓒ Ⓓ Ⓔ

44. Ⓐ Ⓑ Ⓒ Ⓓ Ⓔ

45. Ⓐ Ⓑ Ⓒ Ⓓ Ⓔ

Practice PPST II

Reading

Comprehension

1. Ⓐ Ⓑ Ⓒ Ⓓ Ⓔ

2. Ⓐ Ⓑ Ⓒ Ⓓ Ⓔ

3. Ⓐ Ⓑ Ⓒ Ⓓ Ⓔ

4. Ⓐ Ⓑ Ⓒ Ⓓ Ⓔ

5. Ⓐ Ⓑ Ⓒ Ⓓ Ⓔ

6. Ⓐ Ⓑ Ⓒ Ⓓ Ⓔ

7. Ⓐ Ⓑ Ⓒ Ⓓ Ⓔ

8. Ⓐ Ⓑ Ⓒ Ⓓ Ⓔ

9. Ⓐ Ⓑ Ⓒ Ⓓ Ⓔ

10. Ⓐ Ⓑ Ⓒ Ⓓ Ⓔ

11. Ⓐ Ⓑ Ⓒ Ⓓ Ⓔ

12. Ⓐ Ⓑ Ⓒ Ⓓ Ⓔ

13. Ⓐ Ⓑ Ⓒ Ⓓ Ⓔ

14. Ⓐ Ⓑ Ⓒ Ⓓ Ⓔ

15. Ⓐ Ⓑ Ⓒ Ⓓ Ⓔ

16. Ⓐ Ⓑ Ⓒ Ⓓ Ⓔ

17. Ⓐ Ⓑ Ⓒ Ⓓ Ⓔ

18. Ⓐ Ⓑ Ⓒ Ⓓ Ⓔ

19. Ⓐ Ⓑ Ⓒ Ⓓ Ⓔ

20. Ⓐ Ⓑ Ⓒ Ⓓ Ⓔ

21. Ⓐ Ⓑ Ⓒ Ⓓ Ⓔ

22. Ⓐ Ⓑ Ⓒ Ⓓ Ⓔ

23. Ⓐ Ⓑ Ⓒ Ⓓ Ⓔ

24. Ⓐ Ⓑ Ⓒ Ⓓ Ⓔ

25. Ⓐ Ⓑ Ⓒ Ⓓ Ⓔ

26. Ⓐ Ⓑ Ⓒ Ⓓ Ⓔ

27. Ⓐ Ⓑ Ⓒ Ⓓ Ⓔ

28. Ⓐ Ⓑ Ⓒ Ⓓ Ⓔ

29. Ⓐ Ⓑ Ⓒ Ⓓ Ⓔ

30. Ⓐ Ⓑ Ⓒ Ⓓ Ⓔ

31. Ⓐ Ⓑ Ⓒ Ⓓ Ⓔ

32. Ⓐ Ⓑ Ⓒ Ⓓ Ⓔ

33. Ⓐ Ⓑ Ⓒ Ⓓ Ⓔ

34. Ⓐ Ⓑ Ⓒ Ⓓ Ⓔ

35. Ⓐ Ⓑ Ⓒ Ⓓ Ⓔ

36. Ⓐ Ⓑ Ⓒ Ⓓ Ⓔ

37. Ⓐ Ⓑ Ⓒ Ⓓ Ⓔ

38. Ⓐ Ⓑ Ⓒ Ⓓ Ⓔ

39. Ⓐ Ⓑ Ⓒ Ⓓ Ⓔ

40. Ⓐ Ⓑ Ⓒ Ⓓ Ⓔ

Mathematics

1. Ⓐ Ⓑ Ⓒ Ⓓ Ⓔ

2. Ⓐ Ⓑ Ⓒ Ⓓ Ⓔ

3. Ⓐ Ⓑ Ⓒ Ⓓ Ⓔ

4. Ⓐ Ⓑ Ⓒ Ⓓ Ⓔ

5. Ⓐ Ⓑ Ⓒ Ⓓ Ⓔ

6. Ⓐ Ⓑ Ⓒ Ⓓ Ⓔ

7. Ⓐ Ⓑ Ⓒ Ⓓ Ⓔ

8. Ⓐ Ⓑ Ⓒ Ⓓ Ⓔ

9. Ⓐ Ⓑ Ⓒ Ⓓ Ⓔ

10. Ⓐ Ⓑ Ⓒ Ⓓ Ⓔ

11. Ⓐ Ⓑ Ⓒ Ⓓ Ⓔ

12. Ⓐ Ⓑ Ⓒ Ⓓ Ⓔ

13. Ⓐ Ⓑ Ⓒ Ⓓ Ⓔ

14. Ⓐ Ⓑ Ⓒ Ⓓ Ⓔ

15. Ⓐ Ⓑ Ⓒ Ⓓ Ⓔ

16. Ⓐ Ⓑ Ⓒ Ⓓ Ⓔ

17. Ⓐ Ⓑ Ⓒ Ⓓ Ⓔ

18. Ⓐ Ⓑ Ⓒ Ⓓ Ⓔ

19. Ⓐ Ⓑ Ⓒ Ⓓ Ⓔ

20. Ⓐ Ⓑ Ⓒ Ⓓ Ⓔ

21. Ⓐ Ⓑ Ⓒ Ⓓ Ⓔ

22. Ⓐ Ⓑ Ⓒ Ⓓ Ⓔ

23. Ⓐ Ⓑ Ⓒ Ⓓ Ⓔ

24. Ⓐ Ⓑ Ⓒ Ⓓ Ⓔ

25. Ⓐ Ⓑ Ⓒ Ⓓ Ⓔ

26. Ⓐ Ⓑ Ⓒ Ⓓ Ⓔ

27. Ⓐ Ⓑ Ⓒ Ⓓ Ⓔ

28. Ⓐ Ⓑ Ⓒ Ⓓ Ⓔ

29. Ⓐ Ⓑ Ⓒ Ⓓ Ⓔ

30. Ⓐ Ⓑ Ⓒ Ⓓ Ⓔ

31. Ⓐ Ⓑ Ⓒ Ⓓ Ⓔ

Practice PPST II

32. Ⓐ Ⓑ Ⓒ Ⓓ Ⓔ

33. Ⓐ Ⓑ Ⓒ Ⓓ Ⓔ

34. Ⓐ Ⓑ Ⓒ Ⓓ Ⓔ

35. Ⓐ Ⓑ Ⓒ Ⓓ Ⓔ

36. Ⓐ Ⓑ Ⓒ Ⓓ Ⓔ

37. Ⓐ Ⓑ Ⓒ Ⓓ Ⓔ

38. Ⓐ Ⓑ Ⓒ Ⓓ Ⓔ

39. Ⓐ Ⓑ Ⓒ Ⓓ Ⓔ

40. Ⓐ Ⓑ Ⓒ Ⓓ Ⓔ

Writing

1. Ⓐ Ⓑ Ⓒ Ⓓ Ⓔ

2. Ⓐ Ⓑ Ⓒ Ⓓ Ⓔ

3. Ⓐ Ⓑ Ⓒ Ⓓ Ⓔ

4. Ⓐ Ⓑ Ⓒ Ⓓ Ⓔ

5. Ⓐ Ⓑ Ⓒ Ⓓ Ⓔ

6. Ⓐ Ⓑ Ⓒ Ⓓ Ⓔ

7. Ⓐ Ⓑ Ⓒ Ⓓ Ⓔ

8. Ⓐ Ⓑ Ⓒ Ⓓ Ⓔ

9. Ⓐ Ⓑ Ⓒ Ⓓ Ⓔ

10. Ⓐ Ⓑ Ⓒ Ⓓ Ⓔ

11. Ⓐ Ⓑ Ⓒ Ⓓ Ⓔ

12. Ⓐ Ⓑ Ⓒ Ⓓ Ⓔ

13. Ⓐ Ⓑ Ⓒ Ⓓ Ⓔ

14. Ⓐ Ⓑ Ⓒ Ⓓ Ⓔ

15. Ⓐ Ⓑ Ⓒ Ⓓ Ⓔ

16. Ⓐ Ⓑ Ⓒ Ⓓ Ⓔ

17. Ⓐ Ⓑ Ⓒ Ⓓ Ⓔ

18. Ⓐ Ⓑ Ⓒ Ⓓ Ⓔ

19. Ⓐ Ⓑ Ⓒ Ⓓ Ⓔ

20. Ⓐ Ⓑ Ⓒ Ⓓ Ⓔ

21. Ⓐ Ⓑ Ⓒ Ⓓ Ⓔ

22. Ⓐ Ⓑ Ⓒ Ⓓ Ⓔ

23. Ⓐ Ⓑ Ⓒ Ⓓ Ⓔ

24. Ⓐ Ⓑ Ⓒ Ⓓ Ⓔ

25. Ⓐ Ⓑ Ⓒ Ⓓ Ⓔ

26. Ⓐ Ⓑ Ⓒ Ⓓ Ⓔ

27. Ⓐ Ⓑ Ⓒ Ⓓ Ⓔ

28. Ⓐ Ⓑ Ⓒ Ⓓ Ⓔ

29. Ⓐ Ⓑ Ⓒ Ⓓ Ⓔ

30. Ⓐ Ⓑ Ⓒ Ⓓ Ⓔ

31. Ⓐ Ⓑ Ⓒ Ⓓ Ⓔ

32. Ⓐ Ⓑ Ⓒ Ⓓ Ⓔ

33. Ⓐ Ⓑ Ⓒ Ⓓ Ⓔ

34. Ⓐ Ⓑ Ⓒ Ⓓ Ⓔ

35. Ⓐ Ⓑ Ⓒ Ⓓ Ⓔ

36. Ⓐ Ⓑ Ⓒ Ⓓ Ⓔ

37. Ⓐ Ⓑ Ⓒ Ⓓ Ⓔ

38. Ⓐ Ⓑ Ⓒ Ⓓ Ⓔ

39. Ⓐ Ⓑ Ⓒ Ⓓ Ⓔ

40. Ⓐ Ⓑ Ⓒ Ⓓ Ⓔ

41. Ⓐ Ⓑ Ⓒ Ⓓ Ⓔ

42. Ⓐ Ⓑ Ⓒ Ⓓ Ⓔ

43. Ⓐ Ⓑ Ⓒ Ⓓ Ⓔ

44. Ⓐ Ⓑ Ⓒ Ⓓ Ⓔ

45. Ⓐ Ⓑ Ⓒ Ⓓ Ⓔ

Practice PPST III

Reading Comprehension

1. Ⓐ Ⓑ Ⓒ Ⓓ Ⓔ
2. Ⓐ Ⓑ Ⓒ Ⓓ Ⓔ
3. Ⓐ Ⓑ Ⓒ Ⓓ Ⓔ
4. Ⓐ Ⓑ Ⓒ Ⓓ Ⓔ
5. Ⓐ Ⓑ Ⓒ Ⓓ Ⓔ
6. Ⓐ Ⓑ Ⓒ Ⓓ Ⓔ
7. Ⓐ Ⓑ Ⓒ Ⓓ Ⓔ
8. Ⓐ Ⓑ Ⓒ Ⓓ Ⓔ
9. Ⓐ Ⓑ Ⓒ Ⓓ Ⓔ
10. Ⓐ Ⓑ Ⓒ Ⓓ Ⓔ
11. Ⓐ Ⓑ Ⓒ Ⓓ Ⓔ
12. Ⓐ Ⓑ Ⓒ Ⓓ Ⓔ
13. Ⓐ Ⓑ Ⓒ Ⓓ Ⓔ
14. Ⓐ Ⓑ Ⓒ Ⓓ Ⓔ
15. Ⓐ Ⓑ Ⓒ Ⓓ Ⓔ
16. Ⓐ Ⓑ Ⓒ Ⓓ Ⓔ
17. Ⓐ Ⓑ Ⓒ Ⓓ Ⓔ
18. Ⓐ Ⓑ Ⓒ Ⓓ Ⓔ
19. Ⓐ Ⓑ Ⓒ Ⓓ Ⓔ
20. Ⓐ Ⓑ Ⓒ Ⓓ Ⓔ
21. Ⓐ Ⓑ Ⓒ Ⓓ Ⓔ
22. Ⓐ Ⓑ Ⓒ Ⓓ Ⓔ
23. Ⓐ Ⓑ Ⓒ Ⓓ Ⓔ

24. Ⓐ Ⓑ Ⓒ Ⓓ Ⓔ
25. Ⓐ Ⓑ Ⓒ Ⓓ Ⓔ
26. Ⓐ Ⓑ Ⓒ Ⓓ Ⓔ
27. Ⓐ Ⓑ Ⓒ Ⓓ Ⓔ
28. Ⓐ Ⓑ Ⓒ Ⓓ Ⓔ
29. Ⓐ Ⓑ Ⓒ Ⓓ Ⓔ
30. Ⓐ Ⓑ Ⓒ Ⓓ Ⓔ
31. Ⓐ Ⓑ Ⓒ Ⓓ Ⓔ
32. Ⓐ Ⓑ Ⓒ Ⓓ Ⓔ
33. Ⓐ Ⓑ Ⓒ Ⓓ Ⓔ
34. Ⓐ Ⓑ Ⓒ Ⓓ Ⓔ
35. Ⓐ Ⓑ Ⓒ Ⓓ Ⓔ
36. Ⓐ Ⓑ Ⓒ Ⓓ Ⓔ
37. Ⓐ Ⓑ Ⓒ Ⓓ Ⓔ
38. Ⓐ Ⓑ Ⓒ Ⓓ Ⓔ
39. Ⓐ Ⓑ Ⓒ Ⓓ Ⓔ
40. Ⓐ Ⓑ Ⓒ Ⓓ Ⓔ

Mathematics

1. Ⓐ Ⓑ Ⓒ Ⓓ Ⓔ
2. Ⓐ Ⓑ Ⓒ Ⓓ Ⓔ
3. Ⓐ Ⓑ Ⓒ Ⓓ Ⓔ
4. Ⓐ Ⓑ Ⓒ Ⓓ Ⓔ
5. Ⓐ Ⓑ Ⓒ Ⓓ Ⓔ
6. Ⓐ Ⓑ Ⓒ Ⓓ Ⓔ

7. Ⓐ Ⓑ Ⓒ Ⓓ Ⓔ
8. Ⓐ Ⓑ Ⓒ Ⓓ Ⓔ
9. Ⓐ Ⓑ Ⓒ Ⓓ Ⓔ
10. Ⓐ Ⓑ Ⓒ Ⓓ Ⓔ
11. Ⓐ Ⓑ Ⓒ Ⓓ Ⓔ
12. Ⓐ Ⓑ Ⓒ Ⓓ Ⓔ
13. Ⓐ Ⓑ Ⓒ Ⓓ Ⓔ
14. Ⓐ Ⓑ Ⓒ Ⓓ Ⓔ
15. Ⓐ Ⓑ Ⓒ Ⓓ Ⓔ
16. Ⓐ Ⓑ Ⓒ Ⓓ Ⓔ
17. Ⓐ Ⓑ Ⓒ Ⓓ Ⓔ
18. Ⓐ Ⓑ Ⓒ Ⓓ Ⓔ
19. Ⓐ Ⓑ Ⓒ Ⓓ Ⓔ
20. Ⓐ Ⓑ Ⓒ Ⓓ Ⓔ
21. Ⓐ Ⓑ Ⓒ Ⓓ Ⓔ
22. Ⓐ Ⓑ Ⓒ Ⓓ Ⓔ
23. Ⓐ Ⓑ Ⓒ Ⓓ Ⓔ
24. Ⓐ Ⓑ Ⓒ Ⓓ Ⓔ
25. Ⓐ Ⓑ Ⓒ Ⓓ Ⓔ
26. Ⓐ Ⓑ Ⓒ Ⓓ Ⓔ
27. Ⓐ Ⓑ Ⓒ Ⓓ Ⓔ
28. Ⓐ Ⓑ Ⓒ Ⓓ Ⓔ
29. Ⓐ Ⓑ Ⓒ Ⓓ Ⓔ
30. Ⓐ Ⓑ Ⓒ Ⓓ Ⓔ
31. Ⓐ Ⓑ Ⓒ Ⓓ Ⓔ

32. Ⓐ Ⓑ Ⓒ Ⓓ Ⓔ
33. Ⓐ Ⓑ Ⓒ Ⓓ Ⓔ
34. Ⓐ Ⓑ Ⓒ Ⓓ Ⓔ
35. Ⓐ Ⓑ Ⓒ Ⓓ Ⓔ
36. Ⓐ Ⓑ Ⓒ Ⓓ Ⓔ
37. Ⓐ Ⓑ Ⓒ Ⓓ Ⓔ
38. Ⓐ Ⓑ Ⓒ Ⓓ Ⓔ
39. Ⓐ Ⓑ Ⓒ Ⓓ Ⓔ
40. Ⓐ Ⓑ Ⓒ Ⓓ Ⓔ

Writing

1. Ⓐ Ⓑ Ⓒ Ⓓ Ⓔ
2. Ⓐ Ⓑ Ⓒ Ⓓ Ⓔ
3. Ⓐ Ⓑ Ⓒ Ⓓ Ⓔ
4. Ⓐ Ⓑ Ⓒ Ⓓ Ⓔ
5. Ⓐ Ⓑ Ⓒ Ⓓ Ⓔ
6. Ⓐ Ⓑ Ⓒ Ⓓ Ⓔ
7. Ⓐ Ⓑ Ⓒ Ⓓ Ⓔ
8. Ⓐ Ⓑ Ⓒ Ⓓ Ⓔ

9. Ⓐ Ⓑ Ⓒ Ⓓ Ⓔ
10. Ⓐ Ⓑ Ⓒ Ⓓ Ⓔ
11. Ⓐ Ⓑ Ⓒ Ⓓ Ⓔ
12. Ⓐ Ⓑ Ⓒ Ⓓ Ⓔ
13. Ⓐ Ⓑ Ⓒ Ⓓ Ⓔ
14. Ⓐ Ⓑ Ⓒ Ⓓ Ⓔ
15. Ⓐ Ⓑ Ⓒ Ⓓ Ⓔ
16. Ⓐ Ⓑ Ⓒ Ⓓ Ⓔ
17. Ⓐ Ⓑ Ⓒ Ⓓ Ⓔ
18. Ⓐ Ⓑ Ⓒ Ⓓ Ⓔ
19. Ⓐ Ⓑ Ⓒ Ⓓ Ⓔ
20. Ⓐ Ⓑ Ⓒ Ⓓ Ⓔ
21. Ⓐ Ⓑ Ⓒ Ⓓ Ⓔ
22. Ⓐ Ⓑ Ⓒ Ⓓ Ⓔ
23. Ⓐ Ⓑ Ⓒ Ⓓ Ⓔ
24. Ⓐ Ⓑ Ⓒ Ⓓ Ⓔ
25. Ⓐ Ⓑ Ⓒ Ⓓ Ⓔ
26. Ⓐ Ⓑ Ⓒ Ⓓ Ⓔ

27. Ⓐ Ⓑ Ⓒ Ⓓ Ⓔ
28. Ⓐ Ⓑ Ⓒ Ⓓ Ⓔ
29. Ⓐ Ⓑ Ⓒ Ⓓ Ⓔ
30. Ⓐ Ⓑ Ⓒ Ⓓ Ⓔ
31. Ⓐ Ⓑ Ⓒ Ⓓ Ⓔ
32. Ⓐ Ⓑ Ⓒ Ⓓ Ⓔ
33. Ⓐ Ⓑ Ⓒ Ⓓ Ⓔ
34. Ⓐ Ⓑ Ⓒ Ⓓ Ⓔ
35. Ⓐ Ⓑ Ⓒ Ⓓ Ⓔ
36. Ⓐ Ⓑ Ⓒ Ⓓ Ⓔ
37. Ⓐ Ⓑ Ⓒ Ⓓ Ⓔ
38. Ⓐ Ⓑ Ⓒ Ⓓ Ⓔ
39. Ⓐ Ⓑ Ⓒ Ⓓ Ⓔ
40. Ⓐ Ⓑ Ⓒ Ⓓ Ⓔ
41. Ⓐ Ⓑ Ⓒ Ⓓ Ⓔ
42. Ⓐ Ⓑ Ⓒ Ⓓ Ⓔ
43. Ⓐ Ⓑ Ⓒ Ⓓ Ⓔ
44. Ⓐ Ⓑ Ⓒ Ⓓ Ⓔ
45. Ⓐ Ⓑ Ⓒ Ⓓ Ⓔ

Practice PPST IV

Reading

Comprehension

1. Ⓐ Ⓑ Ⓒ Ⓓ Ⓔ

2. Ⓐ Ⓑ Ⓒ Ⓓ Ⓔ

3. Ⓐ Ⓑ Ⓒ Ⓓ Ⓔ

4. Ⓐ Ⓑ Ⓒ Ⓓ Ⓔ

5. Ⓐ Ⓑ Ⓒ Ⓓ Ⓔ

6. Ⓐ Ⓑ Ⓒ Ⓓ Ⓔ

7. Ⓐ Ⓑ Ⓒ Ⓓ Ⓔ

8. Ⓐ Ⓑ Ⓒ Ⓓ Ⓔ

9. Ⓐ Ⓑ Ⓒ Ⓓ Ⓔ

10. Ⓐ Ⓑ Ⓒ Ⓓ Ⓔ

11. Ⓐ Ⓑ Ⓒ Ⓓ Ⓔ

12. Ⓐ Ⓑ Ⓒ Ⓓ Ⓔ

13. Ⓐ Ⓑ Ⓒ Ⓓ Ⓔ

14. Ⓐ Ⓑ Ⓒ Ⓓ Ⓔ

15. Ⓐ Ⓑ Ⓒ Ⓓ Ⓔ

16. Ⓐ Ⓑ Ⓒ Ⓓ Ⓔ

17. Ⓐ Ⓑ Ⓒ Ⓓ Ⓔ

18. Ⓐ Ⓑ Ⓒ Ⓓ Ⓔ

19. Ⓐ Ⓑ Ⓒ Ⓓ Ⓔ

20. Ⓐ Ⓑ Ⓒ Ⓓ Ⓔ

21. Ⓐ Ⓑ Ⓒ Ⓓ Ⓔ

22. Ⓐ Ⓑ Ⓒ Ⓓ Ⓔ

23. Ⓐ Ⓑ Ⓒ Ⓓ Ⓔ

24. Ⓐ Ⓑ Ⓒ Ⓓ Ⓔ

25. Ⓐ Ⓑ Ⓒ Ⓓ Ⓔ

26. Ⓐ Ⓑ Ⓒ Ⓓ Ⓔ

27. Ⓐ Ⓑ Ⓒ Ⓓ Ⓔ

28. Ⓐ Ⓑ Ⓒ Ⓓ Ⓔ

29. Ⓐ Ⓑ Ⓒ Ⓓ Ⓔ

30. Ⓐ Ⓑ Ⓒ Ⓓ Ⓔ

31. Ⓐ Ⓑ Ⓒ Ⓓ Ⓔ

32. Ⓐ Ⓑ Ⓒ Ⓓ Ⓔ

33. Ⓐ Ⓑ Ⓒ Ⓓ Ⓔ

34. Ⓐ Ⓑ Ⓒ Ⓓ Ⓔ

35. Ⓐ Ⓑ Ⓒ Ⓓ Ⓔ

36. Ⓐ Ⓑ Ⓒ Ⓓ Ⓔ

37. Ⓐ Ⓑ Ⓒ Ⓓ Ⓔ

38. Ⓐ Ⓑ Ⓒ Ⓓ Ⓔ

39. Ⓐ Ⓑ Ⓒ Ⓓ Ⓔ

40. Ⓐ Ⓑ Ⓒ Ⓓ Ⓔ

Mathematics

1. Ⓐ Ⓑ Ⓒ Ⓓ Ⓔ

2. Ⓐ Ⓑ Ⓒ Ⓓ Ⓔ

3. Ⓐ Ⓑ Ⓒ Ⓓ Ⓔ

4. Ⓐ Ⓑ Ⓒ Ⓓ Ⓔ

5. Ⓐ Ⓑ Ⓒ Ⓓ Ⓔ

6. Ⓐ Ⓑ Ⓒ Ⓓ Ⓔ

7. Ⓐ Ⓑ Ⓒ Ⓓ Ⓔ

8. Ⓐ Ⓑ Ⓒ Ⓓ Ⓔ

9. Ⓐ Ⓑ Ⓒ Ⓓ Ⓔ

10. Ⓐ Ⓑ Ⓒ Ⓓ Ⓔ

11. Ⓐ Ⓑ Ⓒ Ⓓ Ⓔ

12. Ⓐ Ⓑ Ⓒ Ⓓ Ⓔ

13. Ⓐ Ⓑ Ⓒ Ⓓ Ⓔ

14. Ⓐ Ⓑ Ⓒ Ⓓ Ⓔ

15. Ⓐ Ⓑ Ⓒ Ⓓ Ⓔ

16. Ⓐ Ⓑ Ⓒ Ⓓ Ⓔ

17. Ⓐ Ⓑ Ⓒ Ⓓ Ⓔ

18. Ⓐ Ⓑ Ⓒ Ⓓ Ⓔ

19. Ⓐ Ⓑ Ⓒ Ⓓ Ⓔ

20. Ⓐ Ⓑ Ⓒ Ⓓ Ⓔ

21. Ⓐ Ⓑ Ⓒ Ⓓ Ⓔ

22. Ⓐ Ⓑ Ⓒ Ⓓ Ⓔ

23. Ⓐ Ⓑ Ⓒ Ⓓ Ⓔ

24. Ⓐ Ⓑ Ⓒ Ⓓ Ⓔ

25. Ⓐ Ⓑ Ⓒ Ⓓ Ⓔ

26. Ⓐ Ⓑ Ⓒ Ⓓ Ⓔ

27. Ⓐ Ⓑ Ⓒ Ⓓ Ⓔ

28. Ⓐ Ⓑ Ⓒ Ⓓ Ⓔ

29. Ⓐ Ⓑ Ⓒ Ⓓ Ⓔ

30. Ⓐ Ⓑ Ⓒ Ⓓ Ⓔ

31. Ⓐ Ⓑ Ⓒ Ⓓ Ⓔ

32. Ⓐ Ⓑ Ⓒ Ⓓ Ⓔ
33. Ⓐ Ⓑ Ⓒ Ⓓ Ⓔ
34. Ⓐ Ⓑ Ⓒ Ⓓ Ⓔ
35. Ⓐ Ⓑ Ⓒ Ⓓ Ⓔ
36. Ⓐ Ⓑ Ⓒ Ⓓ Ⓔ
37. Ⓐ Ⓑ Ⓒ Ⓓ Ⓔ
38. Ⓐ Ⓑ Ⓒ Ⓓ Ⓔ
39. Ⓐ Ⓑ Ⓒ Ⓓ Ⓔ
40. Ⓐ Ⓑ Ⓒ Ⓓ Ⓔ

Writing

1. Ⓐ Ⓑ Ⓒ Ⓓ Ⓔ
2. Ⓐ Ⓑ Ⓒ Ⓓ Ⓔ
3. Ⓐ Ⓑ Ⓒ Ⓓ Ⓔ
4. Ⓐ Ⓑ Ⓒ Ⓓ Ⓔ
5. Ⓐ Ⓑ Ⓒ Ⓓ Ⓔ
6. Ⓐ Ⓑ Ⓒ Ⓓ Ⓔ
7. Ⓐ Ⓑ Ⓒ Ⓓ Ⓔ
8. Ⓐ Ⓑ Ⓒ Ⓓ Ⓔ

9. Ⓐ Ⓑ Ⓒ Ⓓ Ⓔ
10. Ⓐ Ⓑ Ⓒ Ⓓ Ⓔ
11. Ⓐ Ⓑ Ⓒ Ⓓ Ⓔ
12. Ⓐ Ⓑ Ⓒ Ⓓ Ⓔ
13. Ⓐ Ⓑ Ⓒ Ⓓ Ⓔ
14. Ⓐ Ⓑ Ⓒ Ⓓ Ⓔ
15. Ⓐ Ⓑ Ⓒ Ⓓ Ⓔ
16. Ⓐ Ⓑ Ⓒ Ⓓ Ⓔ
17. Ⓐ Ⓑ Ⓒ Ⓓ Ⓔ
18. Ⓐ Ⓑ Ⓒ Ⓓ Ⓔ
19. Ⓐ Ⓑ Ⓒ Ⓓ Ⓔ
20. Ⓐ Ⓑ Ⓒ Ⓓ Ⓔ
21. Ⓐ Ⓑ Ⓒ Ⓓ Ⓔ
22. Ⓐ Ⓑ Ⓒ Ⓓ Ⓔ
23. Ⓐ Ⓑ Ⓒ Ⓓ Ⓔ
24. Ⓐ Ⓑ Ⓒ Ⓓ Ⓔ
25. Ⓐ Ⓑ Ⓒ Ⓓ Ⓔ
26. Ⓐ Ⓑ Ⓒ Ⓓ Ⓔ

27. Ⓐ Ⓑ Ⓒ Ⓓ Ⓔ
28. Ⓐ Ⓑ Ⓒ Ⓓ Ⓔ
29. Ⓐ Ⓑ Ⓒ Ⓓ Ⓔ
30. Ⓐ Ⓑ Ⓒ Ⓓ Ⓔ
31. Ⓐ Ⓑ Ⓒ Ⓓ Ⓔ
32. Ⓐ Ⓑ Ⓒ Ⓓ Ⓔ
33. Ⓐ Ⓑ Ⓒ Ⓓ Ⓔ
34. Ⓐ Ⓑ Ⓒ Ⓓ Ⓔ
35. Ⓐ Ⓑ Ⓒ Ⓓ Ⓔ
36. Ⓐ Ⓑ Ⓒ Ⓓ Ⓔ
37. Ⓐ Ⓑ Ⓒ Ⓓ Ⓔ
38. Ⓐ Ⓑ Ⓒ Ⓓ Ⓔ
39. Ⓐ Ⓑ Ⓒ Ⓓ Ⓔ
40. Ⓐ Ⓑ Ⓒ Ⓓ Ⓔ
41. Ⓐ Ⓑ Ⓒ Ⓓ Ⓔ
42. Ⓐ Ⓑ Ⓒ Ⓓ Ⓔ
43. Ⓐ Ⓑ Ⓒ Ⓓ Ⓔ
44. Ⓐ Ⓑ Ⓒ Ⓓ Ⓔ
45. Ⓐ Ⓑ Ⓒ Ⓓ Ⓔ

Practice PPST I Essay Section

(use additional paper as necessary)

Practice PPST II Essay Section
(use additional paper as necessary)

Practice PPST III Essay Section

(use additional paper as necessary)

Practice PPST IV Essay Section
(use additional paper as necessary)

MAXnotes®

REA's Literature Study Guides

MAXnotes® are student-friendly. They offer a fresh look at masterpieces of literature, presented in a lively and interesting fashion. **MAXnotes®** offer the essentials of what you should know about the work, including outlines, explanations and discussions of the plot, character lists, analyses, and historical context. **MAXnotes®** are designed to help you think independently about literary works by raising various issues and thought-provoking ideas and questions. Written by literary experts who currently teach the subject, **MAXnotes®** enhance your understanding and enjoyment of the work.

Available **MAXnotes®** include the following:

Absalom, Absalom!
The Aeneid of Virgil
Animal Farm
Antony and Cleopatra
As I Lay Dying
As You Like It
The Autobiography of
    Malcolm X
The Awakening
Beloved
Beowulf
Billy Budd
The Bluest Eye, A Novel
Brave New World
The Canterbury Tales
The Catcher in the Rye
The Color Purple
The Crucible
Death in Venice
Death of a Salesman
The Divine Comedy I: Inferno
Dubliners
The Edible Woman
Emma
Euripides' Medea & Electra
Frankenstein
Gone with the Wind
The Grapes of Wrath
Great Expectations
The Great Gatsby
Gulliver's Travels
Handmaid's Tale
Hamlet
Hard Times
Heart of Darkness

Henry IV, Part I
Henry V
The House on Mango Street
Huckleberry Finn
I Know Why the Caged
    Bird Sings
The Iliad
Invisible Man
Jane Eyre
Jazz
The Joy Luck Club
Jude the Obscure
Julius Caesar
King Lear
Leaves of Grass
Les Misérables
Lord of the Flies
Macbeth
The Merchant of Venice
Metamorphoses of Ovid
Metamorphosis
Middlemarch
A Midsummer Night's Dream
Moby-Dick
Moll Flanders
Mrs. Dalloway
Much Ado About Nothing
Mules and Men
My Antonia
Native Son
1984
The Odyssey
Oedipus Trilogy
Of Mice and Men
On the Road

Othello
Paradise
Paradise Lost
A Passage to India
Plato's Republic
Portrait of a Lady
A Portrait of the Artist
    as a Young Man
Pride and Prejudice
A Raisin in the Sun
Richard II
Romeo and Juliet
The Scarlet Letter
Sir Gawain and the
    Green Knight
Slaughterhouse-Five
Song of Solomon
The Sound and the Fury
The Stranger
Sula
The Sun Also Rises
A Tale of Two Cities
The Taming of the Shrew
Tar Baby
The Tempest
Tess of the D'Urbervilles
Their Eyes Were Watching God
Things Fall Apart
To Kill a Mockingbird
To the Lighthouse
Twelfth Night
Uncle Tom's Cabin
Waiting for Godot
Wuthering Heights
Guide to Literary Terms

REA's **Problem Solvers**

The "PROBLEM SOLVERS" are comprehensive supplemental text-books designed to save time in finding solutions to problems. Each "PROBLEM SOLVER" is the first of its kind ever produced in its field. It is the product of a massive effort to illustrate almost any imaginable problem in exceptional depth, detail, and clarity. Each problem is worked out in detail with a step-by-step solution, and the problems are arranged in order of complexity from elementary to advanced. Each book is fully indexed for locating problems rapidly.

ACCOUNTING
ADVANCED CALCULUS
ALGEBRA & TRIGONOMETRY
AUTOMATIC CONTROL
   SYSTEMS/ROBOTICS
BIOLOGY
BUSINESS, ACCOUNTING, & FINANCE
CALCULUS
CHEMISTRY
COMPLEX VARIABLES
DIFFERENTIAL EQUATIONS
ECONOMICS
ELECTRICAL MACHINES
ELECTRIC CIRCUITS
ELECTROMAGNETICS
ELECTRONIC COMMUNICATIONS
ELECTRONICS
FINITE & DISCRETE MATH
FLUID MECHANICS/DYNAMICS
GENETICS
GEOMETRY
HEAT TRANSFER

LINEAR ALGEBRA
MACHINE DESIGN
MATHEMATICS for ENGINEERS
MECHANICS
NUMERICAL ANALYSIS
OPERATIONS RESEARCH
OPTICS
ORGANIC CHEMISTRY
PHYSICAL CHEMISTRY
PHYSICS
PRE-CALCULUS
PROBABILITY
PSYCHOLOGY
STATISTICS
STRENGTH OF MATERIALS &
   MECHANICS OF SOLIDS
TECHNICAL DESIGN GRAPHICS
THERMODYNAMICS
TOPOLOGY
TRANSPORT PHENOMENA
VECTOR ANALYSIS

If you would like more information about any of these books,
complete the coupon below and return it to us or visit your local bookstore.

RESEARCH & EDUCATION ASSOCIATION
61 Ethel Road W. • Piscataway, New Jersey 08854
Phone: (732) 819-8880   **website: www.rea.com**

Please send me more information about your Problem Solver books

Name _____

Address _____

City _____ State _____ Zip _____

REA's Test Preps
The Best in Test Preparation